P9-DEP-235

The Tomb of the Unknown Soldier

CORNERSTONES OF FREEDOM

SECOND SERIES

Roger Wachtel

Children's Press®
A Division of Scholastic Inc.
New York • Toronto • London • Auckland • Sydney
Mexico City • New Delhi • Hong Kong
Danbury, Connecticut

Photographs © 2003: AP/Wide World Photos: 16, 44 top right; Brown Brothers: 6; Corbis Images: 38, 39 (Bettmann), 36 (Wally McNamee), 7, 44 center (Medford Historical Society Collection), 19, 20, 26; Corbis Sygma/Bill Greenblatt: 30; Folio, Inc./Catherine Karnow: 11; Getty Images: 29, 45 top right (Tim Parker/Reuters), 8, 45 top left (Reuters) 3, 42 (Stefan Zaklin); Hulton|Archive/Getty Images: 12, 13 (Scott Swanson Collection), 14; Library of Congress: 18, 23, 24 (National Photo Company Collection); National Park Service/Don Worth: 4, 44 top left; Photri Inc./TWAchs: bottom cover; Robertstock: 21 (W. Bertsch), 5 (D. Corson), 40, 44 bottom (D. Lada), top cover (J. Patton), 10 (H. Sutton); Superstock, Inc.: 9; The Viesti Collection: 35 (Richard Cummins), 32 (Joe Viesti); TimePix/Leonard McCombe: 27; U.S. Army/Shannon Duckworth: 31, 45 bottom.

Library of Congress Cataloging-in-Publication Data
Wachtel, Roger.
  The Tomb of the Unknown Soldier / Roger Wachtel.
    p. cm. — (Cornerstones of freedom. Second series)
  Summary: A description of the history and characteristics of the national monument known as the Tomb of the Unknown Soldier at Arlington National Cemetary, Arlington, Virginia, which was established after World War I to honor an unidentified soldier from each war.
  Includes bibliographical references and index.
    ISBN 0-516-24215-6
    1. Tomb of the Unknowns (Va.)—Juvenile literature. [1. Tomb of the Unknowns (Va.) 2. National monuments.] I. Title. II. Series: Cornerstones of freedom. Second series.
D675.W2W28 2003
355.1'6'09755295—dc21

                                        2003005621

© 2003 Children's Press, a Division of Scholastic Inc.
All rights reserved. Published simultaneously in Canada.
Printed in the United States of America.

CHILDREN'S PRESS, and CORNERSTONES OF FREEDOM™, and associated logos are trademarks and or registered trademarks of Scholastic Library Publishing. SCHOLASTIC and associated logos are trademarks and or registered trademarks of Scholastic Inc.

1 2 3 4 5 6 7 8 9 10 R 12 11 10 09 08 07 06 05 04 03

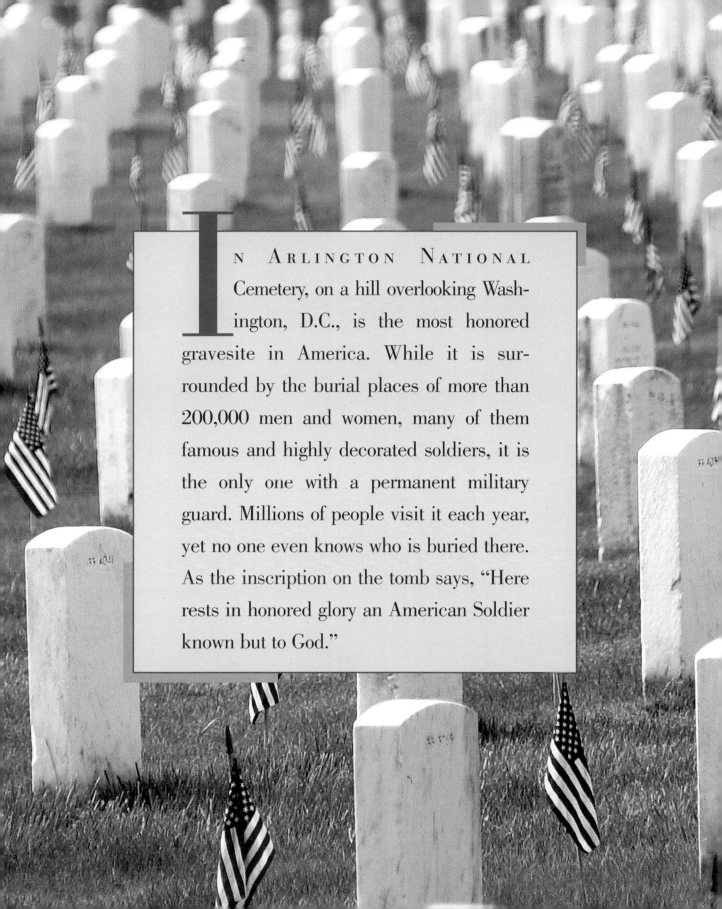

IN ARLINGTON NATIONAL Cemetery, on a hill overlooking Washington, D.C., is the most honored gravesite in America. While it is surrounded by the burial places of more than 200,000 men and women, many of them famous and highly decorated soldiers, it is the only one with a permanent military guard. Millions of people visit it each year, yet no one even knows who is buried there. As the inscription on the tomb says, "Here rests in honored glory an American Soldier known but to God."

Robert E. Lee came to own Arlington House when he married the great-granddaughter of George Washington, Mary Anna Custis. They lived there until 1861, though Lee was frequently away. On May 24, 1861, Union troops occupied the estate. Officers lived in the house while soldiers camped on the grounds.

THE FIRST TOMB OF THE UNKNOWNS

The Tomb of the Unknown Soldier is found at Arlington National Cemetery, the most famous of many American military cemeteries. It is located just across the Potomac River from Washington, D.C. It was established there during the Civil War when General Montgomery Meigs decided to punish Confederate General Robert E. Lee by using his land for the burial of the mounting numbers of Union dead. After the war, the government paid the Lees for the land, but Meigs got his way. The 16,000 soldiers who were buried there guaranteed the Lees would never return.

Although today one must meet certain qualifications to be buried at Arlington, it originally served during the Civil War as a site to bury fallen soldiers whose families were too poor to have their remains shipped home. This often took place without ceremony.

NATIONAL MILITARY CEMETERIES

There are many military cemeteries located in the United States. They are reserved for soldiers, sailors, airmen, and marines who have died in battle and for those who have served with distinction. Their funerals are performed with military honors and the graves are cared for by the U.S. government. Two of the most famous of these are in Arlington, Virginia, and Gettysburg, Pennsylvania. Abraham Lincoln dedicated the Gettysburg cemetery with the Gettysburg Address.

Civil War battles were often furious, and the armies moved on as soon as they were over. Often, old men and boys who were unfit for the army were paid to clean up the battlefields and bury the men. Unless the dead had some identification with them, the gravediggers had no idea who they were. Since the battlefields were usually private property, the bodies could not remain there permanently. They had to be **disinterred** and moved. That led to more problems with identification.

In 1866, the unidentified remains of 2,111 soldiers from the battlefields around Washington, D.C., were disinterred and re-buried in a common grave under a stone monument near Arlington House. An inscription on the monument reads, "Beneath this stone repose the bones of two thousand one hundred eleven unknown soldiers gathered

The bloodiest one-day battle in American history took place on September 17, 1862, at Antietam, in northwest Maryland, in the second year of the U.S. Civil War. There were over 23,000 casualties on both sides. For days, the soldiers were left just as they fell.

It normally took a week to bury all the dead after a battle during the Civil War. When soldiers buried their own, they had to do so quickly in order to move on to the next battle. This led to much confusion in identifying the deceased.

after the war from the fields of Bull Run ... Their remains could not be identified, but their names and deaths are recorded in the archives of their country, and its grateful citizens honor them as of their noble army of martyrs. May they rest in peace." They remain there today in the first tomb of unknown soldiers.

WHO CAN BE BURIED AT ARLINGTON?

Members of the military who die on active duty, those who retire from the military, and reservists with long terms of service are eligible for burial at Arlington. Those who have been highly decorated and anyone who has been held as a prisoner of war can also request burial there. There have been notable exceptions made, including personnel killed in the 2001 terrorist attack on the Pentagon and other notable citizens. The spouses of those buried at Arlington may elect to be buried there as well.

On September 12, 2002, a group funeral was held in honor of the victims of the attack on the Pentagon on September 11, 2001. The unidentified remains buried in Arlington Cemetery were in remembrance of all 184 victims.

TO HONOR THOSE WHO NEVER RETURNED

On November 11, 1918, World War I officially ended. It was a war the scope of which the world had never seen. Then referred to as The Great War, it cost thousands of lives—136,516 from the United States alone. Other countries had their own devastating losses. While many of the dead were returned to their families for burial, many others were never identified. The unidentified men who had lost their lives far from home were most frequently buried in special cemeteries in Europe. Their families never had a chance to properly say goodbye, and the world's governments searched for a way to properly honor those who had given their lives for their countries.

The Battle of Verdun, in World War I, is considered one of the bloodiest in history, with a total of more than 700,000 killed, wounded, or missing on both sides. This blood was shed for a patch of land less than 8 square miles in area in northeast France.

The Arc de Triomphe was commissioned by Napoleon Bonaparte in 1806, but it was not completed until 1836. It was originally intended to honor France's unknown soldiers as well as its generals and major victories from the Revolutionary and Napoleonic periods.

France and England were the first to develop the idea of an unknown soldier. On November 11, 1920, both countries chose and buried one unidentified soldier to represent all those who could not be named. The French placed theirs beneath the Arc de Triomphe in Paris, located at the start of the Champs d'Elysses, Paris' grandest street. The English **interred** theirs in Westminster Abbey, where many of their

A horse-drawn caisson enters Arlington National Cemetery. The tradition of draping the flag over the deceased's casket was adopted from France, where it began during the Napoleonic Wars. In the United States, the flag is always draped so that the blue is at the head and falls over the left shoulder of the deceased.

MILITARY FUNERALS

Military personnel who are buried at Arlington receive military honors at their funerals. Their casket is pulled on a **caisson** or hearse, and draped with an American flag, which is removed and presented to family. A bugler plays "Taps" and a salute is given by a rifle firing team. The higher rank or more honored the serviceman is, the more involved the ceremony. Many funerals are performed at Arlington every day.

most famous artists and leaders are buried. The inscription on his tomb reads, "A British Warrior Who Fell in the Great War, 1914–1918 For King and Country." The Italians soon interred their own unknown, and many felt that the United States should as well.

The original proposal for an American tomb was made by General William D. Connor, commander of American forces in France. He had heard of the French project and was impressed with the idea. His superiors were not. He was turned down for two reasons. The first was the belief that eventually all the unidentified U.S. soldiers might be identified. The second was that the United States didn't

have any place as appropriately impressive as the Europeans did. New York Congressman Hamilton Fish, Jr., decided there was such a place, and he introduced a resolution in December of 1920 to bring an unidentified serviceman from France and bury him with honor at the Memorial Amphitheater in Arlington National Cemetery.

The resolution passed to begin construction of a simple tomb that would serve as the base for a more appropriate monument at a later date. Congressman Fish hoped the burial would take place on Memorial Day in May of 1921. However, Secretary of War Newton Baker told the committee that the date was too soon. Only about 1,200 soldiers were still unidentified and all of those were still being investigated. If they buried a soldier too soon, he warned, he might later have to be **exhumed** when the government finally learned who he was.

Douaumont was part of the battlefield of Verdun in 1916. Over 300,000 unidentified French soldiers are buried at this national memorial to one of the most horrific battles of WWI. This photograph was taken in 1918.

American troops fire from trenches on the western front in World War I. The Germans were the first to use this method of warfare in an effort to hold onto occupied land in France and Belgium. When the Allies realized these fronts could not be penetrated, they, too, began to build trenches. It was in the trenches that some of the most horrific aspects of modern warfare were introduced—machine guns, gas attacks, and landmines.

THE UNKNOWN SOLDIER OF WORLD WAR I

A presidential election brought a new president and a new secretary of war, but still no unknown soldier. Congressman Fish again pushed for a ceremony to be held on Memorial

Day 1921, but the committee finally settled on November 11, 1921, the third anniversary of the war's end. Plans began in earnest for both what form the ceremony would take and how the soldier would be chosen.

In September, the War Department began looking for soldiers buried in France who might represent all those who had been killed and buried anonymously during the war. A body was exhumed from each of the four American military cemeteries in France—Aisne-Maine, Meuse-Argonne, Somme, and St. Mihiel. Each of the four was examined to make sure that he had died of combat wounds and that there were no clues as to the soldier's identity. Then, the bodies were placed in identical caskets and shipping cases.

On October 23, at 3:00 in the afternoon, the four caskets were brought to Chaolons-sur-Marne. There was a large delegation of important officials from the United States military and government as well as France. The caskets were met by a French honor guard and French troops carried the shipping cases to the reception room in the city hall. The caskets were then removed, placed on top of the cases, and covered with American flags. At 10:00 P.M., six American **pallbearers** arrived and began to hold a constant vigil with the French guard.

Making sure the Unknown Soldier was truly unknown was very important. Early the next morning, October 24, 1921, an American officer directed French and American

OVERSEAS MILITARY CEMETERIES

When soldiers, sailors, airmen, and marines die overseas, they are often returned home. Others are buried near where they died. More than 100,000 members of the United States military are buried in American cemeteries located overseas. Some of the best known are in France, near where the D-Day invasion took place, and in Hawaii, where many of the dead from Pearl Harbor and the Pacific Theater of World War II are buried.

15

On Memorial Day in 1930 at Arlington National Cemetery, Sergeant Edward S. Younger honored the fallen soldier whom he had designated nine years earlier as the symbol for all unknown soldiers. Younger was a highly decorated combat infantryman on duty in Germany when he first chose between the four caskets.

troops to move the caskets. That way no one would have any way of even knowing which cemetery each had come from. The officer then designated Sergeant Edward S. Younger to choose the Unknown Soldier. Originally this was to have been done by an officer, but when American officials learned that the French had given this honor to an enlisted man, they decided to do the same.

The ranking French and American generals each made a short speech honoring the dead. Then Sergeant Younger took a **spray** of roses from a Frenchman who had lost two sons in the war. He walked around the coffins several times before placing the roses on the chosen casket. When later asked why he chose the one he did, he replied, "It was as though something had pulled me. A voice seemed to say to me, 'This is one of your pals.'" Younger then saluted the fallen soldier, as did the other officials. The pallbearers took the chosen soldier to another room. The other three were then removed to a cemetery near Paris, where they remain today.

Meanwhile, the body of the Unknown Soldier was placed in its special coffin and sealed before witnesses. It was draped with an American flag and the spray of roses. The utmost care had been taken to guarantee that this was indeed an unidentified soldier killed in battle. Equal care guaranteed that he was treated with honor and respect. It was indeed a perfectly executed and moving ceremony.

The Unknown Soldier was taken on a procession through the town the next day. Soldiers, firemen, policemen, and other dignitaries paid tribute as the honor guard took him to a special train for transport to Paris. The guard watched over him all night, and the next day more dignitaries paid him honor and presented him with memorial wreaths. The route to the ship that would transport him to the United

States was lined with bands playing the American national anthem and military marches.

At the pier, the Unknown Soldier was presented with a French Medal of Honor. American Marines presented arms in respect, and the body bearers took him aboard the USS

The body of the Unknown Soldier is carried from the USS *Olympia* at the Navy Yard while America's highest dignitaries of state, army, and navy stand at salute. General John J. Pershing and the Secretary of War, John Weeks, are among those in attendance.

Army Chief of Staff General John Joseph Pershing visited France in 1921, on behalf of President Warren G. Harding, to present the Congressional Medal of Honor to the French Unknown Soldier. Pershing had commanded the U.S. troops in Europe during World War I.

Olympia. Rear Admiral Lloyd Chandler, commander, escorted the casket to the rear of the ship which had been decorated for the occasion. As *Olympia* left the dock, it was escorted by an American destroyer and eight French navy ships. *Olympia* received a 17-gun salute as it set sail for the United States.

THE UNKNOWN SOLDIER COMES HOME

The plans for honoring and burying the Unknown Soldier were just as elaborate, if not more so, as the ceremonies had been in France. On November 9, the *Olympia* sailed up the Potomac River into Washington, receiving military honors from posts along the way. When it docked, the most distinguished military leaders were on hand to

President Warren G. Harding places a wreath on the casket of the Unknown Soldier in the rotunda of the Capitol on November 9, 1921. Two days later he would give an emotional speech in honor of the Unknown Soldier and plea for an end to war.

receive the honored dead. Among them were John J. "Black Jack" Pershing, the highly decorated soldier and General of the Armies, as well as the Chief of Naval Operations and the Commandant of the Marine Corps. The Secretaries of War and the Navy attended, along with the 3ʳᵈ Cavalry, whose job it would be to escort the soldier to the tomb.

As the casket was taken ashore, it was given the honors a full admiral would receive. A band played Chopin's *Funeral*

20

FAMOUS BURIALS AT ARLINGTON

There are many famous people buried at Arlington National Cemetery. President John F. Kennedy and his brother Robert, both of whom were assassinated, are there. Others include astronaut Gus Grissom, who was killed in a fire aboard *Apollo One*, famous generals Omar Bradley and Jack "Black" Pershing, and polar explorer Admiral Robert E. Byrd. Also in Arlington are boxer Joe Louis and Abner Doubleday, who is often credited with inventing baseball.

The eternal flame that burns at the grave of former president John F. Kennedy was the idea of his widow, Jacqueline Kennedy, inspired by her visit to the memorial of the Unknown Soldier at the Arc de Triomphe in Paris, France, where a similar flame burned.

March and the ship's guns began firing. As he left the ship, a marine bugler played a flourish and the band played the national anthem. The casket was placed on a caisson and the band played "Onward Christian Soldiers." The soldiers and dignitaries then joined in a procession toward the Capitol.

When the procession arrived at the Capitol, the Unknown Soldier was moved into the **rotunda**, where the public could pay its respects. First, however, even more dignitaries visited. This time they were led by President and Mrs. Warren G. Harding, Vice President Calvin Coolidge, the speaker of the House of Representatives, the Chief Justice of the Supreme Court and the Secretary of War, all of whom left flowers. The next day, when the public was allowed to pass by in respect, the crowds were greater than anyone had dreamed. The rotunda was supposed to close at 10:00 P.M., but lines were so long that they were kept open until midnight. By then, 90,000 men and women had passed by to honor the Unknown Soldier.

FINALLY LAID TO REST

The bearers who took the Unknown Soldier to Arlington were all non-commissioned officers. Like everything else done that day, they were chosen so that the symbolism and ceremony of the day would pay due respect to those Americans who had lost their lives in battle. The procession included clergy, the president and vice president, all the military leadership in the country, members of Congress and the Supreme Court, and officials from all over the

The original funeral procession for the first Unknown Soldier commences from the steps of the U.S. Capitol, November 11, 1921. It would take over three hours for the procession to reach Arlington National Cemetery, where over 5,000 attendees would observe the ceremony from the Memorial Amphitheater.

United States. Also in the column was a special group of soldiers who had received the Medal of Honor.

The procession left the Capitol at 8:00 A.M. on November 11, 1921. As it did, an artillery battery began firing once every minute. They would continue to do so throughout the ceremonies, except for a two-minute silence at noon. The

The Unknown Soldier is committed to his final resting place in Arlington National Cemetery. The bottom of the crypt had been lined with a layer of soil from France, where the deceased had first been buried.

procession passed through Washington toward the cemetery for more than three hours, finally arriving at the amphitheater at about 11:40.

The ceremony began in earnest after the moment of silence at noon. The assembled sang "America," and President Harding made an address paying tribute to the soldier and pleading for an end to war. He then placed a Distinguished

Service Cross and Medal of Honor on the casket. Foreign dignitaries also bestowed honors on the soldier, many of which had never been given to a soldier of a foreign nation before. Readings from the Bible and hymns followed. "Nearer My God to Thee" closed the ceremony.

The procession then moved to the tomb itself. The clergy read the burial service and Congressman Fish, the man who had initiated the legislation making way for the Tomb of the Unknown Soldier, placed a wreath on the casket. Plenty Coups, Chief of the Crow Nation representing Native Americans, placed his war bonnet on the tomb. The artillery battery fired three shots as the casket was lowered into the tomb, the bottom of which was covered with soil from France. A bugler played "Taps," and the battery fired a twenty-one-gun salute to honor the Unknown Soldier of World War I.

THE UNKNOWNS OF WORLD WAR II AND KOREA

The World War I Unknown Soldier lay alone for years before the government decided to add more fallen men to the tomb. Meanwhile, changes were made to the tomb's exterior.

In 1932, a large **sarcophagus**, which had been called for but not funded in the original legislation, was added. The marble's engravings hold much symbolism: On the east side are three figures which represent the three allies from World War I. They also represent victory, valor, and peace. The peace figure has a palm branch to reward the devotion and sacrifice that, with courage, "make the cause of righteousness triumphant." The other sides each have

Family members are not allowed onboard military vessels for the burials at sea of a fallen member of the armed forces. However, the next of kin is quickly contacted with information about the ceremony. Here, the ceremony is performed in November 1943 for two sailors who were aboard an aircraft carrier torpedoed by a Japanese submarine.

THE MEDAL OF HONOR

The Medal of Honor is the United States' highest military decoration. It is awarded for soldiers who perform acts of bravery "above and beyond the call of duty." Frequently these acts put the recipients' life in danger, and many are given to soldiers who died saving others' lives. They are also awarded to U.S. Unknown Soldiers. The only Medals of Honor ever given to foreign soldiers were awarded to other countries' unknowns.

three inverted wreaths. The one facing the amphitheater bears the famous inscription, "Here rests in honored glory an American Soldier known but to God."

In 1956, President Dwight Eisenhower signed a bill to honor unknown soldiers from World War II and Korea just as they had been honored for World War I. He had been the commanding general of Allied troops in World War II, so it seemed appropriate that he would oversee these ceremonies. These soldiers were selected and honored much the same

Sergeant Ned Lyle chooses the Korean Unknown Soldier in May 1958 in Hawaii. The Korean conflict ended on June 27, 1953, after 37 months of fighting and 3 million casualties.

way as the World War I unknown had been. The official ceremonies occurred in 1958.

The World War II unknown was selected from soldiers exhumed from cemeteries in Europe and the Pacific. They were placed in identical caskets aboard the USS *Canberra*, and Navy Hospitalman 1ˢᵗ Class William Charette, the Navy's only active duty Medal of Honor recipient, chose one for interment at Arlington. The other was given a burial at sea with full honors.

Four Korean War unknowns were disinterred from a military cemetery in Hawaii. Army Master Sergeant Ned Lyle chose the soldier to be interred. Both the World War II and Korean caskets arrived in Washington on May 28, 1958, and lay in the rotunda until May 30. On that day, they were carried to Arlington National Cemetery on caissons just as their World War I comrade had been. There, President Eisenhower awarded them the Medal of Honor and they were interred on the plaza next to the sarcophagus.

BAKER'S FEARS REALIZED— THE VIETNAM UNKNOWN

In 1920, Secretary of War Newton Baker warned that choosing an unknown soldier too soon would be a mistake. He was afraid that after the unknown had been buried, army investigators would discover his identity and he would have to be exhumed. While it didn't happen then, it did 78 years later.

Advances in medicine and record keeping made finding an unknown soldier from the Vietnam War more difficult

than it had been for the other wars. Though Congress called for a search for a Vietnam unknown in 1973, it wasn't until 1984, some nine years after the official end of the war, that Sergeant Major and Medal of Honor recipient Alan Jay Kellogg, Jr., designated the Vietnam unknown.

President and Mrs. Ronald Reagan and many Vietnam veterans attended ceremonies in Arlington National Cemetery on Memorial Day, May 28, 1984. As tradition dictated, the president presided over the ceremonies and awarded the Medal of Honor to the Unknown Soldier and accepted the interment flag as honorary next of kin. At that point, however, the Vietnam unknown's experience became radically different than the others.

In 1994, a highly decorated Vietnam veteran named Ted Sampley began researching the circumstances around the time and place of death of the soldier whose remains were interred as the Vietnam unknown. He had been declared unknown because of the condition of his body and the fact that several kinds of aircraft had crashed in that area. There

Lieutenant Michael J. Blassie's fighter jet was shot down on May 11, 1972, by North Vietnamese anti-aircraft guns. Because the area was heavily controlled by enemy forces, no recovery attempts could be immediately launched. However, eyewitness accounts eventually led to Blassie's identification.

29

DNA TESTING

DNA (deoxyribonucleic acid) is a set of chemical strands that include genetic material. In short, it is the material that makes humans unique from one another. In recent years, scientists have been able to extract and "look" at DNA. Each person's DNA is different, so it can be used to identify people, even after death. Since humans share a large part of their DNA with their close relatives, DNA can be matched to find out if people are related.

Jean Blassie poses with a photo of her son, Lieutenant Michael J. Blassie. For 26 years he was considered MIA before his remains were identified as the Vietnam unknown. Jean, who could not speak of her missing son for years, said, "In my heart I always knew he was gone, but there's always that doubt."

seemed to be too many possibilities to make a credible guess of the man's identity as far as the military was concerned.

Sampley, however, used evidence that had been found nearby to determine that the body was that of a pilot of a single seat plane. That meant it was probably Lt. Michael J. Blassie. He published his information, which was reprinted by a national news organization. Blassie's family soon learned of the news and asked the Secretary of Defense to exhume the body and test its DNA to make a positive determination. In 1998, the body was positively identified as Lt. Blassie. He was returned to his family in St. Louis and then buried near his childhood home.

The question then was what to do with the Vietnam tomb. After much debate, the Department of Defense determined that it was unlikely that another soldier would ever

A MEDAL REVOKED

The Medal of Honor is a very important honor, and usually there is an investigation to make sure the soldier who receives one performed an act of ultimate bravery. Since the unknowns were meant to represent all those who went unidentified, the government decided to award one to each of them. Since there was no evidence that Lt. Blassie had performed a Medal of Honor action, his Medal was revoked when he was positively identified.

The removal of the Vietnam unknown was an emotional moment for the guards at Arlington, who are honored to protect the unknowns year-round, throughout any weather. In the words of one sentinel, "They gave their identities and their lives for their country and ask for nothing in return."

be truly unknown. Science has simply advanced so far that virtually any body can be identified. Instead, government officials decided to leave the tomb empty and dedicate a new inscription to honor those soldiers who are never found. They are declared "missing in action," and the uncertainty of that designation is very hard for loved ones left behind. For those soldiers and their families, the inscription now reads, "Honoring and Keeping Faith With America's Missing Servicemen." It was dedicated in 1999.

The U.S. Army Drill Team is one of the 3rd Infantry's specialty units. They perform numerous breathtaking drills to the delight of proud Americans, foreign dignitaries, and heads of state. To achieve perfection with their intricate maneuvers, they must practice constantly.

THE OLD GUARD

To most people who visit the Tomb of the Unknown Soldier, the most enduring image is the guards who watch it 24 hours a day. They stand in perfect military posture, ensuring that the men laid to rest there will never be disturbed. Visitors are often surprised to learn, then, that the tomb was completely unguarded from 1921 to 1925. In 1925, a civilian guard was hired to watch the tomb during the day, but it was left unattended at night. It wasn't until March 25, 1926, that a permanent armed guard was posted to the tomb "to prevent any desecration or disrespect." Now, only army personnel can be assigned to that duty. The army was so honored because it is the oldest of the service branches.

For several years, the duty moved from unit to unit, until 1946 when it was permanently assigned to the 3rd U.S. Infantry. The 3rd U.S. Infantry is an old and highly decorated unit of the U.S. Army established in 1784. It is referred to as the Old Guard. General Winfield Scott, impressed with the 3rd Infantry's fierce fighting, gave the unit the nickname during a victory parade during the Mexican War. People who have seen the Old Guard **sentinels** at the Tomb of the Unknowns have been just as impressed.

In addition to providing sentinels for the unknowns, the Old Guard performs other military ceremonies in and around Washington, D.C. That means more than 6,000 ceremonies a year, but the unit is by no means just a ceremonial one. It also provides military security to the nation's capital during any national emergency. In fact, members of the 3rd Infantry were instrumental in securing safety in Washington, D.C., on September 11, 2001, when the Pentagon was attacked by terrorists. It is based at Fort Myer, which is next to Arlington National Cemetery.

The Old Guard is known for two distinguishing characteristics. Every Old Guardsman wears a black and tan "buff strap" on his left shoulder. It is supposed to represent the knapsack strap that members of the 3rd Infantry wore in the 1800s. They also march in parades with fixed **bayonets** on their rifles. This honor commemorates a Mexican War battle when the 3rd routed Mexican troops with a bayonet charge. Only the Old Guard has this honor.

THE SILENT SENTINELS

Guarding the Tomb of the Unknown Soldiers is extremely stressful, difficult duty. The soldiers who do so have to meet extremely high standards and maintain them for their entire period of service. It's not for everyone. In fact, it's not for most people—all the guards are volunteer. If they later find the duty is too difficult, they can transfer to other 3rd Infantry duty, no questions asked.

If a soldier wants to be a guard for the Tomb, or, sentinel, he must meet several requirements. These are so exacting that more than 80 percent of the applicants do not make it through the interview process. He must have a perfect military record and no criminal record. He must be in excellent physical condition and at least six feet tall. He must submit to intensive interviews with the sergeant of the guard, and

Among the various medals awarded for heroic service in the U.S. military is the Purple Heart (far left), established by General George Washington during the Revolutionary War.

officers of the 3rd Infantry. The interviews attempt to determine why he wants to be a guard and that his reasons support and respect the importance of that duty. The interviewers ascertain that the soldiers know how difficult the duty is. Many soldiers only serve as sentinels for

Mourners line the streets of Washington in late November 1963 to get a glimpse of the horse-drawn caisson carrying the body of President John F. Kennedy, who had been assassinated several days earlier. The horse being led behind the caisson bears an empty saddle. This is a tradition to show that the "warrior" will never ride again.

18 months and few rarely serve over two years. As a former sentinel once said, "You have to be perfect."

Once a soldier is selected for guard duty, an intensive period of training begins. The months of training and practicing move each soldier toward the perfection every one of them is expected to achieve. Physical and mental fitness are stressed, and each is expected to become an expert on Arlington National Cemetery and the Tomb of the Unknown Soldier. They are regularly reviewed and tested, inspected and tested again. When they begin their period of duty, the reviews continue regularly to guarantee perfection. Guards are evaluated on uniform, posture, arm swing, heel clicks, timing, and walk, among other things. The intensity of these evaluations is one of the reasons guards serve such a short time.

All Sentinels of the Tomb wear a special insignia. It is a badge with a likeness of the Tomb surrounded by a laurel leaf. Underneath are the words, "Honor Guard." Anyone serving as sentinel for at least nine months is entitled to wear the badge permanently. The guards wear the Army Dress Blue uniforms while on duty. As they march back and forth protecting the Tomb, guards carry their rifles on the shoulder closest to the visitor, as a gesture of protecting the Tomb against any threat.

Even the guard's walk is steeped in symbolism. He crosses back and forth in front of the Tomb on a 63-foot rubber mat (placed there to prevent wear). He must cross in exactly 21 steps. At the end, he pauses 21 seconds, turns, pauses 21 more seconds, and retraces his 21 steps. Each time he stops, he performs a sharp click of his heels. Twenty-one is an honored number symbolic of the highest salute used in military ceremonies.

LAYING WREATHS AT THE TOMB OF THE UNKNOWNS

Many individuals and groups wish to lay a wreath at the Tomb of the Unknown Soldier to honor him and what the Tomb represents. To do so they must request and receive permission well in advance. They schedule their visit to the Tomb and are allowed, with the assistance of Tomb guards, to take part in a brief ceremony. About 2,000 wreaths are laid each year, including Veterans' and Memorial Day ceremonies, usually involving the president.

Members of the Kennedy family mourn at Robert F. Kennedy's funeral in Arlington National Cemetery on June 8, 1968. He had served as attorney general under his brother, President John F. Kennedy, before becoming a senator representing New York. He was slain on June 5, 1968, during his campaign for presidency.

Almost all guard activities are performed in silence. If someone attempts to enter the restricted area around the Tomb, for instance, the guard will stop and bring his rifle in front of him as a warning. If that fails, only then will he speak a warning.

Every hour, or half hour in the summer, the guard is relieved and replaced in a short ceremony that includes inspection of the guards' uniforms and weapons. This is performed in almost total silence by an officer of the guard. At night, the guard changes every two hours.

The Changing of the Guard is one of the military's proudest traditions. The ceremony at the Tomb of the Unknown Soldier happens more frequently in the summertime to give visitors an opportunity to witness the event during daylight hours.

★ ★ ★ ★

While their watch is largely symbolic, occasionally people do stray into the restricted area and have to be warned off by the guard. In 1984, a disturbed civilian briefly took one of the sentinels hostage at gunpoint. In that instance, off duty guards disarmed him from behind and no one was injured.

The sentinels of the Tomb of the Unknown Soldier understand better than anyone the importance of their duty and the sacred nature of the place they protect. So that they never forget, one of their first obligations is to learn the Sentinels' Creed:

My dedication to this sacred duty is total and wholehearted.

In the responsibility bestowed on me never will I falter.

And with dignity and perseverance my standard will remain perfection.

Through the years of diligence and praise and the discomfort of the elements,

I will walk my tour in humble reverence to the best of my ability.

It is he who commands the respect I protect.

His bravery that made us so proud.

Surrounded by well meaning crowds by day alone in the thoughtful peace of night,

this soldier will in honored glory rest under my eternal vigilance.

★ ★ ★ ★

When wars are fought, young men die. Many times they die alone and anonymously far from their homes. The Tomb of the Unknown Soldier recognizes this ultimate sacrifice on what is probably the most sacred ground in the United States. Whether it honors the soldiers who died and went unidentified, those who never came home, or the loved ones who miss their sons and daughters so terribly, the Tomb of the Unknown Soldier will ever remain one of our most important places of remembrance.

Since the early years of Arlington National Cemetery, visitors have been overwhelmed by the sheer number of graves, arranged in military uniformity in honor of the country's war dead. Here, American flags adorn each grave in honor of Memorial Day, 2002.

Glossary

bayonets—knives adapted to fit on the end of rifles to be used in close combat

caisson—a horse-drawn vehicle, formerly used to carry ammunition. Used symbolically in military funeral to bear a soldier's body

disinterred—removed from a grave or tomb

exhumed—dug up

interred—placed in a grave or tomb for burial

pallbearer—one who carries a casket during funeral ceremonies

rotunda—an area underneath the domed part of a building

sarcophagus—a stone coffin

sentinel—one who keeps watch, usually in the military

spray—a bouquet of flowers

Timeline: The Tomb of

1778

John Parke Custis buys the land that will eventually become Arlington National Cemetery and Fort Myer Military Reservation.

1861

Union troops seize Arlington House.

1864

JUNE 15 General Montgomery Meigs proposes the Arlington House property as the site of the next military cemetery.

MAY 13 Private William Christman is the first soldier buried at what would become Arlington National Cemetery.

1866

The remains of 2,111 union soldiers are buried in a common grave as "unknown soldiers."

1919

OCTOBER 29 General William D. Connor proposes the burial of an unknown soldier, similar to the ones being proposed in France and England. His idea is rejected.

1920

DECEMBER 21 Congressman Hamilton Fish, Jr., introduces legislation calling for the tomb of an unknown soldier killed in action in France. The measure is approved the following March.

the Unknown Soldier

1921
1932
1958
1984
1998
1999

OCTOBER 24
Sergeant Edward S. Younger selects a soldier from four exhumed from American military cemeteries in France, to serve as the Unknown Soldier.

NOVEMBER 11
The Unknown Soldier is interred in official ceremonies at Arlington National Cemetery.

A large sarcophagus is placed on the Tomb of the Unknown Soldier, completing the project called for in the original 1920 legislation.

MAY 30
Unknown soldiers from World War II and Korean conflict are laid to rest on the plaza next to the World War I soldier.

MAY 28
An unknown soldier from the Vietnam War is laid to rest with his comrades from previous wars.

After investigation, the Vietnam unknown is exhumed and positively identified as Lt. Michael Blassie. His remains are returned to his family for interment near his home.

A new inscription honoring missing servicemen is dedicated on what was the Vietnam Unknown Tomb. Decision is to leave the Tomb permanently and symbolically empty.

45

To Find Out More

BOOKS AND JOURNALS

Ashbranner, Brent. *A Grateful Nation: The Story of Arlington National Cemetery*. New York, Putnam: 1990.

Bigler, Philip. *In Honored Glory, Arlington National Cemetery: The Final Post*. Vandameer, New York: 1999.

Dieterle, Lorraine. *Arlington National Cemetery: A Nation's History Carved in Stone*. Pomegranate Books, New York: 2001.

James Edward Peters. *Arlington National Cemetery: Shrine to America's Heroes*. Woodbine House, Bethesda, MD: 2000.

Temple, Bob. *Arlington National Cemetery: Where Heroes Rest*. Child's World, Chanhassen, MD: 2000.

ONLINE SITES

Arlington National Cemetery: Tomb of the Unknowns. The official website of Arlington National Cemetery with sections on the Tomb of the Unknowns.
http://www.arlingtoncemetery.com/tombofun.htm

Society of the Honor Guard of the Tomb of the Unknown Soldier. The official website of the men who have guarded the tombs.
http://www.tombguard.org/

The United States Army Military District of Washington Web Page: Fact Sheet: Tomb of the Unknowns. The official website of the military posts in and around Washington, DC.
http://www.mdw.army.mil/FS-A04.HTM

Index

Aisne-Maine, 15

Arc de Triomphe, 10

Arlington House, 4–7

Arlington National
Cemetery, 3, 13

   buried in, 21

   eligibility for burial, 8

   location, 4

Baker, Newton, 13, 28

Blassie, Michael J.,
30–31

Bradley, Omar, 21

Byrd, Robert E., 21

Chandler, Lloyd, 19

Civil War, 7

Connor, William D.,
11–13

Coolidge, Calvin, 22

Doubleday, Abner, 21

Eisenhower, Dwight D.,
26, 28

Fish, Hamilton, Jr.,
13, 14

Fort Myer, 34

Gettysburg,
Pennsylvania, 5

Grissom, Gus, 21

Harding, Warren G.,
22, 24

Kellogg, Alan Jay, Jr.,
29

Kennedy, John F., 21

Lee, Robert E., 4

Lincoln, Abraham, 5

Louis, Joe, 21

Lyle, Ned, 28

Medal of Honor, 26

Meigs, Montgomery, 4

Meusne-Argonne, 15

Mexican War, 34–35

Old Guard, 33–34

Olympia, 19

Pershing, Jack "Black,"
20

Plenty Coups, 25

Reagan, Ronald, 29

St. Mihiel, 15

Sampley, Ted, 29

Scott, Winfield, 33

Sentinels, 33–37,
41–42

Somme, 15

Westminster Abbey,
10–11

World War I, 9–18

World War II, 28

Younger, Edward S.,
16–17

About the Author

Roger Wachtel has been an educator for 17 years, first as a high school English teacher, then as a university instructor. He is now the writing specialist for the Peru Community Schools in Peru, Indiana. He was born in New Jersey, went to high school in Belgium, and now lives in Westfield, Indiana. He is married to Jeanette and has three sons, Thomas, Ben, and Josh. He has a Master's degree in English Education from Butler University. In his spare time, he reads and writes, follows the New York Mets passionately, and goes to automobile races with his sons and brothers. Roger has written three other books for the Cornerstones of Freedom series, *Medal of Honor*, *Old Ironsides*, and *The Donner Party*.

One page torn & taped — noted 8/4/13

11-9-2

Athens Regional Library System

3 3207 00075 2362

I think for a minute.

"Hot air balloon!" I say, and go over to the shelf to get the atlas down again.

The clock on the bookcase chimes as I stand up to replace the atlas.

"Did he get this old clock from there, too?" I call to Aunt Agatha.

Aunt Agatha comes back from the kitchen carrying two vanilla fudge ice cream cones.

"Oh, no, that clock came from France years before my father was even born," she says.

"How did it end up here?" I ask.

"I don't exactly know, Elizabeth," Aunt Agatha says, settling down to eat her ice cream cone. "How do you suppose it got here?"

"On Monday they sold the truck to a used-car-and-truck dealer, and they took all the money they made and opened an antique store in New Brunswick. That is where my father bought this carpet from them one day many years ago. It was the very last of the one thousand carpets," Aunt Agatha says with satisfaction, getting up to clear our lunch dishes.

"And he brought it home in the back of his green station wagon with the real wood trim," I add, not wanting the story to be over yet.

"Pierre finally agrees, and they don't stop again until they get to Somerville, New Jersey. They spend the night at the hotel, and the next morning they spread their carpets out along the sidewalk and start to sell them." I look over at Aunt Agatha to let her know it's her turn.

"Luckily for them it was the weekend of the big bicycle race," she says, "and people were there from all over the world to watch or participate. They sold 987 magic carpets that weekend.

"They spend the night in Seward, Nebraska, where they go to an old John Wayne movie.

"In Shenandoah, Iowa, they get a flat tire and have to change it in the rain.

"When they get to Shoshoni, Wyoming, Pierre says, 'Maybe we should stay in Wyoming and get jobs as cowboys,' but Frank reminds him of the time he fell off a horse when they were in college, so Pierre decides to stay on the trip."

I nibbled apple slices while Aunt Agatha continued, tracing her finger along the page of the atlas.

"They go through Steamboat Springs, Colorado, where they fill up the gas tank and get two free mugs as a gift from a gas station that's having a grand opening celebration.

breakfast the next morning, even though they have to wait
longer for the cook to prepare them special.

"'Why go to Idaho if you don't intend to eat potatoes?'
Frank asks.

"Pierre thinks there might be several good reasons,
but he doesn't think Frank really wants to hear them,
so he keeps quiet.

Aunt Agatha was finishing up her sandwich by the time
I found the right page in the atlas and mapped out a route.
"From Seattle they go south to Salmon, Idaho, where
they eat potatoes six different ways: home fries for
breakfast, au gratin at lunchtime, french fries for a snack,
baked at dinnertime, potato chips when they go bowling
that night, and mashed potatoes with ketchup for

"Well," said Aunt Agatha, "Frank and Pierre drive southeast for a few days through Alaska and Canada, talking over old times and watching for animals. They drive until they've counted thirty-seven polar bears, two herds of caribou, and seven herds of moose.

"'The wilderness is great,' Frank says. 'But let's get back to civilization.'

"So they come up with the idea of driving across the country, stopping only in cities that begin with the letter *S*. They choose *S* because they are near Seattle already, and they want to get a head start on the project."

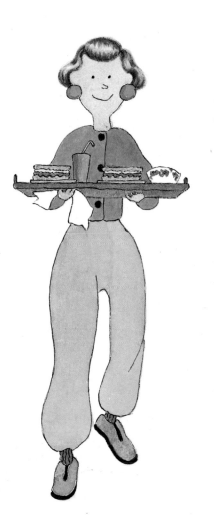

Aunt Agatha got up and went to the kitchen. I could hear her getting out dishes and opening the refrigerator as I continued the story.

"Pierre just happens to be out of work," I said, "so when Frank—did I mention that our truck driver's name is Frank?—shows up in his truck, Pierre says, 'Just give me time to pack a bag and off we'll go.'"

Aunt Agatha came back to her place at the carpet, carrying a tray with lunch: egg salad sandwiches, cucumber and apple slices, and a glass of milk for me. Aunt Agatha never drinks anything with her meals. She says it inhibits digestion.

"The aircraft carrier pulls out into the East China Sea," I told her, "and continues north through the Pacific Ocean toward Japan, and stops in Tokyo for supplies."

"They'll need lots of supplies," she said, "because they're heading for Alaska so our truck driver can visit his old college roommate. He lives in Anchorage and his name is Pierre."

Aunt Agatha stood up to get the atlas, which she keeps on the third shelf of the bookcase near the chiming clock. "And he drove and drove," she said. "He drove through tiny Chinese villages and large Chinese cities with names like Yishui, Linyi, and Qingjiang. At last he drove his truck onto an aircraft carrier that was waiting in Shanghai Harbor." She handed me the atlas already opened to the right page.

"He bought the ring at an outdoor market in Beijing after he loaded his truck with a thousand magic carpets. Then he started the long drive home," I tell her, proud of remembering Beijing from a TV report on China I'd seen recently.

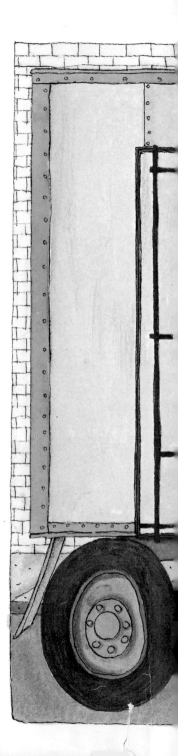

"Truck," I say, leaning back on my elbows.

"An eighteen-wheel semi with red and black letters on the side," she says, reaching for two pillows from the couch.

"And the letters say 'Melrose Trucking—Our Drivers Care,'" I tell her.

"This driver is wearing a black derby, a green corduroy jacket, and has a jade ring on the pinky of his right hand," she says.

My Aunt Agatha has a magic carpet. It's pink and blue with fringe on both ends. And it's just big enough for us to sit on together with our legs folded under us. Aunt Agatha says it came from China.

"How did it get here?" I ask.

Then she gets her smiley eyes and says, "I don't exactly know, Elizabeth. How do you suppose it got here?"

And the game begins.

For Joshua
—A.S.

For Emil—first, last, and always
—P.B.

Text copyright © 1991 by Pat Brisson
Illustrations copyright © 1991 by Amy Schwartz
All rights reserved. No part of this book may be reproduced
or transmitted in any form or by any means, electronic or
mechanical, including photocopying, recording, or by any
information storage and retrieval system, without permission
in writing from the Publisher.

Bradbury Press
Macmillan Publishing Company
866 Third Avenue
New York, NY 10022

Collier Macmillan Canada, Inc.
1200 Eglinton Avenue East
Suite 200
Don Mills, Ontario M3C 3N1

The illustrations are rendered in watercolor and colored pencil.
Book design by Amy Schwartz
Typography by Julie Quan

First American edition
Printed and bound in the United States of America
by Horowitz/Rae
1 2 3 4 5 6 7 8 9 10

LIBRARY OF CONGRESS CATALOGING-IN-PUBLICATION DATA
Brisson, Pat.
Magic carpet / by Pat Brisson : illustrated by Amy Schwartz.
p.   cm.
Summary: Aunt Agatha and Elizabeth imagine the travels of the
rug on which they are sitting, from China across the sea to the
west coast of the United States, and onward in a journey designed
to let its carriers stop only in cities beginning with the letter "s."
ISBN 0-02-714340-6
[1. Carpets Fiction. 2. Voyages and travels—Fiction.
3. Geography—Fiction. 4. Names, Geographical—Fiction.]
I. Schwartz, Amy, ill. II. Title.
PZ7.B78046Mag 1991
[E]—dc20   89-35993

MAGIC CARPET

By Pat Brisson · Illustrated by Amy Schwartz

BRADBURY PRESS · NEW YORK

Collier Macmillan Canada   Toronto

Maxwell Macmillan International Publishing Group   New York   Oxford   Singapore   Sydney

ATHENS REGIONAL LIBRARY
2025 BAXTER STREET
ATHENS, GA 30606

W9-BKB-089

or monastery possessed a wealth of relics, it could be sure of drawing crowds; and no stone was left unturned in order to obtain them. There were regular centres of trade in these commodities, above all Constantinople, which prospered wonderfully well; for to satisfy their wealthy customers the Orientals did not hesitate to divide the bodies of the saints! If honest dealing could not procure the relics one desired, other methods were employed. The monks of Conques, disappointed at their failure to obtain the bones of St Vincent of Saragossa, chose one of their community to go to Agen and get himself appointed guardian of the shrine of St Faith, which he was to break open, and bring back the body. The religious entrusted with this astonishing embassy tells us that although it took him ten years to perform, it was an unqualified success! We read also of the stratagems employed by the sailors of Bari and of Venice in their race for the port of Myra in Asia, where lay the body of St Nicholas.

These coveted relics were of several kinds, but the most popular were naturally those of Christ Himself. The True Cross, which had been removed to Constantinople when the Arabs overran Palestine, was broken up in the course of ages, and pieces were distributed among churches, monasteries, and foreign princes, enclosed in small but richly ornamented reliquaries known as 'staurotheks.' The Latin Emperor Baldwin II, being short of money, sold the Crown of Thorns to St Louis, who built for its reception that glorious 'casket of glass,' La Sainte-Chapelle.[1] In default of objects which had touched Our Lord, the next best were those connected with our Lady, the apostles, and the saints.

Who, then, guaranteed the authenticity of these relics? As a rule, no one; the public was often deceived. We have documentary evidence that there were exposed for veneration a reliquary containing what purported to be a piece of bread chewed by our Lord, the sponge that was offered to Him on the Cross, the baskets used at the multiplication of loaves, His swaddling clothes, some drops of His bloody sweat (at Vienne), and even one of His teeth—which, as some grave sceptics observed, was a little surprising, for His Body must have ascended into heaven whole and entire! On the other hand, it must not be forgotten that the Church frequently expressed her disapproval of these follies, denounced the so-called 'pardoners' who trafficked in bogus relics, and, at the Lateran Council in 1215, forbade the veneration of any object without express permission of the ecclesiastical authorities.

It is not only God, the Blessed Virgin, and the saints who are active

---

[1] According to some writers, the famous shroud of Christ, known as the 'Holy Shroud of Turin,' made its appearance early in the thirteenth century. (*See* Daniel-Rops: *Jésus en son temps.*)

among men. Faith assures us that invisible beings with natures superior to our own play their part on earth. They are often mentioned in the Bible; so here was an attractive theme combining the supernatural with the marvellous, and the angels occupied an important place in popular tradition. Their existence was, of course, unquestionable. But it meant far more to the medieval mind than to the majority of Christians of our own day; and there is no book whose miniatures, no cathedral whose sculpture and stained glass, do not portray these beautiful winged forms. Such are the famous smiling angel on the façade of Rheims, and those on the left-hand tympanum of the Royal Porch at Chartres, flying so gracefully with Christ at His Ascension. The angels are God's messengers: they protect man in peril; they assist the dying to cross the dreaded threshold; one of them weighs good and evil; and a whole battalion is employed to escort the elect to Paradise. How comforting, therefore, it must have been to know that these excellent creatures were always ready to fight under the banner of St Michael; for was there not the ever-present threat of Satan, with all his wicked spirits, 'going about like a roaring lion seeking whom he may devour'?

Fear of the Devil is characteristic of the medieval mind, characteristic of its taste for the marvellous as well as for the supernatural. Hell is part of Catholic dogma, and as such, part of Christian belief. But here too faith may run riot. We shall have occasion later on to speak of the medieval attitude towards sin, and its emphasis upon the virtue of penance. Now fear of hell was a natural consequence of this attitude, and Émile Mâle has demonstrated with much learning the importance of the Devil in medieval psychology. It is enough to read Peter the Venerable's *De Miraculis* in order to understand the power of imagination when applied to the havoc wrought by Satan. He it is who comes to torment faithful souls, his fury proportioned to their virtue; he it is who, in hideous or alluring guise, prowls about the monasteries. As incubus, he forces virgins to his will, and procreates foul offspring in their wombs. As succubus, he tempts men vowed to God. Could one doubt the truth of this when St Augustine [1] said that it is so? Representations of the Devil are numerous. In churches he grimaces from the capitals or assists with his fell legions at the day of doom; he appears in frescoes, in miniatures, and even on the stage.

But if Satan is found everywhere, his figure is not always repulsive; evil may lurk behind a pretty face. Woman is often associated with the Devil, reminding us of Eve's iniquity. At Vézelay, and at Autun, we see the temptress go unrobed, save for an ineffectual streamer that seems to float upon the wind. A young man watches her, absorbed,

[1] *De Civitate Dei*, xv. 23.

while Satan lurks in the background.[1] Still, the Immaculate Virgin protects her faithful servants; an *Ave* saves us from the spell of Eve. If woman is a thorn in our flesh, the Rose of Heaven is not far away.

It is not to be denied that popular demonology included a substratum of fun, and the Middle Ages sometimes laughed at these unholy, monstrous forms. It has been said that whereas the twelfth century depicted demons as horrible deformities, the thirteenth saw them rather as grotesque. All the same, medieval obsession with the powers of darkness, together with an ancient heritage of primitive superstition, was responsible for much psychoneurosis among the credulous.

Superstition, indeed, had been a spiritual leprosy in the barbarian age, and it continued to menace the whole of this otherwise enlightened period. Its origins were many: remote ancestral beliefs, vestiges of Roman mythology, Druidic survivals, Germanic and even Arabic traditions. At the beginning of the eleventh century Burchard of Worms wrote a treatise against those who venerated springs and sacred trees, and who consulted magicians and spellbinders. His book remained in use for many generations. In the twelfth and thirteenth centuries there were still people who dedicated Thursday to Jupiter, who celebrated the new year in pagan fashion, who believed in the Fates and set out banquets for them. When a gale of wind shook porch and roof, it was said the 'Mesnie Hellequin' passed by, the fantastic ride of the Valkyrie; and the Breton legends of Death may yet preserve some memory of ancient fears.

Superstition, a degraded form of supernatural faith, can have dire consequences, by perpetuating the practice of witchcraft and exploiting cowardice. This is where demonology joins hands with age-long magical beliefs which the Church has never managed wholly to eradicate. Strange as it may appear, trust in the efficacy of these rites took on a new lease of life rather than decayed between the twelfth and the fourteenth century. Witch, sorceress, and poisoner were never out of work. It was firmly maintained that one could direct the powers of hell against an enemy by making a small wax image in his likeness and running it through with a bodkin; the practice is called 'imitative magic.' There were also stories of men changing themselves into beasts and running about the countryside intent on every sort of crime; such were lycanthropes and werewolves. Finally,

---

[1] Let us be fair; the Middle Ages knew full well in what handsome guise Lucifer would visit a young woman. Thus in the *Jeu d'Adam*, looking just like Don Juan, he whispers in a charming and too ready ear:

'You are a sweet and tender thing,
Fresher than any rose;
You are whiter than rock-crystal,
Or snow that falls on ice down in the vale.'

it was thought that old hags flew by night to assist at Satan's sabbath!

The Church never ceased to deplore such absurdities. We find Gregory VII rebuking Haakon of Denmark for having burned some women who had been accused of sorcery. A Benedictine monk of Weihenstephan near Freising protested at the execution of three unfortunate women who had been condemned on a similar charge, and he proclaimed them 'martyrs to popular fanaticism.' John of Salisbury, who was Bishop of Chartres at the end of the twelfth century, wrote, not without a touch of humour, that the only way of combating witchcraft was—not to talk about it! Arnaud de Villeneuve, at the request of the Bishop of Valencia in Spain, compiled a treatise (c. 1280) against these aberrations; but they have not yet quite disappeared. They represent the sombre side of that taste for marvel so characteristic of a childlike people.

3. SPIRITUAL GUIDES: SAINTS AND MYSTICS

To recognize only debased forms of religion, and look no farther, would be completely to misrepresent the spiritual climate of the Middle Ages. To insist, as many 'lay' historians have done, upon superstition and witchcraft trials, and to ignore the brighter side of the picture, is a betrayal of the truth. Distortions of Christian faith and practice cannot refute that splendid cloud of witnesses who testify to a creed which has no streak of facile credulity. The true guides of medieval society were the saints and mystics.

Sanctity in the Middle Ages was a commonplace; it flowered throughout the Christian world. There were saints in every land, in every class, at every level of society: monks and priests, popes and bishops, kings and princes, labourers and peasants, scholars and soldiers, contemplatives and men of action. In their search for God some fled the world, to dwell as cenobites, as hermits, and even as recluses.[1] They renounced all hope of tangible success that they might labour for the salvation of mankind through prayer and the merit of their sacrifice. But there were also those who grappled directly with the world, its evil and its unbelief; who spread the word of God, and were even called on to lay down their lives for Christ. It is remarkable

[1] The eremitical life is one of the most extraordinary aspects of God's appeal to the human soul. It answers to a mysterious craving for solitude as experienced by the pioneers of monachism, St Paul of the Desert and St Anthony. St Benedict himself at one time dreamed of following their example. In the days of St Honoratus and St Martin, monastic communities included hermits, and we find them to-day in the 'Republic' of Mount Athos. A hermit is one who, urged by the longing to do penance, or to practise contemplation, withdraws from the society of his fellow men and lives in solitude. Following the tradition of Lérins and Ligugé, later foundations, e.g. Vallombrosa, had sought to *organize* this anarchical form of the spiritual life. The hermit's cell was open

that both forms of Christian effort were often realized in a single individual, who successfully combined the twofold life of action and contemplation. Those who see in every mystic an abnormality—an eccentric dreamer, a 'schizophrenic'—and who look on all contemplatives as 'deserters,' are confounded by a host of medieval saints. Consider St Bernard, St Dominic, and St Louis; is it possible to imagine more balanced personalities? Were souls ever lodged more nobly in flesh? 'The great mystics,' says Bergson, 'have generally been men and women of action, of superior common sense.'

In this section I have only touched upon the subject of medieval holiness. Later on I shall have occasion to treat it in more detail by reference to particular saints. At the root of their heroic endeavour lay a single motive cause—the love of God. The medieval period was above all a mystical age, understanding that word in its proper sense, which is far removed from the material and even sensual connotation with which modern writers have endowed it. Mysticism, strictly speaking, is the act of love whereby a man 'touches' and 'tastes' God. That is its essential element; ignore it, and you distort the whole picture. The faithful in that age observed the mystical act with profound insight, and defined it with extraordinary precision. They recognized and affirmed that this crowning activity of the human intellect does not depend on man alone; it is a grace whose first cause is none other than God Himself, revealing in a very special manner His presence and perfection, and calling the soul unto Himself. They explained that while self-discipline and active prayer are indispensable to all who would attain these heights, neither *constitutes* the mystical act; mortification belongs to an inferior, almost elementary, level of the spiritual life. Though they were models of asceticism, the medieval mystics considered self-denial as a means, not as an end. Medieval society was all too prone to confuse the supernatural with base irrational forms of affectivity or with doubtful probing into the mysterious; yet there are numerous writings which repeatedly emphasize that mystical activity is *not* an extension or, as it were, an overflow of sentimentality, but that it attains its end only outside the sensible, in 'that utter silence, that absolute tranquillity' to which John

---

and accessible. He could come and go at will; he could wander about in silent meditation through the woods, or visit a brother hermit. A recluse, on the contrary, was walled up in an impenetrable cell, a little room of 100 square feet, communicating with the outside world by a narrow slit through which the 'prisoner' received his food. One may say that from the eleventh to the fourteenth century every city in Europe had its reclusery. Remains of one have been discovered at the Tour-Roland in Paris, where the Châtelaine adopted this form of life after her husband's death on the crusade. At Lyons eighteen have been traced. Among these recluses of either sex some may have been *illuminati*, but many appear to have been normal men and women who wished only to live more fully in God, praying for their fellow men. Many have been beatified and even canonized.

of Fécamp refers. External manifestations of mystical activity there assuredly were; [1] but men like St Bernard and St Francis, though they enjoyed such favours, employed the utmost caution when speaking of them. The medieval mystics wrote of the ascent to God and its several degrees in a manner which subsequent ages have amply confirmed. 'There are four things,' says Hugh of St Victor, 'whereby the footsteps of the just are led, four stages whereby they are raised to ultimate perfection: reading, meditation, affective prayer, and the prayer of quiet (that loving disposition which, so to speak, cries out to God). Finally there is contemplation, which we may call the fruit of what has gone before, and by means of which we enjoy in this life a foretaste of eternal happiness.' Such an analysis is sufficient to convince us that as regards the spiritual life the Middle Ages left little for posterity to discover.

This wealth of mystical experience revealed itself in a wide variety of forms. Just as the great composers have written many melodies upon a single theme, so, on the single motif of God's love, several schools have enacted the most diverse codes. Benedictines, Cistercians, Franciscans, and Dominicans follow different roads to perfection. The Benedictines laid great emphasis upon obedience to the Holy Rule; Choral Office was the centre of a peaceful and well-ordered community —life within the monastic enclosure; nor did manual labour, though it occupied an important place in their daily task, interfere with spiritual reading or hinder the love of beauty in God's service. The reform of Cîteaux introduced a different stamp of monasticism. Contemplation occupied a more important place among the White Monks; asceticism was more highly valued; manual labour occupied a large part of their time; while formal beauty yielded to restraint and lack of ornament. But this austerity was counterbalanced by increased devotion to the person of our Lord and to His Blessed Mother. There were similar divergences between the Orders established almost simultaneously at

[1] Mention, however, must be made, in any sketch of medieval spirituality, of the seers and prophets who were so numerous, and whose message may seem to us mere raving. Towards the end of the eleventh century Joachim of Flora, a profound mystic but an austere and worthy monk, interpreted the Apocalypse in the light of visions with which he claimed to have been favoured. He announced the imminent coming of the Holy Ghost, and for two centuries his writings exercised considerable influence. (*See* Chapter XIV, 2.) St Hildegard and St Elizabeth of Schönau, in the twelfth century, declared that they had received revelations in which our Lord had directed them to call their generation to an amendment of life. Blessed Angela of Foligno, a somewhat later visionary, considered her ecstasies rather as lessons in self-improvement. In the thirteenth century, St Mechtild of Magdeburg wrote some most interesting accounts of her mystical experiences. It is to be noted that the number of visionaries increased from one century to the next; it grew in proportion as the perfect equilibrium of the Middle Ages gradually failed and ultimately gave place to the troubled decades of the fourteenth century. In the twelfth century St Hildegard was almost an exception; in the thirteenth we have a regular avalanche of female visionaries; and at the turn of the century Joachim of Flora's influence had terminated in positive aberrations which the Church resolutely opposed.

the beginning of the thirteenth century and classed together as 'Mendicant.' Among the Franciscans, the accent was on renunciation, absolute poverty, passionate love of Christ, and an exquisite reverence for the created world as an image of God. Franciscan spirituality, in fact, was watered with streams of tenderness. That of the Dominicans appears at first sight more austere, directed rather to intellectual achievement. Nevertheless, St Dominic himself was a great contemplative, and it was under Dominican auspices that the Rosary became so popular. The outstanding characteristic of the Dominican way of life was study (considered as a means of self-improvement), and the apostolate (charity in action) regarded as a means of achieving union with God.

We cannot here take account of all the spiritual wealth; the men and their writings are far too numerous, nor is the dividing line always clear between speculative and mystical theology. The most we can do is to cite the more important names in each of the principal schools.

Among the Black Monks there was *Peter the Venerable* (d. 1156), the most celebrated of the abbots of Cluny, who vigorously defended the ideals of his Order. *St Anselm* (1033–1109), a Doctor of the Church, was in turn Abbot of Bec and Archbishop of Canterbury; his influence is apparent in many contemporary events and in several trends of thought. At Cîteaux the giants crowd one upon another: first, of course, St Bernard, whom we shall consider presently;[1] then *William of St Thierry* (d. 1147), whose magnificent *Golden Letter* is one of the most acute and substantial works on mystical theology ever written. The holy life of *Blessed Joachim of Flora* (d. 1202) was perhaps of more importance than his apocalyptic visions. *St Gertrude* (1256–1341) was a great German mystic whose spirituality (both affective and practical), as expressed in her *Exercises*, had a profound effect on her generation; while *St Bridget of Sweden*, a princess of the blood royal, who entered a convent after the death of her husband, had much to do with ecclesiastical reform. And in the school of *St* Victor, established by William of Champeaux at the foot of Mont Sainte-Geneviève, a number of eminent scholars revived the Augustinian system and combined the practice of asceticism with sacred studies, two indispensable prerequisites of the mystic state. The most celebrated member of this school was *Hugh of St Victor* (1099–1141). He wrote an important work on the Sacraments; and every Christian intellectual should bear in mind his twin formulae: 'To be ignorant is to be weak,' but 'Love surpasseth knowledge.' Such figures abound in medieval Christendom. Among the Carthusians were the two *Guigo* (twelfth

[1] See Chapter III. Other great figures named in this paragraph—St Norbert, St Francis of Assisi, St Dominic, and St Thomas Aquinas—will also be studied at greater length in subsequent chapters.

century), one of whom was author of the *Scale of Paradise*. The
Premonstratensians include *St Norbert* with his immediate disciples
Hugh de Fosses, Walter of Saint-Maurice, and *Philip of Bonne Espérance,*
who wrote one of the greatest medieval syntheses. Both *St Francis of
Assisi* (1181–1226) and *Saint Dominic* (1170–1221) inspired a host of
mystics; the Franciscan *St Bonaventure* (*d.* 1274), known as the
'Seraphic Doctor,' was renowned no less for his theological learning
than for his loyalty to the spirit of his master. There were also the
anonymous author of a *Meditation on the Life of Christ*; *David of
Augsburg*; and *Blessed Angela of Foligno* (*d.* 1309), a fashionable lady
who joined the Third Order of St Francis and whose voice still seems
so close to us. *St Thomas Aquinas* (1225–74) and *Blessed Albert the
Great* (*d.* 1280) are the most outstanding of several great Dominicans.
And still the list is incomplete; scores of secular priests and laymen
likewise enjoyed and bore witness to the sublime experience. In
Germany these 'friends of God' included Henry of Langerstein and
Rulman Merswin; in France Honorius of Autun, Richard of Saint-
Laurent, and, even more illustrious, St Louis, that king whose *Instructions to his Son* form a veritable treatise on the spiritual life. The
religion of the masses always reflects the teaching of those who
represent the noblest elements of Christian faith.[1] Judged by these
and similar examples, the medieval soul was far from superstitious,
credulous, and intellectually blind. It shone with the bright flame of
understanding and supernatural faith, the very light of God.

4.   Four Characteristics of Medieval Religion

The Christian religion has at all times been consistent with itself and
loyal to its tradition. But that has not prevented it taking on a
different colour, so to speak, from one generation to another. The
emphasis nowadays, at any rate among French Catholics, is on the
social aspect of the Creed, on the necessity of recourse to biblical and
patristic sources, and on deeper acquaintance with the liturgy. During
the great centuries of the Middle Ages, there were four main characteristics.

The first and most fundamental of these was the profound influence
of Holy Scripture. It is certain that the Bible, considered as a whole,
was familiar to all. Many other books were read in the monasteries
and universities, particularly the Fathers, and above all St Augustine;
but what the masses of the faithful knew best was the Gospel—Christ
Himself manifested through the written word. The remainder of the

---

[1] One need only call to mind, for example, the influence upon their contemporaries of
St Francis of Sales, of Cardinal Berulle, and of M. Olier, in whose image and likeness the
literary and artistic genius of France has at various times expressed itself.

New Testament recalled the earliest beginnings of Christian history or, in the Apocalypse, looked forward to the mysterious dawn of eternity. The popularity of the Old Testament was founded upon a notion inherited from the Fathers of the Church and universally accepted— that the persons and events described therein are prophetic of the later dispensation.

Proof that medieval Christians were thoroughly conversant with the Scriptures is furnished by the glass and sculpture which adorn the great French cathedrals. No craftsman would have troubled to multiply the pages of these 'bibles in stone,' of these 'transparent gospels,' if those who used the buildings had regarded them merely as picture-puzzles. It has been said that the cathedral 'spoke to the illiterate'; and, we might add, the illiterate understood their language.

Men were familiar with Holy Writ because it was studied and taught; not only in religious houses, where the Rule of St Benedict ordained that 'spiritual reading' should occupy one-third of the day; not only among exegetes and scholars, many of whom were so deeply versed in Scripture that their very thought and literary style were moulded by the Bible. The Sacred Books were not reserved to clerics who could read Latin. Educated laymen had translations made of those parts which interested them, and many such vernacular renderings were produced between the eleventh and thirteenth centuries. The four Books of Kings were done into French (c. 1100), and the Proverbs of Solomon into Anglo-Norman (c. 1150). The Oxford and Cambridge Psalters followed not long afterwards, and in 1190 one Herman, a worthy canon of Valenciennes, published a complete edition of the Bible in Alexandrine verses!

This passion for the Bible became, in fact, so strong that the authorities grew uneasy at the prospect of simple folk nourishing their faith upon obscure and often misleading texts.[1] Nor were these apprehensions unjustified; for even the Waldenses and Albigensian heretics based their arguments upon passages of Holy Writ. The fact remains, however, that the faithful drank at the wells of Scripture, which is the Word of God; and that, no doubt, explains the freshness and vigour of their belief.

The second characteristic was devotion to the saints. Though rooted in the deepest soil of Christian teaching, it flourished upon a scale unparalleled before or since. It was, of course, wide open to the abuses of credulity and superstition; but at the same time it was profoundly significant. Medieval man experienced a sense of humility and helplessness in presence of his Creator; he felt the need of inter-mediaries between himself and the Almighty, intermediaries who

[1] Innocent III took steps to meet this danger; somewhat later, Alexander III called attention to the fate of those who turn Scripture to their private ends.

should be men like himself, and who had won their way to heaven by perfecting a nature similar to his own.   Nietzsche has formulated this need in celebrated words: 'Man is a creature who likes to be outstripped'; and the Middle Ages satisfied their craving by devotion to the saints—which at any rate is no more unreasonable than to idolize a boxing champion or a film star.

Lives of the saints vied in importance with Holy Scripture, from which, in fact, they were hardly distinguished by the rank and file. The history of God's faithful servants was looked upon as all of a piece with the Old and New Testaments, and enjoyed almost equal authority. These biographies were innumerable; and although very few of them were admitted to the official literature of the Church, many formed part of the stock-in-trade of *jongleurs* and wandering minstrels, as did the *chansons de geste,* to which indeed they sometimes bore a striking resemblance.   Vincent of Beauvais, in the *Mirror of History,* begins his narrative with the saints of the Old and New Testaments; while the Benedictine Guy of Chartres, and the two Dominicans Peter Calo and Bernard Guy, compiled vast hagiographical tomes which covered every period of history and enjoyed no small degree of popularity. Contemporary lives were not overlooked; and no sooner had Thomas à Becket fallen by the swords of Henry's knights, than a French cleric, one Guernes of Pont-Sainte-Maxence, wrote his life in phrases of impassioned eloquence.   It is true that in the *Golden Legend* of Voragine we find a good deal of fiction mixed with fact; but his famous collection breathes none the less a moving reverence toward the saints.

One could not fail to meet at every turn the countless legions of the Blessed.   Every province, every diocese, counted them by the score; every place, every aspect of daily life, was under their protection. The new-born child received his 'patron's' name, and owed him a particular devotion.   In later life he relied upon the saints rather than the doctor for his continued health: St Geneviève was well known to cure fever, SS. Apollonia and Blaise the toothache, while St Hubert was the guardian against madness.   The peasant at his daily toil invoked St Medard to protect his vine against the frost, St Anthony to watch over his pigs, and many another for such useful purposes.   The journeyman-stonemason prayed to the apostle St Thomas, the wool-carder to St Blaise the tanner to St Bartholomew, the shoemaker to St Crispin; and no traveller would dare to start his journey except under the protection of the archangel Michael or of St John the Hospitaller. Moreover, every season of the year was under saintly patronage. Springtime enjoyed the favour of St Mark and St George; summer of St John the Baptist; winter of St John the Evangelist; autumn of St Martin.   Memories of these and other things still linger in the country-side.

Saints of both sexes are prominent also in the sculpture and stained glass of our cathedrals.   They mount guard at the doors side by side with the great figures of the Bible; episodes from their lives are depicted along with scenes from Holy Scripture, and Christian folk knew every one of them by heart.   The presence of a saint in their midst formed a communal link among the faithful.   Whole towns, whole countries even, are known to have poured out their wealth in order that some venerable bones might be laid up in a worthy casket; and the enamellers, maybe of renowned Limoges, expended all the treasures of their cunning craft upon these reliquaries.   At certain times of the year, or perhaps to ward off the ravages of a plague, the relic, or sometimes a statue of the saint, was carried in procession; and there was much rejoicing as the sacred object passed from street to street on the back of a well-caparisoned horse, surrounded by young clerks clashing cymbals, or blowing ivory horns!

Devotion to the saints was more than simple piety.   First, there was a continual lesson in faith and moral progress; for each of these heroic souls afforded a sublime example of Christian principles in action. As the dogma of the Communion of Saints was better understood, so did the cult increase.   St Bernard describes the spiritual chain which binds together the Church militant and triumphant, and which unites them both with Christ, their head; St Bonaventure lays stress upon the theological bases of this exalted doctrine; the visions of St Mechtild of Hackeborn contain a noble image of the Church forgathered beyond the frontiers of death; while the *Divine Comedy* of Dante is simply 'an epic on the Communion of Saints.'   It is of faith that good works, performed in a state of grace and augmented by the infinite merits of Christ with which they are conjoined, form, as it were, a reserve fund against the immeasurable debt of sin.   This doctrine of the 'reversion of merit' is the background to, and the justification of, a cult which might appear ingenuous and even vulgar, but which was in fact one of the most efficacious means employed by the Church to raise the standards of morality and faith.

Love of Holy Scripture and devotion to the saints had been outstanding factors in the religion of an earlier epoch; but the remarkable tenderness of medieval Christianity arose from two other characteristics—devotion to our Lord's humanity and cult of the Virgin Mary. We must not, of course, exaggerate the importance of this trend to the exclusion of other aspects of the faith; nor must we overestimate its originality.   The outlook of the Middle Ages was certainly Christocentric, but it did not on that account ignore the other Persons of the Godhead.   The Three Divine Persons were often represented together in works of art, and it was during this period that John XXII instituted the feast of the Holy Trinity.   Significant also is the great popularity enjoyed by such hymns as the *Veni Creator*, inherited from an earlier century, and the *Veni, Sancte Spiritus*, written about 1200 by Stephen Langton, Archbishop of Canterbury.   I have said, we must not overestimate the *originality* of medieval devotion to Christ as man; for something like it is already apparent even in the early Fathers, e.g. St Ignatius.   It is none the less true that a new note is discernible. 'Hail, Jesus whom I love.   Thou knowest how I long to be nailed with Thee to the cross.   Give Thyself to me!   Look down upon me from Thy Cross, beloved; draw me wholly to Thee, and say to me: "I heal thee, I forgive thee!"   Meanwhile, though filled with shame, I embrace Thee in a surge of love.'   These phrases, typical of the new devotion, were spoken by St Bernard, who may be truly said to have introduced it.   Before him, St Anselm and John of Fécamp had already given utterance to fine 'surges of love' towards God made Man, but not with such intensity, nor with the same heart-rending pathos. Christianity has never forgotten this poignant song of faith; innumerable devout souls have repeated it, and St Francis of Assisi, who was above all else 'the friend of Jesus,' has sent it echoing down the centuries.

The purpose of this devotion is clearly analogous to that which we recognized in the cult of saints; for insistence on the human side of Christ brings Him closer to man, and emphasizes the fact that He is the supreme intermediary between the sinner and the Judge.   Men spoke of the Babe of Bethlehem, whose very swaddling clothes are mentioned by St Bernard; of the twelve-year-old Boy, upon whom St Aelred of Rievaulx wrote a whole treatise of exquisite beauty; and His conduct during the years of public ministry was analysed in order to discover and expound its lesson.   Above all, there was the contemplation of His Agony and Death—'the passion for His sacred Passion.' [1]

The flowering of love towards the Humanity of Jesus bore fruit of several kinds.   In the liturgy, for example, the consecrated host, as symbol of Christ's body immolated, became the object of very special fervour.   As soon as Christendom learned of the celebrated miracle of Bolsena, St Juliana (a Premonstratensian nun) proposed the eucharistic feast of Corpus Christi.   Instituted in the diocese of Limoges in 1246, it was soon afterwards extended to the universal Church by Pope Urban IV; and it was for the office of this festival that St Thomas Aquinas wrote his masterpiece, the *Lauda Sion*.   To the same current of devotion belongs the familiar monogram of Christ, IXP, which the Swedish order of Seraphins wore upon their breasts.   The Jesuits use the Holy Name itself to designate their Society.

---

[1] It is possible to discover in some of the followers of St Bernard the remote origin of devotion to the Sacred Heart.   Guerric of Igny, for instance, speaks with much feeling of the wound opened by the lance in our Lord's side.

But this cult of Christ's Humanity found perhaps its noblest expression in the arts. Every scene in our Lord's life is found depicted in sculpture and stained glass; and the Royal Porch at Chartres is one of many such façades designed with Jesus as its centre, reminding us in turn of His Incarnation, of His death, and finally of His glorious Resurrection and Ascension. When we admire the intimate humanism of romanesque and gothic sculpture, we should not forget that it was inspired by a faith which taught the love of man in God.[1]

Another facet of medieval religion was an overwhelming devotion to Mary, the mother of Christ. This was not, as has been suggested, a medieval innovation denounced by some as 'mariolatry.' Old almost as the Church herself,[2] it had developed in the course of centuries, particularly in the East where the scurrilous attacks of Nestorius served only to increase the public fervour. But in the West also, from the eleventh century, there was an ever-flowing stream of love towards the mother of Jesus. Why? For the same reason that underlay devotion to the saints and accentuated the human side of Christ: man's longing for a mediator between himself and the dread majesty of God. Who better than the Mother could intercede with her own Son? The cult of Mary is, at all events, closely bound up with that of Jesus. 'All praise of the Mother,' says St Bernard, 'redounds to the honour of her Son'; and Conrad of Saxony remarks that 'there is no better way of praising our Lord than to praise His most glorious and gentle Mother.' It is usual to attribute this devotion to the efforts of St Bernard, to the writings of St Bonaventure, and to the preaching of the mendicant Orders. In point of fact, however, nearly all the great figures in the spiritual life of these three centuries laboured for its propagation. St Anselm, his disciple Eadmer, Richard and Adam of St Victor, Philip of Bonne Espérance, Blessed Hermann Joseph, St Francis, and St Dominic all contributed their share. But in order properly to understand the feelings of the twelfth and thirteenth centuries towards our Lady, we must go to the sermons of St Bernard, to Conrad of Saxony's *Mirror of the Blessed Virgin Mary*, or, again, to the twelve books of Richard of Saint-Laurent's *Praises of the Blessed Virgin Mary*, which might be described as a 'Summa' of Marian devotion.

This period witnessed also the composition of two celebrated anthems, the *Salve Regina* and the *Alma Redemptoris Mater*.[3] It was the period in which the Cistercians began referring to Mary as 'our Lady' (a title borrowed from the usages of chivalry and courtly love)

[1] See H. Daniel-Rops: *Le Porche du Dieu fait homme.*
[2] See H. Daniel-Rops: *Les Évangiles de la Vierge.*
[3] The *Salve Regina* appears to be the work of Adhemar of Monteil, Bishop of Puy and preacher of the first crusade. It was sung by the crusaders at their entry into Jerusalem. The *Alma Redemptoris Mater* is by Hermann Contract, a monk of Reichenau.

and in which *jongleurs* and troubadours sang of her miracles. It was the age in which the 'Hail Mary' first became popular and the Rosary was instituted. Finally, it was during this period that the feast of the Blessed Virgin's Conception, which had been observed in Ireland since the ninth century, took root in England and spread from there all over Europe.

Mary, mother of Christ, held a unique place in the hearts of men : as a mother who listened to her children's woe, as an advocate who would obtain forgiveness of their sins, almost as a supernatural lover. The Franciscan James of Milan, in his *Goad of Love*, calls her 'the ravisher of hearts.' The Old Testament was searched for figures that foreshadowed her. *Eva, Ave!* In that reversal of a name was seen the cancellation of our first parent's fault by yet another woman. But if her joys were hymned, so too were her sorrows; and close by Mary at the Crib stood Mary of the Seven Dolours. *Stabat Mater.*

The extent of devotion to our Lady is revealed in splendid works of art. Innumerable churches are dedicated to her; and the cathedral of Notre-Dame at Paris is surrounded by seven other sanctuaries of the same title, arranged not unlike the petals of a flower. Artists, too, vied with one another to depict her with exquisite grace, and the Virgin Mother appears more and more frequently amid the sculptures of both porch and tympanum. At first she is seen only with her Son, then alone, and even at the last 'in majesty'—an attitude reserved until that time to Christ. From its high place in popular esteem her cult shed upon Christianity a tenderness which has never been surpassed, and which ranks among the fairest of medieval flowers.

5. THE SPOKEN WORD

How did the Church manage to diffuse the great dogmatic concepts which underlie these several devotions? Chiefly by means of preaching, to grasp the importance of which we must forget the pattern of our present world. The twentieth century has at its disposal many sources of information and amusement; but the Middle Ages possessed no radio, no cinema, no newspapers, and there were no political meetings. All these things, which occupy so much of our time and attention, were represented by the rites and ceremonies of the Church. Surprising as it may seem, the medieval substitute for instructive recreation was the Mass and the sermon!

During those troubled times which followed the break-up of Charlemagne's empire, the pulpit had been almost abandoned. While we possess numerous sermons of the fourth, fifth, and sixth centuries, it is hard to find so much as one between this latter date and the twelfth century, when preaching regained some of its importance. The revival was no doubt due to the same impulse which had begun to elevate the human spirit in every domain, a thirst for knowledge of the things of God. It began in ecclesiastical circles. At the beginning of the twelfth century, teachers addressed themselves mainly to a clerical *élite*; but their voices were soon heard beyond the walls of monasteries and chapter-houses. Peter the Bald (*d.* 1197), Maurice de Sully, Bishop of Paris (*d.* 1196), and Raoul Ardent (*d.* 1101), whose 'word was a sword,' all spoke to the masses.[1]

Henceforward preaching made rapid strides, and to it more than one celebrated churchman owed his reputation. St Norbert, St Bernard, St Francis of Assisi, St Dominic, and, above all, the Portuguese St Anthony of Padua, held enormous congregations spellbound. Other famous orators were St Bonaventure, St Thomas Aquinas, Peter the Hermit, Fulk of Neuilly, Guibert of Nogent, Urban II, Innocent III, and Guichard of Beaujeu, who was styled by an indulgent congregation 'the layman's Homer.' Collections of sermons—most of which seem to have been heavy going—were read, studied, and commented upon. Such was the *Mirror of the Church* by Honorius of Autun (*d.* 1129), a collection of sermons for every day of the year. It was written in doggerel and vaguely rhyming Latin, but has been shown by Émile Mâle to have exerted considerable influence among artists.

From the twelfth century onwards there was a sermon on any and every occasion: during Mass, on pilgrimage, at religious ceremonies, clothings, and consecrations of churches; but also at civil functions—coronations, burials, peace conferences, and even tournaments. Preachers spoke on bridges and at street corners, and a stone pulpit or temporary wooden platform was often erected in the public squares.

What was a medieval sermon like? It would certainly not bear comparison with Bossuet's stately art; it was more like those vivid, vigorous discourses which Caesar of Arles or St Hilary of Poitiers had once delivered before enthusiastic audiences. The style was animated, familiar, uninhibited, and sometimes little more than trivial or clownish; for in order to stimulate the interest of his hearers, a speaker would not hesitate to throw in such pieces of news, or mere gossip, as he had picked up in the course of his travels. He might announce the capture of Jerusalem by the crusaders, or the humiliation of the Emperor at Canossa; but he would not disdain to tell of some comic incident that had caused trouble in the neighbouring market-town, or to inform his congregation that a cow had dropped four calves! And if he were the

---

[1] The pulpit as a piece of furniture seems to have been introduced by the Dominicans of Toulouse. Previously there were *ambos*, slightly raised platforms set up in the choir, from which the epistle and gospel were read. It was only in the fourteenth century that the pulpit (movable or immovable) came into general use, a fact of which many liturgists are still unaware. (*See* G. A. Leccy de la Marche: *La Chaire française au Moyen Âge,* 1886.)

parish priest addressing his own flock, he would not gloss over petty scandals or even grave ones. What man but loves a veiled allusion to his neighbour?

The general public, too, enjoyed the same liberty as the preacher. A sermon was a kind of melodrama at which the audience wept or laughed, or (not seldom) interrupted. If the speaker introduced some unfamiliar theme, he was stopped and questioned. Nor was that all. On one occasion a Dominican was insisting that Pilate's wife, so far from having played a creditable part during our Lord's trial, had, by her intervention, risked preventing the crucifixion and thereby placing an obstacle in the way of our salvation. Whereupon the Lady of the Manor rose, indignant, and stalked out declaring she would not listen to this revilement of her sex!

Such piquant sauce, however, helped down the main dish, which, in all truth, was a tax on the digestion. The preacher's aim was to convey the truths of faith; but he had scant regard for their methodical presentation. Most of the sermon consisted of biblical texts thrown off higgledy-piggledy, of patriotic or personal commentaries thereon, of allegories and anecdotes. Pride of place in this hotch-potch was enjoyed by Holy Scripture: 'The Old and New Testaments,' cried Hildebert, 'are twin breasts; ye preachers, drink from them!' Quotations from the Bible were put forward as decisive arguments, and each one was allowed to have at least four meanings. Thus, when a preacher spoke of Jerusalem, he referred to the city itself; to the Church, of which it is a figure; to the faithful soul, which longs to possess God as the Jewish capital possessed the Temple; and finally to heaven, where the elect behold God face to face. This complicated symbolism may sometimes have confused the audience; for, although quite familiar,[1] it was rendered yet more elaborate by a host of subtle allusions to the secret significance of plants and beasts, of precious stones and the heavenly bodies, and by a thousand other curiosities.

By way of light relief, there were, fortunately, 'examples' in the form of anecdotes and apologues. The former were taken from history, contemporary events, or legend. The latter were fables: *The Crow and the Fox, The Cobbler and the Money-lender, The Milkmaid and the Milk Jar*, all occur in medieval sermons. Anecdotes and apologues alike were full of colour, and ended with an edifying moral that was easily understood. It is surely not surprising, in these circumstances, that a good sermon often lasted for two hours.

---

[1] Manuals large as encyclopaedias were compiled to assist inexperienced preachers, e.g. by Alan of Lille, Peter of Limoges, St Anthony of Padua; and somewhat later by William of Mailly, Nicholas of Gorran, and John of San Gimigniano (author of a *Universum praedicabile*). So many would-be orators strove to acquire these books from the library of Paris University that a decree was issued by the Rector, in 1303, appointing a fee payable by each borrower.

6. THE SEVEN SACRAMENTS

It was not, however, sacred doctrine alone with which the Church provided her children. The sacraments offered them supernatural means of union with God. The meaning of the word 'sacrament' was defined in the twelfth century. Until then it often referred to ecclesiastical rites which are not of divine institution; thus the reception of holy water or of ashes is described even by Hugh of St-Victor as 'sacraments.' The necessity of refuting heresy caused theologians to cast their thought in language more precise than hitherto. The recognition of seven sacraments is discovered first in the *Life of Otto of Bamberg* (1139); but it is mainly to *Peter Lombard* that we owe the clarification of this dogma which was sanctioned by the Council of Trent in the sixteenth century, and which has remained the official teaching of the Catholic Church.

Baptism was conferred upon the new-born child. The practice of adult baptism was extremely rare; for the Church had long ago emphasized the importance of baptizing infants with the least possible delay,[1] and it was no longer necessary to wait for the canonical seasons when baptism was traditionally conferred. How then was the sacrament administered? The Greeks still followed the ancient rite of triple immersion; the Latin Church authorized a threefold infusion of water. The older custom, which is more complicated and may be objectionable on grounds of health or public decency, was rarely practised except at Milan and in a few German dioceses. Baptisteries were gradually replaced with fonts, and the ceremony was accompanied with those simple but beautiful prayers which are now recited at the church door.

The act of faith which the god-parents had pronounced on his behalf was later repeated by the child himself, with full knowledge of his responsibility, in the sacrament of *Confirmation*. It was only in cases of danger that this sacrament was administered immediately after baptism. Ordinarily it was postponed at least until adolescence; and to mark its importance it was reserved to the bishop, except in cases where the Pope granted special faculties to a priest.

The *Eucharist* is a sacrament whereby men participate in the Flesh and Blood of Christ crucified; it was considered as the most sacred of all rites, and layfolk were not admitted to frequent communion. The ancient practice of receiving a morsel of leavened bread in the palm of the hand continued in the East. In the West, however, a small disk known as a 'host' was received, as now, upon the tongue; it is unleavened in memory of that which Christ ate at the Last Supper. As

[1] A maximum of forty days was the rule in Italy.

C

to the practice of communion under the species of wine, the precious liquid was at first taken through a reed in order to avoid excess and indelicacy, but was later suppressed altogether.

If communion was rare, the sacrament of *Penance* was extremely popular; for medieval man, as I have said, was acutely conscious of sin. Peter Lombard and Gratian, among many theologians, dwell at great length on this sacrament. Since man is a sinner and knows himself as such, what more valuable rite, they ask, than that which reconciles him with God? It was actually held that in imminent danger of death confession might and ought to be made to anyone available, even to a layman; and we find examples of this practice in the *Gestes* as well as in the Chronicle of Joinville. Confession was made in one of two ways. It was public for such as had given scandal; but this custom was already dying out, and its full rigour was mitigated by commutation, acts of atonement, and indulgences. Private confession, on the other hand, became increasingly common, and was gladly frequented by the faithful. Auricular confession, which had been encouraged by Irish monks during the barbarian epoch, became the general rule. It was made to a priest, upon whom the Lateran Council of 1215 imposed a rule of absolute secrecy; and handbooks known as 'Penitentials' supplied confessors with numerous cases of conscience together with the manner of resolving them. Popular as it became, this sacrament was treated with the utmost respect, and was certainly one of the principal means of the Church's action upon souls.

Those who wished to serve God more directly received *Holy Orders* according to a rite which has never since varied. The solemn ceremonial which attends the conferment of each order, no less than the *interstices*, or intervals, that must normally elapse between the reception of the sub-diaconate, diaconate, and priesthood, are eloquent proof of their importance.

Matrimony, the sacrament wherein the Church both hallows and confirms the union of husband and wife, was hedged about with guarantees. The priest's blessing was then, as it is now, of obligation; and the indissolubility of the bond was unqualified, even in cases of adultery. The Church in her wisdom required express consent of the parties. She never allowed parental opposition to invalidate the union; but she would not recognize a marriage between persons related by ties of consanguinity.[1] The dignity attached by Holy Church to this sacrament was, in fact, one of the principal foundations of society.

When at last the hour struck for a man to depart out of this life, the Church afforded him one last chance in the sacrament of *Extreme*

---

[1] Until the fourth Lateran Council the prohibition extended to the seventh degree in the collateral line; it was then limited to the first four degrees.

Unction, which, sanctifying his body doomed to speedy dissolution, and accompanying his soul with exhortations and prayers for deliverance from evil, constituted the supreme viaticum. Many councils, too, enjoined the clergy to see that it was conferred at all costs upon the dying.

Thus, from birth to death, the whole cycle of events which mark man's passage through the world was sanctified.

7. THE FAITH OF THE COMMON MAN

To what extent, it may be asked, did medieval man embrace this doctrine; and to what extent did he follow the sacramental road to salvation? What was the religious life of the people, of all that unrecorded mass of folk whose names have not come down to us, and who performed no signal deeds? It cannot surely have been mere formality: that those who built the cathedrals and shed their blood in the crusades drank deep at the Fount of Living Water is proved by documentary evidence; but it is rather more difficult to say exactly how they did so.

Certain aspects of medieval faith remind us of the barbarian age, an admixture of light with shadow, and marked by striking contrasts. The superstitious practices to which the cult of saints gave rise might lead us to pronounce it shallow, conventional, and without much foundation. Nothing could be farther from the truth. Side by side with these aberrations there were not lacking examples of intelligent and deep-rooted belief. Prior to the twelfth century, the accent had been rather upon moral conduct and obedience to set principles; but from that time onward the interior life of the soul came to be regarded as all-important in a religious scheme which later found expression in *The Imitation of Christ.*

It is absurd to generalize about medieval religion, to describe it as 'commonplace' or 'naïve.' Then, as now, the Christian faith was one in essence, though its attributes differed according to the intellectual gifts of its adherents; but to say that popular faith was 'gross' and 'devoid of intellectual basis' is to forget that many of the great mystics and theologians came from the lower levels of society, and that traces of those ideological conflicts which troubled the learned world may be detected in medieval folklore. Differences of opinion among speculative theologians were no less striking. They were, if anything, more pronounced than in our day; for the foundations of faith had not been called in question, and a greater margin of freedom was permissible than in present circumstances. To-day the fundamental dogmas of Christianity are under attack, and require stricter interpretation through the mouth of an infallible pontiff. But during the Middle

Ages, when society as a whole was proof against erroneous teaching, there was more scope for the philosophical ventures of Abélard and St Thomas Aquinas.   Both were firm believers, yet differed widely in their points of view, which were in turn as poles apart from the standpoint of St Bernard.

These variations are not without significance: they show that in the Middle Ages faith was by no means naïve, over-simple, and narrowminded.   So far from 'clouding the mind,' it was a source of understanding—*fides quaerens intellectum*, as St Augustine says—and the enthusiastic search for divine truth which it encouraged produced a ferment of intellectual activity in the form of some remarkable debates among the theologians of Paris, Chartres, and Oxford.   But while the Faith thus acted as a leaven, its unchanging principles maintained order amid the clash of ideas and prevented them dissolving into anarchy. All Christians, at whatever intellectual or social level they might be, and however different temperamentally, recognized one overriding purpose—union with God in Jesus Christ.

The spirituality of the Middle Ages expressed itself first and foremost in frequent prayer.   There are numerous examples in medieval literature of prayer in time of danger or at some critical stage of life.   It consisted mainly of such traditional formulae as the 'Our Father' and Creed (which many councils urged that all should know by heart). There was also the 'Hail Mary,' of which the second part was written during the twelfth century, and which was officially recognized for the first time by Sully, Bishop of Paris, *c.* 1196.   It had been a common practice since the tenth century to recite a series of *Paters*, counting them on a knotted cord.   During the twelfth and thirteenth centuries the custom was gradually transferred to the 'Hail Mary' under the twofold influence of Cîteaux and the Dominicans; and this 'chaplet' was the origin of the Rosary.[1]

Medieval Christians, however, were not content with oral prayer alone.   Mystical authors explain that there is another and more interior form, which they describe as 'mental prayer'; nor is it uncommon to find, even in such profane works as the *Chansons de Geste*, the hero 'praying in silence.'   Geoffrey of Vendôme (*d.* 1132) even speaks of the 'prayer of tears,' which seems to have been widely practised.

The importance of prayer in daily life is attested by the large number of books providing samples for every occasion.   To the older *Manuals* of Fleury and the Venerable Bede, to the collections of Alcuin, and

---

[1] The Rosary (Fr. *Rosaire*; Ger. *Rosenkranz*) derived its name from a charming legend. A monk (a Cistercian according to some; others say a Dominican) had just recited fifty 'Hail Marys,' when our Lady appeared to him, crowned with roses.   At first it was called 'our Lady's psalter' because it included 150 'Hail Marys,' corresponding to the number of the Psalms.

John of Fécamp's *Meditations*, there were added the devotional writings of St Anselm and the *Exercises* of St Gertrude, together with prayers by St Francis of Assisi, St Bonaventure, St Thomas Aquinas, and Raymond Lull. We have reliable evidence of the popularity enjoyed by these works; they were, in fact, what we should call to-day 'best sellers.'

Prayer was accompanied by gestures that were so ancient as to be considered almost obligatory.[1] The custom of turning eastward, towards Jerusalem, was still observed. Arms were stretched out so that the body formed a cross, or were raised in supplication like the *orantes* of the catacombs. There were frequent signs of the Cross, genuflexions, prostrations (known as *veniae*, i.e. afflictions); and many a statue in our cathedrals preserves the memory of these dignified postures.

Why did men pray? Chiefly to ask God's protection and benefits. The prayer of praise was not unknown, but it was less widespread than that of petition. Ulric of Strasbourg defines prayer as a 'lifting up of the mind to God as the giver of all good gifts'; and even the great mystic Hugh of St Victor explains that, although the psalms include few petitions, they are a useful form of prayer because they 'obtain so much from God.' We shall have occasion to notice other examples of this realistic outlook of the Middle Ages.

A secondary motive of prayer was man's consciousness of his own misery. John of Montmédy, analysing the two sorts of prayer, emphasizes that the prayer of praise 'is permeated with spiritual joy'; and he goes on to say that 'the prayer of petition springs from penitence.' Herein lies one of the more attractive features of medieval religion. Man felt the heavy weight of sin; mindful of his wretchedness, he humbled himself before Almighty God; and this fact lends a certain charm even to the worst of sinners. Such a one was the 'Knight of the Tub,' a nobleman who had indulged in every form of blasphemy and violence. Having sought out a hermit, he made his confession and was ordered, by way of penance, to fill a little tub with water. He tried for weeks to carry out this apparently simple task, but all in vain; no matter into what spring or well he plunged the vessel, it immediately became empty. One day, however, he let fall a tear of true contrition, and at that moment the tub was filled to overflowing! It was their sense of sin and their innate humility that brought men to repentance and confession,[2] that drove forth innumerable pilgrims on the roads, and furnished the cathedral building-sites

---

[1] St Dominic attached a good deal of importance to the externals of prayer.
[2] The penitential spirit was often carried to excess. The 'discipline' was of ancient usage; but the practice of self-flagellation in public bordered on exhibitionism. The first processions of flagellants took place in Italy, at Perugia in 1260. (*See* Chapter XIV, *infra*.)

with an endless stream of voluntary workers. Notwithstanding his faults, the medieval Christian lived in the full light of Christ.

The Holy Eucharist, strangely enough, was seldom approached by the laity, though priests communicated of necessity whenever they said Mass. In the eleventh century St Peter Damian and Gregory VII had recommended daily communion as 'a principal means of preserving chastity'; their advice went unheeded. The fourth Lateran Council (1215) imposed the obligation to confess and receive Holy Communion at least once a year, and as a general rule the faithful communicated at Easter, Pentecost, and Christmas. St Louis did so six times a year; but it was not until the fourteenth century, when the *Imitation of Christ* was published, that the Blessed Sacrament came to be looked upon as a source of strength against the powers of darkness. Surprising as this abstention from communion may be, it was a sign not of indifference but of profound respect; it was due to fear of sacrilege.

All things considered, the religious life of the common folk seems to have attained a fairly high standard, as is shown also by the custom of 'spiritual direction' which was becoming fashionable at this period. St Bernard gives it explicit approval;[1] and several Chapters of the Dominican order complained that some reverend fathers were so busy directing souls that they had time for nothing else! These facts may be accepted as evidence of an intense religious fervour.

8. THE CHRISTIAN YEAR

Spiritual life was fostered during the Middle Ages by the intellectual climate of that period. Herein modern man is at a serious disadvantage; for to-day, in almost every land, the atmosphere is laden with materialism. God is no longer welcome, unless it be surreptitiously and almost in the teeth of society. Even the most obvious traces of religion, such as the dates of public holidays, are commonly overlooked, so entirely has the world been secularized; and Yuletide revellers scarcely recognize the meaning of a feast which they celebrate with plum-pudding and champagne.

In the Middle Ages things were very different; the whole air was Christian, and no one but could feel himself wrapped round, sustained, and guided by the Faith. The day was regulated by the sound of bells, particularly by the *Angelus*, that lovely prayer which had recently been introduced. The year itself followed the liturgical cycle; holidays coincided with the great religious festivals; and work was sanctified by the religious solemnities of the guilds. Says Paul Claudel, remembering 'the latent murmurs, the eloquent silences, the inexhaustible lesson' of the French cathedrals: 'Christian soul, such is thine

[1] 'He who appoints himself his own guide will listen to a fool.'

inner world, and such thy silence.' It was not only the cathedral, but the entire social scheme, which confronted man with the truths of religion and thereby kept alive the flame of his belief. Our modern calendar bears the stamp of Christ on every page. The year was filled with Him, with reminders of His life and of His death. In December, when nature lies asleep, the Church proclaimed the coming of a Saviour who would triumph over death. The four Sundays of Advent heralded His approach; Christmas Day, marked by solemn rites, was loud with hymns of joy; and the first crib, made by St Francis of Assisi in 1223, was soon copied throughout the Christian world. The feasts of the Circumcision (1st January) and Epiphany (6th January) recalled our Lord's public manifestation, an event which was commemorated during several weeks. But then the central mystery of our Redemption became foremost in the thoughts of men. On Ash Wednesday there began a forty days' fast in memory of Christ's act of self-denial at the opening of His public ministry, and from that date the approaching drama dominated the liturgical scene. Only on the feast of the Annunciation (25th March), which was instituted in the West during this period, did the sad countenance of Mother Church light up with an angelic smile. Next came Holy Week: on Palm Sunday Jesus entered into His city; and step by step, from Wednesday evening, the faithful walked with Him towards Good Friday, a day of dereliction and overwhelming sadness. The Resurrection was accompanied with such joy and such magnificent ceremonial, that in some countries, particularly in France under the Capetian kings, Easter Sunday was observed as New Year's Day. The Paschal festivities lasted forty days and offset the sombre hues of Lent. Finally, our Lord rose into heaven, and ten days later sent the Holy Ghost at Pentecost to comfort and confirm His brethren.

The whole year was thus planned according to the festivals of the Church. Besides the major feasts of our Lord, many saints' days were kept with solemn rites, and those of our Lady took rank above them all. There was the feast of her Nativity on 8th September, the Purification, or Candlemas, on 2nd February, and the Assumption on 15th August.

These landmarks in the ecclesiastical calendar, as well as Sundays, were official days of rest. Public holidays are now regulated by the law of the land, and even when they happen to coincide with Christian festivals, as at Christmas, Easter, or Whitsun, the majority of people are ignorant of their religious origin and significance. The medieval worker, on the other hand, rested on Sunday *because that day was set apart for God*, and on certain other days *because they were appointed for the honouring of saints*. We shall have occasion to notice the importance of this fact when dealing with the Church as a social influence.

Servile work and other profane activities were forbidden on Sundays and holy days of obligation. These latter steadily increased, and a council held at Oxford in 1222 mentions fifty-three, which together with Sundays, the Ascension, and Assumption, gives a minimum total of 107 days. A reaction then set in, tending to diminish their number.

At certain times of the year, also, the duty of fasting sanctified one of man's humblest and purely animal characteristics; I mean the need of food. This venerable custom, inherited from the Jews and widely practised in the early Church, was held in great esteem. To take only one full meal a day was to deny the body for God's sake, and thereby to teach it submission to His will. Fasting was of obligation during Lent, on ember days, on the Vigils of certain feasts, and on Fridays (in commemoration of our Lord's Passion). The Advent and Saturday fasts, common in the preceding era, were gradually abandoned; but no one thought of shirking those which remained in force.

The religious framework of daily life supplied an important psychological requirement. Medieval man, though not in the least standardized, was conscious that he formed part of a whole. The monk in his monastery, the craftsman in his workshop, the burgess in his town, each one laboured for the common good of all; and this communal outlook existed likewise in the religious sphere. Unlike ourselves, every individual realized that he was not alone in the battle for salvation, but was acutely conscious of belonging to *the Church*. That consciousness was born in early Christian times; it was strengthened in the heroic age of persecution; it cemented the unity of Christendom in face of the barbarian invaders; and in the eleventh, twelfth, and thirteenth centuries it took shape in those great Christian enterprises, the Cathedral and Crusade. But the sense of solidarity with one's fellow men found its noblest utterance and deepest spiritual significance in the liturgy.

9. THE LITURGY

The offices of the Church were no less popular than the pulpit. As is still the case in certain Swiss cantons (e.g. Valais) and in French Canada, the entire population attended Mass and took part in the procession. No one, indeed, could neglect this duty without grave scandal. It was not only to Mass on Sundays and holy days of obligation that the people flocked, but to such offices as vespers which are to-day sadly neglected.

Medieval men, feeling at home in church, went there regularly; and Christians were thus brought into contact with that lofty, all-embracing expression of the faith which is the liturgy. Better than the best sermon, better than the most learned treatise, it was the liturgy that made God's presence most keenly felt.   This association of voice and gesture, wherewith the Church conducts her public worship and accompanies the most important events of private life, occupied the forefront of medieval religion.   A modern Catholic will find it almost impossible to appreciate this truth if his participation in the liturgy is confined to attendance at a late Mass on Sunday morning.

The external beauty of the liturgy formed a large part of its appeal. The gorgeous vestments, the unhurried pomp of ceremonial, the organ, and the moving simplicity of plain-chant, all these things conspired to elevate the minds and hearts of those who saw and heard them.   There, in that huge casket of stone, with coloured light pouring from the windows, how could a man not feel himself to have reached 'the heavenly Jerusalem, with walls of precious stone, adorned as a bride for her bridegroom'?[1]   And yet this outward splendour was as nothing compared with what lay beneath the words and gestures, if he would but meditate thereon.   The rites themselves were part of an age-long tradition; each time he went to Mass he was reminded of some event in sacred history or of his ancestors' loyalty to the faith. He found himself confronted with the very drama of his own salvation, with mysteries that matter more than life itself—the Incarnation, the Redemption, and the Resurrection.   It is not to be wondered at that a mystic like St Louis was so penetrated with the grandeur of the liturgy that he once fell into ecstasy while hearing Mass.

Love of the liturgy, however, went hand in hand with a good deal of carelessness; and the behaviour of priest and congregations sometimes left much to be desired.   Cats, dogs, and hawks were taken into church; men remained covered throughout the service; and the time was even spent in dubious conversation.   The Holy Sacrifice itself was in certain cases an object of blasphemous parody, like the Burgundian 'Mass of Bacchus.'   The Church had not only to combat these abuses; she had even to lay down rules for the celebration of Mass.   The presence of at least one server was required; and after 1065 no priest was allowed to say more than one Mass a day,[2] except on specified occasions, as at Christmas.   The failure of some priests to exercise their sacred office at all caused the Councils of Ravenna (1314) and Toledo (1324) to decree respectively that every priest must say Mass at least once and four times a year.   Such customs, far removed from those of our own day, show that medieval religion, for all its admirable qualities, had serious defects.   Of these we shall have more to say.[3]

---

[1] The words are used in the office for the dedication of a church.
[2] Some priests, in order to increase their income from stipends, were in the habit of celebrating twelve times a day.
[3] Chapter IV.

C*

The Roman liturgy had been accepted by the whole Latin Church during the Carolingian era, and allowed of very few exceptions. Variant forms were tolerated in a few dioceses (e.g. Milan, Lyons, and Toledo) on the grounds of immemorial custom, and the Dominicans enjoyed similar privileges. Although the main structure of the Roman rite is of great antiquity, medieval liturgists made a few additions to the missal—notably the three sequences, *Stabat Mater, Lauda Sion,* and *Dies Irae*—and assigned the final blessing to the priest instead of reserving it to the bishop as hitherto. Now that the sexes were no longer segregated, it was judged wise to abandon the kiss of peace; and the practice of genuflecting at the words 'et incarnatus est' in the Creed was taken over from St Louis, who had introduced the custom in his private chapel. The most important liturgical innovation dating from the Middle Ages was the elevation of the Host, a courteous gesture which also enabled those present to see and adore Christ's Body under its sacramental veils. This rubric was intended as a protest against the heresy of Berengar,[1] who denied the Real Presence.[2]

The beauty of the Roman rite lies in its straightforward simplicity; Oriental liturgies involve much complicated ceremonial and an air of secrecy. The Syriac, Coptic, and Byzantine rites [3] seem overcharged with symbolism and protracted ritual, which are apt to confuse the uninitiated. Moreover, the 'eikonostasis,' a screen hiding the altar from the congregation, causes the central act of the sacred drama to take place unseen, in what is known as the 'ritual of silence.' Although the hymns and introductory processions are no doubt of great beauty, they make no direct spiritual impression on the mind, evoking the eternal Logos surrounded by celestial hierarchies rather than Christ crucified. In the West, Mass was a real drama whose familiar stages all could follow and understand; and although the ceremonial has been simplified to some extent since the Middle Ages, many features of our liturgical year still preserve a strong dramatic content; those of Holy Week, for example, or the ceremonies of Christmas and Easter. The alternate responses, the chant, and even the vestments, all tend to arouse in the mind a sense of theatre; and even the sacred text lends itself directly to this treatment.

It was therefore not unnatural that, from the second half of the eleventh century, there developed a sort of dramatized liturgy. The events of Christmas, Epiphany, Holy Week, and Easter were actually

[1] See Chapter XIII and the Index under his name.
[2] On the history of the liturgy see Daniel-Rops, *Missa est* (1951). At this period also there grew up the custom of Solemn Exposition and of carrying the Blessed Sacrament in procession. The purpose in each case was to afford the congregation a better view of the Sacred Host.
[3] The Byzantine rite includes that of St Basil, that of St John Chrysostom, and a Mass of the Presanctified.

represented 'on the stage,' though a certain amount of liberty was taken with the gospel narrative in order to heighten the effect. For example, a sermon wrongly attributed to St Augustine, in which the Apostles are described as having to render an account of their conduct, gave rise to that 'drama of the prophets' which inaugurated the Christmas festivities at Saint-Martial in the diocese of Limoges. Again, to the sober account of the Magi's visit there were added many picturesque details from the Apocrypha. Nor was symbolism overlooked. The disciples at Emmaus were thought of as figures of medieval pilgrims journeying in search of God; they were dressed, as was our Lord Himself, in the familiar habit of pilgrims with hat, scrip, cockle-shell, and bourdon.

Despite their familiarity, these performances made an irresistible appeal to ordinary folk, who watched them for hours with undivided attention. The cast was composed of clerics, and each character had his traditional garments and make-up. Christ always wore a beard, a diadem, and a red robe; Moses was immediately recognizable by the horns on his brow, symbols of the beams of light; John the Baptist was invariably clothed in camel-hair; and (a lasting source of fun) St Joseph was certain to be dressed in yellow. Before long, 'stage-properties' were introduced: Balaam's ass consisted of two men hidden under a skin, which enabled the beast to speak as in the Bible; and Daniel's lions had formidable jaws that really moved. When the Magi spoke in picturesque gibberish that was supposed to be Persian, or when the little publican Zacchaeus climbed up the sycamore-tree, then the crowd would roar with laughter. But there was a solemn silence broken only by sobs as our Lord died upon the Cross.

At the end of the thirteenth century, fashions changed: the play moved from the body of the church and was acted in front of the west doors; episodes and 'effects' were multiplied; and the cast was no longer made up exclusively of clerics. The 'Mystery Plays' of the fourteenth and fifteenth centuries were on the way to becoming a reality. Social historians may discover in these facts undeniable proof of the religious origins of tragedy. The revival of the theatre, which had been buried in oblivion since the fall of the Graeco-Roman Empire, was due to the medieval Church, and is one of the most striking examples of her influence upon all forms of human activity, as well as of her astonishing creative power.

10. THE PILGRIMS

No picture of medieval Christianity is complete without some account of pilgrimages, which were among the most picturesque phenomena of that age. The custom of travelling in groups to some venerable shrine is found in all religions and in every land; it is as old as the Church herself. The Israelites, a nomad people, used to 'go up to Jerusalem' at the great festivals, walking in long files and chanting psalms. Christianity took over this custom, and from the second century onwards pious folk journeyed at considerable risk to pray at the tombs of St Peter and St Paul in Rome. In the fourth century many travelled to the Holy Land, among whom was Silvia Etheria, an enterprising Spanish nun who has left a fascinating account of her journey. Not even the tide of barbarian and Islamic invasion had prevented the satisfaction of this urge. During the whole of that unsettled period thousands of Christians were prepared to face danger in order to kneel at the Holy Sepulchre or at the 'Confession' of St Peter; and with the return of peaceful conditions pilgrimages became still more frequent.

It is hard to imagine the endless flow of those enormous caravans; indeed, such figures as we possess are wellnigh incredible. Half a million people made their way each year to Compostella. Rome was visited by more than two million pilgrims in the first Holy Year; and at no time were there fewer than 200,000 in the Eternal City. In 1064, notwithstanding that Jerusalem was then in Moslem hands, seven thousand pilgrims led by Bishop Gunther of Bamberg undertook the long, difficult journey to the Holy Places. It was considered a moral obligation to go on one of the major pilgrimages at least once in a lifetime, but many did so more than once. Blessed Thierry, abbot of Saint-Hubert in Ardenne, travelled to Rome seven times, and Geoffrey of Vêndome on no fewer than twelve occasions.[1]

God was the final cause of every pilgrimage. The journey was undertaken to obtain from Him some favour, e.g. cure from bodily sickness; to atone for some grave fault; to fulfil a sacramental penance; perhaps merely to express one's faith and happiness; or even, as in the case of Anne Vercors, to tell God of one's restlessness. All these

---

[1] The material organization of medieval pilgrimages would repay detailed study. The question of passage by sea has been discussed by the French naval historian Charles de la Roncière, and the following is his account of their embarkation. 'When a group of pilgrims arrived on the quaysides at Venice, Genoa, or Marseilles, a tremendous clamour rose from the ships, whose destination was written on a scarlet cross upon the sails. The unfortunate travellers were besieged from every side with offers and imprecations, while employees of the various shipmasters strove to obtain possession of their baggage, swore at one another, cursed their rivals, and protested their willingness to be of service. Bewildered and undecided, the pilgrims allowed themselves to be enticed by the display of dainties set out in the stern—Cretan wines and sweetmeats from Alexandria, which the captain himself handed round.' (*Histoire de la Marine française*, vol. i, p. 273). There were regular agencies for the transport of pilgrims; and on board every ship was a *cargator*, the equivalent of our purser, who sold provisions. Etymologists who trace a connection between the word *cargator* and the French *gargotier* (a bad cook) suggest a not improbable picture of conditions on board ship. The *cargator* was not to be trusted; neither he nor any member of his family was allowed to make ship's biscuit, and, in order to prevent him making a profit by issuing short rations, he was obliged on reaching port to throw overboard all unused supplies.

reasons led the 'Jacquots' or 'Jacobites' to Compostella, the 'Romieux' or 'Romites' to the Eternal City, the 'Palmers' to Jerusalem, or— more modest but no less fervent of purpose—the 'Miquelots' to Mont Saint-Michel. Pilgrimage was an act whereby a man placed himself for the time being entirely at the service of Almighty God. It was the highest form of outward prayer and penance, and the whole Christian people was held to benefit thereby: the Church militant, through its suffering *en route*; the dead, who had once travelled the same road and now waited in hope of heaven through the merits of their children; and finally the Church triumphant, in whose honour the laborious journey was made. Every pilgrim, too, was regarded as an object of God's special favour. On the tympanum at Autun Cathedral there is a Doom showing the dead rising from their graves, naked as Adam, all except two pilgrims, each of whom carries a scrip slung from his shoulder. One of these is marked with the cross of the Holy Land, the other with St James's cockle-shell. With such insigna they had no fear of Judgment Day.

Everyone, therefore, went on pilgrimage, or at least meant so to do: high and low, prelates and princes, craftsmen and labourers. There was no class distinction in that vast crowd. Nor was age a bar; for we have record of pilgrimages for twelve-year-old children and of octogenarians undaunted by the long, weary march. Difficulty and danger lay in wait for pilgrims; for, although their sacred character should have afforded them a measure of protection, there were infidel bandits always ready to attack. The long journey on foot, fatigue, and cold were themselves penitential. No doubt there were generous souls who would always welcome a Jacquot or Romite—and even kill a swan in his honour, as in the ballad of *Roland de Cambrai*. No doubt, too, the wayfarer would find shelter in the monasteries and hospices erected for that purpose by means of charitable gifts. All the same, pilgrimage was an arduous undertaking and meritorious in the sight of God.

Let us picture a man starting out on the great adventure. The time has come when he must fulfil his vow, but his wife and family view the whole business with profound mistrust, and protest against his going. Why should he? Surely God does not expect it of him. If the journey is really necessary, why not visit some place nearer home? What about Conques, Vézelay, or Le Puy? Why not take ship and go to Mont Saint-Michel? Compostella is so far away! Our 'Jacquot' takes no notice; in spirit he is already on the road. His friends have told him of the marvels he will see: the stained glass and sculpture, the huge altars, the famous statue of St James on its silver throne, the magnificent ceremonial, and, above all, the very body of the Saint 'ablaze with heavenly carbuncles, wrapped in the brightness of celestial torches.' No, he is not to be deterred. Besides, he has been to confession and has received a diploma which not only certifies that he starts at peace with God and with the Church, but will enable him on his return to use the glorious title 'Confrère of St James.' More than that, he has been received in audience by the bishop, who has given him a letter of introduction to the authorities *en route*. This will prove that he is no impostor, one of those rascals who mix with the holy company—God knows for what nefarious ends! Lastly, he has also made his Will—one never can be sure.

The pilgrim's dress is simple, as prescribed by custom. It consists of a large hat with upturned brim and a band of cockle-shells (symbolic of St James), a leather hood, a voluminous cloak, and a 'scrip' or wallet hanging from his belt. He carries a crooked staff or 'bourdon.'[1]

It is now about Eastertide; the day of departure has come, and the happy pilgrims forgather, say, at the Tour Saint-Jacques in Paris. They hear Mass, and special prayers are recited over them. The priest sprinkles them with holy water, and hands each one his staff and scrip. The remaining hours of daylight are spent in farewell visits, and at nightfall the caravan gets under way. A great shout of 'Alleluia!' goes up, and gradually there is heard along the road that inspiring hymn 'Forward, pilgrim, ever forward!'

The pilgrim routes were established by tradition. Men, women, and children travelled on foot and observed no particular order; very few were able to afford the modest luxury of a horse or donkey. They were escorted by minstrels, whose songs alternated with the pilgrims' chorus; only public penitents (recognizable by their dark gowns marked with a red cross) walked in silent prayer and meditation. The convoy moved from place to place, finding in every town some memorial of ancient belief;[2] for the map of Christendom was in their

---

[1] If he is wise, he will also have learned something about the road. There were handbooks for this purpose, ancestors of *Baedeker* and the French *Guides Bleus*. The best-known of these manuals was one, written in 1140 for pilgrims to Compostella, by Aimery Picaud of Poitou. It gave full particulars of all places of interest through which the reader would have to pass, of the difficulties he might expect to encounter, of rest houses, and danger-points. 'Travel light,' says Aimery. 'When crossing the Landes beware of bogs and horse-flies; and don't touch fried food, it's absolute poison!' He also has something to say about money, which was never safe: 'Don't be too lavish; the journey may last longer than you think. And don't hesitate to sleep out of doors with a view to economy.'

[2] It is curious to note that these Christian memorials on the great pilgrim routes were found side by side with relics of legendary heroes. In Gironde, for example, on the road to Compostella, both Roland and St Romanus were venerated at Blaye; at Bordeaux, Roland's horn was preserved in the church of St Seurin; while in the Alyscamps at Arles the first Gallic martyrs were commemorated together with the warriors who fell at Roncevaux. In Italy too, on the road to Jerusalem, there are many echoes of the *Chansons de Geste*. Thus at Modena we find a picture of King Arthur and the Knights of the Round Table; and on the façade of Verona Cathedral is a statue holding a sword upon which is carved the word 'Durandarla'—Durandal, Roland's sword.

eyes but a network of cathedrals, tombs, basilicas. These journeys lasted many weeks. Compostella was a nine months' march; Rome was not quite so far; but it sometimes took three years to reach the Holy Sepulchre.

The first great centre of pilgrimage, both in dignity and in the merit it conferred, was Jerusalem. It had enjoyed this primacy since the fourth century. The Caliph Hakim, in a fit of rage, had destroyed the church of the Holy Sepulchre and rendered travel in Palestine extremely dangerous. Even so, Jerusalem had lost none of its pre-eminence; and some bold individuals, Count Fulk of Anjou among them, had made several journeys to seek the grace of repentance—of which, it cannot be denied, they stood in urgent need. But pilgrimage to the Holy Places was still beset with difficulties in the eleventh century; for the Seljuk Turks did not hesitate, when they felt so inclined, to massacre the Christian caravans, or sell them into slavery. The indignation roused by this maltreatment of 'God's travellers' was one of the principal motives urged by the Church in support of the first crusade; and the pilgrimage remained a formidable undertaking, even after the establishment of a Christian kingdom at Jerusalem in 1099.

Having travelled across Italy by the Aemilian Way, the pilgrim embarked at Brindisi; not, however, before paying his respects to the Archangel Michael on Monte Gargano. He might, perhaps, decide to take ship at Pisa, Genoa, or Venice; but the distance was still considerable. Once on board, he was faced with a voyage of several weeks in an overcrowded vessel; and after disembarking at a Syrian port, several days' journey lay between him and his destination. But that did not matter; his joy would be all the greater when he knelt at the Holy Places mentioned in the Gospel. There was Bethlehem, where a silver star marked the exact spot of our Lord's birth; the lovely lakeside which had once heard the Master speak; and, above all, the Sepulchre where His Body had rested for three days. He would have so much to tell on his return: he would describe the basilica which was then in course of construction; he would display his precious souvenirs —a little dust from the Tomb, a spray of olive from the Garden of Gethsemane, a medal, a statuette, or better still a palm like those of which the 'palmers' wore an image round their necks.

The journey to Rome, though not so difficult, was considered almost as meritorious. It has been called the 'pilgrimage of the heart,' for a great surge of love carried faithful Christians toward the Eternal City which is the very nerve-centre of the Church. The road, however, was not without its perils; for in proportion as the pilgrims were more numerous, so did a host of robbers lie in wait for them amid the wild passes of the Alps. But such was the unending flow of travellers along every road, that St Bernard of Menthon was moved by charity to build hospices for their reception at the most dangerous points. The French pilgrims, indeed, were so many, that more than one of the routes they followed came to be known as *via francigena* or *via francesca*. In every town there were relics of the saints to venerate, famous churches to visit; but no one failed to turn aside and adore the 'Holy Face' at Lucca. This was a great statue of Christ to which many miracles were attributed; it had eyes of crystal, which gave it an appearance of awful majesty. After a journey of about 1,250 miles the travellers arrived at the summit of Monte Mario, which was also called the Mount of Joy—Montjoie of the old battle-cry. From here they could see Rome spread out at their feet. Caught up on a mighty wave of emotion at the sight of houses, palaces, churches, and vast ruins, all bathed in golden light, they intoned the famous canticle: 'Hail, Rome! mistress of the world, red with the blood of martyrs, white with the lily of virginity; be thou for ever blessed!'

The first visit was to St Peter's, the most ancient church in the city. Here was the statue of St Peter whose big toe they kissed; here was his tomb and that sublime relic, whose authenticity no one questioned, Veronica's veil, with its imprint of our Divine Lord's countenance. They might even be able to greet the Pope himself and kiss his pastoral ring. But there were other places scarcely less venerable: St Paul outside the Walls, where the Apostle was buried after his martyrdom; St John Lateran; the Church of the Holy Sepulchre, reminding them of another at Jerusalem; the Colosseum, with its memories of the early martyrs; and Santa Maria della Rotonda, the ancient Pantheon. Among some excellent guide-books, which told the pilgrim all that he should see, was the *Itinerary of Einsiedeln*. More interesting, however, was the *Complete Description of the City*; it had something to say about every monument and legend, not forgetting the lodging houses, one of which (the Albergo d'Orso) may still be seen on the banks of the Tiber.

Rome's importance as a place of pilgrimage increased steadily throughout the Middle Ages, and was linked with the growing power of the papacy. It attained its zenith in 1300, when Boniface VIII revived the old Jewish tradition of the Jubilee by proclaiming a 'Holy Year.' Responding to the Pope's invitation and the promise of special graces, pilgrims flocked to the city in their thousands. It was difficult to find accommodation for them all; and Dante, who was there, tells us that it became necessary to turn the Ponte Sant' Angelo into a one-way street! These pilgrims were drawn from every land and from every level of society. They included whole delegations representing various nations and cities, that of Florence being distinguished from the rest by its magnificence. What was the result? Evil tongues whispered that the only true beneficiaries of Holy Year were the

Roman tradesfolk; but it can hardly be denied that such a demonstration of piety must have strengthened the links of Christendom and spread devotion to the Church and her supreme head on earth.[1]

The pilgrimages to Jerusalem and Rome were based on such historical facts as the life and death of Christ, or the arrival and martyrdom of St Peter. That Compostella should have attained a position such that its pilgrimage rivalled the other two is not easy to explain. Nevertheless, it did so; and in the *Vita Nuova* Dante goes so far as to say that, 'strictly speaking, a pilgrim is one who travels to the House of St James.' It is odd that the spotlight of history should be focused on the humble fisherman of Bethsaida, son of Zebedee and brother of St John the Evangelist, who, according to the Acts, was first of the Twelve to receive the crown of martyrdom. An apocryphal work informs us that he had visited Spain as a missionary; but it was not until long after his death that his name passed into legend.

Tradition says that in the year 45 a ship from some distant land ran ashore on the coast of Galicia. On board were seven men with a cedar-wood coffin; they were disciples of St James seeking a burial place for the holy relics of their master. Near by was a city surrounded with strong walls and ruled over by a Druid princess known as the 'She-Wolf.' These seven Christians endured many trials, during which the terrible princess was on the point of denouncing them to the Roman governor; but at last, overwhelmed by numerous divine prodigies, she submitted, received baptism, and offered the disciples two bulls to draw the hearse, together with some land on which to build a tomb. Such was the supposed origin of the cult of St James in Galicia. The place was called Compostella, 'Field of the Star,' because the tomb, which had disappeared during the barbarian invasions, was rediscovered by a hermit who dreamed that he was led to it by a star. It is impossible to understand how such traditions could set up so powerful a wave of devotion, unless we associate the pilgrimage with historical fact—the determination of the Christians of Spain to rid their country of the Moslems. St James was reported to have appeared on the battle-field of Clarijo and to have led the Christian charge, on which account he was styled 'Matamore,' slayer of the Moors. There can be no doubt but that the pilgrimage to Compostella was part of the Church's keen interest in Spain, an interest which resulted in the Reconquista. Though it originated in the ninth century,[2] it was not organized on any large scale until 340 years later,

---

[1] The Jubilee of 1300 initiated a custom which has lasted ever since. In 1343 Clement VI decreed that the celebration of Holy Year should take place every fifty years as from 1350. In 1389 Urban VI reduced the interval to thirty-three years in memory of the years of our Lord's earthly life.

[2] The stone sarcophagus had been identified as that of St James about 870; the first great pilgrimage, led by Gottschalk, took place in 950.

by Diego Gelmirez, first archbishop of the new see; but it remained popular throughout the Middle Ages.

Pilgrims came in thousands to Compostella from every part of the Western world. They included Germans, Flemings, English, Poles, and Hungarians; but so numerous were the French, that here, as in Italy, the highways along which they travelled were known as 'French roads.' Four main routes, on all of which there were regular stopping places, led across France. The first of these, starting from the Tour St Jacques in Paris, ran via St Jacques-du-Haut-Pas to Tours, where it was joined by another road from Chartres. The Burgundian route

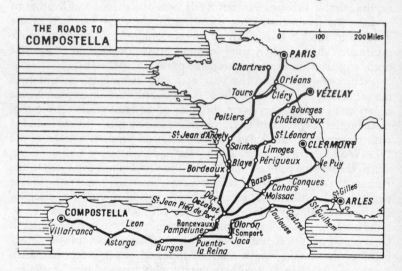

commenced at Vézelay; that of Auvergne at Clermont; while the southern route ran from the Alyscamps at Arles, with Toulouse as its most important halt. All these roads met at Puenta la Reina south of the Pyrenees, from which place the pilgrims journeyed to Compostella by way of Burgos, Leon, and Villafranca. Everywhere there are reminders of their passage, and the Jacobites appear in many a sculptured group, wearing the cockle-shell badge. To the ritual cry of 'Outrée! Susée!' they moved in long columns across scorched plains and frozen plateaux.

Jerusalem, Rome, and Compostella, then, were the three main centres of pilgrimage, but there were others almost as important. Such was the shrine of St.Thomas at Canterbury and that of the Magi at Cologne. Places of less renown also drew enormous crowds. The relics of St Mary Magdalen were believed to have been hidden by St Maximin at Saint-Baume in Provence. No one doubted this tradition after 1279, when Charles of Salerno exhumed a body whose tongue was found to be incorrupt, and the place was visited by popes and princes. There was another shrine of the Magdalen at Vézelay in Burgundy, where some of her bones and hair were said to be preserved. The tomb of St Martin at Tours enjoyed considerable prestige; it was a popular place of pilgrimage, especially on the anniversary of his death (11th November) and on the feast of the translation of his relics (4th July). In Normandy, on the very borders of Brittany, stood Mont Saint-Michel, the inviolable sanctuary of that archangel who is represented in the Apocalypse as protecting the woman's Son against the fury of a seven-headed dragon. He was the patron saint of warriors, and the 'first baron of France'; [1] but the pilgrims who flocked to his chosen isle included artisans, merchants, and even children (the 'Pastoureaux' of 1333), all of whom were fanatically proud of their title, 'miquelots.' In Italy the most popular places of pilgrimage were associated with St Francis, particularly Assisi with San Damiano and the Carceri near by. There were also Monte Alverno, where he received the stigmata, Gubbio, and indeed countless places immortalized by some event in his life.

Innumerable shrines, of course, were dedicated to our Lady: Notre-Dame of Chartres, a venerable foundation in whose crypt stood the Virgin of the Underworld; Notre-Dame of Puy, built to commemorate a miraculous cure; Notre-Dame of Fourvière, set on a hill-top over Lyons; Notre-Dame of Garde, erected by Peter of Accoules about 1210 as a spiritual 'lighthouse' above the port of Marseilles; Notre-Dame of Liesse, the glory of north-eastern France, which was built by the crusaders and became famous when our Lady helped Enguerrand de Coucy to find his two little sons who had been kidnapped by robbers. Notre-Dame of Dusenbach and Notre-Dame of Marienthal were centres of devotion in Alsace. In the south-west, Notre-Dame of Rocamadour, Notre-Dame of Font-Romen, and Notre-Dame of Bécharram were forerunners of Lourdes. The ancient Norman sanctuary of Notre-Dame de la Délivrande was not far from Auray. Here the shrine of St Anne did honour likewise to Mary, whom the Bretons venerated in person at Rumengol, Folgoat, and elsewhere.

These international, national, provincial, and local pilgrimages constituted, in the words of Jacques Madaule,[2] 'a vast arterial system which kept alive the people's fervour and exerted an influence even upon those who never took part in them. The unity of Christendom was evident in the perpetual movement which inspired artists and craftsmen, and provided the minstrels with their songs.' The pilgrimages, indeed, exemplify the driving force of medieval religion,

---

[1] The three fleur-de-lis appear in the arms attributed to St Michael.
[2] *Pèlerins comme nos pères*, 1950.

with its passionate craving for the infinite and its intolerance of boundaries.

11. The Spiritual Armoury of the Church

The outstanding characteristic of the Middle Ages was its unanimous, living, and inspiring faith; a faith whose virtue persisted in spite of blemishes, a faith which explains the determining influence of the Church upon the social and political history of that age. We cannot fail to recognize that secular and ecclesiastical history were more closely linked during these three centuries than in the barbarian epoch.

How was it possible for an essentially spiritual power to dominate the temporal scene? The answer is not far to seek if we bear in mind the unanimous acceptance of the faith. What were the psychological foundations of ecclesiastical authority? First, respect for God's representative on earth. When Pope Innocent IV, speaking as Vicar of Christ, declared all secular power subject to his own, 'as the soul is superior to the body, and the sun to the moon,' he was merely giving utterance to an idea that had long been admitted throughout the Western world.

Moreover, public opinion tended to equate, if not actually to identify, obedience to the law of the land with submission to the law of God. Just as heresy, an offence against religion, was considered tantamount to the civil crime of treason, so, conversely, many misdemeanours which would to-day incur penalties in the civil courts were punished by ecclesiastical tribunals with a 'penance,' e.g. an order to go on pilgrimage. There are few offences in the modern calendar which even a professed Christian would consider as involving sin; but in the Middle Ages life's drama was played out on a stage whose limits were defined by God Himself, and those who overstepped the mark incurred religious guilt. The Church, in fact, controlled the entire mechanism of society; and it was this universal recognition of ecclesiastical authority which had enabled her, since barbarian times, to operate in the twofold character of a spiritual and temporal ruler. The latter may be seen in her creation of new institutions and in her contact with the civil powers; her spiritual function is more difficult to analyse, for it concerned the souls of men. At all events, this dual role produced, as it were, a distinctive human type, a civilization which, in spite of its undeniable weaknesses, does honour to our race.

How, then, did the Church enforce her authority? By means of religious sanctions; those who disobeyed her precepts met with public or with private chastisement, which at that time it was very difficult to escape. But if the Church could order pilgrimages, scourging, alms-giving, fasting, or prayers, she had equal power to mitigate the severity of justice.   For our Lord had said: 'Whatsoever you shall bind or loose on earth shall be bound or loosed in heaven.'   Hence the principle of substitution, which corresponded more or less to the German *Wehrgeld*: a sinner might avoid the full rigour of the law by the merits of a third person, or by almsgiving.   Moreover in the eleventh century the Church began to grant 'indulgences,' i.e. the partial or plenary remission of canonical penances, to anyone who rendered outstanding service to the Christian cause, or even, in certain circumstances, gave evidence of extraordinary piety.   One could, for example, cite numerous instances of an indulgence granted for helping in the construction of cathedrals and hospitals, bridges and dikes, for joining the crusade or fighting with the armies in Spain, or for confessing at some venerable shrine.   It is also known that during Holy Year, in 1300, a plenary indulgence was granted to all pilgrims to the Eternal City who complied with the regulations governing visits to the basilicas, the recitation of certain prayers, and reception of the sacraments.

The execution of an ecclesiastical sentence depended upon no *direct* means of coercion.   The Church had no police force; but she could generally rely upon the support of the civil authorities, since they too were subject to her commands.   Her immediate weapons were exclusively spiritual; that they were effective was due to the faith of her subjects, who believed in hell fire and dreaded the awful consequences of Heaven's wrath.

No one, not even the most hardened sinner, was undaunted by the tide of sacred eloquence.   When a preacher in the pulpit named the guilty person and threatened him with eternal damnation, the most cynical became uneasy.   'Ye are devouring wolves,' thundered Jacques de Vitry to some looting lords; 'ay, and in hell ye'll howl like wolves!'   To Peter de Courtenay, who had insulted the Bishop of Auxerre, Innocent III publicly addressed this awful warning: 'Your conscience will bear witness against you.   Bound hand and foot, you will be cast into exterior darkness to be consumed by the avenging flames.   In vain then will you plead with the Bishop of Auxerre to dip the end of his finger into water and refresh your tongue.   Wretched man, what will you say in your defence when you hear the voice of Christ: "Whatsoever you have done to the least of these my little ones, you have done it unto me"?'

Besides private admonitions of this kind, there were three public sanctions.   The first was the *anathema*, or solemn curse, which was directed against the malefactor in person and did not affect his relations with other men.   Here is the sentence pronounced by the Chapter of Saint-Julien at Brionde upon a thief who stole the priceless reliquary given them by Charlemagne: 'Cursed may he be in life and death, eating and drinking, standing and sitting! May his life be short, and his goods pillaged by his enemies! May an incurable paralysis assail his eyes, his brow, his beard(?), his throat, his tongue, his mouth, his neck, his breast, his lungs, his ears . . .' (and so on for four more lines). 'May he be as a weary stag pursued by hunters; may his children be made orphans, and his wife a demented widow . . . !' The medieval outlook was such that the poor fellow could not help feeling somewhat anxious as to his future.

Excommunication and *Interdict* involved serious consequences in the social and political order. The first of these measures deprived the criminal of association with his fellow Christians. The Church rejected him, and, since the social link was essentially religious, he no longer enjoyed a place in the community. His wife could leave him; his children could defy his orders with impunity. His servants fled the house; and if his property were threatened, no one would lift a finger to protect it, for he was now under the ban of society. The dramatic ceremonial of excommunication was designed to impress the victim with his unhappy state. It was a kind of burial service, read over a living being, and intended not to open for him the gates of heaven, but to bind him fast in death; and no Christian could remain unmoved as the black-clad priests blew out their candles, pronouncing meanwhile the culprit's name. And these measures applied no less if the excommunicated person were the greatest monarch on earth. If he entered one of his cities the churches were closed, the bells were silent, and the streets empty; he might, indeed, have been the plague.

An interdict was even worse, applying as it did to a whole region; and if the guilty party were a king, the entire realm suffered in consequence of his sin. Not only were the churches closed, but the crosses reversed, and no sacrament, except baptism, might be administered. There were no marriages, no burials with religious rites; and since the Church at that time was the equivalent of our public registrar, the very bases of legal existence were thus undermined. Social life came to a standstill, for there were no Sundays or feast days; and the people found it a heavy burden to be deprived of goods which they valued more than life itself. On all sides there were murmurs of rebellion; and if the guilty ruler would not submit, his subjects threw off their allegiance. No wonder that these sanctions proved effective.

Against whom, and in what circumstances were they employed? High and low were subject to excommunication for such crimes as unlawful marriage, brigandage, physical violence upon the persons of clerics, and offences against the law of nations. Among numerous sovereigns who incurred the penalty were Philip I of France, Godfrey of Lorraine, Philip Augustus, Louis VII, and Alfonso IX of Leon. Interdict was applied in cases of recidivism and categorical refusal to obey the laws of the Church. Louis VII, John 'Lackland,' and Frederic II of Hohenstaufen were all punished in this way. It was extremely rare that persons so condemned did not eventually come to a better frame of mind.[1] Their submission might not always be prompt, and might even be accompanied at first with mental reservation; but in the last resort the sense of their own interests and the desire for pardon combined, as in the case of Henry IV at Canossa, to bring them to their knees.

12. SUMMARY

So long as men believed firmly in the gospel teaching, society was dominated by the Christian faith. Practically no aspect of the Middle Ages can be properly understood except by reference to Christian principles. Everyone felt himself to be 'dyed in Christ's blood'; every facet of human life, indeed, bore the sign of the Cross.

Political organization was inseparably bound up with Christianity; for even the feudal chain itself was forged on the anvil of religion in the form of an oath taken on the Holy Gospels. The successors of Charlemagne owed their prestige as delegates of God on earth to their coronation, the repetition of that august ceremony first performed on Christmas Eve in the year 800; and the 'Most Christian Kings' of France, Spain, and England were anointed for no other reason than to lay solemn emphasis upon the fact that they owed their power to God rather than to the accident of birth or the fortune of war. This religious element which underlay the structure of civil authority was the Church's justification for intervening on the political plane, and for exercising her control in matters which might have seemed to lie outside her province.

In the social sphere, Christianity assigned each grade its function in the common task, enabled the lowly to ascend the ladder of success, and relieved the destitute through charitable works, thereby saving them from desperation and rebellion. Christianity alone, we might almost say, stood for the principles of social justice.

Economic life itself was subject to the immediate control of Christian morality, and not on the material plane alone. It is true that the monasteries were centres of production and exchange; and the rising fabric of the cathedrals was the most evident sign of prosperity. But the Church's mistrust of wealth, her condemnation of usury, and her idea of a 'fair wage' produced a spiritual outlook quite different from ours, an outlook whose consequences in the practical affairs of

---

[1] There were cases, however, in which ecclesiastical leaders perished for having used these spiritual arms. Thus, in 1220, Bishop Robert de Meung was assassinated by a knight whom he had excommunicated.

life were immense, notwithstanding widespread indifference to her teaching.

This leads us to the moral influence of Christianity, a decisive factor in the Middle Ages. Men's lives were governed by the faith, by the Ten Commandments, and by the precepts of the Church. Christ's representatives on earth had never ceased from the beginning to insist upon the principles of perfection; and in spite of error, excess, and outright transgression, Christianity had kept alive the highest standards of conduct by imposing on all alike an irrefutable code of morality.

The catholicity of the Church roused in mankind that longing for expansion—that resolute determination in God's cause, which later manifested itself in the Spanish Reconquista, in the missions of St Francis, Raymond Lull, and John of Plan-Carpin, but above all in the crusade, that wonderful epic renewed time and again during a period of two hundred years.

The Church was also the light and guide of man's intelligence; for, as St Bernard says, 'The Word was made flesh and dwelt amongst us; ay, and in our memory and in our thought.' It was Christian doctrine that supplied the theses of philosophy and poetry, that inspired all that was best in the spiritual domain. Nor need we dwell upon its creative function in the realm of art; it is demonstrated before our very eyes by the cathedral, an unchallengeable fruit of faith, 'a great ship towering to the sky.'

Such, then, was medieval faith, and such its works. But we must do more than analyse its several elements; the limbs are not the living body. We must try to see Christianity at work in the stream of life, to understand its influence upon those who for three centuries bore witness for mankind before the Lord. It is difficult to choose one from among so many whose sole purpose was to 'seek the kingdom of God and His justice,' and who, according to the promise, were endowed with gifts that gave them power to determine the fate of their contemporaries.

In choosing St Bernard of Clairvaux, I do so not because I consider him in every way superior to men like St Francis and St Dominic, not because I regard him as having left a deeper mark upon the Church, but because he appears to sum up in himself those numerous aspects under which medieval Christianity is revealed. He laboured with pre-eminent success in many walks of life; and so well does he embody the aspiration of the Middle Ages, that his personality may be taken as representative of the whole epoch.

CHAPTER III

SAINT BERNARD OF CLAIRVAUX

1. THE CALL OF CHRIST

NORTH of Dijon stands the ridge of Fontaines, a spur of Mons Affricus upon which Caesar once encamped his legions. Although not very high, it is fairly steep; from its summit one obtains a bird's-eye view of the Saône valley, the Jura mountains, and, far away on the horizon, the gleaming Alpine snows. A little to the south-west are the hills of Burgundy with their famous vineyards—Richebourg, Pommard, and Corton. But the young man who looked down from his father's terraces upon this countryside in the late summer of 1111 was interested not so much in the splendid panorama, with its harmonious blend of mountain-range and valley, as in a dark forest-patch which concealed a monastery.

He was just twenty-one years old, having been born in 1090, third of the seven sons of Tescelin, lord of Fontaines, and of Aleth, daughter of the powerful lord of Montbard. Both families belonged to the Burgundian nobility; and through his mother, who was descended from the counts of Tonnarre, he had inherited some ducal blood. His ancestry, of which modesty never permitted him to boast, explains some of his outstanding characteristics: his impulsiveness, his courage in face of danger, and his outward bearing, which was ever that of a true knight.

Tescelin was a prominent figure in Burgundy, that region of sharp contrasts, and synthesis of the many diverse elements which go to make up France.[1] He seems to have owned large estates, and to have held

[1] The role of Burgundy has been well described by Pierre Gaxotte in his *Histoire des Français* (Paris, 1950, vol. i, p. 247): 'I would draw attention to one fact of historical geography: the two monastic capitals of Cluny and Citeaux are situated in Burgundy. Is this a mere coincidence? It may be; but the coincidence enables us to understand the soul and nature of that province. It is a region of varied characteristics, a cross-roads, a land of highways, a place of passage and encounter. It is quite the reverse of a barrier, uniting far more than it divides; and the peoples of the West have felt themselves in Burgundy to be on common ground. In this sense it is the key-point of France, whose geographical and historical importance lies in the easy access it affords between the Mediterranean, the Channel, and countries bordering the North Sea. If Burgundy had remained outside the French kingdom, France would not have played so decisive a part in the destinies of Europe. As it was, there were few areas of Christendom so well suited to become a centre of the apostolate, a centre from which men and new ideas were to radiate in all directions.' This observation should not be forgotten when considering St Bernard, a Burgundian who was at once the greatest Frenchman of his age, perhaps the greatest Christian, and the most influential figure of medieval Europe.

high office at the court of Duke Eudes; at all events he brought up his children according to the most lofty ideals, and, above all, set before them the example of his own unblemished life.

Bernard's mother, Aleth, was not only a saint, but a beautiful woman

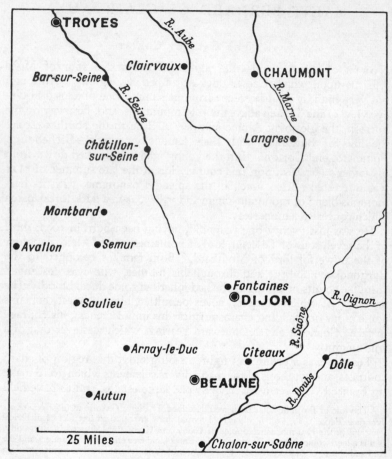

Cîteaux and Neighbourhood

and perfect mistress of a home. Fulfilling with grace and dignity the duties of her rank, she never disdained more humble tasks about the scullery or kitchen; and her charity to the poor was boundless. Her children could not, in fact, have had a more accomplished mother. If she entertained a secret preference for one, it was for her third son, Bernard. One of her biographers relates that while carrying this child in her womb, Aleth had a dream: she saw a white puppy barking furiously, and recognized it as a sign that her child was destined to become a famous preacher of God's word. This charming story is found also in the lives of St Stephen Harding and St Dominic; it need be taken no more seriously than the honey-bees on Plato's lips.

When the time came for her sons to begin their studies, Aleth moved to Châtillon-sur-Seine, where her family owned a house, and where there was a celebrated capitular school attached to the church of Saint-Vorles in the diocese of Langres. If one may judge a master by his pupils, the canons regular who taught young Bernard must have been excellent of their kind; 'for nowhere else could he have acquired that clear, incisive style, which makes him one of the most charming and original Latin prose-writers of the Middle Ages.'[1] At Châtillon he followed what we should call 'secondary studies.' Besides the 'trivium,' which included grammar, rhetoric, and dialectic, he read and expounded Horace, Virgil, Ovid, Cicero, Lucan, Statius, Boethius, and, of course, the Fathers of the Church, especially St Augustine. He did little in the way of higher studies (the *quadrivium*), excepting music; his biographer, however, assures us that at Saint-Vorles he proved himself an attentive scholar, a retiring but obedient pupil, and a friend of delicate susceptibilities. His love of solitude was already apparent, and he was an eager student of Holy Scripture.

Bernard returned to Fontaines in time to be present at his mother's deathbed, and he learned from her one final lesson. Knowing that her end was near, Aleth wished to die in absolute simplicity. She forbade the curtailment of some parochial festivities which had been arranged, and extended the usual invitation for the clergy to come and dine at the castle. Having received extreme unction and viaticum, she made the responses to the Litany of the Saints, and, as the prayer concluded, fell asleep in Christ. No young man could forget such a scene.[2]

In his twenty-second year, Bernard was a noble figure of manhood: slender and dignified, with deep blue eyes that were full of gentleness. His broad forehead proclaimed the keenness of his intellect; and his contemporaries recognized in him that distinguished bearing possessed by most men in whom physical beauty is allied with greatness of soul. Despite these natural gifts, however, there was no trace of arrogance or vanity. The passing years had changed his youthful shyness to that 'extraordinary reserve' of which one biographer speaks, but which never prevented him from asserting his

---

[1] Étienne Gilson,
[2] Aleth richly deserved the honour paid to her by St Bernard's successors when, in 1250, her body was moved from the crypt of St Benignus at Dijon to their abbey church. Her reputation, which rivals that of Blanche of Castile (a lady of far different temperament), has been honoured by the Church with the title 'Blessed.'

authority whenever circumstances required.   He was gentle, modest, and refined; so refined, indeed, that the least impropriety touched him on the raw.   But a modest exterior concealed a soul of fire which no fetters could restrain.   Though the world had many snares for a young man thus endowed by nature and by grace, his biographers are no doubt guilty of some exaggeration when they tell, for instance, of a lady introducing herself into Bernard's bed, or of Bernard throwing himself into the icy waters of a lake in order to subdue temptation excited by the mental image of a girl.   These tales were invented to illustrate the gravity of the danger to which he was exposed; but the truth seems to have been less romantic, the struggle of a more interior kind.

Intellectual temptations are the worst that can assail a brilliant youth; they are not conquered by cold baths.   Bernard was torn between the attraction of profane studies and his growing preoccupation with things divine, a conflict in which the warrior-blood of Tescelin may have played some part.   For a while he suffered the torments of uncertainty; but having confided in his uncle Gaudry, a man of profound insight, he was convinced that God called him to join the company of those who had abandoned all things for Christ's sake.

At this juncture fresh difficulties arose from without.   It was not the first or the last time that a young man in search of his true vocation has found the decision complicated by parental opposition.   Should he go to Germany and continue his studies?   Why not allow his father's influence to obtain for him some lucrative situation half-way between religion and the world?   During those long hours on the terrace at Fontaines, he stood gazing down upon the dense forest, seeing in his mind's eye the humble dwelling of the monks.

In order to appreciate the spiritual conflict whose issue was to determine a soul's fate, we should remember that it was fought out in the unsettled years of youth.   And even when the decision had been reached, Bernard's life continued to the end a battle-field.   He would always have to choose between contraries; there were no half measures and no compromise.

The spring of 1112 was a period of uncertainty and wretchedness, through which every great soul must pass, and from which it cannot emerge except by the narrow gate of an irrevocable choice.   On one side there was 'divine discontent,' and on the other a thousand contrary aspirations, a thousand hopes, upon which he would have to turn his back.   He must decide one way or the other, and accordingly set out for Cîteaux.[1]   Bossuet, in a famous passage of the *Panegyric*, has

[1] 'The Lord spoke to the heart of a young man named Bernard, and although he was young, noble, refined, and learned, he conceived so great a fire of divine love, that, despising all the pleasures and delights of the world, no less than ecclesiastical dignities, he proposed in the fervour of his soul to embrace the rigorous life of the Cistercians.' (*Great Exordium of the Cistercian Order.*)

depicted Bernard at this time. 'Behold a young man in his twenty-second year, filled with ardour, impatience, and the impetuosity of desire! That force, that vigour, that hot, boiling blood, like a heady wine, allows him no rest or relaxation.' Others may turn the restlessness of youth to very different ends; Bernard realized that, since Christ had called him, his gifts would run to seed unless he employed them for the one purpose that ultimately matters. He therefore resolved the forces of contradiction that raged within him by embracing the folly of the Cross.

Fourteen years earlier, on 21st March, Palm Sunday and the feast of St Benedict, a group of novices, moved by the spirit of reform, had left the Cluniac abbey of Molesmes for a dreary solitude among the *cistels* or reeds of the Saône, and established a house of new observance, Cîteaux.[1] Since 1098 the foundation had managed to survive under the direction of St Robert, St Alberic, and St Stephen Harding; but they had had the utmost difficulty in obtaining vocations and providing for their material wants. In 1112 this first Cistercian community deserved its reputation for terrible austerity and extreme poverty which bordered upon destitution, and in these circumstances Tescelin's resistance is not hard to understand; a monastery where the brethren lived like serfs at forced labour, digging the ground and clearing drains, seemed at variance with a nobleman's ambition for his son.

But St Bernard now revealed that extraordinary power of persuasion which characterized his entire life. He enlisted the support of his uncle Gaudry, who afterwards followed him into the cloister; and every one of his brothers was gradually won over to his project. Most of them were soldiers, and one was married; but Bernard predicted that God would contrive a means to gain them all. Gerard was wounded in battle; at the sight of his blood he cried out, as if baptized again: 'Henceforward I am a monk of Cîteaux!' Guy, the young husband, left his wife, who in turn took the veil with their two daughters. There was left only Nivard, the youngest, who at fifteen was below the canonical age for admission. 'See how rich you'll be,' said his elder brothers, referring to the inheritance which they left behind. 'What, you take heaven and leave me the earth?' replied the boy; 'I won't agree to any such arrangement.' And later on he too left for Cîteaux. Tescelin was powerless to stem the tide, and only warned his sons: 'Don't overdo it. I know you so well, it will be difficult to restrain your zeal.'[2]

In April 1112 a troop of about thirty knights (for many of their friends had followed the example of the young men from Fontaines) knocked at the gate of Cîteaux. 'What do you ask?' inquired the

---

[1] We shall study the origins of the Cistercian order in the next chapter.
[2] Tescelin himself subsequently joined the Order.

abbot, Stephen Harding.   And Bernard, in the name of all, fell on his knees and answered in the ritual formula: 'The mercy of God and of the Order.'

2. THE MONK

On entering Cîteaux, Bernard experienced that almost indescribable gladness which reaches to the very roots of a man's being when he has discovered his true calling.   From the first he delighted in the stern asceticism of the new observance.   In accordance with the Holy Rule, he underwent a year's novitiate, although there could be no doubt as to his vocation.   Those first twelve months were not so much a period of physical testing as a spiritual apprenticeship, during which there was born in him a craving that was never satisfied until his death. He prayed unceasingly, and devoted much time to scriptural and patristic literature.   'I used in those days' he said in later life, 'to gather and set up in my heart a sheaf made of our Lord's sufferings, His agony and all His bitterness of soul.'

One fact stands out: Bernard was a monk before all else.   Notwithstanding long journeys, arduous political negotiations, the clash of speculative ideas, and the power and glory of this world, he remained always a monk.   Titles and honours, even the tiara itself, were offered to him; but he refused them all, preferring the humble dignity of a Cistercian.   'St Bernard was no mere writer locked away in his own individuality; he was a monk in a community of monks, praying as they prayed, working as they worked, adhering strictly to the spirit of the Rule and all that it prescribed.' [1]

So, at the age of twenty-two, Bernard was a monk—for ever.   He had donned the plain knee-length tunic of serge and the white woollen cowl, whose hood protected his shaven head against the sun and rain. In his humility he desired nothing better than to live as the most obscure member of the flock; but this was not to be for very long.

One might almost say that Bernard's arrival had attracted God's attention to Cîteaux; for after a somewhat precarious existence the community started rapidly to increase, and twelve months later had grown so large that it was able to found La Ferté, followed by Pontigny, in 1113.   Young Bernard had brought new blood into the Order; his holiness and intellectual gifts endowed him with qualities of leadership that were recognized by all.   When, therefore, in 1115, the Count of Troyes invited the Cistercians to establish a house in his territory, Bernard was made superior of the little community which set out for a high plateau near the headwaters of the Aube.   He was no more than twenty-five years of age, and his appointment might have seemed

[1] V. Berlière, *L'Ascèse bénédictine,* page 101.

unwise. But the selection was that of no less a man than Stephen Harding, and bore witness to the qualities of Aleth's son.

The foundation of this new monastery was the work of several years. The twelve monks from Cîteaux reached their destination towards the end of June 1115, and chose an extensive clearing in the woods at a place called Val d'Absinthe, to which they gave the beautiful name Clairvaux. A cemetery was marked out, an altar set up, and some huts erected. William of Champeaux, Bishop of Châlons-sur-Marne, approved the foundation and raised Bernard to the priesthood. Before long, permanent buildings began to rise, simple and devoid of ornament. There was nothing on the walls, not even on those of the church, and no lamp hung in the sanctuary. The refectory was unpaved, and narrow windows let in a few rays of light. The dormitory was like a row of coffins, for the beds were mere boxes consisting of four planks. As for the abbot's cell, it was a cupboard under the stairs, illuminated by a wretched slit, a hollow in the wall to serve as seat of government.

Bernard had acted upon our Lord's advice and entered by the narrow gate. To conquer his animal nature, according to the precept of St Paul, was in his view the first and indispensable stage on the road to heaven. The monastic vocation involved a total sacrifice: a life of renunciation, fasting, work, and perpetual self-denial. The monastery was a school of sanctity where every monk must forget himself for love of God.

Bernard was to lead this sacrificial existence to the very last. In spite of his exhausting labours, he practised the most extraordinary forms of austerity, which soon began to undermine his health. In the early days of Clairvaux the diet consisted of nothing but bread made of barley, millet, or vetch, together with boiled nettle-leaves, roots, and beechmast. Salt and oil were the only seasoning. It is not to be wondered at that a regime of this kind proved too much for a young man whose health had never been robust. Since Bernard was unwilling to submit to treatment, William of Champeaux intervened, and the chapter was requested to relieve the abbot of his duties for one year so that he might rest. But the doctor engaged to look after him was no better than a quack, whose 'remedies' only increased the suffering of his unfortunate patient; and it was said that the dishes ordered for the sick man were so horrible that they would have turned a healthy stomach. That, however, did not deter the abbot from accepting them with perfect indifference.[1] So far from improving his health, his physical condition deteriorated, and he remained an invalid all his

---

[1] One painful detail will give some idea of St Bernard's constant weakness: whenever he occupied the abbatial chair, a hole was dug in the ground so that he could relieve an irresistible impulse to vomit.

life. It might, indeed, have been said of him, in the words of St Paul, that God confounds the strong by the weakness of His saints.

A man who had obtained such mastery of himself could not but influence others, and there was no one at Clairvaux who did not hold him in admiration. He had proved himself a leader at the age of twenty-one, and a leader he remained throughout his life. He looked upon his exalted situation as one more reason for taxing his own strength; and he never failed to practise that 'purity of heart,' that 'ever right intention,' that determination to set a high example, which typify the religious superior as described in his own sermons.

It was to be expected that one so eager to triumph over the limitations of human nature would demand much of his subjects, and might perhaps require too much. He laid a heavy burden on himself, and there can be no doubt that his monks loved him in return. He spoke of them as a mother of her children, and he used no metaphorical language when he said that they were dearer to him than his own heart. It is impossible to read without emotion those letters which he wrote to the community at Clairvaux, who were always foremost in his thoughts: 'If you find my absence hard to endure, yours is still harder for me to bear. Your lot and mine can never be the same; for whilst you are deprived of me alone, I long for each and all of you.'

But it was not for their sake or for his own that Bernard held his sons so dear. It was for God. The happiness he desired for them was such as will never fade. He asked of them the absolute oblation of their instincts, pleasures, and personal tastes, admitting frankly that the effort was 'above unaided human strength, uncommon, and even contrary to nature.' But the real difficulty in these cases is to see the line where excess begins and where rigour can turn only to frustration. Did the Abbot of Clairvaux overstep that mark?

At first, yes. Seeing in the principle of absolute self-renunciation the only means of achieving the necessary 'reform' of the Church, Bernard imposed upon his monks an existence of undue hardship. St Francis of Sales, who wrote on the subject with his usual perspicacity, says that 'so keenly did he spur these poor aspirants to perfection, that in the endeavour to get them there he merely held them back; for they lost heart, finding themselves driven so hard up the steep and narrow slope.' But Bernard was far too intelligent not to detect faint-heartedness among his own. He questioned himself, asked the advice of his friend, William of Champeaux, and realized that he had gone too far. Some years after the foundation of Clairvaux he discovered the happy medium between extreme asceticism and the requirements of human nature, and this was later embodied in the *Charter of Charity*. St Francis of Sales says that he became 'gentle, amiable, gracious, and condescending—all things to all men in order that he might gain all to Christ.' It is easy to understand that material conditions in the monasteries under Bernard's crozier would have terrified most of our contemporaries!

The marvel is (and it demonstrates the medieval thirst for God) that Bernard's reputation for austerity, far from driving away souls, drew them to him in hundreds. Clairvaux exercised an enormous attraction almost from the date of its foundation. In 1116 the school at Châlons-sur-Marne was half emptied by departures for the Val d'Absinthe. Next came a Benedictine from Chaise-Dieu, followed by the canons regular of Honicourt. Clairvaux might have been described as a heavenly ambush from which Bernard struck down, one after the other, a highwayman, a party of knights on their way to a tourney, as well as numerous monks and priests. Of the saint's family, there now remained in the world only his sister, Humbeline. One day, accompanied by a brilliant retinue, she came to see her brother. Struck by the poverty of the conventual buildings, and suddenly disgusted with her own absurd luxury, she cried out: 'I am nothing but a sinner; but it was for sinners that Jesus died. Bernard may despise my body, but not my soul. Let him come, let him command: I will obey. . . .'

Bernard had but to leave the walls of Clairvaux for this round-up of souls to assume even more astonishing dimensions. His radiance spread everywhere. He appeared, he spoke; and, as at the call of that magic flute in the German fable, thousands were spellbound. Wibald, abbot of Stavelot, has described him preaching: '. . . his visage pale, emaciated by fatigue and fasting, seeming almost ethereal, and so impressive that the mere sight of him convinced his hearers before he had even opened his mouth.' Or again: '. . . his deep emotion, his incomparable art (fruit of long exercise), his clear voice, his gestures always appropriate to his words.'

The result was 'a miraculous draught repeated ever and again.' When he preached at St Quentin, thirty members of his audience begged to accompany him. He visited the students at Paris, and twenty of them left Mont Saint-Geneviève for the Val d'Absinthe. His renown crossed the Channel, and English postulants soon began to arrive at Clairvaux, where the brethren included not a few illustrious persons. Henry, brother of the King of France, came to ask Bernard's advice, but dismissed his retinue and embraced the austere conventual life, as did Philip, Archdeacon of Liége, and Alexander, a canon of Cologne, who later became abbot of Cîteaux (c. 1167). When St Bernard died there were 700 monks at Clairvaux.

Nor was that all. Clairvaux had sown as well as she had reaped. The first daughter-house was established at Trois-Fontaines in the diocese of Châlons (1118); it was followed soon afterwards by Fontenay near Montbard, and Foigny near Vervins. More distant

D

regions too were colonized: Igny in Champagne, Boumont in Vaud, Eberbach near Mainz on the Rhine, Chiaravalle in Italy, and Fountains in England.   By 1153 there were 160 offshoots of Clairvaux, some of them in Ireland, Hungary, Scandinavia, Spain; and these too multiplied in course of time.

Bernard indeed left his mark upon the face of Europe.   Think of the weight on those frail shoulders!   Abbot of Clairvaux until his death in 1153, he never ceased to fulfil the duties of his office, finding time, even amid the cares of state, to decide a question of farming, of enclosure, or of the sale of cattle.   Not only did he personally administer the charity of his house, which relieved thousands of poor people, but, as head of the Order, he kept an eye on all its members, restoring peace to a troubled community, helping another to surmount its difficulties, showing his tireless solicitude for all.   These tremendous labours presuppose, apart from heroic virtue and unflagging energy, unequalled powers of organization, of observation, and of understanding, no less than an abiding determination to rise above himself.   It is the glory of our race that there are a few souls who thirst for 'more,' as there are legion who enjoy an unalterable taste for 'less.'

3.   The Perfect Stature of a Man

The foregoing account of St Bernard's youth and monastic vocation reveals in him a curious admixture of gentleness and passion, of tenderness and fervour, of sensitiveness and forcefulness.   These contradictions, reconciled in God, endowed his personality with rare charm. He has been not seldom represented as his own executioner, and torturer of his fellow men; he has even been described as 'a wicked man.' Actually, he was human in every sense of the word.

We have already noticed St Bernard's affection for his community. This, like many another facet of his character, is frequently misunderstood.   He was no fanatical prophet, no unyielding polemist, as, for example, was St Peter Damian.   In this respect also he was the embodiment of his age: outwardly rough and even violent, but full of that interior sweetness which is known as charity.

True son of the gentle, saintly Aleth, he was devoted to his brothers; and there is no finer instance of fraternal love than his anguish at the death of Gerard, one of his first companions in religion and a close collaborator in his work.   One morning in Chapter, as he was explaining a passage from the Canticle of Canticles, the thought of Gerard welled up in his heart, obliging him to pause.   To the amazement of those present he burst into tears, and then continued: 'You tell me not to weep?   My bowels are torn out; shall I have no feeling? Nay, if I suffer, I do so with my whole being.   I am not made of stone;

my heart is not a heart of bronze. I confess my woe. It is carnal, you say? I know that well, for I know that I am a creature of flesh and blood, sold under sin, delivered unto death, and subject to suffering. What would you? I am not insensible to grief; I have a horror of death, both for myself and for my own. Gerard has left me, and I am in pain; I am wounded unto death.' Is that the cry of an inhuman soul, of a deluded and fanatical ascetic?

Numerous examples of this kind might be adduced to demonstrate St Bernard's tenderness toward his friends no less than toward his brothers. 'Let us rest in the heart of those we love, as they rest in ours,' he would often say; and he practised what he preached. Some of his friendships were models of their kind. Such was the tie that bound him to William of St Thierry: when the latter fell sick, Bernard laid aside even the most urgent business, hurried to the bedside of his friend, and offered to look after him for as long as might be necessary. Nor did he fail in charity towards those with whom he disagreed. At the height of an acrimonious dispute with Peter the Venerable on the subject of Benedictine tradition and the new Cistercian observance, he proved himself so generous that the Abbot of Cluny wrote in a tone of gentle mockery: 'Candid and terrible friend, what could destroy my love for you?' In the famous duel with Abélard, when he felt obliged to discard the last vestiges of pity because the issue was far more important than any human consideration, his final gesture towards his defeated enemy was, as we shall see, one of perfect charity.

It is simply not true that Bernard's austerity prevented the development of his natural gifts, or limited his capacity for love and fellow-feeling. His life provides the answer to those many critics who imagine that the least restraint of natural appetites is detrimental to human character. The farther he travelled on the road of self-renunciation, the greater became his influence for good. The more firmly he controlled himself, the more truly human he was found to be; and that is so, from whatever standpoint his personality is viewed. The famous line of Terence 'I am a man, and nothing human is alien to me' might have been written by St Bernard; and in point of fact, though his eyes were ever upon God, the great mystic used similar words.

To treat Bernard exclusively as the warrior of Christ would be to distort his image beyond recognition. There were many facets to his character: ceaseless curiosity, a deep-rooted but sober craving for knowledge, and the 'sense of time,' that indefinable quality whereby a man not only *belongs* to his age, but understands and gives it expression. St Bernard's interest in human affairs—politics, literature, art, and a thousand commonplaces of daily existence—is among the most attractive elements in his manifold nature. It affected his very outlook upon life, which was always realistic, broad, and sound.

Nevertheless, in common with all who really love mankind, he entertained no illusion about human nature. He knew those shadows which hang over the deep waters of man's heart. This, of course, does not mean that he looked upon our wretchedness as incurable; Bernard was no Calvin. He often alludes to the unhappy fate of Adam's children since the Fall; he points to the sadness of their lives and to the depth of their humiliation; but he never forgets that this wounded and corrupt nature is stamped with the divine image and likeness, that the lamp of God is ever ready to dispel our darkness. This association of clear thinking and supernatural confidence in respect of man is characteristic of St Bernard's humanism. 'Consider thy nobility,' he says, 'and be ashamed at thine own shortcoming. Forget not thy beauty, lest thou be confounded by thy deformity.'

St Bernard has been described as a 'Christian Socrates'; but while the expression is not contradictory in terms, the emphasis must lie upon the adjective rather than the noun. According to him, faith is the means of knowledge and right judgment, and the power directing man's potentialities to their final cause. He realized that in and through God alone can man attain his goal.

4. LIFE IN GOD

It would be misleading to recognize in St Bernard's character and thought only those features which make him like ourselves, for they were magnified by faith and love of God. If he was of the full stature of a man, it was mainly because the human element was illuminated by the light of the Holy Spirit. 'It was almost in spite of himself,' says Montalembert, 'that he was a great orator, a great writer, a great personality. He was, as he desired above all to be, something else besides—a monk and a saint.'

Bernard was a saint in no ordinary sense of the word. His brand of holiness consisted not merely in his refinement of the basic virtues, in his extraordinary humility, in his unfailing charity, or in his continual effort at self-conquest. Sanctity has a more inclusive meaning, which can be applied only in the case of one whose whole being, whose every act and thought, is directed to God who is both End and Way.

The fullness of St Bernard's life and its impact upon his contemporaries stamp him as a mystic. His mystical activity is apparent as the determining factor in all that he did and in every word he uttered. Here again, he is representative of his age, of its profound and unanimous faith, of its submission to the will of God. He is one of the high peaks in medieval society; but a mountain is, after all, part of the surrounding plain, and has its roots therein.

The mystical urge permeated St Bernard's life. Hence his cry: 'My

God! my love! how Thou lovest me! How Thou lovest me!' and: 'Oh, incomparable, vehement, burning, and impetuous Love! Thou wilt let me think of nothing but of Thee; Thou disdainest all things else; and despising all, art sufficient unto Thyself!' The immensity of that love, and of that ineffable exchange of hearts, is nowhere better described than in these few words: 'Understand with what measure, or rather how immeasurably, God is worthy to be loved. He who is so great hath loved us first, gratuitously and entirely, though we are small and miserable! . . . Since our love is related to God, it is related to the boundless, to the infinite, for God is infinite and hath no limits. What then, I ask, should be the measure and the term of our love?'

This man, who has been represented as hard, unfeeling, bases his doctrine upon the notion of God's love for him in spite of his mortality. Mabillon bestowed upon him the title Doctor Mellifluus; and it aptly describes that happy union of tenderness, ingratiating manner, and unvarying politeness which typify his conduct at every stage, and which we might call 'unction,' had not that word come to denote a quality which we abhor. He was bathed in, penetrated and moulded by, a love compared with which all other sentiments are vain.

St Bernard is likewise typical of his age in the fundamentals of his religious outlook. Since God is the *alpha* and *omega*, what other knowledge can there be that does not proceed from Him? Reading, study, and work for the sake of knowledge as such is idle curiosity. The only school is that of Christ. 'Peter, Andrew, the sons of Zebedee, and their companions were not chosen from a school of rhetoric or philosophy; yet it was through them that our Lord accomplished His purpose of salvation.' Hence that almost exclusively scriptural tinge of Bernard's thought and eloquence, which was so prominent an aspect of medieval faith. The Bible was his favourite, if not his only book; he studied it in great detail, and spent some twenty years commenting upon the Canticle of Canticles, comparing one passage with another and endeavouring to elucidate their many problems. If he gave much time also to the early Christian writers, it was only because St Ambrose, St Augustine, St Gregory, and others were themselves steeped in Holy Scripture, and form part of the main stream of Biblical tradition. His devotion to the Bible was so intense, that a number of his sermons consist entirely of scriptural quotations arranged in a rhythmical order which is itself derived from the Psalmist and the Prophets.

His strong mystical tendencies enable us to recognize St Bernard as the source of a current which bore medieval religion towards devotion to our Lord's humanity. 'He who is filled with the love of God is easily stirred by all that concerns the Word made Flesh. When he prays, the sacred image of the God-Man stands before him: he is present at Christ's birth, watches Him grow up, hears Him preach, witnesses His death, His glorious Resurrection, and His Ascension. . . .' Such phrases are a perfect summary of the origin and scope of this devotion, which is so closely associated with the Middle Ages. Christ is not only the supreme model, the archetype; but the Word is truly flesh, our Brother and our Friend. So thought Bernard, who pondered deeply upon every detail of our Lord's human life; and his sermons, taken as a whole, form a complete mystical biography of the Saviour. Speaking of the new-born Babe of Bethlehem, he chooses simple, poignant words, suited to that Babe's humility. The stable, the straw, and even the poor swaddling-clothes, he treats as so many symbols for our edification. But when referring to Christ crucified, his manner becomes stark; his anguished tongue can do more than tell one by one the sufferings of Jesus; and he moves our imagination by the sheer simplicity of his account.

At the centre of St Bernard's spiritual life stood Christ, the God-Man, so near to us and yet so far removed. The great preacher must have carried his hearers along with him, and stirred them to the very depths with this description of our Lord: 'He was beautiful among all the sons of men, both within and without. He, the glory of eternal light, outshone the splendour of the angels. To set eyes on Him was to recognize Him as a man without blemish, flesh without sin, Lamb without spot. O human soul! to think there is conferred upon thee so inestimable a privilege that thou mayest be the spouse of One who is the object of angelic contemplation; that thou mayest gaze upon Him whose beauty the sun and moon adore, and at whose nod the universe obeys!' In order to appreciate how well St Bernard's method was suited to his period, we need only glance at that unforgettable image of the Messiah, known as 'Le Beau Dieu,' on the porch of Amiens cathedral. Or again, that window in the basilica of Notre-Dame du Sacré Cœur at Issoudun. It shows our Lord and St Bernard standing face to face; and in order to express their mutual love, the artist has written above the Heart of Christ the one word 'Bernard,' and on the White Monk's breast the Holy Name.

While on the subject of artistic representation, it is worth while to recall a somewhat different work, illustrating another side of the great abbot's piety. I refer to Murillo's celebrated canvas known as the 'Lactation of Saint Bernard,' a symbolic idea which is found also in a window of the church at Laines-au-Bois in the diocese of Troyes. St Bernard kneels with outstretched arms, his eyes fixed on the Virgin Mary. She is in the act of uncovering her breast (as would a mother for her child) to quench the thirst of her devoted servant. This gracious imagery conveys some idea of Bernard's impassioned reverence for the Mother of Jesus, whom he was, perhaps, the first to call 'our Lady,' and who was never far from his thoughts. There is a tradition that one day, as the community were chanting the *Salve Regina*, the torrent of love which leaped up in his heart overflowed and caused him to cry out: '*Ô clemens! ô dulcis! ô pia!*' Those words now form part of the noble anthem, and perpetuate his memory. Whether or not the story is true, he is known to have composed the *Memorare*. Medieval devotion to Mary is, in fact, inseparable from Saint Bernard.

It would be false, however, to imagine that he set no limit to his veneration. He was strictly orthodox, and never transgressed the boundaries at which Holy Scripture seemed to call a halt. He wisely ignored the apocryphal writings; nor would he call Mary 'Mother,' because the patristic tradition reserved that title to the Church and to sanctifying grace.[1] It was within the strict limits of Catholic dogma and Holy Scripture that Bernard's flaming soul sought out the raw material for those treasures of Christian doctrine which were taken over and recast by later generations. The mystic of Clairvaux rises to his greatest heights in this respect when he discusses Mary's role as mediatrix: 'Needest thou an advocate with Jesus? Fly, then, to Mary. I say without hesitation, Mary will be heard because of the consideration due to her. The Son will hear His Mother, and the Father His Son. Confidence, unflinching confidence, is the stairway of sinners; that is the foundation of my hope.'

The idea of intercession, of man's instinctive longing for a mediator with the Almighty Judge, is an essential mark of medieval piety. Nor, in St Bernard's view, is Mary our sole advocate; for he often speaks of the part played by the Church triumphant. More than one panegyric has survived, preached by him in honour of some saint, wherein he rouses the faith of his hearers by pointing out those of the elect who will represent man's need before the throne of mercy. From this point of view also Bernard was of his time. But he never indulged in those flights of exaggerated fancy to which his contemporaries were so prone; he spoke little on the subject of miracles,[2] and he attached no undue importance to relics.

All these manifestations of Bernard's devouring thirst for God, all his saintly life, culminated in what is certainly the crown of mystical activity—an absolutely pure and disinterested love of God. It is not my purpose here to enlarge upon his mysticism, which combined the

---

[1] On St Bernard's devotion to the Mother of God, *see* Aubron, *L'Œuvre Mariale de Saint Bernard*, Paris, 1935.
[2] There is no doubt whatever that St Bernard wrought a number of miracles in his lifetime, although his fourth biographer, the author of *The Book of Miracles*, seems to have overstepped the mark. He healed the sick and vanquished demons; but his biographers take care to emphasize that he disliked these appeals made by simple folk for the exercise of supernatural power. He was torn between humility and charity.

two extremes of sweetness and austerity. Nor shall I delay to examine those peculiarities which differentiate it from other schools. I shall merely refer to his insistence that all forms of devotion are meaningless unless directed to Almighty God, and that man's end is 'to love God no longer for one's own sake but for Himself alone.' He brought to the supernatural life that urge to seek ever more distant horizons which, as I have said, was among the finest characteristics of the medieval mind. There can be no doubt that he enjoyed at certain rare and privileged moments of his life the ineffable experience of God's presence; but he expressed himself upon this subject with the utmost reserve.[1] But this flight to the summits never caused Bernard to lose sight of earth and human realities. Mystic though he be, your Burgundian has both feet planted firmly on the ground. 'His mysticism,' writes Étienne Gilson, 'was wholly interior and psychological; it was based on self-knowledge and the analysis of our spiritual poverty.' This fact explains how it was that so great a contemplative managed to lead a life of such astonishing activity.

Bernard's impact upon the religion of his contemporaries was enormous. All medieval mysticism derives more or less from him; many writers borrowed from him unashamedly; and he has been read and studied almost as much as St Augustine. All the principal forms of medieval devotion bear the mark of his influence, in respect not only of their content, but also of their outward manifestation—Cathedral and Crusade. It was not simply by prayer, teaching, and personal example that the great abbot sought to achieve the glorification of mankind. We shall presently find him at work in every sphere of life, engaged in the most mundane of affairs. It is indeed of no small significance in the history of religion that one cold monastic cell became the centre of the Western world. As for Bernard, even amid those strenuous duties which, as the conscience of his age, he was obliged to undertake, he never forgot that the one true source of all his strength was supernatural. 'I light my fire,' he used to say, 'at the flame of meditation.'

[1] In the following passage he speaks of the mystical union with as much precision as it is possible to attain: 'Bear for a moment with my folly. I wish to tell you, for I have promised to do so, of my own experience. It is really hopeless to talk about such things; but the Word has entered into me—He has, in fact done so more than once. He may have entered frequently; if so, I have not always been conscious of His coming. But I have felt His presence within me, and I remember it quite well.

'I rose to the topmost part of myself, but still higher reigned the Word. Like some anxious explorer I descended to the very depths of my being, but found Him lower still. I looked outside myself and saw Him to be beyond all things. I looked within, and found Him more intimate than I am to myself. . . . When He enters into me, the Word betrays Himself by no movement or sensation; it is only the secret trembling of my heart which reveals His presence. My vices take wing, my carnal affections are mastered; my soul is refreshed; I am inwardly renewed as it were with the mere shadow of His glory.'

5. St Bernard, the Conscience of his Age

And what a fire! One cannot think of this man's life without recalling our Lord's words: 'I came to bring fire on earth, and what would I but that it be kindled?' Nothing so exasperates a zealous Christian as to see the flame of Christ burn feebly, a pile of smouldering ashes where there should be a furnace of love. 'God's affairs are mine,' he once exclaimed; 'nothing that concerns Him is alien to me.' He felt himself responsible for the truth which he possessed, and desired that all should recognize it. He longed that his Mother the Church might be faithful in all things to her divine Spouse.

So, when 'God's affairs' were imperilled, Bernard was immediately aroused. He cared for nothing and spared no one when God's interests were at stake. At such times he was outspoken to a degree, and his mordant irony was directed at all alike. He once told an archbishop: 'Your conduct is odious; you are so intractable, that I am resolved to have no more to do with you. You prevent the good will of your friends and invite the hostility of others. You know no law but your own whims, and behave like a despot, regardless of Almighty God. . . .' The following admonition was addressed to the Sovereign Pontiff: 'I might as well shut myself away in silence and retreat; for the whole Church will clamour no less against the court of Rome, so long as it pursues its present course. . . .'

The greatness of the Middle Ages is surely apparent in this fact, that the great ones of the earth were prepared to tolerate such language, and usually submitted to the saint's injunctions. It is difficult to imagine one of our modern rulers hearing himself thus denounced without taking immediate steps to silence the offending voice in some secret prison cell.

The Abbot of Clairvaux viewed 'God's affairs' from a twofold standpoint. Those interests were at stake whenever God's law was violated or His precepts ignored. Bernard was at the very heart of that great reforming movement which had been, and would continue to be throughout the Middle Ages, a reviving element in the Church's life. But God's interests were no less imperilled when His Church was threatened in her liberty, her sovereignty, or the reverence due to her. On all such occasions St Bernard intervened.

Count Thibaut II of Champagne was Bernard's immediate over-lord, for Clairvaux lay within his territory. He was among the greatest of French nobles, and his estates exceeded the royal domain of France. Although pious and generous, he was sometimes proud and brutal, and Bernard never failed to rebuke him. Thibaut once refused to do homage to the Bishop of Langres, of whom, under the peculiar anomalies of the feudal system, he held some land in fief.   This was an infringement of ecclesiastical law.   St Bernard at once sat down and wrote so stern a reprimand that the Count submitted.   In another case the principles of charity were involved.   After a trial by battle, the loser had had his eyes put out, and Thibaut's officers had confiscated his goods.   Bernard protested against this barbarism and obtained reparation for the unhappy victim's children.

Remarkable episodes of the same kind are found in his relations with the King of France.   Bernard had experience of two Capetian monarchs, whose characters were very different.   Louis VI, the fat, was a wise sovereign whom the saint loved and esteemed; but he tended to use the Church as an instrument of government, and on that account was called to order by the Abbot of Clairvaux.   Again, in 1127, the king named as his Seneschal (commander-in-chief) a prelate, Stephen de Garlande, archdeacon of Notre-Dame.   Bernard denounced in scathing terms this confusion of dignities, which might be harmful to the Church, and scourged the new seneschal with bitter irony: would he say Mass in armour, or perhaps lead his troops in alb and stole?   So terrible, indeed, was his onslaught, that Louis revoked the nomination.   The same intolerance of abuse appeared soon afterwards in the matter of a dispute between the king and Stephen of Senlis, Bishop of Paris.   Stephen had undertaken the reform of his chapter; but Louis, apprehensive lest he should find the canons less amenable to his wishes, counter-attacked by confiscating the diocesan estates.   Stephen promptly laid them under an interdict and fled to Sens.   He notified St Bernard of his predicament, and in due course the sovereign received a letter from Clairvaux: 'The Church has been driven to lodge a complaint against you with her Lord.   She finds her old friend changed into a tyrant . . .' and so on through four long pages.

In another instance he went so far (perhaps a little too far) as to address Louis VI as 'a second Herod'!   The most extraordinary fact is that the king never ventured to rid himself of so troublesome a prophet.   As for Louis VII, a second-rate monarch, whose divorce from Eleanor of Aquitaine was to prove so detrimental to the kingdom, Bernard had to remonstrate with him ten or fifteen times.   His asperity on these occasions was, if possible, even sharper than that used toward his predecessor; for he had known his sovereign as a boy, had loved him, and been sadly disappointed.[1]

[1] The following passage gives an exact idea of this quiet severity with its undertone of regret for misplaced affection.   'Since I had the honour to know your Highness, I can vouch for my unfailing devotion to your welfare.   During the past year you cannot have been unaware of my repeated efforts, in concert with your ministers, to re-establish peace in the kingdom.   But I fear you render my labours ineffective.   It seems that you are going light-heartedly to cast aside your present advantages, that the Devil has inspired

If St Bernard was the Church's advocate against the secular power, he was no less God's advocate against the Church. The question was, whether the principles governing a monastic order differed in kind from those which all Christians were obliged to follow. Bernard thought not; at the very most, he allowed a difference in the degree of effort required of a monk and of a layman, and in the heights of perfection to which he hoped they might attain. He wished to make the whole Church hear that call to sanctity which he himself had heard.

He appealed first to the head, the Pope; and nothing is more characteristic of Bernard than his attitude towards the papacy, which was one of admiration and respect. He agreed with Gregory VII that the Sovereign Pontiff 'is the only man whose foot all nations should kiss.' But he considered that the holder of so exalted a position should match the dignity of his office with the purity of his life; and no one has better described the duties of a pastor than this austere monk whose humility led him to refuse the tiara. In 1145 he had an opportunity to speak his mind; for one of his monks, Bernard of Pisa, was elected Pope and took the name of Eugenius III. The Abbot of Clairvaux lost no time in addressing to the Holy Father, between 1145 and 1152, five noble letters which now form his celebrated treatise *De Consideratione*, a magnificent work which may be truly described as the Charter of the Papacy. Bernard loved this man, and wrote to him in terms of exquisite grace: 'What matter that you have been raised to the Chair of Peter? Walk on the wings of the wind, if you will; you can never escape from mine affection. Love will recognize a son crowned even with the tiara.' At the same time, however, he reminds the new Pope in solemn phrases of the awful dignity of the title which he bears.

'You are the bishop of bishops; the Apostles, your forbears, were

---

some counsellor to urge upon you the renewal of those disastrous ills of which you had repented. . . . Maybe the inscrutable decrees of Providence have so arranged that Your Highness should view the world from upside-down. You count the dishonourable as matter for self-satisfaction, and you believe that to be honourable which should cover you with shame. . . . For my part, whatever resolution you may take against the welfare of your kingdom, your own salvation, and the glory of your name, I cannot disguise the outrage and the desolation which afflicts Holy Mother Church. I am determined to persevere and, if need be, to combat unto death. In default of shield and sword, I shall employ the arms of my state, which are my prayers and tears.

'I call heaven to witness that I have never ceased to implore God for the peace of your kingdom and the prosperity of your person; and I have used my good offices with the Pope on your behalf. I begin to regret having so far excused you on the grounds of youth. Henceforward I shall take a more realistic view. Sire, if you will not amend, I venture to predict that your sin will not go long unpunished. With all the zeal of a faithful and loving servant, I exhort you to lay aside your malice. I pray you earnestly, remember the Wise Man's saying: "Wounding words from a friend are better than the kisses of an enemy."'

instructed to lay the world at the feet of Jesus Christ. You have inherited that duty; the whole world is your legacy. Pastor of all the sheep, Pastor of all their pastors! In case of necessity, and if the fault deserves, you can bar heaven to a bishop, depose him, cast him out to Satan. You are in very truth the Vicar of Christ.

'What is this your power? An estate to be exploited? Nay: a burden to take up. Be not proud on Peter's throne; it is but an observation post, a high place from which, like a sentry, you may cast your glance over the world beneath. You are not the owner of that world; you are no more than a trustee. The world belongs to Christ.

'Do I, then, say you rule the world, but not as task-master? Indeed I do; for to rule well is to rule with love. You are the servant of Christ's flock; it is not your slave. Yea, and I will add this: there is no iron or poison that I fear so much for you as I fear the pride of power.'

In the event, Eugenius III obeyed these warnings, notwithstanding the magnificence that surrounded him as Pope. He continued to lead the austere life of a Cistercian monk, 'esteeming money no better than a wisp of straw,' and showed himself in very truth one of the 'reformed.'

But that was only a start. Bernard knew that principles which do not pass beyond the realm of ideas are worthless, and so he turned his eye to details. The Pope's entourage was utterly corrupt; the Roman Curia was full of careerists, soft and worldly clerics—it was fast becoming, said the saint, a 'robbers' cave.' Hear with what stinging words he describes these birds of prey. The legates themselves, he cries, are worthless men; 'they will sacrifice the people's salvation for the gold of Spain.' All that must be changed. 'The Pope must choose experienced and disinterested men. Nor must he limit the choice of his entourage to Rome, where corruption reigns; he must select from the whole wide world those who are destined to judge the world.'

His strictures were not confined to the Eternal City, but were heard wherever he thought fit. One of St Bernard's most remarkable achievements was the 'conversion' of Suger, abbot of Saint Denis, where the pomp of a royal court was more in evidence than the austerity of a religious house. Suger, the powerful minister of Louis VI, was told by St Bernard that his luxurious living was a disgrace, that a servant of God should be ashamed to be attended on his journeys by a troop of more than sixty horse; and an astonished court beheld the unwonted spectacle of a prime minister exchanging worldly pomp for monastic observance. The royal policy, which had tended to ignore religious claims, was suddenly reversed; and Suger attained real greatness because Bernard had persuaded him to live as a monk serving God as minister of his king, rather than as a minister who, by chance, happened to be a Benedictine.

Bernard was prominent at every stage of the twelfth-century reform. His notorious dispute with Cluny may be held to have exceeded the strict limits of fair play; for in spite of his criticism, it cannot be denied that the great Order of Black Monks was by no means as lax as he suggested. He was in close touch with the Grande Chartreuse, whose prior, Guigo, was so much attached to him that William of St Thierry assures us that they 'formed but a single heart, a single soul.' He also took part in the reorganization of the canons regular, and remained on the most friendly terms with St Norbert and the Premonstratensians.

The secular clergy were no less an object of Bernard's constant solicitude, and the picture which he draws of them makes sombre reading. From one end of Christendom to the other 'the goods of the Church are dissipated in vanity and extravagance.' The bishops themselves were setting a bad example, at which the Abbot of Clairvaux did not hesitate to point his accusing finger. There was, for instance, Simon, the pluralist of Noyon and Tournai, who grew fat on the revenues of two dioceses; and Henry, Bishop of Verdun, who had secured his appointment by bribery. Bernard's reforming zeal went further still in his treatise on the *Manners and Duties of Bishops*, which was compiled at the request of Archbishop Henri le Sanglier of Sens. 'Why do you get yourselves up like women, if you do not wish to be criticized like women? Be known for your works, not for your fur capes and embroideries! You think to shut my mouth by observing that a monk should not criticize a bishop? Would to heaven you might shut mine eyes also! But were I to remain silent, others would speak—the poor, the naked, and the starving. They would rise up and cry: "Your luxury devours our lives! Your vanity steals our necessities."'

That is the voice of a prophet; and the most surprising thing is that it was heard. Bernard was invited to decide contested episcopal elections at Tours, Langres, Rennes, and York; this simple monk became, in fact, the conscience of the higher clergy. On the other hand, when he praised St Malachy, the great Irish bishop who died at Clairvaux, it was not long before the object of his admiration was canonized.

In Bernard's eyes the Church was more than the clergy; it consisted of the whole army of baptized, a fact which he never overlooked. The flaming zeal of God's advocate could not ignore the needs of secular society. Institutions appeared to him deserving of respect in so far as they conformed with the Christian ideal. Princes hold their power from God; they must govern according to His law, protecting the good, punishing evildoers, and securing justice to the oppressed. To the Queen of Jerusalem, for example, he wrote these splendid words: 'Learn from Jesus how to reign'; but toward those who betrayed this ideal he showed no clemency.

Men of the world, too, came under his lash. Here is a knight, mounted on a horse with gold and silken trappings, his helmet bright with precious stones, the skirts of his finely woven surcoat reaching to his feet. Is that a suitable array for a soldier of Christ? Here are women, tripping along, adorned like some pagan temple, with their heavy trains of sumptuous material, their wimples held in place by golden diadems. Is that a seemly dress for Christian women? The occupations of lax Christians were equally reprehensible. Men, he says, rush headlong into a fight, goaded by love of violence and of danger. They never stop to inquire 'whether the cause is just and the intention right.' They fight innumerable private wars in the shape of tourneys, forgetting that 'the noblest occupation is to render oneself pleasing in God's sight.' As for the ways of women, the least said, the better!

It should not, however, be imagined that Bernard reserved his criticism for the rich. He minced no words when addressing humbler folk, peasant or middle class, and did not hesitate to show them up as greedy, egotistical, or lacking in conjugal fidelity! Nor were these indictments heard as the lofty exhortations of a fashionable preacher; for at the sound of Bernard's voice men were inwardly transformed, and the light of Christ penetrated to their inmost souls. The Abbot of Clairvaux was in truth the conscience of his age, and as such he played no small part in rescuing Earth's salt from insipidity.

6. DEFENDER OF THE FAITH

It was not only in the sphere of moral conduct that St Bernard bore witness to the law of Christ; the same energy is apparent also on the doctrinal plane. His attitude in this respect has been often misrepresented as that of an unbridled fanatic, hot on the scent of imaginary errors, and pitiless toward whomsoever he suspected of upholding them. His detractors, however, are themselves suspect. Berengar of Poitiers, for example, described Bernard's soul as 'filled with rancour'; but Berengar was a disciple of Abélard, and more than prone to rancour.

He has even been called 'torturer,' devotee of the stake, predecessor of Torquemada. True, he maintained that heretics should be delivered to the civil arm and burned, as did most of his contemporaries; but he left no doubt as to what he considered the right procedure of the

Church when confronted with unorthodoxy. She ought not, he says, to take up arms before she has tried by every means at her disposal to recall those who have gone astray. If they persist in error, and thereby show themselves a public menace, then let 'those die who prefer to die rather than return to God.'

Later on [1] we shall examine in some detail those Manichaean tendencies which gave rise, especially in Languedoc, to the heresy known as Albigensianism. In 1143 St Bernard received warning from his friend Evervin, provost of Stanfeld, and launched a vigorous attack on the partisans of these wild doctrines, chief of whom were Pierre de Bruys and Henry of Lausanne. Two years later he accompanied the legate Alberic to the south of France, where his preaching was largely successful. He obliged Henry to withdraw, and made a deep impression on the masses by his example and his miracles; but he took no part in those senseless acts of violence which broke out some time before the spread of heresy called forth a deplorable expedition known as the 'Albigensian Crusade.' [2]

So far was Bernard from fanaticism that he demonstrated on one typical occasion that the defence of Christian truth cannot be divorced from that of charity. On the eve of the second crusade, an anti-Jewish pogrom broke out at Cologne, Mainz, Worms, Spire, and Strasbourg. It was fomented by a Cistercian monk named Rudolph, encouraged by a party of nobles. Immediately he learned of these events, Bernard left Flanders where he was preaching the crusade, and hurried to the Rhineland in order to stop the massacre of Jews.

There is, however, one case, that of his famous duel with Abélard, in which the term 'fanatic' might appear more justifiable, in which he might seem the very type of an 'obscurantist' monk, the enemy of all progress. But it is absurd to call a man ignorant when his writings bear the stamp of erudition, when he enjoys the luxury of a digression to quote Statius, Ovid, and Lucan. Étienne Gilson well remarks that St Bernard 'renounced everything but the art of writing well.' His literary output is surprising both in quantity and in quality. It includes no less than 332 sermons and fourteen treatises, not to mention a correspondence of which we still possess more than five hundred letters. It is marked also by wonderful variety and sometimes by an almost subtle elegance. There is the *Life of St Malachy*, which

[1] Chapter XIII.
[2] St Bernard also disputed with Arnold of Brescia, a Christian democratic leader and apostle of absolute poverty, who held that the clergy had no right to private property, and preached a kind of anticlerical Communism. When Arnold fled to Paris in the train of Abélard, St Bernard persuaded Louis VII not to have him arrested, but to forbid the continuance of his subversive propaganda in France. Arnold of Brescia, as is well known, plunged deeper into heresy and died by decapitation after the defeat of the anti-papal Commune at Rome (1155). On Arnold of Brescia *see* Chapter V, section 6, and Chapter XIII, section 2.

provides much curious information about Ireland in the twelfth century; the enormous *Commentary on the Canticle of Canticles* in ninety-six sermons of inexhaustible richness; two powerful dogmatic treatises *On the Knowledge of God* and *On Grace and Free Will*; scathing polemics; and his 'spiritual testament,' the *De Consideratione*, from which we have quoted some passages on the duties of a pope. All these diverse elements proclaim him an orator and man of letters. Lastly, he was far from despising the human intellect and its activity, as witness his delightful remark that 'It ill becomes a spouse of the Word to be stupid.'

But he ranked intellectual activity second among the ways of knowledge, convinced that neither by dialectic nor by science can man reach to that which alone is worthy of attainment. Like his friend William of Saint-Thierry, he maintained that 'the humble love of a pure heart is worth more than reason and subtle disquisition'; that in order to understand and expound dogma, one should first live it. Such, indeed, is the sole conclusion of his treatise *On the Knowledge of God*.

He adhered firmly to the belief that faith is superior by far to every intellectual process. And it was in order to defend this principle that he engaged in conflict with Abélard, one of the most impressive figures in the history of medieval thought, of whom we shall have more to say.[1] But from the hermitage at Nogent-sur-Seine, where Abélard dwelt with a handful of disciples, there emerged ideas which were hardly compatible with Bernard's view. Not that the great dialectician was an unbeliever, a freethinker; at that period such words would have been meaningless. He had a lively faith, and spoke of Christ with a tenderness that Bernard himself would not have disavowed. Nevertheless, Abélard was consumed with the desire for speculation as other men are with carnal appetites. He himself used to say that he could not remain inactive in face of a problem, but must needs solve it at any cost. This craving, when applied to the mysteries of faith, invited catastrophe. If Abélard, champion of reason and the critical spirit, had prevailed, the clear-cut affirmations of dogma, the very principles of faith, would have become no more than academic theses, to be accepted or rejected at the discretion of individuals. The result would have been a process that ended, as did rationalism, by suppressing the distinction between the legitimate object of reason and that which transcends it, between human knowledge and divine revelation.

We have only to recognize the goal to which Abélard's steps were more or less consciously directed, in order to appreciate St Bernard's motive in joining issue with him. Warned by his friend William of St Thierry, who had sent him Abélard's *Christian Theology* with the

[1] Chapter VIII, section 6.

33568

simple observation, 'Your silence is dangerous,' the Abbot of Clair-vaux tried in the first place to avoid so formidable a task. He questioned his ability to cross swords with so great a master of dialectic; but in 1140, among a crowd of students whom his reputation had attracted to Clairvaux, he met a pupil of Abélard, and forthwith understood the peril. He then made overtures to the philosopher in person; but his appeal was rejected point-blank. Abélard, as if to cut the rods that were to beat his own back, demanded the assembly of a council before which he would defend his thesis. The council met at Sens in 1141, and St Bernard was present.

The two adversaries were far removed in outlook. One was an intellectual, sure alike of himself, of his position, and of his dialectical method; he would immediately pulverize this monk from Burgundy. The other was a mystic whose soul was filled with God, who sought not his own glory, and desired only to bear witness to the word of God. Abélard viewed the council as a debating society where he might indulge his passion for the scrutiny of ideas. Bernard considered it as a tribunal which was to pass judgment on one whose faith was suspect. Nor would he allow his opponent the choice of stations, but came straightway to the point by affirming that the very topics which Abélard proposed to discuss were not open to discussion. The faith must be accepted or rejected; dogma is a whole which cannot be pulled in pieces to suit private whims. Surprised by this attack, disconcerted, crushed at the outset by a torrent of quotation from scripture, compared in turn with Arius, Nestorius, and Pelagius, Abélard saw the ground open at his feet. He could not reply.

In this duel, it was unquestionably St Bernard who represented his age and stood forth as the typical medieval Christian, holding the past exemplary and sufficient unto itself, the faith alone as *alpha* and *omega*. His adversary was the incarnation of a progressive movement whose intellectual courage bordered on audacity. True, Abélard's ideas subsequently played a useful part in the evolution of Christian thought; but in the middle of the twelfth century they constituted a real threat to society, whose cornerstone was unwavering faith. It is not always good to be too far in advance of one's time.

After this defeat, Abélard decided to lodge an appeal from the council to the Holy See; but he was unable to make the journey. On arrival at Cluny he was overtaken by sickness; the Pope approved the decision of the council, and his humiliation was complete. Informed of this, St Bernard hurried to his bedside, in order that his adversary might not carry to the grave the searing agony of those wounds he had felt it his duty to inflict. Peter the Venerable watched the two men exchange the kiss of peace; and soon afterwards, at the priory of Saint-Marcel near Châlon-sur-Sâone, the former master of the Latin Quarter

Lincoln Christian College

was surprised 'by the angelic visitor in holy prayer and the fear of the Lord.' [1]

7.   THE MAN OF AFFAIRS

St Bernard felt in duty bound to leave his cell and join in the battles of his fellow men, simply that Christ might lack nothing of his testimony.   'I never regret,' he once wrote, 'having interrupted a peaceful meditation, if I see God's word take root in a soul.'   This explains the paradox of a contemplative who, from 1127 until his death, wandered over mountain and valley, like 'a fledgling exiled from its nest,' and played a leading part in all the principal events of that time.

It was not that he enjoyed doing so, not that he sought out the occasion for a quarrel.   On the contrary, whenever he was called upon to act, he resisted, hesitated, waited, reflected, and carefully inquired why he had been approached.   And if he at length consented, he did so in obedience to the orders of a superior, through charity towards his brethren and the Church, or through loyalty to truth and justice.   No doubt he was torn between the monastic ideal and the overwhelming load of secular business in which he found himself involved; but he was sure that while thus engaged he was doing what God expected of him without betraying his vocation.   It was precisely because he was a mystic that St Bernard was also a man of action.

It might be said in our modern jargon that the great abbot was a 'man of affairs,' in the sense that he took risks and plunged into the most dangerous conflicts.   But this busy life, wherewith so many men attempt to disguise the void in their own souls, was for Bernard nothing but the logical outcome of another and more exacting duty undertaken when, at the age of twenty-one, he knocked at the gate of Cîteaux. Although he has been officially described as a statesman,[2] or politician, his labours in the temporal sphere had no other purpose than to secure the victory of Truth and Justice.

It is impossible to enumerate the many instances in which St Bernard's intervention proved decisive.   The events which called for his mediation were both great and small, for nothing could be a waste of time when his Lord's teaching was at stake.   Whenever he took a hand, he was always the man of God, free of resentment and personal ambition.   Thus he defended Thibaut of Champagne (of

[1] St Bernard also engaged in a violent dispute with Gilbert of La Porrée, the learned Bishop of Poitiers, who had put forward unorthodox views when treating of the distinction between God and divinity.   Though denounced to St Bernard by two of his own priests, Gilbert enjoyed the influential friendship of several cardinals, and thereby escaped the thunderbolts of his adversary.   But he agreed to alter certain passages in his writing under the direction of Gottschalk, provost of the Premonstratensians.

[2] At Dijon there is a commemorative plaque to 'St Bernard, Statesman.'   Though secular in outlook, the words form a splendid act of homage.

whose conduct he had had several times to complain) against King Louis VII; he protested with the utmost vigour at the devastation of Champagne by royal troops, and brought about a permanent settlement resulting in a marrage from which Philip Augustus was to spring.

Two outstanding events of this period reveal the saint's authority. First there was the Schism of Anacletus, which St Bernard handled in a way so characteristic of his methods and of his influence, that the story deserves to be told in full.

While Honorius II lay on his death-bed, the families of Pierleone and Frangipani set to work on the College of Cardinals. They had the dying man carried to the abbey of St Gregory, and showed him to a restive mob. He died on the night of 13th February 1130, and six cardinals in residence at the monastery elected Gregory of Sant' Angelo, a partisan of the Frangipani, who took the name of Innocent II. Their choice was confirmed by other members of the College. But Cardinal Peter Pierleone, a well-known and popular figure in Roman society, forthwith denounced this hasty procedure; he rallied his supporters, and was elected Pope under the name of Anacletus II. The two pontiffs were crowned on 23rd February, one at Santa Maria Novella, the other at St Peter's. But Anacletus, an astute politician who knew how to distribute gold to good purpose, forced his rival to leave Rome. Innocent took refuge in France.

There were now two 'heads' of Christendom; nor could their respective claims be settled on canonical grounds, for both elections had been invalidated by irregularities. The nations took sides according to their interests. Louis VI convoked a council at Étampes in order to examine the merits of the two claimaints, and the Abbot of Clairvaux was requested to attend. Bernard was reluctant; but a vision from God decided him to obey the summons. He found himself arbiter of the universal Church, and put forward a threefold argument in favour of Innocent II: (1) he was morally the most worthy; (2) he had been designated by 'the most reliable' part of the Sacred College, i.e. by the majority of cardinal-bishops, upon whom a decree of Nicholas II in 1059 had conferred pre-eminence in the matter of papal elections; and (3) he had been consecrated by the Bishop of Ostia according to tradition. The council accepted this ruling, and Louis VI proclaimed his loyalty to Innocent.

The decision, however, could be of no avail if Christendom were divided; and Bernard sought to rally the other Christian states. He saw Henry I of England, and overcame his reluctance; while in Germany, St Norbert, who was then Archbishop of Magdeburg, won over Lothair to the good cause. The Pope and the German king met in March 1131 at Liége, where the monarch held Innocent's bridle and showed him every mark of respect. The gesture was no doubt intended to pave the way for demands of a merely political nature; but Bernard, says his biographer, 'opposed them like a wall,' and Lothair promised to conduct the Pope back to Rome.   Meanwhile, Innocent paid a visit to Clairvaux and was entertained by the monks at their frugal board.   At Rheims, Bernard stood beside the Pope while His Holiness received the submission of Aragon and Castile.   Next, he intervened in Aquitaine, where Duke William, prompted by Bishop Gerard of Angoulême, had recognized Anacletus.   But his success was not long-lived; for Gerard regained the upper hand, and obtained the see of Bordeaux.   Bernard flayed him with merciless irony, and persuaded his suffragans to excommunicate him.

By this time Innocent had arrived in Italy, where Lothair was engaged in military operations.   He sent for Bernard in 1133 to reconcile Genoa and Pisa, whose accord was necessary to oppose Roger II of Sicily, an opportunist who had declared for Anacletus with a view to increasing his own power.   The Cistercian became a diplomat; he arranged a peace, and the people of Genoa gave him a triumphal welcome.   Lothair, however, on reaching a point not far from Rome, found himself short of money.   Bernard asked for and obtained subsidies from the King of England.   Finally, on 30th April, Innocent entered the Eternal City and crowned Lothair on 4th June.   Bernard returned in haste to his beloved monastery, hoping that his task was ended.

But in September, Innocent was again forced to leave Rome, being now deprived of the support of an imperial army, and harried by the troops of Anacletus, who had occupied the Castle of Sant' Angelo. Bernard set out once more.   On his way through Nantes he won over the subjects of William of Aquitaine, whom he reminded that 'there is only one Church, the Ark in which lies the salvation of the world; without it, by the just judgment of God, everything is doomed to perish as at the time of the Flood.'   After hearing Mass (during which he was obliged to stand outside the church, since he was excommunicated), William was reconciled to Innocent.   So far as concerned France, the schism was at an end.

The situation, however, remained grave, for Anacletus was supported by Roger II, who had recently been crowned by the antipope.   At the same time Lothair, who was at war with the Hohenstaufen, was prevented from undertaking an expedition south of the Alps; so it was for Bernard to effect the pacification of Germany, and he started without delay.   At the beginning of 1135 he crossed the Rhine and arrived at Bamberg, where the Emperor received the submission of his enemies.   Then, passing the Alps in midwinter, Bernard descended upon Italy, and in due course reached Pisa, where Innocent II had summoned a council to discover who were his allies.   'St

Bernard,' says an historian of that period, 'was the soul of the council.'

Anacletus was excommunicated, and the domains of Roger II laid under an interdict. The delegates from Milan promised the adherence of that great metropolis provided the deposition of their arrogant archbishop, Anselm, were confirmed. The council agreed, and dispatched St Bernard to Lombardy to forestall trouble. On the way he was jostled by huge crowds anxious to see and hear him, to touch his cowl, and even cut bits from it. He was offered, but refused, the archbishopric; and travelling by mountain passes, along which he was escorted by herdsmen, he at length returned to Clairvaux.

His labour was not yet finished; for while working at his sermons on the Canticle he received another urgent appeal from the Pope, and for the third time turned his steps to Italy. Lothair's army had overrun most of the peninsula; but Anacletus was firmly established in certain parts of Rome, and Roger was invincible in Sicily. Disputes arose between the Emperor and the Pope on the subject of Apulia and with regard to the abbacy of Monte Cassino. Bernard smoothed out these differences, and was even for a short time superior of that famous abbey; then in October 1137, while Lothair, a sick and disappointed man, was journeying northward, he undertook to negotiate directly with Roger. He was in extremely bad health, and likened himself to 'the pale spectre of death'; nevertheless, he hurried on to Salerno to meet the King of Sicily and the canonist Peter of Pisa, who was to present Anacletus's case. His exhortations to re-establish the unity of the Church did not convince Roger; but so great an impression did they make upon Peter that he went and prostrated himself at Innocent's feet.

The end was now in sight. Lothair died on 4th December, Anacletus on 25th January 1138. A few obstinate spirits, including Roger, set up a new antipope, Victor IV, who, in horror at his own sacrilege, fled one night from the palace, joined St Bernard, and appealed to Innocent for mercy. Thus all for which Bernard had striven had been saved. It mattered little to him that Roger II, who had defeated the papal forces and now held the Pope at his mercy, extorted from the latter sacramental absolution and the recognition of his crown. Desiring only that the victor should not abuse his triumph, he urged moderation; but he was unable to prevent those reprisals which overtook the partisans of Anacletus and even Peter of Pisa.

Throughout this struggle, which lasted for eight years, the issue was nothing less than the unity of the Church. Bernard was the great captain and the real victor; but raised as he was upon the pinnacle of honour and success, closeted with kings, and master in so many assemblies, what had been his ambition? To regain the austere tranquillity of his cell. 'Soon, soon I shall be home,' he wrote to the prior of Clairvaux; 'I bring back a reward, the victory of Christ and the peace of the Church.'

Victory for Christ was likewise his sole ambition in the matter of the second crusade. It was at Easter in the year 1146 that St Bernard's preaching rekindled the sacred flame, and launched Christendom upon the second stage of its battle for the Holy Sepulchre.

Almost half a century before, after endless suffering and at the cost of untold heroism, the barons of Godfrey de Bouillon had stormed Jerusalem. But after that triumph, on 14th July 1099, the instability of their conquest had become plain for all to see. The feudal nobility had taken with them to the Holy Land their customary lack of discipline, and, late in 1144, Zengi, the Turkish governor of Mosul, having made himself master of Aleppo, took Edessa from the Christians. Edessa was an outpost controlling the road to Mesopotamia; it was recaptured and held for a very short interval, but fell once more in 1145 to the arms of Zengi's son Nureddin, who massacred the inhabitants. Their cry of anguish reached the West, and Christendom was thunderstruck.

It happened at this juncture that Louis VII was dreaming of some mighty enterprise which should cover him with glory. A first meeting at Bourges showed clearly that the enthusiasm of his barons was not what it had been: they were more chary of the risks entailed, knowing how much a crusade cost in blood and gold. But if Louis VII sometimes lacked wisdom, he was never wanting in courage: he appointed an assembly on the hillside at Vézelay, and invited St Bernard to attend.

Now the Abbot of Clairvaux, with his vast spiritual horizons, had good cause to favour such an expedition; but he was too level-headed to ignore the difficulties involved, and asked for papal sanction. Eugenius III was endeavouring to suppress rebellion and intrigue at Rome, and some time elapsed before he signed the Bull and Bernard could begin his work. We may guess the nature of the saint's appeal from its results: so deeply did he move his audience, that crowds were anxious for the privilege of immediate enlistment; and since there was not enough material for the crosses which so many sought then and there to sew upon their clothing, Bernard had even to divide his tunic among them. Next, he took the road from Vézelay and travelled through Burgundy, Lorraine, and Flanders, to swell the ranks of the crusaders. 'Come,' he urged the Count of Brittany, 'come, my brave soldier! gird up your loins, do not fail your king, the King of France. Nay, do not fail the King of Heaven, on whose behalf your sovereign undertakes so perilous a journey.'

He then went to the Rhineland to protest against a massacre of

Jews, and invited Conrad III to join the crusade. On 27th December 1147 he obtained that monarch's consent to lead the German corps, and solemnly delivered to him the blessed standard; while at St Denis Louis VII received the pilgrim's staff from Pope Eugenius.

No one denies that the second crusade was hopelessly mismanaged and ended in miserable failure.[1] St Bernard, however, was not to blame for the incompetence of Louis VII and Conrad III. He suffered much in consequence, and felt obliged, in the *De Considera-tione*, to justify his conduct. Having explained that the set-back was in no way attributable to Providence, but to the follies of the Christians themselves, he concluded with these noble words: 'I welcome the blows of calumny, the poisoned shafts of blasphemy, so that they may not reach Almighty God. I am glad to lose my honour, provided His glory is untouched.' As evidence that his personal prestige remained unaffected, we may recall that Suger, at the moment when death found him out, was meditating a further expedition with whose effective command he proposed to entrust the Cistercian!

The extent of St Bernard's activity is amazing, especially when we take account of the material handicaps under which he laboured. Travel in those days was arduous and uncertain; and yet this frail figure, emaciated by fasting, journeyed on and on from Paris to Sicily, from Rome to Flanders, from Languedoc to the Rhine, and even crossed the Alps on horseback in midwinter. His health was always failing; he slept badly; his stomach was so disordered that he was obliged 'to sustain it at frequent intervals with a little liquid, for it invariably rejected all solid food'; while his hands and feet swelled for no apparent reason. Nor did the moral atmosphere of the age simplify his task. Remember, this holy man, before whom difficulties seemed to melt away, lived in a society where violence, intrigue, and the lust for power or profit were no less in evidence than they are to-day. No obstacle, however, was too great for him; he never failed to reach his goal.

All this goes to prove that St Bernard was not only a saint, but a genius. No one of mere average ability could have assessed his contemporaries and the passing scene as did the Abbot of Clairvaux. No ordinary man could have shouldered so many tasks at once, keeping in touch with the whole vast network of his Order and making sure that his instructions were carried out. None but a saint and a genius could have maintained a huge correspondence with everyone of importance in Western Christendom, and still remain a man of thought, of prayer, of contemplation. 'His greatness,' says Pascal, 'lies not in his being at the far end of the scale; he is at both ends, and fills the interval between.'

[1] See Chapter X, paragraph 5.

It need scarcely be added that some of the admiration bestowed upon the leader is reflected in that society which submitted to his guidance. Just because Bernard was a superman it seemed natural to take orders from him in the political, diplomatic, and even economic sphere, which would to-day be strictly reserved for 'experts.' Just because he was a saint, whose only weapon was his word, and whom the least petty princeling could have placed under arrest, the greatest sovereigns bowed to his decisions. The twentieth century, in which force is, more than ever before, recognized as the *ultima ratio*, would do well to ponder on these things.

8. St Bernard and the Arts

We have seen the great Cistercian put forth his influence in many different fields; but there is another, in which that influence has been much discussed and adversely criticized. I mean the realm of art.

It has been forcibly argued that he was blind to beauty, and that during the new 'quarrel of images' his part was that of a philistine hostile to all aesthetic achievement. Put like that, the thesis must be rejected. Bernard's attitude towards art cannot be understood except as the outcome of his profound spirituality, of his longing to be of service in God's cause.

When he first appeared on the stage of history, the prevailing force in Western Christendom was Cluny, whose builder-monks were busy throughout Europe. According to their tradition, external beauty was an aid to prayer and, in its several forms, gave praise to God; so that wherever the Cluniacs built, there was a wealth of ornament. Cunning geometrical patterns followed the line of the arcades; arch and cornice were a riot of exquisite detail; capitals became regular menageries; while the lintels and tympana of porches were peopled with kings and saints. Even the interior was rich with frescoes; the cross ornamented with enamel, chased gold, and precious stones. The masterpiece was Cluny itself, an enormous basilica erected by St Hugh. It had seven towers, two transepts, and eight columns of rare marble to uphold the sanctuary. It contained also many priceless treasures, such as the famous candelabrum of Queen Matilda of England, which was eight feet tall and illuminated the high altar.

Against this unheard-of luxury St Bernard protested in his *Apology*. He thought it unfitting that men who had renounced worldly display, who had sacrificed all that delights the senses in order to possess Christ, should be surrounded with a magnificence that could not but lead them into temptation. He therefore condemned 'the enormous height of the churches, their extraordinary length, the useless width of their naves, the richness of polished stone, the paintings which distract attention. Vanity of vanities! nay, worse than vain. The Church's walls may shine, but her poor go naked; she covers her stones with gold, but leaves her children unclothed.'

St Bernard, however, was not the only one to criticize Cluniac ostentation. Peter the Cantor stigmatized excesses in construction, the poet Rutebœuf cried out against the luxury of cloisters, and Suger, himself a Benedictine, adopted the same views after his 'conversion' in 1127. That their words had some effect is clear from the remark of an abbot who, while visiting Suger in his cell at Saint Denis, exclaimed: 'This man puts us all to shame; he builds not as we do, for ourselves, but for God.'

Did spiritual asceticism, transferred to the aesthetic plane, give birth to ugliness? The answer is found in those magnificent Cistercian abbeys which rose throughout the Western world, whose very ruins are overwhelming in their solemn beauty. Look, for example, at Fontenay, Pontigny, Fontfroide, Silvacane, Sénanque, and Alcobaça. Only the cellar at Clairvaux has been preserved from senseless vandalism; but Bouquen, with the noble façade of its chapter-house, is rising once more from the ruins. Gentle restraint, outward austerity, and that 'sober intoxication' which St Bernard desired in the interior life, are noticeable at every turn: in the naves with their perfect lines, in mouldings whose sole ornament is their purity of form, in rays of pearly light that fall through grisaille glass, unmixed with foreign elements, and bring with them a strangely fluid, almost secret quality that speaks to the soul more intimately than does colour. Cistercian art represents an aesthetic far removed from that of the cathedrals with all their wealth of detail; and its refusal to conform with the prevailing ostentation may well have delayed the fall of gothic down that slope of excess and superfluity which was later to become 'flamboyant.'

It should also be remembered that St Bernard's view applied only to the building of religious houses. He never disputed that 'episcopal,' as opposed to monastic, art should 'speak to the ignorant'; and he agreed with the use of such ornament as could stir devotion in carnal men, for whom things spiritual have little meaning. So far from contemning sculpture and stained glass, he encouraged its development, except among those who have abandoned all things for God, and in whose minds a more spiritual outlook should predominate.

St Bernard's views on art spread throughout the West, helped by the elevation of many Cistercian monks to the episcopal dignity, and by the example of Cistercian monasteries which rose in every land.[1] Experts like the monk Theophilus, author of an *Essay on the Several Arts*, were so inspired by his teaching, that parts of this work have been

---

[1] See the album of photographs *Abbayes Cisterciennes*, published by the Marquise de Maillé and Henry de Ségogne (Paris, 1943).

found to correspond exactly with passages from the great abbot's writings.

It has even been suggested that Bernard's impact upon the history of art was more profound than hitherto imagined. The revival of techniques which helped the transition from romanesque to gothic during the thirteenth century was probably due to the influence of Clairvaux. Achard, novice-master in that house, was architect-superintendent of the Order; while the celebrated builder Geoffrey of Ainay was a veteran of the same monastery. Furthermore, several primary features of gothic architecture can be traced to St Bernard. The prolongation of the cathedral choir to form a Lady chapel, more imposing than any of those situated in the apse, would never have taken place had not the White Monk laboured so hard to spread devotion to Mary. The great symbolist's influence, more direct and more pronounced than that even of Suger or Honorius of Autun, is discernible in sculpture and stained glass. His mark is apparent in every detail. For example, a window at Saint-Denis, dating from the time of Suger, shows the chariot of Aminadab surmounted with a green cross and drawn by the evangelists, exactly as St Bernard describes it. And some writers have maintained that the well-known image of God the Father holding the crucifix in outstretched arms is derived from the Cistercian's famous discourse on *Jesus crucified beneath the Father*. Nor is it unlikely that his *Discovery at Easter* gave rise to that custom of depicting the minutiae of the Resurrection (the open tomb, the folded shroud, the angel lifting the stone) which originated in the twelfth century. So far from being hostile to the arts, Bernard helped to give them life; his personality is engraved thereon as upon much else besides.

9.   BERNARD THE KNIGHT

St Bernard's one and only purpose in the temporal sphere was to promote Christianity. His monks were to form a spiritual advance-guard leading society to the light of Christ. But, realist as he was, he understood clearly that this work required co-operation from the laity, who must therefore be inspired with the same ideal if it was to succeed.

When considering the life and labours of St Bernard, one is struck by his resemblance to those great figures who embody the highest medieval ideal in the domain of action. The White Monk, who had 'no weapon but his tears and prayers,' belongs to the same family as Godfrey de Bouillon and St Louis. The son of the lord of Fontaines never lost sight of the ideal inherited from his ancestors: and his contemporaries recognized beneath the Cistercian cowl the invisible armour of a knight.

Numerous instances in his life reveal this peculiar affinity.   We have seen that Suger thought of entrusting him with the effective command of an army; and no one at that time was in the least surprised. In the strategic planning of the second crusade he was asked for and tendered his advice, though it was ignored by Louis VII and Conrad III.   He too showed the German princes how necessary it was for Christendom to smash the pagan Wends.[1]   The Christian spirit which he advocated was energetic, militant, one might almost say military.   His very habit of addressing Mary by the charming title of 'our Lady' was derived from the language of feudalism; he considered himself the Blessed Virgin's liegeman, and served her as a vassal would his sovereign.

Seeking to give this manly form of Christianity a concrete shape, St Bernard dreamed of an institution which should embody it for all to see.   Such was the Order of the Temple.   In 1128, at the Council of Troyes, which he attended at the invitation of Pope Honorius II, he was requested to provide a rule for this military organization whose duty it would be to defend the Holy Land against renewed attack by the infidel.   Accordingly, he drew up the statutes and wrote his *Praise of the new Chivalry*, in which he spoke with unveiled enthusiasm of the ideal which should inspire the soldiers of Christ.   The white habit of the Templars (to which the red cross was a later addition) indicated their spiritual relationship with Cîteaux; and the warrior-monks, unlike the worldly knights despised by Bernard, would pass their lives as 'poor soldiers of Christ' in self-sacrifice and the practice of asceticism.   The ancient seal of the Templars, in fact, showed two knights riding on one horse, reminding them of holy poverty.

Thus, according to St Bernard, knighthood would find its most perfect expression in a body of men who represented both the loftiest temporal ideal of the age (that of the fearless soldier ever ready to die for his cause) and the noblest conception of a Christian soul.   The 'new militia' was the most perfect and most active element in society, for it achieved a union of the sacred and profane; it proved extra-ordinarily effective in the service of the Church generally, but more particularly in carrying out the grandiose designs of the Holy See.

The fate of the Order is well known.   It became a great banking house with strong rooms in every commandery.   It lent money to kings, and its commercial honesty was not always above suspicion. Thus do human institutions decline from their first fervour.   The tragedy which engulfed the Templars is wrapped in such mystery that we cannot deliver an impartial judgment.   One thing, however, may be said.   It was Philip the Fair who, in the shocking 'Outrage of Anagni,' gave the signal for rebellion by the secular powers against the

[1] See Chapter XII, section 3.

spiritual supremacy; and it was Philip the Fair who broke the 'militia of Christ,' which, though fallen from its high estate, was still the living symbol of force subjected to the spirit.[1]   Times had changed; Bernard's two predominant ideas now lay in ruins, and through the mist of centuries to come the modern epoch might already be discerned.

This episode in the saint's life is not one upon which historians have laid much stress; but there is reason to look upon it as of first importance.   At all events, it features prominently in the legend which grew up around this great figure as soon as he was dead.   The main themes of the 'Grail' cycle are probably connected with the tradition of the Templars.   The Knight of the Holy Grail, pure, unselfish, heroic, is no doubt the literary symbol of the 'new militia' founded by St Bernard; and in that part of Wolfram von Eschenbach's poem which links up with the work of the French poet Guyot, Parsifal becomes king of the Templars.   The author continually praises the Temple.   'Happy the mother,' he exclaims in the person of Trevrizent the hermit, 'happy the mother who brings into the world a son destined for such service!'   And many commentators are inclined to think that the prototype of Galahad, the ideal knight, the *preux sans tâche*, was none other than St Bernard.

It has also been noted that, in the thirty-first canto of the *Paradiso*, Beatrice leaves the guidance of Dante's steps, on the last stages of his journey towards the region of eternal bliss, to 'an old man dressed as the glorious family.'   What does this mean?   Some authorities suggest that it is a reference to the Cistercian cowl or to the white mantle of the Templars.   Others think that Dante belonged to one of the secret sects which are supposed to have lingered on after the disappearance of the Templars.   In any case, the guide of whom he speaks is Bernard of Clairvaux.

'That thou mayest consummate thy journey perfectly,' says the old man, 'whereto prayer and holy love dispatched me—fly with thine eyes throughout this garden; for gazing on it will equip thy glance better to mount through the divine ray.   And the Queen of heaven, for whom I am all burning with love, will grant us every grace, because I am her faithful Bernard.'

10. NUPTIALS

Such was Bernard, Frenchman and Burgundian, son of the Church and saint of God.   At intervals in the long course of history there appear these radiant and significant personalities, representing the essential features of the age in which they live and impressing on it the mark of their own genius.   Observing the mysterious accord between

[1] See Chapter XIV, section 7.

the White Monk and the aspirations of the Middle Ages, and remembering the numerous occasions upon which his action proved decisive, we may call the twelfth century 'the age of St Bernard,' even more legitimately than we speak of the age of Augustus or the age of Louis XIV. But if we consider the spiritual heights to which he attained, the impulse which he gave to Christianity and which has lasted until our own day, it must certainly be admitted that his greatness on the historical plane is as nothing compared with the glory that is his in that domain where the uncreated light shines forth alone, and where every figure is but the reflection of God. Following St Paul and St Augustine, a little though not much inferior to them, side by side with his two successors upon earth, St Francis of Assisi and St Dominic, Bernard ranks as one of the major heroes, one of the high peaks of Christianity.

His contemporaries of long ago honoured him as we honour him to-day. Glory, as it were, shone round about him, though he esteemed it but as dust. His biographer does not exaggerate in calling him the 'darling of his age,' for he was loved and fêted everywhere he went. At Milan he was almost crushed to death by cheering crowds, and the students of the Latin Quarter in Paris accorded him a boisterous welcome. When he visited Metz shortly before his death, the multitude was so enormous that he was obliged to take refuge in a boat on the Moselle. A blind man standing on the bank cried out, asking that he might be taken to Bernard; whereupon a fisherman in another boat threw him the end of his cloak, and hauled him to the saint's vessel. When at last the great abbot died, it was thought necessary to keep secret the hour of his funeral lest an excited crowd of relic-hunters should carry off his body.

Such popularity was bound to incur envy and resentment. Nathan stands at his peril before David, Elias before Ahab. It is always dangerous to insist on the principles of truth and justice. 'I know,' said Bernard, 'that by making war on abuses I earn the hatred of evildoers.' He was even denounced to the Sacred College, and received from Cardinal Haimeric an unfriendly letter on the subject of 'these monks who leave their cloister to pester the Holy See and the cardinals.' But he was unmoved by such complaints, no matter from whom they came, and he replied, in terms of respectful irony, that the raucous voices which disturbed the Church's peace were rather those of the noisy frogs which filled the cardinalatial and pontifical palaces.

Nor could he be silenced even by death, before whom his friends and relations had gone down one by one—Malachy the great Irishman; Suger, the minister whom he had reconciled with Christ; Thibaut, Count of Champagne, with whom he had more than once crossed swords, but whom he loved as the first protector of his work; and

Eugenius III, his spiritual son, the beloved Pope. While his health steadily declined, he continued to observe the Holy Rule in all its rigour, and would accept no relaxation. Whether in the monastery or on the road, he lived like the humblest of his brethren. Though in the grip of fever, he travelled to Lorraine on one last mission, to arbitrate between the duke and the people of Metz; but when he returned to Clairvaux his strength was at an end.

With a full heart he watched the slow approach of death. His body was exhausted by suffering, but his spirit seemed to take on new life, his soul to burn with a yet brighter flame. He had looked forward to this crisis as the hour of ultimate illumination; and as he felt his physical powers ebb away, his spirit scaled the final pitch, a supreme effort of which the last sermons on the Canticle of Canticles remain as an imperishable monument. He was about to consummate the mystical marriage, and could not but overflow with gladness as he lay on his truckle-bed in that humble cell, waiting peacefully for the coming of the Spouse.

At nine o'clock on the morning of 20th August 1153 Bernard slept in Christ. He was sixty-three. 'At the moment when he expired,' says the chronicler, 'the merciful Mother of God, his special patroness, was seen at his bedside; she had come to fetch his soul.' Before committing his body to the earth, the monks took a cast of his features, a cast from which all later images of St Bernard are derived: the sunken cheeks are deeply lined, but the high forehead reveals a mighty intelligence, and the whole face radiates a marvellous purity of soul.

It is stated in the *Great Exordium* that immediately after death he worked more miracles than in his lifetime. An epileptic approached the corpse, and was cured of his disease. A young mother laid her paralysed infant on the saint's body, and saw the child leap with joy. These prodigies continued after his burial, and such crowds flocked to the Val d'Absinthe that monastic peace was seriously disturbed. The Abbot of Cîteaux therefore travelled to Clairvaux and, standing by the tomb, forbade the saint in virtue of holy obedience to work another miracle. The humble monk submitted from beyond the frontiers of the grave; a charming story which shows that Bernard was scarcely dead before he passed into legend.

But there was nothing legendary about the work he left behind. The life which he had breathed into his Order continued to flourish long after his death, and Cistercian houses sprang up everywhere. Clairvaux alone gave the Church a Pope, fifteen cardinals, and innumerable bishops. Many a great mystic followed in Bernard's wake: William of Saint-Thierry, Guerric of Igny, Gilbert of Hoy, Alan of Lille, Beatrice of Tirelemont, Mechtild of Hackeborn, and Gertrude, to name but a few. Before the end of the twelfth century four

Lives of the saint had been written.   The *Vita Prima*, edited by his immediate friends William of Saint-Thierry, Ernaud of Bonneval, and Geoffrey of Auxerre,[1] is a mine of carefully selected information; while the *Liber Miraculorum* abounds in marvels which prove at least how greatly St Bernard was admired by his contemporaries.

The Church was very soon obliged to confirm the judgment of the masses.   Nor was he unworthy to be numbered in the calendar of saints, he whom Innocent II described as 'the impregnable bastion of the Church.'   On 18th January 1174, less than twenty-one years after his death, Bernard was canonized by Pope Alexander III.   Anticipating the decision of the nineteenth century, it was decreed that the Gospel for the Mass of the new saint should be that used in the Common of Doctors, *Vos estis sal terrae*; and shortly afterwards, in 1201, Pope Innocent III himself composed a collect in which he spoke of him as 'Doctor Egregius.'

That St Bernard's writings were an object of constant study and meditation until the seventeenth century is clear from the words of Mabillon, who calls him 'the last of the Fathers.'   *The Imitation of Christ* owes much to him, and Pope Nicholas V, a great patron of the arts, whose name is linked with those of Piero della Francesca and Fra Angelico, ordered a splendid manuscript of the *De Consideratione*. Bossuet, Pascal, Fénelon, all drank deep at the wells of his doctrine; but thereafter his glory suffered an eclipse.   It may be that, like St Augustine, who also fell into disfavour for a time, he was found 'too Jansenistic,' as Mme de Sévigné remarked.   Like the Bishop of Hippo, and indeed St Paul himself, he was unlucky in his admirers, among whom were Luther and Calvin!   Did not the dictator of Geneva say of the *De Consideratione*: 'Truth herself speaks by the mouth of St Bernard'?

It was reserved for Pope Pius VIII, the man who said he knew no policy 'but that of the Gospel,' to proclaim St Bernard a Doctor of the Universal Church, in the Brief *Quod Unum* (23rd July 1830).   Since that date his reputation has revived.   Unfamiliar he may still be to the average schoolboy, who cannot be expected to appreciate his tremendous historical importance from a few scattered allusions.   Nevertheless, he has been restored to his rightful place; he is the subject of innumerable books and enjoys a boundless veneration.

In the history of Christ's Church he is the most perfect figure of manhood as conceived by the Middle Ages, one of the supreme guides of Christendom on the road of light, the witness of his age before Almighty God.

---

[1] Geoffrey, once a pupil of Abélard, succumbed to Bernard's fascination and became his secretary.

CHAPTER IV

THE LEAVEN IN THE LUMP

1. Relapse

Not all members of the Church were like St Bernard, not all were saints. It was in the Middle Ages as it is to-day; and he who is surprised or scandalized thereat shows that he has failed to grasp the nature and mystery of the Church.

It is, of course, pitiable and depressing to see Christians fall back time after time into the same old rut. The process may be observed by each one of us as it unrolls against the familiar background of our guilty hearts. But the Church is not only a supernatural reality, the Mystical Body of Christ, associating man with God on the eternal plane through the mystery of Redemption. She is also the lowly mass consisting of all those for whom Christ shed His Blood on Calvary; and that is why a permanent contradiction is apparent between the grandeur of her ideal and the weakness of her members, between 'the dignity of Christianity and the unworthiness of Christians.'[1] We must accept this unhappy paradox: by her condemnation of the heresiarchs Montanus, Novatian, Donatus, and, later on, of the Cathars, Holy Church proclaims that she is formed not only of the just and the predestined, but also of those miserable sinners who are lured to the abyss and stand ever ready to plunge over the edge.

Within this 'assembly' of the baptized, however, some men carry a special responsibility as witnesses of God. They are the appointed guardians of an institution which holds the deposit of faith, the apostolic privileges, and the right to confer the sacraments. The word 'Church,' indeed, is often used to describe those who are invested with such charges and enjoy such powers. Their fundamental role is that of the leaven in a loaf, to give it life and to prevent its collapse. 'A holy clergy makes a virtuous people . . .' says Blanc de Saint-Bonnet; and that was truer in the Middle Ages than at any other period. For the medieval Church, as an institution, was, so to speak, the framework of society; and any weakness on her part reacted upon the whole complex system.

Weak points were inevitable. A cleric is still a man, notwithstanding ordination; he bears within himself the same taint of original

[1] Nicolas Berdyaer.

sin as the remainder of the flock. The invasions, together with the upheavals which followed in their wake, had resulted in a veritable 'barbarization' of society. For six long centuries the West had been wrapped in darkness, nor had the clergy escaped the general contamination. It is true that throughout those six hundred years the struggle had been maintained by relays of holy men and women who had fought against evil both by word and by example; but the barbarian epoch had been ridden by fornicating priests, by prelates who were soldiers rather than men of God, and by brigand-clerks who traded in ecclesiastical benefices. At the turn of the year 1000 victory was not yet in sight; despite notable improvement, too many of those whose duty it was to direct the Church proved themselves unfitted to exercise responsibility, and the situation remained more or less stationary during the next three hundred years. Progress there certainly was, sometimes heroic and decisive. But the contradiction remained, the cruel paradox was still there: although the Church was governed by a long line of splendid leaders, there was not wanting base material even in high places.

It is neither pleasant to dwell upon these shortcomings, nor profitable to multiply examples. A study of the most reliable witnesses provides us with a shameful picture of ignorant, avaricious, lustful, and even criminal ecclesiastics. Few were above criticism. The diatribes of St Bernard, and of others equally severe, were directed against the Roman Curia, which Jacques de Vitry [1] described as 'so busy with temporal and mundane affairs that it had no time for spiritual interests.' They were directed likewise against those parish priests whom St Bernard himself described as 'slaves of avarice, governed by pride, and smearing even the Holy Place with their abominations.' The visitation-book of Eudes Rigaud, Archbishop of Rouen and friend of St Louis, affords an outspoken comment upon clerics who boozed in taverns, kept concubines and children in their homes, and even frequented houses of which morality could not but disapprove. [2] So much for Rouen; but the Normans enjoyed no monopoly of such conduct.

A remarkable anthology, illustrating these undesirable practices, might likewise be formed from the archives of the Church. They reveal that the majority of clergymen were negligent as regards the divine office. Many were unacquainted with the words and made a mockery of their recitation, gabbling the sacred liturgy at top speed. Some took part in orgies, others turned their houses into brothels; and there were even cases of erotic songs in church. The very fact that

---

[1] Patriarch of Jerusalem and later Cardinal. In 1216 he visited the papal court, which was then in residence at Perugia, and was absolutely scandalized.

[2] In one such place a certain reverend gentleman forgot his clothes!

E

popes and councils thought it necessary to condemn such behaviour proves that it existed.

The root cause of these deplorable abuses was undoubtedly the poor quality of those who offered themselves for ordination. Ignorance was rife among the parochial clergy, which was drawn from the lower levels of society. Many parish priests knew no more than the mere outlines or most striking episodes of the Gospel, and even these they mixed with legend. There was no question at all of moral theology. Clerics lived on a level with their flocks; for, despite the efforts of certain bishops,[1] they had never been properly trained. Nor was there much improvement until the advent of drastic reforms, when diocesan seminaries came into being.

An ill-trained clergy, its lower ranks devoid of solid principles and its leaders contaminated by secular influences, could not defend itself against the twofold temptation of the flesh and money. Celibacy of the priesthood, though not originally of obligation, had been proposed as an ideal state since the fourth century. But there had been considerable laxity throughout the barbarian epoch. Married deacons, priests, and bishops were numerous, a fact which could not be disguised by the pretence of chastity; and the general laxity of the ninth and tenth centuries had resulted in a serious increase of such abuses. 'Nicolaïsm,' as it was called, was named after a heretical sect in the early Church. It is mentioned in the Apocalypse (ii. 6–15) as well as by St Irenaeus, and was one of the cardinal points of later ecclesiastical reform. But although official statistics showed a considerable decrease in the number of married clergy, the abuse continued. From the thirteenth century alone at least one hundred unedifying documents have survived, covering a period of less than twenty years. There were married priests at Norwich; others, at Tournai, kept concubines; others again, at Ratisbon, had large families. Nor is it without significance that the Council of Pau (1212) imposed heavy penalties for 'unnatural sins of the flesh' committed by clerics.

Money was a still more dangerous stumbling-block. Simony, so called after Simon Magus who, according to the Acts, offered St Peter money in exchange for the power to communicate the Holy Spirit, is the crime of purchasing an ecclesiastical benefice with temporal goods. Against this disgraceful practice too the Church directed her reforming zeal. A substantial improvement was effected, but the sin was never wholly rooted out. Temporal interests still dictated the appointment of bishops and abbots, and the Church was never able to free herself entirely from this servitude. Generally speaking, avarice, luxury, and dishonesty in certain members of the clergy were denounced, not only by pamphleteers such as Étienne de Fougères and the author of the

<hr>

[1] See Chapter VI, section 6.

Bible de Guyot, not only by fabulists and popular writers, but also by papal Bulls and conciliar decrees.

It is, indeed, depressing to observe this relapse, to watch the leaven become unfitted to fulfil its purpose.   Pope Clement V, William le Maire of Angers, and the Dominican Alvarez Pelajo drew attention at the beginning of the fourteenth century to the same errors as had been deplored in the twelfth by St Bernard, and in the thirteenth by St Dominic and Innocent III.   We need but to peruse Dante in order to find this mass of criticism recapitulated.   The *Divine Comedy* peoples Hell and Purgatory with cardinals 'so heavy that they must be carried,' with 'ravening wolves in shepherds' guise,' and with shameless priests. 'Cephas and Paul, the Vessel of Election,' the poet indignantly exclaims, 'went barefoot and ate when they were able.' [1]   There is, however, something noble and encouraging in these strictures: they were thoroughly deserved, but it is to the Church's credit that she was never indifferent to her defilement.   Time after time she found new leaven that would cause the lump to rise again.

2.   REFORM

If the human lump has a regrettable tendency to fall flat, Christianity contains within itself an indestructible element which periodically supplies the remedy.   I mean the spirit of reform.   In the darkest night of the barbarian age it was manifested in St Benedict, St Columba, and St Benedict of Aniane; later, in the monks of Cluny, in St Romuald, and in St Peter Damian.   All these fiercely and fearlessly set their faces against evils which disgraced the Spouse of Christ; nor did the following centuries look in vain for men to carry on the struggle with like determination.

In what does the spirit of reform consist?   First, in a clear view of those dangers with which the Christian soul is menaced—the danger of routine, of internal disintegration, and of compromise with the world.   Second, in an heroic effort to break with the forces of death, and so recover intact the first fervour of freedom and holiness.   The spirit of reform is for the Church, on the spiritual plane, what it is for political parties seeking a radical transformation of society.   When a revolutionary minority obtains power, it soon finds itself bogged down by self-interest, undermined by indifference and complacency, fixed in the groove of habit.   It becomes 'bourgeois,' and must strive to regain its original condition, to recover its early determination and purity of intention, to break with the perilous advantages of victory. This is what Trotsky, in Marxist language, called the 'permanent revolution.'   Reform is the permanent revolution of Christianity.

[1] See Chapter XIV, section 12.

By what characteristics, then, may we distinguish the genuine reform, so necessary for the historical development of Christianity, from one of those anarchical movements which break out in the Church from time to time only to cause trouble and lose themselves in heresy and schism? The demands of a reformer are admissible only upon certain conditions: they must rest upon an exact appreciation of the errors calling for correction, and upon the true interests of the Gospel rather than on prejudice; they must be conceived within the framework of charity and Christian fellowship. The reformer must not seek innovation, but rather a return to the sources of that institution whose interests he claims to have at heart. He should take his stand upon 'tradition,' in the sense of that which best enables a society to progress while remaining true to the fountain-head of its ideal. Finally, he must not yield to pride; he must preserve humility of heart, submissive always to authority in the persons of the hierarchy, who are responsible before God, who alone may take the initiative, and who alone can bring it to fruition.

Fortunately for the Middle Ages, these conditions were fulfilled on more than one occasion. Heroic souls stood forth from the ranks of Christendom, filled with the love of Christ and respect for the Church, desiring only the kingdom of God and His justice, visibly united with the Apostles and early martyrs, never dreaming of rebellion. Such were Gregory VII, St Bernard, St Bruno, St Norbert, St Francis of Assisi, St Dominic, and Innocent III. Through them the 'permanent revolution' was achieved without dissolving in mere anarchy.

Two circumstances in particular aided the reform. First, the extraordinary latitude permitted, even within the Church herself, to criticism or, to use a political expression, to 'self criticism.' We have noticed St Bernard's independence in addressing himself to bishops and even to the popes. But he does not stand alone; St Bridget was no less outspoken, as were the Poverello of Assisi and many others. Canon Thomas de Chantimpré's curious symbolic work *The Bees* (1248) relates how the Devil visited a certain preacher who was about to address a council, and said to him: 'Don't you know what to say? Just tell them this, that the Powers of Darkness salute the Princes of the Church.' The good canon was *not* arrested and condemned! Grave as were ecclesiastical abuses, independence of this kind made it possible to combat them, and in such a way that criticism of individuals did not lessen men's esteem for the Church and the function of her ministers. These angry prophets had too deep a faith to identify the institution with its faithless servants.

The second favourable circumstance was the hierarchy's ability to see how far criticism was justified, and to act accordingly. Those in authority were free from an all too human weakness which bids them remain silent before such as might take umbrage at their words; and, if a few of them did feel so inclined, they were sufficiently strong-minded to resist the temptation. Herein lay the strength of several great popes: Gregory VII, Paschal II, Innocent III, and Honorius III saw and proclaimed the truth. The reforming movement, in fact, became the very life-blood of the Church, because these popes realized its importance and shouldered their responsibility.

3. GREGORY VII, THE REFORMER

Pope Alexander II died on 21st April 1073, and Cardinal Hildebrand, the most influential figure in the Roman Curia, ordered public prayers for God's blessing on the forthcoming conclave. Next day, however, the crowd attending Alexander's funeral began to shout: 'Hildebrand Pope! Hildebrand Bishop!' and so overwhelming was their enthusiasm that the cardinals, to whom, since 1059, had belonged the duty of nominating St Peter's successor, hastened to confirm this popular election. The new Pope took no pleasure in his promotion: 'The terrible weight of the Church,' he wrote, 'is laid upon reluctant shoulders.' But since God had spoken, he could not refuse, and Hildebrand took the regnal name Gregory in memory of a beloved master. This humble religious, elevated to the highest of all earthly thrones, was still a deacon. He was therefore ordained priest on 22nd May, and on 29th June, the feast of SS. Peter and Paul, was consecrated Bishop of Rome.

He was now a man of fifty-three, and in the prime of life. Corpulent, short-legged, and small of stature, his appearance was not particularly attractive; but immense spiritual power radiated from him. A massive and penetrating intellect, a will of iron, ceaseless energy, and unshakable determination in adversity; such were Gregory's outstanding characteristics. His enemies have represented him as ambitious and unscrupulous, as a politician for whom all means to an end were justified, a violent and, indeed, a wicked man. Nothing is farther from the truth; we have numerous examples of his charity, of his refinement, and of his moderation. 'Love men even while you detest their vices,' he used often to say. He was one of those for whom love of God is the ultimate end of life, for whom 'the whole law is summed up in two words: humility and charity.' Throughout his pontificate he bore in mind that he must render an account of it to the supreme Judge, and he viewed the splendour of his crown as the symbol of terrible responsibility. Few popes have had so exalted a conception of the Church, whose faith he defended by the condemnation of Berengar; whose members, East and West, he longed to reconcile after a separation that had lasted twenty years; whom in his dreams he had already launched on the crusade; whom, above all, he passionately desired to see pure and holy, worthy of her Master.

Legend has represented Hildebrand as having in effect ruled the Church since about 1050, and as having inspired the movement for reform which spread throughout Christendom during the years prior to his pontificate. That is hardly true. But if his friends and enemies alike, though for different purposes, have exaggerated his influence, we cannot but wonder at the meteoric career marked out by Providence for this son of a Tuscan labourer, whose merit alone had made him supreme in the Roman Curia. Born at Sonno c. 1023, he was placed, while still a child, as an oblate in the monastery of St Mary on the Aventine, a daughter-house of Cluny. Becoming secretary to Pope Gregory VI (1045–6), he remained faithful to that pontiff in disgrace, and did much to promote the election of his friend Bruno, Bishop of Toul. It was thus, at the age of less than thirty years, that he came to play an all-important part at the side of St Leo IX (1049–54) who, to make clear his purpose of reform, had entered Rome barefooted on the morning of his coronation. Hildebrand was next entrusted with various missions by Victor II (1055–7) and Stephen IX (1057–8); he manœuvred the election of Nicholas II (1059–61) to the see of Peter, and was the 'right hand' of Alexander II (1061–73), who desired him as his successor. Charged, one after another, with embassies or visitations, adviser to the Pope, and a member of several councils, he had acquired an extensive knowledge of the whole of Christendom; and his influence had more than once proved decisive. It was Hildebrand, for example, who pledged the Church's support of William, Duke of Normandy, in his expedition against England. But above all, his contacts, his observation, and his private meditation had convinced him that reform was of paramount importance.

But the reforms accomplished by Gregory VII had their root in a much earlier movement, initiated more than a century before his birth by Gerard of Brogne, John of Gorze, Erluin of Gembloux, Bruno of Cologne, and others. More than a century had elapsed also since the foundation of Cluny, which became the headquarters of reform and which, during a period of 150 years, played an important part in this connection under its saintly abbots Odo, Maïeul, Odilon, and Hugh. The desire to live wholly in God had already produced the hermits of St Romuald at Camaldoli, St John Gualbert's monks at Vallombrosa, and the enthusiastic crowds of the Pattarines who launched a furious attack upon the luxury of clerical life. Exactly contemporary with Hildebrand, there had grown up St Peter Damian, that hirsute and formidable prophet who had been created cardinal by Stephen IX. The reforming spirit, issuing from the cloister and entering into the hearts of the people, had been welcomed by a succession of popes, who followed a road mapped out by Cardinal Humbert in his treatise *Against Simony* (1057). Clement II, Damasus II, Leo IX, Victor II, Clement V, Nicholas II, and Alexander II had openly embraced the principles of reform. Papal and conciliar decrees had condemned error and denounced abuses; while many a devout soul, urged by the longing for a better way of life, dreamed of restoring the Church to her pristine purity.

Gregory VII, therefore, must not be separated from his age; his merits should not be exaggerated at the expense of his predecessors and contemporaries. The fact remains, however, that his pontificate was of the utmost significance. In him the movement was consolidated; thanks to him, the interdependence of two problems was made clear, and the doctrine formulated which made it possible to solve them both.

When Alexander II first advanced Hildebrand to authority, two, or perhaps three, aspects were discernible in the attitude towards reform. Every right-minded person saw the necessity thereof, but there was some difference of opinion as to the best means of achieving it. Some, especially in Italy, stood for the direct, apostolic, and moral method: to preach against prevalent abuses, above all by example, and to impose heavy penalties upon the guilty. Chief among the representatives of this view was Peter Damian. Others maintained that the real cause of the trouble lay in the poor quality of the clergy, which they attributed in turn to secular interference; and they recommended an institutional and political method which, they argued, would free the Church from the tutelage of kings and barons. Such was the theory of several eminent clerics in Lorraine, good canonists and wise politicians, notably of Cardinal Humbert. But these differences were not irreconcilable, for both sides were agreed as to the essential purpose. Finally, it is not impossible that a kind of nostalgia for the past, especially for the splendid age of Charlemagne, convinced others that it was necessary to restore the Christian order which had suffered during the Carolingian decadence. They felt this to be the surest means of recalling the clergy to their duty and of restraining the power of princes. The great merit of Gregory VII was that he understood, at the cost of bitter experience, that history would reduce these three viewpoints to a single consideration.

At the beginning of his pontificate he tried the first method, and sought to enlist the co-operation of temporal sovereigns. He even attempted reconciliation with such avowed simoniacs and adulterers as the German Emperor Henry IV and Philip I of France, believing that no stone should be left unturned in God's service. A council met at Rome in March 1074, and issued four decrees: (1) Anyone who had obtained ordination or a spiritual benefice by simony was excluded from the ecclesiastical hierarchy. (2) Anyone in possession of a church or an abbey as the result of purchase was *ipso facto* dispossessed. (3) No cleric who was guilty of fornication might celebrate Mass or minister in any way at the altar.   (4) In the event of a cleric publicly disobeying the three preceding ordinances, the faithful were forbidden to attend any service conducted by him, and were to do their best to make him submit.

The decrees of 1074 embodied the principles of a necessary reform, and Gregory VII forthwith sent legates to see that they were given effect.   But these prelates met with general opposition in one shape or another.   Simoniacs were supported by their respective sovereigns in employing every device to frustrate the Holy Father's wishes, and some rebelled outright.   In Germany, for example, Hermann of Bamberg and Lieman of Bremen put themselves at the head of several thousand priests who treated the Pope as little better than a heretic. One meeting of German clergy declared that 'if he won't assure that the divine offices are celebrated by the clergy, he had better apply to the angels!'   The saintly Bishop Altmann of Passau was almost lynched for upholding the pontifical instructions.   Otto of Constance, on the other hand, encouraged the priests of his diocese to marry, and the legates were stoned by fornicators.   In France, Hugh of Die failed to make the least impression.   The Council of Paris was dissolved, and Abbot Walter of Pontoise was assaulted for having argued in favour of reform; while the Council of Poitiers ended in uproar under the super-cilious gaze of Philip I, who, not content with putting up bishoprics and abbeys for auction, organized raids on pilgrims within his terri-tory!   It was not easy to serve God.

Nevertheless, in spite of—one might say because of—this set-back, Gregory's action was to prove of lasting value.   It was now perfectly clear that moral reform was not enough, that the axe must be laid to the root.   Early in February 1075, therefore, he tackled the question of lay influence in ecclesiastical affairs, and set out to achieve a twofold pro-gramme of moral improvement and political measures.   The latter, it was hoped, would free the Church from secular interference.   His legislation, which may be studied in the celebrated *Dictatus Papae*, did no more than re-enact the four decrees of 1074.   But this time Gregory found himself in direct conflict with rulers who benefited by the very state of affairs which he condemned; this time he had raised the issue of relations between the Church and the civil power.   The battle for reform had passed from the moral to the institutional and political plane.   It was the bitter 'Quarrel of Investitures,' which soon became a 'struggle between the Priesthood and the Empire.' [1]

In 1085 Gregory VII was a refugee at Salerno; and it is said that, feeling the approach of death, he cried out in the anguish of apparent

[1] See Chapter V.

failure: 'I have loved justice and hated iniquity; therefore I die in exile.' The story may be an invention, but the words are true enough. For a time, evil seemed victorious; but the great Pope left a mark on history which could never be effaced. Simony had received a mortal wound; the celibacy of priests had been revived; and this effort to give back to the Church her ancient purity, in spite of the difficult circumstances in which the Holy See was placed, had bestowed incomparable prestige upon the papacy.

4. RETURN TO THE SOURCES: THE NEW ORDERS

The primary end of monastic reform was not the abolition of simony and of fornication among the clergy. It went much deeper, and sought to remedy abuses by a return to the sources of inspiration.

We cannot deny that many religious houses were the scene of grave disorders. Cluny herself, the great Cluny who once led the vanguard of reform, had merited reproach. Abbot Peter the Venerable admitted that 'but for a handful of monks the community is no more than a synagogue of Satan, whose name and habit are their only title to the appellation of "religious."' Even in those monasteries, however, where abuses were not flagrant, there was a more fundamental and no less urgent need for reform. In the course of centuries monachism had deviated from the narrow path appointed by the Rule; its very success had caused it to compromise more or less with temporal institutions. Too much wealth, too much property to administer, perhaps also too much study and even too many hours spent in choir, had acted to the detriment of manual labour and the practice of asceticism. Cluny had taken this direction. Rigorists might therefore claim that the true spirit of the Rule had been lost and must be recovered. Moral reform was involved in this 'journey upstream,' this return to what was then described as the 'apostolic life.'

A reaction against the evil habits of the time had already set in, and was still more strongly emphasized by the spread of eremitical life. Many conceived the idea of fleeing not only from the world, but even from the cloister, which they considered as too easy-going; of seeking uninterrupted solitude as did the anchorites of old. A direct link with the Fathers of the Eastern desert had been forged by St Nilus, the great Basilian monk whose austere life had astonished Italy about the year 1000, and whose memory was preserved in the monastery of Grottaferrata. His example had been quickly followed by St Romuald who founded the Camaldolese in 1012, and by St John Gualbert who established Vallombrosa some twelve months later. These men, it should be remembered, had originally no intention of creating new congregations. 'Fools of God,' their one dream had been of total

E*

solitude, a face-to-face communion with the One Unchanging; and it was almost in spite of themselves that they were obliged by the number of their disciples to establish collective discipline.

The same phenomenon was repeated several times in the course of the eleventh and twelfth centuries.   When Stephen of Muret, son of a nobleman in Auvergne, erected his hut in the lonely forest of Limousin (1077), he little thought that his initiative would give rise to a new order [1] which soon numbered 2,000 monks and seventy houses. The same applied to Blessed Robert of Arbrissel, a zealous Breton. Dissatisfied with his life as a canon, he took the road as an 'apostolic missionary,' denouncing clerical vices.   But his rugged appearance attracted such enormous crowds that, in order to accommodate them, he founded Fontevrault (1096), a curious 'double abbey' in Anjou, where men and women were received in twin houses.   Such was the origin (1116) of a congregation which included 3,000 souls in France, England, and Spain.   Stephen and Robert effected genuine improvements in religious life.   The Rule in each case was that of St Benedict with additional austerities; Stephen, in fact, forbade the ownership of land outside the monastic enclosure, and imposed regulations involving extreme self-sacrifice.

It was the same state of mind, the same longing for a return to eremitical life, which inspired the Carthusians, an Order founded in 1084 and still recognized as the pattern of monastic solitude.   St Bruno was a noble Rhinelander, a former student at Cologne and Paris, professor of theology and chancellor of Rheims.   Declining to serve under an unworthy bishop, he resigned his offices and sought a place of absolute silence where he might have leisure to pray alone.   On the advice of his former pupil, Hugh, Bishop of Grenoble, he established himself with six companions in the wild forest that he was to render famous.   Summoned to Rome in 1100 by another ex-pupil, Pope Urban II, he could not endure life in that noisy city, and fled once more into solitude.   This time he chose Calabria, where he founded another house of the Order.   His work in Dauphiné survived and prospered; the constitutions were drafted by Prior Guigo in 1127.

The most remarkable characteristic of the Charterhouse is its combination of eremitical and cenobitical life.   In the little three-roomed house allotted to him, each religious is a hermit; but in choir at matins, lauds, and vespers, as also in the refectory on Sundays and major festivals, he feels himself a member of the community.   Perpetual silence is broken only by short periods of recreation and during the weekly walk.   Fasting is obligatory from 14th September until Easter, and likewise on all Fridays and vigils; meat is absolutely forbidden.   It is, in fact, an existence very similar to that of the hermits

[1] Grandmont, 1124.

proper, but modified and rendered more adaptable to human nature
by the nearness of one's brethren.   That the ideal was well suited to
the age is proved by its success.   The first daughter-house was erected
at Portes-en-Bugey in 1115; and by the end of the twelfth century
there were thirty-seven Charterhouses.[1]   The hard way drew men's
hearts.

Camaldolese, Vallombrosians, monks of Grandmont or Fontevrault, and Carthusians, all looked to the eremitical ideal.   That they
played a vital part in the current of monastic reform was almost
accidental; their achievement in this respect was due rather to the goal
towards which they aspired than to what may be described as 'struc-
tural alterations.'   Quite different was the history of Cîteaux, which
began in a modest way and encountered difficulties that came near to
proving fatal.

About 1075, a few monks had withdrawn to the forest of Collon
near Tonnerre, and Gregory VII had appointed Robert of Champagne,
prior of Montier-la-Celle, as their Superior.   Robert was a strange
personality.   Despite his great reputation for sanctity, some have
charged him with cowardice.   Be that as it may, he was a sensitive,
retiring character, often capable of sudden boldness followed as quickly
by withdrawal; a contemplative unfitted to deal with the contingencies
of daily life.   The new house, Molesmes, soon became famous.   It
was nominally a 'reformed' abbey; but strict Benedictine observance
was marred by 'Cluniac customs,' so called in spite of the fact that
Cluny was in no way responsible for them.   Gifts flowed in; Robert
weakly accepted them, and soon had cause to ask himself in what
respect Molesmes differed from other Cluniac abbeys.   There was no
laxity in the strict sense; but too many small concessions, too many
practices undreamed of by St Benedict, made it difficult to observe the
Holy Rule in its original spirit and simplicity.

A group of religious, led by Alberic and Stephen Harding, planned,
with Robert's approval, to reform Molesmes.   Their attempt was
strenuously opposed by the rest of the community, whose indignation
was such that the abbot was obliged to leave the monastery for a time,
and Alberic was violently assaulted.   The reformers at length determined to secede.   On 21st March 1098, Robert, Alberic, and Stephen
Harding, with about twenty monks, founded a new abbey called
Cîteaux in the valley of the Saône.

The beginnings of this house were beset with difficulties.   At the
end of a year Robert returned to Molesmes on the papal legate's advice
and Alberic took charge.   The young community had to endure
hunger and destitution while they cleared the wilderness and built their

---

[1] Two of these were houses of nuns.   The Calabrian monasteries had adopted the rule
of Cîteaux.

monastery. They lived, however, exactly as they had desired, in absolute poverty, refusing every comfort, devoting themselves to manual labour, fasting, penance, and obedience. The Holy See was informed, and extended its protection to 'the poor monks of the new monastery.' Recruits, however, were few and far between. Cîteaux's austerity caused would-be members to fight shy; nor did the situation greatly improve when Alberic was succeeded by Stephen Harding in 1108.

We have seen [1] how the arrival of St Bernard and his thirty companions in the spring of 1112 altered the situation and began a splendid chapter of monastic history. Cîteaux became so famous that twelve months later the community had outgrown its accommodation and was obliged to found another house. La Ferté, Pontigny, Clairvaux, and Morimond, the four 'elder daughters' of Cîteaux, arose within the space of as many years; and the new congregation, under Bernard's foresight and unflagging energy, set out to conquer the whole world. On Stephen Harding's death in 1134, the Order possessed eighty-four houses; one hundred and fifty when St Bernard died twenty years later; five hundred and thirty in 1199; and seven hundred in the following century. After 1125 there were almost as many houses of women as of men; and the general chapter prohibited further establishment, fearing it might become impossible to provide for the nuns' spiritual direction. In order to assure unity within the Order Stephen Harding had published a constitution known as the *Charter of Charity* (1119), which embodied two fundamental rules: new monasteries were to be subject to the control of their 'mother houses,' and the Order was to be governed by a 'general chapter,' a periodical assembly of abbots and delegates from every monastery.[2]

What exactly was the Cistercian reform? Nothing more or less than a return to the Rule of St Benedict, excluding those elements which had been added in the course of centuries. Everything was forbidden that was not explicitly authorized by the Holy Rule. Built by preference in marshy valleys, not on those towering heights favoured by the Cluniacs, the Cistercian abbeys were intended as homes of total renunciation. The habit of these monks consisted of a plain woollen tunic with scapular and cowl of the same material. Their diet admitted of no meat, fish, cooking fats, milk-products, or eggs. They ate nothing except boiled vegetables; and from 14th September until Easter only one meal a day was allowed. They slept

---

[1] Chapter III.

[2] The custom of holding general chapters was soon afterwards adopted by other orders, e.g. the Carthusians, Templars, Premonstratensians, Canons of St Victor, and later by the Franciscans and Dominicans. The Lateran Council of 1215 made it obligatory for all congregations; the Benedictine abbots and priors were to hold national chapters every month.

fully clothed on straw mattresses without covering. At midnight, roused by the monastery's one bell, the community rose for prayer and matins in a church that was of the utmost simplicity, without ornament of any kind. Above all, no monastery might accept gifts or tithes, and possessed no lands other than what was necessary to supply the monks with their food. Such austerity was unheard of; but still more wonderful was its success. The white habit [1] of the Cistercians was looked upon by the whole Church as symbolic of the perfect life; and the example of this Order born among the marshes of Saône, no less than the labour of her sons, made a deep impression on the Middle Ages.

One of the most curious features of the Cistercian movement was its effect upon the Cluniacs, who regarded the new observance as a reflection on themselves. The ensuing conflict was dignified at the highest level by an exchange of some magnificent letters between Peter the Venerable, abbot of Cluny, and St Bernard; but among the rank and file, it must be confessed, Charity took many a hard knock. By and large, however, this rivalry was not unprofitable, as is shown by subsequent events at Cluny. The great Burgundian abbey had declined since the death of St Hugh (1109), who had been succeeded by an incompetent abbot, Pons de Melgueil. The Order had 10,000 monks housed in 1,450 beautiful monasteries, but she was on the downward path; enormous wealth had inevitably reduced her first fervour to mere routine.

The current of reform, however, had not ceased to flow in Cluny's soul; it had reappeared towards the end of the eleventh century at Rüggisberg near Freiburg, at St Alban at Basel, and at Siegbourg. The torrent was still further increased when Abbot William of Hirschau, instigated by Gregory VII's legate Bernard of Marseilles, decided to transform his community. The primitive observance of Cluny was revived in a spirit of almost combative zeal; and the monks of Hirschau, distinguished by their white habit, sent preachers all over Germany. One hundred and fifty communities affiliated with them to form a congregation which was numbered among the staunchest allies of the papacy during the Quarrel of Investitures.

Peter the Venerable was abbot of Cluny from 1122 to 1156. Apart from his sanctity, he possessed a first-class intellect, and was both a mystic and a man of action worthy of his most illustrious predecessors. In 1132 he tightened up the rules of fasting and silence, re-established the 'ancient and holy practice of manual labour,' and reorganized recruitment. But he took care not to belittle scholarship, the arts, or the

[1] The white habit was also adopted by the Premonstratensians, Carthusians, the monks of Hirschau, and other congregations.

splendour of the divine office, three most characteristic and valuable features of Cluniac life.   His example was infectious, and many houses of the Order adopted these reforms.   The most remarkable instance was that of St Denis, the famous royal abbey outside Paris, which had been inundated by an unhealthy tide of luxury.   In 1127, as we have seen, it was reformed by Abbot Suger, who breathed into his sons the new spirit which, through the operation of grace, he himself had learned from the emphatic but affectionate admonitions of his friend St Bernard.

Nor must we overlook the part played by canons regular in this laborious task of reform.   An important element of religious life in the Carolingian era were those colleges of priests, who lived near the bishop, saw that the choral services were maintained, and formed, as it were, his general staff.   But serious abuses had crept in: many canons were preoccupied with tapping the revenues of the chapter rather than with singing matins; many of them, too, were no better than gyrovagues, constantly absent from their stalls.   Some were guilty of even more deplorable vices—violence and sexual immorality.

Here again, all that was necessary to terminate a sorry state of affairs was the renewal of first fervour.   At Tagaste, and later during his thirty years as Bishop of Hippo, St Augustine had lived in community with a group of friends and collaborators.   Whether or not he actually drew up the so-called Rule of St Augustine is open to dispute; but its principles are certainly discoverable in his works.   The proper course, then, was a return to those principles: the secular clergy must be 'monachized' and rendered worthy of their mission.   The plan, suggested long ago by St Chrodegang,[1] was now revived.   The reformers aimed at persuading canons to live in community, to renounce individual property, and to practise mortification; for it is obvious that life in community precludes concubinage and general dissipation.   The flexibility of St Augustine's 'Rule' was well suited to those groups which had to adapt themselves to circumstances, and they multiplied with wonderful variety.

The movement took several forms.   Some chapters were led by grace to reorganize themselves and adopt the Rule.   The whole chapter of St Martin at Tours, for example, renounced their goods and went to live in poverty on the island of St Cosmas; while at Rome, Pope Gregory VII praised the canons for having 'embraced the communal life after the model of the primitive Church.'   In other cases, bishops imposed reform from without.   Thus at Cambrai the entire secular chapter was evicted and regulars installed in their place. Arnulf, Patriarch of Jerusalem, desired his canons to 'lead the same life as the apostles.'   Elsewhere, a monastic community might choose to

[1] He was Bishop of Metz from 746 until 766.

become canons regular, thinking in that way to lead more useful lives, as did the monks of La Trinité in Vendôme. New centres also were established for bodies of secular clergy who wished to lead the perfect life: Mortain, St Quentin at Beauvais, St Jean-de-Vigne at Soissons, St Victor at Paris, and St Ruf at Avignon. Lastly, a few saints, with an eye to the more distant future, united several of these collegiate groups into congregations. Such was the origin of the canons at Murbach in Alsace, founded by Manegold of Lautenbach, and those of Arrouaise and Artois established by St Gervase.

Three of these congregations—St Ruf, St Victor, and Prémontré— had distinguished histories. The first two are now almost forgotten, but their influence was far from negligible. Founded at Avignon in 1039, the canons regular of St Ruf moved in 1158 to Valence, where they continued until the French Revolution. There is no doubt that they were the first in order of time. Pope Urban II congratulated them in 1095 upon having 'revived the primitive life of clerics,' and Blessed Pons, a Carthusian who became Bishop of Grenoble, told them, in 1129, that they 'had served as a model and norm for all, even the most distant, monasteries of canons.' More than 800 chapters from Norway to Portugal, from Greece to Iceland, were affiliated to this congregation. Three popes came from their ranks; and without in any way neglecting the things of the spirit, they did much for the arts throughout Provence, as also in Catalonia, and even at Chartres. They were likewise an important influence in the framing of the Carthusian constitutions, and served as a model for the famous congregation of St Victor.

The latter was founded by William of Champeaux and named after the nearby hermitage on Mont Saint-Geneviève whither it moved in 1108. Raised to the status of a congregation by Gildwin, Bishop of Châlons, and protected by Stephen of Senlis, Bishop of Paris, St Victor was a regular monastic university. It revived the traditional austerity of religious life with a fervour that attracted thousands; and its glory was enhanced by the fact that reform had as yet made small headway in the neighbourhood of Paris. An attempt was made to rally the chapter of Notre-Dame; but so furious was the opposition that the prior of St Victor was murdered by the archdeacon's nephews; while the secular canons of St Geneviève only agreed to the presence of regulars in their midst when Suger, that determined statesman, threatened to 'cut off their hands and put out their eyes.'

The most outstanding figure in the reform of the canons regular was St Norbert (1085–1134), founder of the Premonstratensians. The story of this young German nobleman is characteristic of his age. Refined and sensitive, he was more concerned with rich furs and hunting than with the Gospel; but having wasted his energies for thirty years, he was suddenly called by God to the accompaniment of a flash of lightning which killed his horse.   As a canon of Xanten, in Prussia, he had preferred the archbishop's palace at Cologne or the court of Henry V to his own chapter; but immediately after his conversion he began to denounce abuses with holy vehemence, imploring his colleagues to reform their lives, and attempting to enforce regular observance.   All in vain: his good intentions earned him nothing but ill will.   One disgruntled cleric spat in his face, and a charge was laid against him in the Council of Fritzlar.   Turning his back on Xanten and his property, he travelled the roads of Germany, Belgium, and France, preaching a return to holy living and the necessity of penance, as Robert of Arbrissel was doing at about the same time.

Norbert had begun to make a name for himself.   We find him acting as arbitrator in more than one feudal dispute, and his contemporaries compared him with Bernard of Clairvaux—sometimes even to the latter's disadvantage.   In 1119 he met Calixtus II, who advised him to settle down.   It was a timely warning; for at this period, when the abbey was still the true centre of religious life, the most effective means of action was to establish a permanent monastic base.   The day of itinerant preachers had not yet dawned.   And so a new house of canons subject to the Augustinian Rule was established in 1121 at Prémontré in the forest of St Gobain.   Norbert, however, was in the grip of apostolic fever.   He set out once more, and continued preaching until called to the archbishopric of Magdeburg, in which capacity he strove to foster the ideals of reform, and crossed swords with the antipope Anacletus II.

His friend and collaborator, Hugh de Fosses, was left behind to draft the Order's constitutions, which included the Cistercian system of general chapters and regular visitations.   It was Hugh also who conceived the brilliant idea of employing the canons regular as an instrument of reform.   The Premonstratensians were to live in community, exactly like monks, singing the divine office and practising mortification.   But they would not remain permanently in the cloister; they would devote themselves to parochial work, and their priories would thus serve as power-houses of Christian endeavour. The Premonstratensian, in other words, was to combine the duties of a monk with those of a parish priest.   The wisdom, and indeed the necessity, of this plan was proved by its success; for in 1350 the Order counted 1,300 houses, devoted principally to evangelizing the German countryside.

5. PASCHAL II

The spirit of reform had come to stay; it could no longer be dis-
owned. None of Gregory VII's successors ventured to turn back;
the majority of them were zealous reformers, and even Victor III
(1086-7), an undistinguished pontiff, renewed his great predecessor's
legislation. When Urban II (1088-99) succeeded to the throne of
Peter, he made this appeal: 'Have confidence in me as you had formerly
in Pope Gregory of blessed memory. I mean to follow faithfully in
his footsteps: I condemn whatever he condemned; I love what found
favour in his sight; I approve all that he considered right and Catholic.'
Certain popes have been accused of 'anti-Gregorian reaction.' The
phrase is inaccurate—except on the political plane, where some of them
felt the papacy had gone too far; but in essentials, i.e. with regard to
the necessity for reform, not one of them is found to have advocated a
different course. Calixtus II (1119-24), Innocent II (1130-43),
Eugenius III (1145-53), and Celestine III (1191-8), all remained
faithful to the ideals of St Gregory VII.

The determination of these popes is even more admirable when we
recall their circumstances. Throughout the twelfth century Peter's
barque was in distress. Five pontificates in succession were disturbed
by conflict with the empire on this very subject of reform. Antipopes
sprang up at the nod of ambitious rivals, but no St Bernard was at hand
to meet the threat of schism that weighed so heavily upon the Church.[1]
Rome was a prey to the factions of Pope, Emperor, and a demagogic
senate of great feudal lords. Lucius II (1144-5) died of wounds
received during an assault on the senatorial palace. A social revolution tinged with heresy broke out in the Eternal City itself, and Arnold
of Brescia proclaimed his republic.[2]

It is indeed astonishing that, in spite of these obstacles, the Church
managed to hold a straight course. The decisive moment of her
voyage was the ninth oecumenical council, which met at the Lateran
in 1123. The question of secular influence upon ecclesiastical appointments having been settled, Pope Calixtus II determined to consolidate
his advantages in a general assembly, the first of its kind to be held in
the West. It was attended by three hundred bishops and other
prelates. No new dogma was proclaimed, no disciplinary laws were
enacted; but the council solemnly defined the principles of reform in
such forcible terms that they could no longer be called in question.

Among these reforming popes there was one who deserves our

---

[1] The schism of Anacletus has been considered in the previous chapter on St Bernard
section 7.
[2] See the following chapter, section 6.

special notice.   Not that he achieved more than others, for in a sense his accomplishment was less than theirs; but his project, though so far in advance of his time as to seem chimerical, was in fact sublime.   He was a monk (whether of Vallombrosa or of Cluny is not quite certain), a contemplative soul, somewhat narrow-minded, and ill equipped for the practical affairs of life.   He took the name of Paschal II, and reigned from 1099 until 1118.   Considering the perilous situation of the Church at that time, with Rome threatened by the armies of Henry V, his qualifications were inadequate; a statesman might have been preferable.

Paschal believed that if the Church was to be rescued from the servitude of politics, she must take her stand exclusively upon spiritual ground; and for that purpose, he considered, only one means would suffice—total renunciation of all her territory, of all those titles which bound her hand and foot within the feudal system.   A poor Church, with no resources other than offerings made by the faithful, would surely enjoy greater freedom of action.   The Pope, in fact, proposed to solve political problems by moral reforms.   He believed that measures suited to personal improvement would be found no less efficacious when applied to the Christian body as a whole.   It was an audacious, if not a fantastic scheme; at all events, it met with scant approval.   This dream of a golden age in which bishops and abbots, relieved of all temporal responsibility, would have only the care of souls, seemed to those dignitaries less attractive than their revenues. His generous proposals were answered with rebellion, an opportunity of which the Emperor at once took advantage.   The Pope was seized and obliged to capitulate.[1]

The majority of Church historians have judged Paschal II unfairly. True, his action retarded rather than advanced the solution of a knotty problem; for to have repudiated temporal power at that date would surely have been to weaken the papacy.   But who can say what would have been the future of the Church if his noble dream had materialized? How many compromises, errors, and even tragedies might have been avoided?

6.   Ancient Errors and New Problems

Relentless effort backed by stern resolve could not, alas, eradicate the evil.   Papal instructions and conciliar decrees met with strong resistance from private interest and personal prejudice.   By the beginning of the thirteenth century simony and the marriage of priests were almost universally condemned, at least in theory; and that was all to the good, but in practice things did not work quite so smoothly.

[1] See Chapter V, section 4.

The moral situation, of course, was in no way comparable with what it had been at the commencement of the eleventh century, or with that miserable state of affairs which had led to the Gregorian reform. But the old errors, the old temptations, were always there; and time had done its customary work. Those who once led the vanguard had since betrayed the ideal of Christ. The great Cluniac abbey at Vézelay was ruled by a simoniacal and incontinent superior who squandered the goods of his monastery to pension off his son and daughter! Nor were the Cistercians much better. We possess a document written in 1202 by Innocent III, addressed to the abbots of Clairvaux, Morimond, Pontigny, and La Ferté, in which the Sovereign Pontiff makes reference to some shameful rumours. At Grandmont, there was brawling during the divine office, and a similar outburst among the Premonstratensians of Saint-Martin at Laon ended in bloodshed. The secular clergy presented much the same kind of picture, especially in remote dioceses where the reforming influence had been weak.

The situation was even more disquieting than in the eleventh century. It must not be forgotten that at the end of the twelfth society was undergoing a radical transformation; new customs were imported from the East by crusaders and travellers, and an enormous increase of trade was causing money to flow more freely. The feudal system was beginning to break up; the serfs were in process of emancipation; towns were developing; and fresh interests brought in their train an altered outlook upon life. The foundations of Europe were crumbling to dust.

It was virtually impossible that the clergy should remain unaffected by this atmosphere of general unrest. Innocent III regretted that 'the shepherd had become a hireling, leaving his flock to the mercy of wolves. The evil which he should destroy, he protects by his treason. Nearly all clerics have deserted the cause of God; and of those who have remained faithful, too many are inept.' Such lamentations speak for themselves.

What would the Church do to meet these new influences? Could she free herself from the many ties that linked her with the feudal regime? It certainly appears that she had allowed the gap to widen between herself and the deepest aspirations of the age. During the barbarian epoch she had assumed the terrible responsibility of preventing chaos, and had taken a leading place in the resulting 'feudal' order. She had made the abbey a replica of the castle; she had sacramentalized the oath, the bond of warrior society; she had blessed the arms of knighthood, instituted works of charity, and created in the shelter of her convents a remarkable system of education. How many men, though dedicated to God's service, could have learned within the space of a few decades to regard as outworn a worldwide organization so clearly blessed by Heaven and guaranteeing them so many concrete advantages? Gregory VII had not attempted to break this link between the Church and the contemporary world; his reform had been erected on moral and spiritual bases, by strengthening the Church's power and by the exercise of her universal authority in every sphere. Paschal II had been looked upon as a fanatic for proposing such a rupture, and it is most unlikely that an exclusively moral reform could have helped the Church in the unsettled climate of that age.

For the tide of intellectual ferment was beginning to invade even the spiritual life. Prophets of both sexes denounced scandals and foretold chastisement. 'Woe betide all nations!' cried St Elizabeth of Schönau, 'for the world is naught but darkness. The Lord's vine has perished; the head of the Church is sick, her members dead!' To which St Hildegarde added: 'The justice of God is about to strike, and His decrees will be your executioners; the papacy and the empire, fellows in corruption, will together fall.' But she went on to say more optimistically: 'From their ruins the Holy Spirit will cause a new people to arise; conversion will be general, and the angels will return to dwell confidently among the sons of men.' The most famous of all these visionaries was Joachim of Flora (1145–1202). Abbot of a Cistercian monastery in Calabria, he was a saintly soul, a mystic whose heart was full of gentleness and poetry. A keen student of the Apocalypse, he had arrived at the idea of a new division of world history. After the reign of God the Father, corresponding to the Old Testament, there was the reign of the Son, intermediate between servitude and full liberty. Soon, however, there would begin the reign of the Holy Ghost, under which men would live according to the 'eternal gospel,' a gospel differing from that of Christ inasmuch as it would proceed not from a written book, but from direct spiritual comprehension of truth. The Church would then be finally regenerated, and would put an end to scandal. She would be pure and holy; the city of men would become the City of God.

So long as these prophecies did no more than encourage pious folk on the road to heaven, they were harmless enough, except perhaps in so far as they ran the risk of unsettling weak minds, as happened later on. But other voices made themselves heard, voices incompatible with Christian doctrine. Criticism was directed against the Church by certain heretics, whose number and influence were on the increase. The Waldenses had been followed by the Cathars,[1] whose leaders, styling themselves 'the Perfect,' had taught a stern lesson to many ecclesiastical dignitaries by the example of their lives. In 1184 Pope Lucius III had condemned the Waldenses, and there was now talk of

[1] See Chapter XIII.

resolving the Albigensian crisis by force of arms. But to what purpose, if the Church would not put her own house in order? The fight against moral degeneracy could not be left, for instance, to the Patarines; nor could clerical ignorance be allowed to continue amid the growing intellectual restiveness. The Church, despite her world-wide authority, might at any moment witness the whole vast mass of her adherents slide from the firm ground of grace and truth.

A new and quite different kind of reform was therefore indispensable. It would naturally have to aim at the restoration of moral values, at the reanimation of the Christian lump with a leaven of enthusiasm and faith; but it would also have to meet new requirements. Once again, Christendom produced men who, understanding contemporary needs, strengthened the Church's authority by adapting her characteristically feudal outlook to a more popular and more universalist conception of society. This work was performed chiefly by a great pope and two saints.

7. INNOCENT III

Pope Celestine III died on 8th January 1198. That same evening the cardinals met, and unanimously chose the youngest of their colleagues to succeed him. It was clear to all that a most important pontificate had begun. Lothair of Segni, who took the name Innocent III, was tall and thin, a fine figure of a man. His countenance radiated intelligence and determination, suggesting at the same time a thoughtfulness that seemed almost to indicate a troubled mind. A former student at Paris, then at Bologna, where he had attended the lectures of Uguccio da Pisa, Innocent had received a solid intellectual grounding both in the classics and in jurisprudence. At the age of thirty he was created cardinal-deacon by his uncle Clement III, and eight years later he succeeded to the Apostolic See, which he was to occupy for eighteen years.

He has been much maligned; and St Lutgard claimed to have seen him, during one of her visions, doing penance in Purgatory until the Day of Judgment! His grand political designs may have overshadowed his truly Christian purpose, but it cannot be denied that his pontificate is one of the most remarkable in the history of the Church. He drove the Emperor from Italy; he appointed himself guardian of Sicily and suzerain of England; he disposed of the German crown; he controlled Hungary, Aragon, and Castile; he revived the crusade; he beat down heresy by armed force. In a word, his manifold activity reveals an exceptionally powerful character. On the other hand, it is no less certain that all his gigantic expenditure of temporal means had in view a single end—the glory of God's Church, whose grandeur was graven deep upon his mind.

He has been called 'proud' and 'brutal.' His style was certainly vigorous, and there was a sharp edge to his tongue. When the interests of the Church were at stake, he would sometimes describe his opponent as a 'conceited ass,' or a 'hog wallowing in muck'; which is not the pontifical phraseology of to-day. But few great administrators are without a tinge of asperity; and a glance at Innocent's correspondence will reveal a man far different from the image presented by historians. His charity was boundless, prompt to bind up wounds inflicted by the inevitable blows of Justice. Apart from deep humility, he had a sincere love of the poor, of captives, and of the sick, together with an almost mystical piety that had been nourished on the works of St Bernard, of Hugh of St Victor, and of St Peter Damian. These qualities mark the finer shades in a portrait of one whom circumstance, as well as his own genius, had raised to the summit of the medieval Church. Innocent III was sometimes mistaken, but he acted in all things for God's glory.

He knew too well the plight of Christendom not to be zealous for reform. As a young priest, and later as a young cardinal, he had travelled much, and had more than once been angered by bishops who dared not proclaim the Gospel truth, and of whom he spoke as 'dumb dogs who can no longer bark.' So deeply had he pondered St Bernard's *De Consideratione*, that its phrases flowed spontaneously from his pen. Moreover, from the very beginning of his pontificate, his Bulls made clear an inexorable resolve to combat the old abuses of simony and Nicolaïsm. In one of the earliest he insisted upon a seemly garb for clerics, forbidding them to dress like dandies, and threatened the visitation of his wrath upon those who indulged in drunkenness. He flayed those who so far forgot their vocation as to carry arms, and took immediate steps to reduce the size of the pontifical court.

Innocent III energetically applied those principles which he had laid down immediately after his election, and his 'reforming' Bulls are legion. The Curia was reorganized by the elimination of noble careerists, forgers of false Bulls, and officials who were suspected of venality. The appointment of bishops was subjected to stricter control, and those who did not fulfil the canonical requirements as to age and learning were rejected. The Pope maintained close contact with the more worthy members of the episcopate, reminding them of their duties, and insisting, as he once wrote to the Bishop of Liége, that 'he who has undertaken the care of souls must bear the torch of learning and example.' Whenever he found that some abuse had crept into a diocese, he notified the bishop, ordered him to take appropriate steps, and, if that prelate proved reluctant, had him reprimanded by trustworthy persons. He railed against incontinent clergy at Norwich in England, at Gniezno in Poland, and in Denmark;

he denounced the accumulation of benefices and the love of money wherever it appeared; nor did the regular clergy escape his stern solicitude. Innocent never acted without the fullest information; but once having obtained it, he went straight to the point. His personal intervention lent weight to the authority of those national and provincial councils whose duty it was to adapt his decisions to local circumstances.

The crowning event of Innocent's pontificate was the fourth Lateran (twelfth oecumenical) Council in 1215, an imposing assembly of 412 bishops, 800 abbots and priors, together with ambassadors from every nation.[1] Questions of reform occupied first place in its deliberations, and the conduct of the clergy was dealt with in a series of more than twenty canons, one of which enacted that every diocese should have a 'master of theology' to instruct those seeking ordination.

The whole of Innocent's teaching on clerical reform was summed up in these canons, which were couched in the most solemn terms. But his legislation, notwithstanding its undoubted value, could have achieved little or nothing by itself; it was simply the re-enactment on a larger scale of principles which had been universally accepted since the time of Gregory VII. Innocent, however, had an intuitive sense of the changes that were taking place around him; he understood that any return to the Gospel must be accomplished by new means.

Characteristic of the pontiff's method was his attitude towards the religious Orders. He relied upon them to preserve vital contact between the Church and the common people, whose future was already in the crucible; he supported the Premonstratensians, who sought personal sanctification through the exercise of parochial duties; and he encouraged those religious who devoted themselves to charitable work outside the cloister. Such was the Order of the Holy Ghost, which received its rule in 1213, and, from quite modest beginnings, grew into an international body with many branches. In 1198, thanks again to Innocent III, St John of Matha was enabled to found the Trinitarian Order whose vocation was to rescue Christian captives from the Moslems.[2] In Lombardy a group of priests, religious, laymen, shopkeepers, and business men formed themselves into a charitable organization bound by vows of chastity and poverty. These 'Humiliati' were mistrusted by the authorities, who considered them more or less as heretics; but Innocent III understood their pious intention and gave them his approval in 1201.

There were also sections of the Waldenses and Cathars who desired to return to the Church, but hoped that, having submitted, they might

[1] See Chapter VI, section 4.
[2] These two Orders will be studied later on (Chapter VI) in connection with the charitable works of the Church.

be allowed to live as heretofore, preaching the moral regeneration of society, subject to episcopal jurisdiction. Innocent III was sympathetic; he welcomed them, and, to the horrified amazement of his court, gladly presented a statute to the 'Poor Catholics' and their superior, Durand of Huesca. Such was the origin of what we call 'the lay apostolate.'

Looking, however, into a more distant future, the Pope realized that old methods would no longer suffice to combat heresy and re-mix the leaven with the Christian lump. He decided, therefore, to institute a new form of the apostolate, closer to the people and better equipped for its task. Innocent saw in his mind's eye a body of men inspired with burning faith and the evangelical ideal, unencumbered by worldly goods, and thus able to approach the poor with open arms, proclaiming once again the words of love and truth.

He thought at first that Cîteaux might adapt itself and provide such men; after all, St Bernard, great contemplative though he was, had proved himself a no less able preacher. Accordingly, he chose two Cistercians, Brothers Regnier and Guy, to whom he addressed the celebrated Bull of 19th November 1206, calling upon them to select a number of 'trustworthy religious who would imitate the poverty of Christ and go forth boldly, in humble guise but with zealous hearts, to seek out and recall heretics from the darkness of their ways with God's help, by their own example, and by the persuasiveness of their words.' But Cîteaux was no longer the Cîteaux of St Bernard. The traditions of the Order had degenerated into mere routine; the Cistercian ideal of poverty was not what it had been a century ago, and Innocent's appeal, with few exceptions, fell upon deaf ears.

Notwithstanding this set-back, the Pope had issued a tremendous challenge, which Providence was soon to answer. It is perhaps, under God, the supreme merit of Innocent III that he understood and encouraged two saints from whom the Church was to relearn the lesson of self-sacrifice—St Francis of Assisi and St Dominic.

8. St Francis, the 'Perfect Image of Christ'

During the summer of 1210 Innocent III received in audience at the Lateran a frail young man with eyes of flame, clothed in the coarse tunic and hood of a peasant. He wore a girdle round his waist, and sandals on his otherwise bare feet. Francis Bernardone had come from Assisi, the chief town of Umbria, with twelve companions poorly clad like himself—twelve disciples like the twelve Apostles. He had come, the Pope was told, to lay before the Holy See his observations on the state of the Church, and his views concerning the apostolate. 'Another of them!' the Pope no doubt exclaimed; indeed, he might never have

consented to receive this vagabond, if Bishop Guido of Assisi and
Cardinal John Colonna had not recommended him. No, the little
Umbrian had nothing in common with those wandering prophets who
crowded the roads at that period, brandishing the Gospels in the face
of Holy Church, upsetting whole dioceses under the pretence of living
an 'integral Christianity,' and of whom one could never be quite certain
that they were not Waldenses or Patarines.

Francis began to speak in vehement but respectful tones, with no
affectation, but with the serenity and persuasive force of those who
have devoted themselves heart and soul to a lofty ideal. He expressed
himself with a kind of eloquent simplicity, full of poetic imagery that
came straight from his heart like an echo of the words of Christ.
Listening in silence, the Pope felt himself carried away on a flood of
strange anguish, and yet of joy; for on the previous night he had
dreamed a dream in harmony with his most dismal thoughts. The
Lateran basilica, mother church of Christendom, was tottering to its
fall; but there came a man sent by Jesus Christ, who leaned against the
crumbling walls and prevented their collapse; a little emaciated fellow,
quite young, with ascetic face and eyes of fire, clothed in rough homespun—the exact image, in fact, of the one who now stood before him.

Innocent III was a good judge of men; he sized up Francis in a
moment. There was no trace of pride, no grandiose ideas which
would probably do more harm than good; he had no wish to found a
new Order, and he made no attempt to expound the merits of a home-
made Rule. When questioned as to his principles, he replied in three
verses of Scripture: Matthew xix. 21, where it is said that to follow
Christ one must abandon all that one has; Luke ix. 3, where the
disciples are ordered to set out on the road without money or change
of clothing, without scrip or staff; and Matthew xvi. 24, which lays
down that unique but all-embracing law—'If any man will come after
Me, let him deny himself and take up his cross.' Moved by such
wonderful simplicity, astonished at the submissiveness apparent in
every word that fell from the mouth of his unwonted visitor, Innocent
III felt sure that Providence had heard his prayer. Here was one after
Christ's own heart, such as he had desired. After a long pause the
Pope exclaimed: 'For sure, this holy man will re-establish the Church
of God on her foundations!' Then, coming down from his throne,
he embraced the Poverello, and addressed the little group: 'Go with
God, my brethren; preach penance according as the Lord inspires you.
And when the Almighty has caused you to increase and multiply, come
back to me, and I will grant you still more than I have done to-day.'

It was thus that Francis, who had come to Rome for no other
purpose than to tell the common father of his hopes and his resolve,
found himself, and his brethren with him, invited to regenerate

Christendom.   These few 'Penitents of Assisi' had become an Order, the Order of Friars Minor, as the founder was to name them six years later.   A splendid page had been opened in the annals of the Church.

Francis was then a young man of scarcely twenty-eight years, short of stature, thin, but of distinguished appearance.   All the known portraits of him agree in showing us a small narrow face terminating in a scanty beard.   The features are regular and refined, with great black shining eyes, and lips slightly parted in a smile; but the most striking of all these portraits, that by Cimabue in the church at Assisi, reveals also a contemplative and exacting soul, an iron will scarcely hidden by a veil of gentleness.

All his biographers who knew him personally describe a character in harmony with these externals.   From youth upwards his noble qualities combined with human shortcomings to render him impulsive in the extreme, and yet of exquisite sensibility.   He was generous almost to a fault, prompt to volunteer his services, and always courteous; one, in fact, whose charm the most surly customer could not resist.   These graces, however, concealed immeasurable reserves of strength, unbending determination, and a temperament which, as his biographers admit, would have led him to all manner of excesses, but for his power of self-control.

In this admixture of restraint and audacity lay the secret of his fascination.   Though invariably polite, he never hesitated to proclaim what he believed true and just.   He was never known to commit the slightest meanness, nor to betray that code of delicate refinement which governed all his actions as a knight of Christ.

This extraordinary man was also a poet.   Like the troubadours from France, whose name he bore and whose language he loved to speak, those troubadours who sang love's joy and the beauty of this world, Francis heard within himself the fraternal voice of creation.   It re-echoed in his heart.   His soul lay wide open to the pure and unspoiled impulses of nature, like Adam in the first springtime.   The faith, which others had reduced to narrow formulae, was not for him dry dogma or stern law, but joyous fervour, mystic gratitude.   The created world stretched before him in its primeval innocence; therefore he looked upon wind, fire, water, and even death itself, as brothers; therefore too larks obeyed his word, and fierce wolves were ready to shake hands with him.   Through him a new tone was introduced into the Christian symphony, a tone of ineffable purity and depth.   He was the very model of those whom Jesus loved.

When Francis knelt before the Pope in 1210, some years had elapsed since he discovered his vocation and set out on the heavenly adventure. Nevertheless, God had been obliged to knock loud and call several times before the son of Bernardone, a wealthy wool merchant, became

'Il Poverello.' It had taken many a dream, the miracle of the talking crucifix, and even the less spectacular experience of imprisonment and sickness, in order that this handsome, hot-blooded young man, whom the wild youth of Assisi had acclaimed as one of its leaders, should be transformed into a humble penitent, clothed in homespun and on his knees before the Sovereign Pontiff to receive the tonsure.

Born in 1182 in Umbria which seems to consist, as it were, of red ochre and light, in that Italian Galilee where nobility strikes the eye from near and far, and in the city of Assisi which stands so proudly on its hill, perched on the tawny flanks of Monte Subasio, Francis had lived hitherto as do most boys of his class. Although a Christian by baptism and faith, he cared less for prayer than for singing and dancing, earning money, and fighting in those petty but ferocious wars in which the towns of Italy at that period were constantly engaged. It was, in fact, one such quarrel that gave him his first taste of enforced inactivity. While a prisoner of war at Perugia, Francis began to consider his own heart. After a year in jail he returned home, but in so precarious a state of health that he was obliged to take to his bed. There followed long hours of silence, which are more favourable to the Lord's approach than is the dissipation of an active life. It was then, at the age of about twenty-one, that he heard the call of God.

Francis remained henceforth and for ever a captive in the Master's hands. He made up his mind to join the crusade, hoping thereby to win knighthood; but on two occasions Christ warned him against such a course. Torn between past pleasure and present duty, he was wandering one day in the Umbrian plain along a hillside planted thick with cypress. Suddenly, and with overwhelming certitude, he realized that our Lord was there beside him, in him, bowed down with sorrow and humiliation, pierced with five wounds. The die was cast.

When God speaks, says the prophet, who can turn away? Yes, it was the Lord whom Francis recognized in that putrid leper, whom he met by the wayside and kissed upon the mouth. It was the Lord whose ineffable presence he felt during those hours of solitary prayer spent in the mountain caves. It was the Lord whom, while on a pilgrimage to Rome, he longed to serve, humbling himself to beg among the beggars. Above all, there was that wonderful and mystic day when, praying before an old Byzantine crucifix in the dilapidated chapel of San Damiano, he had heard the Lord say to him in a gentle but irresistible voice: 'Francis, go and rebuild my house; it is tumbling down.'

Too modest to believe that Christ would ask him to rebuild a Church whose walls are not of stone but of immortal souls, he spent some time restoring with his own hands a number of chapels, oratories, and other sacred buildings that had fallen into disrepair. His destiny, however, lay elsewhere; and God, who uses all things to fulfil His purpose, employed other means to make him understand. The elder Bernardone, furious at the sight of his boy now aged twenty-five neglecting his plain duty to sell woollen goods and earn a living, intervened. The chaplain of San Damiano, a good old priest who had treated the young devotee as his own son, heard himself abused for a thousand imaginary offences, and particularly for having fostered the credulity of a half-wit! Summoned to return home, and even hailed by his own father before the magistrates, Francis remained adamant. At last he understood the Lord's command: he must abandon everything, even his own property, and follow Him. He now took that decision once for all, and the population of Assisi beheld with deep emotion an extraordinary scene in the piazza. Francis, the one-time dandy, appeared almost naked before Bishop Guido, who had been invited to pass judgment on the case. Flinging his garments and what little money he had left at Bernardone's feet, he cried out that from now on he would recognize no father but the Father who reigns in heaven. The bishop, covering the young man with his cloak, welcomed him on behalf of Holy Church.

There are certain steps in a man's life which, no matter what befalls, can never be retraced. Sacrifice of self and of one's earthly goods, in obedience to that command heard but rejected by the rich young man, is the only means of becoming a disciple of Him who desired to be, on earth, as the least of men, a traveller without possessions, having nowhere even to lay His head. From the age of twenty-five Francis never forgot that his vocation was to be poor with the Poorest of the poor; he was indissolubly wed to holy poverty.

This was his constant theme during the remainder of his life. Poverty, the absolute refusal to possess worldly goods of any kind whatsoever, was the kernel of his teaching. Insistence on this precept, the most difficult of all Gospel precepts, was his unique contribution to the reform of a Church threatened by her wealth with utter ruin. Poverty meant more to him than it had done, for example, to St Bernard, more than it would do later to his great contemporary St Dominic. They looked upon it as the means of liberating Christian men from all external cares that they might better serve the Lord. For Francis, on the other hand, total renunciation, utter destitution, was the supreme goal, not only the means to but the very end of sanctity. 'Seek ye first the kingdom of God and His justice, and all things else shall be added unto you.'

But that was not sufficient. The life of solitude and contemplation chosen by the son of Bernardone was no doubt of great merit in God's sight. But it lacked, so to speak, the power of radiation; and the Church at that date had need of more than the hermit or recluse. One

day in February 1209, Francis was hearing Mass alone in the chapel of
San Damiano, which his own hands had rebuilt, when a verse from the
Gospel swept him off his feet: 'Go ye forth and preach, saying: "The
kingdom of heaven is nigh. . . ."' Go! . . . Preach! . . . He must
leave this blessed solitude where God had sought him out amid the
peace of meadows and the song of birds. He must wander far and
wide, crying the Good News. So, wearing the grey tunic of a peasant,
his loins girded with a cord, Francis climbed the hill leading to Assisi,
and there, in the piazza of his home-town, began to speak. His
vocation to poverty was enlarged by a call to the apostolate, and the
twin foundation stones of the Franciscan Order were thus laid.

Those were mysterious and splendid times. Morality was no
higher than it is to-day; but there was something spontaneous, something instinctive, in the spiritual atmosphere. Francis began his
mission with a French song in order to attract the crowd; then he
began to tell of God and His justice, of the necessity for repentance and
self-denial. Many a heart was stirred, and there were not wanting
men to follow in his footsteps: Bernard of Quintavalle, Peter of
Catana, Giles, Sylvester, Morico, Barbaro, Labbatino, Bernard of
Viridante, John of San Costanzo, Angelo Tancredi, Philip the Tall,
and even John of Capella, who was to prove himself the Judas of this
new 'apostolic college.' Their number included rich bourgeois and
peasants, a knight, a labourer, and two priests who enjoyed no special
privilege. With twelve disciples at his side, Francis resolved to submit
himself to the judgment of the Pope and seek his approval of their
undertaking.

Innocent III's encouragement gave them vital energy. Once the
Pope had authorized them to preach, the Grey Friars were able to
approach parish priests and obtain leave to instruct their flocks. From
the humble monastery at Rivo Torto under the hill of Assisi, where
they had built their own huts, the friars went in pairs through the whole
countryside, to Spoleto, Perugia, Gubbio, Montefalco, and even
farther afield towards Arezzo and Siena. A new aura of fraternal
charity spread around them wherever they appeared. At Assisi, the
factions were reconciled by the young saint's voice, and put an end to
their quarrels. Vocations were so numerous that Rivo Torto was
quickly followed by the establishment of another house, St Mary of the
Angels, which was to become famous through the 'Portiuncula'
indulgence. Before long the whole of central Italy had grown used to
seeing these Grey Friars on the highway, begging their daily bread,
with no fixed dwelling place, but singing well of Christ in joyous,
fervent voices.

Among the most remarkable of Francis's adherents was Clare, a
girl of exquisite form and feature, whose very name seemed to spread

light around her, and whose portrait on the walls of the basilica at Assisi still moves us with its mysterious and penetrating charm. Rich, beautiful, and of noble lineage, she too might have embraced the gentle life marked out for her. But hearing Francis, in the cathedral at Assisi, speak of God and His love in words that were not of this world, she resolved to abandon all things and follow him. On Palm Sunday, 1212, she left home, confided her vocation to Bishop Guido, and set off in the radiant brightness of an Umbrian spring to dwell alone in a forest of holm-oak not far from Rivo Torto. Such was the origin of the Poor Ladies, or Poor Clares as they are known to-day. The first community was established soon afterwards at San Damiano, an Order which the poet in Francis had called 'my little plant,' but which was to increase rapidly and put forth many shoots.

When the Lateran Council met in 1215, Francis revisited the Eternal City in obedience to the Pope's injunction of five years ago. Innocent was delighted; and when the Council, alarmed by the mushroom growth of new religious Orders, decreed that all such associations must adopt an existing Rule, he declared that the Penitents of Assisi had already been approved.

This official act of recognition marks the third important stage in the history of the Friars Minor. At first there was no need for elaborate organization; Francis admitted anyone who desired to serve God and proclaim Him before the world, and clerics ranked no higher than laymen. It was an Order of religious, unencumbered with rich abbeys, travelling the world in that freedom wherewith Christ had made them free. Vocations continued to pour in, not excluding many learned men who gladly humbled themselves with the humblest, and sacrificed the pride of intellect as all their brethren had sacrificed the pride of fortune. Soon the Friars Minor, as they were now called, became so numerous that Francis was able to send them still farther afield. The first mission to France, Germany, Spain, and the East was a failure; they were not discouraged, but tried again, and with such determination that the grain at last took root. By 1221 the Order had spread throughout Christendom.

Meanwhile, another shoot had begun to flourish on the parent stock. This was the 'third Order,' which enabled persons of both sexes, whose duties kept them in the world, to observe a Rule similar to that of the friars. Many laymen desired a life of self-sacrifice; but their craving had fallen into disrepute as suggesting kinship with the Waldenses and Cathars, while the Humiliati of Lombardy and the Poor Catholics provided no satisfactory framework. Now that craving found an outlet within the great Franciscan Order. Important consequences flowed from the institution of this 'lay militia.' The Franciscan ideal spread deep among the masses, increasing the effect of the new leaven and raising up sublime figures such as St Elizabeth of Thuringia and St Louis, who were both members of the Third Order of St Francis.

Nevertheless, the extraordinary achievement of the Poverello was offset by many trials. Success is an obstacle not easily surmounted. What had been suited to the first community of friars, whose only governor was God, and even to the conventual groups at Rivo Torto and the Portiuncula, was hardly sufficient for the direction of an Order which had assumed gigantic proportions, which had branches in every land, and to which thousands of souls looked for spiritual guidance. Some system of regular administration was clearly indispensable; but herein lay a difficulty. How could the work be organized without losing its essential freedom?

The free-lance preacher is all very well when he happens also to be a saint; but it was doubtful whether such work could be safely entrusted to all and sundry who were attracted by the new Order's splendid reputation. Francis had long since realized the necessity of being able to rely on someone with administrative experience, and in 1218 the saintly Cardinal Hugolin (afterwards Gregory IX) had become Protector of the Order. Again, in 1220, he had agreed that all who wished to join the Friars Minor should undergo a year's novitiate. Notwithstanding his dislike of innovation, which was apparent in his refusal to appoint only clerics to positions of authority, or to accept several offers of exemption from episcopal and other jurisdiction, he was obliged to allow some modification. This process may be seen by comparing the Rule of 1221 with that of 1223. The latter version laid smaller emphasis on manual labour, forbade secession from the Order, and insisted more firmly on the duty of obedience. As a precaution against vagabondage, all friars were to have fixed residence when not actually engaged upon the mission. Each house was subject to a 'guardian'; all houses within a given area were placed under the authority of a 'custos'; several 'custodiae' constituted a province governed by a 'provincial minister'; while the provinces together formed the Order of Friars Minor under a 'minister general.' The arrangement proved satisfactory. Later, as more priests joined the Order, clerical duties became prominent, and from 1223 the Franciscans were obliged 'each day to celebrate the divine office according to the Roman rite.'

These changes, however, troubled the saintly founder's soul, causing him profound unhappiness. Was this, he asked, the will of Christ; had not his ideal been betrayed? 'Who are these men who have dared to separate my brethren from me?' he would murmur in his sorrow, torn between the poles of inspiration and efficiency. Weary, and in broken health, he had handed over the government of his Order to Peter of Catana as minister general; but Peter soon gave place to Brother Elias, whose genius for organization was not always in accord with the simple and unsullied promptings of grace. Francis himself returned as it were to his origins. He lived more and more in God, sometimes on an island in Lake Trasimene, sometimes in the cave at Subiaco where St Benedict had once dwelt as a hermit, sometimes on the glowering summit of Monte Alverno, which a friend had given him for his meditation. He desired as never before to live in Christ and to resemble Him. Beside that, what mattered the vitality and success of of his Order?

At long last God gave him the mystic answer. In September 1224 he climbed Alverno, amid the glory of sunlight and birdsong. On the morning of the 17th, after days of burning prayer that was a veritable anguish of love, suddenly, in that blinding ecstasy, he beheld a seraph flying with six wings and bearing in its supernatural form the image of the Crucified. How long did the vision last? What was the visionary's experience? We do not know. But on returning to his senses, he found himself bathed in agony—pain terrible yet exquisite; for imprinted in his hands and feet and side were the wounds of our Lord's sacred Passion, bleeding. The witness of Jesus Christ now bore in his own flesh the stigmata of his God.

Upon this ineffable privilege the soul of Francis fed throughout his closing years. Onward from that tremendous hour he seemed to live only that he might sing of God and praise Him in a thousand ways. As if inspired, there flowed from his lips poems that spoke of God's glory manifested in creation, poems like the *Canticle of the Sun*, which is one of the most beautiful hymns uttered by the mouth of man. Sick, exhausted, almost blind, and tormented by barbarous physicians who pretended to cure ophthalmia by the application of red-hot irons to his temples, Francis still maintained his joyful serenity and sublime peace of soul, praising God for his tribulations. Having dictated his last will and testament, in which he recalled the substance of his message to the Church, his tenderness increased until he seemed transmuted into love.

As the final agony drew near, he asked to be carried to St Mary of the Angels, which reminded him of his youth. In sight of the convent he made his bearers halt, and for the last time blessed Assisi. Then he asked Bro. Angelo and Bro. Leo to sing for him once more his *Canticle* to which he had added a verse in praise of 'our sister death.' On Saturday, 3rd October 1226, being now almost speechless, he managed to intone the Psalmist's words: 'I have cried to the Lord with all my voice.' He died immediately afterwards; and it is said that a great flight of larks rose into the sky, bearing his soul company.

So fruitful was his labour that Pope Benedict XV described him a 'the most perfect image of our Lord that ever lived.' He had supplied the Church with a new fighting force, adapted to contemporary needs. To the powers of disintegration he had opposed the irresistible might of the Gospel in its original simplicity. He had offered Christendom a form of piety more human than that even of St Bernard, more closely linked with the marvels of creation, a piety full of enthusiasm and gratitude. Francis was canonized two years after his death, in 1228. Innumerable books and works of art have been devoted to his memory; but it is perhaps to an apostate from the faith that we must go for an all-embracing tribute. No man, says Renan, has been more acutely conscious than was Francis of Assisi that he was the son of his Eternal Father.

9. St Dominic: God's Athlete and Builder

While the Poverello fought his heroic fight against the love of money, another man faced up to the second danger that beset the Church, the peril of complacency, of intellectual routine, of ignorance which opens wide the door to doctrinal error. His work resulted in an Order capable of disputing on equal terms with the adversaries of truth. But this Order was not based upon any preconceived plan or abstract ideal; it arose, as do most of the Church's institutions, from necessity and the dispositions of Providence.

One day in the summer of 1205, Innocent III was visited by Dom Diego de Azevedo, Bishop of Osma, a humble and little-known diocese of Spain. Two years previously he had been sent to Denmark by Alfonso VIII of Castile to bring back a bride for the Infante; but the young princess had died, and Diego was unwilling to return home without having prayed at the Apostle's tomb. He was a holy man, an excellent priest, who hoped to do still more for God. The little diocese had been 'reformed' by his predecessor, Martin de Bazan, and the canons of his chapter followed the usages of Prémontré. Now Dom Diego was not satisfied with merely doing his best in the peaceful occupation of a bishop. He dreamed of those millions of souls wandering in darkness, souls whom his Lord desired should see the light. He had heard tell of the Cumans, a barbarian tribe encamped on the borders of Hungary, who were said to be particularly ferocious; and he now sought the Pope's leave to resign his episcopal charge in order to visit and baptize these savages. One of the principal members of his suite was Dominic of Calahorra, the young sub-prior of his chapter, whom Dom Diego loved as his own son.

The Pope's conversation with his visitors has not been recorded; but we may guess its tenor from subsequent events: 'Why travel that distance to evangelize the pagan when so many precious souls are being

F

lost to Christ right on your own doorstep, just across the Pyrenees? The formidable mission you desire to undertake awaits you in Christian Languedoc, which is prey to heresy!' Innocent III was already concerned at the progress of Albigensianism; he had determined to recruit an army of preachers who would fight the Cathars on their own ground, and had recently approached the Order of Cîteaux. Diego saw the point of this argument. He returned to Spain, but made a détour through Burgundy in order to visit the great Cistercian abbey and don the white cowl of St Bernard's sons. Later, he was to rank, with his disciple Dominic, among the forty or so papal missionaries who worked in Languedoc.

The situation throughout southern France was one of immense difficulty for the Church; and the struggle upon which he now entered at the Pope's request proved for Dominic, youthful and enthusiastic as he was, a wonderful experience, a time of trial and formation. The Catharist leaders, who called themselves 'the Perfect,' were challenging the Catholics to public disputations, for which the latter were not always well qualified. The simple and coherent fashion in which the heretics presented their dogmas made a deep impression on the masses, as did the austere simplicity of their lives and their undoubted charity. The papal emissaries, Regnier and Guy of Cîteaux, Peter of Castelnau (Archdeacon of Maguelone), and even Abbot Arnaud-Amalric of Cîteaux, had despaired of success.

Our two Spaniards quickly sized up the difficulties involved; for they appreciated the dialectical skill of their opponents, who were more than a match for the arguments brought against them. But Diego and Dominic reached a still more important conclusion, though it is uncertain which of them first put it into words. At any rate, while attending a chapter of Cistercian abbots and other dignitaries of that Order at Castelnau near Montpellier, in the summer of 1206, they gave free vent to their view. The papal legates, they said, travelled in comfort with a retinue of horses, carriages, baggage, servants, and all the paraphernalia deemed necessary for persons of their rank. 'The Perfect,' on the other hand, lived poorly and journeyed on foot, as befitted those who moved in humble society. Which of these two groups, the Spaniards asked, would strike the people as more representative of the Gospel teaching? There was no need to look elsewhere for the cause of failure. Such too was the conclusion reached by Innocent III a few weeks later in his famous Bull of 19th November Diego and Dominic were indeed 'tried men determined to imitate the poverty of Christ.' They practised what they preached, sent their attendants back to Osma, and gave out that in future they would travel the roads unaccompanied and on foot, after the manner of our Lord's apostles. Dominic had learned a twofold lesson from this initia experience: he was clear as to his life's purpose—the establishment of a firmly grounded intellectual system to support the truth of Christ—and saw that he must bear witness to that truth by the example of renunciation and holy poverty.

He was now a man of about thirty-five years, calm and yet passionate, like all the best of his countrymen. Most of those who have left their mark upon the pages of Spanish history have sprung from Old Castile, a sublime but ruthless territory, the highest point in all that lofty plateau. Castile is a province of intense vitality and tragic violence. The deep blue dome of sky seems to press down with all its weight upon the desert floor; dark shadow contrasts with dazzling light; and night, twinkling with millions of stars, alternates with blinding noon. It is a province that hardens the body and forges character. Cid Campeador, Guzman the Brave, and the Conquistadores, as well as St Teresa and St John of the Cross, were all Castilians.

Dominic, third son of Felix and Juana Guzman, was born in the Douro valley about 1171. His birthplace, Calahorra, could offer little in the way of education; so Dominic was sent first to reside with his uncle, the archpriest of Gumiel, and later to the University of Palencia, in Leon, where he remained for about ten years. His parents could not fail to notice his keen intelligence, which clearly deserved an opportunity for higher studies. It was also related that, during her pregnancy, Doña Juana had dreamed a prophetic dream like that of St Bernard's mother. She saw issue from her womb a young hound carrying in its jaws a blazing torch which set fire to the whole countryside. The prophecy appears to have been fulfilled in Dominic from youth upwards; for he joined the canons regular at Osma, and soon dominated the cathedral chapter. When less than thirty years of age he was elected sub-prior, and took his seat as a member of the bishop's council.

All Dominic's biographers agree with his spiritual daughter, Blessed Cecilia Cesarini, that he was a fine-looking man, well built, of no more than medium height, but perfectly proportioned. His manly countenance was rendered even more striking by the lustre of his eyes; his hands were long and thin. His dignified bearing was enhanced by a certain radiant tranquillity that emanated from his person, inspiring both affection and respect in all who met him. Never refusing a challenge, anxious to come to grips with his opponent, he was a spiritual athlete, the athlete of Christ crucified. Admired for his extreme simplicity, for his compassion towards the unfortunate, for his delicate and generous sensibility, and for his abiding charity, his character was no less persuasive than his dialectic.

His genius, quite different from that of St Francis of Assisi, lay not in lightning intuition backed by gentle obstinacy, but in the lucid study of facts and their assessment.   Once the end was clearly defined he devoted himself with unhurried energy to its attainment.   Dominic has been called a 'builder'; [1] his flair for organization and creative method, combined with fearless energy, were the marks of a singularly productive intellect.   Moreover, he possessed the art of expressing his ideas, his plans, and the stages of an argument with remarkable eloquence.   His biographers agree likewise in telling us that when he spoke, in a voice that was by turns affectionate and menacing, none could resist the beauty of his language, the force of his logic, or his infectious enthusiasm.

It was not without reason that Dominic came to be regarded as the very mouthpiece of God.   A man of action, a thinker, and an able administrator, he was an even greater mystic, a soul devoted to Christ, upon whom he desired above all things to model himself; and his thought was steeped in the Bible, particularly in the Gospels, which he always carried with him.   He possessed the faith of those to whom it has been promised that they shall move mountains; and it is therefore not surprising to learn that he worked numerous miracles and even raised four persons from the dead.   St Dominic was at once a man of affairs, a mystic, and an intellectual, according to a pattern of which the Middle Ages produced so many examples from St Bernard to St Louis. Together, those three characteristics make the perfect man.

After Dom Diego's return to Osma, where he died in December 1207, Dominic, helped no doubt by a few companions, assumed sole responsibility for the apostolate.   These strange missionaries visited the towns and villages of Languedoc, where their self-denial, modesty, and charity rivalled the corresponding virtues of 'the Perfect.'   We find them at Caraman near Toulouse, at Carcassonne, at Verfeil, and at Fanjeaux not far from Pamiers.   Public disputation with the heretics became more frequent, turning more often to the profit of the Christian faith; and God Himself bore witness to His faithful servants.   One day, by way of experiment, a treatise written by the saint was thrown into the fire together with a heretical book.   Dominic's was rejected unharmed by the flames; the other was burned to ashes, and conversions began to multiply.

Shortly before Diego returned to Spain, but no doubt on his own initiative, Dominic made his first religious foundation.   At Prouille, a small town situated at the foot of the Pyrenees between Montréal and Fanjeaux, there was a shrine of our Lady, a place of pilgrimage, where Dominic had often prayed.   Here he conceived the idea of establishing a convent for women and girls who had abjured their heresy but who wished to continue living the same chaste and austere life that they had known among 'the Perfect.'   It was an excellent plan; for these

[1] By Mgr Gillet, formerly Master-General of the Dominicans.

religious exercised a powerful influence upon women of the upper classes, and were later entrusted with the education of children. The convent also provided the itinerant missionaries with a centre from which they could reach the heretics in country places and still remain in contact with Toulouse.

On 15th January 1208, soon after the foundation of Prouille, the papal legate Peter of Castelnau was assassinated. The result was the Albigensian crusade.[1] Horror swept down upon Languedoc with the armies of the North; but in this terrible war—which he might justify in principle, but of whose inhuman cruelty he could never have approved —Dominic took no part. He may, in the course of his duty, have taken a hand in the 'conviction' of certain heretics, that is to say in discriminating between them and the faithful. But this was part of his vocation; there is no proof that he ever sat on a criminal trial, and it is quite certain that he never participated in an act of war.[2]

Leaving Prouille, where he fulfilled the office of 'nuns' prior,' Dominic resumed his work as an itinerant preacher. He was virtually alone, for most of the Cistercians had departed. People were amazed at his energy, and impressed by his resolve to keep open the gate of the fold for those sheep who had gone astray. The newly appointed Bishop of Toulouse, a Cistercian named Foulques, appealed to Dominic and his companions. A wealthy citizen of that place gave them a house near the church of St Romanus, and another milestone had been reached. Dominic now governed a community of diocesan missionaries subject to episcopal jurisdiction. This arrangement agreed well with papal policy; it was also the seed of a new Order which the saint already had in mind. His community numbered only seven, but they knew God had called them to a formidable task. Bishop Foulques called them 'Friars Preachers,' a name which was afterwards ratified together with their Order by Pope Honorius III.

By the time the oecumenical council met at Rome on 1st November 1215 Foulques and Dominic had decided that they ought to enlarge the sphere of their activity. Innocent III had prayed for just such an apostolate as they were about to propose, but there was a difficulty. The council had decreed that all who wished to serve God in the religious life must adopt one or other of the already sanctioned Rules; Dominic and his friends received a good deal of encouragement, but nothing more substantial. It was necessary, then, to choose an existing Rule. That of St Augustine was familiar to the canon of Osma, and its flexibility allowed of its adaptation to altered circumstances. The Friars Preachers accordingly embraced a constitution

[1] See Chapter XIII.
[2] During the battle of Muret, at which the crusaders routed the King of Aragon, Dominic remained in church upon his kness.

very similar to that of Prémontré. They were to be canons regular in virtue of their Rule, monks in spirit, and missionaries in their mode of life. Such were the fundamentals of the Order which now awaited canonical recognition.

On 12th July 1216 Innocent III died at Perugia, where the conclave met without delay and chose Cardinal Savelli to succeed him. This astonishing old man took the name of Honorius III, and died in 1227 at the age of more than one hundred years. At the time of his election Honorius was active both in mind and body. He recognized the Cathars as a most dangerous sect, and had learned of the part played in Languedoc by the little community of St Romanus. On 22nd December he sent them his warm approval, and wrote to Dominic that his brethren would become 'champions of the faith and true lights of the world.' The Pope formally 'confirmed the Order, taking it under his protection'; and this act, repeated in January 1217, marks the institution of the Friars Preachers, who thereby reached the third and most important stage of their development.

They were as yet a mere handful, sixteen to be exact: half a dozen Spaniards together with recruits from Normandy, England, France, Provence, Navarre, and Languedoc. The international outlook of the Dominicans was thus clear from the very start. Their habit—the white woollen robe of canons regular and the large black travelling-cloak of Spanish priests—was suggested by the circumstances of their origin and institution.

The principal characteristics of the new Order were now firmly established: it was to consist of preachers and scholars, of men devoted to poverty and the spoken word. First and foremost they were preachers, spokesmen of Jesus Christ, and soldiers of the Holy Ghost. They would go forth and teach not only in those churches to whose clergy the diocesan authorities recommended them, but wheresoever occasion offered, in the universities and schools, and even in the public squares. The Order had scarcely been ratified before Dominic dispersed his brethren to the four corners of Christendom. He had his eye principally on the great intellectual centres, where the conflict of ideas, if more prolonged, would be more fruitful.

Now victory in this struggle required the necessary weapons. St Dominic, recognizing the value of his own theological training at the University of Palencia, had determined that the brethren must improve their education preparatory to embarking on their mission. Before leaving for Rome in September 1216 he had asked the master of theology at Toulouse to undertake the instruction of his subjects; but as soon as the Pope's approbation had been obtained, the Order turned to the great universities for the training of its members, many of whom attained professorial rank.

The Friars Preachers owed their third outstanding characteristic to St Dominic in person. During his struggle with the Cathars, he had realized the need of poverty and self-sacrifice; but there was danger that, as the Order grew, its work might be hindered by endowments, or by the gift of churches which it would then have to administer. In other words, their functions as canons regular might interrupt their freedom of movement. At Toulouse, as early as 1216, Dominic had sought to impose the principle of absolute poverty; but he had been prevented by the opposition of Foulques, who foresaw 'his' missionaries scattered beyond the confines of his diocese. In Rome, however, Dominic met St Francis of Assisi, probably at the house of Cardinal Hugolin. Though different in so many respects, the two men understood one another's point of view completely; and it is said that at the second Franciscan chapter in 1217 a solitary white-robed figure was present among the grey Franciscan ranks. A painting by Andrea della Robbia, in the Loggia of San Paolo at Florence, shows St Dominic at the moment of parting from Il Poverello, asking the latter for his hempen girdle to commemorate their friendship. Confirmed by the example of St Francis in his ideal of poverty, St Dominic raised the question once again with his Order, and in a general chapter held at Bologna at Pentecost, 1220, it was resolved that the Friars Preachers should own no churches, convents, or landed property; they too would live as mendicants, and thus be free to wander in God's service.

Such, then, were the essential marks of the new Order in 1220. The Dominican Rule had not as yet been codified, and would not be until 1228; but the founder saw clearly what was indispensable if the tiny seed were to become a tree. That he did so is enough to prove his genius. Organization preceded expansion; and his successors had only to follow his design in order to avoid those tragic disputes which troubled the Franciscans. His broad views, his realism, his understanding of contemporary needs, and his determination to make straight for his goal, reveal St Dominic as one of the ablest of all religious founders.

The Order, as conceived by him, was really a synthesis inspired by, but more highly developed than, the hierarchy of Cîteaux. It was a synthesis of personal authority and dependence upon subordinates; for it had points in common both with monarchy and with the commune, two political institutions which were evolving at that time. The government of each house was vested in a prior elected by the whole community for a given period. When his term of office had expired, he became once more a simple religious; meanwhile, the conventual chapter acted as a brake upon abuse of power. One stage higher, the provincial chapter confirmed the election of priors and itself elected the prior provincial, whose chief task was to make the visitation of all his subject houses. This provincial chapter consisted of conventual priors, each of whom was assisted by an elected 'definitor' and a number of 'preachers general,' friars who had been licensed to preach in all dioceses. The part played by these 'definitors,' reliable men chosen by their communities, was of great importance, for they were counsellors of the priors provincial, between whom and their own brethren they served as intermediaries. Finally, there was the master-general, elected by a general chapter composed of priors provincial and definitors. In order to assure constant vigilance from above, and to provide as it were a safety-valve for discontent, the general chapter consisted of two groups: the priors provincial assembled once every three years, the other two were reserved for meetings of the definitors, who investigated such complaints as had been laid before them. The Dominican constitutions were so flexible that they were easily adapted to new requirements, yet so secure that they have never been revised; and there is no stronger testimony to the founder's inspiration and foresight than the fact that his institution has remained practically unaltered since the thirteenth century.

St Dominic was also responsible for what is known as 'individual dispensation,' a system which was to prove of great value to the Order. The Dominicans sprang, as we have seen, from the canons regular, and were therefore bound by the traditional duties of choral office and other monastic observances; but it was not easy to reconcile such duties with the demands of an active life. Suppose, for example, that a friar was so far distant from his convent that he could not be present at sung prime or terce; what was he to do? The nature and duties of his vocation necessitated some kind of compromise, and this took the form of 'individual dispensation,' whereby the superior had power to exempt a religious from the obligations of the Rule, and thus make it easier for him to carry out his mission as a preacher.

Side by side with the Order of Friars Preachers, there grew up a number of kindred organizations. The female community at Notre-Dame de Prouille developed into a contemplative Order, whose reputation was still further enhanced when the nuns of Santa Maria in Trastevere at Rome placed themselves under Dominican jurisdiction. This contemplative Order was later supplemented by 'regular third Orders' devoted to teaching and care of the sick. The influence of Dominican ideals was strengthened by the creation of another kind of third Order, whose original purpose was rather different from that of the corresponding Franciscan institution. At first it was described as an 'Army of Jesus Christ' charged with the defence of Holy Church, then as a 'Fraternity of Penance.' But its aim was before long indistinguishable from that proposed by St Francis to his lay disciples: it sought to apply the Order's religious principles in secular life, and the Dominican scapular was worn alike by warriors and kings.

Papal approbation was the signal for a decisive thrust. Vocations became more numerous, and included a high percentage of scholars and intellectuals. Four years later there were several hundred Black Friars on the road; but even more striking than this numerical increase is the accuracy with which the first Dominicans summed up the current situation and appraised its need. Here again, we cannot help but see the founder's penetration. His Order established itself at those very points where lay the destiny of Christendom: Rome and Paris and Bologna. At Rome, under the Sovereign Pontiff's eye, there was the priory of St Sixtus, followed soon afterwards by that of Santa Sabina on the Aventine. At Paris, the theological capital of Europe, and at the great legal centre of Bologna, Black Friars attended lectures by the most eminent teachers and soon reached professorial status. That Dominican learning was so soon qualified to rescue the beleaguered fortress of the intellect, that it was able to incorporate with Christian doctrine those yearnings which could otherwise have led only to rebellion and heresy, was due in no small measure to the fact that Dominic himself had placed his sons at these strategic points. Without him the Church would never have produced St Thomas Aquinas.

Success had crowned his labour, and he was ready to resume the life marked out by his vocation. Simple as ever, with the same humility as of old, he set out once again upon his mission. The Plain of Lombardy, the Tyrol, the valleys of Switzerland, and the highways of France saw him come and go. Then, as though urged by a presentiment of death, he determined to revisit the land of his childhood, Spain, which he had quitted fifteen years ago. Reaching Segovia at the foot of the Sierra Guadarrama, not far from Osma and the castle of the Guzmans, he took up his abode in a cave. The good folk of the neighbourhood flocked to him in hundreds, and he made his first Spanish foundation, Santa Cruz. Leaving the new convent under the direction of Corbolan (who was afterwards beatified), he pushed on to Madrid, always preaching, travelling almost without rest, in spite of failing health.

On his return to Bologna, Dominic was exhausted. He might indeed have contemplated his work with pride, had his humility allowed him to glory in aught else but Christ; for there were now eight Dominican provinces—Spain, Provence, Lombardy, Rome, Germany, England,[1] and Hungary.[2] But the servant of God had been warned by an angel that he must soon depart out of this life. He

---

[1] Bro. Gilbert of Fraxineto had recently arrived in England, and a Dominican priory had been established at Oxford.

[2] The Hungarian foundation had been made by Bro. Paul.

F*

foretold that his death would occur before the feast of our Lady's Assumption, and set out on a final journey, this time to visit Hugolin at Venice. Having commended the affairs of his Order to the cardinal's benevolence, he returned to the priory of St Nicholas at Bologna towards the end of July 1221. By this time he had fallen victim to incurable headache and the ravages of dysentery.

Dominic's end had all that calm and simple dignity which had accompanied him through life. He delivered a parting discourse to the young novices, and called twelve senior brethren to his bedside. Having given them his final directions with a view to the Order's prosperity, he made public confession before them all. His biographer, Blessed Jordan of Saxony, who describes the scene, gives us a striking picture of Dominic's grave visage as he spoke these words: 'Divine goodness has preserved me from all stain until this hour; but I must admit that I have not escaped the weakness of discovering more pleasure in the conversation of young women than in that of aged crones.' On Friday, 6th August, shortly before noon, he bade the community range themselves on each side of his couch as if they were in choir. As the supreme moment drew near, he had the strength to bid them start the prayers for those *in extremis*; and at the words 'Come to his assistance, O ye saints of God,' he rendered up his soul. At that same hour, according to tradition, the saintly Prior Guala of Brescia was wrapped in ecstasy. Like Jacob, he saw heaven open, while angels ascended a ladder to the throne of Christ carrying a man clothed in the Dominican habit, but whom he could not identify because the hood was drawn down over his face as is done for a dead friar.[1]

10. The New Leaven

The appearance of the mendicant Orders was the most significant event of the Church's interior life during the thirteenth century. Not from the seclusion of their cloister, nor even through the lecture-room, would this new class of monks influence the mass of Christians. Their approach was more direct; their method a form of preaching better suited to the aspirations of mankind at large.

The extraordinary success of the mendicants goes to prove that they satisfied an urgent need. The stream of vocations soon became a torrent: in the second half of the thirteenth century, for example, the Franciscans had 25,000 religious and 1,100 houses; by 1316 there were 30,000 friars in 1,400 convents. The growth of the Dominican Order was not quite so rapid. Its emphasis upon intellectual attainments and its relative indifference to popular forms of devotion tended to limit

---

[1] St Dominic was canonized in 1234.

the number of vocations. Nevertheless, it counted 7,000 members in 1256, 10,000 friars with 600 priories in 1303, and 12,000 in 1337.

These facts, however, are not meant to suggest that the two Orders suffered no growing pains. First, there were internal problems arising from an inevitable clash between pure ideal and practical exigencies. It seems that absolute renunciation of all worldly goods is incompatible with the efficient working of a great institution; and there is constant danger that intellectual labour, necessary though it be, may finish as an end in itself, rather than as a means to the knowledge and love of God. Personal ambition and mutual jealousy took advantage of this tension; nor indeed could it be hoped that among so many thousands all would prove exempt from human weakness simply because of their profession.

So far as the Dominicans were concerned, such crises had no grave repercussions. To begin with, their organization was such as to prevent disagreement on many points. Again, St Dominic had shown both firmness and sagacity in his attitude towards two basic principles of religious life. When St Thomas Aquinas remarks that poverty is a means to but not the essence of perfection, he shows himself a true disciple of the founder who, while directing his sons to the universities, made it clear that the sole end of study is knowledge of God and the victory of the Cross. Finally, as an Order of clerics, the Dominicans were not confronted with the delicate problem of relations between priests and laymen in the same community. It must not be imagined, however, that they enjoyed continual fair weather. Faults against poverty and obedience were not infrequent, and the deposition of a master-general by the Holy See in 1291 caused a good deal of trouble.

But these squalls were as nothing to the storms through which the Grey Friars passed. Here conflict was inevitable from the outset. The sublime folly of the Poverello, already manifest in his early years, was repeated in his Testament: 'I expressly forbid any brother to accept money in any way whatsoever, whether in person or through a third party. . . . He who is not learned must not try to learn.' An arrangement of that kind was scarcely suited to a worldwide organization.

The first Franciscan crisis, however, was not provoked by differences of principle; it was the result of a defective constitution. Bro. Elias of Cortona, appointed minister-general in 1232, behaved so autocratically that he was deposed in 1239 by the general chapter, which took this opportunity to reshape the Order and place it on a more democratic basis. The general chapter would henceforth meet every three years, and provincials were to be elected by provincial chapters. The same period witnessed a further modification, which brought the Order of St Francis into closer line with the Dominicans by reducing the status of its lay members.   It was not long before these were disqualified from acting as superiors,[1] and in course of time lay membership was virtually prohibited.

There was also an acute divergence of opinion on the subject of poverty.   Those who advocated the primitive austerity of the Rule met with violent opposition, both in theory and practice, on the part of those who stood for evolution.   A marble offertory-box which had been placed on the site of the new basilica at Assisi was smashed to pieces by one of the Poverello's dearest friends, Bro. Leo, who thereby earned himself a public whipping.   In Germany, Bro. Caesar's devotion to the saint's ideal cost him his life.   But the force of circumstance was irresistible, and there were further mitigations.   In 1230 the Bull *Quo elongati* lent authority to a juridical fiction according to which 'no one is considered to *own* what he merely *possesses*, so long as he does not in conscience *consider* himself as owner, so long as he does not *refuse to give it up* or *lay claim to it*.'   The Friars Minor remained 'poor' in principle, while a number of 'spiritual friends' or 'nuntii' were *considered as* owners and administrators of their property, and accepted money on their behalf.   In 1245 Innocent IV tried to resolve the problem by declaring all property held by the mendicants to be vested in the Holy See.   St Bonaventure, who was minister-general from 1257 until 1273, came nearest to finding a solution.   He endeavoured to save the vestiges of poverty by interpreting it as the 'indispensable measure of control over indispensable goods.'

From the second half of the thirteenth century Dominicans and Franciscans were both clerical Orders.   They had now abandoned their hermitages and taken up residence in the towns, where they combined parochial work with the task of itinerant preachers—a form of activity which contributed much to their practical efficiency and immediate success.   It is not improbable, on the other hand, that they would have achieved still more by adhering to the letter of their Rule, leaving the secular clergy to exercise its customary duties and learn from them the lesson of asceticism.   Such a course would certainly have avoided other difficulties which the mendicant Orders were destined to encounter.

For it cannot be denied that they were not always well received. Not every parish priest was prepared to welcome these religious among the flock which had been committed to his care, and upon which he depended for his livelihood.   An anonymous treatise, probably the work of a Picard priest, gives vent to this complaint: 'Here are men who seek to forestall the clergy in their ecclesiastical functions.   They claim to administer the sacraments of baptism, penance, and extreme unction of the sick, and also to bury the dead in their own churchyards.

[1] Elias was the last minister-general who was not a priest.

Worse still, in order to bring us into disrepute and keep the faithful from our pious reunions, they have created two new confraternities, which are joined by men and women in such numbers that nowadays one can scarcely find a single Christian whose name does not appear in one or other register.' Nor were the friars regarded with much greater favour by the monks. The bishops frankly mistrusted men whom they suspected as agents, if not as spies, of the Holy See, and whose centralized organization was exempt from episcopal control. The Archbishop of Sens, for example, long refused them admission to his diocese.

In spite of these difficulties, the numbers and power of the mendicants grew steadily throughout two centuries. The Picard's lament, indeed, describes both the extent and the cause of their success. Many a 'Rue Cordelier,' 'Marché des Capucins,' and 'Place des Jacobins' bears witness to their influence. Encouraged by the Holy See, popular with the middle and lower classes (who found them more approachable than the monks in their fine abbeys), they were able to establish one house after another. Within a quarter of a century, twenty-five Franciscan and twelve Dominican convents were founded in Belgium and northern France. The Dominican priory of St Jacques at Paris, the Sacro Convento or 'Great Convent' of the Franciscans at Assisi, Santa Sabina of the Black Friars, and Ara Coeli of the Minors at Rome together sheltered hundreds of religious; while Padua, Bologna, Lyons, Oxford, and Genoa were scarcely less important. Before long, the Church began looking to the new Orders for her senior officials. No less than 450 bishops, twelve cardinals, and two popes were to issue from the ranks of St Dominic; and if the Franciscans produced only two hundred bishops and eight cardinals, this smaller proportion may be attributed to the tradition of humility bequeathed to his Order by St Francis, and also no doubt to its having contained fewer men of learning.

Further evidence of the friars' impact upon ecclesiastical life may be seen in the fact that their organization and methods of training were copied by more ancient congregations. The canons regular, especially those of Prémontré, were influenced in matters of theology and pastoral work by the Dominicans, who were their offspring. The example of both Black Friars and Franciscans attracted Cluniacs, Benedictines, Cistercians, Premonstratensians, and Trinitarians to the universities; while the secular clergy were shamed into a more diligent exercise of their sacerdotal functions. Monastic life in general was stimulated by this form of apostolate; and despite the famous thirteenth canon of the Lateran Council, which forbade the introduction of new Rules, the first half of the thirteenth century reaped a veritable harvest of religious Orders.

In Palestine, a number of crusaders had determined to live as hermits in the celebrated caverns of Mount Carmel. About the year 1156, under the direction of St Berthold of Malifay, they had founded a small association which prided itself upon having thereby revived a tradition of immense antiquity, dating from the prophets Elias and Eliseus. In 1209 the patriarch Albert of Jerusalem gave these 'Hermits of Carmel,' or Carmelites, a permanent Rule which was approved by Pope Gregory IX in 1228. It was an austere code, enjoining solitude and penance of the utmost rigour. Within twelve months, however, the Turks had rendered life on Carmel quite impossible; the Order there-fore removed to Europe (1229), built a number of convents, and devoted itself to missionary work. In 1248 Innocent IV recognized it as the third mendicant congregation, named after 'Our Lady of Mount Carmel.'

A fourth mendicant Order, which came into being at about this time, was known as 'the Hermits of St Augustine.' The Rule of St Augustine had been adopted not only by the canons regular, but also by small eremitical communities such as the Guillelmites, founded before 1157 by St William of Maleval; the Jeanbonites, instituted about 1229 by Blessed John Bon of Mantua; and the Brittinians who dwelt near Fans with the hermitage of St Blaise of Brittino as their centre. In 1256 Pope Alexander IV united these three groups under the title of 'Augustinians.' Though described as hermits, they resided in towns and became almost as numerous as the Dominicans. It has been said that in the year 1300 the Order had some 30,000 members. This is probably an exaggeration; but many a street-name, such as the 'Quai des Grands-Augustins' or 'Rue des Petits Pères,' still preserves their memory. They too found their way into the universities, which they supplied with several distinguished teachers, among whom was Blessed Augustine Trionfo. So great indeed was their influence that in 1319 they held the offices of Sacristan, Librarian, and Confessor to the Pope.

These Orders of men had their female counterparts, with whom they formed the rallying point of the third Orders; but there were many more such congregations. One of the most interesting, as showing the effect of the new leaven among simple layfolk, was that of the 'Servants of the Blessed Virgin,' or Servites, instituted on 15th August 1223 by Blessed Bonfiglio Monaldi, a Florentine merchant to whom our Lady appeared while he was singing lauds. Six of his friends believed the vision, and these 'Seven Founders' withdrew to Monte Senario. They too were recognized as a mendicant Order in 1255, and soon afterwards took up residence in the towns; they too held more than one chair in the universities; they too gave rise to an Order of nuns and a third Order; and it was they who spread devotion to our Lady of Seven Dolours. But if the Franciscans and Dominicans had competitors in the work of reform, which was in a special sense their own, we must not forget that its success was mainly due to them, not only because they were pioneers in the field, but also because of their numerical superiority.

No one can fail to recognize the influence, direct or indirect, of this new leaven upon the clergy. Its effect upon the Christian masses, however, was still more remarkable. The Benedictine chronicler Matthew Paris and the miniaturists of that period give us a picture of the mendicants, travelling barefoot, with no baggage other than a kind of cylindrical pouch slung from the shoulder and containing a manual of piety, a book of sermons, a *summa auctoritatis* (i.e. selected passages from the Fathers), and a volume of those *exempla* or anecdotes which were so prominent in their teaching. They halted everywhere—at churches, convents, castles, and tournaments, as well as in the public squares and harvest fields. Simple, austere, and poor, living on such alms as they received, they made a deep impression on the common people. They spoke the truth as they saw it, without fear or favour; and some of them, e.g. the Portuguese Saint Anthony 'of Padua' and Berthold of Ratisbon, acquired extraordinary fame. Their rough and ready speech together with their penitential lives made a powerful appeal to those who heard them.

It is difficult to say just how far their ideal of poverty influenced society. Gustave Schnürer affirms that it 'checked the undue growth of a materialistic civilization' and that 'the Church in the thirteenth century received from them a timely warning not to concern herself with temporal questions to the point of forgetting her divine mission.' The work of the mendicants was no less fruitful in the field of charity. The 'Great Devotion' of 1233, when Dominicans and Franciscans made a concerted effort on an international scale, brought about spectacular results in the way of reconciliation between families, clans, and cities. At Paquara especially, the Dominican John of Vicenza spoke so beautifully on the subject of fraternal love that hundreds made their peace then and there. The mission of 1233 survived in those 'associations of peace' which are often confused with the two third Orders whereby the Dominicans and Grey Friars maintained their hold upon society.

The activity of the mendicants took numerous forms. One of the most curious was the promotion of certain friars to what can only be described as theocratic dictatorships. Thus John of Vicenza, following his phenomenal success in 1233, was appointed Podestà, then Rector, and finally Duke of Verona and Vicenza with plenary powers; an innovation which, repeated elsewhere, foreshadowed the rule of Savonarola at Florence. These were exceptional cases, but innumerable friars undertook court duties which gave them a hand in politics. Many, for example, acted as confessors to princes and their families;

and when St Louis, resolving to base his administration on the principles of charity and justice, revived the Carolingian 'Missi Dominici' in the form of 'Grand Inquisitors,' it was the mendicant friars whom he invited to undertake these delicate functions. While providing spiritual directors and advisers to temporal sovereigns, they showed themselves no less friendly towards the free towns; and their convents —built not upon the Cluniac hill-tops or the solitary marshes of Cîteaux, but in the heart of cities—became centres of intellectual, spiritual, and even political life. Their 'democratic' regime, which enabled every religious to exercise a measure of responsibility in his conventual chapter, was not unlike the communal system; for the mendicants not only rejected the paternal jurisdiction of the abbots at a time when the cities were repudiating feudal autocracy, but they represented a new concept of the common good.

St Dominic had realized his vocation in the struggle against heresy; and it was to the friars that the Church continually appealed to defend the purity of her doctrine. Thus, the mendicants found themselves engaged in the unpleasant duties of the Inquisition; [1] especially the Dominicans, upon whom fell most of the odium roused by that tribunal. Moreover, when Christendom became aware that Islam could not be subdued by force of arms, it was the mendicants who led the great missionary crusade, going among the infidels whom they hoped to win for Christ by love. [2]

Finally, their exertions were of capital importance on the intellectual plane. At a time of intense spiritual ferment, the new Orders were found more capable than were the secular clergy or the old monastic congregations of identifying themselves with and giving direction to the interests of their contemporaries. Their entry into the great seats of learning, however, was not effected without opposition; and the annals of that period tell of ceaseless conflict in the university of Paris. The triumph of the Dominicans Roland of Cremona and John of St Gilles, and that of the Franciscan Alexander of Hales, as teachers of theology, let loose a storm of protest. A pamphlet entitled *Perils of the Present Time* (1256), by William of Saint-Amour, denounced the teaching of the mendicants with impassioned vehemence. It was not merely a question of jealousy or profit; a new way of thinking and of reasoning, a new approach to theology, was in process of formation. The contest centred upon Aristotle, whose most illustrious and ultimately victorious champion was St Thomas Aquinas. [3]

In short, it was to the mendicant Orders that the sixteenth-century reform owed both its origin and its success. It is not difficult to see that the 'return to the Gospel,' for which they strove, exercised no less profound an influence upon canon law, upon the notion of criminal justice, and upon social life, than upon devotional practices.   True to that lasting and mysterious paradox that is the Church, the mendicants laboured not only to re-establish the pristine purity of Christian morals, but also to breathe the Gospel spirit into the new framework of life. We owe it to them that the necessary transformation was accomplished not outside and in opposition to the Church, but deep within her womb.

We come now to the part played by the Holy See in this colossal undertaking.   During the twelfth century reform had been *attempted* side by side with, but independently of, Rome; in the thirteenth it was *accomplished* in close collaboration with the Sovereign Pontiffs and under their direction.   Franciscans and Dominicans had, from the very first, placed themselves unreservedly at the disposition of the Holy See; and St Francis once beheld a vision of his Order (represented by a brood of chicks) defended by the Roman eagle against attack by sparrow-hawks.   Neither St Francis nor St Dominic asked for 'exemption,' but a succession of Bulls regulating the affairs of the two Orders made them exempt *de facto*; they were answerable to none but their own Generals, who worked in strict harmony with the Lateran.

We may also observe that every thirteenth-century pope favoured the mendicant Orders.   The kindly eye of Innocent III presided over their birth.   Honorius III (1216–27) gave them canonical status. Gregory IX (1227–41) showed himself, on Peter's throne, no less well disposed than he had been as Cardinal Hugolin; and his successors, whether Italian, French, English, or Portuguese, manifested the same interest and goodwill.   Even those who cared less for the Church's well-being—e.g. Innocent IV who, notwithstanding the blamelessness of his private life, was dominated by unworthy counsellors—continued to protect the advocates of an indispensable reform.[1]

Two outstanding events of this period were the Councils of Lyons in 1245 and 1274.[2]   They concerned themselves with the reorganization of the new Orders in view of their encroachment on the rights of secular priests, but did not impede their work.   A union of interests between the mendicant Orders and the papacy was sealed once and for all [3] in 1276 by the election of a Dominican, Peter of Tarentaise, as Pope Innocent V.

[1] It was two mendicants, the Franciscan St Bonaventure and the Dominican St Thomas Aquinas, whom Urban IV (1261–4), 'political' Pope though he was, instructed to compose the office of Corpus Christi.
[2] The second of these Councils was summoned by the reforming Pope St Gregory X (1271–6).
[3] Except towards the end of the pontificate of Innocent IV, who appeared for a time to be influenced by his entourage and to fear that the success of the mendicants would overshadow the prestige of the papacy.   His alarm, however, was short-lived, and he later paid splendid homage to the new Orders by describing them as 'Sons of Obedience, ready to brave all perils in defence of justice.'

The mendicants thus formed an army devoted to the Sovereign Pontiff, a useful instrument for the dissemination of his views, and a diplomatic corps which might safely be entrusted with the most difficult and dangerous embassies.   We find them, for instance, under orders from the Pope to support Charles of Anjou in Sicily, to arrange the peace between St Louis and the English king, and to subvert the power of Frederick II.   This latter achievement incurred savage reprisals; for in 1249 the Emperor actually decreed the penalty of death by burning for the Dominicans and Franciscans who, 'under the cloak of religion, play the game of Lucifer'!

The coming of the friars, therefore, was a landmark not only in the field of moral reform.   They upheld the cause of successive popes in their struggle with the temporal power.   But they also represented a new conception of the Church and of her function in the world: a Church in whom the brilliance of feudal power would give place to interior prestige; the Church of the missions, and of the universities wherein human thought was to make notable advances; a Church in closer sympathy with the aims of an enlarged society.   Thus, once again, as has happened so often in the course of history, the permanent message of Christ was embodied in a particular form of Christianity; once again the leaven had done its work.

CHAPTER V

THE CHURCH AND THE POWERS

1. IN THE WORLD BUT NOT OF THE WORLD

THE spiritual and moral problem which the Church endeavoured so courageously to solve was not the only one with which she was confronted; for in order to accomplish her supernatural mission, it was necessary that she should clarify her relations with the civil power. The two realms of authority appear at first sight to be unconnected; actually they are inseparable. Christ Himself emphasized that the Church is 'not *of* this world'; her essential purity tends to raise her above the things of earth. Nevertheless, her work lies *in* this world, among men, within the framework of their interests and institutions. She can no more be indifferent to the laws upon which her freedom depends than to those material resources which enable her ministers to carry out their supernatural function. She is a spiritual society, foreshadowing the City of God; but she is obliged to maintain close contact with the City of the World, and that is no easy task.

The problem is everlasting. It is the most difficult of all those which Christendom has been called upon to solve; and if no satisfactory solution has yet been found, it is surely because none exists, because it is in the nature of things that there should be continual tension between the spiritual and the temporal order. Three situations are possible. The secular power may be opposed to the Church upon ideological or political grounds, which means persecution; or the State may ignore religious activity and treat the spiritual society as nonexistent, which means neutrality. But persecution had ended in the fourth century, and neutrality was quite unthinkable in the Middle Ages; so there remained a third possibility, collaboration.

The pre-eminence of the Church throughout the Dark Ages, the universality of the faith, and the submission of temporal leaders to the Christian creed, had resulted in an unhealthy influence of the secular on the spiritual domain. The Church had set her seal upon the brow of emperors and kings; she had provided them with agents and administrators; she had received from them lands and other material benefits; and she had enjoyed their protection at a time when it had been of considerable value. By the same token, however, she had largely curtailed her freedom, until at last she found herself subject to those with whom she had meant only to walk hand in hand. During the barbarian epoch she had scored a notable success; but that same victory now threatened her with ruin. The moment had come when she must awake and act.

It should not, on the other hand, be thought that there was permanent antagonism between the medieval Church and State. Many a page of history is occupied with the Quarrel of Investitures and with the struggle between Priesthood and Empire, regrettable conflicts in the course of which St Thomas à Becket suffered martyrdom and a French envoy insulted the Pope. But such was not the normal state of affairs. A vast majority of people thought with St Bernard: 'I am not one of those who say that the peace and freedom of the Church is harmful to the Empire, or that the Empire's prosperity is harmful to the Church. On the contrary, God, who is the author of both, has linked them in a common destiny on earth, not for the sake of internecine strife but that they may strengthen one another.' For the most part there was concord between the spiritual and temporal powers; disagreement, no matter how violent a form it might assume, was the exception.

The gravity and the ferocity of these disputes must be sought in the fact that they involved the entire historico-social complex. To call in question the Church's ownership of material goods was to deny fundamental principles, and perhaps to overthrow the established order. Excessive zeal on behalf of temporal concerns was not hard to justify in the name of supreme spiritual interests. We may deplore clerical participation in the feudal regime; but in the circumstances which then prevailed, a Church without lands, a papacy without territorial sovereignty, would have been bound hand and foot at the mercy of rival factions. Moral, economic, and political considerations all played their part in the conflict between Church and State, not to mention the egotism, self-esteem, and other passions of antagonists in either camp.

It is therefore a false view to see the conflict simply as an affair of politics, as a struggle between powers equally determined to subdue the world. Political ambition was never the prime motive, even of the most theocratic popes. The true origin of that strife, which continued at intervals for a period of almost three centuries, was the deep-rooted longing of the Church to stand fast by her vocation. She resolved to put an end to secular interference, which was an obstacle in her path; and once having joined issue with her opponents, she was led to ask herself whether the divine law might not be more perfectly observed on earth through the predominance of spiritual over temporal authority. The question was not one of politics, national or international. The contest may appear to us marred by violence and by sordid intrigue; but what was at stake? The unity of Christendom, the primacy of the spirit, and freedom of the human conscience.

2. THE PROBLEM OF INVESTITURES

In the early Middle Ages relations between Church and State were founded on a spirit of co-operation. Three dates are of capital importance. In 380 Theodosius decreed that all his subjects should embrace 'the faith delivered to the Romans by the Apostle Peter'; in 490 the hierarchy of Gaul baptized Clovis, the young Frankish king, and thereby determined the fate of the barbarian world; while at Christmas in the year 800, Pope St Leo III conferred the ancient crown of empire upon Charlemagne, a descendant of the invaders. Throughout six hundred years and more, by means of unending courage and endurance, the Church had kept a restraining hand upon those turbulent princes who dominated Europe, with the result that society had returned step by step to the light of civilization.

There was another side to this tremendous achievement. Though herself a spiritual power, the Church had worked well upon the temporal plane; but in doing so she had failed to put first things first. Her leaders had grown deaf to the Gospel precept; by mixing with the world they had lapsed into worldliness. The history of the barbarian epoch is that of continual co-operation between the spiritual and the temporal, a co-operation which Charlemagne treated as a principle of government.

Nor could the Church escape the rise of seignory and feudalism. By virtue of donations from the faithful, every bishop and every abbot became head of an enormous territorial domain. He was *ex officio* a rural landlord like other landlords, having his 'reserve' and tenants, exacting labour, and dispensing justice. Moreover, an unavoidable system of 'recommendations' involved him in that network of dependence and allegiance which was the feudal system. His lands were fiefs, held from an overlord to whom he owed the customary duties of a vassal—even that of military service, which he fulfilled through a lay deputy (the *vidame*) since divine law would not allow him to bear arms. The Carolingians had granted territorial rights to certain prelates, provided the latter agreed to exercise them as vassals; and it was not uncommon for laymen to obtain control of ecclesiastical domains. The result was that the Spouse of Christ lived on terms of intimacy with the established feudal order.

The union was not a happy one. The prelate bore a strange resemblance to his temporal neighbour. Like him, he had vast buildings, domestic officers, administrators for his estates, tax-gatherers for his revenue. One can hardly be surprised that his life was often 'lordly,' surrounded with pomp and far from the spirit of the Gospel. The moral problem was inextricably bound up with social and political factors.

The Church tried hard to free herself, not by withdrawing from the feudal system, but simply by attempting to gain a privileged position within it. Some clerical landowners were dispensed from homage, and thus avoided open recognition of an overlord. An abbey might enjoy 'exemption,' which meant that it was dependent immediately upon the Holy See and therefore free from seignorial or even royal interference. But this privilege did not remove the essentially feudal character of ecclesiastical principalities, which continued to form part and parcel of the system, and from which churchmen still collected 'regalities.' There was another so-called remedy known as 'advocacy'; but it often proved more burdensome than the evil it was supposed to remove. 'Advocates,' whose duty it was to protect a clerical domain against attack by neighbours, gradually became permanent and hereditary, and they frequently behaved as if they owned the property entrusted to their care. Temporal rulers, however, united with the clergy to abolish this institution.

Generally speaking, then, the medieval Church was engulfed by feudalism; consciously, or more often unconsciously, she had committed the mistake of linking her fortunes too closely with prevailing sociological factors. This was the sole cause of the many crises which she survived and of the disaster which finally overwhelmed her. Nevertheless, there was a point at which collaboration became so dangerous that it could no longer be ignored, for it affected the deepest loyalties of the Church, imperilling her very soul; and it was on this point that there broke out the first great political conflict of the Middle Ages, the Quarrel of Investitures. The problem may be formulated thus: was the Church to compromise so far as to entrust laymen with the appointment of bishops? Surely the Church alone, as depositary of the faith, should choose those who were to speak in God's name. To understand the gravity of this question, we must go back and consider how the early Church nominated those who were to govern her.

In Africa, for example, in St Cyprian's day, the process of appointment was twofold. The bishop was *elected* by the people, but he could not enter upon his duties until he had been *consecrated* by another bishop. Divine investiture, by virtue of uninterrupted tradition dating back to the Apostles, made him the direct heir to powers conferred by Christ. Under the Christian Empire, and before the barbarian invasions, the civil power had taken no part in the appointment of bishops. Clovis was the first to do so. That cunning chieftain, newly elevated to the royal dignity, foresaw the advantages of alliance with the hierarchy, and made sure that every diocese within his dominions was governed by a man whom he could trust. He exerted no pressure upon the clergy or the faithful; but he took care that no

one should be ignorant of which candidate he preferred.   His successors went still further.   Notwithstanding the opposition of several
councils, the Merovingians did not hesitate to control the elections in
their own high-handed way, until it was agreed that no bishop should
be chosen without the sovereign's consent.   Charlemagne, that
'pious guardian of the episcopate,' regularly nominated them; and the
fact that his choice was invariably good made the principle no less
dangerous.   From the ninth century bishops were to all intents and
purposes chosen by the king, the clergy and people dutifully acclaiming
the prelate thus appointed; so much so that we find instances of a
temporal sovereign granting the clergy *permission* to elect!

This undesirable custom was so firmly established by the tenth
century, when the feudal system began to take shape, that it became
almost an integral part of the new regime.   Bishops continued to be
appointed by the emperor, the king, or some other temporal overlord;
but there was worse to come.   Of the two constitutional elements in
the process of appointment, i.e. the choice of the new titular and his
consecration, it was not merely the former which was usurped by
laymen.   In theory, the overlord delivered to the chosen candidate
only the territorial possessions annexed to his title; in practice,
however, it was not easy to distinguish the remission of temporalities
from the spiritual election.   There was a ceremony known as 'investiture,' during which the overlord handed the new bishop his crozier and
ring with the words 'Receive the Church'; and one chronicler records
Otto the Great as having delivered to a certain bishop the 'pastoral
charge,' i.e. the right to guide souls, which only sacerdotal authority
can confer.   The result was intolerable confusion.   In the middle of
the eleventh century even those temporal overlords who were good
Christians considered bishoprics and monàsteries as fiefs analogous to
other fiefs, the holders of which were exclusively bound to religious
duties, but over which they claimed indisputable rights.   They never
suspected that spiritual interests were thereby placed in jeopardy.

Similar interference had been going on at the parochial level.   The
method was somewhat different, but its consequences were much the
same.   The parish church had in many cases been built and endowed
by the local landowner, whose descendants considered themselves its
absolute master.   They expected, in particular, to enjoy part of its
revenues, which consisted of tithes, and taxes paid on the occasion of
baptisms, weddings, and funerals.   The church, in fact, belonged to
the lord as did the common bakehouse, mill, and winepress; and he
took care to put it in charge of a cleric chosen by himself, one who
would take an oath of fealty to him and whom he would invest.

Nor did the papacy itself escape lay interference.   Since the day
when Charlemagne's firm hand ceased to preserve order in the Eternal

City, the see of St Peter had too often been the stake of warring factions; and the majority of popes from the pontificate of Sergius III (904–11) until about 960 had been creatures of ambitious aristocrats or even of licentious females.   The restoration of the Empire by Otto the Great in 962 had put an end to the tyranny of the Roman nobles, but it had not freed the papacy.   Officially indeed, by virtue of Otto's 'declaration,' the Sovereign Pontiff could not be consecrated before he had sworn fealty to the emperor; and since that date the German emperors, whether they were simply well-disposed like Otto III, or saints like Henry II, had held the Holy See in a dependence that was tantamount to subjection.

It is most remarkable that a great number, and even a majority, of these popes, bishops, and parish priests chosen by emperors, kings, and local landlords, remained true to their vocation and lived good priestly lives.   But there was always danger that unworthy men might be appointed to positions of authority.   Simony and Nicolaïsm, two evils which afflicted the medieval Church, had been due to secular influences; while the disposal of the Apostolic See by a group of Roman nobles had resulted in the appointment of John XII, who, says the *Liber Pontificalis*, spent his life 'in adultery and vanity.'   The emperors, in general, had acted for the best; but it had only required a ruler such as Conrad II (1027–39) to succeed St Henry for the appointment of bishops to become an object of disgraceful barter.   How were feudal chiefs to be prevented from selling investitures; and how persuade their nominees to live worthy of their calling?   As for parish priests, how were their moral qualities, or even the minimum of priestly learning, to be guaranteed, if the overlord who appointed them could secure their ordination by subservient bishops?   It was precisely this moral and spiritual danger that roused the conscience of the Church.

The desire for reform, which had first appeared during the tenth century,[1] was at the root of a political crisis which brought the Church into collision with the civil powers; but many years elapsed before men perceived a connection between moral and spiritual problems on the one hand and political issues on the other.   St Peter Damian, for example, believed that royal support was indispensable to bring about the reform which he desired.   Nor did those who, like St Romuald and St John Gualbert, preached the lesson of example imagine that a return to the practice of evangelical virtue must have repercussions in the political sphere.   Others, however, saw more clearly.   Long ago, in the tenth century, Rathier of Liége (afterwards Bishop of Verona) had proclaimed that the episcopate must be free from all secular influence and dependent upon none but the Holy See.   A hundred years later, Wason, Bishop of Liége, defended the rights of the

[1] See also Chapter IV.

episcopate against temporal princes, and went so far as to rebuke the Emperor Henry III for having deposed Gregory VI; while Cardinal Humbert of Moyen-Moutier, in his book *Against Simony* (1057), wrote these words: 'What right have laymen to dispose of ecclesiastical benefices and invest with the crozier and ring, a ceremony which is the climax of episcopal consecration?' The Quarrel of Investitures was implicit in the cardinal's forthright question, and events were soon to prove him right.

3. PAPAL ELECTIONS ENTRUSTED TO THE CARDINALS

The first of a series of acts that were destined to liberate the Church was accomplished during the short pontificate of an energetic Burgundian, Nicholas II (1059–61). It deprived the Emperor of his right to nominate the Pope. Circumstances were favourable; for on the death of Henry III, in 1056, his son Henry IV was no more than a child, whose guardian was the Empress Agnes. When Leo IX died, in 1054, the clergy of the Eternal City stole a march on the German court and the Roman aristocracy by electing a pope of their own choice, Frederick, abbot of Monte Cassino, brother of the Duke of Lorraine, friend of Cardinal Humbert, and a zealous advocate of ecclesiastical independence. This pontiff, Stephen IX, reigned for only a few months; but a precedent had been created—a Pope had been elected without reference to the Emperor, who had simply been invited to approve the choice.

On Stephen's death the factions combined to nominate one John, Bishop of Velletri, who took the name of Benedict X. The great Burgundian monk Hildebrand, afterwards Gregory VII, was then in Germany. He made contact with Agnes, who was indignant that the tyrannous Romans should have dared to appoint a pope; and, assisted by the Marquis Godfrey of Lorraine, he secured the election of his compatriot Gerard, Bishop of Florence, as Pope Nicholas II. A few weeks later, in order to prevent a repetition of these intrigues, the new pontiff promulgated his famous decretal of 13th April 1059.

'We have decided,' so ran this momentous document, 'that on the death of the Sovereign Pontiff of the Roman and universal Church, the cardinal-bishops shall take the utmost care for the appointment of his successor; after which they shall invite the cardinal-priests together with the remainder of the clergy and the people to confirm the new election. . . . They shall confine their choice to the Roman Church provided they can find a suitable man; otherwise they shall choose someone from elsewhere, saving the honour and reverence due to Henry at present king and, God willing, future emperor.'

It should be noticed that there are two parts to this decree. The first is definitive and categorical; it withdraws the choice of the pope from laymen and confides it to a group of dignitaries known as 'cardinals,' who, since the tenth century, had occupied an increasingly important situation in the Church. The second part consists of a respectful tribute to the Emperor.

No one could mistake the meaning or the import of this decision. The Roman nobility made a display of force, while the German court refused to entertain the legate sent to notify it of the decree. But Nicholas II was not to be caught napping. Reversing the whole policy of his predecessors, he made an alliance with the Normans who, though little more than bandits, had established themselves in the south of the Peninsula.[1] Seven years earlier, under the command of Robert Guiscard and Richard of Capua, they had defeated Leo IX and taken him prisoner. Later, fearing German ascendancy, they had agreed to negotiate, and had proclaimed themselves vassals of the Pope at the Council of Melfi in 1059. The oath taken by Guiscard to Nicholas II contained a clause expressly binding him, in the event of the Pope's death, to assist the cardinals in the election of his successor. Nicholas capped this manœuvre with a French alliance, and the Roman nobility, on sight of the Norman troops, abandoned their antipope. The German court maintained an attitude of reserve, confining itself to the publication of a false decretal in which the rights of the Emperor were affirmed.

Encouraged by the effects of his diplomacy, Nicholas II confirmed it in August of the following year (1060); but this time there was no mention of 'reverence due to Henry,' nor even of popular consent. Henceforward the papal election belonged to the cardinals alone; and well-informed people studied the sixth canon of a council held in 1059. It ran as follows: 'No priest or cleric shall in any wise receive a church from the hands of a layman, whether for payment or gratuitously.'

Nicholas II died after a brief reign of thirty months; but his pontificate left its mark on history. Would his work survive? At one moment there was cause to doubt; for his successor, Alexander II (1061–73), who was elected in accordance with the decree of 1059, met with violent resistance both from the Roman aristocracy and from the German court. Once more an antipope arose in the person of Cadalus, Bishop of Parma, and the future seemed wrapped in uncertainty. The new Pope, however, was no weakling. He knew how to make numerous 'concessions' while remaining firm in all essentials. At his side Archdeacon Hildebrand stood fast by the principles of reform, and he it was who was predestined to renew the struggle.

---

[1] The settlement of the Normans in southern Italy will be dealt with in Chapter X, which is devoted to Byzantium, since it was amid the ruins of the Byzantine Empire that they established their domain.

4. THE QUARREL OF INVESTITURES

At the end of February 1075 the atmosphere in Rome was tense. A council, which had been in session for a week, had taken stern measures against many persons of high rank: five members of the German king's council had been excommunicated; and an archbishop, together with a dozen Italian and German bishops, had been suspended 'by reason of their stiff-necked disobedience.' Decisive events were in progress under the leadership of a swarthy little man with a will of iron, who for ten years now had occupied the Apostolic See. Momentous results were anticipated, and they were not long delayed.

In the preceding year another synod had promulgated the famous decrees for the moral reform of the Church, ordering the deposition of simoniacal priests, and forbidding clerics guilty of fornication to approach the altar. But these steps, as we have seen, had met with fierce resistance. In Germany especially, and in France, the papal legates had been everywhere rebuffed. This set-back at first caused the Pope 'immense grief, boundless sorrow'; but a man of his mettle could not yield to such emotions. Harsh experience had taught him a lesson: it was not enough to inflict penalties, to excommunicate or suspend recalcitrants; since his reforming policy had proved inadequate, he must go farther and attack the root of evil. Gregory VII therefore changed his method and promulgated a fresh decree: 'No ecclesiastic shall in any wise receive a church from the hands of a layman either gratuitously or by onerous title, under pain of excommunication both for the giver and the receiver.' This clause repeated almost word for word, but with the addition of dire threats, the sixth canon of 1059, whose application had been prevented by the untimely death of Nicholas II. Its terms, though perfectly clear, involved some confusion. Its purpose was undoubted; but in forbidding every cleric 'in any wise' to receive a church from the hands of a layman, the decree surely absorbed the temporal in the spiritual, and confused clerical functions with the temporalities attached to them. It is possible that Gregory was conscious of the mistake and foresaw the injustice to which it might give rise; but fifty years were to elapse before the distinction was properly understood. The situation, however, was extremely grave, and only drastic measures could provide a remedy. The decree of 1075, which condemned all lay investiture, was something quite new, and was to involve the Church in the most serious political conflict she had ever known.

For the issue was ultimately political. Temporal landlords would inevitably feel they had been robbed. To renounce the investiture of bishops, abbots, and parish priests was to give up rights which were considered at that time to be perfectly legitimate. For some it would have spelled ruin; for others, e.g. the German emperor, it meant the dismemberment of their States. Did Gregory VII take account of this? The decisions of 1075 admitted of no exception in principle, and he repeated them in 1078 and 1080, with even greater precision; but at first he was not invariably strict in their application. In countries such as England, which was ruled by his friend William the Conqueror, or in Spain, where simony was practically unknown, the decree was never promulgated; and even in France, where Philip I was not above criticism in this respect, he showed himself lenient. Outwardly his policy was dictated by the determination for reform; but so long as the sovereigns were not opposed in principle to this goal, they found the Pope ready to mitigate the full rigour of the sacred canons.

In Germany the situation was altogether different owing to the nature of its institutions and the character of its rulers. The great feudal clerics constituted a fundamental part of the imperial regime; for the bishops, who were responsible for much of the administration, were the mainstay of the central authority against the baronage. For the Emperor to renounce their investiture would have been to forgo the right to nominate his chief officials, to jeopardize the fulfilment of military duties by his vassals, and to imperil the financial resources of his government.

The young Franconian prince, Henry IV, who had worn the crown since 1056, was least of all prepared to make these sacrifices. Intelligent and tenacious, realistic and astute, he had derived from the spectacle of those disorders among which his youth had passed a consciousness of his imperial rights and pride in his royal dignity. He had been engaged since the first days of his reign in a hard struggle with the German nobility; he had come near to defeat by the Duke of Saxony in 1073, and had been obliged to flee at dead of night from his castle in the Hartz. But he had restored the situation; and while Gregory VII was presiding over the famous council at Rome, Henry IV was mopping up the rebel troops whom he had routed on the banks of the Unstrutt. Such a man was unlikely to cede his rights. His ancestors had appointed popes; what was all this talk about a campaign against simony and fornicating priests? He had more important things in hand. Thus the promulgation of this decree, which was otherwise quite uneventful, was to bring about something like a state of war between Pope and Emperor, Priesthood and Empire.

Since the conflict was in fact political, it is natural to inquire what forces the antagonists controlled. Those of the Empire were exclusively material, and absolutely unreliable. The memory of Charlemagne persisted, though somewhat vaguely. The Emperor might look to Germany for troops, to Italy as a source of revenue; but along the highways leading from the Rhine to Rome there were powerful men who sought an opportunity, as the saying went, 'to pluck the imperial eagle.' His enormous territory, centred upon the Alps, included Germans, Italians, and French; it was not easy to govern, and suffered constant variations of frontier. Two institutions in particular placed its holder in an unenviable situation; to become Emperor, the King of Germany required to be anointed, which only the Pope could do; while the three crowns of Germany, Italy, and the Empire were elective and made the Emperor dependent upon those who raised him to that dignity.

In appearance, the papacy was weaker still. Its territory was minute, smaller than the Duchy of Saxony or that of Normandy, consisting of the Patrimony of St Peter on the Tiber, the Romagna, and the March of Ancona. True, it was protected on the north by fiefs belonging to Matilda, widow of Godfrey of Lorraine, who was devoted to the papal cause; and on the south, since the pontificate of Nicholas II, by the Normans, who had established themselves in Apulia about the year 1030 and had recently taken Sicily from the Moslems. But Robert Guiscard and his fellow brigands were uncertain allies, and, on the whole, a source of danger to the papal states. Tuscany and the March of Ancona, on twin routes to Sicily, lay open to the imperial armies; civil war was rife throughout the papal territory; while Rome itself was prey to the ambitions of the Senate, of the Commune, and of an aristocracy that would not be overshadowed. But to this unpromising material there were added the far more effective weapons of excommunication and interdict, and these were to prove decisive. The Pope's right to crown the Emperor showed on which side real power lay: there could be no emperor without the pope, whereas since 1059 there was no need of an emperor to make a pope. Besides, the idea of Christendom at that time was an infinitely stronger motive force than the nostalgic concept of imperial glory. The spiritual arm would prove more effective in the approaching conflict.

The decree of 1075 caused a great stir in the dominions of Henry IV. Hitherto relations between prince and pontiff had been cordial; annoyed, however, by the new measures, and urged no doubt by his entourage, which included a number of churchmen who had been excommunicated for simony, Henry flouted the papal decisions. He appointed one of his creatures to the vacant see of Milan, and subsequently repeated this gesture at Fermo, Spoleto, Spire, Bamberg, Liége, and Cologne. An angry letter from Gregory VII ordered him to desist. It reached Henry IV at Goslar on 1st January 1076; and before the month was out the indignant monarch replied in his own fashion.

On the 24th a synod of priests and prelates hostile to the Pope met at Worms. 'The false monk Hildebrand' was loaded with insults, accused of having disturbed the peace of the Church, of usurping powers to which he had no right, of attempting to steal the crown of Italy, and even of immorality. He was declared deposed, and envoys were sent to Rome to invite the clergy and people to choose his successor. In the north of Italy a group of prelates, many of whom were simoniacs, assembled at Piacenza and confirmed their decision.

But Gregory VII was not the man to be upset by such insolent defiance. At a synod held in Rome on 14th February, he stood up and spoke as follows: 'King Henry has presumed with insensate vanity to defy the Church; wherefore I bar him from governing the kingdom of Germany and of Italy. I absolve all Christians from the oath which they have taken to him, and forbid anyone to recognize him as king.'

This was an unheard of sentence: the Pope was deposing a sovereign prince! Its effect was astonishing. The partisans of reform took heart, and those who had hurried to obey the royal command at Worms began to think it imprudent to quarrel with so energetic a Pope. The earth seemed to open at Henry's feet, and his enemies once more raised their heads. An assembly of nobles and bishops met at Tribur, recognized the Pope as having justice on his side, and agreed that Henry IV should no longer reign. The German nobility was restive; some bishops set out for Rome; and at the beginning of 1077 there was question of holding an assembly to confirm the monarch's deposition and appoint his successor. Henry IV had learned his lesson.

There followed a prodigious scene which was to make a deep impression on the age, and whose memory still survives in a proverbial phrase after the passage of nine centuries. On 25th January 1077 Henry IV went to Canossa. He crossed the Alps and travelled through northern Italy with a small escort, turning a deaf ear to those few flatterers who would have encouraged him to remain firm, and letting it be known to all that he was now but a prodigal son returning to his Father's house. The Italian winter in that year was cold, and snow covered the Apennines where the Pope had taken refuge. The castle of Canossa, an eyrie in territory belonging to the Countess Matilda, might have withstood a siege. But he who now appeared before its walls was a penitent, stripped of the emblems of royalty, clothed in sackcloth, and barefoot.

The Pope himself tells us of what followed: the three days' wait outside the fortress, the supplication of the defeated king, the intervention of the Countess Matilda and various cardinals, and then the final scene when the heir of the Ottos, 'of a stature and beauty worthy of an emperor,' prostrated himself before the stocky little man in whom shone forth the power of the Apostle. Christendom stood amazed;

but the vanquished monarch swore a vague oath in which the words
'Henry, King' seemed to annul the political consequences of a year ago.
The excommunication was lifted; and the crown, though shaken,
seemed once again to sit securely on the Salian's head.

Many historians regard Henry as the true victor of Canossa; they

maintain that the Pope, for all his strength, was worsted by the royal
cunning, and that the pardon marked a political defeat. True, the
absolution, couched as it was in equivocal terms, compromised
Gregory's manœuvre. But Gregory was a saint, and in his eyes the
gesture had been no mere act of policy; it was an expression of God's
infinite mercy, to which no sinner can appeal in vain. The pontiff
was never more sublime than at that moment.

On the political plane, however, the results were disastrous. The

German princes, shocked by a reconciliation which upset their plans, declined to recognize the penitent monarch, though he had been absolved. On 13th March they assembled at Forcheim, and there, in spite of the papal legates, proclaimed the deposition of Henry IV, who was to be succeeded by his brother-in-law, Rudolph of Rheinfelden, Duke of Swabia and Governor of Burgundy. Civil war broke out; and its fury was aggravated by Henry's renewed defiance of a Pope whom he now considered the ally of his enemies. Deposed once again in March 1080, the king replied with a decree of the Council of Brixen, deposing Gregory, 'false monk, ravisher of churches, necromancer,' and proclaiming in his stead Wibert, Archbishop of Ravenna, who took the name of Clement III.

For a moment it seemed that the issue must be determined by force of arms. Henry IV was defeated at Grona, between the Elster and the Saale; but Rudolph was left dead upon the field. Sweeping into Italy, the king seized the Iron Crown at Milan, and marched on Rome in company with his antipope. Gregory's situation was critical. Robert Guiscard had been excommunicated for his shameless looting, and would not stir; while in Tuscany the towns subject to Matilda sided with the German, who restored to them their privileges. Gregory VII hastened to negotiate with Guiscard, and agreed to invest him with such lands as he had overrun; but all in vain. The Norman was at war with the Byzantines, and would not intervene. Two years sufficed for Henry to establish his authority over the whole of northern Italy. After a prolonged struggle he entered Rome, and enthroned his Pope, who, in turn, crowned him Emperor on 31st March 1084.

The confusion may be imagined. The Emperor and the antipope occupied St Peter's and the Lateran. Between those two points, Gregory VII held out in the Castle of Sant' Angelo, while two groups of his partisans defended the Capitol and the Palatine. There was some bargaining, in which farce was enacted side by side with tragedy. The Pope refused to leave his stronghold, but was prepared to lower the crown by rope on to Henry's brow! In the narrow streets of the city, however, both parties resorted to gang warfare. The Capitol was taken, and Gregory awaited a final assault upon his fortress, when Robert Guiscard, realizing at last that he had everything to lose by Henry's success, advanced in force. The king decamped; but the remedy proved far worse than the evil. Hordes of bandits (Moslems for the most part), of whom Guiscard's army was composed, gave themselves up to pillage, murder, sacrilege, and rape. The population retaliated under the leadership of Henry's supporters; but Robert Guiscard drowned the insurrection in blood, and thousands of innocent folk were massacred. Others, including women and children and a number of senatorial families, were sold into slavery. It is even said that a marabout recited Islamic prayers in the half-ruined basilica of St Peter.

The Pope was overwhelmed with grief. He knew his principles to be sound; but his tender conscience was afflicted by the disasters brought about through their application in the political field. He could stay in Rome no longer, and allowed himself to be carried off to Salerno in Norman territory. When he died there soon afterwards, on 25th May 1085, it seemed that his efforts had entirely failed. But the bright light of his saintly soul preserved him from despair. His last encyclical had recalled his fundamental principles, and proclaimed in the nave of St Peter's his indestructible belief that though the tempests of this world may shake the Church she can never be submerged.

It had now to be decided whether the struggle should be continued, or whether some basis for agreement should be sought. After the short pontificate of Victor III (1086–7), which witnessed a clash between the moderates and intransigents, an energetic Frenchman, Eudes de Châtillon, was elected to the papal throne and took the name of Urban II (1088–99). He declared himself a disciple of Pope Gregory, and thereby revealed his purpose; but the situation remained confused for years. Sometimes travelling the length and breadth of Italy to encourage his supporters, sometimes living at Rome in danger from the antipope's intrigue, Urban was the embodiment of loyalty to principle. Little by little fortune returned to the Church's camp, thanks to the subtle diplomacy of the Pope. Roger of Sicily, brother of Guiscard, who had just completed the conquest of that island, proclaimed himself, and was recognized as, papal legate within his dominions; so that Rome was no longer threatened from that quarter.

With Milan as their centre, the Italian towns in the north formed a league against Henry IV, in alliance with the Countess Matilda, who had recently been married to the Duke of Bavaria. Lorraine and Saxony rallied to Urban II, while the king's eldest son Conrad revolted against his father and submitted to the Pope. At the celebrated Council of Clermont, in 1095, it seemed that Urban II had restored to the papacy its ancient prestige. But the problem of investiture was far from settled. It had lately been revived in England, where William Rufus carried on open traffic in ecclesiastical benefices, and also in France, where Philip I, at loggerheads with the Church on account of his adulterous marriage, had resorted to the old practices of simony.

Paschal II (1099–1118), as we have seen,[1] was a holy monk, full of good intentions, but no statesman. From the moment of his accession he was confronted with a maze of difficulty. In England the way became easier on the death of Rufus. His successor, Henry I (1100–1135), guided by St Anselm, adopted a policy of reconciliation with the

[1] See Chapter IV, section 5.

G

Church, and the concordat of 1107 established an acceptable *modus vivendi*. France did likewise under the influence of Philip's son Louis (later Louis VI). In Germany, however, the situation deteriorated, although at first there were high hopes. Henry IV's second son, appointed heir in place of Conrad, rebelled in 1104; and Paschal II saw this as a means to break his adversary. The old Emperor died of disappointment and grief on 7th April 1106, but Henry V proved still more dangerous. Crafty and avaricious, so successfully had he posed as a devoted son of the Church that he had secured a promise of the imperial crown. Now, securely seated on the throne, he claimed the same rights as his father. In 1110, having quelled an Italian revolt, he entered Rome, full of honeyed words but with hatred of the Pope in his heart. Paschal was already dreaming of his mighty project, the Church's total separation from the feudal regime provided the sovereigns would renounce all claims to investiture. Their mutual antagonism flared up on the very day when the Pope was to crown Henry V as Emperor (12th February 1111). The *casus belli* was an insurrection on the part of those who feared the damage they might suffer in consequence of Paschal's offer. Arrested and held captive for two months, the unfortunate Pope's nerve gave way; he capitulated, recognizing Henry's right to invest with ring and crozier. Nevertheless, as soon as he regained his liberty, Paschal revoked his concession and excommunicated the Emperor. From that time until his death he showed no more weakness; he refused to temporize, and would not lift the censure.

This troubled pontificate, in which so much goodwill did nothing but increase disorder, came no nearer to finding a solution. The world, however, was growing impatient; while diplomats argued and armies fought, philosophers took a hand. Chief among these was a Frenchman, Bishop Yves of Chartres, who died in 1116 without beholding the triumph of his theory. The solution he put forward was a simple one: it consisted in distinguishing the spiritual element of an ecclesiastical benefice from its concomitant temporal advantages. A bishop or an abbot was both a man of God, a depositary of powers handed down from the Apostles, and at the same time a tenant of lands, etc., granted by laymen. In any investiture, therefore, it was necessary to separate consecration, with delivery of the crozier and ring, from the remission of temporalities. *Spiritual* investiture could be performed by none but the religious authority; *temporal* investiture belonged of right to the overlord. This solution, so clear and so logical, obtained gradual recognition. It was favoured by Calixtus II (1119–24), who, soon after his election, wrote to Henry V: 'Let the Church hold what belongs to Christ, and let the Emperor have all that belongs to him.'

Agreement was reached on this basis by the Concordat of Worms, 23rd September 1122. The Emperor renounced all claim to invest with ring and crozier, which was reserved to the Pope or to the consecrating bishop, and also promised freedom of canonical elections. The Pope, in turn, recognized Henry's right to take part in the election of bishops and abbots, but without recourse to violence or to simony: 'The prelate-elect shall receive his temporalities from the prince, and shall faithfully perform his duties as a vassal.' In the following year these wise decisions were confirmed by a council held at Rome.

The Quarrel of Investitures was ended, and the Church free from lay tutelage. Not least of the benefits resulting from this settlement was the regular appointment of bishops who upheld the principles of reform. This did not mean that every problem had been resolved. The Church being still an integral part of the feudal system, there were repeated lapses in the moral sphere, while the political situation was doomed to end in a renewal of the conflict.

5. THE PRIMACY

The battle revolved about this question: Where lies the primacy? Gregory VII had a very high notion of the papal authority, the highest that any pope had yet conceived. 'The Pope,' he wrote in all sincerity, 'is the only man whose foot all peoples should kiss; provided he is canonically elected, he is rendered sacred by the merits of St Peter.' Anticipating by eight centuries the dogma of infallibility, he went so far as to affirm: 'The Church can never err: Scripture bears witness she will never err.' Whence he concluded that 'he who wishes to obey the commandments of God must not despise *our* commands, where they interpret the decisions of the holy Fathers; he must receive them as if they came from the Apostle himself.'

From such convictions it was natural to conclude that 'kingly power was invented by human pride; the power of bishops is established by divine compassion.' From this essential superiority of religious jurisdiction there followed consequences which Gregory VII did not hesitate to declare. At the beginning of his pontificate, early in 1075, he drew up a series of twenty-seven concise propositions, known as the *Dictatus Papae*, summarizing his intentions with a view to reform, and formulating the papal doctrine of Roman primacy. Since the Pope, as representative of Christ on earth, is the heir of powers given to the Apostles, no other power on earth can rival his. All are subordinate to him. The twelfth proposition expressly stated: 'It is lawful for the Pope to depose emperors'; and by punishing Henry IV, Gregory was merely giving effect to this axiom. Papal theocracy, i.e. the government of men by God through a supreme hierarch, the Pope, was implicit in this formidable sheaf of propositions.

Contrary to general belief, these ideas did not originate with Gregory VII; they had been current in the Church for centuries. The theory, known as 'Political Augustinianism' since it can be traced to St Augustine, had been slowly and painfully evolved and given shape over a very long period. In the seventh century, St Isidore of Seville had affirmed the subordination of the secular power to religious authority; and even at the height of Charlemagne's ascendancy, in 800, when Leo III was utterly dependent on the Frankish king, Alcuin, though devoted to his sovereign, had assured the Emperor that 'the Holy See is subject to no one's judgment!' During the Carolingian decadence the Church had obtained control over the Emperor, affirming that the duty of princes is to 'provide for the service of God.' She had, in fact, established the imperial power in subjection to herself. Smaragdus, Hincmar, Agobard, and Jonas of Orleans had all upheld this theory, whose development had been made possible by the weakness of the emperors; and the *False Decretals* had formulated it so clearly that Gregory VII's *Dictatus* owed much to them. The great Pope, therefore, could claim to found his argument on venerable tradition.

But the Emperor too had considerable authority on his side. When Henry IV notified Gregory VII of his deposition in 1076, he wrote: 'You have struck at me although I am, despite my unworthiness, among those who have received royal unction, and although, according to the tradition of the holy Fathers, I can be judged by none but God and cannot be deposed for any crime unless—which God forbid!—I have erred in matters of faith.' This last reservation shows how lively a layman's faith could be, even when he opposed the Church; but the Emperor's words allowed of no misunderstanding. As the Lord's anointed he was subject to the judgment of God alone; the Pope had no power to depose him. Theocracy was face to face with imperial absolutism, and the Church's claim was answered in these words uttered by one of Barbarossa's henchmen: 'What pleases the prince has the force of law.'

Hence, during the Quarrel of Investitures, far-sighted ecclesiastics realized that it was necessary to insist upon the superiority of spiritual jurisdiction. Admittedly, the spiritual and the temporal power were essentially different and operated in different spheres; but this surely could not mean that the Church had no right to intervene in matters of state. The reasoning was perfectly logical: a government's first duty is to labour for the world's salvation, and in that respect it is clearly subject to the Church. Now it cannot be denied that in human affairs spiritual principles are sometimes violated, that politicians commit sin;

and therefore, *ratione peccati*, the Church may justly claim to exercise control. True enough; but in politics it is hard to distinguish what constitutes moral guilt from what pertains to the defence of legitimate interests.

This doctrine found expression in a famous theory known as the 'Two Swords,' which attained its full significance under the auspices of St Bernard. The two swords mentioned in St Luke's Gospel (xxii. 38) represent, so he maintained, the spiritual and the temporal power. 'Both belong to Peter: one of them he actually wields, the other is at his disposal as and when circumstances require. Referring to the latter, our Lord told His Apostle: "Put up thy sword in its scabbard." It was Peter's sure enough, but not to draw with his own hand.' These scriptural arguments seem to us mere hair-splitting; but in the Middle Ages they carried a good deal of weight. St Bernard was expounding the one and only theory which his contemporaries believed valid. On the spiritual plane, the Church, in the person of her head, the Sovereign Pontiff, enjoyed a plenitude of power, and therefore the right to judge all Christians (sovereign princes included) whenever they sinned. But side by side with this *direct* right went an *indirect* right to compel the obedience of lay rulers, in order that earthly institutions might conform with divine principles.

Such was the attitude of every pope during the twelfth and thirteenth centuries. As years passed, their situation became increasingly uncertain, and they felt obliged to lay more and more stress upon this doctrine. If Gregory VII claimed right of control over the civil power, Innocent III (1198–1216) went so far as practically to usurp the imperial dignity. Because he 'represented Him to whom belongs the earth and all that is or dwells therein'; because he was 'the ambassador of Him by whom kings reign and princes govern, of Him who dispenses kingdoms to whom He will'; the Pope claimed 'power to overthrow and destroy, to disperse and scatter, to build and plant.' He was 'above all princes, since it belongs to him to judge them.' The spiritual primacy claimed by Gregory VII tended later to become *total* primacy—in the Empire as in the Church, where the Vicar of Christ would share his power with none.

Moreover, the theory of two powers, each with its exclusive sphere of jurisdiction, was nullified by the Church's view of her superior dignity and importance: 'The royal power borrows its splendour from the papal authority in the same way that the moon reflects the brightness of the sun.' Here we have a disastrous misunderstanding. To push the theory to its logical conclusion would necessitate a vast governmental machine at once spiritual and temporal, with the Pope its head and secular princes as no more than his viceroys. This 'theocratic Utopia,' resulting from a distorted view of political

Augustinianism, would inevitably tend to absorb the whole of secular society in the Church, so that the City of God would become identified with the City of men. No temporal sovereign could accept a proposition of that kind.

Around this doctrinal issue there were enacted a succession of dire events which brought the Church into renewed conflict with the civil authority. Right up to the terrible crisis at the beginning of the fourteenth century the popes held fast by their claims. Innocent IV (1243–54) expressed them more categorically even than had Innocent III; and Boniface VIII in his famous Bull *Unam Sanctam* (1302) reaffirmed the Church's right to wield both swords.

The havoc caused by these contending ambitions may incline us to judge severely of the doctrine involved, to condemn the notion of a 'theocratic Utopia' which is so repugnant to our psychology, and which the Church has now abandoned.[1] We must not forget, however, that the popes were activated by lofty intentions; they were not led on by vanity, but by a profound and lively faith in their supernatural mission, and by legitimate pride in bearing witness to the Holy Spirit.

The theory was acceptable to the medieval mind; it seemed to follow naturally upon a universal faith, and to crown the grand ideal of Christendom. 'It corresponded to men's aspirations at the same time as it safeguarded Christian justice and created law in that society of Christian nations which formed medieval Christendom.'[2] That it did not succeed was not due to lack of goodwill or of right intention; there was a much deeper cause. 'We have been appointed prince over all the world,' wrote Innocent III; but a more authoritative voice than his had long since murmured: 'My kingdom is not of this world'— and thereby given him an answer.

6. FREDERICK BARBAROSSA

Less than thirty years after the Concordat of Worms the question of primacy emerged from the realm of theoretical discussion into the harsh light of day. 'Since by Divine Providence,' wrote Frederick Barbarossa, 'I call myself and *am* Emperor of the Romans, I have but the shadow of power unless I govern Rome.' Was he going to revive the pretensions of Charlemagne and the Ottos? The popes could not agree to that.

Frederick had succeeded to the German throne in 1152, at the age of

[1] The present attitude of the Church is quite different. Leo XIII, in his encyclical *Immortale Dei* of 1st November 1885, expressly declared that the temporal and the spiritual power are sovereign, each in its own sphere which is bounded by clearly defined limits.
[2] These words were written by Mgr Arquillière, a leading authority on this problem

thirty years. His sense of grandeur and his passion for glory were strengthened by remarkable gifts. Tall, upright, and slim, he was the very type of those young Germans in whom moral instability combines with physical fitness to further their ambition and combative instinct. There was nothing about him to suggest the complex personalities of his son and grandson; he was a soldier, a leader of men, a creature of boundless energy, though not without intelligence and judgment. We cannot but admire his character, in which cruelty could not overshadow an essential nobility, and in which violence ran side by side with generosity. A firm believer, he was devout and charitable; his faith was never in question, even at the height of his struggle with the Holy See. He had a clear skin, keen blue eyes, well-formed red lips, and fine teeth surrounded by a thick beard with glints of gold and flame. 'Barbarossa'—Red Beard—the Italians called him; the nickname passed into history, and from 1152 until 1190 the political scene was dominated by the tall figure of Frederick I Barbarossa, the greatest of the German emperors.

For thirty years the Germanic world had been in eclipse. Henry V's death without issue in 1125 was followed by a period of confusion, during which feudal ambition had enjoyed free rein. Three families had vied for supremacy: the house of *Saxony*, which had threatened the imperial government since the minority of Henry IV; the house of *Welf*, which had held the hereditary dukedom of Bavaria since 1170, and whose power extended over a wide area around Lake Constance; and finally the house of *Hohenstaufen*, which was also known by its territorial name of *Weiblingen*. The rivalry between 'Guelfs' and 'Ghibellines' (as the Italians pronounced 'Welf' and 'Weiblingen') had made way for the accession of Lothair (1125–37); but on the latter's death, a Ghibelline, Conrad III (1138–52), had quickly overcome his adversaries, assumed the crown, and put down an insurrection of the Guelfs. Conrad's victory was followed by a marriage between his brother and the widow of the vanquished leader. This union ended the struggle for the time being, and from it Frederick was born. Half Ghibelline and half Guelf, he seemed predestined to lead a reunited Germany in a career of magnificent achievement.

Meanwhile, the papacy also had lost something of its prestige. Rome, together with the whole Christian world, had passed through a period of storm and stress. On the death of Calixtus II an antipope had opposed Honorius II, upon whose death Innocent II had been confronted with another, Anacletus. The result had been more than ten years of schism, to heal which St Bernard had laboured with all the might of his authority.[1] Two insignificant popes had followed, Celestine II and Lucius II. The Cistercian Eugenius III (1145–53)

[1] See Chapter III, section 7.

had done much to rehabilitate the papacy, to strengthen the moral and intellectual life of Christendom, to revive enthusiasm for the crusade, and to bring about the submission of heretics. But after him the aged Anastasius IV (1153–4) lacked strength to withstand the German king.

The Italian situation had been complicated by two new elements.

(1) Roger I was succeeded by his son Roger II (1101–54), an able diplomat and warrior, a true descendant of Tancred de Hauteville. With him the Norman adventure reached its high-water mark: conqueror, then heir, of his cousin William, Roger II unified southern Italy regardless of papal protests. Honorius II intervened; but his army was beaten, and Roger was invested (1128) with the duchy of Apulia at Benevento amid barbaric splendour and the glare of torches. In spite of this success, he took advantage of difficulties created by the schism of Anacletus. Notwithstanding several appeals addressed to him at Salerno by St Bernard, he continued to support the antipope, and was crowned king on 23rd December 1130. On the death of Anacletus he raised up another antipope, Victor IV; but the latter quickly submitted to Innocent II. This pope, too, attempted to break his adversary by force of arms; but he was decisively beaten, and obliged to invest Roger as King of Sicily, Duke of Apulia, and Prince of Capua. Henceforward the Norman kingdom, which was subject to a discipline unusual at that time, became an important factor in Italian politics.

(2) The beginning of the twelfth century witnessed a movement towards communal independence. There was fierce hatred between neighbouring cities; Milan detested Pavia, while Venice, Genoa, and Pisa vowed one another to destruction. Within the towns themselves, also, antagonism ran high; and a bitter feud between the Montecchi and Cappelletti has been immortalized in the legend of Romeo and Juliet. Both Church and Empire were hostile to the growth of free towns, with whom they were constantly embroiled; and the quarrel between Guelfs and Ghibellines was transferred to the peninsula, where it came to represent the struggle of papal against anti-papal factions.

In Rome itself the communal movement issued in extremes of violence. Until then the Pope alone had exercised authority, nominating the city prefect, directing the police, and trying criminal cases. The 'Roman consuls,' despite their grandiose title, were no more than his hirelings. But, powerful though he was, the Sovereign Pontiff had numerous enemies, including the Roman aristocracy who looked back with regret to the old days when they made popes, and the common folk whom anything could rouse. In 1143 a mob stormed the Capitol and elected a Senate. Lucius II was mortally wounded in a fruitless attempt to recapture this strong-point, and in 1145 Eugenius III agreed to recognize the Senate. The situation deteriorated still further with the appearance in Rome of a brilliant demagogue. Arnold of Brescia was an austere canon regular, obsessed with apocalyptic dreams. His ideas were not unlike those which had inspired the generosity of Paschal II; but they included social and political elements which made him heir to the Pattarines, a ferocious rabble of self-styled reformers who had caused much trouble in Italy during the preceding century. Arnold insisted that temporal power must be exercised by none but laymen; the clergy must surrender their wealth and landed property, and live henceforth exclusively on tithes and public charity! Condemned by his bishop in 1139, he had gone to France, where he was welcomed by his old friend Abélard. St Bernard, however, had secured his expulsion from that kingdom, and the champion of revolution came to Rome at the very moment (1146) when Eugenius III was obliged to leave the Eternal City. His inflammatory tirades against ecclesiastical abuses made a deep impression. Most of the common people, and even a number of the clergy, rallied to his side. Arnold became a sort of dictator, and excited the mob with promises to restore the ancient glory of their city. The Republic of all-conquering Rome was to be revived along with the Senate, the equestrian order, and the tribunate; and even Eugenius III was obliged to compromise with the fiery tribune when he returned from exile. A third form of universal domination was thus conceived in opposition both to the papacy and to the Empire.

Immediately after his accession, Frederick Barbarossa, following the example of Charlemagne, turned his gaze towards Rome. His consuming ambition would not be satisfied by the unification of his German and Italian dominions; what he had in mind from start to finish was nothing less than to restore the worldwide authority of the Roman Empire. With this end in view he proclaimed himself *Romanorum imperator semper Augustus, divus, piissimus, imperator et gubernator urbi et orbi*. Charlemagne had never gone that far. In 1133 Frederick had inherited the kingdom of Arles, a remnant of ancient Lotharingia, to which there were added later not only Provence, but also Franche-Comté, Burgundy, the Lyonnais, Viennois, western Switzerland, Savoy, and Dauphiné. He did not simply annex these French territories; they came to him through marriage with the heiress of Upper Burgundy in 1156, when he assumed the crown of Burgundy at Arles. He regarded all sovereign princes simply as his lieutenants. Boleslav of Poland agreed to kneel before him; the rulers of Hungary and Denmark acknowledged themselves his vassals; and he himself created the kingdom of Bohemia by conferring on Duke Ladislaus a golden crown which had in it more of symbol than reality. Only the

G*

kings of France and England, Louis VII and Henry II, refused submission, though they displayed no small degree of respect towards this
mighty prince.   Frederick himself referred to them as 'provincial
governors' or 'petty kings.'

A man of Barbarossa's outlook necessarily viewed the Pope's claim
to primacy as an obstacle to be removed at any cost.   The government
of Rome was indispensable to the accomplishment of his grandiose
design; two years after his accession, therefore, he set to work.   It
seemed for a moment that he might reach agreement with the Roman
demagogue; for Arnold of Brescia, together with the 'Senate and
People of Rome,' recognized Frederick and offered him the crown of
empire.   Barbarossa's reply was contained in a celebrated letter: 'Why
vaunt the glory of your City, the wisdom of your Senate, the quality of
your youth?   Rome is no longer to be found in Rome.   Would you
see again her former greatness, the majesty of senatorial purple, the
strength and discipline of an equestrian order?   Behold our State.
Those things belong to us already in virtue of our imperial dignity.
We are your lawful master.'

The Roman Commune could do little in face of the German army;
the aged Pope Anastasius lay dying, and it appeared that Frederick must
have his way.   But at this critical juncture Providence sent one who
would call a halt to his pretensions.   Nicholas Breakspear was an
Englishman, of rough exterior but keen intelligence, tenacious as a
mastiff.   His father, it was said, had been an ignorant peasant who
ended his days as a lay-brother in some religious house; but he himself
had grown up among clerics, and had become a canon regular of
Saint-Ruf at Avignon.   Eugenius III had created him cardinal and
sent him as legate to Scandinavia.

Anastasius IV died on 3rd December 1154.   Forty-eight hours later
a unanimous vote of the Sacred College elected Breakspear, who took
the name of Adrian IV and reigned until 1159.

Frederick was at this time in northern Italy.   He had assembled his
vassals and representatives of the cities in the plain of Roncaglia near
Piacenza, where he promised reforms and announced his intention of
assuming the Iron Crown of Lombardy.   After that, he would go to
Rome.   At present his interests coincided with those of the Pope; for
Barbarossa had no love for Arnold, and Adrian IV had just laid the
Eternal City under an interdict following the assassination of a cardinal.
But their apparent friendship could not disguise mutual suspicion.
At their first meeting, Frederick declined to perform the office of
marshal by leading the Pope's horse and holding his stirrup, which for
centuries had been a duty of strict etiquette; nor would he do so until it
was explained to him that the tradition went back as far as Charlemagne.

Accompanied by the Pope, Frederick then set out for Rome.   He captured the Leonine city by surprise, but the commune still occupied the remainder.   The imperial coronation took place on 18th June behind locked doors in St Peter's; and when the populace, warned by the soldiers' acclamation, rushed to the basilica, they were driven back before a murderous charge.   'See,' said one of the Emperor's suite, 'you get iron instead of gold; that's the coin we Germans use.'   Not long afterwards, Arnold of Brescia was seized and hanged; his corpse was burned, and its ashes thrown into the Tiber.   The Pope re-established his authority upon the ruins of the Republic, and Frederick departed, alarmed by the ravages of malaria among his troops; but his arrogance and cruelty had aroused general mistrust.

Relieved of his embarrassing associate, Adrian IV took stock of his position.   He needed allies.   Milan, the chief city of Lombardy, viewed the Emperor with feelings similar to those of the Pope.   Moreover, William the Bad of Sicily (1154–66),[1] who had been at loggerheads with the Holy See and had routed a joint force of papal and Byzantine troops under Manuel Comnenus, was alarmed by the German menace.   Adrian IV gladly confirmed the titles and privileges inherited from his father, including an unusual degree of independence enjoyed by Sicily in ecclesiastical affairs.   The imperial court looked with a jaundiced eye on a *rapprochement* whose significance was plain for all to see.   After Barbarossa himself, the soul of antipapal policy was the chancellor, Rainald of Dassel, a diplomatic adventurer who had scant respect for promises; and tension between the two masters of Christendom rapidly increased.

The first clash arose from the Emperor's arrest of the Archbishop of Lund.   Adrian wrote an outspoken letter, which was carried by two legates to Besançon.   Frederick was holding a Diet there in the spring of 1157, and the assembly treated this epistle as an insult.   In ambiguous terms, which were no doubt intentional, the Pope reminded Frederick of the benefits (*beneficia*) which the latter owed to him, including the imperial crown which he had conferred (*collata*).   Rainald of Dassel protested at this outrage.   *Beneficia!*   That was the word used to describe fiefs granted by an overlord to his vassal.   The Diet re-echoed his indignation; but the legates refused to be intimidated.   'From whom,' asked Cardinal Roland, 'does the Emperor hold his crown if not from the Pope?'   Upon which, an equerry rushed at him with drawn sword, and would certainly have killed him, had not Frederick himself stepped between them.   This outburst of wrath may have suggested to Adrian that he had gone too far; or he may have thought his gesture had achieved its end.   At any rate, he made it clear that he had used the word *beneficia* in the sense of benefits and not of fiefs (*beneficium non feudum sed bonum factum*).   The legates, however,

[1] He was the son of Roger II, and merited his nickname.

were forbidden to visit Germany, and Rainald set about the organization of antipapal propaganda. High words were exchanged with growing frequency, and war was soon inevitable.

The issue at stake became apparent at the Diet of Roncaglia (1158). Frederick engaged the four most celebrated jurists of his time to expound the doctrine of imperial absolutism as conceived by Roman Law, which was then on the flood-tide of its renascence.[1]   By way of giving effect to his thesis, which was diametrically opposed to the papal view, the Emperor next decreed that Italy was to be reorganized on the basis of Justinian's *Pandects* and Byzantine methods. He insisted on the imperial authority, forbade the federation of towns, and even provided for a common coinage. A grandiose plan, indeed, but one which could not be applied except by force. Such were the opening moves in this titanic struggle.

In order to subdue the Italian cities, Frederick placed them under the rule of officials known as podestats. Genoa, Brescia, Cremona, and Piacenza became restless. Milan openly revolted, and for two and a half years held out against the imperial army. Supplies failed, and she was obliged to capitulate in the spring of 1162; not, however, before the Milanese had solemnly destroyed the symbol of their freedom, the *carroccio*, a car drawn by four oxen and carrying the communal standard. Frederick vented his cruel rage by delivering the whole city, with its churches, to the flames. The population was dispersed and condemned to forced labour, while German soldiers amused themselves playing bowls with the heads of slaughtered prisoners.

From Rome, Adrian IV had watched the conflict with grave anxiety. The Countess Matilda had died, and her estates had been seized by the Duke of Bavaria, notwithstanding her bequest to the Holy See. A number of important archbishoprics, including those of Cologne and Ravenna, were granted to imperial favourites; and when the Pope protested, Rainald answered that possession of Rome was necessary for the fulfilment of plans adopted at Roncaglia, and that the Emperor would soon take possession of the city. Adrian fled for refuge to Anagni, and was about to excommunicate Frederick when he died on 1st September 1159.

By an overwhelming majority, the conclave elected none other than Cardinal Roland, who had braved the German's wrath at Besançon. The new Pope, Alexander III (1159–81), was gentle but firm, a leading jurist, and a brilliant diplomat such as Tuscany had frequently produced. The Emperor did not misjudge his adversary; but three dissenting cardinals had elected an antipope, Victor IV, who was recognized forthwith by Barbarossa.

[1] See Chapter VIII, section 10.

In the long run, however, this attempt to create schism met with no success. Germany alone rallied to the antipope. As a refugee at Salerno, Alexander III was treated with the utmost respect by Louis VII; he was also recognized by Henry II of England, and, in fact, by almost the whole of Western Christendom. Frederick, though shocked by this display of unanimity, could not draw back. When Victor IV died he was replaced by Paschal III,[1] who was in turn succeeded by yet another antipope, Calixtus III.

These puppets, however, were of no avail, and Alexander now resolved to show his hand. Returning to Rome in November 1165, he was welcomed as a liberator; and before long his diplomacy made him the centre of resistance. Sicily confirmed its alliance, Venice asked for one. Several urban leagues came into existence, one with Verona, another with Cremona as its nucleus; and Milan, now rising from its ashes, joined the latter. Alexander managed with great skill to form them into a single bloc with Venice, and the alliance was governed by a council of Rectors drawn from sixteen towns. The Pope had given his answer to the Diet of Roncaglia.

For the fourth time (1166) Frederick crossed the Alps and moved through northern Italy. Entering Rome, he conceived the strange idea of a second coronation, while Alexander fled, disguised as a pilgrim. But the Emperor was overtaken by a catastrophe that seemed like a divine retribution; for a terrible epidemic carried off half his army and many of his close associates, including Rainald. With great difficulty he made his way back to Germany. Here the Empress assumed control, while he escaped into hiding and thus saved his life (August–September 1167). In the following year an attempt was made to bar future German invasions by the erection of a new fortress at the confluence of the Tanaro and Dormida. It was called Alexandria after the Sovereign Pontiff. 'A town of straw!' Barbarossa exclaimed contemptuously; but all his fire could not subdue it.

For the next seven years Frederick nursed his wrath, but his third antipope did no more to secure for him the protection of Heaven than the other two had done. In 1174 he undertook a final expedition which ended in disaster. His subjects were tired of these costly descents upon Italy; he scarcely managed to assemble 8,000 men, and they were defeated before Alexandria. He summoned reinforcements, but his new army amounted to no more than 6,000. On 29th May 1176, at Legnano, between Lake Maggiore and Milan, the city militia and papal forces, numbering 10,000 men, encountered Barbarossa's

[1] Paschal III decided to canonize Charlemagne, whose bones had recently been discovered at Aix-la-Chapelle. Frederick had them deposited in a golden barrel, surmounted by a tabernacle crowned with lamps. Gigantic feasting took place on this occasion (29th December 1165) at Aix, the magnificence of which astonished contemporaries.

host.   During an action which lasted for several hours, Frederick was thrown from his horse, and was only saved in the nick of time by one of his officers, who gave him his own charger.   The imperial standard-bearer lay dead upon the field, the standard fell into enemy hands, and the imperial troops disbanded.

Legnano is an important date in medieval history, for it confirmed the primacy of the Holy See.   After signing a treaty of peace, the Emperor assisted Alexander to mount his horse, while the Pope, as a sign of forgiveness, gave him the kiss of peace.   Never, perhaps, had a successor of St Peter appeared so truly great; and the third Lateran (eleventh oecumenical) Council, which met in 1179, sealed his triumph.[1] But the troubles which disturbed Alexander's pontificate were not yet concluded.   Barbarossa was meditating his revenge.   He had prepared his way by the Peace of Constance, by exacting an oath from the Italian communes, by heaping favours upon the city of Milan, by defeating Henry the Lion in Germany, and by reaching an understanding with Sicily.   Rome was once more on the verge of revolution when the Pope died in exile at Civitacastellana on 30th August 1181.   But six years later Christendom was shocked by the fall of Jerusalem to the arms of Saladin; and Frederick Barbarossa, who was fundamentally a good Christian, set out on the crusade.   It may be, also, that he hoped thereby to satisfy a thirst for power which he had failed to quench in Italy.   He never returned.[2]

7. THE ZENITH OF THE PAPACY

The dream of imperialism was not submerged with Barbarossa in the river Cydnus; his son and grandson both revived it, though in a different form.   These two men, in whom there was a streak of genius, realized that so long as central Europe was a prey to anarchy it could no longer serve as the foundation of that colossal edifice which they intended to create.   Moreover, in consequence of an economic revolution, the gateway to power was now in the Mediterranean and on the Channel coast.   Henry VI, and after him Frederick II, conceived the idea of a Mediterranean empire.   They were inspired not so much by the tradition of Charlemagne as by that of Trajan, Hadrian, and Constantine.   Antagonism between the Holy See and the Empire assumed fresh significance: Italy was no longer the key to papal independence.   The papacy hoped to preserve the unity and orthodoxy of Christendom by increased centralization of power in its own hands; while the emperors sought to extend their authority over the whole

[1] It was the third Lateran Council that decreed, among other things, the necessity of a two-thirds majority at papal elections.
[2] See Chapter XI, section 7.

Mediterranean area by reconciling a variety of religions and by establishing a civil authority independent of the Church.

As a matter of fact, the nucleus of this idea may well have been present to the mind of Barbarossa when, in 1184, he arranged a marriage between his eldest son Henry and Constance of Sicily. Ten years older than her husband, who never loved her, she was the post-humous daughter of Roger II and heiress to the Norman kingdom. Although she was under religious vows, Pope Lucius III (1181–5) did not openly object; and when his successor, Urban III (1185–7), a Crivelli who, like all Milanese, detested Frederick, ventured to protest, he was silenced by an invasion of the papal states. The popes had good cause to fear this policy of encirclement.

The situation became still more ominous when Henry VI succeeded his father in 1190, at the age of twenty-four. Ambitious, short of stature, pale, and with a lofty brow, he had inherited all his mother's Provençal refinement. He had scarcely mounted the throne when he descended upon Sicily in order to lay hands on the inheritance of his father-in-law, William II, which was disputed by Tancred, an illegiti-mate brother of William I. After an initial defeat, he was crowned Emperor by Celestine III, and returned to continue the struggle. But success was not easy; the Sicilians had no wish to be Germanized, while the Pope, who had begrudged him the imperial crown, secretly upheld the cause of Tancred. It was only when the latter died, in 1194, that Henry won the day. His enemies were burned in pitch, flayed alive, crushed between boards, or buried alive up to the neck and their heads shorn off like grass. The Empress Constance, a true Norman at heart, expressed her disgust at these abominations. She was promptly accused of adultery, and he who was supposed to be her lover suffered death with a circlet of red-hot iron fastened round his head. A centralized government, modelled upon that of the Capetians, made Sicily as it were the pattern of a modern monarchy; and the German emperor, in possession of rich territories, could set about the realiza-tion of his vast design, of which he made no secret. He married his brother, Philip of Swabia, to a daughter of the Basileus Isaac Angelus; and when the latter was dethroned in 1195, he gave out that he would be 'revenged on these Byzantine traitors.' Then he took the Cross, hoping that his army would return victorious from Jerusalem by way of Constantinople. Contrary to international law and without the slightest justification, he imprisoned Richard I of England on his way back from the crusade and forced him to do homage, tactics which gave Philip Augustus food for thought. Step by step, it seemed, Henry would become master of the whole white race; the popes at any rate could do nothing to stop him. Neither Gregory VIII, who occupied the chair of Peter for only two months, nor Clement III, who had to meet renewed troubles at Rome, nor the venerable Celestine III, who was elected at the age of eighty-five, left much evidence of their passage through the Lateran.   Providence, however, intervened to snap the thread of Henry's dreams and destiny.   A pernicious fever—aided, so rumour said, by poison from the hands of Constance—carried off the young Emperor on 28th September 1197.   He was thirty-two.   His fleet, which had gathered at Messina, never sailed for the conquest of the East.

A few weeks later, on 8th January 1198, there ascended Peter's throne one of the most powerful figures in the medieval Church, Lothair of Segni, Innocent III.   His age, his nobility, his wide culture, all those many gifts which have been recognized by later historians no less than by his contemporaries,[1] enabled him at the most favourable juncture to play a vital part.   Through eighteen years and with tireless energy he acted on the principle that the Holy See enjoys absolute supremacy.[2]   Perhaps his knowledge of men was not his strongest point; perhaps, too, his feudal origins prevented him from seeing the real issue and sometimes caused his view to seem outmoded.   This much, however, is quite certain: he had the interest of Christendom at heart; he was determined to make God victorious; and, even in the exercise of a theocratic policy, when pride might well have had its say, he never forgot that he was simply an instrument of God, and showed himself a humble Christian.

Innocent III found Rome in the hands of an insolent commune, the papal states occupied by Germans, and Sicily administered by imperial officials.   If Henry VI had been alive, it would have been impossible to remedy this perilous situation, but his death made all the difference. The Romans had no allies, and Innocent took advantage of this fact to destroy the Senate (which was reduced to two, and then to a single member), and to deprive the Prefect of his powers.   The commune retained its autonomy, its assemblies on the Capitol, its army and finances, and even its right to coin money, which it exercised concurrently with the Pope; but so long as Innocent sat in Peter's chair, demagogy stood no chance in Rome.

The papal states were recovered; Spoleto, Ancona, and Ravenna were reoccupied; and Innocent was supported by the Tuscan cities in driving the Emperor's vassals from the former territories of Matilda. Having pacified the north, he accomplished a master-stroke of diplomacy in Sicily.   In order to safeguard the rights of her young son Frederick Roger against the Germans, the Empress Constance offered to recognize the Pope as overlord.   She died soon afterwards, bequeathing the guardianship of her child to Innocent III, whose

[1] See Chapter IV, section 7 (ad init.).
[2] See section 5 of the present chapter.

legates henceforward administered on his behalf a splendid kingdom which in times past had caused the Holy See much anxiety.

Nor was the situation in Germany less favourable. Young Frederick Roger was styled 'King of the Romans'; but the princes did not want a child as their sovereign. Some had already chosen Otto of Brunswick, others Philip of Swabia. Innocent III did not hesitate between the Ghibelline Philip, who was arrogant like all the Hohenstaufen, and Otto, a Guelf, who seemed accommodating and full of good intentions. Philip had been excommunicated; but in choosing Otto the Pope chose one who, though a brave soldier, was unreliable. Besides, Otto lacked the financial resources of his adversary, and was therefore a less valuable ally. He suffered one defeat after another; but Philip, who had begun overtures to the Holy See, was assassinated in a family quarrel. Whereupon Otto, recognized by the whole of Germany, asked for the imperial crown, which Innocent conferred upon him in 1209.

'Well beloved son,' the Pope wrote to him, 'behold us united in one heart and soul! Who can resist us, now that we bear the two swords which the Apostles once showed our Lord, saying: "Behold two swords," to which our Lord replied: "It is enough!"' Applying a theory familiar to all, Innocent III undoubtedly intended to show that he was owner of the temporal sword and was merely entrusting it to Otto. But events soon gave the lie to these fair words. If Otto had seemed modest and conciliatory before his coronation, he now revealed himself as a worthy successor to Barbarossa. He occupied the Tuscan cities, placed his own vassals in charge of Ancona and Spoleto, and set his podestats over Vicenza, Ferrara, and Brescia. He also claimed homage from the Prefect of Rome, and even led an army as far south as Naples. Innocent III retaliated by excommunicating the Emperor in 1210, and recognizing as king his own ward Frederick Roger, who was then aged seventeen and took the style of Frederick II. Finally, the Pope took vigorous steps to counteract Otto's advantage by rousing Italian patriotism against German interference, but chiefly by siding with the French king Philip Augustus in his quarrel with Otto's ally, John of England. The French victory at Bouvines (27th July 1214) was no less his own, and the fourth oecumenical council held at the Lateran in 1215 crowned this triumph.

The papacy was once again victorious, and Innocent stood forth, in accordance with his theocratic doctrine, as the first man of his age. But Otto's strength was as yet by no means exhausted, and continued to preoccupy his thoughts. Meanwhile, however, he laboured to reform the Church and launched Christendom against the Albigenses. He exercised sovereign rights in England, created the kingdom of Portugal, and imposed his authority on Aragon as also, to some extent, upon Leon and Castile.   His influence was felt in Norway, in Sweden, on the Baltic shores, and in Poland, while Hungary became a papal fief. Innocent, in fact, was overlord of western Europe.   It may be that Christendom could not otherwise have opposed the forces of disintegration, but how long could this situation last?   Could the priesthood really govern the world?   The answer was to come from Frederick II (1218–50).

Otto IV was gathered to his fathers on 19th May 1218, two years after the death of Innocent.   Frederick was now master of Germany. Already king of the Romans, and heir to Sicily, he held all the trump cards, and knew how to play them.   Hitherto he had shown himself so gentle, so polished, always ready to obey the Holy Father.   If there was talk of a crusade—why, of course, he would join up at once.   He had been told to create a diversion in Germany on Otto's rear, and had carried out that task with undeniable courage.   How, then, could Innocent have suspected on his deathbed that this beloved youth would prove an even more dangerous enemy of the Church than Barbarossa?

Frederick II in no way resembled his great Swabian ancestor.   He was so small, he looked so frail; even as a young man he stooped, and became prematurely bald.   An Arab chronicler, in fact, remarked that he would not have been worth ten shillings as a slave; but his face revealed great strength of character, and few could endure his piercing gaze.   Highly strung, unstable, stubborn yet easily discouraged, his personality was a mass of contradictions.   He delighted to recall his Norman-Sicilian ancestry, compounded of high courage and strong passion.   That was his mother's legacy; he was the son of Constance, a Viking, who was said to have been revenged upon her spouse by poison.   Frederick's intelligence was of the highest order, but he wanted restraint and, still more, the sense of personal guilt.   He was too prone to believe that cunning compensated for lack of principle. His energy swept all before it; he was always ready to exert himself to the utmost, and one of his contemporaries, torn between admiration and disgust, referred to him as 'the Wonder of the World.'   Frederick was a genius, but unbalanced.

The most surprising note in his character, one that became more apparent with age and experience, was his attitude towards religion. He is among the very few medieval men in whom we can detect a strain of scepticism.   All religions were equal in his eyes—equal in their worthlessness.   While thirsting for knowledge, he would accept none but experimental and logical demonstration.   The Moslem scholars whom he invited to his court introduced him to the study of physics and chemistry, and thereby persuaded him that Christian dogmas had no meaning.   Among the numerous legends which have gathered round his name, one tells how he shut up a man in a hermetically sealed barrel in order to prove that when it was opened no soul would fly up to heaven! It is not surprising that his contemporaries took him for antichrist, 'the beast rising from the sea, its mouth full of blasphemy, with the claws of a bear, the body of a leopard, and the fury of a lion.'

Nevertheless it is facile to regard him as a commonplace anti-Christian, or a mere fanatic. Though logical enough, he was extremely complex. He had been brought up under the Church's wing and never created an antipope, but he was excommunicated several times. He was pleasure-loving, but still admired St Francis of Assisi. He was more or less an atheist, but made war on heretics. Though anathematized by the Holy See, he went on the crusade, even though, as a crusader, he had dealings with the Moslems and remained on friendly terms with them. Nor must it be forgotten that he died and was buried in the Cistercian cowl. No character of the Middle Ages is quite so enigmatic, and none, we must admit, has quite his fascination for those interested in psychology.

The Church would clearly have her work cut out to handle such a man. 'The whole earth,' he used to say, 'looks forward to imperial domination.' And again, 'Is not the Emperor the embodiment of Law?' His chancellor, Pierre de la Vigne, later addressed him as 'Caesar, bright Light of the World.' Like his grandfather, he wished to be a second Charlemagne; like his father, he dreamed of reviving the ancient Mediterranean empire of Rome, 'her victorious eagles, her fasces, and her triumphal wreaths.' Conflict between him and the papacy was inevitable.

Frederick II was hardly seated on the throne when he began to prepare Sicily as the starting-point of his tremendous scheme. He was passionately fond of that island where natural beauty and historical tradition formed a perfect synthesis, where four civilizations one after another—Greek, Roman, Byzantine, and Moslem—had left their impress and were ultimately fused in the crucible of Norman culture. Palermo, his capital, became a glorious city with its crown of towers and domes, and with the fragrance of its gardens. The glow of golden mosaics mingled with delicate Arab lattice-work; in the basilicas, marble columns supported cupolas imitated from those of Byzantium; and gothic churches were enriched with Saracenic ornament. Frederick lived like a caliph, surrounded with Moslem sages and the mamelukes of his bodyguard. He even kept a harem full of oriental beauties. Within four or five years Sicily had become a centralized monarchy, where the least resistance met with massacre and deportation. The Constitution of Melfi formed a code inspired by Byzantium and rivalling the masterpieces of Roman Law, while the system of taxation was rigorously enforced.

Frederick turned next to Germany.   Realizing that he could not annihilate the baronage, he sought to divide it.   For this purpose he relied upon the Holy See, which had supported him in his contest with Otto, as also upon the Teutonic Order, which was then in its heyday and whose Grand Master, Hermann of Salza, was his willing agent. Apart from the short-lived revolt of his son Henry, his dominions in this part of the world caused him no anxiety.   His marriage with Isabel of England enabled him to keep France at arm's length, while he employed Raymond IV of Toulouse as a further threat to the Capetian monarchy.   He was virtually omnipotent; and when the newly formed Lombard League defied him in 1237, it was crushed by Swabian and Moslem cavalry at Cortenuova.   The carroccio was captured and borne in triumph to the Capitol.   And now, with Machiavellian cunning, Frederick strengthened his hold on Italy by quartering German veterans in the towns and using local collaborators, Ghibellines, to carry out his policy.

The papacy, meanwhile, had made no move.   Honorius III (1216–1227), convinced that an understanding was possible with a ruler who was so emphatic as to the necessity of reform, who persecuted heresy, and who swore three times to take the Cross, had even crowned him Emperor (22nd November 1220).   But it is not unlikely that, towards the end of his life, Honorius realized the truth.   His successor, at any rate, was under no delusion; it was not the first time a militant and resolute Pope had followed a peaceful trimmer.   Gregory IX (1227–1241) was none other than the great Cardinal Hugolin, whose vigour had not been impaired, let alone destroyed, by the advent of his eightieth year.   This fiery old man could never have sat by and watched Frederick entangle the whole of Italy in his web.   The Emperor was vulnerable in that he had not kept his oath to take the Cross.   Gregory therefore excommunicated him and, when Frederick at last set sail, followed him even to Jerusalem with maledictions because of his extraordinary behaviour in negotiating with instead of fighting Islam.   In due time the Pope learned of Frederick's success in the Holy Land, and for a short period the two were reconciled.   But their enmity quickly revived.   Following the defeat of the Lombard League, Gregory allied himself with Genoa and Venice; he excommunicated his adversary a third time when the latter occupied papal territory in Sardinia, and finally absolved the Emperor's subjects from their allegiance.

But the days had gone when one word from the Pope could bring an emperor to Canossa.   Frederick II was firmly in the saddle, and his excommunication proved of no effect.   How, indeed, could it restrain the mamelukes whom Frederick had let loose upon the papal states? Driven from Rome, which was on the verge of revolution, Gregory trembled as he beheld the imperial armies sweep through Italy unchecked, and Frederick name his bastard Enzio governor of the peninsula.[1] In desperation, he offered the imperial crown to St Louis for his brother; but the French king prudently declined to thrust himself into a hornets' nest. At this juncture, the Mongol invasion under Genghis Khan struck terror into Europe. The yellow cavalry, having annihilated the Russians, the Poles, and the Teutonic Knights, rode headlong for Vienna and the Adriatic. Rivalry between the two heads of Christendom looked very much like double suicide; but how to find a basis of agreement? Gregory resolved to break his adversary, and summoned a council. Most of the prelates who were to take part embarked at Genoa, but they were intercepted by the imperial navy; and the fathers of the council, instead of passing judgment on the rebel, were forced to kick their heels in prison until such time as he might choose to free them. The Pope died on 22nd August 1241 at the age of almost one hundred, and it seemed the temporal power must triumph.

For two years Frederick II dominated the West. Gregory's successor, Celestine IV, reigned for only fifteen days; and two years elapsed before the election of his successor, for the Sacred College was a prey to pestilence and harassed by imperial intrigue. Besides, the Emperor assumed full responsibility for the defence of Europe, and devised a strategy so remarkable that it exhausted the effort of the Mongols and obliged them to withdraw. At the same time, he strengthened his hold upon his dominions, purposely setting aside the feudal lords of Germany, and even the ecclesiastical princes, in favour of the towns whose fortunes he established. But the tireless adventurer was growing old. His hatred of the Church had become an obsession: he persecuted the mendicant Orders, bullied the Teutonic Knights, and boasted to the Egyptian ambassador that he had founded a caliphate in direct line from the Prophet, 'far superior to the absurd Christian institution of electing anyone at random as their head.'

The situation, however, altered unexpectedly. St Louis would not stand idle and watch a man like Frederick II obtain control of Europe. He began by requesting him to release the French cardinals whom he had imprisoned. 'Let not your imperial wisdom surrender to the intoxication of your own sweet will,' wrote Louis to the despot of Palermo; 'for the kingdom of France is not so weak that it cannot kick against the spur.' He then called upon the Sacred College to proceed with the election of a Pope.

Innocent IV (1243–54) was a lawyer, a Genoese aristocrat, and a man of unrelenting determination, who was destined to save the Church at a

---

[1] Frederick's eldest, and legitimate, son Henry had rebelled against his father, but in vain.   He was now dying of grief, a prisoner in Apulia.

moment when her cause seemed hopeless.   It was no mere chance that
he had assumed the name of a great theocratic pope, and his encyclical
Aeger cui levia formulated the doctrine of papal primacy in terms more
definitive than those even of Innocent III.   He was prepared for mortal
combat with the Emperor.

Innocent took up residence at Genoa for greater security, and summoned a council to deal with Frederick II.   In vain did Frederick
plead the yellow peril which he must oppose, and the renewed Moslem
threat which had culminated in the recent fall of Jerusalem to the
Sultan of Egypt.   The council met at Lyons in 1245; Frederick dared
not retaliate for fear of French intervention, although Lyons was an
imperial city.   The assembly would not even hear the message of this
'Proteus,' as the Pope described him.   A lengthy indictment set forth
his usurpations and his crimes.   Convicted of perjury, sacrilege, and
heresy, Frederick II was excommunicated and declared no longer
emperor or king.

This sentence had profound repercussions.   The Emperor was
desperate, and tried to enlist the support of other rulers by pretending
that their interests were identical with his own.   Then he had recourse
to social revolution in the name of evangelical principles, but failed
completely.   Together with his son Conrad IV, whose election he had
secured, he managed to hold his own in Germany; but the patriotism
of the Italian towns proved fatal to his cause.   Parma revolted, and the
disaffection spread to Florence, Milan, Ferrara, and Mantua.   Frederick
tried to recapture Parma, but his camp was surprised and he was
obliged to flee.   This spelled ruin.   Enzio, his beloved Enzio, was
taken prisoner, and all his friends began to fade away, even the chancellor Pierre de la Vigne, whom he blinded in revenge.   At the height
of his rage, the beaten monarch was gathering his forces for a final
throw when he was carried off by dysentery on 13th December 1250,
in the camp of his Moorish troops.

Innocent IV declared the race of Hohenstaufen accursed, and Heaven
heard his imprecation.   Conrad IV died prematurely four years later
(21st May 1254), followed soon afterwards, on 7th December, by his
redoubtable opponent.   Southern Italy was drenched in fire and blood
through the rebellion of Manfred, an illegitimate son of Frederick by an
Italian woman.   But he was already doomed, and met his death at
Beneventum in 1266 at the hands of French troops under Charles of
Anjou, brother of St Louis.   His naked body was paraded through the
streets astride an ass; and the tragic story closed with the execution of
Conrad's sixteen-year-old son Conradin in 1268.

8. A Dangerous Victory

The Church's victory, won at so great a cost, brought with it serious disadvantages. Scarcely had the papacy attained its zenith in the temporal sphere than it was stricken wellnigh as grievously as its rival. The struggle of the Priesthood and the Empire proved fatal to both.

There could be no doubt as to the Empire; after the deposition of Frederick II, a succession of puppets wore that most illustrious of crowns. First there was one William of Holland, set up by a couple of archbishops. On his death in 1256, seven princes met to elect an Emperor; they were the origin of an electoral college to whom the right henceforward belonged. These rulers had an eye to business, and put up the imperial throne for auction. Alfonso of Castile and Richard of Cornwall pretended to have obtained it; but so little importance was attached to their respective claims that no Pope would crown either of them. This period (1250–73), when the throne was, to all intents and purposes, without an occupant, is generally known as the Great Interregnum. And even the election of Rudolph of Hapsburg (1273–91), who was preferred by the Electors to Philip the Hardy, if only by reason of his weakness, did not terminate the imperial decadence. Both Rudolph and his son Albert I (1291–1308) failed to make the throne hereditary in the house of Austria, as did Henry VII (1308–1313) in that of Luxembourg, and Louis IV (1313–47) in that of Bavaria. Germany and Italy, in the throes of feudal anarchy and communal unrest, were to find the heritage of Barbarossa, Henry VI, and Frederick II a long and painful burden.

Nor did the Holy See fare much better. There was no immediate cause to suspect that the papacy would not continue to dominate Christendom; but among the twelve popes who succeeded Innocent IV, few were equal to their task. Some, like Alexander IV (1254–61), were no more than the puppets of unworthy counsellors. Some, like Nicholas III (1277–80), were guided by their nephews. Others, like Urban IV (1261–4), Clement IV (1265–8), and Martin IV (1281–5), were not, to say the least, of consummate ability. Providence seemed to bear a grudge against the papacy. Three pontiffs died in less than a year (1276–7): the Dominican Innocent V, a nephew of Innocent IV; Adrian V, who reigned for only thirty-six days; and the unfortunate Portuguese John XXI, who was killed after a pontificate of six days when the ceiling of his room collapsed. Honorius IV (1285–7) befriended the University of Paris, and Nicholas IV (1288–92), a Franciscan, was likewise interested in the advancement of studies; but neither had means or time to change the course of Peter's barque.

Only St Gregory X, who was elected in 1271, had the qualities of a leader and a large-scale plan.   He meant to revive the crusade, to end the Greek schism, and to reconcile the Ghibellines and Guelfs; but he reigned for no more than five years.   A two-year interregnum (1292–4), when the cardinals split up into gangs and fought one another in the streets, was followed by the curious election of Celestine V in 1294; [1] and these two events are characteristic of the spiritual disorder prevailing at the end of a century during which the papacy had been so great.

Its political influence continued to decline.   In Germany, the towns asserted their independence, while the feudal lords prepared to strike a blow which fell in 1356, when the Pope was excluded from all share in the appointment of an emperor, and confirmed this decision by the Golden Bull.   The lawlessness prevailing in the towns of northern Italy had similar results.   Obedience to the Holy See was the object of perpetual conflict between Ghibellines and Guelfs.   At Rome, there were repeated outbreaks of violence.   Sicily had been conferred upon Charles of Anjou by the Holy See, which soon repented of its choice.   That scatter-brained but ambitious ruler publicly opposed his Angevin cardinals to those of Italy, while his manifold injustice exasperated the Sicilians.   When, therefore, on 31st March 1282, the bells of Palermo sounded the 'Sicilian Vespers,' resulting in the massacre of all Frenchmen resident in the island, the French Pope Martin IV was unable, even by means of excommunication, to prevent Peter of Aragon, Manfred's father-in-law, from assuming the Norman crown. The papacy had lost its ancient fief.

The Church's struggle and her hard-won victory had consequences even more profound, one of which was not at first apparent.   The Popes, in order to achieve their goal, had been obliged to concentrate power in their own hands.   By doing so, however, they had altered the ancient structure of a Church which, though it had for centuries recognized the Roman primacy, had never considered that primacy synonymous with centralization.   'An instrument of reform, though useful at a given time, may afterwards become a fruitful source of evil,' writes an eminent Jesuit historian; 'and ecclesiastical centralization, which in the thirteenth century freed the Church from the trammels of feudalism, opened the door at a somewhat later date to serious abuses.' [2]

By their defence of an ideal, which was essentially feudal in that they proclaimed themselves suzerain of all suzerains, the Popes had already shown their failure to understand a process of evolution which had begun during the twelfth century.   The future of the Church lay with the mendicant Orders.   The free towns and centralized monarchies

---

[1] See Chapter XIV, section 1.   [2] Fr. Joseph Leclerc, *Études*, September 1951.

stood outside the theocratic sovereignty; while the insult hurled at Boniface VIII by a French minister in 1303, together with the 'Babylonian' exile at Avignon, may be thought to have avenged the discomfiture of Henry IV, of Barbarossa, and of Frederick II.

9. THE CHURCH AND THE COMMUNAL MOVEMENT

From about the year 1150 onwards urban civilization counted for more and more in the destinies of Western Christendom.   The towns were now the centre of social life; they played a vital part in production and distribution, as well as in the intellectual domain.   What attitude would the Church adopt in face of this new movement?

She herself had contributed to the development of urban centres,[1] many of which had grown up round a place of pilgrimage or an abbey. The people were glad of clerical protection; they enjoyed the greater leniency of clerical courts, and need pay taxes to no one but the abbot. St Denis, Vézelay, La Charité-sur-Loire, Conques, St Sernin, and many other towns originated in this way; and by means of franchise or exemption the monasteries had given birth to many a 'new town' where citizens and clergy benefited by mutual exchange of services. Urban institutions were, in principle, not unlike those of the Church. Like her, the townsfolk wanted peace, though chiefly for commercial reasons; the parochial militia, raised to defend the Truce and Peace of God, were the germ of communal associations; mass movements in the form of pilgrimages and crusades, though religious in origin, served as means of distribution, thereby furthering the development of urban trade; while the liberty afforded by the Church to those who dwelt within her shadow gave them both the longing for independence and the means wherewith to attain it.

Nevertheless, when the communal movement began, the clergy were hostile.   For two reasons, one ideological and the other practical.   A cleric, used to spiritual command, was unlikely to sympathize with this claim to freedom, which seemed to him nothing less than rebellion and a door to anarchy.   Besides, the position of the Church within the feudal system caused her to mistrust these townsmen who would prey upon her goods.   The mitred lords did not hesitate to oppose what they considered as unpardonable disobedience.   Hence those brief but bloody convulsions which, first in Italy and then in France, marked the beginning of the communal movement, and in which the senior clergy

[1] The great historian Henri Pirenne denied that the abbeys (which were often situated miles away in the country) had anything to do with the growth of medieval towns.   Mlle Françoise Lehoux, in her work *Le Bourg Saint-Germain*, a masterpiece of erudition, shows how the case of the abbey of Saint-Germain-des-Prés, cradle of the town of that name, disproves his thesis.   Pirenne's view is far from general acceptation among historians, many of whom consider the abbeys to have been 'seeds of the towns.'

behaved so high-handedly.   Such episodes occurred at Cremona about 1030; at Parma, Milan, and Mantua shortly before 1050; at Cambrai in 1077; and at Beauvais in 1099.   Most famous of all is the tragedy of Laon in 1112, a detailed account of which is given by Guibert of Nogent.   It shows the harm suffered by the Church through her entanglement in the feudal system, and explains the opposition of the communes to ecclesiastical authority.

The city of Laon was subject to Bishop Gaudry, a perfect specimen of those mitred barons who were unworthy of their titles.   Supported by his negro steward, of whom the inhabitants were terrified, his conduct was that of a petty tyrant.   Not a week passed without some member of the episcopal clique waylaying one or other of the citizens and holding him to ransom; while the burden of fines, tithes, and taxes was intolerable.   Profiting by the absence of their master, the townsmen reached agreement with the clergy and nobility, and purchased for hard cash the right to organize themselves as a free town.   Gaudry, on his return, was furious.   The citizens hoped to appease his rage with a donation.   He pretended to accept it, but took immediate steps to abolish their association.   The king was called upon for judgment. 'Four hundred *livres* if you recognize the commune!' cried the citizens. 'Seven hundred if you suppress it,' answered the bishop.   Louis VI took the last-named sum, but left the inhabitants to fight it out with their tyrant.   This they quickly did.   A general strike was declared. Cobblers and shoemakers shut up their shops, innkeepers and publicans refused to sell; and when the bishop declared his intention of recovering in the shape of taxes those seven hundred *livres* paid to the king, the population was seized with murderous rage.   Gaudry was warned, but only laughed at the threat.   'Well, well!   So those people mean to kill me?   Why, if my negro John tweaked the nose of the bravest man among them, the fellow would not dare to make a sound!' Rioting broke out, and the avenging cry 'Commune!   Commune!' was heard in the streets.   Armed with swords and two-edged axes, the townsfolk rushed into the episcopal palace.   The terrified Gaudry took refuge in his cellar and hid under a barrel.   He was found, and there ensued a lamentable and disgusting scene: the bishop was hacked to pieces, while the mob set fire not only to his house but even to the cathedral.   Only the arrival of royal troops could bring back calm to Laon.

The communal movement as a whole, then, was looked upon with disfavour by the Church.   Time and again the popes expressed their disapproval.   Thus in 1139, Innocent II invited Louis VII to support him against the citizens of Rheims, begging him to 'dissolve the criminal associations of the Rémois'; and Eugenius IV wrote to the same king, asking him to intervene at Vézelay and oblige the citizens 'to abjure the commune which they have set up and return to the obedience of their abbot.' Innocent III, though he looked to the Italian cities for help in his struggle with the Emperor, inflicted penalties on the commune of St Omer; and Gregory IX later described the townspeople of Rheims as 'more savage than vipers.' Preachers thundered from the pulpit against 'these communities, or rather these conspiracies, like heaps of tangled thorn; these conceited people who, confident in their numbers, oppress their neighbours and subdue them by violence.' Such too was the opinion of Abbot Guibert of Nogent, of Bishop Yves of Chartres, of the preacher Jacques de Vitry, and of St Bernard himself—none of whom resembled Gaudry.

Antagonism between the Church and the cities continued throughout the thirteenth century.[1] The higher ranks of the clergy not seldom had good cause to charge the communes with extortion, with encroachment on ecclesiastical property, and with attempting to impose communal taxes upon the clergy. The townspeople, on their side, were conscious of their strength, and endured with dwindling patience what remained of episcopal or abbatial tutelage. They were also aware that they enjoyed the tacit approval of the Capetian monarchs, who, while restraining the communal movement within their own dominions, were not dissatisfied at its growth in the territory of their vassals, and who, from Philip Augustus onward, appointed burgesses to governmental posts. Hence those numerous incidents which foreshadowed the anti-clericalism of the French Revolution: monasteries were pillaged, bishops were insulted, and men took part in sacrilegious masquerades. Jacques de Vitry denounced the communes as 'modern Babylons.'

This antagonism was widespread in Germany, where the urban movement was a key-piece in the contest between Emperor and Pope. The towns were on the imperial side. Thus we find Henry IV and Henry V conferring many privileges on the citizens of Worms and Spire, while the 'new town' of Fribourg-im-Brisgau was granted so liberal a statute that many cities—Frankfort, Munich, Vienna, Aix-la-Chapelle, Dortmund, and others—demanded equal rights. When Frederick II entered upon his decisive combat with the Holy See, he was able to rely upon the towns; and even the episcopal cities, which

---

[1] The parochial clergy often sided with the communes, an alliance which foreshadowed that of the clergy with the Third Estate in 1789. The same was true of many bishops, a fact which makes it possible for Petit-Dutaillis, the historian of the communal movement, to refute the opinion of Luchaire who, in a work entitled *Les Communes françaises*, exaggerated the hostility of the Church. Petit-Dutaillis hits the nail on the head when he explains that the clergy misunderstood the communal movement, 'just as Renan misunderstood the Paris commune of 1871.' At all events, there are cases in which a bishop fostered the growth of a commune in opposition to some local tyrant. Thus, at Le Mans, in 1069, the bishop was party to a conspiracy against Geoffrey of Mayenne. At Beauvais the bishop was supported by the commune; while the Bishop of Noyon prided himself upon having 'made a commune.'

had been held in check so long as the Emperor was in alliance with the higher clergy, set out on the road to independence and soon became virtual republics. During the Great Interregnum the emancipation of the towns made still further progress, urban leagues proving the only real force that remained in Germany, which was otherwise a prey to anarchy. Emancipation was often achieved in face of the Church and at the cost of violence. At Cologne, for example, between 1263 and 1266, the rebellious townsfolk attacked the property and even the person of their bishop, for which they were condemned by a council. At Liége the population rose against Bishop Henry of Gueldre, a prelate so pitiable that not even Rome would support him.

In Italy the situation was rather different. It was complicated by the Pope's struggle with the Empire, an Empire that represented Germanism. Here the Church was looked upon as the champion of patriotism or local privilege; and that is why the communal movement, which had emerged during the eleventh century in opposition to the bishops, now sided with the Pope. But if the urban leagues were his allies, their relations were still founded on mistrust. That much is clear from the history of the Roman commune under Arnold of Brescia and later. Innocent III's control of the Senate was not destined to survive him; and we shall find his successors often obliged to leave the City when its one Senator spoke as master, in the name of 'the Roman people.'

It would be wrong, however, to conclude that the communal movement was anti-Christian. It may be that certain elements—for political reasons rather than from conviction—used the Catharist heresy as a lever against the Church; but a great majority of the urban population had no idea that by resisting their bishops they were attacking the Church. Cologne, while in rebellion against its bishop, still bore inscribed upon its seal: *Sancta Colonia Dei gratia Romanae Ecclesiae fidelis filia*. Men might mock the clergy, scorning their prerogatives; yet, as Henri Pirenne rightly observes, 'this secular spirit was linked with a more intense religious fervour.' Having bullied their bishop, townsmen continued to frequent pious confraternities and to multiply charitable foundations, while the most glorious testimony of their youthful vigour was seen in the cathedral.

As years went by their vast increase of wealth gave the cities a new outlook upon life. Business was often their main preoccupation, until materialism contended (sometimes victoriously) with the spirit. In the towns of Italy and Germany, on the eve of that golden age known as the 'Quattrocento,' materialism was much in evidence. The same was true of France, where the towns experienced a rapid decline due to bad management and lack of unity, to internal dissensions between the great burgesses and smaller craftsmen, and to the influence of an all-powerful monarchy. Contrary to what has some-times been alleged, the Church was not hostile to trade, and the arguments of certain canonists, such as Pancapalea of Bologna, who condemned all commercial profit, were never taken literally. The trading class was unreservedly praised by men whose orthodoxy cannot be called in question, e.g. the hermit Honorius of Strasbourg and the preacher Berthold of Ratisbon. Excessive wealth, however, became a source of anxiety to those who proclaimed the Gospel message; and from the beginning of the thirteenth century money was one of the chief pulpit-themes. It was no mere coincidence that the Church's emphasis on poverty, as represented by St Francis, and the establish-ment of the Friars Minor in the cities, was exactly contemporary with plutocratic expansion. But while the 'new leaven' did much to reanimate religious fervour, it was unable to prevent the gradual ascendancy of riches and the consequent growth of materialism.[1]

About the year 1300 tension between the Church and the towns took on a new and graver significance. The bourgeois mind was at the root of that movement which pretended to emancipate the human conscience from faith. The great urban universities revived the study of Roman Law, and thereby furnished arguments against the doctrine of papal sovereignty. They too produced a number of theorists, and even theologians, who taught the independence of temporal affairs. Such were Marsilius of Padua, William of Occam, Peter of Ailly, and the celebrated John Wyclif, who eventually lapsed into heresy.[2] Nor were politics the only subject of discussion in the towns. It is signifi-cant that in 1270 the Bishop of Paris was obliged to condemn certain propositions embodying ideas current in his diocese but incompatible with Christian doctrine upon such matters as the creation of man, the immortality of the soul, free will, and the resurrection of the body. It was in the towns also that there took root a new spirit from which the Church would one day have much to suffer.

10. MONARCHY AND THE CHURCH

At the beginning of the fourteenth century the medieval equilibrium was broken, the primacy of the Holy See was called in question, and the Church's authority defied. The reason for this was not so much the social and psychological transformations of that time as the growth of nationalism, a phenomenon of great importance in the political field. Like all changes that disturb society, it was slow to appear, and we can follow its development in the relations of the Church with various monarchs over a period of three hundred years.

Throughout the barbarian age the Church had been the auxiliary of

---

[1] See the final section of the previous chapter.   [2] See Chapter XIV.

kings; and that is no less true of the troubled days when the Capetians set out on the steep path to glory than of the momentous morning when Clovis was baptized.   The alliance of Church and monarchy in feudal times is among the determining factors of history.   Clerics appealed to the king against baronial oppression, and the system of advocacy [1] gave place to royal patronage.   It was common during the twelfth century for kings to issue letters, declaring that they took such and such a church or abbey under their protection.   This privilege was extended to all churches during the thirteenth century, and was considered by the great Capetian monarchs as entailing the most solemn obligations on their part.

Protection of the Church, however, was only one aspect of a more general function—that of keeping peace.   The Church desired peace, and did her best to secure it.   Realizing that the organic weakness of the central power had been a constant source of disorder throughout the Carolingian decadence, she looked for a strong political regime, a single unit capable of guaranteeing peace.   The kings thought likewise; and when, at a later date, St Louis declared that his mission was to assure the 'tranquillity of order,' in fulfilment of the Beatitude 'Blessed are the peacemakers,' he was only formulating a rule of conduct which had been observed by all his ancestors.   Philip Augustus added the 'Quarantaine-le-roi' to the Church's two pacificatory institutions, 'God's Truce' and 'God's Peace.'

This alliance between Church and monarchy is apparent in the rite of coronation, a ceremony which is said to date back to the kings of Israel, and which had been in use throughout most of Christendom since the eleventh century.   Its three elements are all religious: the *oath*, whereby the prince swears to protect the Church and uphold justice; the *election*, proposed by the archbishop, ratified by the assembled prelates, and then by popular acclamation; and the *anointing*, which confers upon the sovereign his character as elect of God.

In England the royal coronation was even regarded as a sacrament, and one chronicler, known as Anonymous of York, goes so far as to suggest that the king is a member of the clergy!   In France he was supposed to have supernatural powers of healing, especially in cases of scrofula.   The Oriflamme, or royal banner, which appears in history as early as 1100, was an explicit symbol of the monarch's Christian faith; he bore it as 'attorney of St Denis,' and tradition held that it originated either from a legacy of St Peter or from St Martin's cloak.

The French coronation was a magnificent rite to which the Church brought all the pomp at her disposal, and an *Ordo* compiled at Rheims during the reign of St Louis describes the ceremony in detail.   It took

[1] See section 2 of the present chapter.

place on a Sunday in Rheims Cathedral,[1] which was adorned with tapestries, and where a lofty daïs had been erected in the middle of the transept.

On Saturday evening the prince was solemnly received by the chapter, and spent some hours in prayer. Next morning, at dawn, matins, lauds, and prime were sung while the barons and other dignitaries assembled at the main doors. Archbishops and bishops were grouped around the high altar. The prince entered the cathedral at nine o'clock to the sound of pealing bells. A long procession of monks from the abbey of St Remi escorted a canopy beneath which was carried the sacred ampulla said to have been brought from heaven by an angel for the baptism of Clovis; the archbishop received it at the great west door and laid it on the high altar. Mass then began and was celebrated with full liturgical splendour. When the time came for him to take the oath, the king laid his hand upon the Gospels and swore to uphold the rights and observe the laws of Holy Church, to do justice, and to combat heresy. Meanwhile, there had been laid upon the altar the sceptre, the long slender rod of justice, the sword in its sheath, and finally the crown. A little apart from these were laid the silken shoes embroidered with golden fleurs-de-lis together with the violet tunic and cope brought by the Abbot of St Denis from his monastery, where they were carefully preserved. Piece by piece the king was arrayed in his magnificence. The Great Chamberlain tied the silver shoe-strings; the Duke of Burgundy attached the spurs; the archbishop girded him with the sword, which the Constable immediately took and carried unsheathed during the remainder of the ceremony, upright before the king. And now came the most solemn moment. With the point of a golden needle the archbishop took a little chrism from the ampulla, while the king knelt before the altar to receive might from Heaven through the holy oil applied to his forehead, breast, back, shoulders, and elbows. Meantime there was sung the anthem: 'Thus was king Solomon anointed.' Vested now in tunic and cope, almost like a priest, holding the sceptre in his right hand and the staff of justice in his left, he mounted the throne so that the whole people could see and acclaim him, while the archbishop and the peers of the realm together took the crown, and placed it slowly on his brow.

From this alliance with the Church, sealed with liturgical solemnity, the kings derived considerable advantages. The first of these was political: by agreeing to crown the heir during the lifetime of his

---

[1] Sens also claimed this honour, as did Orléans. When Louis VI decided to be crowned at Orléans, the Archbishop of Rheims protested, asserted that Rome had conferred upon him an exclusive right to crown the king; to which Yves of Chartres replied that the *efficacy of the sacrament* (note the expression: the rite is likened to a sacrament) cannot depend on those who administer it.

father, as was done during the first two centuries of the Capetian
dynasty, the Church established that house on foundations such as no
feudal rebellion could undermine.   There were also military benefits,
for the kings enjoyed ecclesiastical support in their struggle with
robber-barons or revolted princes.   Thus in the famous episode of
Castle Puiset the wicked baron Hugues was defeated by the troops of
Louis VI assisted by the local peasantry under their parish priest.
Finally, there were economic considerations: in return for their protection of the Church the kings obtained subsidies which, though at
first occasional, became gradually more regular.   And these were paid
with the approval of the Holy See, which preferred to assist local
monarchs rather than the Empire.

The Church expected those kings who enjoyed her patronage to live
as good Christians, as representatives of God on earth.   There was a
celebrated formula which originated at the Council of Paris in 829 and
was repeated on many subsequent occasions: 'It is the duty of a king to
govern and rule his people with equity and justice, and to see that they
enjoy peace and concord.'   All Christian thinkers from St Bernard to
St Thomas Aquinas lay it down that 'the people does not exist for the
prince, but the prince for the people.'   Later on the poet Eustache
Deschamps (c. 1340–c. 1406) would enumerate the duties of a Christian
king in these words:

> First, he must love God and the Church;
> Let him have a humble heart, pity, and compassion;
> Above all things he must prefer the common good;
> He must hold his people in great affection;
> He must be wise and diligent.
>
> Let him have truth, such must the ruler be.
> Far from punishing the good, he must do them no harm;
> But let him do justice on the wicked,
> So that all goodness may be manifest in him.

Fine principles, indeed.   What if a sovereign failed to abide by them?
Ratione peccati, the Church claimed a right to censure monarchs in
order to recall them to right ways.   The theory of 'Two Swords'
applied to them no less than to the Emperor.

But where did royal wrongdoing begin and end?   In some cases
there could be no doubt, and when the king sinned in his private
capacity he fell under canonical sanctions.   Nor was that uncommon
for many princes treated matrimony in a far from Christian manner
repudiating their wives and remarrying, living in concubinage, or
ignoring the canonical impediments.   There was no royal family that
did not provide examples of this kind, and the list is wellnigh interminable of those who were excommunicated upon such grounds.   Th

principle was quite clear: the Church would punish king and com-
moner alike.   In fact, however, a monarch's guilt involved questions
of private morality and of politics that were inextricably interwoven.
Excommunication for open adultery might drive a whole kingdom into
the camp of those hostile to the Church, and it sometimes happened
that the Pope had to close his eyes to scandal if he wished to avoid so
disastrous a consequence.   The case of Philip Augustus illustrates to
perfection the link between private morality and political interest.

It was not only against the sixth and ninth commandments that
royalty sinned.   A king might be guilty of violence or injustice; what
would the Church do then?   To intervene might be to take sides in
the political game.   Here again the principle was never in doubt.   It
was expressed by Innocent III in unambiguous terms: 'We, whom
divine Providence has entrusted with the government of the Church,
are resolved that neither death nor life shall prevent Us embracing and
upholding justice.'   But when it came to dealing with hard facts, this
doctrine raised a thousand difficulties.   When, for example, the Pope
tried to prevent war between France and England, he considered
himself as acting not by virtue of a feudal right, to exercise which
belonged to the king, but by virtue of a superior duty, that of preventing the misery and injustice which follow in the train of war.   All
the same, ecclesiastical intervention could have political consequences
and provoke political retaliation.   The Church was led almost
inevitably to take a hand in the affairs of kings.   Her quarrels with
them, unlike her struggle with the Empire, were not concerned with
universal primacy; but she often had cause to dispute claims which
they believed legitimate.

Theoretically, the solution in such cases was the doctrine of 'Two
Swords': the Church enjoyed a twofold power, one direct over the
souls of men, the other indirect over their bodies by reason of the sins
which men commit and which the secular arm must punish when
called upon by the spiritual authority.   Many kings, in fact, submitted
to ecclesiastical control in such matters as the fight against heresy.
But their obedience was not so prompt when more mundane interests
were at stake.   Although disagreement with the various kingdoms in
the matter of investiture was less acute than with the Empire, this fact
did not eliminate tension between the papacy and certain monarchs;
for the principles of reform were not welcomed by all rulers with the
same degree of enthusiasm.   During the twelfth and thirteenth centuries the papacy became aware of its own strength; it tended, therefore,
to exert direct pressure on the kings, treating them sometimes as little
better than vassals.   The Pope was virtual head of a federation of
states, or League of Nations, upon which he endeavoured to impose the
rule of Christ for the benefit of Christendom as a whole.   This led, in

H

effect, to the absorption of the feudal system by the Church, culmin
ating in that confusion of spiritual and temporal affairs the inheren
dangers of which we have already seen.   There were cases in which
this theocratic ideal was actually applied.   Kings who felt themselve
imperilled by their neighbours' avarice, or who needed a trump card in
the diplomatic game, were prepared to recognize the Pope as overlord
and to pay him annual tribute, as also were those princes who wishe
for the royal title.   The classic instance was that of Aragon, one o
five small kingdoms manœuvring for power in Spain.[1]   In 1204 King
Pedro II, who had come to Rome for his coronation by Innocent III
laid upon the Apostle's tomb in St Peter's the crown and sceptre he ha
just received, and made what can only be described as a deed of gift to
the Pope.   'I declare this kingdom,' he said, 'tributary to Rome in th
sum of 250 gold pieces payable each year from my treasury to th
Apostolic See; and I swear on behalf of myself and of my successor
that we shall remain your vassals and obedient subjects.'   Severa
kingdoms did homage in analogous terms, and we have already see
the Norman rulers of Sicily employ this means of assuring papa
support against imperial ambitions.   Hungary was almost a replica o
Aragon, in its subjection to the Holy See, its first king, St Stephen
having received his crown from Pope Sylvester.   A papal legate ha
delivered the crown of Bohemia to Ottokar; and Portugal became
kingdom in 1179, when Alexander III conferred the royal dignity o
Alfonso I, the Conqueror, in return for his victories over the Moor
John of England, at war with France and threatened with baroni
unrest, declared that he meant thenceforward to hold his kingdom 'as
vassal of the Pope and of the Roman Church,' and offered to pay th
Holy See an annual tribute of £1,000.   The Latin Empire of Con
stantinople, the kingdoms of Jerusalem, Serbia, and Denmark, togethe
with the dukedom of Poland and a number of lesser states did likewise
while the Pope enjoyed nominal suzerainty even over the distar
kingdom of Kiev.

It is not difficult to understand how dangerous for the Church wa
this 'League of Nations' with the papacy at its head.   As tempor
sovereigns, the popes were involved in all those financial and othe
entanglements which are the lot of rulers; even Sancho I and Alfons
II of Portugal were excommunicated for arrears of tribute.   Nor coul
the Holy See stand aloof from the political differences of its vassal
In England, for example, King John, who had recognized the Sovereig
Pontiff as his overlord, enjoyed the protection of Innocent III.   Force
by his rebellious subjects to sign Magna Carta in 1215, he was sup
ported by Innocent, who condemned the proceedings and rebuke

---

[1] Aragon, whose frontiers marched with those of Languedoc, was half Spanish and h
French.

those prelates who had defied their king. Again, when the barons
and clergy threw off their allegiance and proposed to crown the son of
Philip Augustus, they were excommunicated by Innocent III, who
solemnly forbade the King of France to launch an attack on England.
Nor is it certain that the Pope was influenced in these matters by purely
spiritual motives.

Papal authority was effective only in those states that were relatively
weak or constrained by circumstances to obey. As soon as a monarch
had learned how to keep a firm hold upon his subjects through strong
central government, he thought no more of declaring himself a vassal
of the Holy See. National consciousness began to develop as
monarchy made headway, and did much to undermine the concept of
Christendom as a single unit. The result was increasing tension
between Rome and the leading monarchies, especially England and
France.

The kingdom of England as established by William I had proclaimed
its devotion to the see of Peter in thanksgiving for the moral assistance
rendered by the Church through Hildebrand's good offices in 1066.
But England had never acknowledged the Pope as overlord; and the
Conqueror, while observing the formalities, had used a free hand in
the appointment of bishops. When William II 'Rufus' (1087–1100)
succeeded his father, matters came to a head on the subject of investitures. The new monarch was 'more ferocious and more wicked than
any other man,' and his unblushing simony merited a stern rebuke from
Urban II, of whom he took no notice whatsoever. The champion of
Christian principles in this crisis was St Anselm (1033–1109), a nobleman from the Val d'Aosta. After thirty years as abbot of Bec in
Normandy, he had won such renown by his theological writings as
well as by his remarkable personality that he had been promoted to the
archbishopric of Canterbury in 1093. Anselm withstood Rufus, who
refused to apply the decrees against lay investitures and would not
listen to those timid prelates who urged him to submit. He preferred
exile to surrender; and it was not until Henry I (1100–35) showed better
dispositions than his predecessor that the saintly archbishop consented
to reoccupy his see. The contest between the English monarchy and
the Church reached its climax in the death of St Thomas à Becket, an
event which made so deep an impression on the contemporary mind
that we find it depicted by sculptors and glass-workers in the cathedrals
of Coutances, Sens, Paris, and elsewhere.

With the accession of Henry II in 1154 the Anglo-Norman monarchy
became the most powerful in Europe. Heir to England and Normandy, and, through his father, to Anjou, he married Eleanor of
Aquitaine, divorced wife of Louis VII, who brought him the greater
part of France. He was a heavily built man, broad-shouldered, with a

leonine head and powerful limbs. Tireless, always in the saddle, h
travelled the length and breadth of his dominions. He was also a goo
Christian, heaping wealth and favours on the Church. But he did no
intend that his clergy should escape the policy of absolutism upo
which he had resolved; and being a foreigner who never learned t
speak the English language, it is hard to see how he could have mair
tained a grasp on his enormous territories without some measure o
despotic rule. He subdued the baronage with the help of Thomas
Becket, a man of culture, high intelligence, and subtle pride, a ministe
experienced in business and of unlimited devotion to duty. Appointe
Archbishop of Canterbury by his devoted sovereign, in spite o
ecclesiastical opposition, Becket, the one-time politician, underwent
psychological transformation due to the promptings of divine grac
He was now a churchman, and devoted himself body and soul to th
interests of the Church; henceforward the royal tyranny would hav
no more able or more zealous an opponent. When the king dete
mined to raise a tax on ecclesiastical lands, Becket protested. Whe
he sought to reorganize the administration of criminal justice so as
make the clergy answerable before secular tribunals, the archbishc
would not agree. Henry, enraged, instituted proceedings again
him; but Becket refused to appear, and was declared a felon for h
contumacy. The fearless prelate withdrew to Sens, from which ci
he directed the resistance, devoting himself meanwhile to fasting ar
mortification, feeding his mind upon Holy Scripture and theolog
In 1170 he was given a safe-conduct and returned to England, only
protest once more. Henry II had had his eldest son crowned
defiance of ecclesiastical regulations and tradition. Becket no
excommunicated those prelates who had taken part in the ceremon
and the royal anger knew no bounds. 'What!' exclaimed Henry,
there not one among all these cowards whom I support that will r
me of this wretched priest?' His words proved fatal; for on 29
December the archbishop was set upon in his cathedral by a band
ruffians and brutally murdered. Disgusted with himself, and conscio
of the growing horror at his deed, the king hurried to meet the legat
who were on their way to inform him of his excommunication. F
met them at Avranches, humbled himself before them, and did pub
penance. The same day it was learned that his army had won
victory in Scotland, and men concluded that the martyr had forgiv
him; but the Church had scored.[1]

She scored again fifty years later when King John attempted a poli
of despotism which he had no means to support. He launched viole
attacks upon the Church, forcing the Archbishop of York into exile f

---

[1] We may compare the martyrdom of St Thomas à Becket with that of St Stanislaus
Cracow, who fell victim to Boleslav II of Poland in 1079.

efusal to pay a subsidy, declining to recognize Stephen Langton who
had been appointed to the see of Canterbury at Innocent III's request,
and even confiscating the temporalities of the English clergy. But
these measures ended in disaster; for the prelates, uniting with the
barons in a revolt which ended at Runnymede, obliged him to give
way. John planned to escape from his predicament by declaring
himself a vassal of the Holy See; but this act of submission was short-
lived, and the English never took it seriously. Henry III (1216–72)
maintained a close alliance with the Church as a counterpoise to
baronial influence; but his successor, Edward I, would admit of no
dependence upon Rome, and by 1300 the English monarchy had
become no less secular than the French.

The Church had lent the full weight of her support to the Capetian
kings, who, though they were not all of St Louis's calibre, were without
exception convinced and practising Christians. Yet it was in France
that the problem of relations between Church and State was most
acute. French history is darkened by no tragic drama such as that of
Becket. Nevertheless, it was in France that the monarchy became
most keenly conscious of its political independence. This is a remarkable fact when we consider the importance of Capetian France in
medieval Christendom; nor is it without reason that we use the word
'Gallicanism' to describe theories and practices which tended to limit
the papal authority in several countries.

France had shown herself friendly towards the popes, who had
always found a refuge in French territory when driven from Rome.
Many French theologians, from St Bernard onwards, had upheld the
papal primacy; and this was unanimously recognized by the French
prelates assembled in the Council of Lyons (1274). The French
people, too, had been most generous in their support of the crusades.
On the other hand, as the Capetian kings awoke to their increasing
strength, they became progressively hostile to papal interference.

Their desire for independence is shown by numerous events. The
first Capetian to become conscious of his power was Louis VI (1108–
1137). He was a good Christian, and heaped privileges upon the
Church; but he kept a close watch upon bishops and abbots, intervened
in ecclesiastical appointments, and never lost an opportunity to prove
himself master in his own house. Thus, when his friend Suger was
elected abbot by the community of St Denis without reference to
himself, Louis imprisoned those monks who brought him the news.
When Calixtus II claimed that the Archbishop of Lyons (which was at
that time an imperial city) was primate of all Gaul and had rights over
the Church at Sens (to which Paris was subject), Louis protested and
gained his point. Strange as it may seem, we find the same independent spirit in Louis IX, the holiest of kings. That great Christian

did not hesitate to speak his mind to the Curia upon excessive increases of ecclesiastical taxation; he allowed his bishops to air similar grievances against the papal exchequer, and would permit no interference from Rome with his own policies. He withheld assistance from Innocent IV when the latter joined issue with Frederick II; and although he pressed for the release of some French cardinals who had fallen into Frederick's hands, he made no move to join in the celebration of that Emperor's defeat.

St Louis, in fact, was a true scion of his grandfather, Philip Augustus (1180–1223), who, in the course of a long and acrimonious dispute, had clarified the principles governing relations between the French crown and the papacy. This man of steel, in whom a high sense of his royal duties was allied with somewhat unscrupulous ambition, had conceived a notion that was later formulated by French jurists: 'The King of France is Emperor in his own dominions.' Good Christian though he was, he would not be ruled by clergymen. The quarrel between Philip Augustus and Innocent III was further complicated by the monarch's private life, which fell under ecclesiastical censure. In 1193 Philip had married Ingeborg of Denmark, but quickly divorced her for reasons which did not entitle him to remarry. Immediately after the accession of Innocent III he received this stern note from the Lateran: 'The royal dignity cannot take precedence of Christian duties and in this matter it is impossible for us to distinguish between a prince and his subjects. If, contrary to our hopes, the King of France ignores our present warning, we shall be obliged, in spite of ourselves, to raise our apostolic hand.' The Pope's position was unassailable. The king refused to put away his 'second wife,' and Innocent laid France under an interdict. But the extent to which the royal strength had developed is shown by the fact that a majority of bishops ventured to disobey the Pope and formed a solid bloc around the throne, while those who carried out the papal instructions suffered loss of property. Here, then, although the Pope was indubitably right, the king had scored a diplomatic victory.

The problem became still more involved when the issue was one of public morality. Following the capture of Jerusalem by Saladin Clement III called for a crusade, and Philip seized this golden opportunity for an attack on England. The Pope intervened with threats of a new interdict, to which the French King replied: 'The Roman Church has no business to impose censures when the king chastises a rebellious vassal. The legate no doubt smells English sterling. . . I do not fear your sentence; it is unjust.' And there for the time being matters were allowed to rest. But when, in 1203, Innocent resolved to terminate the Anglo-French affair at any cost, the royal answer was more forcible than ever: Philip required of all his barons an oath to support him, *even against the Pope*, and took his stand upon the principle that 'in feudal matters, the king is not bound to take instructions from the Holy See; the Pope should not interfere in disputes between sovereign rulers.' Innocent III forthwith replied that he had nothing to say from the feudal standpoint; but *ratione peccati* his jurisdiction was absolute, and he had a right to condemn war between Christians. Notwithstanding his strength, he could not bring his adversary to heel; and John 'Lackland' was deprived of Normandy, Anjou, and Touraine. The claims of the monarch prevailed over those of the Pope, for spiritual and temporal interests were so closely linked that the former were at an inevitable disadvantage. Innocent III failed to overcome the French king's resistance: Ingeborg remained a prisoner, while Philip protested against the election of Otto IV, and accepted on his son's behalf the crown of England.

In this way the interests of Church and State drifted farther apart. The breach opened by Philip Augustus in the majestic edifice of the papacy grew ever wider until, in the next century, Philip the Fair tore down a whole wall. The irresistible current of history dissolved the feudal mass, transforming it into a number of centralized monarchies which could develop only by means of a proud self-assertion. Meanwhile, the secular ideal of Christendom as a theocratic Utopia had involved the popes so deeply in political disputes that the Holy See was correspondingly affected by this universal tide of change. In order to defeat the Emperors, Rome had had to rely upon the youthful vigour of new-born kingdoms; but these same kingdoms had rapidly become 'as a reed that wounds the hand that grasps it.' By confusing (though from the highest motives) its spiritual function with the exercise of earthly power, the papacy may be said to have betrayed its mission. Its future was undoubtedly compromised.

CHAPTER VI

A SOCIETY WITHIN SOCIETY

1. A State without Frontiers or an Army

WE have watched the Church engage in bitter struggles, waging war, sealing alliances, and taking her place at the head of a 'League of Nations.' It may therefore be asked, was she herself a State? By virtue of her territorial possessions, yes.[1] True, she was a State without frontiers, a State unarmed amid the most military of societies; but she could still command the obedience of warriors. The members of this State were not unlike the rest of men. They were of equal birth; and their dress at that period differed little from that of laymen, except during Mass and other liturgical ceremonies. The clergy, however, though part and parcel of medieval society, was clearly distinguishable therefrom.

It was distinguished in the first place by its sacred character and peculiar function. Next, it formed a learned hierarchy, firm but flexible, and governed by clearly defined principles. Again, it was international; 'the class that prays' became a veritable super-State. Above all, its purpose was neither temporal dominion nor the securing of man's temporal happiness; but because of the confidence it enjoyed, and because of its reasonable approach to human problems, it excelled in the art of government and made its authority not only acceptable to, but even loved by, mankind at large.

The medieval Church had many faults, but during the eleventh century she evolved that harmony and that enduring system of government which we admire in the thirteenth. Her methods and institutions came into being under pressure of events; but when compared with other political systems of that age, she appears always in advance of the time. Though guided by supernatural principles, her management of affairs was remarkably practical and realistic.

[1] See the preceding chapter. The States of the Church involved her in many difficulties; but at that time temporal power was considered indispensable, and until the organization of their financial system in the thirteenth century, the popes derived therefrom the chief part of their revenue (see section 10). Innocent III tried to form this State into a single barrier stretching from the Tyrrhenian Sea to the Adriatic. Its elements were disparate: the Patrimony of St Peter, the Plain of Perugia, the March of Ancona, and the Romagna, all given by the Carolingians; then there were Tuscany and territories north of the Apennines bequeathed by the Countess Matilda in 1155.

2. ENLISTMENT OF THE CLERGY

The medieval clergy represented a far larger proportion of the total population than is now the case. They were perhaps ten times as numerous. This fact must be constantly borne in mind; it was partly due to unanimity of faith, but there were other causes. The Church attracted innumerable vocations because her function was so highly esteemed, apart from the fact that men in holy orders enjoyed many privileges. There was no problem of vocations. Candidates for the priesthood were plentiful; chapters were never below strength; and the smallest parish had its vicar, often assisted by several curates. This great stream of aspirants naturally contained elements of unequal value, but there was abundant material from which to choose. Those who could not hope for military command gravitated towards the Church.

The regular clergy were particularly numerous, and formed a *corps d'élite* upon whom the Church mainly relied. The growth of the monastic orders is wellnigh incredible. Thus, in the year 1100, Cluny, which had been founded in the tenth century, numbered 10,000 monks in 1,450 houses, most of them in France and the remainder scattered throughout western Europe. The Cistercians founded 348 monasteries within a period of fifty years; nor does St Bernard's biographer exaggerate in describing the great abbot as '. . . a terror to mothers and wives, for, wherever he spoke, husbands and sons embraced the religious life.' When St Francis and St Dominic invited men to follow in Christ's footsteps, they were heard with no less enthusiasm. In 1316 the Franciscans had 1,400 houses and more than 30,000 religious; the Dominicans, in 1303, had 600 houses and 10,000 friars. Other Orders were almost as flourishing. Furthermore, congregations which admitted lay brothers (lay monks not destined for the priesthood but bound by the threefold vow of chastity, obedience, and stability) received crowds of postulants. These *conversi*, or 'bearded brethren,' relieved the choir-monks of material duties and external business. Oblates, too, were numerous. They were semi-seculars, better educated than the lay brethren, living as it were on the outskirts of the community and taking part in the divine office. Religious houses, in fact, though sometimes below standard, were unfailing nurseries whence the Church drew many of her greatest rulers.

From what class of society did the clergy spring? From every class without exception. Intelligence, study, and practice of the virtues could lead anyone at all to the highest offices in the Church, thus ensuring the continuity of culture which is necessary for the life of any society but is seldom found in worn-out civilizations. The famous

H*

Carolingian Archbishop Adalberon had expressed the principle in these words: 'Divine law admits of no distinction of rank or birth; before God, the son of a labourer is not inferior to a monarch's heir.' True, the Church was an aristocratic society, a monarchical organization; but she recruited her clergy on a democratic basis, reviving herself unceasingly at the living springs of the people. Here are some examples. Suger, abbot of St Denis, was the son of a serf; Maurice de Sully, the Bishop of Paris who built Notre-Dame, was the son of a beggar; St Peter Damian, a future cardinal, had been a swineherd, as had Bishop Wazon of Liége. More remarkable still is the list of those who occupied the papal throne: Gregory VII, son of a carpenter; Benedict XII, son of a butcher; Urban IV, son of a cobbler; Benedict XI, son of a goatherd; not to mention others such as Urban II and Adrian IV whose origin is most obscure.

The Church, therefore, enabled each and all of her sons to be revenged upon the accidents of birth and fortune, attracting to herself the finest elements in society. She was, indeed, no 'closed shop'; but that does not mean to say that there were no ties of affection and mutual interest, no 'class-spirit,' among the clergy. All those ecclesiastical dignitaries who took part in political life, who built the cathedrals, who led the masses on pilgrimage or crusade, all were conscious of belonging to a ruling caste. They held together, forming within each State a spiritual unit isolated from, and not seldom opposed to, the feudal world. They also secured places for their friends; thus Eudes of Paris had Aubry de Humbert appointed to the see of Rheims, and Hervé to that of Troyes. The clerical vocation, too, sometimes ran in families; thus Peter of Nemours had three brothers who were respectively bishops of Meaux, Noyon, and Chalon.

The bishops and abbots, as leaders and administrators, were the main sources of ecclesiastical influence; but they were by no means the only workers in that field. Priests and monks occupied situations of every kind—as statesmen, civil servants, diplomats, professors, warrior-chiefs when need arose, and spiritual advisers to the barons on crusade. Not even monks were wholly separated from the world. For monachism had roots throughout society, to which it rendered service in exchange for men; and when God's interest required, as in the case of St Bernard, a monk might be granted leave of absence from his monastery.

The Church, then, was incarnate in society. We do not deny that 'clericalism' of this sort had defects, that the counter-influence of laymen upon the clergy was detrimental to the latter. But the activity of the Church cannot be ignored if we would understand medieval institutions as a part of history, if we would explain the beneficent influence of Christian principles in every walk of life.

3. The Head of the Church

At the head of the clergy stood the Pope, common Father of all the faithful. During the three great centuries of the Middle Ages the Church tended more and more to organize herself upon the pattern of a strongly centralized monarchy, with her own government, local executives, inspectors, and diplomats. The papacy, though criticized and abused in the game of politics, continued to increase in stature.

By whom was the Pope elected? After the decree of Nicholas II, in 1059, by the cardinals. This word 'cardinal,' already of great antiquity in the Church, was used at first somewhat vaguely to designate those clergy who were so to speak the hinge (*cardo*) of the Church. To 'incardinate' a cleric to a church was to fix him to it like a hinge to a door. In the course of the tenth century the word took on the more general sense of 'principal' or 'very important,' and was applied to ecclesiastics of high rank—archbishops or patriarchs of various sees. It was at Rome, however, that the 'cardinal clergy' attained supreme importance and became associated with the ancient glory of Peter's city. The cardinal-bishops were the 'suburbican' bishops of seven dioceses around the capital, of which the farthest, Palestrina, was less than fifty miles from the Lateran. The cardinal-priests were rectors of the chief parishes in Rome; they also served the basilicas of St Peter, St Paul outside the Walls, and St Laurence. Finally, the cardinal-deacons claimed to represent the regional deacons who had once administered the seven wards of the City, but their number had already exceeded this traditional figure. Altogether, the College of Cardinals consisted in the thirteenth century of fifty-three members: seven bishops, twenty-eight priests, and eighteen deacons. Alexander III was the first to confer the title of cardinal upon foreigners, appointing them to real or fictitious duties in the Roman Church.

The importance of the cardinals gradually increased. Not only was it their duty to elect the Pope, but they formed a sort of Council, or Senate, of the Church. By the end of the eleventh century cardinal-bishops took precedence of all other bishops; and at the two Councils of Lyons, in 1245 and 1274, even cardinal-priests and deacons enjoyed this privilege. In 1245 Innocent IV conferred a red hat upon his legates, and this was slowly adopted by all cardinals.[1] 'Pillars of the Church' and 'Successors of the Apostles' became current terms denoting these high dignitaries.

---

[1] The red robes were not introduced before the pontificate of Paul II (1464–71), nor the title 'Eminence' before that of Urban VIII (1630). Cardinals belonging to religious orders continued to wear their habits, and it was only in the reign of Gregory XIII 1572–85) that they were authorized to wear cardinalatial insignia.

Curious to relate, the solemnities of the Conclave have an almost comic origin. Though entrusted with the papal election, it sometimes happened that the cardinals could not make up their minds; and the decree of Alexander III (1179) requiring a two-thirds majority made their choice still more difficult. Between 1241 and 1305 the papal throne was vacant for a total period of ten years. After the death of Clement IV, in 1268, the Princes of the Church deliberated for seventeen months without result. They were then shut up in the palace at Viterbo, where their meetings were held; but as they were still undecided at the end of two years, the mob rushed the palace one pouring wet day, and tore off the roof in hopes that the rain might bring them to their senses. At the same time, a semi-ultimatum from St Louis called upon them to make a choice. They elected St Gregory X, who, in order to prevent a repetition of the scandal, caused the second Council of Lyons (1274) to make strict rules governing the election. It was decreed that within ten days of the Pope's death the cardinals should assemble at the papal palace, each accompanied by one servant only, and should not leave until they had given Peter a successor. Inside, there was to be a single 'conclave' where all would live together. The door was to remain closed, and none might go out on pain of excommunication. If there were no election at the end of three days, the cardinals would be entitled to no more than one meal a day for five days, after which they were to subsist on bread and water. Except for the restrictions on food, and a somewhat longer period to allow for the arrival of foreign cardinals, this canon of 1274 is still in force.

These rules show to what humiliation the papacy at that time might be exposed, but in no way detract from its greatness. The popes were threatened, insulted, exiled, and even imprisoned; but they had so strong a sense of the dignity of their exalted position that even their enemies were conscious of it. We have heard Gregory VII assert that 'the Pope is the only man whose foot all peoples should kiss,' and his statement was accepted more or less throughout the Middle Ages.

A pontificate was certainly a splendid episode when he who sat upon the throne of Peter was one such as Gregory VII or Innocent III. Ever anxious for God's glory and the good of souls, the Pope watched over the universal Church both as ruler and as father. He wished to see all, to know all, and to do all. By summoning bishops and abbots to his presence, often from far away, he kept himself informed upon men and affairs. An enormous correspondence flowed from his chancellery, ranging from affairs of the highest importance to the smallest details. His chosen legates made known his views and saw that his instructions were carried out. Firm but cautious, he knew how to restrain their ardour as well as how to fire their zeal. He attended also to administrative, diplomatic, and even military business; he was the life of the whole Church. Meanwhile, he renewed his strength at the deep wells of prayer and contemplation, for the greatest of the medieval popes were saints.

The authority of such a pope was almost unlimited. Subject to Holy Scripture and conciliar decrees, he was absolute sovereign in the realm of dogma and of discipline. Papal infallibility was not yet an article of faith, but it was in fact admitted. 'The Roman Church cannot err, and Scripture bears witness that it will never do so.' This formula of Gregory VII, to which we have already alluded, is precisely that of Pope Hormisdas in 516. St Thomas bases the infallibility on Luke xxii. 32, in which our Lord tells Peter: 'I have prayed for thee that thy faith fail not, and do thou in turn strengthen the faith of thy brethren.' He also quotes 1 Corinthians i. 10, where St Paul requires unity of faith, a unity of which the Pope is both guardian and measure. To rebel against him, therefore, is to rebel against God and deserve terrible chastisement. Thus, all those rulers, except Frederick II, who opposed the Pope, made clear that their action was directed not against the papal authority as such, but against a man; they pretended to show him up as a bad pope.

Let us now take a look at some of the main points in the growth of papal power. An oath of canonical obedience was exacted by Gregory VI from certain prelates with a view to the reform. It was imposed on all metropolitans by Gregory IX, and extended to all bishops by Martin IV. The right of confirming episcopal nominations, which was already reserved to metropolitans, belonged henceforward to the Pope, who often himself appointed *motu proprio* the titulars of dioceses and exempt' abbeys. Canonization, which was formerly done by the bishops at their own discretion, was reserved to the Pope by Alexander II in 1170. Authentication of relics was also reserved to Rome. Absolution from certain grave sins, e.g. the sack of churches, fraternizing with excommunicated persons, and forgery of papal documents, belonged exclusively to the Pope. We shall have something to say later on about his right to hear appeals.

The Sovereign Pontiff's dignity was emphasized by numerous external signs. It is true that in official acts proceeding from his chancellery he took the lowly title 'Servant of the servants of God'; but he often referred to himself more proudly as 'Vicar of St Peter' or 'Vicar of Jesus Christ.' The form of address 'Holy Father' was common; likewise 'Your Holiness,' borrowed from the imperial liturgies of the East.

He did not yet wear the white soutane,[1] but he already had the *tiara*,

[1] This dates from the pontificate of Pius V (1566–72), who was a Dominican and retained the white robe of the Friars Preachers.

a special kind of mitre which distinguished him from other bishops. It was probably Nicholas II who to the lower rim of the *frigium* or *camelaucum*, which he wore in common with all persons of high rank at Rome, added a golden crown as symbol of his sovereign power. At the beginning of the fourteenth century Boniface VIII added a second crown, and one of the Avignon Popes—Clement V or Benedict XII— a third. Thereafter it was claimed that these three crowns represent papal sovereignty over the Church militant, suffering, and triumphant. Besides the tiara, the Pope had various liturgical ornaments peculiar to himself. Such was the *subcingulum*, a kind of maniple marked with three crosses and suspended from the girdle. On his right hand he wore the Fisherman's Ring, the stone of which was engraved with an image of St Peter casting his nets. When he celebrated pontifical High Mass, the ceremonial, though distinct and splendid, was not so magnificent as that introduced during the Renaissance, and which is still in use to-day. His audiences were already governed by strict etiquette: it was customary for all visitors, even royalty, to kiss his hand or the hem of his robe; and when he was on horseback the most exalted of the princes present held his stirrup and led his mount.

The papal residence was worthy of its occupant. This was the Lateran, where the popes had lived since the beginning of the fourth century. The Emperor Constantine or his second wife Fausta presented them with the ancient house of the Laterani, which had long since been taken from its owners by Nero's exchequer; and the papacy had for so long been associated with the place that its possession was looked upon as tangible proof of legitimate election. It was a splendid and well-planned group of buildings, comprising the palace, the basilica, and the baptistery with its enormous hall of five apses where councils met. There was also a priceless collection of relics, including memorials of the Old Testament, and the *Scala Sancta*, a staircase which was claimed to be that of Pilate's praetorium, the very staircase which Jesus had ascended to His trial.

Outside the city [1] stood St Peter's, built over the tomb or 'Confession' of the Apostle, on the spot where he confessed his faith by martyrdom. St Peter's was also the basilica of Constantine, with its 'quadri-portico' beneath which lay so many popes, its glorious apsidal mosaic, and its twelve twisted columns adorned with vine and supporting the *pergula* or rood loft. The church was crowded with so many small sanctuaries, altars, and tombs that the whole formed a picturesque medley quite unlike the orderliness of St Peter's to-day. Near by, on the site of some modest houses erected by Pope Symmachus about the year 500, and rebuilt in 800 for Charlemagne, Innocent III raised a palace standing amid gardens. This was the

[1] The Lateran was within the Aurelian wall.

Vatican, where his successors preferred to live until their departure for Avignon.

The government of the Church necessitated a great number of departments, for the weight of business steadily increased. There was the examination of candidates for ecclesiastical dignities, there were appeals to be heard, there was the drafting of Bulls and other papal documents, besides a host of miscellaneous matters in which the Pope's intervention had been requested. Together, these numerous departments formed the *Curia*. The consistories, which replaced annual synods formerly held in Rome at the beginning of Lent, consisted of cardinals, whose duty it was to keep the Pope informed and to assist him with their advice. In turn, he revealed his plans to the consistory, and notified them of his principal appointments, especially of nominations to the Sacred College.

The most important office in the Curia was the *chancellery*, which dealt with all the most vital affairs of Christendom. From the beginning of the thirteenth century it was directed by a chancellor and vice-chancellor, who were assisted by notaries charged with the drawing up of Acts, and by subordinate officials both clerical and lay. The chancellery was divided into four offices: (1) 'Minutes,' where the schema or draft of the Act was prepared; (2) 'Engrossment,' where the original document was written; (3) 'Registers,' where a copy was taken in order to keep a record of everything that went out; and lastly (4) 'Bulls,' where the seal (*bulla*) was affixed. This seal was a disk of lead marked on one side with the Pontiff's name between the arms of a cross, and on the other with images of St Peter and St Paul. Extraordinary care was taken to guarantee the authenticity of papal documents; their drafting and presentation was in itself an art and a tradition. The formulae varied according to the type and purpose of each; the style was metrical, rhythmic, sometimes almost poetic; and there were rules governing the manner of dating, of affixing the seal, and of choosing the ribbons to which it was attached. He was a devilish clever forger who could imitate such models, but it was quite often managed. The rules of the papal diplomatic service were copied by all the chancelleries of Europe. No state, except England, had such well-preserved archives, and none, of course, were of such universal application.

To provide for the execution of its orders and to control the bishops, Rome employed the services of legates. This idea, which was borrowed from the Carolingian *Missi Dominici*, had begun to take shape in the Gregorian period. St Peter Damian, Cardinal Humbert, and Hildebrand had all sent out 'legations' to settle particular affairs. After his election to the papacy, Hildebrand extended and improved the system. Hitherto the appointment of legates had been temporary, and the popes continued in certain cases to entrust a special envoy with the delivery of instructions.   These *Legati Apostolicae Sedis* or *Legati Sanctae Romanae Ecclesiae* were vested with superior authority during their mission; their powers superseded all others; and they had the right of deposing bishops, even though they themselves were simple priests or monks.

Notwithstanding, however, the importance of their function, temporary legates could not achieve lasting results, for the very nature of their appointment made their presence in any one place short-lived. Gregory VII, therefore, decided to make some of them permanent; and in this way the legate became the Pope's personal representative or ambassador in a particular locality.   Very often he took the archiepiscopal title of the country wherein his duties lay; and in many cases it was the result of this procedure that an archbishopric attained 'primacy,' an ancient dignity which had more or less fallen into disuse. Thus Gregory VII's Grand Legate became 'Primate of the Gauls'; while Urban II conferred the primacy of Belgium on the Archbishop of Rheims, and that of Narbonnais on the titular of Narbonne.   The Archbishop of Canterbury was created primate of England, and the Archbishop of Salerno primate of southern Italy.   There was no question of a mere honorary title, but of real jurisdiction; and the Archbishop of Aix was sternly rebuked for having shown too little *obedience* and *reverence* towards his primate.

Naturally, the appointment of a permanent legate, especially if he became a primate also, was not to everybody's taste.   Protests were frequent; and the letter sent in 1078 by the clergy of Cambrai to those of Rheims is nothing less than an indictment charging the legates with aiming at personal despotism, with tyrannical behaviour, with corruption, and with disrespect for venerable diocesan customs.   But if centralization tended to destroy the fruitful variety of the Christian world, it enlarged the Pope's sphere of action and strengthened his authority.

Nor were the clergy alone in their experience of papal jurisdiction. Legates, like modern 'nuncios,' were sent to kings; papal ambassadors were attached to the imperial court, to those of England and of France, but above all to those realms which recognized the suzerainty of the Holy See.   Here the legates exercised enormous power, claiming, and often obtaining, 'Peter's Pence.'   No other sovereign at this period controlled such efficient means of government.

4. OECUMENICAL COUNCILS, THE ASSIZES OF CHRISTENDOM

We may now ask whether the Pope's authority was restricted by those assemblies which formed the assizes of Christendom and which are known as oecumenical councils.   No.   Theories which were later described as 'conciliar,' and which maintained that councils are superior to the Pope, were first put forward by William of Occam at the beginning of the fourteenth century. From the eleventh to the thirteenth century there were isolated cases of resistance to papal authority, but these never amounted to doctrinal disputes.

An oecumenical council was always summoned by the Pope; and he did so only when he felt the need of support from the whole Church in determining some point of dogma or in taking some grave decision. The careful preparation of agenda, and not seldom the drafting of 'canons' which the fathers of the council would have to approve, was done by the Curia. The Sovereign Pontiff presided over sessions with all the pomp of Roman ceremonial. The council appears to a large extent as a consultative chamber rather than as a parliament giving expression to its will. At the same time, there are no grounds for treating this fact as an instance of unjustifiable authoritarianism. for the council was almost always in full agreement with the Pope upon essentials, and no one disputed his *de facto* authority.

The traditional list of oecumenical councils includes no more than twenty since the foundation of the Church, and seven of these were held during the Middle Ages. The Lateran Council convoked by Innocent III in 1215 is considered as the twelfth. The first eight were common to the Eastern and Western Churches, but after the ninth, in 1123, the Orientals ceased to take part. Moreover, while these assemblies were 'oecumenical' in principle, the number of delegates who attended them varied enormously. In 1215 more than 3,000 clerics of all ranks and nationalities met at the Lateran, but at the Council of Lyons in 1245, which was part of the war against Frederick II, there were only three patriarchs, 140 bishops (most of whom were French or English), and a few hundred priests and monks. Any pope who summoned a council when in difficulty had far less chance of welcoming large numbers than had a strong pope who was feared and respected by all.

We may say, then, that the typical general council, the supreme assembly of the Middle Ages, was that of the Lateran in 1215, which marked the zenith of Innocent's pontificate. On 19th April 1214 the Pope sent invitations to all patriarchs, archbishops, bishops, abbots, princes, and kings throughout the Christian world, asking them to meet at Rome on 1st November 1215. The delay of eighteen months allowed between the convocation and the assembly is significant: no pains were spared in preparation, and no one could excuse his absence. The Pope had also given strict orders regarding attendance at the council: only two prelates in each province might remain at home to deal with urgent business, and even they would have to send representatives. The same applied to chapters and religious congregations. Apart from these cases, no excuse would be accepted; and the

Archbishop of Lund in Denmark, who tried to evade his obligation, was quickly called to order.

The early autumn of 1215, therefore, found all Christian Europe on the road to Rome. Four hundred and twelve bishops answered the papal summons. Eight hundred abbots and priors were likewise on their way—the whole of Western monachism. The secular powers were also present in this assembly of Christendom, represented by ambassadors chosen from among princes of the blood. The Latin Emperor of Constantinople, the Kings of Germany, France, England, Jerusalem, Aragon, Portugal, and Hungary each sent the highest member of his entourage. Many barons came in person. Among these was the Count of Toulouse, for the Albigensian affair was on the agenda. From the East, there were only three or four hundred Greek bishops, but the magnificent delegations from Poland and Dalmatia proclaimed the attachment of those countries to the Church. As for the clergy of subordinate rank, there were at least three thousand.

The opening session on 11th November may be imagined. The basilica of St John Lateran proved too small to hold the crowd; and when Innocent III appeared he was greeted with a tremendous and prolonged ovation. In the presence of Christendom gathered in that place the great Pope seemed to embody the supremacy of Mother Church over all other powers. Business was concluded in three public sessions, on 11th, 20th, and 30th November; for the debates had been so well prepared that there was no long-drawn-out discussion. The fathers voted with exemplary dispatch and in accordance with the Pope's wishes upon the liberation of the Holy Land, upon the reform of morals, upon the Albigensian affair, and upon many more thorny questions. Between times, a number of smaller groups were at work on the seventy canons for approval in solemn session. The twelfth oecumenical council, in fact, was a striking manifestation of the Church's unity, and set its seal upon the glory of the papacy.

5. Bishops and Dioceses

The regional organization of the Church had rested from the very beginning upon a fundamental unit which was both spiritual and administrative. This was the church, a community of persons governed by a bishop and afterwards identified with a distinct geographical area. Long before the barbarian invasions, the bishop was a man consecrated to rule a given territory corresponding to the Roman *civitas*. In fact, the bishop's authority was almost always associated with a city or town behind whose ramparts he had his cathedral and his palace, the seat of his administration. But as Christianity penetrated the countryside, and rural parishes grew up, his authority became more extensive by the addition of a country 'suburb.' During the tenth century the region included within a bishop's jurisdiction came to be known as a 'diocese,' an imperial administrative term which has survived until to-day.

Dioceses varied greatly in importance, and first as to their dimensions. That of Nantes, for example, covered 3,800 square miles as against Laon with 965 square miles in the same province; nor can the diocese of Bourges with 9,290 square miles be compared with that of Orange, which included no more than 168 square miles.[1] Numbers also varied, not only in relation to area, but also according to density of population. In Normandy there were about thirty people to a square mile, but at least sixty in Flanders. Hence there were dioceses large and small, rich and poor; that meant to say there were differences of 'kudos' among the bishops, which personal merits might lessen but never eliminate.[2]

But whether his diocese were large or small, rich or poor, the bishop always enjoyed great prestige, and exerted considerable influence. He spoke as an equal of the greatest barons, who generally respected him no less than did the common people. His cathedral was the church of his 'cathedra' or chair; and as he mounted the steps of his throne, the crowd beheld a splendid figure. He wore an alb of fine linen, a stole fringed with gold, embroidered dalmatic and chasuble, and, on his head, the tall pointed mitre as seen in the sculptures at Chartres. His left hand grasped the crozier, while the right, adorned with a golden ring, was raised in benediction. If he were an archbishop, or a bishop specially favoured by the Holy See, there hung on his breast the pallium.

The bishop's powers were extensive, embracing those of order and of jurisdiction. It was he who conferred major orders and the sacrament of confirmation. As a rule, it was he who consecrated every new bishop, who blessed new abbots and abbesses, who consecrated the oil and chrism, who blessed bells, sacred ornaments, new churches, and cemeteries. He possessed administrative and judicial powers over his clergy, and could even degrade them for serious faults. Directly or indirectly he supervised education; charitable works were subject to his control; and his was the last word in all matters concerning faith and morals.

Over the bishop there was generally a metropolitan archbishop (France had eighteen of them) who had jurisdiction over his 'suffragans,' i.e. the bishops in his province. Since the Carolingian epoch, however, the powers of metropolitans had steadily decreased, and they

[1] See the interesting paper read to the International Congress of Historical Sciences in 1950 by J. de Font-Réaulx on the 'Comparative Structure of a Diocese in the thirteenth and fourteenth centuries,' and published in the *Revue d'histoire de l'Eglise de France* (July–December, 1952).

[2] Hence the curious proverb *Blé vaut mieux que sac* (Bayeux, Lisieux, and Évreux are worth more than Séez, Avranche, and Coutances).

continued to do so until the sixteenth century, when the Council of Trent virtually abolished them.   If they confirmed the appointment of and consecrated their suffragans, it was by virtue of ancient custom rather than by right; and their visitations of all dioceses in their province were, with certain exceptions,[1] chiefly a matter of etiquette. They continued to act as judges of second instance, before an appeal to Rome, and they retained the right to preside over provincial councils; but this did not amount to much.   The pyramidal notion of the Church, so dear to Boniface VIII and some of his contemporaries, did not last.   Notwithstanding the respect accorded to a bishop, he can hardly be said to have preserved the importance, the freedom, or the means of action that he once enjoyed.   The formula *Ecclesia in episcopo* was certainly not as true in, say, 1200 as it had been in 400 or 600.   The extension and centralization of papal government brought about the decline of episcopal authority; so that the bishops, even when they were not primates or legates, gradually became representatives of the Pope in their own dioceses.   Rome's ascendancy over the episcopate is particularly noticeable with regard to the choice of bishops and the conferment of benefices attached to the see.

The whole purpose of the Church in her quarrel over investiture was to deprive laymen of their right to nominate bishops.   Would she return to the ancient method of election in which the canons of the chapter, the monks of the diocese, and the people all took part?   The Council of Lyons in 1245 entrusted elections to the chapters alone; but in point of fact the canons were not always in a position to nominate their bishop, for the Pope reserved the right to decide a candidate's merits and to regulate the election.   Bishops were often elected 'by the grace of God and of the Apostolic See.'   When the chapter was unable to choose between several candidates, the matter was settled by an appeal to Rome; and the Council of Lyons in 1274 stated that the number of these appeals was 'inconceivable.'   Since a bishop-elect frequently sought consecration not from his metropolitan but from the Sovereign Pontiff,[2] it is not difficult to estimate the extent of papal influence in the dioceses.   Such influence reached its climax in Castile, where Alfonso X recognized the Pope's exorbitant claim to depose and reinstate bishops, and also to annul an election 'even when the chosen candidate was worthy.'

Again, the ceaseless flow of events drove the papacy to claim (and

---

[1] See the observations of Cardinal Baudrillart in his Introduction to M. Andrieu-Guitrancourt's *L'archevêque Eudes Rigaud et la Vie de l'Église au XIIIᵉ siècle.* Eudes Rigaud, archbishop of Rouen, made several visitations of every diocese in his province, and kept a close watch on the administration of his suffragans.

[2] It was at this period that there grew up the custom of journeys *ad limina* by newly elected bishops.   The Pope wished to make his acquaintance in person; and if that were not possible, he desired a representative to come and do him homage.

not seldom to obtain) the right to dispose of benefices at its sole discretion. Either to reward some faithful servant, or to please a monarch, the Pope would grant the revenues of an ecclesiastical charge by appointing the titular. This practice began on a modest scale with Innocent II; it was a good deal more common under Alexander III and Innocent III, and many a clerk of the chancellery or other Roman employee received benefices in various parts of Christendom. In 1225 Honorius III decreed that 'in every church and every cathedral one prebend shall remain at the disposal of the Holy See,' and the Pope sometimes went so far as to promise a benefice during the lifetime of its present holder! Urban IV extended this form of advowson, and Clement IV laid down the principle that 'the free disposal of ecclesiastical charges, whether before or after the death of their holders, is an Apostolic prerogative.' The importance of this fact is obvious: the immense wealth of the Church was in the papacy's control. Naturally, there were protests. Robert Grosstete, for example, is celebrated for his outspoken denunciation of this abuse at the Council of Lyons in 1245. He accused the Holy See of granting benefices to unworthy persons; and even allowing for the Bishop of Lincoln's irascible temperament, we may agree that his criticism was not wholly unjustified. For the most part, however, resistance proved ineffective; and in this respect the episcopate lost nearly all its privileges.

There was also opposition to the power of bishops, first from the cathedral chapters. The canons had a right to administer the diocese while the see was vacant, and the bishop was supposed not only to take their advice, but to allow them some share of his authority. Disputes were inevitable. The most famous of these occurred at Bordeaux, where Archbishop Geoffrey de Loroux was actually obliged to flee for his life. Generally speaking, however, the canons cared little for their rule; most of them lived alone and received a part of the chapter's revenue known as the 'prebend.' Sometimes, in order to increase the prebend, the chapter would reduce its own numbers, arranging for the divine offices to be sung by substitutes called 'vicars'; and this was one of the abuses which the canons regular, especially those of Prémontré, strove to remedy.[1] Again, it was from among the canons that a bishop chose his officials—the cantor, the chancellor, the theologian, the inspector of schools, the penitentiary, and the custos or treasurer. It is not difficult to see that two neighbouring powers so closely associated might easily become rivals.[2]

[1] See the paragraphs on the canons regular in Chapter IV, section 4.
[2] There were also groups of canons unconnected with the cathedrals, serving a church and living on its temporalities. They were not obliged to observe a rule or to live in community. Such groups were described as 'collegiate.' Thus the canons of La Charité-sur-Loire were collegiate before becoming regular. The collegiate canons of Saint-Ours at Aosta were the true spiritual centre of that region.

During the barbarian age, bishops were assisted by archdeacons, who inspected, supervised, and presided at certain functions in their name. But in course of time many of these dignitaries acquired benefices which gave them independent rights and revenues. Having their own interests and duties, they found it difficult to remain mere deputies of the bishops, who accordingly had sometimes to complain of their abuse of power. Their authority decreased, and the office was abolished by the Council of Trent.

Meanwhile, at the end of the twelfth century, a new figure made his appearance in the diocese. This was the vicar-general. Originally he deputized for the bishop when the latter was travelling or absent on crusade; but from the pontificate of Gregory IX onwards he was entrusted with regular duties, and served his chief more directly in administrative and judicial business. Finally, a bishop who was aged or sick was given a coadjutor who succeeded him at his death. The coadjutor often received the title of a bishopric which had been created in the East during the crusades but had vanished beneath the tide of Moslem conquest. Holders of these honorary and commemorative titles were known as bishops *in partibus infidelium*.

Lastly, the bishop had his *diocesan council* or *synod*, in which parish priests and representatives of religious orders assembled at irregular intervals. Metropolitans were likewise entitled to summon *provincial councils*, which had been of great importance during the preceding era. In Spain, for example, the Council of Toledo had ranked almost as a national senate. But the growing power of popes and kings left such institutions with little part to play.

6.   PRIESTS AND PARISHES

The elementary division of Christian society was the *parish*. Like the diocese, it varied in extent: some parishes covered a very small area, others were enormous. Historical circumstances, too, gave rise to different characteristics. Thus, in southern Italy, which was often ravaged by war and constantly threatened by the Saracens, parishes were described by the significant word *castra* (forts) and were closely concentrated. In northern Italy, on the other hand, they were known as *plebes* (peoples), and had many chapels remote from the centre. In peaceful Normandy they were subdivided into numerous self-contained units.

The parochial clergy were variously named. '*Presbyter*' and '*rector ecclesiae*' were terms of great antiquity. The latter still survives in Britain, where we speak of the 'rector.' During the thirteenth century 'curate' was a more common designation. The curate (not to be confused with the modern English sense of the word) was a priest who had the cure or charge of souls—a *pastor*. But there were other terms in use, without necessarily implying any particular function or dignity; e.g. *dean, chaplain, prior*, and *vicar*.[1]

Generally speaking, the bishop was entitled to appoint these lower clergy, although landowners claimed the right of 'patronage' and 'presentation.' A canon of the third Lateran Council had forbidden the erection of 'cures' except with the bishop's approval; but there were many violations of this rule, and the parish priest was often little more than an employee of the castle.

Nevertheless, strenuous efforts were made to remedy abuses. Alexander III laid down that only the bishop could appoint a parish-priest, though he agreed that the choice should be made from candidates nominated by the overlord. The fourth Lateran Council insisted that the parochial clergy must be sufficiently educated in matters pertaining to their duty; and it was decreed that the bishops were to provide for their instruction. The Council of Lyons (1274) went still farther, and wisely forbade the appointment of anyone below the age of twenty-five years. The one appointed must already be in priestly orders, or must seek ordination within a year. Anyone who obtained the appointment of an unworthy candidate was subject to heavy ecclesiastical sanctions. It cannot, however, be denied that these regulations were often treated as somewhat elastic.

The rural clergy were extremely poor. Most parishes had funds for the use of their clergy; but apart from the fact that such funds were often embezzled by some temporal overlord or prelate, they were in many cases quite insufficient. The study of royal taxation in France has revealed the existence of many parishes not subject to assessment because their annual income was less than ten and even than seven livres (scarcely one-third of a sou per day), though a labourer earned at least half a sou. There were numerous parishes of this kind in mountainous country and in the barren regions of Champagne. As for vicars, they frequently had nothing at all upon which to live, except the *droit d'étole*, i.e. freewill offerings.

We can hardly, therefore, be surprised that under such conditions the behaviour of the clergy sometimes left much to be desired. Even those who were not open to criticism on grounds of ignorance or immorality must often have been tempted to obtain a little money in exchange for their spiritual services. The Lateran Council of 1215 was hard put to it to discriminate between the necessity of free administration of the sacraments and the natural desire of clerics not to die of hunger. All the same, it is rather surprising to find a priest demanding the baptismal robes of new-born children in order to re-sell them, and

---

[1] The *archpriest* (or dean) usually supervised a number of parishes; but this duty was somewhat vague. The same title was held by the parish priest of a cathedral.

even carrying off the bedclothes of a dying man to whom he had just given extreme unction! The bishops were obliged to lay down a regular scale of charges: the diocesan of Noyon, for example, allowed a parish priest to take three sous for a marriage, but twelve for a reconciliation!

This last item is an indication of the parish priest's authority and manifold activity. The parish was a far more closely knit unit than it is to-day. The clergy alone had the right to baptize, preside at marriages, and to conduct funerals. It was expressly forbidden to attend Sunday Mass in any but one's own parish church; and an Archbishop of Bordeaux threatened with excommunication any priest who received a parishioner not faithful to his or her own parish. In Brittany the offence was punished with a fine of twenty sous—a very large sum, equal to at least two months' salary. The priest was there-fore in constant touch with his flock. He knew each one individually. He was the common receptacle of petitions and complaints. He had charge of the health as well as of the morals of his parish, keeping an eye on lepers, and acting as a sort of police-superintendent in the matter of lost property and day-to-day upsets. Above all, he kept the register of baptisms, marriages, and deaths. Since he came from the same social stratum as most of his parishioners, it is not surprising that he intervened on familiar terms in their personal affairs, and would even denounce a thief or an adulterer from the pulpit. Thus, in spite of obvious faults, the medieval clergy was the link of Christian society; it kept alive the faith of simple folk.

7. THE REGULARS

The immediate task of the secular clergy, from archbishop to parish-priest, was to lead the people to salvation; and for this purpose they lived 'in the world' among their flocks. But there was another body of clerics who exercised no less important duties in the Church, and about whom we have already spoken.[1] They were distinguished by the fact that they lived according to a Rule (*regula*), and were therefore known as 'regulars.' The regular clergy numbered thousands of religious, who were governed by superiors entitled, according to circumstances, *abbots*, *priors*, or *provosts*. The twelfth and thirteenth centuries were the golden age of monachism, the summer-time of a tree whose countless blossom was of infinite variety. The number of religious; their influence upon the civil and ecclesiastical authority; their contribution to the secular hierarchy in the form of bishops, cardinals, and even popes; and, not least, their economic and social activity, made the regular clergy one of the foundation-stones of Christendom.

[1] See Chapter I, section 4.

These numerous Orders are difficult to classify. We may distinguish the more ancient institutions, which followed the Rule of St Benedict, from those observing one of more recent date, e.g. the Franciscans. But there were also much later foundations, such as the Premonstratensians and Dominicans, whose way of life was based upon the venerable Rule of St Augustine. Even setting aside the Benedictines, Cistercians, Franciscans, and Dominicans, the whole complexus of 'lesser' Orders was of great importance. A more logical basis of distinction is that of proximate ends—contemplation or the active life. But while the Carthusians fell within the former category, the Cistercians joined activity with the apostolate of prayer. Besides, the active life was of several kinds. The Premonstratensians and other canons regular, for instance, devoted themselves chiefly to the work of reform; the Antonine Hospitallers, the Brothers of the Holy Ghost, the Brothers of St Lazarus, and the Croisiers to works of charity; the military associations of the Temple and Teutonic Knights to armed contest in the cause of Christ and Holy Church. And when St Francis and St Dominic instituted the two great mendicant Orders, they established an entirely new form of religious life.

Let us try to draw a picture of one of those great monasteries belonging to the most celebrated observance—that of St Benedict—in its heyday: Cluny, say, or Saint Gall, or Fulda. It was a world within itself, a human society of which no modern religious house can give the least idea. The conventual buildings were surrounded by high walls and covered an enormous area. They were arranged according to a strict plan, and each one was suited to the purpose assigned to it by the requirements of community life: chapter-house, cloister, *scriptorium*, cells or dormitories, guest-house, and infirmary; not to mention storehouses and farm-buildings. The whole of this vast agglomeration was dominated by the abbey church, whose several towers thrust proudly towards heaven.

Around the monastery, with its hundred or two hundred monks, there lay a whole *familia*, a regular monastic city, where the dwellings of the *famuli* encircled the conventual buildings and were in many cases the origin of a town. There were agents, *vicarii*, *villici*, and stewards who managed the estates of the abbey; there were hereditary administrators of the kitchen, of the bakehouse, and of the tannery; there was a crowd of hired servants employed on the hardest work in place of the monks, who were now more concerned with the divine office and copying manuscripts than with ploughing and reaping; there were the oblates, who had pledged themselves and their goods to the abbey in return for the privilege of living in cloistered peace and wearing the habit of the Order; and finally, there were *voluntary serfs*, free men and women who had literally enslaved themselves to the community in order to satisfy their piety, and about whose necks, in the course of a symbolic rite, the abbot had passed the rope of the conventual bell. All together, these various categories included at least as many souls as the monastic population.   They all worked in the immediate neighbourhood of the abbey, from which, however, they were separated by the 'enclosure' so as not to disturb the recollection of the monks. Thus, at Corbie there was a cloister between the apartment where the domestics prepared the food and the kitchen where the religious cooked it according to prescribed regulations and to the accompaniment of psalms.   That all these busy folk were content with their lot is indicated by the proverb: 'It is good to live under the crozier.'

So much for the *familia* proper.   There was another and still larger *familia* which included those pious Christians who had been enrolled in confraternities of prayer or in charitable 'societies' attached to the monastery.   Membership of such groups authorized them to be present at the offices recited on their behalf, and to be buried in the holy ground of the monastery.   Lists of these confraternities [1] have been preserved, and that of Saint-Gall contains more than 1,700 names. Nor must we forget the members of those numerous bodies which, though not so closely connected with the abbey, visited the hallowed spot on major festivals in tens of thousands.

The abbey was governed by an abbot who was elected for life and whose authority over his flock was in theory absolute.   All those qualities demanded by St Benedict, and described by Pope Gregory the Great in his life of the holy founder, made the abbot a leader in every sense, a true father, a spiritual guide, and an administrator.   Assisted by two subordinate officers, the prior and novice-master, he was relieved of temporal cares by the cellarer or bursar, who, in turn, was assisted by the refectorian, cook, *custos panis*, *custos vini*, and guestmaster.   But in point of fact the whole weight of responsibility rested on the abbot's shoulders.   The worth of his community depended on his own merits, and there lay the problem.

In theory an abbot was elected by all the professed monks.   The fourth Lateran Council accepted this principle, specifying three methods of election: by 'inspiration' in the case of unanimity, by conventual scrutiny, or, finally, *via scrutinii mixti*, i.e. in two stages. This latter form meant that the whole community appointed ten or twenty delegates by whom the final choice was to be made.   But in the election of abbots, as in that of bishops, secular interference was a notorious evil.   Princes would send ambassadors to a community which had just lost its abbot, in order to suggest the name of his successor, and in some cases even enthroned their own candidate by force!   Intervention of this kind was often nothing short of scandalous.

---

[1] The list was usually entitled *Liber Vitae*.

Thus at Hautmont we find a monk named Guy, who had been installed by the Countess of Blois, holding the monastery with a garrison of 127 men and imprisoning such religious as opposed him.   Needless to say, no good could come of a contested election.   It was fraught with inextricable difficulties which could only be resolved by a costly appeal to Rome, unless some neighbouring baron put paid to the quarrel by stronger methods.

Generally speaking, every great Benedictine monastery was autonomous; Cluniac centralization was on the decline.   Autonomy, however, did not mean isolation.   Communities 'fraternized' to the extent of exchanging spiritual and even material services, hospitality, and mutual assistance, without question of the Order exercising control over each house.   But the reforming movement and the example of Cîteaux [1] gave rise to a more closely knit organization.   The Benedictine abbots of the province of Rheims were the first to meet in plenary assemblies.   This practice spread in face of opposition, and Innocent III resolved to make it of universal obligation.   In 1215 the Lateran Council ordered the establishment of provincial chapters to be held every three years, but appointed no central authority capable of exercising strict control.   The Benedictines never adopted the hierarchical system of Cîteaux, and it is to this lack of centralization that we must attribute the decline of the Black Monks from the fourteenth century onwards.[2]

Meanwhile, however, the religious Orders served as a moral link between one diocese and another, until the thirteenth century when relations between the universities became a far more potent agency of intellectual exchange; and this is true alike of those Orders which were modelled on the pattern of Cîteaux, of the Franciscans or Dominicans with their central government, and of the more independent Benedictines.   Their influence may be traced in many lands: the Norman Benedictines had priories in England, the Cluniacs in Spain; and if we could draw a map of those regions which were affected by the Parisian abbey of St Denis, it would cover an area equivalent to that of France.   St Norbert and La Cluze in Italy, St Ours in the Val d'Aosta, and St Maurice in Valois all remained in close touch with their daughter-houses and with laymen whom they counted among their friends, despite the fact that they were often separated by difficult mountain ranges.   Later, in the thirteenth century, houses of the mendicant Orders served, one might almost say, as barracks where shock-troops awaited call-up for the Master's service; and having once established themselves in the towns, they formed a network of influence 'more or

[1] See Chapter IV, section 4.
[2] The mendicants were organized on lines different from those of the more ancient Orders; see the final section of Chapter IV.

less closely woven, but careful never to leave too many gaps.' [1]   Side by side, then, with the secular clergy who had charge of the Christian flock, the regulars were the motive force of medieval Christendom.

8. ECCLESIASTICAL JUSTICE AND CANON LAW

The Church's elaborate organization and hierarchy of rulers made her a society within society, a state above other states.   Her independence and authority were still further increased by the twofold fact that, as a state, she had her own courts of law and her own finances.

Ecclesiastical justice [2] is wellnigh as old as Christianity.   The early Christians, under imperial persecution, could not submit their differences to the tribunals of their executioners; disputes were therefore argued before the religious authority.   Judicial functions had also been assumed by bishops during the barbarian epoch, when they upheld the principles of equity against the rough and ready procedure of Germanic law.   Charlemagne, who combined religion with politics, followed the same practice and often appointed clerics to act as judges.   In the troublous days of the ninth and tenth centuries the Church alone enjoyed sufficient prestige to command that degree of respect which is necessary for the effective running of any legal system.   From the eleventh to the fourteenth century, therefore, we find ecclesiastical tribunals which occupy a place proportionate to the Church's role in medieval society.

What was the scope of ecclesiastical jurisdiction, and what the powers of ecclesiastical courts?   The principle was clear enough: the Church claimed an exclusive right to try her own members.   This was known as the *privilegium fori*, which removed from the competence of lay judges all who were dedicated to God.   It was a matter of jurisdiction *ratione personae* (by reason of the subject to be judged), to which the Church clung tenaciously.   In 1279 the Council of Avignon decreed excommunication against any lay official who arrested a cleric,

[1] J. de Font-Réaulx.

[2] *Ecclesiastical justice* must not be confused with *clerical justice* which developed from the feudal system.   A bishop who was a lay overlord had legal rights over his territory, similar to those enjoyed by every overlord and quite independent of those which belonged to him as a spiritual ruler.   Such was the case, for example, with the bishops of Metz, whose temporal domains included the city of Épinal, which lay outside their diocese. Likewise, the archbishops of Rouen were Lords Chief Justices of Louviers, which came under the spiritual jurisdiction of Évreux.

It sometimes happened that this justice, which, though essentially laic, was 'clerical' inasmuch as it was exercised by churchmen, came into conflict with that of the Church. Thus, M. Maurice Veyrat, in his remarkable study *La Haute Justice des Archevêques de Rouen, Comtes de Louviers* (Rouen, 1948), shows us the bishop of Évreux demanding in vain the delivery of a cleric arrested at Louviers.   In this town, the strongest evidence of the archbishop's jurisdiction was a four-posted gallows capable of 'holding a dozen criminals at once.'   A realistic symbol of the Church's part in temporal affairs!

even *in flagrante delicto*, and refused to deliver him to ecclesiastical judges. Moreover, the term 'cleric' was given the widest possible application. Slowly but surely the Church extended the privilege of her tribunals even to married and degraded clerics, leaving to the civil courts only those who were guilty of bigamy, forgery, or inveterate heresy. Others so entitled, on grounds of the 'Church's interest' or the 'charity of Christ,' were widows, orphans, students, crusaders, and pilgrims. Now ecclesiastical justice was an improvement upon that of the civil courts: its procedure was more exact, more rapid, and also more humane, inasmuch as in criminal matters it recognized neither the 'Judgment of God' nor 'Trial by Ordeal.' On that account, vast numbers posed as 'clergy,' and towards the end of the thirteenth century the competence of ecclesiastical courts was almost unlimited.

There was yet another cause which tended to increase this jurisdiction. The ecclesiastical courts enjoyed authority not only *ratione personae*, but also *ratione materiae*, i.e. by virtue of the object of an offence and of the matter at issue. This second basis of competence was less clearly defined than the *privilegium fori* which had been laid down in several Carolingian capitularies. In practice, however, it was made to cover a very wide field. The Church normally claimed jurisdiction in all cases where her interests were at stake (e.g. tithes, benefices, donations, and wills). Normally, too, she made it her business to pass judgment upon crimes that bore a religious character, such as sacrilege, blasphemy, and the practice of withcraft, as well as all offences committed in holy places. Since her jurisdiction included all spiritual causes—both those related to vows and ecclesiastical discipline, and also those involving a sacrament or affecting her as guardian of oaths—and the right to sentence those guilty in any of these respects, there was scarcely a limit to her intervention; for in medieval society wellnigh everything was connected with a sacrament or depended upon an oath.

By the same token, there were strong protests and some open resistance; e.g. in England, where Henry II attempted to restrict the sphere of clerical privilege. In France, under Philip Augustus, it was the barons who leagued themselves against the tribunals of the Church and addressed a formal complaint to the king. St Louis settled these differences by a series of concordats. In Germany, Frederick II could not resist so fair an opportunity of injuring the Church, and obtained from his jurists a solemn declaration of the State's superiority in legal matters. As the monarchies became stronger, the privileges of Church courts declined. Thus, in 1349, the famous assembly of Vincennes lodged sixty-six objections against them; and shortly afterwards, in the middle of the fourteenth century, the Parlement of Paris claimed the right to hear appeals against abuse of power by ecclesiastical tribunals.

Custom, in fact, tended to limit the Church's competence to cases that were exclusively religious.

It may now be asked, Who administered justice in the Church's name? We need scarcely remark that the increasing complexity of legal business prevented the bishop from hearing all cases in person as he had done until the beginning of the twelfth century, giving judgment 'in his synod' or 'in his court.' The *official* (professional judge), acting on the bishop's behalf, made his first appearance during the pontificate of Alexander III; and before long a regular judicial system was evolved.[1] The judge sat with a number of assessors; the 'keeper of the seal' acted as clerk of the court; the 'promoter' was perhaps the origin of our public prosecutor; and there were also advocates and notaries. The arrangement was gradually improved as follows. Over the judges, whose jurisdiction was confined to limited areas, was the chief justice. His powers extended to the whole diocese, and he might hear appeals. In course of time heresy was removed from the competence of ordinary tribunals, and special courts were established 'to seek out heretical perversity.' These formed what is known as the 'Inquisition,' whose procedure helped to bring the Church's legal system into disrepute. Lastly, at the summit of the whole edifice, the papacy had its own courts to which every convicted Christian had the right of appeal; in principle at all events, for this right was for a long time somewhat vague. Under the stronger popes the number of appeals was enormous. Even in the twelfth century St Bernard complained that the pontifical palace 're-echoed every day with the noise of Justinian's laws rather than with Christ's,' and that there was heard 'from morning to evening the shrill cry of pleaders.' Innocent III and Innocent IV eventually took steps to define the right of appeal and restrict its use.

This huge mass of judicial business had at least one fortunate result, which was also partly due to the Holy See's resolve to secure its own rights. The Church became the leading jurist of that age, and her law —the *Canon Law*—attained a degree of importance similar to that enjoyed by Roman Law in the ancient world. Theoretically, the 'canons' were disciplinary regulations decreed by councils ($\kappa\alpha\nu\acute{\omega}\nu=$ rule or regulation). In practice, since nearly all private and secular affairs were dependent on religious principles, Canon Law enlarged its scope to include many precepts and prescriptions which we should now regard as having little or nothing to do with priests.

The golden age of Canon Law extended from the twelfth to the thirteenth century. The Church was for long without a code; but since the sixth century she had used a collection of canons compiled by a Scythian monk, Denys the Little, who also fixed the beginning of

---

[1] After the fourteenth century the system was known in France as *officialité*.

the Christian era. Later, Charlemagne had prescribed a more elaborate 'corpus,' called 'Hispana' because it originated in Spain. Next, we have a celebrated forgery known as the 'False Decretals,' which attributed to former popes a number of decisions and decrees which in themselves reveal no small degree of wisdom. In the middle of the eleventh century the Church decided to systematize her legal text-books, and a start was made by French canonists, notably by Yves of Chartres. But their work was quickly superseded by that of Gratian, the great Master of Bologna University, who in 1152 published his *Concordia discordantium canonum*, a regular treatise of canonical lore which completed, corrected, and pruned the ancient corpus. Though not official in the strict sense of that word, Gratian's work became a classic in the Law schools, and was adopted by the courts. Innocent III brought the Canon Law under papal supervision by appointing a commission of notaries to revise Gratian. They added several more recent canons and decretals, and presented the result of their labours to Bologna University. The new publication, however, was both diffuse and defective; about 1230, therefore, Gregory IX requested his chaplain, the Dominican Raymond of Pennaforte, to draw up a systematic code of Canon Law. This epoch-making work, entitled *Quinque Libri Gregorii IX*, was completed within four years; it was adopted by the whole Church and received no additions until the Sixth Book of Boniface VIII. The *Clementines* of Clement V were published by John XXII in 1317. These three works, forming the *Corpus juris canonici*, continued to represent the Church's law right down to the promulgation of the present *Codex* in 1917.

We must also say a few words about the human aspect of ecclesiastical justice. It is true that the Church borrowed much from Roman Law, especially with regard to procedure; [1] it is also true that she was influenced to some extent by Germanic custom. But if we consider her legal system as a whole, we shall recognize it as an original creation. She was the successful guardian of principles far more liberal than those of Roman or Germanic Law. It was she who fixed the limits of power, and who first laid down the rules of war. It was she who first guaranteed the rights of the weak, of widows, and of orphans. It was she who distinguished the sacramental and contractual elements in marriage, and who admitted the equality of spouses without undermining

---

[1] The Church's attitude to Roman Law was complex. The popes and the great (religious) universities, especially that of Bologna, encouraged its study; and St Yvo, a future judge of Trégniers, attended the school of Orléans. At the same time, however, there was a noticeable tendency to forbid clerics the study of Roman Law, on the grounds that it inculcated non-Christian principles and favoured the power of princes (Lateran Council, 1139). Later, Roger Bacon lampooned the clergy for their preoccupation with Digests and Pandects. In the thirteenth century the renaissance of Roman Law was encouraged by temporal sovereigns, and even used by them as a weapon against the Church. See Chapter VIII, section 10, and Chapter XIV, section 3.

the husband's headship.   It was she who restricted parental authority;
and it was she who enforced respect for a man's last wishes as expressed
in his Will.   Canon Law was the pioneer in many fields of jurisprudence.   We should not, for example, possess our modern ideas of
delinquency and punishment, were it not that the canonists studied the
difference between *crimen* and *peccatum*, between felony and mis-
demeanour.

Modern society has in some respects moved far from the principles
of medieval jurisprudence, notably in regard to the right of asylum.
If a malefactor, a political opponent, or a condemned criminal managed
to reach 'asylum,' he was inviolable; and 'asylum' included not only
the fabric of a church or religious house, but any centre under ecclesiastical control, even the cross which marked its extreme limit.[1]   This
merciful provision might, of course, save some jail-bird from the
gallows upon which he should rightly have been hanged; but it
rendered justice less implacable, and safeguarded that last chance of
repentance and forgiveness which the legal systems of our day are more
than ever inclined to withhold from those within their clutches.

9.   The Finances of the Church

As the Church administered her own justice, so she had her own
finances.   During the great centuries of the Middle Ages her wealth as
a whole increased considerably, though somewhat irregularly.

The Holy See had its particular sources of revenue.   These consisted, first, of income from the papal states, a detailed account of which
was drawn up in the *Liber censuum* by Cencio Savelli, a Roman cleric
and a good financier who later became Pope Honorius III.   Next,
there was *Peter's Pence*, contributed chiefly by those countries which
acknowledged themselves vassals of the Holy See.   Thus, in the reign
of King John, England paid a tribute of £700 and Ireland £600; while
Frederick II promised one thousand gold pieces on behalf of Sicily.
The papal budget was further augmented by 'fees for protection' paid
by churches and religious houses which had applied for direct dependence upon Rome.   There were also dues paid by high dignitaries for
the confirmation of their appointments, and by archbishops on receipt
of the pallium.   Finally, there were payments for Bulls and other
papal documents, as well as for various dispensations and indulgences,
not to mention certain extraordinary clerical taxes levied on a variety of
occasions.   It must be admitted, finance was far too prominent a
feature in the history of the medieval papacy, especially from the

---

[1] This is the origin of the calvaries often found at the entrance to continental villages
and whose memory is preserved in the street-names of certain towns.

middle of the thirteenth century. Innocent IV's exchequer became notorious for its repeated demands, for its skill in raising 'voluntary donations,' and for its co-operation with Florentine bankers in fleecing archbishops on their visits *ad limina*. These methods were continued by Innocent's successors, and the amounts of 'gratuitous offerings' were fixed with minute precision by the Curia of Alexander IV, Urban IV, and Clement IV. At the end of our period the popes at Avignon had developed an even more elaborate though not altogether edifying system.

The remainder of the Church had four sources of revenue: *tithes*, *perquisites*, *donations*, and *benefices*.

The tithe, or gift of the faithful to their clergy, was an ecclesiastical institution of great antiquity which had been codified by the capitularies of Charlemagne and then by the Council of Paris in 870. Theoretically, it was payable by all laymen from their revenues of whatsoever kind; and the amount, as shown by its etymology (Lat. *decima*, Fr. *dîme*) was one-tenth. It was collected locally and brought to the tithe-barn. In practice, however, things did not work so simply. Many of those from whom tithes were due obtained dispensation by purchase or favour. Rates varied considerably; the tithe on corn, for example, was in some cases 'one sheaf in ten,' in other cases every eleventh, twelfth, or even thirteenth sheaf. As to the duty of carriage, many peasants excused themselves, and the parish-priest had to go and fetch what was owed to him.

Perquisites, known in some districts as 'altar money,' were an off-shoot of the '*droit d'étole*.' In order to save priests from destitution, with which many of them were threatened, the authorities had been obliged to allow remuneration for pastoral duties which, in canonical theory, were gratuitous. Presents made to the parish-priest on the occasion of a wedding or baptism became almost everywhere fixed charges.

The principal source of ecclesiastical revenue took the form of donations, some of which were imposed by Canon Law. Clerics were bound to bequeath to the Church whatever they had managed to acquire through their priestly functions; but this rule was less strictly observed as time went on. Many laymen, on the other hand, made valuable bequests to the Church, sometimes from piety, sometimes out of gratitude, or in order to assure prayers for their souls.

Benefices were the revenues of property attached to an ecclesiastical office. Bishops and abbots frequently had at their disposal great wealth derived from land, farms, town-property, workshops, and other real estate belonging to the see or monastery. In principle, no one was allowed to 'cumulate,' i.e. to touch the revenues of an abbey or bishopric other than his own, and this rule was stressed over and over

I

again by councils in the eleventh and twelfth centuries. But in the thirteenth century this wise regulation was relaxed, together with that of 'residence,' according to which a cleric was bound to reside in the see to which he had been appointed. Henceforth we find canons enjoying the benefit of cures in which they never set foot, and fulfilling their duties through poorly paid vicars, while many a high dignitary collected the profits from appointments in which he was not otherwise interested. The strictest theologians and canonists, especially those of the University of Paris, vehemently condemned such practices, but in vain.

We must not infer from this account of ecclesiastical revenues that all clerics lived in opulence. Disparities were often so great as to be nothing short of scandalous. The priest in charge of a parish whose beneficiary lived miles away had to make do on what was called 'adequate emolument,' which never represented half the benefice and often not so much as a third. That meant destitution. Between the income of a vicar and a wealthy bishop the proportion was in many cases as much as 300, and sometimes 1,000, to one.

Even if we consider them as a whole, the finances of the Church varied greatly from one region to another. Where it is possible to refer to documents of the French royal exchequer, we find that diocesan revenues varied from three to thirty-five livres per square mile. Yet, France was 'the paradise of God'; in Italy or Spain the Church's income was far less.

Moreover, these resources were not without enemies or over-zealous friends, first among whom were the temporal sovereigns. The revenues of the clergy were theoretically exempt from taxation, but not in practice. Kings who were proud to call themselves protectors of the Church did not hesitate to ask her, in terms no less imperative than polite, for all kinds of subsidies. In France alone we find heavy taxes laid upon the clergy, now for the crusades, now to stamp out the Albigensian heresy, now to provide for war in Aragon. Until the end of the thirteenth century these subsidies were never raised without permission from the Pope; but after that date governments levied taxes on the clergy with unfailing regularity, and Philip the Fair did so whenever he pleased. The practice soon became general everywhere. The Italian clergy were oppressed by the communes; but the popes could do nothing about it, since they needed assistance from the urban leagues against the Emperor.

Another ingenious method employed by secular princes to lay hands on Church property was the so-called royal prerogative. This curious custom was a relic of secularization as practised by the Carolingians, a relic of the privilege of investiture once claimed by temporal rulers. On the death of a bishop or abbot the king took his place for as long as the see remained vacant, and collected its revenues.[1]   The practice was not universal, nor was it employed in every province of a kingdom such as France; but those who could hope to benefit thereby seized every chance to do so.   It is not difficult to imagine with what solicitude the holders of such privileges hurried, while the see was vacant, to hew down forests, empty fishponds, sell the flocks and harvests, so long as they formed no part of the deceased prelate's personal estate.   Official protests, such as were heard at the Council of Lyons in 1274, fell for the most part on deaf ears.

This method of taking from the clergy part of their wealth was a recognized procedure.   But many laymen succeeded in making handsome profits.   Barons in search of money, especially during the eleventh and twelfth centuries, preyed upon bishoprics and monasteries, nor was the communal movement blind to its opportunity. Others acted in a more underhand fashion, embezzling tithes and even converting them into dowries for their daughters!   With the collusion of civil governments and certain members of the clergy, this practice was so well established that Innocent III was obliged to tolerate 'enfeoffed tithes.'   The tithe, in fact, became an article of trade.[2]

These losses were, after all, no more than occasional; but there was another, infinitely more far-reaching in its effects, and in certain cases much more severe, which the Church unwittingly incurred.   The urban renaissance and the growth of trade gave rise, as we have seen, to ever-increasing monetary exchange, resulting in a general fall in the value of coinage.   This phenomenon corresponded to what we should now call 'inflation,' and it is well known that during a period of inflation fixed incomes tend to fall.   The fact made little or no difference to those ecclesiastical beneficiaries who had been wise enough to exact payment in kind; but those who had preferred money to goods suffered an inevitable loss of income, for it was, of course, practically impossible to persuade debtors to accept a higher scale of charges.

[1] C. Laplatte, in his essay on 'The Administration of Vacant Bishoprics' (*Revue d'Histoire de l'Église de France*, 1939), has shown that the temporal prerogative was not a rich source of revenue for the kings; but it was accompanied by the 'spiritual privilege' (i.e. the right of nominating to benefices normally enjoyed by the titular), which enabled them to pension off many a favourite.

[2] This explains why the tithe, which was not in itself exorbitant (especially if we take account of the public services rendered by the Church), soon became unpopular.   The common people were angered by this diversion of their pious offering from its lawful ends and by this misuse of the 'goods of the Crucified.'   From about the year 1200 payment of tithes was stoutly resisted, complaints were made to the king, and organized strikes occurred.   A judgment of the ecclesiastical court at Sens condemned certain persons who had not paid their tithes for four years, and the monks of St Bertin wrote to the Pope asking him to apply ecclesiastical sanctions to those who would not pay.   There is record of still more serious incidents: priests were beaten up when they came to collect tithes, and in 1226, at Dunkerque, some were actually murdered.

The principal victims of this situation were the great Benedictine abbeys, and it was largely responsible for their decline towards the end of the thirteenth century.

The revenues of the Church, therefore, were not altogether secure. Considered as a whole, she was possessed of great wealth and must be recognized as the leading financial power; but against that must be set her enormous expenditure. The papacy had to meet the salaries of a host of officials, the upkeep of the pontifical palace, and that traditional splendour which the most saintly popes could not forgo. It had to subsidize crusades, missionary work, and religious building schemes. Gigantic sums of money were consumed by such undertakings as the chimerical attempt to restore the Latin empire of Constantinople, which was pursued by the Holy See from 1261 onwards.[1]   The clergy were alone responsible for services which to-day are provided by the State and for which the twentieth-century taxpayer has to find sums he might well wish reduced to a tithe rent-charge. Education, charitable institutions, hospices, parochial administration, and certain public works were among the numerous activities which fell to the clergy but which we now regard as the province of lay officials. Ecclesiastical revenues were by no means earmarked for the comfort and recreation of the clergy.[2]

10. THE CHURCH AS AN ECONOMIC POWER

The Church was indeed a society within society; but she must not be thought of as a foreign body, drawing upon the common stock of men and money and giving nothing in return. She took a prominent share in the daily round of life; and no historian, however anti-clerical his bias, has ever denied her civilizing influence. None has failed to recognize her vital part in the work of production and exchange, or that her impact upon human culture, vast and permanent as it has proved to be, was not intentional. The Church's purpose was neither to increase production, nor to make profits, nor to extend her commercial sphere. True, all these things were added unto her, but only because she was concerned first and foremost with 'the Kingdom of God and His justice.'

The economic doctrine of the medieval Church could not have been

---

[1] See Chapter XIII.
[2] It is worth while to notice the means whereby the papacy rewarded its servants. It was concerned with remunerating the more important among them by granting benefices, but left the salaries of inferior executives to these beneficiaries of apostolic favour. Again, until 1310 payment was in kind: officials of the Curia drew 'rations' from the kitchen, while the Marshal's office issued hay and oats for horses which were indispensable in an age when the papal court was always on the move. Equerries received their liveries. In the fourteenth century money came into its own. Accounts show that wars fought in Italy represented the greater part of papal expenditure.

further removed from modern theory and practice. It was an economy devoid of avarice, in which wealth was never sought for its own sake, in which commercial transactions had no profiteering motive, in which production was proportionate to demand, and in which expenses (gratuitously incurred for God's sake) were always ahead of savings or capital deposits. It was, moreover, an economy close to those who laboured for it. A century ago Disraeli praised it in these words: 'To-day we deplore absentee owners. But the monks were always in residence; they spent their income among those who produced it by the labour of their hands.' We might vary his observation and say that the Church had nothing in common with capitalist bosses, who are entirely cut off from the masses responsible for production. Ecclesiastical economy was at any rate man-sized.

We know what was the economic role of the monasteries in barbarian times. Whereas the barons and other temporal landowners only just managed to preserve the (mainly rural) centres of economic life in the Roman world, the monks undertook an immense task of colonization. The sons of St Columban, followed by those of St Benedict, completely altered the appearance of huge tracts of land, turning woods and swamps into arable and pasture. A religious house, established in the most impenetrable of German forests, became at once a nucleus of culture, of production, and of exchange; the whole countryside was transfigured.

Monks in the eleventh and twelfth centuries had, of course, less need than their predecessors to work as pioneers, except on the borders of Germany and Poland and Central Europe. The early economic stage was passed; but each abbey continued to exercise important economic functions, thanks to the Holy Rule of St Benedict, which requires every monastery to be self-supporting.

Again, it must be remembered that monastic life itself was favourable to the growth of intense economic activity. The monks, especially the Benedictines, most of whose time was devoted to spiritual reading and the divine office, could not be 'producers'; their manual labour, though ordained by the Rule, was fast falling into disuse and was quite inadequate to the needs of a large community. A monastery was therefore a wage-paying corporation, distributing money in its neighbourhood.

What did these expenses cover? First the subsistence of the monks, their food and clothing—often a considerable item when we consider the size of communities. Next, there was the heavy cost of divine worship: material for vestments, wax for the candles, oil for the lamps. Far heavier was the cost of building. One need only visit the ruins of medieval monastery to realize the sums necessary to erect and maintain it, more especially as the monks built on the grand scale for

God's glory and the benefit of future generations.   Without seeking comfort, they had an eye to hygiene and convenience, as may be seen from a glance at the latrines of Fontenay.   A monastery in the twelfth century had a better supply of flowing water than has the Palace of Versailles.

The expenses of building and upkeep were by no means the limit of monastic economy.   The monks' vocation included works of charity no less than contemplation.   We may be sure that the greater part of their revenues was employed for purposes other than religious.   For *what* purposes?   Mainly for charity in its several forms.   We shall have more to say about the importance of this branch of monastic activity in the sphere to which it properly belongs—that of human relationship; but it was clearly no less considerable on the economic plane, and here the secular clergy vied with the regulars.   Think what the Church as a whole must have spent in works of charity at a time when she alone was responsible for social security and public assistance, not to speak of education.   Even the business of hotel-keeping, which appears to us strictly commercial, was part of Christian charity; most places of call on the roads were hospices, religious establishments for the convenience of travellers and pilgrims.

There were even cases in which the charitable funds of the Church were strained to breaking point, e.g. in times of public calamity, plague, or famine.   The civil authority was extremely short-sighted and held no reserves; so that men looked to the Church, and especially to the religious houses, whose granaries, fishponds, and resources of every kind were forthwith placed at their disposal.   There are numerous instances of dioceses and monasteries selling their treasures, even the sacred vessels, in order to save the neighbouring people from starvation.

One of the most curious undertakings of the Church in the economic field was that of bridge-building.   Here we have a surprising and little-known chapter of history, obscured by legend.   It begins about 108⟨ in the south of France, where the confraternity of St Sibert constructed a bridge at the place long known as Maupas but thereafter as Bonpas. Their example was followed elsewhere, and enterprising laymen undertook to bridge the Rhône.   Thus in 1177, so it is said, there came to the city of Avignon a pious shepherd named Benézet, whom God had instructed to build a bridge at that point where the river is particularly wide and difficult to cross.   St Benézet and his 'bridging brethren' worked at the job for seven years, and it was their hands that produced the famous bridge whose ruins may still be seen.   In 1265 the Cluniac Benedictines decided to erect a bridge somewhat farther north.   They probably called in the confraternity of the Holy Ghost, which originated at Nîmes; whence, no doubt, the legend that the Third Person of

the Trinity took a hand in the work.[1]   At all events, the bridge took
nearly a hundred years to build; it was called Pont-Saint-Esprit, and
gave its name to that delightful town.   Many more examples of this
kind might be cited.   At Lyons the wooden bridge collapsed and was
rebuilt in stone by a religious confraternity; the same was done at
Saumur by the monks of St Florentin; while in Portugal, Blessed
Princess Mafalda instituted an order of builders to bridge the Tagus.
The whole Church became interested in these useful projects, and
special indulgences were granted to bridge-builders.   When in 1275
the bridge at Maestricht gave way, carrying with it an entire procession,
as many as forty days indulgence were promised to anyone who helped
to reconstruct it.   Nor, on such occasions, were the hierarchy slow to
act.   Thus, at Grenoble, in 1219, Bishop John himself raised the
money to rebuild the bridge destroyed by the Isère, as was also done at
various times and under other circumstances by the bishops of Rodez,
Bourges, Metz, Basel, Minden, York, Durham, Orvieto, and many
others.   The most remarkable instance was that of Conrad von
Scharfeneck, Bishop of Metz, who in 1233 ordered that the best suit of
clothes belonging to each person who died in his diocese should be
sold, and the proceeds used for building a bridge over the Moselle.
This was the Bridge of the Dead, which is still standing.   Those
bridges which the Church helped to build were often sanctified by the
erection either of a chapel at one end or midway, or of a cross, or
even of a simple niche from which the figure of a saint might watch over
the structure.   The saint, of course, was invariably St Christopher, a
poor ferryman of whom the Golden Legend relates that he was once
privileged to carry on his shoulders none other than Jesus Christ.

The Church's vital role as a medium of exchange was represented
not only by building bridges and mountain-hospices, nor even by the
construction of roads and river-embankments.   The ordinary course
of monastic life involved a number of activities which affected the
neighbourhood, sometimes over a very wide area.   For example,
monastic workshops, mills, forges, saw-mills, etc., gave rise to large-
scale industries in many places; and we have a striking instance of this
in Dauphiné, where the Carthusians were the first ironmasters.
Certain abbeys had business interests far from their own walls: e.g.

[1] The bridge at Avignon was the first to be made of stone; its completion, therefore,
marks an important date.   The building of the bridge at Pont-Saint-Esprit is the object
of a learned study, entitled *Un Pont au Moyen Âge*, by M. Guy Dupré (1947).   This work
was undertaken by the prior and apparently entrusted to a confraternity.   Some of the
workmen were dedicated (*donati*) to the task by way of penance; they wore a white dress
ornamented on the chest with a bridge in crimson material.   About 1349, priests were
allowed to take part in the work, thus foreshadowing the modern worker-priests.   The
labourers were often at loggerheads with the prior.   Leopold Delisle, a great French
scholar, doubted whether there was an Order of 'Bridgers'; history has not yet spoken
her last word upon this matter (*Académie des Inscriptions*, vol. xix (1892), p. 540).

seaside fisheries, or the vineyards around Laon which belonged to the abbey of Lobbes in Hainaut.

Again, the crowds who flocked to a religious house, to a shrine, or to some place of pilgrimage, might begin a considerable flow of trade. Nearly all the great fairs were of ecclesiastical origin: Lendit, not far from the abbey of Saint-Denis, Tarascon-Beaucaire, Provins, Troyes, Frankfort, Cologne, even Wisby on the Baltic and Novgorod in Russia. Since all fairs were held on religious festivals, it is no mere accident that French peasants still speak of St Martin's or St John's market; and that the same word (*Messe*) is used in German to signify both 'Mass' and 'fair.'

To sum up, the economic activity of the Church throughout the eleventh and twelfth centuries was principally monastic. It coincided with the full flowering of religious life; and when, during the thirteenth century, the monastic edifice was undermined by causes that were at once moral and financial, there set in a twofold decline, not only of its spiritual vitality but also of its economic force, so that former opulence gave way sometimes to actual distress. At that juncture, however, there appeared another great economic phenomenon in the Church, side by side and largely connected with the growth of urban centres; I mean the building of cathedrals.[1] Although it was no longer the monks, but the bishops and Christian people generally, who were at the helm, the economic result was just the same. Year after year the building sites drew to themselves an endless stream of manpower, ensuring thousands upon thousands of working hours, and calling for the services of every guild. Imagine the quickening of economic life in France, say in 1250, when some fifty cathedrals or large churches were in course of construction. There again, as the monasteries had done in preceding centuries, it was the Church who took the lead in what we should now describe as an 'extensive programme of public works.'

11. THE CHARITY OF CHRIST AND SOCIAL SECURITY

If we would estimate the benefits conferred by the medieval Church upon the society in which she lived, we must take into account her labour in a field which is now described by such phrases as 'public assistance' and 'social security.' Here she stood practically alone. The State as such, whether described as empire, kingdom, or republic. did not consider itself bound by any duty towards its subjects even though they were helpless, destitute, or sick. By the end of the period

[1] For the present we need only refer to Chapter IX on the cathedrals, which deal at length with the causes and progress of this phenomenon in the twelfth and thirteenth centuries (pages 347–92).

in question only very few municipal or royal hospitals had come into existence, and these were administered by religious. The Church, however, taught her children that each one is answerable for all.

There you have one of the paradoxes of the Middle Ages: a society which was, on the whole, more violent and more indifferent to suffering than that of western Europe in the twentieth century, could behave with extraordinary generosity ànd refinement, working the constant miracle of Christ's charity. It is astonishing that, with no official organization and no help from the Government, Christian generosity sufficed to run welfare institutions upon a scale which would have done credit to ourselves. Private charity, about which it is, of course, difficult to learn much, was both widespread and open-handed. So much at any rate is clear from biographies, the heroes of which make gifts to those in misfortune; from chronicles which refer to 'God's table,' meals for the poor, and portions left over for any unfortunate who happened to knock at the gate; and also from innumerable wills containing bequests in favour of the poor.[1]

This tide of charity continued to increase, reaching its high-water mark in the time of St Francis of Assisi and St Louis. Encouraged by the concession of indulgences, and prompted by the mendicant Orders, it resulted in a veritable flood of donations and in the founding of congregations dedicated to the service of 'our lords the poor.' [2]

The Church, through the medium of her clergy, had opened up the way, and she carried on the task with unfailing devotion. There had been an organized system of poor-relief in every parish at least since the eleventh century; and a register, known as *matricula*, was kept of all those who received help. The parish priest and his curates administered the fund, which, in accordance with an Act of 818, was supplied by one-fourth of the tithes and one-half of all donations made to the parish. But it was not easy to protect this budget against cupidity, and a rule was made that only those in genuine trouble might receive assistance, and then only on condition that they were local people. Each monastery had its own *matricula* in charge of an 'almoner.' In general, there were two classes of assisted persons: a body of poor folk (usually twelve in number) who were lodged, fed, and clothed within the convent walls, and a varying number of destitute men and women who were provided with the necessities of life. In some cases

---

[1] In Germany the word *Seelegerat* was used to designate gifts made by a Christian for the sake of his salvation. It occurs in many wills.

[2] This observation was suggested by Dr Fleurent's most interesting article 'Une assurance-maladie à Colmar pendant le Moyen Âge' in the *Annuaire de Colmar* (1950). It deals with the administration of a 'sick fund' belonging to the journeyman tailors of Colmar. Members who fell sick had a room reserved for them in the hospital under an agreement between the latter and the confraternity. The head of the confraternity was bound to visit his sick at least once a day to 'hear complaints, console, and encourage them.'

I*

the number was very great.   St Riquier, for example, served more than
five hundred meals each day; Corbie distributed fifty loaves; while
Cluny kept an annual reserve of five hundred sides of salt pork for the
use of the poor.   The work of relieving poverty was so fundamental
that St Bernard never delegated it, even when burdened with those
heavy cares which made him the arbiter of Europe.

In the eleventh century there sprang up simultaneously religious
Orders expressly vowed to works of charity, and joint benevolent
societies.   The earliest and most widespread Order of hospitallers was
that of the *Antonines*.   It was founded in 1095 near Vienne (Dauphiné),
in the parish of Mota, where relics of St Anthony the Hermit were
preserved.   The district had recently suffered from an outbreak of
that mysterious disease known as 'burning sickness' which is thought
to have been caused by the use of spurred rye.[1]   Those affected turned
black and died almost at once.   Two noblemen, Gaston de Valloire
and his son Guérin, were miraculously cured, and, as an act of thanksgiving, founded a congregation known as the Hospitallers of St
Anthony to nurse those afflicted with this disease.   It was reorganized
in 1297 by Boniface VIII as a congregation of canons regular.   The
Antonines were celebrated as far afield as Livonia and Transylvania.
These begging brethren, with their black mantle marked with a Tau-
cross (called St Anthony's cross) and their small hand-bells, were
welcome everywhere.   If they entered a country that lay under
interdict, the terrible sanction was suspended; and if anyone gave them
a pig, it was marked with St Anthony's cross, a bell was tied round its
neck, and it was allowed to wander freely, eating whatever it pleased.[2]
The Antonines, however, were not alone in tending the sick.   An
Order of the Holy Ghost, founded in 1178 by Guy of Montpellier,
worked in the hospitals and also took in foundlings.   Though a
religious institution, it was governed by a lay grand master, and
towards the end of the thirteenth century possessed more than eight
hundred houses.   Two other 'crutched' orders vied with the
Antonines, though on a more modest scale.   These were the *Cruciferi*
instituted at Bologna about 1150 and approved by Alexander III in
1160, and the *Stelliferi* of Bohemia and Silesia.   They were distinguished respectively by a red cross and a six-pointed star of the same
colour.   In 1099, after the capture of Jerusalem by the crusaders, a

---

[1] Doctors nowadays call it ergotism.   During the summer of 1950 in the neighbourhood of Pont-Saint-Esprit on the Rhône, cases of bread poisoning were attributed to
ergotism.   The *Burning Sickness* has been exhaustively studied by Dr Henry Chau-
martin (Paris, 1947).   Grünewald's famous reredos at Colmar illustrates the work of the
Antonines.

[2] Such is the origin of St Anthony's pig, which is still proverbial.   Medieval artists
often depicted the great hermit accompanied by a porker; more recent theologians, in
search of a learned explanation, have claimed that this useful animal was symbolic of the
carnal temptations overcome by the saint!

group of nobles founded the Order of St Lazarus to care for lepers in the East. Louis VII, who saw them at work, brought twelve brethren to France; and the Order spread rapidly until it possessed, in Europe and Asia, no fewer than three thousand lazar-houses. It was reorganized by Innocent IV, as the Order of Knights of St Lazarus, and survived into modern times. Finally, there was a congregation of canons regular known as *Brethren of the Cross*, founded about 1210 by Theodore de Celbes, a canon of Liége. Their duty was to visit countries ravaged by heresy, especially Albigensianism, in order to nurse the sick and thereby reveal the true charity of Christ.

Thus, by the conjoint efforts of the hierarchy, the new Orders, and private generosity, there came into being a host of charitable institutions. That is why, until quite recently, French hospitals were called *Maison-Dieu*, or *Hôtel-Dieu*. Many of them were established by a bishop, a monastery, a religious Order, a rich layman (king or prince), or, later on, by a commune. But their character was always markedly religious; the staff consisted of men or women dedicated to God and styled 'brothers' or 'sisters,' who, even if they belonged to no recognized congregation, followed a Rule inspired in most cases by that of the Hospital of St John of Jerusalem, and were almost always governed by a cleric, priest or monk. The majority of hospitals were vast buildings—that of Milan was renowned for its beauty—where the sick, the infirm, and the aged alike were received and cared for. Treatment, however well-intentioned, might be far from scientific, but at least the destitute found shelter and consolation.

Among these hospitals, there were already some that specialized in particular diseases. That opened at Paris by St Louis was intended for the blind; it took the still-famous name of *Quinze-Vingt* because it could provide for $15 \times 20 = 300$ cases. William the Conqueror had long ago established one in England, and about 1220 the Bishop of Chartres built the *Six-Vingts* for 120 patients in his cathedral city.[1] Abandoned children, according to ecclesiastical law, were to be laid at the door of a sanctuary or religious house as a precaution against their being killed. They had their own hospital, run by the Order of the Holy Ghost, or were sheltered by Hospitallers of Jerusalem who had left their normal duties in Palestine so as to carry on this holy work in Europe. Some of these children's hospices were enormous, and the inmates were looked after until they reached adult age, when work was found for the boys and a dowry provided for those girls who did not wish to take the veil.

Most impressive of the specialized hospitals were the lazar-houses. Leprosy, which was far more widespread than to-day, was the terror of

---

[1] There appear to have been no mental hospitals before 1375, when the *Tollkiste* (madhouse) was opened at Hamburg.

the age; so much so that Joinville told St Louis that he would rather commit thirty mortal sins than be afflicted with the dread disease! But Christianity had learned to respect the brethren of Christ in these hapless folk covered in revolting sores.   St Francis's kiss bestowed upon a leper, not to mention the solicitude for lepers shown by St Louis, St Elizabeth of Hungary, and St Hedwige, is sufficient proof that in this domain also the saints preached by their example.   The leper (Lat. *misellus*), that supreme example of misfortune, was likened to the unhappy Lazarus who, the parable assures us, will find joy in heaven.   Hence the word 'lazar' and 'lazar-house.'   We have all read some account of the heart-rending ceremony with which the leper was conducted to a house which he might henceforward never leave without his rattle and a distinctive mark sewn on to his clothes.   The same methods have been used in modern times; and the story of Father Damien shows how inhuman the seclusion of lepers can be.   In the Middle Ages they were at least accompanied with words of super-natural hope.   Innumerable establishments were reserved for them; and in 1225 a census ordered by Louis VIII revealed that there were more than 2,000 lazar-houses in France alone.   The patron of this struggle against the frightful scourge was *St Roch* (1295–1327), son of an illustrious and noble house at Montpellier, from whom the present family of Castries descends.   He spent his whole life caring for lepers, so far forgetful of himself, says the legend, that his faithful dog had to beg bread for him.   Roch himself died of the horrible disease.   His radiant personality became one of the best known in medieval times, and remained so into a later age, if we may judge from the many pictures of him by Tintoretto, Carracci, Rubens, David, and others.[1]

It is impossible to enumerate all the forms assumed by Christian charity, or the institutions to which it gave rise.   Some of the most curious were devoted to the *recovery of prostitutes*.   This social sore existed throughout the Middle Ages, but increased during the thirteenth century with the growth of towns and universities.   Prostitutes were found everywhere, even in the crusading armies!   St Louis took steps to regulate their trade, and an encyclical of Innocent III in 1198 promised total remission of his sins to any pious man who married a harlot with a view to her rehabilitation.

In 1204, Fulk, parish priest of Neuilly who was afterwards celebrated as Peter the Hermit of the fourth crusade, began, with his curate Peter of Rossiac, haranguing fallen women in the public squares and in the streets.   Later, he founded a congregation for the purpose of reclaiming them; and his devoted efforts soon brought into being an abbey which

---

[1] Cf. Prof. Jeanselme: 'Comment l'Europe au Moyen Âge se protégea contre la lèpre in *Bull. Hist. de la Médecine*, 1931.   For life in a lazar-house, *see* C. Schmidt: *Notice sur l'église rouge et la léproserie de Strasbourg* (Strasbourg, 1879).

adopted the Cistercian Rule. Fulk was not alone in this work; in 1272, Bertrand, a citizen of Marseilles, established a similar community which was recognized as a monastic Order by Nicholas III. Their example was imitated at Rome, Bologna, Messina, Bourges, Dijon, and even at St Jean d'Acre in Palestine. But the most interesting and most successful of these undertakings was that of Canon Rudolph of Hildesheim, who was asked by the Archbishop of Mayence to reclaim the *fahrende Weiber* (street-walkers). He founded the Order of Penitent Sisters of St Magdalen, under whose austere rule these ladies might walk the road to heaven.

Not even so generous an outpouring could exhaust the fire of Christian love. If the sick and the infirm were dear to God, there was yet another class of men for whom our Lord demanded succour in the parable of the Good Samaritan. These were travellers, especially pilgrims, who journeyed in search of Christ, and for whose benefit several congregations were founded. In Italy, the Hospitallers of Altoparcio guided travellers through the dangerous marshes around Lucca; in Spain, the Knights of St James protected pilgrims on the road to Compostella; and a like duty was performed by the Templars in Palestine. In the Alps, where the passes were especially difficult in winter, hospices were established by St Bernard of Menthon (996–1081), a young nobleman from the Val d'Aosta, whose father resided on the lake of Annecy and who had already spent a long life in the apostolate. His memory is preserved by the Great and Little St Bernard, whence (until 1953) the canons regular and their famous dogs guaranteed the safety of travellers in those parts. In the thirteenth century, when a new road was opened from Central Switzerland towards Italy, the monks of Disentis built a hospice and named it St Gothard in memory of the holy bishop whose charity had shed light on Hildesheim. So hospices sprang up on all the highways of Christendom, centres of Christian welcome where travellers and pilgrims found food and lodging, where they could mend their clothes and shoes, get a shave and haircut, and confess their sins.

All this provides tangible proof that the idea of Christendom was no abstract notion, and that the Church imparted to secular society the very strength of Christ. If we desire one more proof of her boundless charity, we shall find it in the *Redemptive Orders*, whose founders were inspired by the most sublime of motives. In Africa and Asia the infidels treated their Christian captives as slaves, who were not seldom in peril of their lives. A number of heroic souls combined in an attempt to deliver these unfortunates: they begged money for ransom, and even visited Moslem territory, offering themselves as substitutes for any captives whose salvation was thought to be in danger. This extraordinary undertaking involved grave risks, as witness St Raymond

Nonnatus, who was martyred in 1240 by the Bey of Algiers on account of his unrelenting zeal. Two great Orders were vowed to this work. The *Trinitarians* were founded in 1198 by St John of Matha and Felix of Valois with encouragement from Innocent III. Their white habit with its red and blue cross soon became famous. The chief house of the Order in France was the convent of St Mathurin at Paris, where they became known as Mathurins, or 'Donkey Brothers,' because those of them who went on begging missions were content with this humble form of transport. The *Ransomers*, otherwise known as the Order of Our Lady of Ransom, was founded in 1223 by St Peter Nolasco and St Raymond of Pennaforte, who introduced into their Rule the vow of self-substitution for captives. Between the date of their foundation and the French Revolution, these two orders delivered more than 600,000 captives, among whom was Cervantes.

Such was the splendid service rendered by the Church in return for the privileges granted to her by medieval society. Nevertheless, we shall misunderstand her economic and institutional role unless we bear in mind that her charitable work was not the fruit of cold calculation on the part of statesmen anxious to maintain order and to avoid misery which begets trouble. Her work in this field had nothing in common with the regimentation of Social Security or with the anonymity of Public Assistance. The Rule of the Paris hospitals in 1230 stated that they were to receive 'the poor and wretched as our Lord Himself,' that they must be 'honoured and served as if they were God.' Our lords the poor were loved indeed. For when the Church taught her children to be charitable, she was not taking her stand on the merely administrative plane; she was teaching them how to obey Christ's command.[1]

---

[1] The Middle Ages had a mystic nostalgia for poverty, and came within an ace of treating it as a sacrament. In every medieval will made at Paris we find a bequest in favour of the Hôtel-Dieu. (*See* E. Coyecque, *L'Hôtel-Dieu de Paris au Moyen Âge.*)

CHAPTER VII

MAN UNDER THE EYE OF GOD

1. 'Wherever there is Man, there is Human Nature'

The Church asked nothing more of her children than to be faithful to Christ's message; but at no time has it been easy to obtain this fidelity. 'Wherever there is man, there is human nature,' says Montaigne; and no matter how strong religious faith may be, it cannot avoid the fact that man is a creature of flesh and blood, full of sin and disobedience. Human nature was of no higher quality in the Middle Ages than it is to-day.

The barbarian epoch had witnessed an alarming decline of moral values and of civilization. Pillage, rape, and murder had long been fashionable occupations. The law of force, *Faustrecht*, prevailed; it was impossible, therefore, that violence and immorality should vanish from the earth within a few brief decades. Though profoundly Christian from many points of view, medieval society was none the less brutal, merciless towards children and defeated enemies, while its sexual life left much to be desired. In this atmosphere the Church strove untiringly to inculcate the civilizing principles of justice, human dignity, and peace.

Violence was the most striking feature, represented by the armed and armoured warrior galloping at the head of his men. When a creature of that kind is roused, men do better to avoid its path. Now fury was the only sentiment a true warrior thought worthy of himself; 'to think is to make oneself ridiculous' was a common saying. To rush upon his neighbour, upon Church property, and upon helpless peasants was considered almost a professional duty, whereby the soldier trained his hand for operations on a larger scale. How else, indeed, could he avoid boredom in his thick-walled castle, half fortress and half barracks, when chase and tourney, both images of war, did not suffice to occupy his days?

'They preferred combat to fine gold and food,' says the *Chanson d'Antioche*; while a knight confesses outright: 'If I had one foot in Paradise and the other in a castle, I would step down from above to go and fight.' Read any of the *Gestes*, and you will at once smell fresh-spilled blood and 'earth bestrewn with brains'; you will see widespread massacre on every page, dying men at their last gasp on the field, the wounded forcing back 'their guts into their bellies.' Family ties were no obstacle to such deeds, and it was often the warrior's own brother, his father, or his cousin whom he dispatched in this way.   A man who clove his enemy in two, or opened his breast and tore out his heart; a hardened old soldier who dashed children against a wall, or boozed on the ruins of a convent whose nuns he had just slaughtered; neither of these types was looked upon as a savage brute, but rather as a hero who deserved pardon for his whims.   Such are the chief characters, for example, in the lays of Raoul de Cambrai or in the Lorraine Cycle. There was little protest, unless a whole population was massacred, or the soldiers behaved with abnormal cruelty.   The Sire de Coucy was a bestial figure, as was Bernard de Cahuzac, who put out the eyes of 150 prisoners at Sarlat while his wife amused herself by cutting off the breasts and tearing out the nails of a female prisoner.

Such practices were not confined to the feudal class; urban wars were every bit as frightful as those waged by the barons.   Quarrels between the Italian cities were full of unimaginable violence.   Whole provinces were laid waste and devoured by fire; the utmost refinement of torture was visited upon the losers; [1] and men were put to death in pitch, in boiling oil, and by still more hideous means.

It was often impossible to excuse these acts of violence on grounds of war, for many 'soldiers' were no more than highway robbers.   Suger says of the Sire de Coucy that he 'devoured like a ravening wolf.' The monks of St Martin at Canigou used ten pages of a large folio volume to recite the cruelties inflicted upon them by the lord Pons du Vernet.   Many families of noble extraction descended to the level of feudal brigands, taking up their abode on some mountainside and lying in wait for travellers.   The very name of Hohenzollern (high customs-officers) is suggestive!   These bandits, too, were orthodox Christians. Abélard, speaking of the Count of Blois, says with disillusioned irony: 'Thibaut gives plenty of money to the religious orders; the more he steals, the more he has to hand out.   It would be better if he stole nothing and gave nothing.'

Violence and cruelty, then, were part of medieval life.   Men were so accustomed to it that their sense of indignation had become atrophied. Nothing is more striking in this connection than their system of criminal justice.   For example, there was a feudal law which reserved the right of chase to the landowner on his own property, and Enguer-rand de Coucy once applied this law by hanging three boys who had poached a rabbit.   St Louis summoned him to court and punished him severely for this outrageous act of cruelty.   Whereupon several barons protested that there had been no miscarriage of justice.   The use of torture after condemnation as an increase of punishment, as well as beforehand in order to extract a confession, steadily increased.   The

---

[1] e.g. at Forli, where prisoners were shod like mules.

Germanic custom of trial by ordeal continued in use, whereby the accused had to plunge his hands into boiling water or walk barefooted on live coals.   There was also the judicial duel, a strange method of settling differences by allowing the parties to cut one another's throats and leaving Providence to point out the winner.

We might at least expect to find that women behaved better.   They may not all have gone so far as the hideous torturess of Sarlat; but many of them, living in their castles as in a guard-house, seem to have been formidable viragos.   We find them leading armies into battle, as did Blanche of Navarre, Countess of Champagne, who burned Nancy. Aubrée d'Ivry built a stronghold during her husband's absence, and shut him out on his return; but a dagger put an end to her pretensions.

It need scarcely be said that sexual morality fared little better.   We have just been speaking of women, and it is an admitted fact that the women of any period are the true gauge of its moral standards. Judging by medieval literature (which, by the way, was often so out-spoken and realistic as to take the heart out of any twentieth-century novelist), female manners seem to have been deplorable.   We are assured that women spent so many hours at their toilet that they arrived for Mass 'long after the consecration'; and as for their dress, a little poem by Robert of Blois describes a technique of coquetry that seems not yet to have grown old:

> Aucune laisse desfermée
> Sa poitrine, pour ce qu'on voie
>   confaitement sa chair blanchoie.
> Une ses jambes trop descœuvre . . .
> Prudhomme ne loue pas cette œuvre.

Nor was there only question of peccadilloes; the *fabliaux* and *gestes* make constant reference to adultery.   Documentary evidence suggests that society as a whole showed scant respect for sexual morality. Preachers never ceased to inveigh against the corruption of manners; and even allowing for the professional character of their invective, we cannot suppose that it was all mere imagination.   We must likewise assume that the detailed lists of carnal sins found in confessors' manuals were not dictated simply by a taste for classification.

It stands to reason that men were no better than women.   If proof be needed of the moral chaos, there is plentiful evidence in the matri-monial fantasies of kings and emperors.   Examples of divorce, remarriage, and public concubinage are numerous.   Some of-them have a certain quaintness, such as that of the Capetian Philip I deserting his wife Bertha of Frisia.   Premature stoutness had diminished her charms, and the monarch, in his hurry to replace her, carried off Bertrade, Countess of Anjou, the wife of one of his chief vassals. Others kept a mistress—sometimes more than one; and the Emperor

Henry IV was notorious for the indignities with which he loaded two successive wives, Adela of Turin and Praxede.   One of the counts of Poitiers bundled his wife and children out of doors, and installed a younger woman who was herself already married.

The kings of Sicily also distinguished themselves in this respect. No son of Roger II made any secret of his harem, and we know that Frederick II imitated their example.   Well-behaved sovereigns, such as William the Conqueror in England, and St Louis in France, were considered anomalies.   Noblemen, of course, followed in the footsteps of their rulers; and after the capture of Barbastro, in Spain, the Moslem chroniclers were horrified at the licentiousness of the French barons. In the East, the crusaders gave a shameful exhibition of Western morals.   Incidentally, too, the crusades and wars in general were often a severe test of conjugal fidelity, as were pilgrimages in general. Absent husbands frequently returned to find themselves supplanted. Enguerrand de Coucy was renowned not only for his barbarous justice, but also for his rape of Sibyl, Countess of Namur, while the count was fighting elsewhere.   Nor were clerics themselves altogether free from guilt.   The satiric poet Mahieu assures us that the clergy of 'St Geneviève, Notre-Dame des Champs, and St Maur seduced the women of Paris.'   Nor was it without reason that in 1231 the synod of Rouen forbade the keeping of vigils in churches, or that another assembly referred more explicitly to 'wolves' who profited by these occasions to 'sollicit' the pious females of the flock.

It is foolish to generalize, for documentary evidence in any period is more often concerned with evil than with good; and while History names the profligates, she overlooks the mighty host of those who remained true to the laws of chastity and to their marriage vows. Nevertheless, the upper classes of medieval society as a whole impress us no more favourably than do their counterparts of to-day.   As for the lower orders, what little we know of them through *fabliaux* or chronicles suggests a level of morality scarcely higher than that of brute beasts.

The Church strove manfully to stem this degrading current, calling her children to the practice of those Christian virtues which are depicted on the sculptured porches of cathedrals in the form of chaste, simple, and heroic girlhood.   Men did not reject her lesson outright; human nature is weak in the presence of temptation rather than fundamentally bad.   All the same, those who bore witness to the teaching of Christ often went in peril of their lives.   Bishop Robert de Meung, for example, was assassinated in 1220 by a robber-baron whom he had recently excommunicated, and Bishop Robert of Clermont was thrice imprisoned by Guy II, Count of Auvergne, a notorious raider of abbeys.   Seculars and regulars alike were hated by all the riff-raff of society.   It would be impossible to set down the revolting details of cruelty and blasphemy to which so many churchmen were subjected by these brutes; yet, in spite of repeated set-backs, and at the cost of age-long effort, the Church persisted in her formidable task.   Slowly she raised the moral standards of society, and put an end to numerous horrors and injustices, by forcing the animal in human nature to feel itself continually in God's sight.

2.   Respect for the Human Person and Liberation of the Serfs

At the root of her endeavour lay one vital factor: respect for man, i.e. for the human person.   Had not Christ said that God cares for each and every individual, that God, whose solicitude extends even to the humblest sparrow, is interested in each and every one of us?   The idea that man's importance consists in his being a unique and personal entity was seen by the Church to derive support from the whole feudal regime, within which all social relationships were personal, as between man and man, and within which nothing counted apart from the individual (*nihil praeter individuum*).   The terrible notion of mankind as an anonymous mass in which the individual is annihilated, or reduced to a mere number in the mechanism of administration and production, would have horrified medieval men, who were closer than we are to reality and to life.

To-day we think of slavery in the ancient sense as the ultimate degradation of human personality.   It was a system under which one man belonged to another, as does an animal or lifeless chattel.   This melancholy institution had not disappeared in the Middle Ages.   The slave-traffic was a black spot on the period; Saracens and Jews were the principal commodity.   These human cattle came chiefly from Illyria, Dalmatia, and the Slav countries.   But German barons were not ashamed to deal in pagans from the Baltic; and when Rome was taken by the Normans, all the efforts of Gregory VII failed to prevent the sale at a low price of thousands of inhabitants to the Moslems. There was still a slave-trade in England and Ireland in the twelfth century, and also at Lyons, Florence, and even Rome itself; nor was it regarded as unlawful, provided the individuals sold were not Christians at the time of their capture.

The early Church, while reminding masters that their slaves were also their brethren, had not condemned slavery, and Patristic writers followed Plato and Aristotle in admitting that it was part of natural law.   'The slave should be resigned to his lot, in obeying his master he is obeying God,' wrote St John Chrysostom; and according to St Augustine, 'God introduced slavery into the world as punishment for sin.' But in the fifth century churchmen began to protest against the iniquity of slave-owners, and at least fifty regional councils between 451 and 700 enacted canons for the protection of slaves. Many bishops refused to allow them on their estates, and urged their masters to enfranchise them; while a council held at Toledo was obliged to check the zeal of certain holy prelates who were on the way to ruining their dioceses in order to meet the cost of manumission.

The anti-slavery movement increased from the twelfth century onwards; and councils, such as that held at London in 1102, forbade 'this ignoble trade whereby men are sold like beasts.' The popes also did their utmost, and with some success, to ensure that slaves who embraced the Christian faith were granted freedom. In France, under Philip Augustus, it was declared that 'any slave who passes within the frontiers of the kingdom and receives baptism is free,' and the same was done at Florence in 1289. There were, of course, always a number of bishops who closed their eyes to this disgraceful traffic; but Christendom as a whole tended to condemn slavery as immoral and to improve the lot of its victims, for whose deliverance the orders founded by St John of Matha and St Peter Nolasco put no bounds to their charity.[1]

Side by side with the slaves properly so-called (and these were not very numerous) there existed a class of men known as serfs, who are often confused with them because their name is derived from Latin *servus* (slave). The serf was in no sense a slave; he was treated not as an animal but as a person; he possessed his own family, home, and plot of land, and he was quits with his master once he had paid his dues. He was not the property of a man, but was attached to a domain in accordance with the essentially medieval concept of an association between men and land, an association which, at the other end of the scale, forbade even a nobleman to alienate his domain. While the *villein*, or free peasant, had the right to 'move out,' i.e. to leave his land, the serf was tied to it. On the other hand, his land was not distrainable, and he owed no military service in the event of war. He was therefore proof against those vicissitudes which threatened his 'free' neighbour. His position was, from many points of view, so advantageous that one collection of usages speaks of the 'privilege enjoyed by serfs of being guaranteed against eviction from their land'; and there are numerous instances of free peasants making themselves serfs for the sake of peace and security. It has been held[2] that serfdom, by

[1] See the preceding chapter, section 11.

[2] By G. Roupnel in his excellent *Histoire de la Campagne française*. Some historians go even farther and maintain that the burdens of serfdom, viz. formariage, mortmain, and *chavage*, were common to serfs and to villeins holding land from an overlord. These charges were in origin purely domanial. It has even been denied that the serfs formed a distinct class. Thus in Champagne 'all villeins were regarded as serfs.' Whatever the truth may be, it appears that in the Middle Ages serfs were a small minority. (Cf. Jean Imbert, *Histoire du droit privé*, p. 42.)

keeping families on the same parcel of land generation after generation, did much to create the sturdy French peasantry.

A serf's attachment to the soil, however, entailed certain restrictions. His lord had a 'right of pursuit,' i.e. he could bring him back by force if he absconded. He had also the 'right of formariage' which originally enabled him to prevent a serf marrying outside the fief, but which was later reduced to monetary compensation for any loss the master might suffer in consequence.[1] Finally, when a serf died his lord possessed a 'right of mortmain,' i.e. could sieze any goods acquired by the serf during his lifetime. In theory this was an oppressive right, but in practice it was often mitigated by permission to make a will. Such permission was expressly granted, or was exercised by virtue of a custom which recognized the whole family as joint owners and therefore exempt from mortmain.

The Church was not slow to take an interest in serfs and their condition. The first bishop to promulgate a decree determining their rights was Burchard of Worms (d. 1025), who forbade the imposition of fresh burdens; and his example was followed in many dioceses. During the crusades, the Church recognized that every serf had a right to take the Cross, that his lord could not prevent him doing so, and that, having done so, he was *ipso facto* free. One matter in which she acted with the utmost vigour, in order to enforce respect for human dignity in the serf, was the question of his marriage. She opposed the separation of married couples by the sale of one spouse together with the land on which that spouse resided. The *Concordia* of Gratian declared that 'the marriage of serfs cannot be dissolved, even when the two partners belong to two different masters'; and Pope Adrian IV, in a decretal of 1155 which was afterwards included in the *Corpus Juris Canonici*, went still further by declaring the indissolubility of marriage between serfs, even if it had been celebrated without the master's leave. Marriage between a serf and a freeman, to which landowners were evidently opposed, was authorized by the Church; it was even encouraged in many monastic and other ecclesiastical domains, and in 1135 Pope Urban III decreed that all children born of such unions were free.

The Church, then, laboured to ensure respect for the servile class; and there is a remarkable difference between the treatment of serfs in religious documents and in the *chansons de geste* or *chantefables* which speak for the governing classes. The story of Aucassin and Nicolette

[1] Hence the 'right of thigh,' about which so much nonsense has been spoken and written. The serf (male and female) required the lord's permission to marry; and since in the Middle Ages everything took the form of symbolic gesture (e.g. delivery of a fief was effected by handing over a clod of earth), the lord, in order to signify his agreement, placed his hand on the serf's leg or on the marriage-bed. From that fact, much has been imagined. . . . (Cf. L. Venillot, *Le droit du seigneur*.)

in *Garin de Lorrain* represents the serf as nothing better than a beast and utterly contemptible. But at the beginning of the eleventh century Archbishop Adalberon of Rheims, in his *Poème satirique*, speaks with tender feeling of these folk 'without whom no free man could live, and of whom the very king and bishops are in a way servants, so much do they depend on them for everything.' And what finer homage could the Church render to the serfs than to admit their sons into her ranks? She never barred them from the religious Orders, and many reached the summit of the hierarchy.[1]

The Church did more than this. She was not alone responsible for the great movement which, between the tenth and the thirteenth century, succeeded in abolishing serfdom in the West, but she is known to have given it a powerful impetus. Circumstances were favourable; for, as we have seen, the Middle Ages were a period rich in material achievement, and certain medieval inventions placed at man's disposal a store of accumulated energy. The hard horse-collar attached to the animal's body, instead of a soft collar around its neck, enabled it to draw loads weighing two or three tons as against a maximum of nine or ten hundredweights by the old method; while the introduction of horseshoes still further increased its hauling power. A new style of cart with independent front wheels made it possible for drivers to turn more easily, and helped to increase the volume of overland transport at the same time as carriage by water was facilitated by the invention of lock-gates. This increase of energy resulted in the use of animal-power instead of manpower in mills. At sea, the stern-rudder, which supplanted the steering-oar, permitted the construction of larger sailing-ships, and partly did away with the use of slaves as rowers. These technical advances had their repercussions upon social life. 'After the tenth century, complete mastery of animal driving-power freed men from work in that capacity, caused great strides in land-travel, and favoured the use of water-power with all its mechanical possibilities. . . . The inspired invention of an unknown man (probably a Frenchman during the so-called darkness of the Middle Ages) was destined to change the face of the world. . . .'[2] It was during this same period that serfdom died out in the West; and if we add that the increased wealth of the towns worked in the same direction by encouraging the acquisition of money rather than of land, it is easy to recognize the disappearance of serfdom as a sign of the times.

Here, again, we have an illustration of the Church's insight, of her readiness to seize an opportunity, and of the vigour with which she employed circumstances in the interests of faith. Technical achievement had reached a point from which mankind could make decisive

[1] See Chapter VI, section 2.   [2] Lefebvre des Noettes.

progress; the Church applied her basic principles to new historico-social conditions, and took a leading part in the liberation of the serfs.

The list of wide-scale enfranchisements carried out by the Church and affecting whole populations or estates is too long to set down in full. In France alone there were many such occurrences, which created a considerable stir. In 1197 the Abbot of St Rémy at Sens liberated all his serfs at Vareilles and Liége; in 1200 the Abbot of Vézelay set free all those who lived on the estates of that great abbey; in 1225 the chapter of Sainte-Croix at Orléans emancipated 500 serfs at Étampes; and in 1246 the monks of St Denis accorded the same privilege to their serfs. Next, in 1249, the Abbot of Saint-Germain-des-Prés enfranchised all those at Villeneuve-St-Georges, and in 1250 those at Thiais. Finally, in 1290, the Abbot of St Gildas at Châteauroux gave every serf at St-Marcel-lès-Argenton his freedom. Enfranchisement on a smaller scale was still more frequent. The abbots of Saint-Père at Chartres and Marmoutier each liberated more than 1,000 serfs; while in Normandy all the great abbeys followed suit, so that by the end of the thirteenth century there was hardly a serf left on their estates.[1] If we allow personal freedom to be a recognized privilege in any civilized society, we must likewise admit that the Church, together with the monarchy,[2] was a potent factor in the task of civilization.

3. THE HOLINESS AND DIGNITY OF LABOUR

While the Church looked upon man as a free and responsible agent, she was far from teaching him individualism. It is undoubtedly to Christian influences, to the doctrine of fellowship as taught in the Gospel, that we must principally attribute what Père Mandonnet[3] has described as 'the most characteristic phenomenon of European life in the twelfth and thirteenth centuries, the strength of fellow-feeling'; by which he means the remarkable aptitude in men to form themselves

---

[1] The Church has often been blamed for observing the custom of that time and requiring compensation from liberated serfs. But the practice is explained by the fact that enfranchisement involved her in a very heavy loss of revenue and the risk of labour-shortages. That is why, in many cases, manumitted serfs were required to put in so many days of work, on the 'instalment plan.' The amount of compensation has been greatly exaggerated; it was generally one sheaf of corn in every twelve and was known as the 'gerbe libératrice.' Serfs very often resisted emancipation, but such cases were rare on ecclesiastical estates. Laymen, on the other hand, frequently demanded enormous sums by way of compensation and taxes.

[2] Louis VI was the first Capetian king to free serfs in his domain; Louis VII went so far as to declare that liberty was part of French law. St Louis, in particular, enfranchised many serfs and encouraged his vassals to do likewise. These grants of freedom were almost always onerous, for the king and barons were in great need of money to resume the crusade. See G. Tenant de la Tour, L'homme et la terre de Charlemagne à saint Louis (Paris, 1942).

[3] In his Saint Dominique.

into groups and work together. Time and again we find in the charters of free towns and trade associations reference to the law of Christ's love.

Medieval man, aware of a higher law binding him to others, was fully conscious of his obligations to the community. He looked upon work, therefore, not merely as the means of earning his living, but as an activity worth while in itself and productive of virtue. In this matter, too, the Church was foremost in the field. She respected manual labour, which St Benedict had enjoined upon his sons both for their personal sanctification and for the common good; she taught men to value it by pointing to the example of Joseph the carpenter, Crispin the shoemaker, Eloi the goldsmith, and many another working man whom she herself had canonized. Everyone was familiar with St Paul's warning: 'He who worketh not, neither let him eat.' The labourer tilling his field, the craftsman producing wrought iron, dressing wood or leather, were each and all engaged in charitable work, preparing for themselves a place in heaven. Contempt for manual labour, which is felt by many intellectuals to-day, had no place in the age of the cathedrals; nor was it until the eighteenth century that men came to recognize a difference in meaning between the words 'artist' and 'artisan.' [1] Now since labour was a form of Christian virtue, the very organization of the working-class was specifically Christian. Theoretically there were two kinds of association, the *confraternity* and the *guild*. In practice, however, there was not much difference between them. Confraternities were originally indistinguishable from those many devout societies which had sprung from the cult of a saint, from companionship on pilgrimage, or from the wish to benefit by prayers after death. They were sometimes known as 'candles' or 'clubs,' after the candle offered by members to the church or the meal for which they 'clubbed' together. When the confraternity united men who followed the same trade it had this twofold character of a religious brotherhood and mutual aid society. Members were required

[1] It is important not to misunderstand the nature of the medieval working-class movement, which was often tinged with anti-clericalism. Banter and ridicule at the expense of monks and canons was only part of a small quiverful of arrows which the common folk loved to let fly against the clergy, simply because they were top-dogs and children have always enjoyed a joke against their elders. That it did not amount to much is shown by an amusing thirteenth-century poem entitled *Dit des fèvres*:

> In my view the workers are
> The folk for whom one should pray more.
> Believe me, workers do not live
> To dawdle; that's the very truth.
> Their property is not let out at interest.
> Workers live honestly by honest toil;
> They give and spend more open-handedly
> Than usurers who do not a stroke of work—
> Canons, provosts, or monks.

to attend certain offices, especially on the patronal feast-day; while pensions were paid from the common chest to those who were aged, sick, or unemployed. Moreover, these brotherhoods or confraternities gave rise to a system whereby travelling members might be lodged and fed by the local branch in almost every Christian country.

The guilds were organized on hierarchical lines, comprising masters, companions, and apprentices. Note, however, that this hierarchical system did not become widespread until about the fourteenth century with the ascendancy of the middle class; in the twelfth and thirteenth it was easy to rise from the degree of apprentice to that of master. The guild was essentially a professional body, uniting all workers employed in a given trade and subject to no authority. When St Louis instructed Étienne Boileau to draw up the *Livre des Métiers*, he intended no more than to codify established custom, not to make new regulations having royal authority.

For the most part, these associations of working men were fostered by the Church, who, it has been suggested, preferred that her children should emphasize their purely professional solidarity, since brotherhoods or confraternities tended to beget the Chapel spirit, and ran a risk of sowing tares in her midst. Christianity, then, kept a firm hold upon the guilds and other trade groups, many of whose statutes have a strong religious tone: 'Brethren, we are images of God; that thought is the keynote of our association. With God's help we shall achieve our purpose, provided fraternal charity is found among us; for it is by love of our neighbour that we rise to love of God.'

Actually, the guild modelled its pious customs, its liturgical traditions, and its charitable works upon those of the confraternity. In the stained-glass windows of our cathedrals we can still recognize both the collective labour and the faith of medieval workmen. Coopers, furriers, tanners, or bakers would subscribe to do honour to their patron saint, and present a window at the bottom of which was a panel showing them engaged in their particular occupations. In the reign of Philip Augustus, when Eudes de Sully presented Notre Dame with relics of his illustrious predecessor, St Marcel, the goldsmiths of Paris presented a valuable casket for their reception, and this was the origin of a custom known as 'may des orfèvres,' which lasted until the Revolution.[1]

Work thus performed beneath the eye of God ennobled man, and satisfied his heart's desire by giving him that 'pride in a job well done' which Péguy praised in ancient France, and of which there are many examples in the stories of the guilds. We read, for instance, in Thomas Deloney's tales of the weavers and shoemakers of London,

[1] Cf. P. M. Auzas, *La traditionelle offrande de la Corporation des orfèvres*, Ecclesia (Paris), May 1951.

that 'Every son of a shoemaker is a prince by birth,' and the art of mending shoes is called a 'noble trade.' The guilds also made rules governing manufacture. It was important to avoid the production of shoddy workmanship by unscrupulous individuals; and these regulations (which prescribed, among other things, the number of threads that should go to an ell of cloth, the thickness of stones used to build a house, and even the wood from which coffins should be made) bore witness to the dignity of labour.

The application of religious principles to labour organizations benefited the public by ensuring the production of sound commodities. It was likewise advantageous to the workers themselves, providing for their spiritual and moral welfare but also improving their material circumstances by forbidding unfair competition, preventing too low a level of wages, and condemning undue extension of the working day.

All the main feasts of the Church were what we should now call 'bank holidays.' Sunday (which included Saturday afternoon), together with many liturgical feasts, each of which frequently took in two or three days besides, were recognized holidays. The number of days thus set aside for prayer and rest from work varied from one diocese to another; they might be as few as thirty-three days (excluding Sundays) and as many as fifty-three or even seventy-four. But this number was clearly excessive; in the thirteenth century a reaction set in, and it was gradually reduced. Rules concerning rest from work were obeyed to the letter. Woe betide anyone who worked on Sunday or a feast day! Ecclesiastical penalties descended on him like a ton of bricks. Exceptions were extremely rare: the goldsmiths of Paris, for instance, were allowed to work during the morning on Sundays and feasts of the Apostles, but only in order to meet the expenses of an enormous banquet which they provided for all the poor of Paris at Eastertide.

A whole body of labour-laws thus came into being, not imposed by the State but arising spontaneously from the collective soul of Christian people. This code governing the production of goods was so effective that no one can confidently claim superiority for our modern regulations.

4. THE CHURCH AND MONEY

It may be asked, What was the position of wealth and profit in a society which treated work both as a means to individual progress and as a service to the whole community? Here again, the fundamental idea entertained by medieval Christendom appears full of common sense: it respected the existing order of things, even though practice was often enough opposed to doctrine. It is one thing for society to stand by and watch certain of its members yield to the temptation of huge profits (more or less justly acquired), even while it condemns the abuse of money; but it is quite another thing for that society to prostrate itself before wealth and to recognize, in Péguy's terrible phrase, 'money as master in the place of God.' In the first case, man retains his dignity, his liberty in face of mammon; in the second, he is riding headlong towards servitude and degradation. The Middle Ages certainly had their quota of wicked millionaires; the economic principle, however, on which society rested was not the familiar cry, 'Get rich!' but our Lord's saying, 'Blessed are the poor in spirit.'

Generally speaking, the notions of property, work, and profit were not so clearly defined as they are to-day, from a strict economic point of view, but in relation to services rendered. Landed property did not belong to a man simply because he had inherited or bought it, as is now the case. A modern owner of real property may be dispossessed in order to settle his debts, *but not because he misuses it or does not use it at all.* In the Middle Ages the exact opposite was true: a landowner, though up to the neck in debt, could never *on that account* be dispossessed of his estates, but he could be if he proved himself unequal to his responsibilities or broke his feudal oath. The moral principle took precedence of economic considerations.

The same thing applied in the case of work. Nowadays, money is the measure of labour; transactions between one man and another are in essence monetary, i.e. a certain sum of money passes in exchange for a certain amount of service or merchandise. Medieval man based his dealings and justified his services on wholly different grounds— fidelity, devotion, protection, charity, and, above all, on the notion of the common good. Granted there were many exceptions; avarice was plentiful, but the principles of human relationship were moral and not economic.

Exactly what part the Church played in this respect may be seen in the famous question of *loans at interest,* or, as theologians and canonists described it, *usury.* This word did not refer merely to interest above a legal rate, but more generally to all interest obtained by lending money. Usury included a number of transactions which political economy distinguishes. There were loans at interest in the strict sense, coalitions or monopolies of production and sale, time bargains, and indeed every kind of speculation.

From her very inception, the Church had been opposed to usury. Lending at interest was quite common in the Roman world, and Cicero tells us that in his day the rate was as high as 12 per cent. But it seemed intolerable that a man should profit by lending money to his brother in time of need. The Fathers of the Church had answered transactions of this sort in our Lord's own words: 'Give to one another without expecting a return' (Luke vi. 34); and in the fourth century many councils had forbidden usury on the part of clerics. At the end of the eighth century and the beginning of the ninth this prohibition had been gradually extended to laymen; clerical usurers were even threatened with dismissal, and all (both clergy and laity) with excommunication. But the fact that these measures were repeated time and again throughout the medieval period suggests that they were not altogether effective. In 1049 the Council of Rheims, presided over by Pope Leo IX, included in one censure both usury and fornication. Later, in 1139, the Lateran Council declared usurers 'infamous.' This severe canon was repeated at the Lateran Council in 1179, at the Council of Lyons in 1214, and in 1311 at the Council of Vienne, which condemned as heresy the doctrine that usury is permissible. Names of usurers were posted on church doors, and the third Lateran Council excommunicated any Christian who did business with them. Innocent III favoured punishment of those who lent money at interest on a large scale, hoping that by these few well-chosen examples others might be brought to think again.

All our evidence points to the Church having had principally in mind those material abuses which were the more intolerable because they involved (at least at the beginning of the period) poor people who found themselves obliged by some misfortune to seek cash loans. The financial or speculative loan hardly as yet existed. Besides, the Church herself lent money: her treasures formed a rich storehouse; she had only to melt down a few pieces of plate, and there was money to lend to the unfortunate. But these were loans *without interest*—if not in effect free gifts, for there could be little hope in such cases of getting anything back. Such loans could not encumber the borrower. As Henri Pirenne [1] remarks: 'By forbidding usury upon religious grounds, the Church rendered signal service to the farming community during the early Middle Ages. She spared it the crushing burden of increasing debt which had so grievously afflicted the ancient world. Here Christian charity managed to apply in its full rigour the precept of lending without interest; and the saying "*mutuum date nihil vice sperantes*" was well suited to the character of a period when money had not yet become an instrument of wealth, so that all remuneration for its use must necessarily have seemed extortion.' [2]

---

[1] *Histoire économique de l'Occident médiéval.* The Church's economic role has been closely studied by R. Genestal, *Rôle des monastères comme établissements de crédit* (Paris, 1901). He has shown clearly that the Norman monasteries had become veritable farming banks advancing money to smallholders. Their work in this respect was of considerable importance.

[2] In fact, the prohibition of loans at interest and speculative practices gave rise to semi-clandestine, or at least officially unrecognized, groups of people who devoted themselves entirely to these forbidden trades. Such were the Northern Italians or 'Lombards' and, to a less extent, the Jews. These did not become really important until about the twelfth century when big business began to spread its tentacles, and with it the bank.

The Church condemned not only lending at interest, but all excessive profit from business.   On the other hand, the Lateran Council of 1123 threatened with excommunication those who oppressed merchants with excessive tolls and taxes, a decree which passed into Canon Law. The Church was also first to condemn the universally accepted law of piracy.   She intended to set a limit to commercial ambitions.   A sixth-century document, included by Gratian among his canons, expressly stated that 'Whoever buys a thing in order to re-sell it intact, no matter what it is, is like the merchant driven from the Temple.' Literally interpreted, this sentence would have prevented trade altogether.   The Canonists, and especially Rufinus, who studied the question in his *Summa Decretarum*, wisely decided that what was forbidden was purchase and sale *without work or risk*.   Commerce was licit so long as it required some financial outlay or personal labour. But there is no doubt that the general tendency at that period was to bring buyer and seller into direct contact without a middleman, and also to keep an eye on merchants so as to deter them from trickery, fraud, and misrepresentation.   The Church considered every commodity as having a *just price* based on the work necessary to produce it, an indubitably better idea than that which leaves prices dependent on capital and advertising.

This doctrine was evolved during the Middle Ages under pressure of circumstances.   Big business had never ceased to operate, even in the worst days of the barbarian epoch.   Towards the beginning of the eleventh century we discover tycoons like the famous St Godric (or Goodrich) of Finchale.   He made a fortune in the coasting trade along the shores of England, Flanders, and Denmark, as well as by lucky speculation, but was then touched by grace, gave his goods to the poor, and became a hermit.   It was chiefly in the twelfth century, however, that commercial undertakings assumed really gigantic proportions. The millionaire type began to multiply, producing men like the Venetian Romano Mairano, who invested the equivalent of twenty or

---

The natural ill-feeling of debtors towards their creditors was visited upon the Lombards and the Jews, especially upon the Jews, who were held at arm's length like criminals, and more or less confined within their Ghettos.   Such is the origin of 'pogroms' to which Jews have so often and in so many lands fallen victim, and which constitute one of the least lovely pages in the history of medieval Christendom.   But as a whole the Church, through the voices of her rulers, opposed these outbreaks of popular fury.   We have already seen St Bernard going to the rescue of persecuted Jews in the Rhineland; the Popes often took Jews under their protection; and when Duke Henry of Brabant ordered in his Will (1261) that all Jews should be expelled from his domains, St Thomas Aquinas told his widow to do nothing of the kind.   For the discussions that raged around the prohibition of usury, and the casuistry to which it gave rise, see an article by M. Louis Vereecke entitled 'Licéité du *cambium bursae* chez Jean Mair' in *Revue historique de droit français et étranger*, 1952 (p. 124).   He prints the text of an opinion given by the Faculty of Theology at Paris in answer to a question as to the lawfulness of engaging in the money-trade.

thirty million francs (1928 standard) in naval armaments, and profited to the tune of 50 per cent.   Widespread commercial networks such as those operated by Rhenish or Flemish weavers, who dealt in bales of wool by the hundred, could no longer be run on a cash basis; so that commercial credit, i.e. banker's loans, by means of drafts, discount, and bills of exchange, became necessary.

The Church adapted her principles to the new situation by deepening their foundations.   What was it she meant to condemn?   Mere speculation, money gained without work or risk.   Surely it was no more than fair that a lender who risked eventual loss or obvious failure should have a right to be indemnified; and likewise if his debtor purposely delayed repayment.   Canonists of the thirteenth century recognized this fact and distinguished the *titulus morae* (right in case of delay), the *titulus poenae* (right in case of loss), the *titulus periculi* (right in case of certain danger to the capital), and the *titulus lucri cessantis* (right in case of failure to succeed).   At the beginning of the fourteenth century a theologian named Alvarez Pelayo declared that the prohibition of usury could not extend to these cases.

The fact remains, however, that the Church upheld her principles. All profit derived from moneys lent without work or risk was unlawful; nor did she hesitate to free debtors from liabilities which seemed excessive, and we know of contracts in which borrowers engaged not to use this cunning method of escape.   It cannot be denied that in some cases the Church closed her eyes to abuses, that the popes were sometimes obliged to seek aid from financiers and allowed them to handle the papal revenues in a manner far from consistent with morality. But those cases were exceptions which prove the rule.   The Church did her best to destroy the primacy of gold, or at any rate to bring it within the principles of divine law.   And it was at that very time when she upheld those principles and when her greatest saints preached the ideal of poverty that she reached the zenith of her glory.

5.   THE CHURCH OPPOSED TO VIOLENCE

We come now to a more fundamental, more elementary, and far worse danger threatening the human person, that of unrestrained violence issuing in massacre and assassination.   It is to the Church' honour that she headed a movement that was gradually to elevate the conscience of mankind until public order was restored.   Amid the chaos of the ninth and tenth centuries, when Norman and Saracen spread terror far and wide, and when feudalism was becoming more or less a hierarchy, the Church had both the courage and the perseverance to instruct man once more in the principles of peace.   The worst menace at that time was, and continued for another century to be, the private war, which respected neither place nor age nor person, and often resulted in those deeds of almost inconceivable horror to which we have referred. The principal victims of these conflicts were, of course, the weak and innocent, defenceless villeins and serfs, priests and monks whose resources covered the cost of such enterprises. It was against these repeated acts of private war that the Church launched her campaign for the 'Peace of God.'

The movement began unpretentiously towards the end of the tenth century when the Councils of Charroux in Poitou (989) and Narbonne (990) re-enacted the prohibition against armed attack and pillage. In this latter year also the Council of Puy founded a 'league of the friends of peace' which was supported by both clergy and laity. The Church had early recognized an oath taken upon relics or the Gospels as a means of restraining violence. Faith was so firmly rooted in the souls of men that she was able to assume that most warriors who took such an oath would observe it; in any case, it brought the offender within the Church's jurisdiction, for she was the guardian of oaths. The Council of Verdun-sur-Saône (1016) had been the first to apply this method. It had been followed by a number of others, at which supporters of the Peace of God had undertaken 'not to attack the clergy; not to seize the peasant's ox, cow, etc. (a long list of animals follows); not to kill; not to attack travellers; and not to encourage any kind of brigandage or violence.' The Council provided for sanctions, and after 1031 any district in which the Peace had been violated was laid under interdict.

The movement, once initiated, swept away all resistance. Opposition, however, was sometimes keen, and came from unexpected quarters; for certain bishops frowned upon the Peace of God, arguing that, whatever happened, they could not excommunicate every baron in their dioceses! The idea, however, caught on in Italy, Spain, and the Germanic lands. In 1081 the Bishop of Liége obliged all those in his diocese to swear to observe the Peace of God, and almost all his colleagues in the Empire quickly followed suit. In Italy, the synods of Melfi (1089) and Troïa (1093) applied it to Apulia and Calabria. In Spain, it was promulgated by a council held at Gerona in 1068. The great territorial princes had too much interest in the maintenance of order within their domains not to side with the Church. As long ago as 1021 Robert the Pious and Henry II of Germany, who dreamed of universal peace, had taken steps to give the institution official status. All the Capetians, too, were zealous supporters of the Peace of God. Thus, in 1155, Louis VII proclaimed a general and absolute peace of ten years, and he discussed it at an interview with Frederick Barbarossa in 1164.

The Church went still farther and recruited volunteers for the defence of peace.   These formed a militia whose duty it was to punish offenders and enforce their submission.   'War upon those who cherish war!' was the watchword to which thousands from every class of society answered with enthusiasm.   The experiment seems not to have been at first an unqualified success.   These champions of peace, ill trained in the art of war, were often badly mauled by the veterans whom they sought to convert.   In 1038, for example, on the banks of the Cher, the warrior-bandit Eudes of Déols easily annihilated the holy militia sent against him by Aimon, Archbishop of Bourges.   But the system was gradually improved; peace associations hired professional soldiers, who formed a kind of Territorial army paid from the proceeds of a special tax known as the *paxagium*.   The volunteer militiamen were often commanded by royal officers, and we know what help they gave the Capetian kings, particularly Louis VI the fat, against the robber-barons.

The institution of a militia in defence of peace shows that the Church recognized that war might be justified in principle.   She was far from professing what to-day we should call 'pacifism,' and Pope Gregory VII himself declared: 'Cursed be the man who will not dip his sword in blood.'   What she did do was to introduce the notion of justice into warfare.   The *Liber. feudorum*, a code of Christian chivalry, expressly states that a vassal is not a felon, i.e. does not violate his feudal oath, if he refuses to assist his overlord in an unjust war.   If the Church not only permitted but even encouraged the use of arms, she did so in the name of higher principles: the principle of justice which defined the aggressor and obliged him to keep the peace, and the principle of charity which requires us to help the weak against unjust aggression.   Such were the ideas expressed in many councils and papal documents studied and sifted by jurists and canonists from Manegold of Lautenbach to Yves of Chartres.

In virtue of this second principle, that of charity, the Church instituted another movement, more or less connected with the first and called the 'Truce of God.'   Her purpose was to suspend fighting altogether for a certain time without inquiring whether a particular war was in itself legitimate.   The idea had been mooted in 950, though without success, by Pope John XV at the time of a quarrel between the Duke of Normandy and an English king.   A synod held at Elme, near Perpignan, in 1017 had decided that all military operations must cease 'from the ninth hour on Saturday until the first on Monday'; while the synod of Nice in 1041 had prescribed a truce from Wednesday evening to Monday morning, since Thursday was the day of our Lord's Ascension, Friday of His Passion, Saturday of His Burial, and Sunday of His Resurrection.   The Truce had been gradually extended to two whole periods of the liturgical cycle, Lent and Advent; then to certain feasts of our Lady, St John the Baptist, and the Apostles; and lastly to vigils and ember days. In 1054 the Council of Narbonne embodied this regulation in the splendid formula that 'a Christian who slays another Christian sheds the Blood of Christ.'

The 'Truce of God' became increasingly popular. It penetrated into northern France and the Rhineland, then into England, Italy, and Spain. It was adopted by the papacy in the second half of the eleventh century; and at the celebrated Council of Clermont, in 1095, Urban II called for a general truce. 'You have seen,' he said, 'that the world has long been troubled by these injustices, so much so that in certain parts it is impossible to travel safely on the roads. By day there is little or no security against brigands, or at night against thieves who lie in wait for you both within doors and without. That is why the so-called *treuga*, instituted long ago by the holy Fathers, needs tightening up. Each one of you must enforce it in his diocese; and if anyone, urged by cupidity or rashness, should violate the Truce, let him be punished with the appointed penalty of excommunication through the authority entrusted to you by God and on the strength of decisions reached in this council. . . .' In 1123, 1139, and 1179 the first three Lateran councils prescribed the Truce of God for the whole Church, and their resolutions became part of Canon Law.

The question was, whether these lofty ideals would prove effective. It is certainly true that they often did so, that many great lords overcame the temptation to violence and submitted to rules of conduct which a purely moral authority claimed to impose on them.[1] The problem became infinitely more complicated when there was no question of private wars or of relatively unimportant differences between nobles, but of clashes between kings or national interests. Even in these difficult cases the Church did not hesitate to intervene.

At such times the cause of peace was upheld chiefly by the papacy. The papacy by definition, at least in theory, transcended political strife and party quarrels, because its authority was of divine origin, and because it enjoyed universal prestige. It was therefore eminently fitted to act as arbitrator, inasmuch as one man could hear and decide the case. If we would understand the attitude of those who admitted the papal claim to judge between belligerents, and that of the popes to whom it belonged, we must bear in mind all that has been said in a previous chapter concerning the doctrine of Two Swords, which gave the Holy See both a direct and an indirect right to intervene in temporal affairs. But the popes were not the only ones who acted in this way. Several men, notably St Bernard and St Louis, were accepted as

[1] Even before the kings approved these measures, as did Philip Augustus and his successors by introducing the *Quarantaine le Roi*, a truce which suspended hostilities and thereby gave their own forces time to take a hand.

political arbitrators merely because they were saints: their judgments were considered as proceeding from the Almighty Himself.

Much has been written concerning the Church's function as peacemaker.[1] 'To mention only a few of the cases summoned before the court of Rome,' says Drouard, 'there was the affair of William the Conqueror and Harold of England, followed by the Quarrel of Investitures. There was the intervention of Clement III between the kings of France and England; of Innocent III between Philip Augustus and Richard Cœur de Lion, to whom threats and exhortations were alternately addressed; and between John Lackland and Philip Augustus. The Emperor Frederick was condemned by Gregory IX in 1236, and deposed by Innocent IV in 1245. Boniface VIII endeavoured to make Philip the Fair observe his truce with England; while John XXII sided with Ludwig of Bavaria against Frederick of Austria, and spoke in a letter to Philip V of "exercising the right of imposing truce which belongs to the Apostolic See." Next, there was the general intervention of Nicholas V, who, in order to provide for large-scale recruitment against the Turkish invaders, proclaimed peace throughout the Christian world, conferred authority on ecclesiastical dignitaries to negotiate the same, and required at least that armistices should be concluded and observed.' Drouard's list of papal arbitrations in the strict sense is no less impressive. He cites 'that of Gregory VII between Philip I of France and William the Conqueror, of Innocent III between England and Scotland, and the mediation of Clement III and Celestine III between France and England. Innocent III likewise intervened in the affairs of Italy, Portugal, Serbia, Armenia, and Bulgaria.'

All these efforts, it need hardly be said, failed to establish an indefinite reign of universal peace. But they did enforce the recognition of a Christian Peace similar to the *Pax Romana*, preferable to armed conflict, and which so impressed the minds of men that we are justified in claiming that, by and large, the great medieval centuries enjoyed a season of international tranquillity far superior to anything known in the barbarian epoch or during the succeeding period. Thanks to papal Bulls and conciliar decrees, there grew up slowly but surely a framework of International Law embedded in those canonical treatises which alone could give it universal application.

The Church's activity was not confined to the realms of public and private law. She attempted, in a more general way, to train the conscience of mankind away from cruelty and violence. The majority were in favour of and anxious for peace, and the collective conscience was both formed and directed by the Church. Insisting on the Gospel

[1] See especially the essays by Père Delos in *La Société internationale* (1928), and C Drouard, 'La Paix médiévale' in *Cahiers du Monde Nouveau*, 1, 2, and 4, 1945.

precepts, 'Love one another,' 'My peace I leave unto you,' she created a body of opinion the strength of which was eventually recognized by the warrior class.   If there had been no such thing as public opinion, or if the collective conscience had not been Christian, it is unlikely that the spiritual weapons would have been so effective, or that so many excommunicated rulers would have submitted to an unarmed clergy.

This endeavour to stem the tide of violence and atrocity is immediately discernible in two particular instances.   First there was the matter of ordeal and judicial duel, methods of trial which were so much part of an accepted system that the Church could not at once abolish them.   They were even recognized by some provincial synods, though the papacy always disapproved of them both in theory and in practice. They were never employed by ecclesiastical tribunals, and the Lateran Council of 1215 expressly forbade priests to bless those who had recourse to them.   The judicial duel had long since been condemned as a monstrosity.   Archbishop Agobard of Lyons (779–840) declared it to be 'no law, but murder'—*non lex sed nex*; and Pope Nicholas I (858–67) added that it was equivalent to tempting God.   In 1216 Honorius III prohibited its use, and St Raymond of Pennaforte's great juridical compendium contains these words: 'The duel and every other form of ordeal are forbidden, because they lead to the condemnation of innocent persons; to have recourse to them is to tempt God.'

The second instance was the tourney, an often bloody sport in which the nobility indulged with unbelievable brutality.   It was originally fought with blunted arms, but early in the thirteenth century the use of sharp weapons was introduced, and every meeting became a sort of miniature battle in which the two sides confronted one another before a bevy of fair ladies who would be their reward.   Combatants were often wounded, and sometimes killed.   The Church took a firm stand against this form of entertainment,[1] which, as the Council of Clermont said in 1130, 'endangered both body and soul.'   The Lateran Council in 1179 forbade these 'detestable festivities,' and instructed priests to refuse Christian burial to those killed in a tourney.   It must, however, be conceded that in this matter the Church's denunciation fell mostly on deaf ears.   Those taking part cared little for excommunication, for this mock warfare was already too much part and parcel of contemporary life.   No matter with what energy and patience the Church might set to work, violence was so deep-rooted in the medieval mind that any attempt to eradicate it altogether was bound to meet with failure.   Therefore, with characteristic common sense, the Church,

---

[1] There were rare exceptions to this rule; in 1200, for example, the great tourney at Éry-sur-Aisne was blessed by the episcopate because the victors had promised to join the fourth crusade.

having done all she could to loosen the stranglehold of brutality adopted another method intended to Christianize force and its employment. This method was twofold. First she offered her warlike sons the crusade as an outlet for their passions. 'Now,' cried Urban II at the end of his great sermon at Clermont, 'all those who have abused their right of challenge against the faithful must embark on a worthy undertaking that will end in victory. All those who have lived as brigands must become soldiers of Christ. Henceforth they will fight the good fight against barbarians, and those who have been in one another's pay for the sake of a few pence will reap an everlasting reward.' If 'to kill a Christian' was 'to shed the blood of Christ,' to slay an infidel now became a sacred duty, a work deserving of salvation Here was a splendid opportunity for hot-heads itching to use their swords.

As regards the other means adopted by the Church with a view to hallowing the arms of war, it occupies so prominent a place in Christian society that we must consider it at some length. I refer to the institution of Chivalry.

6. CHIVALRY: A CHRISTIAN IDEAL

Of all familiar types representative of the Middle Ages, none is more likely to captivate our imagination or to move our hearts than is the knight. All the animal passions in man, all his will to power, all that issues from the dark regions of his soul, driving him to violence and destruction, is satisfied and transcended in this noble image of the just and upright warrior, haloed with virgin purity; whose aim is rather sacrifice than victory, blood offered than blood shed.

Chivalry was not born on Christian soil. It sprang from the traditions of Germanic tribes in which no young man bore arms until he received them (helmet, buckler, javelin) from the hand of his father or his chieftain; [1] and the Church laboured with undying patience to endow this military investiture with the quasi-sacramental character of knighthood. Centuries were needed in order to effect a complete merger of the two traditions, that of the savage north with that of the Roman and Christian south, a synthesis of which knighthood was the perfect symbol. It was in the middle of the barbarian epoch that the Church began to accomplish this union, by blessing the weapons of those who went to war and by giving them appropriate battle-cries About the year 1000 priests used to say the following prayer over youths who were ready to take arms: 'Hear, O Lord, our petitions and bless with Thy majestic hand this sword wherewith Thy servant

[1] See Tacitus, *Germania*, Chapter XIII.

desireth to be girt, so that he may be enabled both to defend churches, widows, orphans, and all servants of God against the cruelty of pagans, and also to strike fear into the hearts of traitors!' From about 1050 this ideal grew still deeper and more Christian. By the beginning of the twelfth century the institution had come to stay, and in fully civilized countries was recognized and respected by all.

What was a knight? What qualities and virtues were demanded of one who bore this title? He was a soldier—a cavalryman (*chevalier*), for to fight on horseback was a privilege. He was a warrior, whose primary vocation was armed combat; but he was also expected to live up to certain moral principles, and bound himself by oath to do so. He was a man who believed that over and above force there existed values to which he dedicated himself. In this way, the commandments which regulated his conduct bore a military and a Christian character indissolubly linked. As a soldier, he must above all be brave, never give ground, and meet the enemy wherever his leader bade. Such were the duties of his state. And in order that he might fulfil them to the letter, he was required to possess physical strength, perfect health, and skill; no dwarf or bandy-legs might be a knight. These qualities were indispensable; but they were not enough, and there was an old saying: 'Tant est prudhomme si comme semble qui a ces deux choses ensemble valeur de corps et bonté d'âme.' [1]

'Goodness of soul' meant the whole scale of virtues, religious as well as secular and social. At the summit was faith, which gave the others meaning and importance. Because he was a believer, the knight was obliged to respect the Church and to defend her at all times; but he was assured that whatsoever he accomplished in the rough school of arms, he did it for God. If ever a man was conscious of living in the presence of God, it was the perfect knight. Such were Godfrey de Bouillon, Baldwin the Leper, and St Louis, soldiers whose life and death were committed from the outset into God's hand.

The qualities demanded of a knight were really the fulfilment of a Christian's obligation. He was faithful, devoted to his leaders, strict in the observance of his feudal oath. He was loyal, hated deceit, and faced up to the truth as he faced up to the enemy. He was loyal, nay more, an unflinching servant of the ideal of justice, 'in order,' says William Durand's *Pontifical* (a code of chivalric liturgy), 'that Justice may find a champion here below.' He was also charitable, vowed to defend the weak, the clergy, widows, and children; generous to his subordinates and even to the enemy. Chivalry was a sublime ideal which no civilization has managed to surpass. True, it was seldom realized, and frequently obscured by human covetousness; even so,

---

[1] He, it seems, alone is worthy who has these two things together, strength of body and goodness of soul.

there is merit in the fact that a whole society acknowledged the worth
of that ideal and strove, in the persons of its noblest representatives, to
spread it far and wide.[1]

Entry into the ranks of Chivalry was effected by means of an
elaborate and spectacular ceremony known as *dubbing* (*adoubement*).[2]
Its fundamentally religious character shows the institution to have been
a true Order; it was, as we have seen, in the nature of a sacramental.
In the eleventh century this rite, which might almost be described as a
liturgy, was quite simple, but it was gradually improved and enriched
with symbolism. The ancient Germanic elements, e.g. the purifying
bath and delivery of the sword, were retained; but they became part of
a mystical ceremony calculated to impress upon the candidate his future
responsibility before God.

It is night, a holy night—the vigil of Easter, say, or some other great
festival. Locked in the silent church, alone with a few candles to
accompany his prayer, the young squire keeps watch and meditates
He is twenty years of age, strong and courageous. For some time
past he has resided in his overlord's household, learning to ride, to
handle a sword, and to tilt at the 'quintain.' Earlier this evening he
has confessed and taken a ceremonial bath, so as to be pure in soul and
body; he has also donned a long white tunic as if for second baptism
A new life is now opening before him.

At length the great day dawns, and hour by hour the long ceremony
will unfold its pomp. Witnesses are there, usually twelve distinguished knights, together with his family and neighbours. Mass i
celebrated by some high dignitary of the Church surrounded by a vas
assembly of clergy; and when Holy Communion has confirmed him in
the pious resolutions taken during his vigil, the ceremony of admission
begins. Facing his sponsor, the candidate 'lays claim to knighthood.
Next, the witnesses clothe him in his new attire: two of them help him
on with the heavy linen acton, each one lacing a sleeve; another with
the coat of mail; two more with iron hose; and the last buckles on hi
spurs. As he receives each of these insignia he is reminded that thi

---

[1] Gustave Schnürer has some penetrating remarks on the history of the word 'honour'
'Knightly honour,' he concludes, 'was attended by particular prestige. A great mora
advance was involved in the Church's development of this concept, an advance not onl
upon the immediate past but also upon antiquity. In pagan antiquity the word signifie
no more than the rendering of external honours. This idea was subsequently elaborated
external honour was due only to one who was interiorly worthy, i.e. the man of honou
whose worthiness resided in himself. The essence of the new conception of honour
then, was the link established between exterior honour and interior worthiness. For th
knight, honour of rank was only a particular form of Christian honour. His honou
must consist in rendering the honour due to Jesus Christ and to God; for Them he wa
bound to fight, suffer, and die. The knight remained faithful unto death to the cause o
Christ; and thus fidelity, which was a particular obligation of knighthood, became
Christian obligation.'

[2] From Old German *dubban*, to strike.

arming should 'righteously serve justice,' and he replies 'God grant
that it may do so.'

The sponsor then advances with a drawn sword, extends the blade for
the young squire to kiss, and gives him a sharp blow on the shoulder
with the flat.   This is the accolade or *paumée*,[1] a survival of the old
Germanic rite.   Finally, he pronounces the formula of dedication,
beginning with an invocation of St Michael and St George, and admits
the youth into the order of Chivalry.   Girt with the sword, the new
knight stands before the altar, stretches forth his right hand, and takes
the oath.

Such was the ritual of 'dubbing,' a solemn mingling of military
symbolism with the sacred liturgy; and there is no better illustration
of the method whereby the Church introduced her spiritual ideals
into what was, after all, no more in substance than a formality of
incorporation.   Who could be admitted to the ranks of Chivalry?
Contrary to widespread belief, the privilege was not dependent upon
birth or fortune.   'No one is born a knight,' ran the adage, and in
theory even commoners could be knighted [2] as a reward for courage
and devotion.   'Knighthood,' it was said, 'confers nobility,' and 'the
means of attaining nobility without titles is to be made a knight.'
Moreover, the institution stirred enthusiastic longings of youth.
Francis Bernardone dreamed of knighthood at the age of twenty years,
before Christ called him to another service; and the kudos attaching to
that title was largely responsible for the eagerness with which many a
young man embarked on the crusade.   Not before the second half of
the twelfth century was it decided in certain countries [3] that, apart from
exceptional cases, only the sons of knights should be granted knighthood.   But this step perverted the very meaning of the institution,
which, through lack of members who had proved their worth, atrophied
and lost its essential character.

Knighthood could be lost just as it could be won.   He who failed in
his duties, violated his oath, or was cowardly or cruel, ran the risk of
degradation.   This took the form of a humiliating ceremony at which
the delinquent's spurs were hacked off flush with his heels.   'Honni
soit hardiment où il n'a gentilesse'; nobility of soul went hand in hand

---

[1] *Accolade* from *colada*, the Provençal form of *colée*.   *Paumée* because the blow was
originally given with the hand.

[2] I say 'in theory,' for in fact this was very seldom done.   Until the thirteenth century,
soldiers of fortune and seigniorial officers were admitted to knighthood.   When the
urban bourgeoisie rose to power, its members coveted the honour; but the original
warrior class, fearing the encroachment of these people, gradually created an 'order of
Chivalry,' so that *de facto* nobility gradually became nobility of right.   Kings, however,
reserved to themselves the privilege of authorizing a man to be knighted, and their
instructions were conveyed in what was significantly called a 'letter of ennoblement.'
In this way Philip the Fair rewarded a butcher who had fought bravely at Mons-en-
évèle.

[3] Norman Sicily was the first, *c.* 1160.

with valour in the field.   The higher degree of refinement represented by Chivalry took a long time to evolve and reach perfection.   It began with Roland of the *Chanson*, which was written about 1120, but included traditions of much greater antiquity.   Roland, however, was still a fierce fighting man who delighted to cleave his enemy in two or beat out his brains, and whose faith rested on the quiet assurance that to triumph over pagans was the most sacred of all duties.   Nevertheless, there is already apparent in this crude way of thinking a definitely Christian element—the idea of sacrifice, of man offering his life to God, as expressed by Roland in the hour of death.   According to the *Chanson*, the knight should be a powerful influence for good, and many crusaders made it a point of honour to imitate these lofty examples. Before long, the *Cantar del Cid* put forward a new but exaggerated model in the person of that great Spanish adventurer who had courage-ously done battle with the Moors towards the end of the eleventh century.   About the same time also (*c.* 1200) the *Niebelungenlied* roused ancient memories of German heroism.   The ideal knight, in conse-quence, lost none of his nobility or purity; he became more realistic, more concerned with results obtained than with mere gallantry.   At this date the Holy Sepulchre was once again menaced by Islam; a new generation was called upon to defend it, and the crusading spirit varied according to the personality of individual knights.   Some laid emphasis not so much upon military qualities and temporal ends as upon loftiness of spirit; the knight, in fact, no longer considered him-self as a 'Christian soldier,' but as a Christian who would serve God before all else, even in battle.   Such is the mystical type of knighthood which we find in the story of the Grail as told by the Provençal Guyot and the German Wolfram von Eschenbach (twelfth century).   Around the mysterious vessel which had held the Precious Blood of Christ, and which, say the poets, is really the 'Grace of the Holy Spirit,' are grouped the figures of Parsifal, 'toute candeur et toute niceté'; of Bohort, who expiates his sins so thoroughly that Paradise opens for him; and finally of Galahad, the incarnation of Purity itself.   These are sublime embodiments of Chivalry, who lived almost as monks, in whom was reflected the living image of St Bernard or the crusader-founders of the Temple, and of whom St Louis was the heir.

Roland, Cid, and Galahad stand for three periods and three varieties of a single splendid ideal which dominated the political and social order of the Middle Ages.   So powerful and so enduring was this ideal, that in the days of Luther and Machiavelli, long after Christendom had disintegrated, it fashioned the outlook of a man who died facing the enemy as Roland died at Roncevaux—Pierre du Terrail, Seigneur de Bayard.

7. THE CHURCH AND HUMAN LOVE

There was another sphere of life in which the Church played a decisive part, more decisive perhaps than in her struggle against violence. This was the sphere of human love. To the profligacy which was rife in feudal society she opposed those very principles upon which Europe was ultimately stabilized. She insisted, first, upon obedience to the commandments of God, to Christ's precept of chastity, and to that doctrine which she had made her own since the days of St Paul. She insisted also upon respect for the human person, which led her to place woman on a level of spiritual and moral equality with man.[1] It was respect full of tenderness and mercy, of which our Lord Himself had given numerous examples; the same respect which so many heroic and saintly women had helped to implant in Christian consciousness from the time of the Persecutions down to the worst days of the barbarian epoch. Moreover, by raising the moral standard in general, the Church did much to tighten relationships within smaller groups, to strengthen the family, and to establish it as the unit of society.

She laboured with obstinate determination to give marriage its true dignity. Adultery, a veritable plague in the feudal world, was condemned time and again, even when the guilty sat in high places, even when the sin disguised itself as second marriage. 'So long as his wife lives,' wrote St Anselm of Lucca in the eleventh century, 'it is never lawful for a man to marry another woman.' The same applied to women; in fact, the Church tended to regard adultery on the part of a woman as more serious than in the case of a man. But she never condoned the killing of an adulteress, for 'two wrongs do not make a right.' Wherever there was flagrant guilt, her first concern was to remove the scandal, then, if possible, to bring the parties together in repentance and forgiveness, a matter upon which one of the Hungarian councils delivered itself of much sage advice.

Both in books and sermons the Church loved to praise marriage; she looked upon it as sacred and indissoluble. Jacques de Vitry (d. 1240) went so far as to say that married people 'also belong to an Order, the Order of Matrimony.' His words were echoed by the Dominican Henry of Provins: 'The Order of Matrimony is by no means of recent origin, but has existed as long as humanity itself. Our Order and that of the Friars Minor have been recently established; indeed, all religious Orders are later than the Incarnation. But the Order of Matrimony is as old as the world. I will go even further:

[1] See Fr. Claude Schall, *La doctrine de fins du mariage dans la théologie scolastique*, Paris, 1948, and the article by Fr. Riquet entitled 'Christianisme et population' in *Population*, October 1948.

K*

our Order is the work of a mere mortal, but God Himself founded the Order of Matrimony at the beginning of time.' And the good Dominican concludes with this irrefutable argument: 'At the time of the Deluge, those whom God preferred to save were married people.' Robert de Sorbon (1201–74) described marriage as a 'sacred Order,' of which, said Pérégrin, God alone is the Superior; while Guillaume Péraud enumerated the 'twelve heads of honour' proper to marriage. St Thomas Aquinas, in his *Summa Theologica*, rounds off these eulogies of marriage with a shrewd observation: 'Although the state of virginity is better than the state of matrimony, a given person may still be more perfect in the married state than another in that of virginity.'

Theologians and canonists, however, did more than simply condemn violations of conjugal morality or praise the merits of that state. They produced a whole body of legislation; and, from Anselm of Lucca to Gratian and his successors, no canonical work of any importance omitted to deal with this subject, which occupies a large section of the present *Codex*. Marriage is a sacrament, but in what exactly does it consist? The canonists replied: 'Its essence is the consent of the parties'; they themselves administer the sacrament. The priest, they maintained, acts, so to speak, as witness on behalf of God and blesses their union; and some went so far as to say that his blessing is no more than an 'ornament' or 'flourish.'

The Church also set her face against feudal marriages, whereby a man gave his daughter to some vassal whom he desired to invest with land. They were marriages lacking genuine consent, and were therefore considered invalid. In order to preclude all doubt as to consent the Church forbade clandestine marriages, and required the presence of witnesses.[1] She likewise condemned the influence of wealth in this connection. 'Are we going to publish the banns of marriage between my Lord Such-and-Such and my Lady So-and-So's purse?' cries Jacques de Vitry. The keen interest displayed by so many modern churchmen in problems of conjugal relations is nothing new; that much is quite clear from medieval documents. Some rigorists tried to limit free intercourse between husband and wife by forbidding the marital act on certain days, e.g. Friday, or during certain periods such as Lent; and the example of St Louis suggests that these prohibitions were sometimes taken seriously. Those with more common sense protested at this undue severity in which Peter the Cantor, a twelfth-century preacher, saw 'an indirect means of bringing marriage into disrepute.'

---

[1] The Church was particularly watchful in the matter of impediments. She would not allow marriage between persons related by consanguinity up to the twelfth degree, nor (on grounds of spiritual relationship) would she recognize the marriage of a godfather and godmother who had together held a child over the baptismal font.

The administration of the sacrament was attended with a wealth of beautiful and elaborate ceremonial which we have inherited; and even betrothal, whereby the parties bound themselves *per verba de futuro*, was a solemn rite. The Church blessed the ring, of which the episcopal or abbatial ring, as also that worn by nuns, is a symbolic replica. Wedding rings came into general use during the twelfth century; they were tokens of fidelity and love, 'worn,' says Honorius of Autun, 'on that finger wherein beats the vein of the heart.' The nuptial Mass, too, was accompanied with expressive symbols: a single veil was held over the young spouses, and the first loaf of bread they would eat together was blessed by the priest, together with the first measure of wine they were to share. In some countries there was even a custom of incensing the marriage-bed and sprinkling it with holy water, what time the couple sat therein side by side and prayed.

Thus hallowed, the matrimonial bond was indissoluble. Unlike Roman and Germanic Law, according to which divorce could be effected by mutual consent and even at the wish of one party, Canon Law stubbornly refused to recognize it. Even in cases of adultery, the Church repeatedly quoted St Augustine's famous dictum which occurs in his *De bono conjugali*: 'The marriage tie cannot be broken except by the death of either party.' Nor could a marriage be dissolved even 'in the cause of religion.' There were conciliar decrees ordaining that if a wife took the veil against her husband's will she must be returned to him, for according to St Paul (1 Cor. vii. 4) it is the husband and not she who has command over her body. Grounds for annulment recognized by the Church were very few; there were, and still are, only three: (1) if the husband had been ordained before the marriage; (2) if the parties were related within prohibited degrees (and even then ecclesiastical jurisprudence hesitated to apply the letter of the law for fear it should be made a pretext for divorce); (3) if there were infirmity of the flesh,' but in this case an interval of two or three years was required as well as the testimony of at least seven relatives that there had been no intercourse between the parties.

The Church, then, was at pains to honour marriage as it deserved. She likewise undertook the training of mankind in love, and laid down rules wherever there was danger that instinct might break loose. Important consequences followed, of which two in particular should be noted. The first of these concerned the family, which would infallibly have been ruined by lustful imagination and unbridled passion if Christianity had not stemmed the tide. By this means the very framework of society was strengthened in such a way as to endure for centuries; and it is no exaggeration to say that the enormous increase of population during the Middle Ages was partly due to the Christian view of marriage.

The Church's attitude towards human love had another consequence which made a deep impression on the mind of Europe, and helped to distinguish Western civilization from those, say, of India, China, and Islam.   This was the raising of woman's status, a truly remarkable phenomenon.   It is clear that at the beginning of our period woman occupied an insignificant place in a society where force reigned supreme; she did not count, except for her reproductive function. She had to submit to her lord and master; and if she criticized his behaviour she was likely to receive what the *Geste de Lorraine* describes as 'the big fist fair and square on her nose,' or to be dragged by the hair as was Blanchefleur by her husband William of Orange (future saint).   As for a personal opinion, she was not supposed to have one; and if she tried to speak her mind, she was quickly sent about her business.   This attitude underwent complete transformation between the eleventh and thirteenth centuries.   The Church obliged man to respect the dignity of woman, who ceased to be his property, the plaything of his passions or his interests.   Woman's maternal role in society was still regarded as fundamental, but society now recognized her right not to be absorbed in it.   Both the slavish type of female and the virago were superseded by another kind infinitely more delicate, the kind imagined by a twelfth-century troubadour in these gracious words:

> Work of God, worthy, praised
> As is no other creature;
> Endowed with all blessings and virtue
> Both of spirit and of nature.

There is a well-known and apposite remark of Charles Seignobos 'Love?   An invention of the twelfth century!'   And Gustave Cohen an expert on the medieval period, is of the same opinion.   'Love,' he says, 'is a great discovery of the Middle Ages, especially of twelfth century France.   Before that time it had not savoured so fully of eternity and spirituality.'   Here we meet a question that has produced two fascinating but widely different interpretations: [1] How far was this metamorphosis of love, or rather this appearance and impressive growth of the love-passion in Christian consciousness, due to specifically Christian influence?

During the twelfth century there grew up, especially in the south of France, where manners were more refined, a new ideal known as courtesy.   It was popularized by the Provençal poets or troubadours Guillaume de Poitiers, Macabru, Jaufre Rudel, Bernard de Ventadour and Arnaud Daniel, many of whose exquisite verses have come down

[1] Denis de Rougemont: *L'Amour et l'Occident*, Paris, 1939; Pierre Belperon: *Jo d'Amour*, Paris, 1948.

to us. In what did courtesy consist? In a code of delicacy, of politeness, and fidelity by which love was regulated. So defined, love could perfectly well be included in the Christian outlook; it constituted an advance on sexual beastliness, and it reached fulfilment in God. Thus we find the celebrated but tragic love of Abélard and Héloïse striving painfully to tear itself away from carnal temptation, and rise towards eternal consolation. In the wonderful story of Tristram and Iseult, passion seems wholly to enslave the lovers; and yet there is a sublime Christian echo in their repentance, the high light of that pathetic scene in which the compassionate hermit reveals to them the ways of God.

But did courtly love retain these Christian characteristics? In practice, it is open to doubt whether the impassioned urge that drove man towards woman was always platonic; and even when the intention was pure, we cannot be certain the devil did not play his part in their effusions—notwithstanding Macabru's uncouth assertion that 'true love and sexual love cry out for one another.' What part, though, did Christianity play in love's transformation on the historical and psychological plane? Denis de Rougemont maintains that 'the love-passion appeared in the West as a counterblast to Christianity (and especially to its doctrine of marriage) on the part of souls inhabited by natural or inherited paganism.' And he goes so far as to advance a theory, which other historians (among them Pierre Belperron) have warmly denied, that the troubadours who sang of courtly love had been contaminated by Albigensianism. On this view, the love-passion is heresy. Others believe there may have been Arab influences at work in its development, e.g. the court of Cordova, where manners had reached a high stage of refinement, or certain examples picked up by crusaders in the East. We can only say, without pretending to decide these questions, that it was precisely in the heyday of courtly love that the raising of woman's status (which was certainly the Church's doing) effected a complete reversal in the order of values, making woman, weak and helpless though she remained, no longer dependent on the warrior but the object of his veneration.

It may also be asked whether or not the Church took account of woman's glorification. There is no question of her having as it were situated courtly and mystic love, so as to treat the former as a kind of substitute for the latter. It is a fact, however, that both were developed at the same time, and that the two impulses (one spiritual, the other carnal) often met, even in speech. 'The Middle Ages,' writes Gustave Cohen, 'drew no hard and fast line between divine love on the one hand and human love on the other, between heavenly and earthly love, between love spiritual and carnal; love was there with all its complexity, the motive power of life.' Surely Christianity set its seal upon the glorification of womanhood when it offered mankind the purest and the fairest of all women, Mary, Virgin full of grace. At a time when all earthly loves were failing, it was the Church who could alone console mankind, offering them a love which knew no weakness or decay. Thibaut IV of Champagne wrote many a verse in honour of the lady whom he loved, Queen Blanche of Castile; but when about to leave her and set out on the crusade, he penned these lines:

> Lady of heaven, great and powerful queen,
> Be thou my succour in my most need.
> May I be fired to love thee aright!
> When I lose my lady, do thou, Lady, me assist.

This work of training men in love accomplished by the medieval Church culminated in the worship of Mary.

8. St Louis

To live in the presence of God: such was the ideal offered to medieval society by the Church in spite of many difficulties and set backs.   There were men and women who, without leaving the world or joining the ranks of the clergy, managed to live accordingly and practise heroic virtue.   If we would learn by the example of one among the lay saints, we may do so by considering the most typical, a prince who with sovereign splendour occupied the throne of France from 1226 until 1270—Louis, the ninth of that name, whom history remembers as Saint Louis.   In him were assembled and expressed all those virtues which twelve hundred years of Christianity had developed in mankind.   He dominated his age, and shed upon it so much lustre that our vision is apt to be deceived.   We tend to see him as representative of the thirteenth century as a whole, whereas those hundred years were less truly Christian than the twelfth.   In the eyes of posterity, St Louis is not only the type of manhood at its best, according to medieval standards, but one of those transcendent figures which, through generation after generation, vouch for the grandeur of our race.   It is impossible to speak of him otherwise than on a note of respect mingled with affection.

The monarch's physical appearance is easily imagined.[1]   He was tall and thin, rather frail, with regular features, fair hair, and clear blue eyes.   His strength and goodness of soul were reflected in his every look.   Morally,[2] he was a saint, but there was nothing sanctimonious

[1] From contemporary descriptions, principally that by the Franciscan friar Salimbene, who saw him in 1248 at his departure for the crusade; and also from works of art, above all the beautiful statue at Maineville (Eure) which was no doubt inspired by contemporary records.

[2] The psychology of St Louis is familiar from the Chronicle of his intimate friend Joinville; but also from documents used in the process of his canonization, especially the evidence of his confessor William of Saint-Pathus.

or bigoted about him.   On the contrary, he was gay; he could both make and take a joke, and preferred conversation to books.   There was, indeed, a patriarchal atmosphere about his court.   But he had none of those easy-going ways which often veil inherent weakness, none of that undue familiarity which is often the concomitant of bad manners.   He never thrust himself on others, was never casual in his address; and when need arose he could prove himself tough as tempered steel.   Few men have been so keenly aware of their eternal destiny; few mystics have been such accomplished men of the world or taken so active a part in public life.

The keystone of his career was rock-like faith, critical but unshakable.   'Dear child,' he warned his eldest son Philip in a testamentary letter, 'I beg you set your heart upon the love of God; for without that no one can be saved.   Avoid doing anything that will displease God.' And Louis observed these principles throughout his life; they were the source of all his merit.   He had grown up under the wise tutelage of his mother, Blanche of Castile, who used to tell him, almost as a truism, that she would rather see him dead than in sin.   He never forgot this lesson.   Despite the crushing burdens of office, he found time each day to recite the liturgical hours, to search the Scriptures, and to read the Fathers.   He confessed often, and his penitential practices included fasting as well as the discipline and hair-shirt.   His diet was frugal, his dress simple—except when the duties of his rank obliged him to wear ceremonial robes.   One of his biographers observes that he 'combined the manners of a king with the habits of a monk'; he was, in fact, a Franciscan tertiary.

It may be suggested that St Louis was guilty of excess in this direction, and Voltaire unworthily accuses the 'crowned monk' of negligence.   That is manifestly absurd, when we consider the state in which he left France.   'The throne shone like the sun which sheds its rays far and wide,' says Joinville; and his is not the language of a courtier.   Louis was a grandson of Philip II (1180–1223), whose success in consolidating his dominions had earned him the title of 'Augustus' after the victory of Bouvines.   He was also the son of Louis VIII, whose brief reign had sufficed to prove his courage and his intellectual gifts.   St Louis, therefore, never had to admit that his faith conflicted with his duty as trustee of the French kingdom; the wonder is that while working for his realm he was able to reconcile its best interests with the supernatural demands of religion.   His outward expression of that faith may sometimes cloy; but it was only his manner of proselytizing in and out of season, of preaching, and of moralizing. We may be tempted to smile at the thought of a father sending his favourite daughter a hair-shirt and discipline for Christmas; but the gift signified a transcendent love, and Isabel accepted it as such.   On one occasion, certainly, he was tempted to go beyond the requirements of his faith by shirking the responsibility laid on him by God. He talked of joining the Cistercians or Franciscans, whose humble board and labours he delighted to share. His wife, however, who acted on this occasion in a manner worthy of her dignity, reminded him that his duty lay not in withdrawing from the world, but in governing according to God's law. At once he put aside his dream.

St Louis considered the Faith as no 'garden enclosed,' no remote and secret region of the soul unrelated to conduct. It should, so he believed, govern man's every act; and since to believe in Christ and to follow his example is, first, to love one's fellow men, his generosity was unbounded. 'He had charity towards his neighbour,' wrote William of Saint-Pathus, '*together with orderly and virtuous compassion*'—words deserving of remembrance and meditation. 'He practised works of mercy,' William continues, 'by lodging, feeding, clothing, visiting, and comforting the poor and the infirm, whom he relieved and supported by personal service. He ransomed friendless prisoners, buried the dead, and assisted all both virtuously and abundantly.' St Louis setting out to walk through the streets of his cities and distribute alms by the handful; St Louis at the Maison-Dieu at Compiègne tending the worst cases, oblivious of his defilement by pus oozing from lupus-sores; St Louis inviting to his table twenty poor folk whose filth and stench revolted the soldiers of his guard; St Louis making straight for a leper, whose distant rattle had attracted his attention, and giving him a fraternal kiss: these anecdotes and many more are derived not from some 'Golden Legend,' but from the most reliable histories. More-over, France was indebted to him for countless charitable institutions: the hospitals at Pontoise and Versailles, the 'Quinze-Vingts' for blind people at Paris, besides guest-houses and orphanages. Nor must we forget his numerous Benedictine establishments. Joinville tells us that he 'adorned his realm with many a Maison-Dieu of his own founda-tion,' and adds by way of conclusion: 'Many priests and prelates might envy the king his manners and his virtues.'

Above all, these virtues, which were essentially religious, never detracted from his natural qualities or impeded the development of his character. He realized, in fact, that they were fraught with peril. Joinville records that one day when the king was in a merry mood he asked him and Master Sorbon whether it is better to be '*prudhomme* or *béguin*.' He listened, smiling, and then, more gravely, said: 'Well, I would prefer to be known simply as "*prudhomme*"; you can have all the rest. It is so great and grand a thing to be *prudhomme*, that even the very word itself is a mouthful to pronounce.' What did he mean? He meant what the whole Middle Ages understood the word to mean; he meant what the *Gestes* mean when they refer to Roland and Percival

as *prudhommes*, viz. *integrity*.   Integrity is achieved by the fulfilment
of those duties arising from the situation in which God has placed
one; it demands submission to the moral law, and whole-hearted
striving after perfection.   St Louis, on account of his royal birth, was
required not only to cultivate the inner man, but to prove himself a
knight 'sans peur et sans reproche,' a king who realized his duty; and
such indeed he was.

St Louis was a true knight all his life, a soldier in whom courage was
a second nature, because it rested on the certainty of everlasting life.
He faced the enemy with fervent joy, and was always in the forefront of
battle, never yielding, never resorting to guile.   He might have
stepped from the *Grail Quest* rather than from the pages of history.
Even his enemies were affected by the radiance of his personality; and
when he was taken prisoner by the Moslems, the Sultan's leniency not
only did honour to a Moor but revealed the stature of a Christian.
Many stories bear witness to his prestige.   One day a Moslem chief,
one Faress-Edin, who had brutally assassinated his master, sought out
the captive king and begged him for the honour of knighthood as
reward.   St Louis refused—not without irony, since he asked the
murderer whether he intended first to renounce the Koran.   To everyone's surprise, the criminal bowed his head and withdrew without a
sign of resentment.   Such was the saint's authority.

St Louis, however, was no mere paragon of knightly valour.   He
never failed in the virtues of humanity and refinement, whereby the
knight was recognized not only as an accomplished warrior but as a
witness of God.   His gentleness towards children, his longing to
protect the weak, all those qualities, in fact, which are now covered by
the word 'chivalry,' are so characteristic of him that one is apt to forget
how much their practice must have cost a man so quick-tempered and
so highly strung.   He possessed also, to an eminent degree, that
quality which the poets assign to Parsifal and Galahad: he was 'single-
minded'; which means to say he was a gentleman, upright in mind and
heart, rejecting all that tends to drag men down into the mire.

This quality of single-mindedness is outstanding in St Louis's
relations with his wife.[1]   Unlike so many princes whose matrimonial
and extra-matrimonial whims fill the chronicles with scandal; unlike his
contemporary Frederick II; unlike several of the Capetians too, such
as his beloved grandfather; St Louis showed that it is possible for a
king to obey the sixth and ninth commandments without being at
the same time either a prude or physically impotent.   He had no
fewer than eleven children.   God alone knows the merit of his loyalty
to Margaret of Provence, whom he had married while still a boy.   At

[1] See my study of St Louis's marriage in *En cet annel tout mon amour*, Ecclesia, July
1951, and in the collective work, *Le couple chrétien*, Paris, 1951.

that time she was a pretty little girl of fourteen, but after several years of flaming passion for his charming spouse, Louis realized she was light-headed, coquettish, and unsympathetic towards his mystic aspirations. Although she could show herself every inch a queen, as she did during the crusade, she was likewise capable of petty intrigue, if not of down-right treachery, which caused him some anxiety.   Their union was little more than a prolonged and often painful misunderstanding; but the saintly king remained faithful to his marriage vows.   No act on his part, whether in the eyes of God or before the gaze of men, betrayed the motto he had had engraved on the inside of his wedding-ring: 'En cet annel, tout mon amour.'   ('In this ring is all my love.') [1]

However great a man's interior virtues, they cannot be called truly Christian unless they are in some way manifested, made apparent, in day-to-day conduct, amid the duties of his state.   St Louis never forgot the principles taught him by his mother, who, during her regency, had also accustomed him to be present at council-meetings, to listen to the jurists, and to go in person wherever his people suffered in consequence of poverty, epidemic, flood, or bad harvests.   Even at the end of his life, when it was clear he desired nothing but union with Christ, to live and die in His love, he continued to fulfil these tasks with unflagging ardour because his Lord expected it of him.   So great, indeed, was his sense of responsibility, that he considered himself one with his people, as sharing in their destiny.   On 4th June 1249, before Damietta, he summed up his idea of a Christian king in these memor-able words: 'My friends and trusty subjects, we shall be unconquerable so long as we are united in charity; *I* am not King of France, *I* am not Holy Church; it is you who, because you are all the king, are Holy Church.'   Surely no ruler has defined his mission in more splendid terms.

The policies which these ideals led him to adopt made the reign of St Louis one of the happiest in French history.   The following short sentence may still be read in the letter of advice bequeathed to his son Philip: 'You must see to it that your people, who are your subjects, live under your rule in peace and equity'; and such was the whole purpose of his government.   Equity demanded, first, the repression of those who endangered public order and brought suffering to the common folk.   Private wars were strictly forbidden; and although St

---

[1] We know from evidence given during the process of his canonization, especially that of the king's confessor, that St Louis abstained altogether from intercourse with his wife not only during Advent and Lent, but also on Fridays and Saturdays, vigils, and even on feast days whenever he received communion.   He was clearly something of a rigorist; but Margaret offered no objection.   Instead, therefore, of scoffing at his austerity, we should perhaps see it rather as proof of a lofty determination on the part of both spouses to spiritualize even carnal pleasure, an outlook which is similarly reflected in the fact that so splendid a Christian communicated very seldom, four or five times a year at the most.

Louis did not succeed in preventing them altogether, at least they were the exception during his reign. Equity demanded likewise that he should recognize, and oblige others to respect, human personality even among the humblest and most destitute of men; which explains the leading part taken by St Louis in emancipating serfs. Some words spoken by Jacques de Vitry in a sermon penetrated deep into his mind: 'True nobility resides in the soul. We have not been fashioned some of us from gold or silver, others from clay; we have not come some of us from the head, others from the heel. We are all descended from the same man, all sprung from his loins.' In 1246 he began the enfranchisement of serfs in his private domain; and whenever possible he encouraged his vassals to do likewise, compensating from his own resources those who were deterred by the prospect of financial loss. The working classes had no firmer friend, none more attentive to their needs or more generous to their occupations, than the king who took Étienne Boileau [1] as his confidant and appointed him to one of the highest magistracies.

Peace and equity, however, entailed a more stringent obligation. The Capetian monarchs had been long renowned as 'rois bon justiciers,' royal judges upon whose scrupulous fairness all were able to rely; and Joinville has left a famous description of St Louis going straight from Mass to sit in the woods at Vincennes, where, leaning against an oak, he would hear 'without impediment of court-procedure' anyone who desired to put his case. The picture is symbolic; for even though he could not always administer justice in person, it was his constant preoccupation. As a judge, however, he was by no means indulgent, as some people discovered to their cost. A cook, for example, who had committed robbery with violence thought he could escape the gallows because he belonged to the royal household; St Louis personally sentenced him to death. Then there was a noblewoman of Pontoise who had persuaded her lover to murder her husband. Franciscans, Dominicans, ladies in waiting, and even the queen herself, all interceded on her behalf; but Louis had her burned on the site of her crime, 'because it is good that justice should be seen to be done.' Many cases were celebrated in his day for the firmness and independence which he showed. The affair of Enguerrand de Coucy astonished his contemporaries. An illustrious baron, connected by marriage with all the nobility of the realm, was arrested, thrown into jail, condemned to pay a heavy fine, and obliged to expiate his crime by pilgrimage— simply because he had had three boys hanged for poaching on his land. In the light of thirteenth-century customs, the sentence was unthinkable. Another case, though seldom quoted to-day, caused no less sensation at the time. The king's own brother Charles, Count of

[1] It was Boileau who had organized the trade-guilds in days of Philip Augustus.

Anjou, had been convicted of imprisoning a knight travelling through his territory, and appealed to Louis against the verdict.   Summoned to appear at Vincennes, he thought it as well to take with him a select body of jurists; but at the king's order they were opposed on behalf of the plaintiff by the most eminent crown counsel, and the result was such as might have been expected.

The influence of St Louis in the field of justice was as profound as it was lasting.   Judicial duels were abolished by a decree of 1260, and 'instead of battle, proof was to be based on evidence.'   Cases in which an appeal lay to the king, subject to the Parlement, were explicitly defined and their number increased.   Great care was taken in the appointment of judges, who were obliged to take an oath to receive neither gold nor silver nor any other fee from interested parties, and forbidden to frequent taverns or to play at dice.   The provostship of Paris had been hitherto a fief of the wealthy bourgeoisie, who sold it to the highest bidder.   It was now made a salaried office and entrusted to Étienne Boileau, of whom Joinville says that 'he filled it so thoroughly that no malefactor, thief, or murderer dared remain in Paris but he was soon hanged or otherwise removed; neither family connections nor gold nor silver, could save him.'   And the chronicler adds that 'people were henceforth drawn to Paris by the fairness of its courts.'

St Louis adopted the same equitable policy with regard to money. He spent very little on himself, and, in his will, advised his son to follow his example.   True, the level of taxation was not reduced during his reign; that was due partly to the wars he was obliged to undertake against rebellious vassals and the King of England, and partly to the crusades, which were financed almost exclusively by France.   But in this respect also he showed himself scrupulously just; he declined the services of moneylenders, and saw to it that there was no unfair assessment.   He would undertake none of those profitable currency-deals which marred the reputation of his grandson Philip the Fair.

Thus, while living up to his duties as a Christian, St Louis attained the full stature of kingship.   In his day, too, France was regarded by the whole of Christendom as 'the most blessed and most happy land'; a country where, since peace and harmony went hand in hand with an effort to achieve efficiency, the 'conjuncture' (as modern economists would say) was most favourable.   Throughout his reign France was the scene of intense creative activity.   At this period Master Robert of Sorbon, the king's chaplain, founded a still famous college—the Sorbonne.   All the realm of France, indeed, and especially Mont Sainte-Geneviève at Paris, was covered with institutions, colleges, and houses for students.   At this period also, the towers and side-chapels of Notre-Dame were constructed; Chartres cathedral was rebuilt after its destruction by fire in 1194; and the scaffolding at Rheims, Bourges, Amiens, Beauvais, and Rouen was alive with workmen. Finally, it was in the days of St Louis that there soared to heaven, symbolic of his reign, the Sainte Chapelle, a marvel of delicately carved stone and mysterious glasswork, destined to receive that most sacred of all relics—the Crown of Thorns.

In his day men were able to distinguish those among their masters who wielded power for their own interests and those who sought to exercise authority for the common good alone. None doubted that St Louis was of this latter class; and when he died, the grief of France was echoed in a moving lay: 'To whom will poor folk cry out, now that the good king is gone, who loved them so?' Long before Boniface VIII issued his official Bull in the Church's name, the common people had already canonized him in their hearts.

St Louis was the admiration not of France alone, but of all Christendom, which knew him while still on earth as a man of God. For he applied the same principles which governed his life to the sphere of international relations, a sphere in which they have too frequently been misinterpreted. He believed, and on more than one occasion openly declared, that there are not two moral codes, one for the individual and another for the community. He considered such precepts as 'Love one another' equally binding on the international as on the personal level; and his attitude in this respect has been falsely judged if not completely misunderstood. The extravagances of present-day nationalism have so distorted man's sense of values that otherwise honest men are ready to embrace the worst elements of Machiavellianism for the sake of quick returns, while Christian policies are denounced as chimerical and dangerous—with results that are plain for all to see.

Did Louis's 'policy derived from Holy Scripture,' to quote a phrase of Bossuet, do harm to the French monarchy? There is some difference of opinion; but we do know that, so far as this most saintly of the Capetians was concerned, it involved no servility towards the Church, no indifference to the welfare of France. On many occasions he adopted a policy of absolute independence with regard to 'Mother Church,' whose most obedient son he nevertheless styled himself in his private capacity. He was once approached by a group of bishops who wanted help from the secular arm to enforce a sentence of excommunication. Louis replied that, in his opinion, those penalties were often undeserved, and he would therefore not interfere. On the contrary, he got the Pope to request that they would in future think twice before imposing sanctions of this kind. Certain high Roman prelates, and even some popes, e.g. Innocent IV, took such licence in the matter of ecclesiastical property as amounted almost to rapine.[1]

[1] Chapter VI, section 9.

St Louis gave full support to the protests of the French clergy, and approved the terms of a memorial addressed by them to the Lateran. He acted in still more characteristic fashion during the tragic conflict between the Priesthood and the Empire.   He would not for a moment play second fiddle to the papacy.   When, in 1240, Gregory IX offered him the Roman crown for his brother, the Count of Artois, he joined Blanche of Castile in refusing it; and later on he tried to arrange a settlement between the two adversaries.   In 1245 Innocent IV summoned an oecumenical council at Lyons to depose Frederick II; but St Louis refused to attend in person, and did all in his power to mitigate the Pope's severity.   He could not prevent the sentence of excommunication being read from the pulpits, but at least he took care to make no comment which might suggest that he approved.   When we consider the results of this unhappy quarrel, we are surely justified in believing that his appeal for a general reconciliation and a united effort in the crusade shows him to have been more clear-sighted than the Roman pontiff.

There is one case, however, in which St Louis's impartiality in international affairs deserves particular attention; for the course he chose to follow in his dealings with Henry III of England appeared contrary to the best interests of his crown.   Philip Augustus, in return for the injury done him by his vassal John 'Lackland,' had seized most of that monarch's French possessions, including the paternal estates of the Plantagenets.   The English made repeated protests against this confiscation, and prepared to resume war at the earliest opportunity.   St Louis asked himself whether his ancestor had acted fairly; 'his conscience pricked him.'   Henry was supported by his brother Richard, Earl of Cornwall, whose election as 'King of the Romans' had been secured by the Pope; but the title was purely nominal, and, in any case, the English baronage were constantly at loggerheads with their sovereign.   Henry, therefore, was not much to be feared; and if St Louis had consulted none but political interests, he need only have drawn his sword to sweep France clear of English influence—or what was left of it.   The solution upon which he decided was altogether different.   He told Henry: 'If you will unconditionally renounce your claim to Normandy, Anjou, Touraine, Maine, and Poitou, recognizing these provinces as unquestionably French and at the same time doing homage to me for Guienne, I will grant you as fiefs (in return likewise for your homage) all my possessions in Limousin, Quercy, and Périgord.   Furthermore, if Alphonse of Poitiers should die without issue, I will allow you to take Saintonge and Agenais, again as my vassal.'   This proposal astounded the king's advisers, who asked him what end he had in view.   The saint replied: 'To establish love between my children and his children, who are first cousins.'   This extraordinary arrangement has been criticized not only by his contemporaries, but by many historians down to the present day.   In order to understand it, we must try to share the outlook of that period, when the fact of doing homage for land was an extremely serious matter, and when a great overlord such as the King of France exercised a very real power of control over fiefs held by his vassals.   There was not a handful of French soil which the King of England would occupy as an independent sovereign; Normandy and all the Loire valley was restored unreservedly to France, while distant Guienne, which would in fact have been very difficult to conquer, was made subject to France in such a way that Bordeaux came under the appellate jurisdiction of Paris.   On 4th December 1259, in the royal orchard on the site of what is now the Place Dauphiné, the King of England, bareheaded and without mantle, belt, or spurs, knelt before St Louis, in whose hands he placed his own, swearing faith and loyalty.   By acting thus on Christian principles, Louis had not done badly for France.   This was proved by the English themselves, who showed the greatest indignation: 'It is beyond the bounds of reason!' exclaimed John Peckham, Archbishop of Canterbury.

Deeds such as this, at all events, raised the king's prestige by capturing the public imagination.   At a time when moral principles counted in international politics to an extent which they no longer do, St Louis enjoyed universal respect because he was a thorough-going Christian.   This much is evident from the fact that he was called upon as 'elder statesman' to arbitrate between one nation and another, rather as St Bernard had done in the preceding century and for the same reason.   In one sense, too, his intervention was a great deal more effective than the similar efforts of Innocent III and other great popes. For St Louis spoke not as enjoying *de facto* authority, nor as having power to condemn and to constrain, but only by virtue of that wisdom which he had received from God.   We find him adjudicating on the succession to Hainaut and Flanders, ignoring altogether the private interests of his own brother Charles of Anjou.   Again, at the expense of his future son-in-law, Thibaut V of Champagne, he judges who shall occupy the throne of Navarre.   Between the Count of Chalon and his son the Count of Burgundy, between Burgundy and Champagne, between Henri de Luxembourg and Thibault de Bar—in each case it is Louis who decides; and no one could suspect him of an unjust end. When his advisers suggested he should leave his vassals and their neighbours to tear one another to pieces, he was indignant and replied that by so doing he would 'earn the hatred of God.'   He was called upon to intervene in the home politics of foreign states.   Thus, in 1258, when the great barons of England defied their king, St Louis— in a manner perhaps somewhat tactless and abrupt—condemned and rejected the Provisions of Oxford as unfair. As regards Italian politics, he had tried to prevent his brother Charles of Anjou from accepting the Sicilian crown, and having failed, he refused to send his own troops to occupy that dangerous realm.[1]

The culmination of St Louis's Christian policy was the crusade, upon which he twice embarked. The undertaking failed on each occasion, and we may ask whether this was due solely to the French king's unpreparedness and tenacity, or to the fact that the rest of Christendom, including the papacy, withheld assistance. The two expeditions have much to commend them; but they mark the one single point at which St Louis's holiness, blinding him to a sense of reality, led him into dreamland and disaster. We might on this account harbour resentment, were it not for his heroism during the Egyptian campaign and the sublimity of his death at Tunis, which endow his portrait with an aureole of splendour.[2]

Such, then, was Louis de Poissy,[3] King of France and witness on behalf of man before the face of his Eternal Father. We cannot doubt that in whatever station of life he had been placed by birth, he would have been what we have seen him to be—a perfect Christian, a just man after Christ's own heart, a saint. Providence had ordained that, in the position which he held, he should move as a figure of outstanding influence and significance. We may recognize in him the most complete example of what Christian faith, which dominated the Middle Ages, could do with one prepared to give it his whole obedience and thereby reach the full stature of a man.

---

[1] If St Louis had had his way, the atrocity known as 'The Sicilian Vespers' would never have occurred.

[2] The crusades of St Louis will be studied in Chapter XI.

[3] This was the way he liked best to style himself, for it was at Poissy that he had been baptized.

CHAPTER VIII

THE CHURCH AS GUIDE OF HUMAN THOUGHT

1. PROTECTRESS OF CULTURE

CHATEAUBRIAND, in a famous passage commemorating the Church's work during the night of barbarism, speaks of the monasteries as 'almost like fortresses in which civilization took refuge under the banner of a saint.' He goes on to say that 'they fostered learning, together with philosophic truth which was reborn from religious truth. Without the inviolability and leisure of the cloister, the works and languages of antiquity would never have come down to us; the chain which links past with present would inevitably have been broken.'

Historians of all shades find no difficulty in agreeing to recognize the medieval Church as a stronghold of culture. From the days when Cassiodorus made his *Vivarium* in Calabria at once a place of spiritual elevation and an asylum for learning, to the dark years of the early eleventh century when the religious houses had actually become 'fortresses' though at the cost of many vicissitudes and in some cases disastrous eclipse, culture had belonged exclusively to the Church, and the monks alone had cared for spiritual things.

We may ask whether their effort to safeguard the intellect was altogether disinterested. Not in the modern sense of this word; its end was not the search for knowledge. It was, however, disinterested inasmuch as churchmen, who laboured with their brains no less than with their muscles, never had in view their personal satisfaction but only the glory of God. To this end all intellectual activity, in common with every form of human endeavour, was subordinate: culture was dependent on religion. There could be no understanding of Scripture and no splendid liturgy without the study of Latin; there could be no sound belief without close scrutiny of the Sacred Books and Patristic writings. And because they appreciated this truth, popes, bishops, and abbots strove to preserve culture in the midst of a society which regarded it with absolute contempt. The Church was also aware that she could not defend her position unless she were armed for intellectual combat; and the great pagan authors owe their survival to a few religious who decided to use the vast experience embodied in ancient literature and philosophy as a means to the knowledge of God.

Moreover, the interpenetration of intellectual and religious activity had left its mark upon the vocabulary. 'Clerks' were not simply men dedicated to God; they were also intellectuals, specialists in culture, and deeply respected on that account. They formed a 'third class of people,' the other two being knights and labourers. The word *clerici* signified not only 'clergymen' in the narrow sense, but also professors and students. Nothing indicates better than does this confusion of terms the responsibility undertaken by the Church at a time when culture, together with all human values, was in direst peril; and she continued, though not in quite the same way, to exercise this function after 1050.

The mind of Europe no longer required protection against the threat of barbarism; but it still needed guidance towards its true end, the service of God. She had likewise to make sure that, so long as Christian society was in the melting-pot, man should not be diverted from his path by intellectual pursuits. She endeavoured, therefore, to provide a safeguard by making faith the basis of culture and of thought. From the eleventh to the fourteenth century, with very rare exceptions, all culture was fundamentally religious. Education and letters were almost a monopoly of the Church, whose representatives devoted themselves to fostering the specifically Christian aspect of intellectual studies, until such time as they began to assert their autonomy and claimed to dispense with faith.

But the essential factor, one which in this respect was to differentiate our period from its predecessor, was that the Church, while maintaining her hold upon intellectual life, did not *seek* to preserve her monopoly therein. Learning was no longer the apanage of a theological clique or of enclosed monks; men were invited by the Church in ever increasing numbers to enjoy its benefits, especially in those urban settlements which were in process of regeneration through social and economic changes. It was the Church, in fact, who was responsible for the splendid flowering of those intellectual values which she herself had saved from shipwreck.

2. LIBRARIES AND COPYISTS

In her effort to protect man's intellect, the Church first of all taught him respect for books. Here, for example, is a heavy parchment volume containing the words of God or one of His servants; it is rare, costly, and therefore an object of love, of veneration, and of jealous care.[1] 'He rightly dies disgraced who loves not books,' ran a proverb; and St Bernard says that 'a cloister without books is like a castle with no armoury.' These precious works were passed from one religious house to another for re-copying, and in the dark days of the

[1] A library of 900 manuscripts was considered enormous; it staggered the imagination.

Norman invasion, the loss of libraries was among the most keenly felt of many great disasters.

We have all seen pictures of a copyist-monk bent over his desk, engaged through long hours in beautiful lettering, or in illuminating the pages of some liturgical book. There were thousands of such men, of whose names we are ignorant but to whom we owe our knowledge of Boethius, St Augustine, and St Jerome no less than of Virgil, Terence, and Ovid. Thanks to these scribes of God, the human intellect has kept contact with its past; they have bequeathed to us a living memory for which we are rightly thankful. There had existed for many generations, and there continued to exist from the eleventh to the fourteenth century, certain great centres of the copyist's art: St Gall, Reichenau, Fleury-sur-Loire, Corbie, Mont-Saint-Michel. Others grew up within that period, e.g. St Germain-des-Prés at Paris, and St Martial at Limoges. Each had its own style of lettering (antique or, before long, uncial derived from the Carolingian minuscule) and, above all, its own style of illuminating ornamental capitals or designing as full-page illustrations those wonderful miniatures which hold us spellbound.

The style of Corbie, for example, was in the Carolingian tradition, an extraordinary mixture of living and abstract forms. Again, it is clear that the illuminators of St Martial at Limoges sought inspiration from the local school of glass-painters and enamellers; the result was a new *genre* of small, familiar scenes. The Parisian workshops, on the other hand, produced masterpieces of easy realism, e.g. the Psalters of St Louis preserved in the Bibliothèque Nationale and in the Musée Condé at Chantilly.

It is hard to imagine the time taken to complete such works. The number of lines in certain copies of the Bible is staggering; and the colouring of miniatures, which was done in successive layers, each of which had to dry before the next could be applied, involved weeks of slow labour on the smallest detail. But this delay gave the copyists more leisure, and their joint achievement, with its brilliant gold, vivid blues, purples, and deep violets, may still be seen in all the perfection of eternal youth.

During the thirteenth century, when culture stepped from the monasteries and cathedral workshops to establish itself in the universities, copyists followed in its wake. Laymen set up their own studios and worked under the direction of clerics. Paris, the intellectual centre of Europe, did an enormous trade; and we learn from Gilbert of Metz that 60,000 copyists were engaged on this work in or around the capital. But although the production of manuscripts, and therefore also of miniatures, had developed into something like an industry, genuine masterpieces could still make their appearance. Such was the

'Belleville Breviary,' prepared by Jean Belleville and his school about 1320.[1]

3. PAROCHIAL, MONASTIC, AND CATHEDRAL SCHOOLS

It is commonly believed that most people in the Middle Ages were ignorant; and we are too often presented with the picture of illiterate folk ready to lap up superstition from the hand of a tyrannical clergy. Medieval man, on the contrary, has bequeathed to future generations abundant evidence of his astonishing intellectual vitality. Historians have failed, if they have not actually refused, to see the truth.

First let us inquire whether there were as many illiterates in the Middle Ages as is so rashly supposed; whether their number exceeded that which is found to-day in certain countries of western Europe. Our archives contain thousands of deeds to which the witnesses have fairly and squarely appended their signatures. Furthermore, when we recall the numerous clerics and famous teachers of plebeian origin, we are forced to conclude that the instruction of children, even in the lowest strata of society, was by no means neglected.

Again, when considering this period, we must be careful not to identify education with knowledge of the alphabet. Whereas to-day learning and culture rest chiefly upon visual data acquired through reading and writing, in the Middle Ages, when books were rare and costly, hearing played a much greater part than now. A chapter of the municipal statutes of Marseilles, dating from the thirteenth century, enumerates the qualifications of a good lawyer, and concludes: '*litteratus vel non litteratus*' (whether literate or not). In other words, a thorough grasp of law and custom was more important than to be able to read and write.

To say that the Church tried to foster ignorance in order to strengthen her authority is to admit a downright lie in face of known facts. In the sixth century we hear St Caesarius of Arles explaining to the Council of Vaison (529) the urgent need of schools in country places; while page after page might be filled with the names of

---

[1] In recent years some interesting light has been shed upon the methods used by copyists. The model (*exemplar*) of the work was first authenticated by masters specially appointed by the university, and then lodged in a kind of central library. It was divided into numbered sections rather like a modern 'fold.' Any master, student, or professional scribe who wished to take a copy of a particular work borrowed the *examplar* section by section, returning each one as soon as he had finished with it. Every now and again, for some reason or another, he was issued, say, with section 3 before section 2; in which case he either left the necessary space (which might eventually take in the margins), or, if he were less scrupulous, copied each section as it came to hand regardless of the correct order. This second method was destined to puzzle generations of scholars! In Italy, the list of *exemplaria* available in a library was announced by the school beadle; in French Dominican and Franciscan houses it was posted up on days when university students were to attend an office.

later bishops who took the same view. St Nizier of Lyons, Theodulph of Orléans, Leidrade, and Hincmar, all distinguished themselves in this respect. The Church likewise dictated Charlemagne's scholastic policy, the first of its kind to be tried out seriously in the West. During the tragic tenth century schools declined together with all civilized activity; but when conditions improved the Church resumed her task, reopened schools, and insisted once more upon the necessity of education. It is impossible not to admire such canons as those of the Lateran Council (1179), which direct the clergy to establish as many schools as possible for the free instruction of all children, even of 'poor scholars.' The theory that in a well-ordered society the people should be left to wallow in ignorance was propounded not by the Church, but by Voltaire!

Our familiar grades of education—primary, secondary, and higher —were already recognized in the Middle Ages. At the bottom of the scale were parochial or 'little' schools. Wherever a parish depended on the landlord, it was he who founded the local school. We still possess a deed, dated in the year 1200, whereby the lord of Rosny-sur-Seine agrees with the parish priest to open a school on his estates; it is a model of understanding and good sense. The parishioners themselves often subscribed towards the maintenance of a schoolmaster; and there still exists an amusing little document in the form of a petition made by a group of parents for the removal of a master who was ragged to such an extent that the pupils bombarded him with their pens. In theory, all children were required to attend lessons, and many contracts of apprenticeship contain a clause whereby the employer agrees to send the boy to school.

Instruction was given in a room adjoining the church, or even in the church itself. The master was often a layman who acted at the same time as cantor, sacristan, and, as we should say to-day, parish clerk. The children paid a small fee, generally in kind, e.g. beans, fish, or wine; very rarely he might receive a few pence. Before taking up his appointment he was supposed to have ecclesiastical approval; and in certain dioceses, such as Paris, Rheims, Lyons, Toulouse, and Montpellier, he had to pass an examination. What were the subjects taught in these schools? First and foremost religious knowledge, i.e. the catechism, but also reading, writing, the art of 'tallying' (i.e. arithmetic by means of counters), a little grammar, and sometimes a few scraps of Latin. Since books were unobtainable, mural pictures were used instead. These were made of calf- or sheepskin and painted with Old Testament genealogies, catalogues of the virtues and vices, or specimens of handwriting. A few have survived.

We can thus be certain that during the twelfth and thirteenth centuries, at any rate in the more advanced countries of western Europe.

there was a fairly widespread system of primary education, which provided moral training as well as factual information.   On a higher level, there were the monastic and cathedral schools, corresponding to our secondary schools and offering, for the most part, a slightly higher course of studies.   Religious houses, true to their vocation as 'citadels of the mind,' had been the first to open schools which provided a rather more advanced curriculum.   Famous educational centres included St Riquier, Gembloux, Reichenau, Luxeuil, Marmoutier, St Wandrille, and St Remy at Rheims.   Later came Fleury and St Martial at Limoges; while at Paris there were St Geneviève, St Victor, and St Germain-des-Près.   King Robert the Pious was a pupil at Fleury; Gerbert, the future Pope Sylvester II, who began his education at St Geraud d'Aurillac, was afterwards the glory of St Remy.   At the beginning of the twelfth century there were seventy monastic schools in France.   Among the most celebrated of these were Bec-Hellouin in Normandy, rendered famous by such masters as Blessed Lanfranc and St Anselm; St Denis, which produced Louis le Gros and his minister Suger; and Cluny, where Peter the Venerable attached great importance to this side of monastic work.   Argenteuil, where Héloïse was educated and Abélard lectured, was a well-known school for girls.

In the middle of this century, however, the monastic schools already showed signs of deterioration; advocates of reform were opposed to the coexistence of an 'interior' school for the novices and an 'exterior' school for lay pupils.   After Peter the Venerable, Cluny made no effort to save its own school from extinction; while at Cîteaux, children were no longer admitted 'within or in dependence upon the monastery.' The regulars abandoned educational work, which, owing in large part to the urban renascence, passed to the secular clergy, who very soon proved themselves excellent teachers.

Episcopal and capitular schools were established soon after their monastic counterparts.   Most of the great bishops founded institutions of this kind, e.g. at Orléans, where St Aignan himself condescended to teach.   Early in the twelfth century France possessed no fewer than fifty episcopal schools, and the third Lateran Council obliged every diocese to open one.   Some of these institutions enjoyed remarkable success.   Fulbert, Yves, and John of Salisbury adorned the school of Chartres, which was a melting-pot of ideas, not a few of them suspect. Avranches shared the glory of St Anselm and his school at Bec. Besançon received innumerable favours at the hands of Frederick Barbarossa.   William of Champeaux taught at Châlons-sur-Marne. St Bernard was a pupil of Châtillon-sur-Seine.   Finally, the school of Paris, grouped around Notre-Dame, was a veritable nursery of bishops and other distinguished men, the seed whence sprang that most famous of medieval universities.   Outside France, there were celebrated cathedral schools at Canterbury and Durham in England; at Toledo in Spain; at Bologna, Salerno, and Ravenna in Italy.

These establishments were subject to the control, or to the direct influence and inspiration, of ecclesiastical authority. The headmaster, who was generally a canon appointed by the bishop or dean, had a whole-time job; and we may be sure he had his work cut out, for school-life at that time was by no means a holiday.[1]

Both the monastic and the episcopal schools were open to all comers between the ages of seven and twenty, without any class distinction. The only difference was one of fees. Originally, and in theory, instruction was given free of charge. It continued to be so in the monastic schools. In diocesan establishments the rich were generally expected to pay; but those who possessed nothing were not excluded, and teachers who demanded money from all their pupils indiscriminately were reprimanded by a number of councils. Examinations were free, and the Lateran Council prohibited the taking of fees 'from candidates for professorship in return for granting licences.' Education was also available to girls; generally speaking, however, it was of a lower standard, as was natural since there were fewer female schools and some earlier councils had forbidden the attendance of girls at male establishments. Certain institutions, however, which were reserved to them reached a very high standard, as may be judged from the fact that at Argenteuil Héloïse studied not only the Scriptures and Fathers of the Church, but also medicine and surgery, apart from Abélard's courses in Greek and Hebrew from which she derived so much pleasure.

Studies followed the traditional courses as arranged by Alcuin at Charlemagne's request: the *trivium* (grammar, dialectic, rhetoric) and *quadrivium* (arithmetic, geometry, astronomy, music). Nevertheless, it appears from medieval treatises on education, e.g. those of Hugh of St Victor and John of Salisbury, that masters often went beyond these narrow limits; and one famous teacher, Thierry of Chartres, used quite rightly to say that the *trivium* and *quadrivium* were only means to an end, which was to guide young footsteps in the paths of truth and wisdom. Their main ambition was to devise and inculcate a method which would open up the entire field of human knowledge. For this reason, dialectic, which sharpens the mind and renders it more supple, was a much-honoured branch of learning; while those sciences which

---

[1] It appears that discipline was not easy to maintain in these schools. There were no special premises; students sat on the ground and wrote with a stylus on wax tablets propped up on their knees. The number of students, too, obviously made discipline still harder to enforce. St Bernard sharply criticized the behaviour in schools of his time, accusing pupils in the cathedral school of many vices and crimes, including fornication, adultery, and even incest. Stories of the 'Goliards' echo these disorders, which were perpetuated by university students down to the time of Villon.

were as yet outside the classical curricula were taught by masters who, since they enjoyed much more discretion in their choice of subjects than is the case nowadays, exercised a far stronger influence upon their pupils. So long, for example, as Bernard of Chartres taught in that city, grammar was a general course of literature. Some schools even provided technical training, e.g. that of Vassor near Metz, where students were taught how to work in gold, silver, and copper. Specialization in the true sense gradually made its appearance: Chartres was the home *par excellence* of letters, Paris of theology, Bologna of law, Salerno and Montpellier of medicine; and we shall rediscover this tendency to specialize in the major universities.

Higher education came into being about the year 1200, at the climax of a tremendous intellectual ferment, when the older cathedral schools turned their eyes towards more fruitful pastures. Before that date, a man determined to enlarge his outlook had no alternative but to attend the Arab schools in Spain,[1] or those of Constantinople, where many students from the West attended lectures by the 'first philosopher,' Michael Psellos. Henceforward, those in search of higher culture found all they needed in the West. Episcopal schools limited themselves to secondary education, while more advanced studies began to thrive in the atmosphere of a novel institution called the University.

4. THE UNIVERSITY

The rise of the universities, pride of medieval Christendom and spiritual sisters of the cathedrals, marks an epoch in the history of Western civilization, a milestone on the road of human thought. Their origins were in each case very similar, and each developed along the same lines. Though born in the shadow of the cathedrals, it was not long before they sought to escape from the rather meddlesome control of episcopal chancellors and chapters, in order to pursue their own way toward a more vigorous culture. In this they were encouraged by the supreme ecclesiastical rulers; for the popes, who were then at the zenith of their power, naturally desired to control these intellectual power-houses as an aid to strengthening their own authority. Thanks to the repeated intervention of the papacy, higher education was enabled to extend its boundaries; the Church, in fact, was the matrix that produced the university, the nest whence it took flight.

It may be helpful to examine the evolution of a university by means of a concrete example, and Paris may be considered typical. In the closing years of the twelfth century, cathedral schools were on the decline, even that of Chartres which had been once so famous. A host of keen young students were crowding into Paris, the Capetian capital

[1] e.g. at Toledo, where Gerbert studied.

which was then in its full flower. The episcopal school was full to overflowing; those at the abbeys of St Victor and Ste Geneviève were no less popular; while innumerable private teachers offered instruction at any convenient point along the streets that wound down from the hill whereon the shrine of Ste Geneviève kept watch over the city she had saved from Attila. Masters and students were everywhere to be seen: on the still grassy slopes around St Julien-le-Pauvre; in the Clos Garlande, the Clos Bruneau, and the Clos du Chardonnet; along the Rue St Jacques, the Place Maubert (whose name re-echoes that of 'Magnus Albertus,' Albert the Great), and the Rue Lemoine, called after the great cardinal who did much to benefit the student race.[1] The agitation caused by this seething mass of people was felt not only on the intellectual plane, and the Chancellor of Notre-Dame tried without success to bring the noisy throng under his authority. The urban communes were multiplying rapidly, trade-guilds were in process of development; and so, in order to resist the Chancellor more firmly, masters and students followed their example by forming, as it were, a scholastic union, the *Universitas magistrorum et scholarium Parisiensium.*

In the year 1200 some German students sacked a tavern and left the landlord half dead; the townsfolk, assisted by the royal provost and his police, flew to arms and retaliated, killing five students. The University appealed to the king. Philip Augustus, realizing the advantages conferred on his capital by the presence of so learned an institution, degraded the provost, punished the regular inhabitants, and granted the University 'privilege of clergy,' which freed it from police control. But masters and pupils thereby found themselves subject to the episcopal chancellor. There was only one way to get rid of him, and that was by appeal to higher authority. Pope Innocent III agreed to take the infant University under his protection; and his legate, Robert de Courson, gave it a statute whereby the bishop's rights were so curtailed as to be henceforward virtually non-existent. The University was now in a position to throw off the yoke of Notre-Dame; she laughed at the excommunications which were fulminated by successive Ordinaries only to be annulled by Rome. The University had indeed become a formidable power. In 1229 there were fresh brawls; Blanche of Castile's police intervened with undue severity, and the masters joined their students in a strike. Worse still, they emigrated to Toulouse, Angers, Rheims, Orléans, and even to

[1] All this quarter of Paris preserves the memory of medieval scholars: there is still a passage du clos Bruno (11 Rue des Carmes) and a church of St Nicolas-du-Chardonnet. The Rue des Fossés-St-Bernard recalls the great monk who was idolized by the University; the Rue St Victor reminds us of the abbey where so many famous masters taught. Some hold that the Rue du Fouarre (i.e. of straw) takes its name from the straw which students used as bedding.

England, Italy, and Spain. Far from punishing them, Gregory IX issued his Bull *Parens Scientiarum* (1231), which made the University of Paris an international association, responsible to the Holy See alone, a small state within the Church and also within the State. After an absence of two years, professors and pupils returned victorious to Paris.

Under cover of their secession, however, a new element had made its appearance. The mendicant Orders, both Dominican and Franciscan which were then on the flood-tide of popularity, had found their way into the ranks of the University. The Dominican Roland of Cremona opened a school of theology in the Convent of St Jacques; a distinguished teacher, John of St Gilles, took the white habit of St Dominic while the famous Alexander of Hales became a Franciscan. The University had welcomed papal authority so long as it was exercised from a distance; but these new Orders were a disturbing factor—they were the Pope's 'yes-men.' Violent conflict broke out between clerical members of the University and the mendicant friars. The seculars wished to deny professorial status to the regulars, and for five years (1252–7) there was constant rioting. Innocent IV hesitated in face of this opposition; but when Alexander IV, a former Dominican ascended Peter's throne, he took a stronger line, and even threatened the recalcitrants with excommunication. All notorious enemies of the friars were removed from office, including William of St Amour who had defamed them in a written work, and the University was thereby forced to yield. Henceforward she admitted Franciscan and Dominican teachers, a step she never regretted since it added to her illustrious roll of members the names of Bonaventure and Thomas Aquinas.

In this way the trials sustained by the University brought about a advance in higher education. Her interests were often short-sighted and too material; but by freeing them from the control of episcopal chancellors and cathedral chapters, she enhanced the value of her academic degrees, and was enabled to grant teaching licences to those alone whom she considered worthy. Moreover, her submission to the Holy See attracted a better class of teacher, while she herself benefited by the youthful vigour of the mendicants. Towards the end of the thirteenth century, as papal authority weakened, the University acquired more freedom. This does not mean that she represented an effort towards emancipation as opposed to the Catholic faith; her masters and students still consisted almost entirely of tonsured clerics and her seal bore in its upper compartment an image of our Lady enthroned with the Infant Jesus in her arms. The University was, as it had always been, a religious corporation; it had merely secured recognition of intellectual and cultural autonomy in so far as this did not conflict with dogma, and by so doing it had taken a decisive step on behalf of all mankind.

The universities enjoyed worldwide respect.   Innocent IV spoke of them as 'rivers of science which water and make fertile the soil of the universal Church,' and Alexander IV compared them to 'lanterns shining in the house of God.'   The University of Paris, renowned above all others for her theological school, was commonly called the 'New Athens' or 'the permanent Council of the Gauls.'   She was governed by a rector, elected at first for one month and later for three. His office was of the highest dignity; he was styled 'Amplissime Seigneur,' and on ceremonial occasions he took precedence of nuncios, of ambassadors, and even of cardinals.   When a king of France entered his capital, it was the rector who received him and read an address of welcome.   Every year, followed by all the masters in their robes, hoods, and caps, and by an enormous crowd of students, he went to the June fair to buy parchment for the whole University, and none might purchase any of that precious material before him.   If he died in office, the humble professor received honours due to princes of the blood, and was buried at St Denis.   We can scarcely require more cogent proofs of the veneration with which the Middle Ages treated learning.

The celebrity of the great universities drew incredible numbers of students not only from every province of France, but also from Germany, Flanders, Italy, and even from Syria, Armenia, and Egypt. Many princes granted bursaries to those of their subjects who wished to pursue higher studies.   Thus, in 1192, Sancho I of Portugal allocated 00 *morabitinos* to the monastery of Santa Cruz at Coimbra 'to support such canons as are studying in France.'   What was the total number of students?   We need not accept Philip of Harvengt's statement that at Paris 'they outnumbered the inhabitants,' but we may reasonably suppose that there were between three and four thousand of them in a city which at that time had a population of no more than about 50,000. It must have seemed, as it does to-day at Coimbra or at Cambridge, that the city's life depended on the University.

Nor, indeed, must we think of a medieval university as having the outward appearance so familiar to ourselves, with its own buildings, libraries, technical apparatus, and other facilities.   Thirteenth-century scholars enjoyed no such advantages.   No hall could accommodate the University of Paris in full session, and it was necessary to beg hospitality from the Mathurins or from the Dominicans of St Jacques. A fashionable professor had often so many pupils that he was obliged to lecture from the pulpit in a church; and the Collège de Sorbon owed much of its immediate success to the fact that it possessed an enormous hall, so that meetings could be held 'at the Sorbonne.'

Studies were divided into four Faculties, each under the direction of a dean. They were Theology, Law, Medicine, and Arts. The latter covered subjects taken by the higher classes in modern French schools —philosophy,[1] elementary mathematics, and higher rhetoric. The faculty of arts attracted three times as many students as all the others, and its dean soon became master of the whole University. Teaching methods were identical in all four Faculties: the masters lectured while the students sat (generally on the floor) and took notes, except in cases where the professor entrusted the exemplar manuscript of his course to copyists for reproduction and sale. Teaching was done in three stages: *lectio*, in which the text was read; *quaestio*, a commentary thereupon; and *disputatio*, when students and masters together criticized the thesis. This final stage became increasingly important, and masters such as Abélard and St Thomas Aquinas excelled at it. The *quodlibet*, a free discussion on all sorts of subjects and much enjoyed by young students, was an extension of the *disputatio*. As for the methods employed in private study, they were not very different from those now in use. Robert de Sorbon, in his *De Conscientia*, lays down six rules as follows: an ordered time-table, concentrated attention, memory-training, note-taking, discussion with one's fellow students, and finally prayer. By following his counsel, which is valid in every age, the student could climb the steps of learning and acquire the three recognized degrees: *déterminance*, which qualified him to undertake more advanced studies; the *baccalauréat*, which entitled him, after he had reached the age of twenty, to do a little teaching without abandoning his own studies; and lastly the *licenciate*, which was solemnly conferred and entitled him both to enrolment on the syndicate of masters and to open his own school whenever he desired. The *doctorate* was rather an honorary and complimentary title.

That de Sorbon's principles too often went by the board is shown in contemporary documents, from which it appears that the behaviour of students left much to be desired. These crowds of young people were very difficult to manage. There was an administrative system which, for convenience, grouped them according to nations. At Paris, for example, they were divided into French, Picards, Normans and English;[2] but this was a very broad distinction, since Italians and Spaniards were classed with the French, while all northerners, Germans included, were counted as English. At Bologna the distinction was twofold—Cismontanes and Transmontanes.

Students in the thirteenth century differed scarcely, if at all, from

---

[1] In the French secondary schools philosophy follows the *classe de première* and prepares for the second part of the *baccalauréat* examination.

[2] The Rue des Anglais between the Boulevard St Germain and the Rue Lagrange doubt preserves their memory.

their modern counterparts.   They were critical but warm-hearted, enthusiastic but excitable, devoid of malice but full of mischief.   All feast days were occasions of rowdyism by day and even more so by night; to empty a dung-cart over the city militia, or to fire a train of gunpowder under the feet of the night-watch on its rounds were the least of their pleasantries.   Among these hundreds of youths there were some, of course, who took work seriously; but there was also the vanishing type, upon whom the professors seldom set eyes, not to mention those tenth-year students who, under pretext of continuing the most improbable studies, wandered from tavern to tavern, more interested in wine and girls than in Latin conjugations.

The student's greatest problem was then, as it is to-day, one of money.   We possess a number of letters written by medieval under-graduates to their parents, in which money-matters are always promi-nent.   Wealthy youths rented chambers, and the smarter set even had their own men-servants.   The poor lodged where they could, worked as copyists or bookbinders, and were hard put to it for a meal.   Study was a costly business, and it was in order to solve the grave social problem created by destitution in the universities that colleges were established by pious souls in almost every centre of learning.   The first was that of the Dix-huit, founded in 1180 by a wealthy citizen of London on his return from a pilgrimage to the Holy Land, for the maintenance of eighteen poor and deserving students.   Others fol-lowed his example.   When St Louis became king there were already several colleges at Paris; Robert de Sorbon, acting by order of his sovereign, founded yet another which was to immortalize his name— the Collège de Sorbon for sixteen Masters of Arts who wished to study theology.   The whole area which now adjoins the Boulevards St Germain and St Michel was soon built over, and most of the great schools in this quarter stand on the sites of medieval colleges.[1]   In the fourteenth century there were fifty of them, and when certain charitable hostelries formed a body of teachers to prepare their inmates for the higher Faculties, they became the equivalent of secondary schools and were the forerunners of modern French *lycées*.

The same thing applied to other universities which arose simul-taneously and in almost every land.   France alone had ten: Mont-pellier (1125) was certainly established before Paris, though it was not really organized until 1220; Orléans was founded in 1200, Toulouse in 1217, Angers in 1220; even such modest townships as Gray and Pont-à-Mousson had their universities; while those of Lyons, Pamiers,

---

[1] The Lycée St Louis on the site of the Collège d'Harcourt, the École Ste Barbe on that of the Collège des Cholets (founded by Cardinal Cholet), the École Polytechnique on that of the Collège de Navarre (founded by the wife of Philip the Fair), the Lycée Louis-le-and on that of the Collège de Plessis (founded by Geoffrey du Plessis), etc.

Narbonne, and Cahors existed early in the fourteenth century. About 1350, the University of Paris began to decline, weakened from within by the pernicious custom of selling degrees and by the great crisis of the Hundred Years War; but others were ready to take over the torch.

There was no region of Western Christendom that was not proud to possess a university, often at the cost of heavy sacrifice.   In Italy, the ancient school at Salerno became a university in 1200; Bologna's glory dated from 1111.   There were also Padua, Pavia, Naples, Palermo, and even the *Studium Curiae*, a 'flying university' that travelled with the papal court.   England had Oxford and Cambridge.   In Bohemia, Prague was celebrated long before the rise of the imperial university at Cracow (1362), Vienna (1366), and Heidelberg (1386).   The venerable University of Salamanca in Spain was contemporary with Paris, while Coimbra in Portugal quickly established its high reputation and was favoured by every Portuguese monarch.

These citadels of the intellect were celebrated throughout Europe. All knew where such and such a master taught, and the presence of an eminent professor sufficed to draw a crowd of pupils, wherever he might be.   The cosmopolitanism of medieval universities, like that of pilgrimages and crusades, brought about an interchange of men, of knowledge, and of ideas, the importance of which is plain for all to see.

5.   THE TRAVAIL OF THOUGHT

Such an interchange, however, was but the outward sign of a prodigious ferment in the domain of thought which occupied the whole great period of the Middle Ages.   Nothing is more absurd than the common belief that thought was at a standstill, held down by ecclesiastical directives, paralysed by fear of the Inquisition, and even hesitant in face of its own demands.   The exact contrary is true.   The universities were centres of keen intellectual activity, where the greatest minds confronted one another in passionate argument, where complex influences swayed opinion this way and then that, and where men did not hesitate to grapple with the thorniest problems so far as their means allowed.   Faith was no sterilizing force, but a leaven that caused the lump to stir and rise.

First, the cosmopolitan spirit of Christianity rescued the raw material of speculation from those watertight compartments in which it had been imprisoned since the rise of nationalism and to the detriment of Europe.   The students were an international body; so too, as we have seen,[1] were the professors.

In the second place, this fruitful exchange of knowledge and ideas was saved by the ideal of Christian unity from the confusion which

[1] See Chapter I, section 8.

must otherwise have resulted from linguistic differences. The Church, as guardian of schools and universities, gave them her own language, Latin. To-day, when international assemblies are obliged to use headphones and simultaneous translations, revealing thereby the Babel of our tongues, we can appreciate the benefits of a single language understood by all educated men. St Thomas Aquinas, an Italian, left his native Campania for Cologne, where he attended lectures by a German, Albert the Great, and afterwards delivered his own course at Paris. While masters taught in Latin, students voluntarily adopted the same medium to distinguish themselves from lesser breeds, and even translated their own names into Latin. Thus, the Chevaliers and Caballeros became *Militis*; the Tisserands, Tissiers, and Webers called themselves *Textoris*; the Oudendycks pretended to forget their Dutch origin and styled themselves *De Veteri Aggere*; the Hammerleins, an Alsatian family, preferred *Malleolus*, a faithful rendering of 'little hammer'; and it was owing to this unanimous adoption of the language spoken long since by Cicero that the scholastic quarter of Paris became known as the *Quartier Latin*.

Apart from the use of Latin as a language, Latin literature was the gateway to learning. The study of grammar was based upon St Jerome's master Donatus, upon the sixth-century Byzantine Priscian, and upon Capella, whose encyclopaedia was all the rage. Critical judgment was naturally derived from Cicero, Quintilian, and Boethius, as well as from Latin translations of Porphyry and Aristotle. No one could claim to be a mathematician unless he had studied Frontinus, Columella, Gerbert, and the Latin versions of Ptolemy; while every musician made constant reference to Boethius's *De Musica*.

As for the quality of Latin in the Middle Ages, most accomplished writers used a style so good that it was often barely distinguishable from that of classical models, and at its best bordered upon plagiarism. Every sort of composition was represented, from theological treatises to sacred and profane poetry, and even comedy. The beauty of medieval Latin is enshrined in many a sublime masterpiece such as the *Dies Irae* by Thomas of Celano, St Thomas Aquinas's *Pange Lingua*, and the great *Stabat Mater* of Jacopone da Todi. But this high standard was by no means invariable. We can still read numerous documentary records, schoolboy exercises, and administrative reports, in which the Latin is as macaronic as in Rabelais; and modern French preserves its quaint charm in such phrases as 'être a quia,' 'couper sibus,' and 'aller pedibus cum jambis.'

These defects notwithstanding, Latin was a sure means of conveying ideas; its outward uniformity was the symbol and cement of an internal unity arising from the acceptance of common principles. Desire for a universal culture was felt by all alike; they achieved it by submission to appropriate influences, and by drinking deep at every source from which it sprang. But their very acceptance of common principles saved them from the twofold peril of agnosticism and eclecticism. Just as medieval art, which evolved from the most diverse elements, cannot fail to impress us with its originality, so also the intellectual life of the Middle Ages, as it flowered in the great cosmopolitan universities, retained a striking harmony. There lies the advantage of a vigorous civilization, sure of its own strength and of itself.

Such was the nature of medieval learning which is so frequently decried. It was founded on firm principles, yet insatiably curious and in unceasing labour. It is hard to realize the staggering productivity of those thinkers. How many, for example, know that the Jammy edition of Albert the Great occupies twenty-one large volumes; the Vivès edition of St Thomas, thirty-two; and that of Duns Scotus twenty-six? It has been calculated that if we were to assemble all the works of the 305 masters of theology who taught at the University of Paris during the first century of its existence, their pages would exceed in number those of Migne's *Patrologia Latina*.

The period, in fact, is outstanding not only by reason of its material achievement,[1] but also on account of the profundity and extent of its knowledge. Masters who excelled in a particular field were not confined within its boundaries; the practice of specializing in one subject was as yet infrequent. Men like Abélard in the twelfth century, or Alexander of Hales, St Thomas Aquinas, and Roger Bacon in the thirteenth, made a thorough survey of contemporary learning. Nothing is more characteristic than the word *Summa* which occurs so often in the titles of great medieval works. The *summa* was encyclopaedic in its range; it strove to set forth knowledge from the standpoint of eternity by supplying a definitive answer to every question however inconsiderable. Behind the austere process of question and answer we may perceive the passionate craving after ideas which inspired these men, a craving which tormented Abélard, pathetic and altogether supernatural in the case of St Bernard, outwardly serene though secretly violent in that of St Thomas.[2]

Before the beginning of our period, intellectual life had been

[1] The invention of paper contributed enormously to the spread of knowledge by substituting a fairly cheap material for the ruinously expensive parchment. It is known that the method of manufacturing paper from old rags, which had long been familiar to the Chinese, was introduced into Africa and Spain by the Arabs. It became common in Italy and France during the twelfth century.

[2] This passion for ideas was not without its dangers, for pride can all too easily play a part therein, as happened to Abélard and Sigier of Brabant. Simon of Tournai is a still more flagrant warning. In 1200, while lecturing in Paris, he ended a discourse with these words: 'O little Jesus! little Jesus! how I have strengthened and exalted Thy doctrine in this address. Yet, were I Thine enemy and wished to do Thee harm, I would be just as capable of weakening and refuting it with even stronger proofs and argùments.' Was this, perhaps, the source of Baudelaire's poem *Châtiment de l'Orgeuil*?

nourished almost exclusively on crumbs from the Roman table; letters, philosophy, and the sciences were for the most part derived therefrom. But from the twelfth century onwards Europe was consumed with a youthful longing after new conquests, and, being convinced that the heritage of the past was infinitely richer, strove to possess it.   Students went out from every university, and in the course of their travels gleaned new harvests.   Fresh information and new methods of thought were brought back from the East to serve as the bases of original ventures. The intellectual substructure of Europe was about to undergo a change.

Whence came the decisive impulse? From Byzantium? Partly, but in a much greater degree from Islam.   For Islam was the true heir of Greek science and philosophy, which had been taken over and translated by Moslem scholars.   There were many points of contact between the West and the Arab world.   Islamic culture was discovered by the crusaders in Syria; its precious relics were gathered up by the Normans in Sicily; Constantine 'the African' and Leonardo of Pisa studied it in Africa; but above all, the Universities of Cordova and Toledo in Spain attracted many research students, and enjoyed so great a prestige that Arabic was still used at Toledo for purposes of teaching even after the Reconquista.   In the twelfth century a number of translations from Arabic were made by enthusiastic Christians and converted Jews at Toulouse, Béziers, Narbonne, and Marseilles. Other keen workers in this fruitful field were the Englishmen Adelard of Bath and Michael Scot, the Italian Gerard of Cremona, the Spaniard Gondisalvi of Segovia, and the German Hermann.   Raymond Lull was sufficiently well versed in Arabic to write books in that tongue. Arabian science thus became widespread.   Astronomical tables, medical treatises by the celebrated Ibn Sina (Avicenna), text-books of algebra, geometry, and even trigonometry, together with the so-called Ptolemaic geography, all reached the West and proved their value. Eventually the philosophy and theology of Islam penetrated the Universities of Paris and Oxford, where they stirred up fierce controversy; so that men were for or against Avicenna, Ghazali, Maimonides, and Averroes, just as nowadays they are for or against Freud and Heidegger.

It was mainly due to Arabian influence that Greek thought was rediscovered. This was an event of capital importance; for besides original Islamic works, scholars were now able for the first time to translate Arabic versions of Greek masterpieces into Latin. The craze for Greek mounted steadily from about 1150, when Archbishop Raymond of Toledo engaged a team of translators. Its study was resumed in southern Italy and Sicily, where it had never quite died out; and the West soon became familiar with Plato's *Timaeus*,[1] together

---

[1] *Timaeus* was the only one of Plato's Dialogues known at this period.

L*

with the writings of Galen, Archimedes, Hero of Alexandria, and the Greek Fathers.   The recovery of Aristotle's works caused an intellectual revolution.   In the thirteenth century every available item from the Stagirite's pen was translated, often twice, either from the original or from an Arabic version; Archbishop Robert Grosseteste and Roger Bacon were keenly interested in this task.   From 1250 Greek was taught in Dominican schools, and from 1312 in the Universities of Paris, Oxford, Bologna, and Salamanca.   A whole new field of thought had been opened up.

The consequence of these acquisitions was to let loose a wave of philosophical inquiry.   Earlier theologians generally confined themselves to 'positive theology'; their sole aim was to prove doctrinal propositions by the argument from authority, i.e. by collecting evidence from Scripture, tradition, and conciliar decrees.   Scholasticism, the theology and philosophy of the schools, had a different end in view.   Its ancestry may be traced to St Augustine, Cassiodorus, St Isidore of Seville, and (somewhat later) to Alcuin and Rabanus Maurus.   Taking their stand upon philosophy, the scholastics endeavoured to show that dogma is consistent with reason, and that no objection could invalidate it.   'Speculative theology' had now been born, and philosophy became 'the handmaid of theology.'   All the most influential thought of the twelfth and thirteenth centuries derived from scholasticism.   Scholastic philosophy applied itself to the rational study of many problems, while scholastic theology strove to combine the whole of revealed truth in a single body of doctrine (a *summa*).   The principal method used for the advancement of learning was dialectic, the art of reasoning, which seeks to deduce the logical consequence of a given idea.   The syllogism was held in great honour; and if this method of inference sometimes degenerated into vain discussion and verbal hair-splitting, no one can deny that it also contributed to the progress of thought and to the study of fundamental problems.

We must, indeed, never forget that such problems were the main concern of the scholastics; and this is one of the most striking and admirable characteristics of intellectual life in the Middle Ages.   The form in which they were cast may be sometimes disconcerting; but if we manage to penetrate beyond an obscure terminology and discern what was at stake, we shall find that it concerns ourselves.   For example, the great dispute which lasted throughout the Middle Ages was that of Universals.   Now what was this all about?   It was an attempt to decide whether general, or universal, ideas, which we express by such words as 'humanity,' 'class,' etc., correspond to types that really exist, or whether they are simple abstractions, mere invention of the mind.   At first glance, nothing seems more pointless than this discussion upon words, in which arguments were opposed to arguments, realism to nominalism, Plato to Aristotle. But stop and think, what was the real issue? Nothing less than the validity of knowledge, the possibility of man's knowing truth through the medium of reality, the antagonism between essence and existence. Have these questions ceased to trouble us? Surely, if it is the *genus* or *species*, and not the *man*, which *is*, the individual has no right to autonomy, to freedom. This question is at the very heart of our present tragedy; the scholastics long ago realized its importance.

The problem of being, of general and particular, of knowledge, of freedom, and so on, were the subject-matter of ideological clashes in which passion could attain to extremes of violence. Far from stagnation, medieval thought strikes us as a splendid effervescence of which few periods can show the like. It was in this stirring climate that St Anselm, Abélard, and St Bernard worked. They were followed by Albert the Great, St Bonaventure, St Thomas Aquinas, and finally by Roger Bacon and Duns Scotus—an imposing array of genius, or at least of extraordinary talent, and produced by Christendom within a period of less than two hundred years.

6. The First Period of Scholasticism

At the root of all this immense intellectual labour, as of the whole medieval edifice, lay the Faith. No problem at that time had any meaning, except in so far as it was related to a higher problem, to the knowledge of things divine. Theology was therefore, beyond all doubt, the queen of sciences, the science *par excellence*, one from which all else started and to which it ultimately returned. But faith was no hindrance to the mind; on the contrary, by providing man with a basis of certainty it enabled him to strike out boldly into the unknown. And these scholastics knew well how to venture; they knew that their foundations were unshakable and would not let them down. They have been justly compared [1] to 'highly skilled rope-walkers who, holding the balancing-pole of Revelation to give themselves confidence up to the last moment, perform the most daring acrobatics on the narrow cord of speculation.'

The crucial problem, therefore, was the relation between reason and faith. Should reason assist faith, or vice versa? To believe in order to understand, or to understand in order to believe; that was the alternative with which medival thinkers were very soon confronted. Thanks only to the determined labour of our scholastic forbears, we are no longer obliged to choose between two alternatives. Both propositions are true: faith assists the working of reason, while reason

[1] By Mme L. Lefrançois-Pillion in *L'Esprit de la cathédrale*, p. 208.

supports faith on the defensive.   St Augustine and St Thomas Aquinas
are complementary, not mutually exclusive.   But in the excitement of
discovery the scholastics took one side or the other: belief for the
sake of understanding, understanding for the sake of belief.   Broadly
speaking, we may say that between the eleventh and the thirteenth
centuries the accent shifted from the former to the latter half of what is
really an indivisible formula.   About the year 1050 emphasis was on
the first alone, but by about 1250 opinion had veered in favour of the
second.   The history of medieval religious thought is the history of
this transformation.

In the eleventh century St Peter Damian (1007–72) insisted that
'God has no need of rhetoric to draw souls unto Himself.   Those
whom He sent to evangelize the world were not philosophers.'   The
question was, could so categorical an assertion be upheld?   Without
abandoning the primacy of God, some of the most penetrating intellects had already begun to suspect that there was no hard and fast line
between faith and reason, and that philosophy could help dogma.
Among these thinkers was the Saxon monk Gottschalk whom Hincmar
had opposed.   There was also the great John Scotus Erigena (c. 815–
c. 877), who likewise tended to heterodoxy, maintaining that true
philosophy is true religion, and contrariwise; and the most characteristic feature of St Augustine's thought was that it explained all things
by reference to God as their first principle.

Such was the attitude adopted in the first period of scholasticism.
The most eminent teachers believed it a mistake to reject the assistance
of philosophy; if reason could help them better to apprehend the
mysteries of faith, why set it aside?   *Fides quaerens intellectum.*
Taking dogma as a starting point, the scholastics strove to enlarge
their field.   Lanfranc (1005–89), headmaster of Bec and later Archbishop of Canterbury, made brilliant use of this method.   In order to
combat the eucharistic errors of Berengar, he did not hesitate to
employ philosophical arguments and dialectic as well as tradition.

One man, however, was responsible for the birth of orthodox speculation: St Anselm (1033–1109), who is sometimes called the Father of
Scholasticism.   Here was a great intellectual for whom love was
among the chief ends of knowledge, a bishop whose exquisite sensibility was unaffected by the rough and tumble of political warfare.[1]
Scion of a noble family from the Val d'Aosta,[2] he loved, as a child,
to gaze in raptured meditation upon the mountains of his native land;
and while still at school he was saved by Lanfranc from dangerous
aberrations.   Becoming a monk at Bec, he was in due course elected

[1] See Chapter V, section 10 for an account of St Anselm's political dealings with
William Rufus and Henry I.
[2] His father was a cousin of the Countess Matilda of Tuscany.

abbot, and finally Archbishop of Canterbury.   Throughout his life
Anselm had, as he used to say, 'only one consolation, only one satisfaction,' the love of God.   His intellectual pursuits, his scholasticism,
and his dialectic form part and parcel with his mysticism.   His guiding
principle was 'to love what one knows,' to learn more in order to love
more.   'I do not seek to understand,' he used to say, 'in order to
believe; I believe in order to understand.'   True, he sometimes failed
to distinguish objects to which reason can attain from those which faith
alone reveals.   For example, posterity could not accept the arguments
with which he tried to prove the existence of the Trinity, the necessity
of the Redemption, and the Resurrection of the body.   His famous
argument *a priori* for the existence of God, still known as St Anselm's
ontological argument, is not irrefutable, in spite of the fact that its
essentials were adopted by Descartes, by Bossuet, and (in a modified
form) by Leibniz.   According to St Anselm, since every man carries
within himself the concept of supreme greatness, of absolute perfection,
therefore this immense and perfect Being exists.   St Thomas Aquinas
demonstrated the weakness of that proof; but St Anselm deserves
credit for having approached the theological problem from a rational
standpoint, for having opened up the way to philosophical investigation, and for having understood the possibility of a fruitful marriage
between reason and faith.   His works are perhaps more celebrated
than any others dating from that period.   They are not in the form of
a *summa*, but they cover logic and dialectic, the criteria of truth and
free will, besides the mysteries of God (in the *Monologion and Pros-
logion*), the Trinity, the problem of Evil, and the Redemption.   We
also possess many of his sermons, prayers, and letters.   First of the
great medieval Christian thinkers, he lived too early to effect the new
synthesis required by altered circumstances; all the same, we should be
grateful to him for his pioneer labours.

It was unlikely that St Anselm's wisdom and moderation would be
found in all philosophers and theologians at a time when thought was
in the melting-pot.   Dogma was imperilled by recourse to reason.
At Tours, for instance, the headmaster of St Martin's, Berengar (1000–
1088), fell into heresy through trying to subject the mystery of the
Holy Eucharist to an artless rationalism.   His teaching was condemned, but he returned to his error 'because he could not mistrust his
own reason.'   At Compiègne, there was a Breton canon named
Roscelin (1050–1120), who had thrown himself heart and soul into the
dispute about Universals on the side of nominalism.   He wished to
apply to the mystery of the Holy Trinity his theory that only individuals are real, genera and species being mere 'names.'   The result was
to deny that there could be one God in three Persons, and Roscelin was
condemned by the Council of Soissons in 1092.   Again, the celebrated

school at Chartres, founded by Fulbert, provided without doubt the most liberal and intensive education available at that time. But it enjoyed close relations with Toledo, and was therefore open to the winds of semi-heresy and suspect opinions which were disseminated by such masters as William of la Porrée, Thierry of Chartres, William of Conches, and Bernard Sylvestre, until the pantheism of that school was likewise condemned. Even these difficulties, however, have their significance by pointing to the labour-pains of medieval thought. It was no easy matter to harness reason with faith, as the twelfth century was well aware; and this truth is nowhere better shown than in the conflict between two of the most brilliant intellects, Abélard and St Bernard.

We have already seen the nature of this conflict; [1] its surpassing interest lies in the fact that it was a head-on collision between men who embodied most completely the twin tendencies of their age. It is difficult to do justice to Abélard (1079–1142); his genius lacked balance, but his intellectual daring contributed in no small measure to the progress of thought, and helped to bring about the glory of the thirteenth century. This young aristocrat from Nantes, whose ignorance of mathematics caused him to be nicknamed 'bon à lêcher le lard,' Abélard, gave evidence in boyhood not only of a craving for knowledge, but also of a disquieting itch for personal renown and originality at any price. Having studied, first, under the nominalist Roscelin at Compiègne and then under the realist William of Champeaux at the school of Notre-Dame in Paris, he had, at the age of barely twenty-three years, discredited the teaching of both masters. Attracted to Laon by the fame of a professor named Anselm, [2] he soon abandoned him with the charitable remark that 'this man's fire makes a lot of smoke but gives no light!' Abélard now began teaching on his own, and the school of Ste Geneviève under his direction soon eclipsed Notre-Dame and St Victor. He had five thousand pupils, men who had already made their mark or would do so later on: future bishops and cardinals, and even a future pope. As might have been expected, success went straight to his head; he had reached the age of forty when he began to lose his balance. We are all familiar with the tragi-comic drama of his lust for Héloïse, a girl of eighteen but the most brilliant of his pupils. We know also the terrible revenge taken upon him by the uncle of his willing victim. Ordained priest at the Abbey of St Denis, he could not endure the silence of the cloister. After teaching for some while in a priory at Brie, he was condemned for the first time by a provincial council, ordered to burn his book on the Trinity, and to remain in his cell. He soon emerged, however, and built a hermitage called 'The Paraclete' at Nogent-sur-Seine; students flocked to him in

---

[1] Chapter III, section 6. [2] To be distinguished from St Anselm of Bec.

thousands; and Héloïse established a community of women near by.
Eventually he returned to Paris and welcomed once again, at the age of
fifty-seven, the vast audiences of his youth.   Such was Abélard's
personality that none could be indifferent to him; he was exalted by
some, hounded to death by others, and only the direct intervention of
St Bernard could suffice to overwhelm him.

Abélard's output was enormous.   It included philosophical treatises
on dialectic, on morality, and on Porphyry; exegetical essays, notably
on the Epistle to the Romans; but above all his theological treatises
Sic et Non, *Christian Theology* (1138), and *Introduction to Theology*.
Nor must we overlook his correspondence with Héloïse, which
contains many beautiful passages.   On the other hand, a bare enumeration of his writings can convey no adequate idea of the influence
exerted by this dazzling teacher who breathed life into the dry bones of
abstract thought.   As a dialectician he was in a class of his own; he
did much to perfect the scholastic method, and it was he who introduced the *disputatio* or criticism of the thesis.[1]   His theory of knowledge was certainly at the root of an effort towards the concrete and the
real, which, as we shall see, was accomplished by his successors.   Why,
then, was Abélard condemned?   Certainly not for unbelief; he was
profoundly Christian and proclaimed himself a dutiful son of the
Church, 'accepting all that she teaches, rejecting all that she condemns.'
Nor, strictly speaking, can we say it was on account of heresy.   St
Bernard accused him of 'speaking like Arius of the Trinity, like
Pelagius of grace, and like Nestorius of the person of Christ'; but that
referred rather to his general outlook than to any explicit statement.
Some minds are never happy except on the edge of an abyss.   The
basic problem lay in his concept of the relations between reason and
faith.   'You cannot believe what you don't understand,' he used to
say; and that was in direct opposition to St Anselm.   For the formula
fides quaerens intellectum he substituted *intellectus quaerens fidem*.   Did
he sufficiently distinguish the reasons for belief from the truths to be
believed?   Did he take into account the fact that there is a point to
which the unaided intellect never will attain?   Pushed to its extreme,
his doctrine would have deprived dogma of all substance and reduced
faith to nothing.   His efforts might have been salutary, had he
remained within the framework of dogma and agreed to recognize that
there are such things as mysteries.   But this equilibrium was not
achieved until the appearance of a man far less proud than Abélard,
far more aware of God, and submissive to grace, St Thomas Aquinas.

Face to face with Abélard, who looked to the future and whose
boldness knew no bounds, it was natural that those who perceived the
danger should take a contrary standpoint, clinging for dear life to the

[1] See above, page 312.

lessons of the past.   The school of St Victor, that nursery of saints,[1] was a fortress of the traditional spirit; and William of Champeaux, disgusted with the tumults of the school of Notre-Dame, had sought peace within its walls before his appointment to the bishopric of Châlons.   Hugh of St Victor also taught there, arguing that the profane sciences should be treated merely as food for meditation. Richard of St Victor, another professor in this school, echoed St Paul's warning, that contemplation alone enables us to see God, and then only 'as in a glass, darkly'; while Gauthier even wrote a book against scholasticism.

St Bernard also was a man of the past, but with a difference; he possessed genius and foresight.[2]   His tireless intellectual activity is sufficient proof that he was no voluntary ignoramus, as his critics have alleged.   He never rallied to the battle cry 'Be ye therefore fools.' Now St Bernard recognized four classes of scholar: those who treated learning as a source of pride; those who set little value upon it; those who used it to do good to others; and those who sought it merely to improve themselves.   In the last two categories he saw nothing of which to complain; but that was not the point.   'What,' he asked, 'does philosophy matter to me?   The Apostles are my masters; they have not taught me to read Plato or to unravel the subtleties of Aristotle, but they have shown me how to live.   And believe me, that is no mean science.'   To know God is one thing, to live in Him is something quite different and far more important.   By his constant emphasis on this truth St Bernard exercised a considerable influence upon catholic doctrine.   His theology may have suffered eclipse, but his attitude carried a great deal of weight, even in the development of thought.   His mysticism permeated rather than opposed the scholastic outlook.   It was a useful counterpoise to the forces of dialectic, acting as guardian of traditional truths, without which theology would have soon become a purely human science, and correcting by its sweetness those elements of the scholastic method which were not seldom dry as dust.   While defending a position that seemed altogether out of date, St Bernard was in fact helping to prepare the future.

On the eve of the thirteenth century the long labour of a hundred years bore fruit.   Religious thought was now more certain of its method as well as of its goal, and a number of great epitomists had already tried to set forth the whole science of God in one *summa*. Among these was Peter Lombard, the 'Master of the Sentences,' whose work was a recognized text-book in his own day.   There were also Gandulf of Bologna, Peter of Poitiers, Robert of Melun, and several

[1] See Chapter III, section 4.
[2] Ibid.   I shall not repeat my observations on St Bernard's work; it is dealt with sufficiently in that place.

others whose names we do not know. It was not long before Vincent of Beauvais gave new form to this dream of universal synthesis in his *Speculum Majus* (a fourfold work covering nature, science, morality, and history), in which he proposed to lead knowledge step by step from terrestrial life right up to the Last Judgment. Controversialists included John of Salisbury, Alan of Lille, that arch-enemy of heretics, and Peter of Blois, who was looked upon by some, even during his lifetime, as another Father of the Church. The time was ripe for the last step toward the peak, where men of genius would find an auspicious climate in which to spread their wings.

7. THE ZENITH OF SCHOLASTICISM: ST BONAVENTURE

A new age was beginning, in which the highest hopes would be realized: the age of Albert the Great, St Bonaventure, St Thomas Aquinas, Duns Scotus, and Roger Bacon. With the appearance of these giants, intellectual life was completely transfigured. Within the period covered by their lives the universities were born. Within that period also the Franciscans and Dominicans attained professorial status in those same universities, and were soon followed, though on a lesser scale, by representatives of the more ancient Orders. Rivalry between the regular and secular clergy, keen to the point of violence, was yet another important factor of progress. But it was above all in the fundamental approach that intellectual life underwent a change. The speculative method triumphed; the ground which Abélard had trod at dreadful risk was henceforth safe. Theology, the 'queen of sciences,' watched her handmaid, philosophy, grow in importance. Teachers continued to rely upon authority, and to this extent remained 'Augustinian'; all the same, they made every endeavour to scrutinize the data of revelation and appealed more often to logic. At that time most thinkers tried to *understand in order to believe*, but this did not mean to say there were no opposing tendencies. How was one to understand; by the light of reason alone or by recourse to more subtle means, intuitive and similar to mystical contemplation? Man is able to set up a strictly rational philosophy, as the ancients did, but has he the right to do so as a Christian? On this grave question St Bonaventure and St Thomas Aquinas disagreed.

The rediscovery of Aristotle was another event of capital importance, for it influenced the whole history of thought. Broadly speaking, most Christian philosophers since the Fathers had been Platonists; the majority had been affected by Plato's Ideal Theory, as well as by his views on intuition, on the spiritual life, and upon ecstasy. The realism and rationalistic methods of the Stagirite had been practically unknown. Aristotle's reappearance in the West was due mainly to the

Arabians Avicenna and Averroes, and to some Jewish scholars, of whom Maimonides is the most famous. From 1162 translations began to multiply, and Aristotle's treatises upon natural science and metaphysics were studied by all the most eminent philosophers. The movement began with Alexander of Hales, William of Auvergne, Vincent of Beauvais, and St Albert the Great. At first the Church was alarmed at this influx of strange views, and at the still worse fact that these views arrived under an escort of suspect commentaries by Averroes. A council held at Paris in 1210 excommunicated the Aristotelians, who were again censured six or seven times without effect. Led by Gregory IX, the Church then altered her mind. She decided to adopt the more useful elements of the Stagirite's philosophy; and this inspired undertaking reached its logical conclusion in the *Summa Theologica* of St Thomas Aquinas.

Three generations succeeded one another in the intellectual life of the thirteenth century. First, the precursors who, while looking back to an older tradition, did not close their eyes to the new tendencies and the results of more recent study. William of Auvergne (1190–1245), the learned Bishop of Paris, remained an Augustinian in his theory of intellectual knowledge, but championed everything that might enlarge the mind. Alexander of Hales (1175–1245), an English professor known to his students at Paris as *Doctor irrefragabilis*, compiled a *summa* which was greatly esteemed in his own day. He was one of the first of many scholars whose humility led them to join the Franciscans. Though an heir of St Augustine, St Anselm, and Hugh of St Victor, inasmuch as he attached great importance to inspiration, Alexander upheld the right of philosophy to explain the nature and attributes of God, and he thus prepared the way for St Bonaventure.

St Albert the Great, a prodigy of learning, belonged to an aristocratic German family. While a student at Padua, he had joined the Friars Preachers, and after teaching for some while at Paris, he was appointed head of the Dominican 'Studium' at Cologne. There his authority was such that one short sentence could terminate any discussion: 'Magister Albertus dixit.' The 'Universal Doctor' had spoken, and all would hold their peace. Natural science, physics, morals, philosophy, theology—nothing escaped his inquiring mind. Though faithful in many respects to Augustinianism, he nevertheless grappled fearlessly with the delicate subject of relations between faith and reason, showing that while reason cannot explain mystery, it does help to make straight the way of the Lord. A whole-hearted admirer of Aristotle, he maintained that the Stagirite could be used just as St Augustine had used Plato; but at the same time he was quick to discover and to reject anything in Aristotle's teaching that was contrary to Christian doctrine.

St Albert's immense achievement [1] bore fruit in the person of his lineal successor, St Thomas Aquinas, who, with St Bonaventure, dominated the intellectual climate of the thirteenth century.   These two men were the principal representatives of the second generation, and even to-day their joint reputation is enormous.   We must not, however, treat them as mutually hostile.   To begin with, they were both saints and united in the bonds of deep affection.   Each of them, moreover, was an infinitely complex unit; so that we shall be hopelessly in error if we see the one merely as holding a mystical, intuitional, anti-intellectual philosophy, and the other simply as a strict rationalist. The truth is that they are inseparable and complementary.   Each embodies one of the two currents of Christian thought, which can be fully understood only by considering them together.

John of Fidenza was born in 1221 near Viterbo of a noble Tuscan family.   According to tradition, the Poverello himself worked a miracle on his behalf, and, foreseeing the child's glorious destiny, gave him the surname 'Buona ventura.'   Few lives have been so harmonious; seldom have such brilliant intellectual gifts accorded so well with the leaning of their owner's heart.   Having joined the Friars Minor at the age of seventeen, he studied at Paris under Alexander of Hales; but his youthful genius was so quick to appear that, as soon as the quarrel between regulars and seculars was ended, the University opened its doors to him.   He was then aged thirty-six.   His outstanding reputation caused him to be elected master-general of his Order, and he had to abandon teaching so as to devote himself, in the most awkward circumstances, to problems of administration, arbitration, and appeasement.   Though constantly preaching or presiding over assemblies, this friend of popes and adviser to many a great personage continued to labour at the task he had begun in the University.   It may well be that external affairs weighed heavy on a soul thirsting for knowledge; but he was too submissive to God's will to refuse whatever Providence required, even the many honours that were conferred upon him.   He accepted the Red Hat from Gregory X in 1274, because the Pope insisted; then he set out for the Council of Lyons, but died on his way back (14th July) at the age of fifty-three.

All those who were acquainted with St Bonaventure give the same picture of refinement, of exquisite and unequalled sensibility, together with a kind of supernatural radiance.   'It seems that Adam has not sinned in him,' said his master, Alexander of Hales.   He was, indeed, a true son of that saint whose habit he wore and whose life he wrote in terms of fervent admiration.   Meanwhile the sweet fire of God's imperious love flamed from his mystic soul, the root and crown of all his thought.

[1] Recognized in 1931 when he was proclaimed 'Doctor of the Church.'

Étienne Gilson has described St Bonaventure's work as 'powerful and complex,'[1] and it is indeed surprising that it flowered in so few years amid the thorny hedges of administration. His exegetical writings include commentaries on Ecclesiastes, Wisdom, St Luke, and St John; we also possess more than one hundred lectures and nearly five hundred sermons. His *Threefold Way, Soliloquy, Five Feasts of Jesus, The Mystic Vine*, and ten other treatises deal with the spiritual life; while his theological *Commentaries on the Sentences of Peter Lombard, Disputed Questions*, and *Itinerary of the Soul to God* are masterpieces of their kind. The whole of his work is inspired by the one single purpose of leading souls to God. For him, intellectual pursuits had no sense or value except in so far as they were directed to faith and love; and herein lies the difference between St Bonaventure and St Thomas, who was convinced that demonstration of the truths of faith sufficed. St Bonaventure has more recourse to the ways of the Holy Spirit and of grace. He does not admit that unaided reason can be a road to God; philosophy must be subordinate to those supernatural ideas which illuminate the mind of man and which are nothing else than faith and wisdom in God. Thus, his philosophy and theology are closely linked in a mysticism exalted by supernatural craving for God. Herein he is the heir of his favourite teacher St Augustine, of St Anselm, and of St Bernard. But this fact certainly did not prevent him proving his point by every useful means. He borrowed arguments from Aristotle, and, though he would not allow the pre-eminence of reason, he understood clearly that when enlightened by grace it could help man to his final end. Just because created things are signs of God, it is important to know them well. And so this coherent and subtle combination produced a theory of knowledge, a metaphysical doctrine, and a rule of life united together in a single impulse, an impulse that snatches man from the earthly level and bears him away to the empyrean of grace. Speculative mysticism found its fulfilment in St Bonaventure, and he has never been surpassed.

Although he has been recognized as a Doctor of the Church since 1587, his work has not enjoyed an equal reputation with that of his Dominican rival. But St Bonaventure is an important milestone on that road along which so many minds, from St Paul and St Augustine to Bergson, have tried to discover a certain something which is more than reason, more even than intelligence, and which enables man to lay hold upon the mysteries of God and of the world; that certain something which Christians receive through the grace of Jesus Christ.

[1] *L'Esprit de la philosophie médiévale*, 1932.

8. The Zenith of Scholasticism: St Thomas Aquinas

Among the students attending St Albert's lectures at Cologne in 1248, one was remarkable if only for his physical dimensions. A great massive fellow with a placid face, he seemed somehow to be always absent-mindedly chewing the cud. With his incredible tranquillity and his astonishing gift of remaining silent, he appeared to his fellow students so dull-witted that they nicknamed him 'the dumb ox.' But on one occasion, during a debate, the ox broke loose, and with ten words silenced all his adversaries. St Albert, however, knew him well and, it was even whispered, had invited him to share his own prodigious labours. At all events, a day came when the Master, echoing their sarcasm, cried out: 'Dumb ox if you like, but I tell you that he will bellow so loudly that the whole universe will be amazed!'

St Thomas was then twenty-four. The Campanian family of Aquinas, into which he had been born in 1224, was one of the noblest in Italy. The Emperor Barbarossa was his uncle, Frederick II his cousin. As a layman he would have been entitled to bear four or five royal quarterings on his shield. While still an oblate at Monte Cassino, and no more than six years old, he had astounded his masters with an unexpected question: 'What is God?' At the age of fifteen, when a schoolboy at Naples, he had discovered the new stripling stream of Dominican enthusiasm, and it had captivated his imagination. Nothing had been able to deter him from a vocation which he knew to have been sent by God, neither the indignation of his father, nor the cajolery of his sisters, nor the violent means adopted by his brothers, none of whom were pleased at the idea of a mendicant Aquinas. His family confined him in one of their castles, where he was visited, on their instructions, by a damsel of supposedly irresistible charm. But Satan's envoy came out with a flea in her ear, having narrowly escaped the burning log with which Thomas had threatened her. He wished to be a Dominican, and a Dominican he would be; not Abbot of Monte Cassino or Archbishop of Naples. Nothing could break his saintly determination.

Thus it came about that he spent six years at Paris, and just over two years at Cologne. By 1251 his education was complete; his scholarship was immense and his judgment extraordinarily mature. No sooner was he appointed to teach than crowds flocked to hear him. Peter Lombard's famous *Book of Sentences* had never been the object of such original commentary or fruitful development, a fact far from welcome to those who, with increasing displeasure, observed the mendicants assault the bastions of learning. In 1256, by express command of Alexander IV, St Thomas entered the professorial ranks of

the University at Paris, together with his Franciscan friend St Bonaventure.

Recognized by many of his contemporaries as a shining light, he
would henceforward, and with the same tremendous urge that was
characteristic of his manner, carry on a threefold task as teacher, writer,
and adviser to three popes.   After three years at Paris he was summoned to the papal court, where he assisted Alexander IV, Urban IV,
and Clement IV as a kind of official theologian to the Curia.   He then
spent another three years in Paris before going to found the University
at Naples, continuing meanwhile to lecture before excited audiences.
Yet, by some miraculous means, he found time to write; his commentaries and expositions fill thousands of pages which bear the mark
of originality and genius.

His destiny seemed assured when, in 1274, Gregory X, whose
purpose could not be mistaken, ordered him to attend the Council of
Lyons along with St Bonaventure.   The Franciscan was able to
be present in that assembly before rendering his holy soul to God.
Thomas was less fortunate; his gigantic frame could not resist disease.
He was obliged to halt at the Cistercian abbey of Fossanuova, and
there he died on 7th March at the age of less than fifty years.

Any attempt to portray the psychology of such a man is doomed to
failure, for the conflicting aspects of his character are so cunningly
blended as to defy analysis.   This placid giant, with his large, calm
countenance and candid look, would speak his mind in no uncertain
terms whenever some favourite issue was at stake; and on days when
thought stirred keen within him, he would pace hurriedly up and down
the cloister.   This intellectual juggler, whom we may sometimes
imagine busied solely with the paragraphs of his *Summa*, was the same
man who, having a difficult problem to resolve, would lean his brow
against the door of the tabernacle; the same man whom the mystery of
Christ's Passion drove to tears; the same who, with schoolboy
simplicity, placed his work under our Lady's protection; the same who
confessed that in mystical contemplation he had 'learned things compared with which all writings are mere straw'; the same, lastly, who
when on the point of death had read to him the most tenderly spiritual
of all scriptural books, the Canticle of Canticles.   It is hard to know
what most to admire in this tremendous genius: the extent of his
learning, his powers of organization and exposition, or his wellnigh
unbelievable output together with an almost Napoleonic capacity for
grappling with four or five problems at once, of dictating the most
pertinent answers to four or five abstruse questions to four or five
secretaries.   Nor must we forget his wonderful insight, which
enabled him to go straight to the point, to recognize what was transcendent in the evidence of sense, and the absolute simplicity with

which he accepted the real and learned its lesson.   Yet all that constitutes his greatness in the eyes of men is nothing beside that which
ennobled him before the face of God: his modesty, his faith, his angelic
purity, his supernatural charity, the visible light of a true Christian
which shone in his every word and deed.

It is nearly as difficult to grasp St Thomas's literary achievement.
The clarity of his style, the sharpness of his mind, his remarkable gifts
of expression and lucid exposition, are too well known to need further
comment.   But consider the amount of study his writings must have
involved.   His works contain 48,000 references or allusions; only the
most brilliant intellect could have formed from this huge mass of
erudition not a mere hotch-potch, but an organic whole.   If we are
inclined to think of him as a dusty professor or an outsize bookworm
eating up dry parchment chapter after chapter with his arguments, we
shall do well to remember him also as the poet (for such he was) who
wrote the *Pange Lingua* and the *Lauda Sion*.

The mere catalogue of his writings would fill several pages.   There
is practically no subject which he did not handle in his own splendid
fashion.   The dream of transcending particular sciences in order to
attain a universal science in which all that is of interest to man should
be arranged in order of importance was not new; but no one had
conceived it on so large and brilliant a scale as did St Thomas Aquinas.

His exegetical works are devoted to Isaiah, Job, and the Canticle of
Canticles, as well as to the Gospels and St Paul.   Of his innumerable
sermons we know little, except that they sometimes reduced those who
heard them to tears.   His ascetical and mystical treatises include the
Two Precepts of Charity and the *Angelic Salutation*, both of which are
gems.   Then there are the *Summa contra Gentiles*, a great apologetic
work refuting heretics and pagans; philosophical books dealing with
logic, physics, the natural sciences, morals, and metaphysics; and those
unfinished *Commentaries on the Works of Aristotle* which are the
foundation of all the rest.   Most of his theological works grew from
the *Quaestiones Disputatae* which he had discussed with his pupils.
This list alone shows that the *Summa Theologica* is only a part of St
Thomas's work, though it is certainly the most important; it is the
nave and choir of the whole edifice, but the side chapels and precincts
are not to be neglected.

It was at Rome, in 1265–7, that St Thomas, feeling himself no longer
at home within the official limits of commentary on Peter Lombard,
determined to write a *summa* along the lines customary at that date.
He spent nine years at the task, which was interrupted only by his
death.   The *Summa Theologica*, whose extent is no less remarkable
than its profundity, was intended by the author himself as a concise
introduction to theology, which he would no doubt have expounded at

much greater length had he lived.   His purpose, then, was to provide
students with a precise and systematic body of teaching, unlike
previous works of this kind, which had been disorderly and incomplete.
With this modest end in view, however, he produced a work of
unequalled stature.

The *Summa Theologica* takes the usual scholastic form of question
and answer; it is a work both of analysis and of synthesis.   Of
analysis, because the relevant questions, following one upon another
in regular succession, are dissected with astonishing insight.   Of
synthesis, because the elements thus identified are in some sort re-
arranged in a new order and given perspectives hitherto unknown.
God, the object of all theology, is present throughout every chapter;
He alone is always in question, directly or indirectly.   In the First
Part He is studied as *Being*, first in Himself—the One and Triune God
—then outside Himself as principle, i.e. in so far as He can be known
in His works (God the creator and ruler of the world) and through the
behaviour of the spiritual and temporal universe, including man.   The
Second Part treats of God as the *Good*, i.e. as the end of rational
creatures; and this leads the author to examine not only human acts
and passions, but also the principles of conduct, the law by which God
teaches us, and grace by which He assists us.   Then, viewing together
those moral obligations to which man must submit if he is to attain
God, St Thomas analyses the virtues (theological, cardinal, and human)
together with the vices opposed to them.   This leads him to conclude
by analysing various ways of life and those gifts which enable us to
practise virtue and avoid vice.   Finally, in the Third Part, he meant
to show God as the *way*, not only for man as such, abstract and
theoretical, but for *fallen* man, a creature of sinful flesh, but redeemed
by Christ's Incarnation and Sacrifice.   This is the shortest part of the
Summa, for St Thomas left it unfinished.   It was supplemented from
his notes and other writings by his friend and disciple Reginald of
Piperno.   Judging by the completed questions on Christ and the
sacraments, it would have surpassed the earlier sections in emotional
intensity.

The enormous scope of the *Summa Theologica* omits none of the
great problems which bewilder men.   St Thomas's motive in undertaking it seems akin to what the Holy See itself had in mind at that
period: to unify the whole Church in a single, living body with the
Pope as its head.   Just so, the *Summa* aimed at unifying the mind of
Christendom.

On one point at least St Thomas was in full accord with the wishes
of the sovereign pontiffs.   After 1231, instead of rejecting Aristotle,
they proposed, as we have seen, to use what was most valuable in his
writings for the benefit of the Church.   St Thomas went even farther,

much farther than his master Albert the Great. Having studied the entire Aristotelian *corpus*, which had been faithfully translated for him by his fellow Dominican, William of Moerbeke, he conceived a profound admiration for the Stagirite, whose dialectic and experimental method seemed to render him the most powerful and most useful among ancient philosophers; and one of St Thomas's main ambitions was to place Aristotle's teaching at the service of Christ. Far from endangering the truths of faith, Aristotelianism could support them by furnishing arguments in their favour. Conversely, the school of Aristotle could arrive at a perfect understanding of the world only by steeping itself in the Gospel and in the light of Revelation. Thomism is not merely a Christianized Aristotelianism, for the great Dominican contributes much that is his own; but St Thomas rendered incalculable service to the Church by fusing Aristotle with the stream of Christian doctrine and thereby affording her new means of knowledge and of demonstration.[1]

He was indebted to Aristotle chiefly for the idea of man as a rational being. The Augustinians, like the neo-Platonists, viewed reason as a stage in religious life, a foreshadowing of supernatural illumination. Aristotelianism treats it as valid in its own right: man's vocation here below is not to comprehend things supernatural and divine, but to proceed by abstraction from results acquired by the senses. Hence, *reason and faith have each their respective sphere of activity*, so that the old problem of their relations is solved once and for all. 'The philosopher considers in creatures that which characterizes them according to their proper nature; the believer considers in them only what characterizes them in relation to God.'[2] But, since God is absolute truth, there can be no opposition between reason and faith, because truth is *one*. Truth as known by reason and truth as known by faith must therefore coincide and assist one another. Just as the astronomer and the physicist conclude by different means that the world is round, so the undivided truth is attained both by natural reason and by supernatural revelation.[3]

Hence Thomism is at once a philosophy and a theology, which, though they have each a different subject matter, strive towards a

---

[1] St Thomas made himself the champion of Aristotelianism, which he defended on numerous occasions against two kinds of adversary. The traditionalists looked upon it as a dangerous novelty, more or less heretical; and this 'old guard' of Augustinians and neo-Platonists had friends in high places, e.g. Stephen Tempier, Bishop of Paris. Others, more dangerous in many ways, were extreme Aristotelians, fanatics who endeavoured not so much to subject Aristotle to the Gospel as subordinate Christ to the Stagirite. Powerfully influenced by the Moslem Averroes, they were heading for rationalism pure and simple, and, by the confusion which they created, compromised all the saint's teaching. He had some hard battles with the most notorious of them, Sigier of Brabant.

[2] *Contra Gentiles*, II. 4.

[3] *Summa Theologica*, Pars I[a], q. I, art. 1.

common good. Like an intellectual pyramid, it rests firmly on concrete and sensible reality, while the summit pierces into the infinite invisible. It takes man as he is with his mortal life, his faults, and limitations. Since he is both body and soul—ontologically associated —there is no reason to despise his carnal rags, as the disciples of Plato tended to do. On the contrary, since God has endowed man with sense, sensible experience must be the starting-point whence he comes to understand the world and discover God in creation. Whereas St Bonaventure thought that to bother with things of experience was to 'taste the forbidden tree of good and evil,' St Thomas advocated respect for the created, the carnal, the human. This new attitude was to reanimate Christian morality; Christian sociology and economics would follow much later.

Reason works upon sense-data by a process of abstraction, distinction, and conclusion. It helps the advance of knowledge *in its own particular sphere*, taking no account of faith and revelation. Its whole purpose is to establish truth upon so solid a basis that nothing will be able to overthrow it; and St Thomas thought that since God is Truth, a lucid exposition of the truth in all its aspects would render it unchallengeable. Without denying the part played by supernatural revelation, he attached less importance thereto than did St Anselm or St Bonaventure. He knew well that God *can* be attained by flight of the soul and spiritual self-surrender; but these ways are often subjective, on which account they appeared, in his eyes, to have a more limited value than has clear reason. Everything is not explicable by reason, and there may seem to be discrepancies between it and faith; that is because the human mind belongs to a finite being, and cannot penetrate the infinite invisible which is properly the domain of revelation. Faith, towards which the whole intellectual effort is directed, is thus its crowning glory.

Within this gigantic system all the major problems are discussed and answered: the existence of God, knowledge, freedom, the relation between natural and supernatural. Questions of conscience, be they moral, sociological, or political, are solved by the application of principles; for there is nothing that Thomism is not ready to explain. The incomparable strength of the system lies in the firmness wherewith everything, from the lowest to the highest, is arranged, set out, and balanced by the hand of genius. It is no laborious tracing of ancient philosophy on to Christianity, nor a mere mosaic of ideas and references. Thomism was actually a new synthesis meeting the urgent needs of Christian thought; it did not create dogmas, but enabled men to grasp them more firmly.

So magnificent an edifice calls forth unbounded admiration. We may hesitate to allow reason so important a place as does St Thomas, and we must agree that some of his scientific references are out of date; but we cannot refuse to recognize his work as one of the high-water marks of Western genius.   Even during his lifetime many considered it as such, as is clear from a letter addressed by the masters of Paris University to the Dominican General Chapter immediately after the saint's death.   He was, it says, 'the star which guided the world, the *luminare majus* spoken of by Genesis, the sun which presides over the day.'   He was canonized in 1323, fifty years after he died; in life he had been known as the 'Angelic Doctor,' and in 1567 he was officially ranked among the Doctors of the Church.   Since the encyclical *Aeterni Patris* of Leo XIII, he has been, in fact, the official guide of philosophical and theological studies, and every succeeding Pope has exalted his wisdom, his charity, and his genius.[1]

In the inmost courts of heaven where three Divine Persons are enthroned, St Thomas stands between Aristotle and Plato with Averroes prostrate beneath his feet, while an assembled council does honour to his greatness; his steady gaze seems concentrated inward as he soars, contemplative, in time and space.   Thus he is shown by Benozzo Gozzoli in a celebrated painting now in the Louvre; so too may all Christian generations think of him.

9.   THE THIRD GENERATION OF SCHOLASTICISM AND DUNS SCOTUS

It could not be expected that St Thomas's work would find immediate favour or meet with no resistance.   Original thinking invariably provokes lively opposition, just as one generation usually asserts itself by opposing its predecessors.

No sooner was St Thomas laid to rest than the partisans of Augustinianism and neo-Platonism raised their heads, not only among the Franciscans and secular clergy, but even in the ranks of the Dominicans.   They found no difficulty in playing up resemblances between Thomism and Averroism so as to include propositions from the *Summa* with others that were obviously unorthodox, and their ruse succeeded on more than one occasion.   At Paris, in 1277, Bishop Tempier drew up an anti-Thomist syllabus of 219 articles, and the same was done at Oxford that year by order of the Dominican Archbishop of Canterbury, Kilwardby.   In 1278, William de la Mare, a disciple of St Bonaventure, declared war on Thomism, which he claimed to 'correct,' and all teaching members of the Order of Friars

---

[1] The Church, however, does not impose Thomism as the one and only philosophy. Following the *Motu proprio* of Pius X (29th June 1914), the Congregation of Studies replied, in answer to a question, by summarizing Thomism in twenty-four propositions and declaring that it was 'put forward as a reliable body of doctrine but not imposed.'

Minor were ordered not to use the *Summa* without this famous
'Correctory.' As condemnations increased, the Dominicans realized
how much was at stake, and prepared to defend their position. Two
general chapters rallied the Order in defence of Thomism, and a
number of 'anti-correctories' appeared in answer to the Franciscan
compilation. Their numerous allies included the Cistercian Humbert
of Brouilly and the Carmelite Gerard of Bologna, but above all Giles
of Rome, who was the first to think of showing that St Augustine and
St Thomas were not irreconcilable but complementary, that the *Summa*
could be used as a starting-point for the Bishop of Hippo's soaring
genius. The conflict was prolonged and ended in a victory for
Thomism, which does not mean to say that the Church ultimately
rejected the doctrines upheld by the Franciscan school. St Bonaventure has joined his friend and rival in the catalogue of saints; nor
did the encyclical of Leo XIII, which glorified St Thomas, withhold
from the great Minor his fair share of praise.

The problem which brought the two most able minds of the mid-
thirteenth century into conflict was not ended by their departure from
the scene. It was almost certainly in the very year of St Thomas's
death that there was born in Scotland a man whose intellect, no less
penetrating than that of the Angelic Doctor, stood in direct opposition
to Thomism. John Duns Scotus (*c.* 1265–1308), a young genius
whose short life did not enable him to prove his worth, has never been
accorded the recognition he deserves. Surnamed already by his own
contemporaries the 'Subtle Doctor,' he astounded audiences by the
rapidity of his thought, by the compact logic of his argument, and by
the marvellous dexterity with which he handled ideas. First a student
and then a professor in the University of Oxford, he afterwards taught
at Paris and Cologne. We do not know much about him; as a young
combatant in the lists of intellectual warfare he was original to the
point of paradox, but capable of discovering new fields of thought in
brilliant flashes of illumination.

The canon of his writings is still incomplete, but it falls into two
main sections, the *Opus Oxoniense* and the *Opus Parisiense*, based
respectively on his teaching in the Universities of Oxford and Paris.
The *Opus Parisiense* was handed down by one of his pupils. Though
a dialectician like St Thomas, and like him also a champion of the
critical method, he starts from different principles and reaches different
conclusions. According to Duns Scotus, man's will takes precedence
of his intellect; hence the term *voluntarism* which is often used to
describe his system. He maintains that the submission of all men to
the law of truth cannot be achieved simply by demonstrating truth.
His divergence from Thomism in this view of the part played by the
two faculties, leads him to differ likewise as to the role of free will and

grace. He insists on the active character of the soul, upon that freedom which he defends as a first principle in the spiritual domain. His general conception of the world is thus far removed from the imposing system elaborated in the *Summa Theologica*. Is St Thomas so sure that, in speaking of the real, man can truly understand and know that there are in Creation fixed laws which reason can discover and analyse? Surely the freedom of divine Omnipotence is opposed to such fixity. Granted, science has its own domain; but what is its value outside that domain? Is it not essentially useless? Thus the strain of mysticism introduced by Duns Scotus to the detriment of reason is even stronger than St Bonaventure's contribution.

In this sense, Scotism is a useful corrective to a certain intellectualism of which St Thomas himself was not guilty, but to which many of his disciples undoubtedly yielded. This, however, is not to say that everything in the doctrine of Scotus is acceptable. As Émile Bréhier remarks, his principles 'tend, willy-nilly, to dissolve the organic union of reason and faith, of dogma and philosophy.' Worse still, his youthful audacity often sails too close into the wind. He deserves credit as almost the only thinker of his age to contemplate a theology of the Blessed Virgin (including her Immaculate Conception) and to foreshadow the doctrine of her part in the scheme of redemption; but his theories on the motives of the Incarnation, on the necessity of man's redemption, and on what he considers the purely moral function of rites and sacraments are, to say the least, peculiar. His disciple, William of Occam, by pushing some of his ideas to their extreme, reached a kind of anarchical empiricism;[1] and there are elements of Scotist doctrine among the roots of Protestantism.

For two centuries the Church was the protectress of thought. She took human reason by the hand and guided its footsteps within those boundaries beyond which faith forbade it to venture. But as soon as children grow up they escape from the influence of those who have formed them. Reason, becoming self-conscious, yielded to the temptation of pride, and knowledge acquired in the lap of Mother Church ended by turning men against her. Then indeed the Christian Middle Ages were in mortal agony and a new page was turned in the history of mankind.[2]

10. FROM CANON LAW TO ROMAN LAW

While theology, accompanied by and afterwards allied with, her handmaiden philosophy, held first place in the esteem of medieval thinkers, her growth gave rise to many other branches of learning.

---

[1] See Chapter XIV, section 3.
[2] See Chapter XIV for a discussion of this dramatic turning-point

These branches were studied with keen interest precisely because they were more or less identified with the sovereign science until the day when they were recognized as autonomous and could strike out on their own.

Such was the case with jurisprudence, or, as it was then described, the 'science of decrees.' During the barbarian age jurisprudence existed only as a slender offshoot of rhetoric or of moral theology. It was afterwards given new impulse by the theology of the sacraments, and especially (at a still later date) by that of the Church which received a good deal of attention during the contest between the Priesthood and the Empire. Theology and law were indissolubly mixed in the writings of Burchard of Worms (*d.* 1025), and even in those of Yves of Chartres (*d.* 1116). It was Irnerius (*d. circa* 1139) who first understood that law is a separate discipline, to be cultivated for its own sake.

Moreover, at the beginning of the twelfth century, lawyers were in great demand. The Church needed a body of competent men for her chancelleries and tribunals, and papal legates were required who could hold their own with the representatives of hostile powers. We have already commented [1] on the birth and development of Canon Law during the twelfth century, when Gratian employed the scholastic method of question and answer in the compilation of his authoritative *Concordia discordantium canonum.* Roland Bandinelli (afterwards Pope Alexander III), Raymond of Pennaforte, and many others helped to enrich and complete Gratian's work until the establishment, at the beginning of the thirteenth century, of a *Corpus Juris Canonici* which the Church was to retain unaltered for a period of five hundred years.

The chief centre of legal studies was Bologna; its University had no rival in Christendom, eclipsing the old schools of law at Rome, Pavia, and Ravenna.[2] The University of Bologna was of a somewhat unusual type. Though controlled by the Church, it was subject also to the hostile influence of a wealthy commercial group who considered the study of law as a purely secular means to good business; and the history of legal education is fraught with picturesque or violent incidents due to antagonism between the two elements.

At Bologna also a new factor came upon the scene, or rather, a forgotten science reappeared in the shape of Roman Law. In their attempt to give order to the Canon Law, jurists followed the pattern of the great Roman treatises which had been arranged, by order of Justinian in the sixth century to form the *Code*, the *Novels*, the *Digest*, and the *Institutes*. Irnerius laboured to revive the *Corpus Juris*

---

[1] Chapter VI, section 8.

[2] At Paris, where jurists had long worked in the shadow of Notre-Dame, the Faculty of law, established early in the thirteenth century, was far less important than that of theology.

Civilis early in the twelfth century; but the principal agent in restoring the prestige of Roman Law was Accursus, author of the *Great Gloss.* From Bologna the science, thus revived, spread rapidly. Vacario taught at Canterbury, Placentin at Montpellier, James of Revigny, Peter of Belleperche, and others in the recently erected Faculties of Law at Toulouse and Orléans.

This revival met with vigorous opposition. Roman Law was essentially imperial law, and provided the emperors with arguments in favour of their claim to universal dominion. Kings were alarmed, and even forbade the teaching of Roman Law, as did Philip Augustus at Paris. They recommended instead customary law, which was closer to national traditions and had been carefully evolved and solidly established in France and England during the twelfth century. Not until later did they decide that by a simple substitution of the word 'king' for 'emperor' Roman Law could be made a powerful instrument of despotism. Thus it is that legal history under Philip the Fair, Louis XI, Richelieu, and Louis XIV, right down to the French Revolution, is marked by the continuous ascendancy of Roman Law. As for the Church, she too watched with serious misgivings the growth of a jurisprudence not one of whose principles were founded on the Gospel, and in which the papal authority had no chance to intervene. Besides, the Germanic emperors had no better allies than the Roman lawyers of Bologna; and the struggle of the papacy against the Empire was to some extent a struggle between Canon and Roman Law. In 1219 Honorius III forbade priests to study Roman Law; [1] but resistance proved futile. Here again, by encouraging the human intellect to perfect its methods the Church had done much to undermine her own strength. It was the jurists who were destined to organize the secular power against the Pope in the unhappy days of Philip the Fair.

11. Was there a Medieval Science?

Did the schools and universities represent a scientific movement in our sense of that phrase? Strictly speaking, they did not. Mathematical, physical, and natural sciences were associated, and sometimes practically confused, with branches of study far removed from them. When Hugh of St Victor, who considered theology as an art, tells us that the seven basic sciences are weaving, arms-production, navigation, agriculture, hunting, medicine, and the theatre, we get some idea of this

[1] This step, however, was only an extension of measures taken by the Council of Tours in 1163 against religious who had left their cloisters to study law and physics. Further, this prohibition was capable of dispensation. In 1235 Gregory IX authorized laymen to study Roman Law at Orléans. *See* G. Digard: *La Papauté et l'étude du droit romain au XIII* siecle*, Bibliothèque de l'École des Chartes, 1890, p. 381.

inability to distinguish the sciences. It is characteristic that the universities included no scientific Faculty, except that of medicine, which became the glory of Montpellier after the school of Salerno had been ruined by internal troubles and by war. Yet in this case, as in that of law, the confusion was not altogether unserviceable to the cause of science. How could a Thomist theologian, anxious to explain the system of the world created by God, disregard the sensible aspects of creation? Whether he were Peter Lombard, Albert the Great, or St Thomas Aquinas, all of whom varied in the extent of their knowledge, he was obliged to have some scientific bases.

What were these bases? Medieval science appears to us so grotesque that we generally confer upon it no more than an indulgent smile. In order to understand it, we should perhaps try to place ourselves against the psychological background of the Middle Ages, so different from our own, where the supernatural flowed in from every side, where reason and logic had not yet invaded the whole field of consciousness, and where faith caused man to live, as the poet says, in a 'forest of symbols.' [1] In one medieval Bestiary we find an elephant, quite correctly drawn, side by side with a dragon in full flight. Here is a striking image of medieval science, in which the imaginary rubbed shoulders with the real.

This, however, is not meant to suggest that there were no minds able to grasp the nature of true scientific research. Even some churchmen, pondering on questions raised by faith, were led to foreshadow later methods. St Anselm, Yves of Chartres, and Abélard, for example, were in this sense precursors. The rediscovery of Aristotle caused an increase of scientific curiosity; the leading translator of his works in fact was none other than Leonardo da Pisa, the founder of mathematics.

The use of Aristotle's dialectical and realistic method altered the whole spirit of inquiry. Hitherto, argument had rested mainly upon authority, as it had done among the old school of theologians. 'I tell my pupils,' said a medieval professor, 'here is what Aristotle teaches, here is what Plato says, this is how Galen expresses it, thus says Hippocrates. In this way they have confidence in my words which represent the opinion of so many famous men.' The introduction of Greek and Arab treatises on astronomy, geography, physics, alchemy, and medicine began by hindering sound research; for textual commentary took the place of observation and reasoning. But as men's minds became steeped in Aristotelianism, they were obliged to adopt a fresh attitude.

The first scholar to do so was a saint, Albert the Great, whose influence upon the development of philosophy we have already noticed. His encyclopaedic intelligence, which drove him to experiment on

[1] See Chapter II, section 2.

plants as well as meditate upon the most abstruse problems of metaphysics, renounced ancient errors once for all. 'Natural science,' he
used to say, 'does not consist in ratifying what others have said, but in
seeking the causes of phenomena.' A logical conclusion which is
proved contrary by observation must be rejected; a principle denied by
facts is a false principle. And the whole future orientation of scientific
thought, distinct from theology, is summed up in these words: 'It is
not our business to search nature for the means whereby the Divine
Creator, through the immediate intervention of His free will, uses the
works of creation to work miracles which reveal His omnipotence; we
should rather try to understand what happens in the realm of nature by
reason of inherent causes.' When we speak of medieval science, we
are too prone to cite in evidence a crowd of racy anecdotes from
Vincent de Beauvais's *Speculum*, forgetting men like Albert the Great.

It would be outside our scope to enumerate facts which prove that
the Middle Ages possessed at least the elements of science; to recall
such discoveries as the so-called Arabic numerals, the magnetic needle,
the convex magnifying-glass, the mathematical principles of acoustics,
the function of mineral salts in living organisms, of alcohol, of sul-
phuric and hydrochloric and nitric acid, etc.[1] We shall be content to
suggest that apparently futile researches, e.g. for the 'philosopher's
stone,' may have had a purpose not so very different from those of
modern science; as Paul Tannery so justly says, 'false science saved
the true.' Urged by the Christian craving to win souls for Christ as
well as by scientific curiosity, the Middle Ages made an invaluable
contribution to the discovery of the world. What matters from the
Christian point of view is the evolution of new methods, and the
appearance deep within religious thought of an attitude which was to
be that of modern times. St Albert the Great was not the only one to
take this road; in spite of his greater caution, St Thomas Aquinas had a
similar outlook, and that strange person Raymond Lull was of the
same lineage.

The new trend, however, found its genius in the person of Roger
Bacon, who overwhelms us with astonishment no less than with
admiration. To call him enigmatic is an understatement; he is a living
contradiction. On the one hand he represents the most backward
characteristic of the Middle Ages, what with his pharmacopoea
employing dragon's head, dung, and mirabelles; what with his naïve
belief in the influence of stars and elementals. On the other hand,
certain lightning-flashes of inspiration make him in many ways the
forerunner of modern science. Obviously, one does not agree with

---

[1] Incidentally, we need only think of a cathedral to realize that men who were able to
calculate the curve of an arch, the resistance of materials, and the size of stones could not
have been ignorant of mathematics or of physics.

M

him when he asserts that mathematics may be applied in the domain o
metaphysics; but it cannot be denied that his method is at the roo
both of Cartesianism and of researches which have borne fruit in th
shape of present-day science.

Roger Bacon was born of a good Somerset family in 1214.   H
soon abandoned soldiering in order to study mathematics, theology
and languages, first at Oxford, then at Paris, where he worked unde
the direction of Alexander of Hales and Albert the Great.   His restles
mind craved for truth; and in 1251, at the age of thirty-seven, believin
that the only way to satisfy his intellectual hunger was to abandon th
world altogether, he took the grey habit of St Francis.   It mus
however, be admitted that the Poverello's meekness did not sink ver
deep into his heart; for Bacon hurled himself with unrestrained ferocit
upon all whom he suspected of upholding erroneous opinions.   Alex
ander and Albert both came under fire, as did St Bonaventure, th
master general of his Order.   He caused trouble everywhere, eve
among his own brethren.   Nay, he went so far as to cast the horoscop
of Christ, maintaining that God could not have saved the world excep
by virtue of certain heavenly conjunctions!   Denounced as magicia
sorcerer, and associate of the Devil, he was on the point of being dea
with as such; and it required the intervention of Popes Clement I
and Nicholas IV to save him from the consequences of his ow
audacity.   Some think he was kept in close confinement for fiftee
years; certainly a number of his propositions were condemned in 127
But all these tribulations did not prevent him continuing his gigant
task and living to the ripe old age of eighty.   He died at Oxford in 129

There is scarcely a science which Bacon left untouched: mathematic
optics, and medicine were but three of those which roused his insatiab
curiosity.   His book on *The Secrets of Art and Nature* is filled wi
visions of the future—steamboats, railways, balloons, cranes, su
marines, microscopes, telescopes, and the terrible effects of gunpowde
In optics, long before Galileo and Newton, he formulated the laws
the reflection and refraction of light.   It was he who suggested
Clement IV a reform of the Julian calendar, though this was not do
until three centuries later by Gregory XII in 1582.   He wrote a whc
book to prove the absurdity of magic.   But his most brilliant achiev
ment was the *Opus Majus*, published at the Pope's request in 1266,
which he explained the true nature of scientific method.   The ch
cause of error, he maintained, was undue reliance on the opinions
certain men; the only means of arriving at truth was precise observati
and the closest possible reasoning.

Bacon sought to apply these principles for the first time in the doma
of Holy Scripture.   In order to understand Revelation, he said, beg
with the sacred text itself.   For that purpose, study the languages

which it was written; make use of such profane sciences as chronology, geography, computation of the calendar, and astronomy. There you have the complete pattern of modern exegesis. Did he appreciate the danger in which his method would involve the faith if wrongly employed? He must have done. As a convinced Augustinian and Franciscan, he repeatedly denounced the abuse of philosophy (which he described as one of the capital sins), and proclaimed that faith comes before all research. He was an anti-Thomist and anti-Aristotelian who held that ultimate truth is not attainable by knowledge, and that scholasticism could not demonstrate the existence of God. This great scholar who helped to found the rational method, admitted that, beyond science, of which he constituted himself the zealous champion, there lies a region inhabited by mystery and the unknowable. It was the outlook of a true Christian and a mystic; but what would happen when science turned its back on dogma, when it claimed independence and would recognize no authority superior to reason? Though a Christian genius, Roger Bacon carried within himself forces that were hostile to his faith.

12. THE BIRTH OF VERNACULAR

We have observed the process whereby the Church, having stimulated thought in the realms of philosophy, law, and science, saw them kick against her; and it is natural to inquire whether the same thing happened in the sphere which we now call literature. Slowly, unobtrusively, side by side with Latin literature but tending gradually to supplant it, there grew up first in France and England, then in Spain, Germany, and Italy, a literature in the vulgar tongue. It appealed not so much to clerics, who knew Latin, as to the common people as a whole. Next, we may ask, what was the connection between this literary revival and the simultaneous intellectual movement within the Church herself? Undoubtedly, the source of inspiration was quite different. Non-Christian influences were clearly at work in the formation of these new *genres*: Germanic in the *chansons de geste*, Oriental in poems of courtly love, immemorial tradition and shreds of ancient folklore in the *fabliaux*. This process, however, seems to have taken place not wholly outside the bosom of the Church.

One fact is certain: vernacular literature arose at a time when all educated men were clerics, and we may safely assume that the first vernacular poems were also written by clerics. The excellence of this poetry, even in its earliest days, suggests it was the work of men familiar with the great models. The famous Théroulde, whose name occurs tucked away in a line of the *Chanson de Roland*, seems to have been a Norman bishop or priest of whom traces survive in the chronicles. Clerics were no doubt interested in popular language just as specialists in semantics nowadays study dialect. One English bishop, for example, is said to have been so fascinated by Anglo-Saxon poetry that he stood disguised on a bridge and sang the adventures of a sea-king; while at the school of Fécamp clerics and minstrels formed a single 'brotherhood.'

Besides, the background of medieval society was completely Christian and influenced every form of thought. Joseph Bédlier has proved that many elements in the *chansons de geste* are derived from pilgrimages or from the moral atmosphere of the crusades. The places said to have been visited by the heroes of the *Guillaume d'Orange* cycle lie along the roads leading to Compostella; and scholars have been able to identify more than fifty churches mentioned in the *chansons de geste*.

Much, indeed, of this vernacular literature is itself religious. The earliest French poems, e.g. the *Cantilène de Sainte-Eulalie*, written in Picard dialect shortly before 900, and the tenth-century *Poème de la Passion*, are Christian. Verse-lives of the saints were fashionable throughout the Middle Ages; so were the *Miracles de la Vierge*, edited by Walter of Coincy about 1210 and including the well-known story of the Juggler of Notre-Dame. The *chanson de geste*, begun soon after 1050, was gradually enlarged over a period of more than two hundred years; it is alternately tragic and powerful in *Roland* and *Guillaume d'Orange*, harsh and brutal in the Lorraine cycle and *Germont et Isembart*, realistic and even trivial in the *Pèlerinage de Charles* and the *Couronnement de Louis*. But the Christian faith is present throughout; it puts sublime words into the mouth of dying Roland, it inspires William with the ideal of self-sacrifice, it breathes the crusading spirit into the actions of the king and of Garin de Monglane; and even in the *Geste de Dovom* or the *Geste de Lorraine*, where the villain is prey to the most violent and shameful passions, the end of the tale shows him punished for his crimes, and is therefore in accord with Christian teaching. In early specimens of courtly romance, telling of adventures inspired by love, the Christian spirit is by no means prominent; but it occupies a large place in the *Round Table* cycle, where the Grail theme is outstanding among a host of Gallic symbols. Gustave Cohen has proved beyond all doubt that drama originated in the Church. It was an offshoot of liturgical plays on such themes as the Christmas story, the lives of the saints, or biblical episodes. Performances, which first took place in the sacred edifice, were afterwards held outside the west door. Drama became semi-liturgical with the twelfth-century *Walloon Nativities* and the play of *Adam and Eve*. Later it expanded to take in the *Miracle à Personnages*, which, in the thirteenth century, included such masterpieces as the *Jeu de saint Nicolas* by Jean Bodel

nd Rutebœuf's *Miracle de Théophile*. Even some elements of
omedy, as Cohen shows, are in direct descent from liturgical or
paraliturgical representations.[1]

It is therefore no exaggeration to say that vernacular literature was
to a large extent born in the lap of Mother Church, though it tended
to break loose from her apron-strings. Side by side with Christian
influences, other elements crept in that were certainly not founded on
the Gospel; and even the cycle which idealizes Lancelot, Galahad, and
all *preux chevaliers*, includes 'ancient romances' that are equally
unchristian. *Tristram and Iseult*, the most beautiful of medieval
stories, which was seven times revised between 1150 and 1200, is but
the tale of a disastrous love; nor is there much Christianity in the
wonderful adventures told in *Aucassin and Nicolette* or the *Roman de la
Violette*. Much also of the *Miracle à Personnages* is secular in outlook,
e.g. the moving story of Griselda; and we have seen [2] how the poetry
of the troubadours, though not exactly heretical, lies far beyond the
Christian horizon.

The satirical fable and *fabliau* had a popular tang and represented, as
Sainte-Beuve remarks, 'the taste for gaiety and pleasure in the passing
show of life.' They too were utterly unchristian, not only because of
their derisive anti-clericalism, which delighted to present the clergy as
miserly, gluttonous, and even worse, but also because their morality
was too often completely amoral. True, there were religious *fabliaux*,
e.g. the *Chevalier du barillet* and the *Dit du vrai armeau*; but for the
most part this popular literature, in proportion as it increased and
spread among the masses, deserted its once Christian home.

Take, for example, that most successful of medieval books, the
celebrated *Roman de la Rose*. It forms a 'poetic *summa*' of 22,000
lines, and was compiled at different periods by two poets, Guillaume de
Lorris (*fl. c.* 1225–40) and Jean de Meung (*fl. c.* 1275–1300). Both of
them were clerics, and the second a doctor of theology. Is their work
Christian for all that? The authors were evidently on their guard;
for 'if there be any words of which Holy Church disapproves' the
writer was prepared to alter them. But consider the subject-matter:
it deals with the art of love, and in such a way that scholastic methods
are employed for the most unedifying purposes. In the part written
by Guillaume de Lorris there is so much complicated symbolism that
it is unsafe to represent the poem as a mystical allegory.

In Jean de Meung's contribution there can be no doubt whatever;
his courtly scholasticism advocates a code of morals which in no way
squares with the Commandments. The Rose is Joy, symbolizing the
excitement of life. Of course, the poet assures us, there is heavenly
joy as well, but the best means of attaining it is to know earthly joy.

[1] See Chapter II, section 9.   [2] Chapter VII, section 7.

Though himself a priest, Jean de Meung lampoons ecclesiastical celibacy. He also considers marriage absurd, contrary to the law of nature; a view which is nothing more or less than sexual communism All women for all men, and all men for all women; every woman for every man, and every man for every woman!' It is by perfect conformity with nature, he says, that we lay hold on Paradise: 'tant beau tant délectable d'herbes, de fleurs, tant beau fleurables, de violettes et de roses et de toutes bonnes choses!' Nothing illustrates better than does this masterpiece of Christian eroticism the extent to which, in the late thirteenth century, men were a prey to forces drawing them away from Christian tradition in every department of intellectual life.

Had the Church, then, abdicated her leadership; could Christianity no more emit the vital juice? This twofold question was to be answered on the threshold of the fourteenth century, one of the turning points of history; and that answer was to be given by a genius Dante Alighieri.[1]

[1] See Chapter XIV, section 12.

CHAPTER IX

THE CATHEDRAL

I. THE FLOWER IN WHICH THERE BLOSSOMED A WHOLE AGE

THREE or four times in the course of history—three or four times, but certainly not more—has a civilization managed to embody itself in imperishable monuments which reveal to posterity the creative strength, the profound religiousness, the technical capacity and talent of their builders. Such trees do not grow unless the sap is pure and plentiful; such flowers do not blossom unless society is fertile and in harmony with itself, unless its members possess the creative instinct and breathe that spiritual fervour which, by raising mortal man above himself, secures his immortality. Such works do not come about accidentally; they emerge in the fullness of time through secret patience and unbounded hope, marking the high tides of human history.

These monuments enable us to understand the whole civilization from which they originated. In the Parthenon of Pericles it is Athens we behold, leader of art and mistress of clear thought. Brahmin India unveiled amid the chaotic order and exuberance of Borobudur. A single glance at the Palace of Versailles tells us what France was under the Great King. The Middle Ages in western Europe likewise expressed themselves in a form that has never been surpassed. This perfect flower of medieval culture is known as the Cathedral;[1] unique and irreplaceable, it bears witness as does no other single factor to the spirit of that time.

If *nothing* of medieval Christianity had survived excepting the cathedrals, they alone would tell us all, or nearly all, that matters about the period in question: its spiritual life, its moral code, its day-to-day existence, its methods of work, its literature, and even, to some extent, its political beliefs. Suppose, however, that *everything* except the cathedrals had survived the vicissitudes of time; suppose that Rheims, Amiens, Beauvais, and Chartres had not endured; it is certain that much of our inheritance would have been lost, that we should know far less about the Middle Ages than we do.

[1] The word must be understood here in a broad sense so as to include abbey churches, which, as I shall explain, were often prototypes of cathedrals, and also simple parish churches whose naves were, so to speak, offshoots of the giant cathedral trunk.

The cathedral, then, is the embodiment of an epoch; and yet, at first glance, it looks like a boulder broken loose, crushing all that had preceded it, annihilating all that lies around.   As we gaze upon its enormous mass towering above the city, it seems for a moment to weigh too heavily upon the humble dwellings in its neighbourhood. That, however, is mere illusion.   If its appearance on the stage of history overwhelms us as an almost miraculous event, the fact remains that it was the product of a particular region, of a particular period, of one clearly defined form of the age-long human effort.   Péguy realized this when he drew near to Chartres and beheld her spires rising from the cornfields; he said they were like plants soaring from perennial roots deep down in the soil of Beauce.   Amiens seen from Moreuil, or Laon glimpsed from afar off in Champagne, give the same impression of deep-rootedness; and if we look more closely at the cathedrals of Paris, Rouen, and Bourges leaping from among the housetops, it is remarkable how their gigantic shapes form one body with those nameless dwellings which they crown and whose deepest aspirations they proclaim.

Offshoot of earth, earthy, and bound to earth by innumerable ties, the cathedral is no less a product of man's slow resolve.   Its appearance, swift as the blooming of a flower, was in fact preceded by long centuries of germination and organic thrust.   Coming into being as the result not only of technical improvements but also of the ceaseless and more powerful urge of communal inspiration, it blossomed at a time when the sap was most abundant and most fertile.   The cathedral is contemporary with the crusades, the universities, the pilgrimages, and the *summa*, all of which proceeded from the same vital source, and with which it has evident connections.   But the cathedral transcends all the rest, first by the sublime selflessness of its purpose as the very house of God, then by the imperishable and poignant quality conferred by beauty on the outpourings of man's soul.   Purer than the crusade, more moving than any written work, the cathedral stands alone as the perfect expression of a faith.

2.   THE REVIVAL OF CHRISTIAN ART

The men who built the cathedrals did not start from scratch; behind them lay the tradition of a long past.   When the ancient world collapsed, most of what constitutes civilization, including the majority of art-forms, was swept away.   But enough seeds remained to regenerate life once the deluge had passed.   Christianity saved art, and much else besides, by her determination to provide buildings for public worship.   Her basilicas were founded upon Roman models, of which many fine examples had survived. These were imitated by the barbarian settlers, and their plan may still be seen. Fruitful influences came also from Byzantium. Quite soon, therefore, Christian art reappeared in the West, though hesitant at first, and inevitably clumsy. Merovingian churches were poor in structure, but richly decorated; e.g. the Ostrogothic basilicas at Ravenna with their brilliant mosaics. The Carolingian 'renaissance' tried to harness this endeavour, thus foreshadowing, for a while, the great achievements of the future, as well as giving art its pride of place in human activity.

By the year 1000 this patient and gradual awakening, which had been going on throughout the West, though with varying success in different lands, had effected an amazing revolution. It was at this date that the Burgundian chronicler Raoul Glaber referred to a 'white mantle of churches' covering the world. Churches had sprung up everywhere; they were still small, but their outlines heralded the main features of our great cathedrals. A number of technical inventions went hand in hand with artistic inspiration. The art of stone-dressing had been rediscovered, and stone walls could now be made as smooth as brick. As the height of the church increased it had become necessary to find a substitute for the column, which had been copied from those used in ancient temples, and often taken bodily from their ruins. Blocks of stone had therefore been arranged to form pillars. The roof was another serious problem, for the dimensions of a wooden beam cannot be indefinitely enlarged. Hence builders had begun to study the art of vaulting, which, after being long forgotten, had reappeared in Merovingian times, though on a very small scale.

Events threw long shadows before them in those days of trembling expectation, when, as fools pretend, Christendom was bowed beneath the 'terrors of the year one-thousand'! Sculptors, with unskilled hand but, for all that, with love, did their utmost to rediscover the lost secrets of form; and the first ornamented capitals abounded with a whole conventionalized array of flowers and beasts. Fresco painting was introduced to illustrate the Bible story on church walls, and stained glass made its first appearance, 'telling,' said Archbishop Adalberon of Rheims, 'all manner of tales.' A new world was about to come forth from the womb of Art.

It is difficult to grasp this wonderful rebirth which began about 1050 and continued for three hundred years. Never had there been so prodigious an outpouring in any part of the world. Wherever the Catholic Church held sway, building-sites attracted craftsmen inspired by joyous rivalry, afire with a creative fever. The cathedrals of Cremona, Piacenza, and Ferrara, the exquisite church of Santa Maria in Trastevere at Rome, and many more, were exactly contemporary with St Gilles-du-Gard, St Trophime at Arles, Poitiers, and St Denis.

M*

Later, while Noyon, Laon, Bourges, Chartres, Paris, Rheims, and Amiens soared into the skies of France, the same enthusiasm was manifested at San Lorenzo fuori le Mura at Rome and the basilica of Assisi in Italy; at Rochester, Worcester, and Westminster in England; at Magdeburg, Frankfort, and Cologne in Germany; at St Gudule at Brussels in Flanders; and elsewhere.

What lay behind this extraordinary proliferation? There were no doubt incidental causes, of which the most common was fire. Churches of the old type had wooden roofs and were easily set alight; there was scarcely one which had not been burned more or less to ashes four or five times before the final reconstruction. Sometimes replacement became necessary through increased attendance. Suger, for example, tells us in his pithy style how people flocked to his abbey at St Denis in such numbers that the clergy whose business it was to show the relics had to flee through the windows before an excited crowd of faithful. On such occasions so many women fainted that a special team had to be organized to pass them out from hand to hand above the heads of the congregation. We need only think of the vast crowds that gathered at pilgrim shrines to realize why naves were built on a scale hitherto unknown. Hence the size of St Martial at Limoges and St Sernin at Toulouse; hence too the basilica of St James at Compostella.

In many cases, however, the replacement of an old cathedral by a new had no such cause. It was prompted only by the desire of one generation to excel its predecessors, or by the urge to give God a more worthy and more beautiful dwelling; and this intention is well set forth in an extant document written by William de Seignelay, Bishop of Auxerre, explaining the decision to rebuild his cathedral while the present structure, no more than a hundred years old, was still in good condition. He merely wished to emulate what he had seen at Paris and in the cities of northern France, so that, 'discarding its ancient form, his cathedral might shine with all the beauty of restored youth and be inferior to no other in beauty or perfection.' William de Seignelay was not the only one to hold this view: before rebuilding Notre Dame, Maurice de Sully pulled down a church that had been completed only seventy years earlier; while at Laon, in 1160, Bishop Walter de Mortagne substituted a gothic cathedral for the romanesque building which had been erected no earlier than 1114. In Rheims cathedral we can now see the foundations of at least four earlier churches. Surely there is no better argument for the vitality of an age whose belief in God spelled progress.

We of the twentieth century may well stand amazed before the very speed of this achievement, we whom reinforced concrete has made familiar with structures far less enduring than was romanesque.

Western Europe may be conceived at this date as one huge building-site: Noyon 1140, Angers 1145, Le Mans 1150, Senlis 1153, Laon 1160, Poitiers 1162, Sens 1168, Bayeux 1175, Agde 1180, Bourges 1192, Chartres 1194, followed by Rheims, Amiens, Troyes, Mont-Saint-Michel, the Sainte Chapelle, etc. So the list continues, right through the twelfth and thirteenth centuries. Mme Lefrançois-Pillion reminds us that a master-craftsman who began his career at the age of twenty on the scaffolding of Laon or Paris, and moved perhaps to Chartres about ten years later, might have worked on the early stages of Rheims and lived to see the bold experiment at Amiens. Four stupendous buildings would thus have been completed within the span of a single lifetime.

Now this incredible achievement was the outcome of deep-seated energy, not of mere passing whim. So much is clear from the surprising but constant striving away from servile imitation and pattern-book style towards originality. If the comparison with organic evolution has any meaning whatsoever, we may apply it to this amazing process which enabled great artists, over a period of more than two centuries, to be ceaselessly inventive and yet remain true to a common source of inspiration. They set no store by the famous law of 'unity of style.' One generation did not consider itself bound to follow in its fathers' footsteps and do in 1250 what it had seen done in 1200; but since all drank at the same source and lived according to the same tradition, their several works are subject to a higher unity. At Le Mans, for example, a splendid gothic choir stands side by side in perfect harmony with a grand romanesque nave. To this universally accepted rule, unwritten as yet but not to be denied, we owe the continuous unfolding, like some noble tree, of Christian art in western Europe.

To what, then, must we attribute such extraordinary fertility? It was part of that general stirring [1] which characterized the Middle Ages during three hundred years of glory. France, in those days, was first among the nations; and her part in their immense creative achievement was therefore unsurpassed. It was on French soil that romanesque attained perfection; on French soil also gothic was evolved. France was Christian, and her creative urge, which spread throughout western Europe, was set in motion and given its direction by the Christian faith. She who inspired these undertakings, she who led the artists to their goal, and very often taught them how to work, was none other than the Church. For the glory of her God, the Church proclaimed and caused men to recognize 'the unique value of art.' [2]

---

[1] Cf. Chapter I, section 2.   [2] Jacques Maritain, *Art et scolastique.*

3. BUILDING FOR GOD

The clergy were also the immediate originators of these gigantic schemes. Here, as elsewhere, the monastic orders were the spearhead of a movement destined to put new life into civilization. Until at least the middle of the twelfth century, art was chiefly monastic; the abbey church preceded the cathedral, laying down the principles of construction and foreshadowing their boldest achievements. At Cluny, for instance, the vaulting was carried to a height of 98 feet, while the nave was extended to well over 100 yards. The romanesque cathedrals of Rheims, Limoges, Perigueux, and Toulouse, to name only four typical specimens, were of quite modest dimensions compared with the neighbouring abbey churches of St Remi, St Martial, St Front, and St Sernin.

At the head of the monastic architectural movement stood Cluny. Throughout the eleventh and at least the first half of the twelfth century, the great Burgundian abbey, under Hugh and Peter the Venerable, was really the source of all that mattered in Western architecture; and it is not one of the least merits of the Black Monks that they set before their contemporaries the ideal of beauty in the service of Almighty God. Besides doing much to perfect the art of vaulting, Cluny was responsible for the renaissance of sculpture and its intimate association with architecture; while investigation as to the origin of stained glass shows that in this respect also her influence was paramount.

Built between 1088 and 1130, Cluny was the victim of atrocious vandalism. Only a heap of ruins and a few old engravings survive to give us some idea of the prodigious mass with seven glorious towers that was once the largest abbey in Europe. But Cluny bore fruit in many fields, often far from her native Burgundy; and many a work derived from her bears present witness to her grandeur. Vézelay, tall and pure on her acropolis, was built about 1140 by Abbot Ponce de Monbaissier, brother of Peter the Venerable; St Benoît-sur-Loire, the ancient Fleury, was founded to be 'a model for the whole of France'; in Normandy, the ruins of Jumièges still speak of ancient majesty, as do the twin abbey churches at Caen, and those of Fécamp, St Pierre-sur-Dives, and Lessay.

Of the many great monastic builders whose genius is proved by an almost interminable catalogue of works, one calls for our particular attention. Suger, abbot of St Denis, was the son of a serf; but he raised himself by sheer ability to the highest offices of State. A slight figure of a man, he devoted his unflagging energy with equal success to theological speculation, to politics, to diplomacy, and to all the arts. There is a priceless document, dictated by the great abbot himself, which gives us a detailed account of his work in this last respect. First, he determines to rebuild the abbey church, which was evidently too small; and he sets about the task with those gifts of judgment and administration that were peculiarly his own. Columns from some Roman ruin are brought by sea; he himself chooses the tree-trunks from which the main beams are to be hewn; and so forth. The newest techniques, the most 'up-to-date' art-forms, the richest materials, the most skilled workmen, everything in fact that can ennoble the house of God, is harnessed to the work. The longer we study this noble figure, the more we shall appreciate his importance in the realm of art. But his distinguished services were shared to some extent by most abbots of the greater monasteries, few of whom escaped the building craze. In Germany, Hirschau and Maria-Laach exercised an influence similar to that of St Denis in France. St Bernard and his followers, rejecting what they considered useless and sinful luxury on the part of Cluny, recommended a more sober form of monastic architecture. But even so, it is quite wrong to maintain that the Cistercian attitude was retrograde and unintelligent; for, as we have seen,[1] it gave rise to those austere masterpieces whose whole beauty is their purity of line, and which we can still admire at Fontenay or Pontigny, at Front-froide or Alcobaça.

Monastic architecture endured as long as did the Middle Ages, and even outlived them. Its plan was fixed by tradition and perfectly adapted to the requirements of conventual life: chapter house, parlour, refectory, dormitory, library, and kitchen continued to be arranged in the same splendid harmony as of old; while those innumerable cloisters which, in every part of western Europe, impress the modern visitor so poignantly with the calm loveliness of things divine, continually multiplied. The style remained for a long while romanesque, so much so that some writers have drawn a false distinction, claiming that all abbey churches were romanesque and all cathedrals gothic. In point of fact, monastic architecture developed in course of time and adopted new techniques; but from the mid-twelfth century it no longer led the way.

The social and political evolution which gave urban civilization pride of place in the Western world had repercussions in the domain of art. As towns began to outstrip the monasteries and castles, men did not cease to build for God. Responsibility for the work, however, was now in other hands; the abbey church was superseded by the cathedral.

Who, then, was responsible for building the cathedral? The

[1] See Chapter III, section 8.

bishop, in almost every case.   The cathedral was his seat, his *cathedra*. Liturgically, it was his church and that of his chapter (just as the abbey was the church of an abbot and his monks), and it was natural that he should wish to make it as beautiful and large as possible; for human pride was no less powerful in this matter than glory in the sight of God. The history of these episcopal builders in the twelfth and thirteenth centuries has yet to be written; it should prove instructive.   Generations and even families of bishops [1] devoted themselves heart and soul to this task, moving heaven and earth for its success, and employing every instrument of holy rivalry to attract the best workmen available. On the tympanum of the porch at Sainte-Anne de Notre-Dame at Paris there stands an image of Maurice de Sully, one of the most active of the cathedral-builders, who occupied the see of St Denis from 1160 until 1196; and through him, in that place, we may render homage to the whole medieval episcopate.

It stands to reason that no bishop could have accomplished so vast a labour single-handed.   He needed the people's support, and he obtained it.   A legend fostered by Michelet, and even by Viollet-le-Duc, makes out that the cathedral was, so to speak, a weapon used by the townsfolk to make war against the tyranny of episcopal overlords. The facts prove otherwise.   It is true enough that the middle classes looked on the cathedral as evidence of their city's prosperity, that they were proud of its nave and of its dizzy towers; but this more or less democratic spirit never went so far as to persuade them that they could build a cathedral without the very man whose presence alone justified its construction and who would one day preside within its walls. Bishop Geoffrey d'Eu, one of the builders of Amiens, records, in 1236, that the rebuilding of the cathedral 'was decided with the full support of the clergy and people of Amiens'; and it has been remarked that even in those cities where the communal movement was directed against episcopal authority, the builders carried on uninterruptedly with their work.[2]

The celebrated miniature of the 'Jewish Antiquities,' in which Jean Fouquet, in order to represent the construction of Solomon's Temple, has painted a cathedral building-site, is later than the great period with which we are at present dealing; but it gives us an exact idea of what the scene must have been like at Chartres or Laon, Paris or Rheims, at a time when the whole population laboured at these stupendous works with hand or at least with heart.   One wonders how relatively small cities, numbering only a few ten-thousand inhabitants, managed to finance the building itself and to provide board and lodging for the workers.   No less surprising is the fact that while so many yards were opened at the same time, each was able to procure sufficient skilled

[1] See Chapter VI, section 5.   [2] See Chapter VI, section 5.

labour. The cathedral was a social undertaking; from an economic point of view it may be compared with our modern dams or motor-roads, and the people as a whole felt that by sharing in the work they were benefiting themselves as well as glorifying God.

In some cases the population took a direct part in the building operations, and these voluntary 'fatigues' are mentioned in a letter from Aimon, abbot of St Pierre-sur-Dives, to a community of monks in England. Notre-Dame de Chartres, says Aimon, profited by this unselfish fervour: 'We saw powerful men, proud of their birth as of their wealth, and accustomed to a life of ease, harness themselves to a cart and haul a load of stone, lime, wood, or some other material. . . . Sometimes the load was so heavy that more than a thousand persons, men and women, were required to draw the cart. They worked so quietly that one heard not so much as a whisper. When they took a rest by the way, one heard nothing but confession of faults and a humble prayer to God for remission of their sins. The priests exhorted them to be of one mind; hatreds were silenced, enmities vanished, debts were cancelled, and men's hearts returned to unity one with another. If anyone was so confirmed in wickedness that he would not forgive and listen to the priests, his offering was thrown from the cart as impure, and he himself driven with ignominy from the society of that holy people.' [1] A beautiful scene indeed; but was it rare or frequent? We do not know for certain. The system of voluntary fatigues seems to have been dropped about the middle of the thirteenth century, although traces of it are found in records concerning work on the cathedral of Troyes and at Châlons-sur-Marne. But Christians had still another means of sharing in the *Opus Dei*—by their gifts, of which there was no lack.

When it was decided to rebuild a cathedral, the bishop, the canons, rich townsfolk, and neighbouring landowners made the first offerings. The king was next approached, and usually gave a large sum. Collections were then made throughout the city and surrounding country-side, and no one, not even the poorest, dared shirk so high a duty. 'The Cathedral of Paris,' said the papal legate, Cardinal Eudes de Chateauroux, 'was largely built with the farthings of old women.' The Pope was invited to grant indulgences; and the most precious relics of the sanctuary to be rebuilt were sent out, often to great distances, in the care of preachers who would address the crowds preparatory to making a collection.[2] These preachers, incidentally, were always welcome, and entertainments were sometimes arranged in their honour. For good measure, God and His saints would combine to grant miracles on behalf of generous donors. The Blessed Virgin

---

[1] Migne, *Patrologia Latina*, vol. clxxxi, p. 1707.
[2] Collections were made as far afield as Prussia for St Martin of Colmar.

herself, for example, appeared to a certain English student who, returning from abroad with a golden brooch 'for his dear lady-friend,' was moved to give it so that Mary might have her cathedral.   Sometimes a wealthy benefactor would undertake the whole cost of some part of the edifice.   More often one of the trade guilds would offer a stained-glass window; at Chartres nineteen of them together presented no fewer than forty-seven.   Only public sinners were excluded from this means of doing penance, and usurers were thus enabled to restore ill-gotten gains.   At Paris even the 'guild' of prostitutes asked the bishop to accept either a window or a chalice; and the theologian instructed to look into this ticklish business agreed—subject to the gift being made unobtrusively. A wonderful display of mass enthusiasm!

Historically, indeed, the cathedral may be regarded as an indication of society in full process of expanding, of society overflowing its old boundaries and feeling itself strong enough to place its exuberant vitality at the service of an ideal.   For there was certainly an ideal associated with and giving meaning to this upsurge of vigour.   If, like Claudel in *The Satin Slipper*, we ask 'What had happened to them, to these clodhoppers, these yokels, these sharpers, these dirty-tails,' that they adorned the world with so many marvels, the one and only answer lies in two words: they believed.   It seemed natural enough to build for God, so natural, in fact, that no one wished to boast about it.   As André Michel observes, medieval literature in its several forms is almost completely silent on the prodigious strides made by architecture.   There was also humility, the sure guarantee of faith.   Some writers, e.g. Louis Gillet, see in the cathedrals a recoil from the crusades, a middle-class answer to that other sublime folly whose aim was to reconquer the Holy Sepulchre.   There seems, however, to have been no interaction or mutual influence between the two.   Both undertakings proceeded from the same spirit and expressed the same outlook; they bore witness to one faith.

4.   The Hands that built the Cathedrals

There were able hands in the service of that faith.   Just as we must cease to look upon medieval masterpieces as miracles of art, struck out in a moment of time without pattern or preparation, so also we must be careful not to view the cathedral-builders as inspired artists extemporizing under pressure of their own genius.   They were fervent souls, to be sure, but they were also clear-headed, down-to-earth fellows, experienced craftsmen with a definite technique.   That is precisely why they built these imperishable works.   'The spiritual,' says

Péguy, 'is itself carnal,' and his words might well have been written by St Thomas Aquinas.

Who were the men whose hands fashioned these wonders? They were not yet known by the more dignified name of 'architect'; they were called 'foremen of works,' 'masters of masons,' or more simply 'master-masons.' As the professions became more highly organized, they were included in the guild of 'mortar-men and stone-dressers'; for at this period there was no distinction between an artisan and an artist, while respect for manual labour was on a level with that enjoyed by the highest artistic inspiration. For, of course, they were not 'labourers' in the modern sense of the word, still less country bumpkins; some of them were quite well educated, and even knew Latin,[1] though the knowledge they managed to acquire in the course of their many journeys was naturally based rather on experience than on books. The epitaph of one of them, Peter of Montereau, who lived for a long time at St Germain-des-Prés, describes him by the dignified title *doctor lithotomorum*, teacher of stone-dressers, i.e. master-mason.

These foremen and masons (the two jobs were often done by one man, the architect turning sculptor during the long winter nights) who built the cathedrals are not altogether unknown to us. Many of them, though unfortunately not all, have left their names engraved on some part of the edifice; others were immortalized by their children who buried them in the churches they had helped to raise. We have mentioned Peter of Montereau who worked on the new abbey of St Denis; he was succeeded by his son Eudes, whose monumental effigy used to lie in the Cordeliers between those of his two wives. Another magnificent tombstone shows the architect of Saint-Nicaise at Rheims, Hugh Libergier, proud and elegant in his hood and beautifully folded cape. At the central crossing of many cathedrals there was an area of paving curiously inlaid with black marble or lead, like an elaborate game of goose. It was called the Labyrinth and had an esoteric meaning which is difficult to unravel; indulgences could be gained by following it on one's knees. Actually it represented the builders' names: at Rheims, for example, the Labyrinth bore those of the first four architects, John of Orbais, John the Wolf, Gaucher of Rheims, and Bernard of Soissons; at Amiens those of Robert of Luzarches, Thomas and Renaud of Cormont. Elsewhere contemporary documents provide us with this information. Thus we find William of Sens travelling to Canterbury and throwing himself heart and soul into the work, while Master Jean Mignot of Paris was consulted by the people of Milan with regard to their famous cathedral. We learn also

[1] The latest commentator on Villard of Honnecourt points out, however, that the Latin notes to his manuscript are not in his own hand.

of the adventurous life led by John Langlois, builder of the choir of St Urbain at Troyes.   This gifted craftsman was something of a nomad; after constructing several churches in France, he took the Cross and ended up in Cyprus, where he was responsible for the Cathedral of Famagusta.   We know much less about the sculptors, but a few names have been preserved: Robertus on the porch at Chartres, Bruno on that of Saint-Gilles, Gislebert at Autun.   John of Chelles has left his name on the foundations of the south transept at Paris, Jehan Ravy and Jehan Boutellier on the choir screen in the same cathedral.

Of all these artists, however, one is more familiar than the rest; by an extraordinary piece of good fortune we have his private note-book, an album in which he set down his observations and ideas, illustrating them with rough sketches.   In its present state it consists of thirty-three very old parchment sheets, and is preserved in the Bibliothèque Nationale at Paris.   His name was Villard de Honnecourt, a Picard from the neighbourhood of Cambrai, who lived in the middle of the thirteenth century and no doubt belonged to the aristocracy of his craft.   He is credited with part at least of the cathedral at Cambrai, the abbey of Vauxcelles, and the church of St Elizabeth at Cassovia in Hungary, where he was summoned between 1241 and 1247.   An attractive personality, he was passionately interested in everything, and turned everything he saw to his advantage.   Villard's reflections and sketches supplement one another, representing a vast frieze of those familiar figures which the medieval world presented to his eager mind. Here is a window at Rheims, which he drew 'because he rather liked it'; here is the tower of Laon which so astonished him; here are beasts sketched in a few lines, a lion 'done from life,' and all kinds of objects, especially people such as jugglers or soldiers, clerks or musicians, all observed with the same keen eye.   He had also studied the great monuments of his age: the cathedrals at Rheims, Laon, Cambrai, St Quentin, Chartres, Meaux, and numerous abbey churches, of which he speaks with enthusiasm and expert knowledge.   If evidence be required to prove what stares us in the face, viz. that no cathedral was built by ignoramuses, Villard de Honnecourt's sketch-book will provide it.

No one, indeed, could reasonably suppose that buildings of such perfection were constructed by rule of thumb, haphazardly.   Suger himself employed the exact sciences to calculate the curve of vaulting, and diagrams have been found on the walls of Clermont, Limoges, Narbonne, Rheims, Strasbourg, etc., which show that the builders understood mathematics, three-dimensional geometry, and trigonometry.   Before a cathedral began to take shape, it had passed through the drawing-board stage in the foreman's office.   The same kind of preparatory work was done in the case of sculpture; Villard's note-book contains sketches of solid bodies broken up into geometrical figures (rather like those affected by cubists and 'abstract' painters), triangles, cones, and parallelepipeds. The difficult science of stereotomy, which is now fast disappearing, and the laws governing the resistance of materials, were equally well understood. It is not absolutely certain that we have penetrated all the secrets of medieval knowledge.

How did the foremen and stone-dressers acquire their skill? It was not taught in the universities, and there is no trace of anything like a 'School of Fine Arts.' Nevertheless, it is unthinkable that men who achieved so high a degree of accomplishment should not have wished to train others. Some authorities have even put forward a theory that Villard de Honnecourt's album was in fact a kind of manual intended for reproduction and distribution among his pupils. It is also remarked that the foreman's craft ran in families, e.g. the Montereaux, to whom we have already made reference, the Chelles, Chaumes, and Valrinfroys; while at Amiens, the Cormonts, uncle and nephew, both of whose names occur in documents relating to the same work, may well have belonged to different generations. Be that as it may, pupils must have learned their craft in close association with a master. He would begin by making them carry hods of mortar; next he would initiate them into the art of measuring and assembling stones, then into the difficult calculation of vaulting and the art of stone-dressing. Their formation would be completed by long journeys which amounted to veritable tours of Europe.

The cathedral-builders were principally craftsmen, but they were also men of faith. Not saints, indeed, for there is reason to think some of them did not lead very edifying lives; but, like all men of that period, they did believe. They travelled from one site to another, working 'for God and Holy Church' with that simplicity of heart which characterizes those who know they are on the right road. Loving their craft, they felt that they served the Master well and were laying up for themselves a heavenly reward. After all, was not God Himself the great architect? On the title page of the *Bible moralisée* at Vienne, was He not shown, compass in hand, measuring the universe? Their faith formed part and parcel of their art, of their craft, and of their daily

[1] It is well known, for example, that our modern glass-painters are at a loss to explain by what methods romanesque stained glass was endowed with its amazing brilliance. Climb up into the roof of Notre-Dame at Paris, and you will find that the ancient beams are much thinner than those of more recent date. You will also discover that those erected by Viollet-le-Duc have already been attacked by insects while the thirteenth-century timbers are still immune; what preservative was used? Some have boldly suggested the transmission of immemorial secrets within the building confraternities. We know at any rate that in the Middle Ages the normal standard of measurement, the cubit, varied from one country to another; that used in building the cathedral of Strasbourg was exactly the same as that used on the Great Pyramid.

round; a long cry from those modern artists who 'practise sacred art' while they proclaim their want of faith.[1]

Such, then, were the artists called in by promoters, donors, or bishops when embarking on their solemn enterprise.   One question remains to be answered: How were they engaged, maintained, and paid? Here again, medieval custom was vastly different from our own.   The money question was less prominent than it is to-day.   Among all the documents which we possess relative to the building of cathedrals, there is no single reference to a wage-dispute.   The most renowned foremen were paid yearly.   Like simple workmen, they received a modest wage in pence and halfpence together with agreed rates for work done.   If the promoter were a religious congregation, the artist fed with the monks, though it was stipulated that on fast-days he should be served with better rations than his hosts.   He was often given benefits in kind, e.g. clothes and especially 'gloves to protect his hands from the lime.' [2]   Simplicity is a Christian virtue; labour for God's glory is its own reward, and the merit thus acquired is not easily assessed in terms of money.

5. ROMANESQUE ARCHITECTURE

The busy hands of master-craftsmen produced forms whose evolution constitutes perhaps the most thrilling in the whole history of art.   That story does not fall strictly within the limits of this book; but no historian of the Church can disregard the appearance of those temples in which the faithful of the Middle Ages prayed, especially when so many of them are in use to-day, when our own prayers rise to to same roofs that once received Christian voices in the days of St Bernard and St Louis.

About the year 1000 there emerged from the Carolingian chrysalis

[1] It has often been maintained that, since the characters of medieval faith are found in the art of that period, medieval man's love of symbolism and mystery must have influenced his art.   Huysmans, indeed, strongly upheld the symbolic explanation of Christian art in the Middle Ages.   There seems to be a certain amount of truth in this, especially in the suggestion that some influence was exerted by the 'science of numbers,' which attributes a secret significance to every numeral: for instance, 3 is the divine number; 4, the number of matter because there were four recognized elements; 7, the number of man, was arrived at by adding the other two; and so on.

Researches into the famous *golden number* known in antiquity have not yet been pursued scientifically with regard to architecture.   Again, why were the cathedrals orientated so that the choir lay to the east?   Was it because that was the direction of Jerusalem or of Paradise?   Or was it because tradition held that our Lord had faced eastward on the Cross?   It is highly probable that the slight obliquity which is to be noticed in certain choirs was entirely accidental in origin, and was not done on purpose to suggest the bowed head of our Lord at the moment of His death.   As for such theories that the windows represented the Doctors, the columns the Apostles, or that the northern rose window was an allusion to hell and that in the south transept to Paradise, they seem to have been of a much later date.

[2] Hence the French expression 'se donner des gants' (to take credit for a job).

an architectural style which was subsequently propagated through almost all the lands once ruled by Charlemagne.   It was by no means a 'primitive' art; on the contrary, it was full of memories showing the varied influence of Rome, of Byzantium, of the Asiatic East, of Islam, as well as of the Scythian and Sarmatian steppes.   All these elements were gradually absorbed, digested, and new forms were imposed to give us what we now call early romanesque.   Splendid examples of this style, dating from the year 1000 or soon afterwards, are to be seen in St Philibert at Tournus (928–1019), the Abbey of Ste Foy at Conques (1030–80), and St Hilaire at Poitiers (1045–80).

The most recent studies of romanesque art pay particular attention to a group of churches belonging to this period which are found along a line drawn from Catalonia to Switzerland through Savoy, Lombardy, and Burgundy.   Massive and generally squat, these edifices are built with a curious arrangement of broken stones, while the exterior is adorned with a system of blind arcades running in festoons below the cornices.   This ornamentation is called 'Lombard,' because its main centre of diffusion was northern Italy.   It seems, however, that Catalonia was an equally powerful force in the spread of early romanesque, Catalonia, where the abbey church of Santa Maria at Ripoll (consecrated in 1031) was already monumental.

Builders very soon became more ambitious, and whereas the first romanesque edifices were of quite modest proportions, from the middle of the eleventh century they grew larger.   Naves were extended and became immense.   At first the tendency was to build round churches based upon Asian models or on the Pantheon at Rome.   The Palatine Chapel at Aix-la-Chapelle was a magnificent example of the round style.   It no longer exists, but its memory is preserved in smaller buildings on French soil, e.g. the exquisite little church at Germigny-les-Prés and that at Ottmarsheim in Alsace.   The first church of St Benignus at Dijon (c. 900) was also a rotunda.   This plan was everywhere abandoned, but reappeared after the crusaders had seen circular mosques in the East and the Templars had made the celebrated mosque of Omar at Jerusalem their headquarters.   The temples at Paris and at London (both now destroyed) were also round churches, as were the churches of the Templars at Laon, Metz, Montmorillon, and Segovia. But all these were exceptions.

The type which ultimately prevailed was modelled on the basilica; it consisted of a central nave with twin aisles, and could more easily hold large crowds.   Simple and solid, these early romanesque naves have an air of calm strength which characterizes the style from beginning to end.   The transept, or transverse nave crossing the main axis so as to form a cross, had already been used in ancient basilicas [1] and

---

[1] So had the deambulatory, a kind of passage-way round the apse.

endowed the edifice with more complicated perspectives together with a more subtle play of light and shade. The nave gradually became longer and taller, while the towers—which had existed for many generations, often apart from the church itself—became an integral part of the façade and lent the building an appearance of sovereign majesty.

Increasing dimensions, however, raised an awkward technical problem—the roof. The simplest and most obvious means of covering a nave was to lay beams from one wall to the other in such a way that they could either be left visible or hidden by a coffered ceiling. This method of roofing was never completely abandoned; old St Peter's at Rome consisted of five naves roofed with wood, and some Roman basilicas still have richly ornamented wooden ceilings. But the method involved a twofold disadvantage: the size of the nave was strictly limited, and the mass of dry wood was liable to catch fire. Another means of roofing was already known, viz. the stone vault borrowed by the Romans from the East and frequently employed by them. It had likewise been used in Carolingian times, though in a somewhat rudimentary form; specimens may be seen in the low narrow vaulting at Jouarre and Vénasque, in St Laurent at Grenoble, and in the semi-dome of the baptistery at Poitiers. It was this stone vaulting of which foremen and monastic architects of the eleventh and twelfth centuries made increasingly deliberate use.

The art of vaulting consists in the arrangement of previously dressed stones in such a way that, when the scaffolding is removed, their own weight holds them in place. It was a costly process (fifteen to eighteen times more so than a wooden roof), but a sure protection against fire. Two main kinds of vault, both Roman in origin, were used by romanesque architects. There was the 'barrel,' or semi-cylindrical, and the 'groined' vault. The latter is obtained, in mathematical parlance, by the intersection of two 'barrels'; it may be described more simply as consisting of four convex compartments whose bases rest upon supports. But the great drawback of a romanesque vault was the tremendous weight of so large a mass of dressed stone. Even when reinforced with arch-bands, which divided the thrust, the weight still tended to force the walls outwards. The abbey church at Bec collapsed in this way three times in a hundred years! There was only one means of avoiding such accidents, and that was to strengthen the walls by making them so thick-set and heavy that they could easily support tons of limestone or granite. But if the walls were to be made as much as 1½ or 2 yards thick, what about window-openings? How was the nave to be lit? Architects of the romanesque period attacked these two problems, bearing in mind the necessity of adequate support and light.

Vaulting, however, must not be considered the outstanding characteristic of romanesque.   Other solutions were discovered or retained.
We shall find brilliant romanesque architects in Normandy, who,
though by no means timid, steadily refused to employ the vaulting for
which their splendid naves seemed to call.   In the south of France,
many surviving Roman temples, baths, and aqueducts provided useful
models.   Moreover, the West had long been familiar with Byzantine
work; and this is why the naves of Périgueux, Souillac, Angoulême,
and other churches in that region are covered not with beams or
vaulting, but with cupolas.   These structures are curiously reminiscent
of Santa Sophia and the Holy Apostles at Constantinople, or of St
Mark's at Venice, though at Puy they assume an entirely different form
and suggest Moslem influence.

The period between 1000 and 1200 was one of tireless experiment
and of intense activity in the realm of creative art.   After the first wave,
which produced the abbey churches of Cluny (1088–1109), Conques
(1030–80), Holy Trinity (1062–83) and St Stephen (1064–87) at Caen,
St Sernin at Toulouse (1076–1119), and which had repercussions at
Cologne (1065), Spire (1030–1106), Lincoln (1072–92), and Pisa
(1063–1118), a second and more powerful wave took shape in Vézelay
(1104–32), St Lazare at Autun (1120–78), St Front at Périgueux (1120–
1173), Salamanca (1120–78), Parma (1130–50), and Worms (1171–
1234).   Earlier models, seen by pilgrims and merchants, and afterwards by the crusaders, were studied, and their lessons absorbed.

It is not, therefore, surprising that, unlike gothic with its remarkable
unity of forms, romanesque architecture is extraordinarily diverse.
Unity there certainly is, but interior, concealed, transcending the forms
themselves; a spiritual unity which enables us to recognize at first
glance the relationship in style and period between buildings that look
completely different one from another.   Romanesque remained an
experimental style; when the ogival intersection came into use, it was
found adaptable to all plans, to all dimensions, and there was no need
of further experiment.   Thus the phrase 'romanesque architecture'
covers buildings which have no resemblance, though archaeologists
try to group them in 'schools.'   How many 'schools' were there?
Seven, according to Arcisse de Caumont; Anthyme St Paul said fifteen;
while Viollet-le-Duc hesitated between seven, fifteen, or thirteen.
Others counted no fewer than twenty-four.   Some experts prefer a
local division based on the arrangement of naves and aisles, or on the
method of roofing.   We shall only say with Louis Gillet, an artist as
well as an historian, that in the concert of faith and enthusiasm which
arose from medieval christendom 'each province struck its own note
which was echoed by its neighbour.'

In the small district of Auvergne we have such masterpieces as

Notre-Dame du Port at Clermont, St Julien at Brioude, St Paul at Issoire, and St Nectaire at Orcival, with their continuous barrel-vaulted naves and groined aisles where light falls obliquely through the tribunes; with their sturdy central towers and deep-coloured materials —sandstone, lava, basalt, limestone, and arkose. Viewed from without, the side chapels and apse are massed in a series of curves around the central tower, poised as if in imitation of the nearby mountain-range. Poitou, with neighbouring Anjou, Angoumois, and part of Guienne, is a land of fair abbeys: St Radegonde and St Hilaire at Poitiers, St Eutropius at Saintes, Fontevrault, and St Savin at Aulnay. Above all, there is that jewel, Notre-Dame la Grande, where the monotony of barrel-vaulting is relieved by the use of arch-bands, where the lateral vaulting rises almost as high as the nave, and where the amazing exuberance of sculpture, not unlike that found on some ancient monuments in India, somehow gives the whole edifice the appearance of an oriental casket. Languedoc, together with a large area reaching as far as Portugal and Spain, borrows elements from all its neighbours, interpreting them in its own favourite medium, brick, and employing them with a sense of harmony, a taste for simplicity and light, that are truly sublime. Languedoc also contains some of the most perfect examples of romanesque sculpture, e.g. at Moissac. Within the narrow limits of Provence, we have St Trophime at Arles, St Gilles du Gard, St Guillem du Désert, St Victor at Marseilles, not forgetting Montmajour, Maguelonne, and the fortified church at Saintes Maries. Their austere beauty is revealed in the simplicity of their plan, in the peasant roughness of their pillars, in their flattened roofs, and in much else that looks back to the traditions of an ancient past. But now take Burgundy, a land of bold experiment in the field of architecture, home of the Cluniacs and later of the Cistercians, whose influence was destined to spread throughout Christendom. Burgundy raised her naves as high as they would go and extended them to enormous lengths;[1] she multiplied them even to excess, contrived to admit plenty of light, and adorned them with so many sturdy towers that it is hard to say whether their purpose was to glorify God or to flatter human pride. Cluny, the masterpiece, is gone. But in Burgundy we can still admire her rival offspring, e.g. at Autun, Paray-le-Monial, Saulieu, Bourbon-Lancy, and Beaune, as well as in St Benignus at Dijon, at Pontaubert, but above all at Vézelay, that rare marvel high upon its hill. We have already mentioned that most curious of romanesque schools, which scattered domes and cupolas in Périgord and a wide region round about. These structures not only cover the transept-crossing, but are repeated along the whole length of the building. To this school belong St Front and St Étienne at Périgueux:

[1] The nave of Cluny was just over 561 feet long.

Cahors, Souillac, and even churches so far afield as Angoulême and Saintes. Burgundy, indeed, contributes a chorus of originality, exoticism, and traditionalism to the varied concert of romanesque. As for her rival, Normandy, she has a wealth of noble abbeys at Jumièges, Caen, Fécamp, and St Pierre-sur-Dives, besides the churches and cathedrals of Évreux and Ouistreham. She preferred not to grapple with the problem of vaulting, and remained faithful to the timber roof; all the same, it was she who set an example of enormously tall naves filled with light, of the splendid, many-staged central tower open to the crossing, and of that wonderful type of gabled façade flanked by towers which afterwards became a feature of so many masterpieces. At Jumièges and St Étienne, as at Vézelay and Paray-le-Monial, gothic was already on the threshold. Lastly, we must make special mention, on account of their historical and religious no less than their artistic importance, of a group of churches on the road to Compostella. These are the pilgrim churches of St Martial at Limoges, St Sernin at Toulouse, and Conques. St Martin at Tours, on the same route, has since disappeared.

The diversity of romanesque as seen in France is noticeable elsewhere. In Spain, for example, whereas St James of Compostella and St Isidore at Leon are strikingly reminiscent of St Sernin at Toulouse, Notre-Dame de la Sierra near Segovia resembles a Burgundian church, St Vincent at Avila is related to the edifices of central France, while the cloister of Gerona cathedral is closely akin to that of St Trophime at Arles.

These influences are often combined with local elements, resulting in new forms, particularly in Italy, which is the home *par excellence* of romanesque, and which resisted gothic for several centuries. The wonderful variety of this 'Lombard' architecture can be studied in St Ambrogio at Milan, St Zeno at Verona, as well as in the cathedrals of Parma and Modena, whose simplicity belongs to the old tradition. South of the Apennines, the Badia at Fiesole and San Miniato at Florence are rich with marble; the façades of Pisa and Lucca are covered with a lace-work of small columns and blind arcades which give a most delicate effect. At Rome there is little or no ornament; the twelfth-century basilicas are almost as austere as those dating from the fifth century. In southern Italy, however, the glory of architectural style is heightened by the soft colouring of beautiful stone; here the Lombardic style was subject to Byzantine-Arabian influences from Sicily.

Meanwhile, in England, Norman architecture, which came over with the Conqueror, had issued in the splendours of Lincoln, Winchester, Durham, Chester, and Canterbury. Later, it varied according to district and period. It penetrated even into Norway in the shape of St Mary at Bergen, competing with the technique of the old Viking carpenters. In Germany, ancient Carolingian traditions and Lombardic influences gave rise to a number of strange cathedrals which might be said to have no face, for there is an apse at both ends. They are enormous buildings with massive towers reaching up like so many arms, and their timbered naves rival those of Normandy. German cathedrals are sturdy and yet charged with poetry, especially those built of an exquisite rose-coloured sandstone. From Worms, Mainz, and Spire this art spread along the Rhine and even farther afield, to Tournais with its fine steeples, to lovely Bamberg, and to Saxony, Poland, Denmark, and Sweden.

Such, then, was romanesque, the first fine flower of medieval architecture. How far can we compare it, as it has often been compared, with gothic? Though perhaps less perfect in form, it did at any rate escape the danger that was to threaten its successor, the danger of sterility, of a beauty so purely mathematical that it could not appeal for ever. It is less graceful, but it conveys a wonderful impression of ordered bulk; it is less harmonious, but it suggests organic growth and almost enables us to see the creative sap at work. From the complexity of age-old elements and local influences it managed to produce a coherent system, a fresh harmony, in which beauty of mass and line is heightened by the ornaments of fresco, glass, and sculpture. Romanesque has a certain 'horizontal' feeling; it is profoundly religious and makes one think of a monk's silent meditation. It corresponds to an altogether interior spirituality whose dominant virtue is faith. The style went out of fashion not because it had failed, but because its technical achievements had helped to solve architectural problems in new ways, and also because its restraint no longer roused an echo in the hearts of men. Christendom, spurred now by new-found confidence in itself, preferred to make stone speak of its favourite virtue, hope, which raises man above himself and draws him towards God.

6. GOTHIC ARCHITECTURE

Stand in any of the great gothic naves, drink in the atmosphere of the place, and you will enjoy a twofold experience: physical sensation and spiritual emotion. You will inevitably be struck by the vertically soaring lines, and feel yourself penetrated by, enveloped in, light. Unlike the romanesque basilica planted firmly on the ground, crouching, so to speak, on its foundations, the gothic cathedral is erect, upstanding.[1] Unlike the heavy, semicircular barrel-vaulting which necessitated enormously thick walls and narrow windows, making the

---

[1] The comparison has been ably developed by Mme Lefrançois-Pillion in *Maîtres d'œuvre et tailleurs de pierres*. The German archaeologist Wörringer speaks of the gothic church as an 'upstanding edifice.'

nave darker in proportion to its length, gothic technique satisfied the craving for light, which was allowed to pour in and flood the whole building. The two characteristics recognized by our senses awaken a corresponding echo in the soul. Supernatural joy is called forth by this appeal of soaring height; instinctive happiness is shed by these vast areas of light, which seem to promise the ultimate elucidation of life's problems and to reflect here on earth the brilliance of uncreated splendour.

Nevertheless, it would be wrong to imagine that these spiritual qualities which we recognize in a great gothic masterpiece were first and foremost in the minds of the builders. No architect ever designed a nave of such dizzy height merely to keep pace with the mystical ideals of his contemporaries, or added one bay to another simply in order that the light falling through them should symbolize knowledge of God. At the root of every great artistic achievement there lies a technical invention. The ogival arch, which alone makes the gothic cathedral possible, has in itself no religious meaning; besides, it was used to cover all kinds of building, e.g. dormitories and cellars. But herein lies the mystery of art: a technical discovery is made at the very moment and under the very conditions when a whole combination of circumstances and aspirations enables it to realize to the utmost its potentialities and to assume spiritual significance.

The ogival arch is formed by two sectors of a circle meeting at a more or less acute angle. It existed during the romanesque period, just as the semicircular arch, which is generally regarded as characteristic of romanesque, remained common during the age of gothic. The ogive, or, to speak more correctly, the intersection of ogives, is simply a means of roofing the nave in a more satisfactory way than that employed by romanesque builders.

Consider a bay, i.e. the space (usually quadrangular) formed by four supports in the shape of columns, retaining walls, or pillars. Now throw two intersecting diagonal arcs to join opposite corners and linked at their point of intersection by a keystone, a specially cut stone shaped like a sort of four-leaved clover. Lastly, fill the four resulting compartments with some light material, and you have a section of ogival vaulting. The romanesque groined vaulting had helped to divide the pressure; but it was still a solid block of enormous weight. The gothic technique not only avoided a large part of this weight, but also made the four compartments absolutely independent of one another. Above all, it localized the thrust, assembled it, so to speak, and confined it exactly to the four points on which the two arcs rested. The result was that vaulting, which weighed relatively little, could be raised to any height; and the walls, being no longer required as supports, could be devoted almost entirely to window-space.

The only remaining problem was how to keep the pillars erect under the fourfold thrust of the vaulting. The solution presented no difficulty whatever; it was based on the elementary principle of shoring. If a wall threatens to collapse, it can be held in place by a framework of beams set slantwise against it. Similarly, the thrust which tended to force the edifice apart was collected and carried away by means of flying buttresses, to be received by heavier masses in the shape of close buttresses, i.e. pillars so solid and so deeply embedded in the ground that there was no risk of their yielding. To make assurance doubly sure, these pillars were given added strength by the imposition of a kind of stone cap, the pinnacle, just as, in order to prevent a cane falling, one need only press one's hand on the knob.

This astonishingly simple method respected the laws of matter. Among the leading paradoxes of gothic architecture is the fact that it appears to soar heavenward though in fact the whole structure is based on a downward thrust. As we gaze awestruck at the lightness of the whole, we must not forget that this fantastic arabesque rests on foundations of enormous volume, driven as much as fifty feet below the surface.

Gothic architects managed to derive beauty from the necessity of submitting to the inescapable effects of weight. The cathedral is a marvel of logic, which Maritain has compared to the *Summa* of St Thomas. It is an elegant solution of a problem in geometry and physics, a thing of beauty precisely because there is nothing false or artificial about it. By calculating exactly the dimensions and design of pillars, by tracing perfectly the curve of flying buttresses, the architects proved once again the great aesthetic law that any object fully adapted to its purpose is beautiful. The gothic cathedral has never been more rightly described than in these words of Mme Lefrançois-Pillion: 'A diagram clothed in beauty.'

It is just here that we feel the mysterious meeting between technical data and the highest spirituality. The cathedral architects, or at least the great majority of them, were certainly not inspired by any mystic urge, nor can we even be sure that they expressly intended to create beauty. Nevertheless, because the sap of Christian faith and hope ran in their veins, they inevitably produced the beautiful, the great, the spiritual. Once the problem of roofing had been solved, naves grew taller even to the point of rashness, and by an elementary law of proportion their length also increased beyond anything before attempted. They multiplied, too; triple and fivefold naves led crowds through triumphal avenues to the altar of the Lord. Towers, as if driven by the ascending force that elevated the whole building, reached heights never before attained: 269 feet at Rheims, 304 feet at Chartres, 466 feet at Strasbourg, and 525 feet at Ulm.

All the same, gothic architecture, though born of superhuman ambition, remained essentially human; it had none of those excessive dimensions which may be seen in Roman temples of the decadence. Just as the sculpture of gothic cathedrals remained closely linked with man's life and the objects familiar to him, so their architecture kept within human proportions, as may be seen by glancing at the doors, galleries, balustrades, and steps, all of which are man-sized, conceived in relation to man.[1] Surely the profound humanism of Thomist thought had much to do with this.

Such was the art to which the Renaissance attached the word 'gothic' as an epithet of opprobrium, in which, during the age of Louis XIV, Fénelon could see no more than a confused heap of eccentricities. The nineteenth century has not received the credit due to it for having restored to gothic its rightful place as one of the greatest episodes in the history of art. Chateaubriand made it loved, and Viollet-le-Duc revealed its grandeur. The word 'gothic' remains in use, and is perhaps in some sense justified; it reminds us that the origins of western civilization, and therefore of its aesthetics, included non-Latin, non-classical elements equally powerful but rooted in a wholly different tradition.

It would be historically more correct, however, to describe this form of architecture as the 'French style,' as in fact was done by the Renaissance architect Philibert de l'Orme, who spoke of 'the old French mode.' The ogival style was fashionable in France about the year 1200; but elsewhere, in Germany for example, it did not appear until the end of the thirteenth century, and no masterpieces were produced before about 1350. Moreover, it was in France, especially in the neighbourhood of Paris, that we find the greatest achievements of gothic, which were destined to serve as models everywhere.

Gothic architecture has been traced to remote and often strange origins, e.g. Armenian. But one need only examine the romanesque vaulting at Moissac, with its awkward supporting-arches like intersecting ceiling-beams, to find oneself asking whether the discovery of the ogive may not have been made in several places at once. Where, in fact, was the first ogival bay constructed? British archaeologists have claimed priority for the cathedrals of Durham and Peterborough, where, they say, the new technique appeared in very humble forms and can be dated by textual evidence from 1093. But the most numerous examples of primitive ogival vaulting are found in a small area between the Somme and the Oise on the borders of the Île-de-France. There,

[1] This is why one receives an impression of immensity at Rheims or Amiens more easily than at St Peter's in Rome: the human scale is absent from the typical Renaissance building. The angels supporting a holy-water stoup are 6 feet 6 inches high, but how can one appreciate the fact when there is no standard of comparison?

in the poor churches of Cambronne and Airanes, we still find undoubted examples, however clumsy and ungainly they may be.   The
most ancient are probably those of Moriental Abbey on the edge of the
Forest of Compiègne; they date from 1115.   On the other hand, it is
fairly safe to say that the first large-scale attempt was made at St Denis
during the abbacy of Suger, who, at the time of the opening in 1144,
referred in an extant document to arches built in the new style around
the choir, 'upheld by no support or rest' and quaking, while still
unfinished, in a sudden gale.

Having invented the ogive, architects did not look upon it as a final
solution incapable of improvement.   On the contrary, their resource-
fulness is nowhere better shown than in this respect.   Now that the
problem of vaulting had been solved and architecture established on
rational foundations, builders, far from submitting to the slavery of set
forms, felt themselves more free than ever to experiment boldly so as to
perfect their methods.   One generation after another came nearer to
the ideal.   Just as romanesque thrills us with its diversity in space, so
does gothic with its variety in time, with its perpetual transformations,
with its evolution.   We have only to compare a great abbey church
like Fontenay, Pontigny, or Fontfroide (where Cistercian austerity
agrees so nobly with the unadorned technique of early gothic) with
such perfect examples as the nave of Amiens or Rheims in order to
gauge the distance travelled, and to realize the extent to which unity of
style managed in the course of years to express itself in countless
different ways.

Noyon (1151–1220) heads the list of 'major' cathedrals; Noyon, so
despised that she was stripped of all her sculpture and is now covered in
a hideous yellow wash, yet still so solid, so powerful in the perfect
balance between mass and empty space.   Used for worship—at least
the choir—since 1157, Noyon has a somewhat dumpy, unobtrusive
appearance suggestive of romanesque; it is only 72 feet high, less than
Cluny.   The bays are very small; the supports, consisting alternately
of columns and stout pillars, are massive; the intersecting ogives, each
of which covers more than one bay in 'sexpartite' vaulting, give one
a curious sense of timidity.   Next comes Sens, consecrated in 1164
by Pope Alexander III during his exile in France.   Its restraint is apt
to pass unnoticed by those visitors who have eyes for nothing but the
marvellous flamboyant façades of the transept which were added in the
fourteenth century.   The vaulted tribune above the side-aisles, which
gives Noyon such a heavy appearance, is replaced by a light gallery
known as the triforium, a celebrated example of which appeared at
Chartres thirty years later.   Sens enlarged the architectural vocabulary, suggesting that upward flight which was henceforward characteristic of the whole style.   Next in order stands Laon (1160–1207), the

cathedral so much admired by Villard de Honnecourt.   Dominating
the whole city and even the whole province, it seems at first enormous,
cyclopean, with a strange barbaric quality heightened by the figures of
oxen which protrude from its towers.   But on closer examination one
realizes the advances made by its builders.   The plan is of rare proportions; the façade is flanked by two strong towers looking down upon a
triple doorway of calm and stately elegance; the light can almost be
felt in this lofty nave which it enters through vast windows.   Laon is
indeed the work of an original architect of first-rate ability; it is at once
the goal of prolonged effort and the herald of future perfection.

Notre-Dame at Paris (1163–1260) is the first in time of four great
masterpieces (the others are Chartres, Rheims, and Amiens), not to
mention all those 'minor' cathedrals which, from Rouen to Bourges,
form as it were a crown of loveliness around the jewel of Notre-Dame.
How different, too, are these marvels one from another!   Paris, begun
in 1163, is solid and reflective, meditative and calm, as befitted the
genius of her kings; no other church, except Chartres, has such an air
of fervour, symbolizing in its strength and sadness the virtue of
Christian hope.   The façade, though severe, is perfectly balanced.
The nave was not particularly well lit until about 1260, when the
transepts were completed with their glorious rose-windows.   Notre-
Dame breathes an atmosphere of serene majesty with its plain cylindrical
pillars, its superb flying buttresses, and a roof that has been justly
compared to 'a ship taking flight.'

Chartres (1194–1260) marks the zenith of gothic architecture.   It
was rebuilt after the destruction of an earlier cathedral by fire, and its
builders made use of all that had been learned from previous experi-
ments at Noyon, Sens, and Paris.   The triforium greatly facilitated the
elevation of the nave, which, together with the side-aisles, is lit by
windows of hitherto unequalled size and consist of twin lancets topped
with a rose.   The effect of height is increased by sheaves of columns
encircling the pillars, while the vaulting rises to 131 feet.   Viewed
from outside, with its sturdy flying buttresses, the exquisite curve of its
choir, the skyward leap of its western towers, and its perfect spire,
Chartres, perhaps more than any other French cathedral, evokes the
spirit of Christian joy and of invincible hope.   As for the interior, no
one has ever managed to convey in words that warm, mysterious
atmosphere created by a union of perfect line with the splendour of
stained glass.

Rheims (1214–1300) may be considered more impressive than
Chartres, with its greater wealth of marvels in the grand style.   Its
flying buttresses seem not intended to support the structure, but to have
been built, so to speak, for amusement; and what a delightful idea to
have topped each pinnacle with a little niche from which an angel is

ready to take wing! Rheims is a wonderful, a glorious cathedral, realizing every potentiality of gothic, but with unfailing good sense. It marks the point of equilibrium beyond which the craving for height, light, and length would endanger the whole structure. The builders did not dare to lessen wall-space as was done at Amiens, Beauvais, and the Sainte-Chapelle. The boldness of Rheims consists not so much in its architecture as in its matchless sculpture; and it enjoyed special prestige as the scene of the French coronation.

The supreme point of audacity was reached at Amiens (1220–70). After that, there was only the experiment at Beauvais, where the builders attempted to carry the vaulting to a height of 157 feet and to make the supports as slender as possible. Their purpose failed; for the choir, which was the only part completed, collapsed in 1284 and the piers had to be doubled. At Amiens the builders respected the laws of equilibrium. The vaulting is about 138 feet high, but the rise of clustered pillars is so imposing that it looks still higher and appears to hang in mid air. Waves of light pour into the church, and the choir consists almost completely of open bays. Outside, the system of flying buttresses is so exactly right that it could scarcely be imagined otherwise. Here it is no longer, as at Chartres, a harmony of form and colour that strikes the eye, but sheer perfection of line. Begun in 1220, Amiens is the last word of gothic architecture, in very truth a 'diagram clothed in beauty.'

This progress, whose milestones are Noyon, Sens, Laon, Paris, Chartres, Rheims, and Amiens, can be traced far beyond the narrow confines of the region which contains those seven masterpieces, though it constitutes hardly a seventh part of France. Side by side with the 'major' cathedrals are a host of 'lesser' but still shining lights. Rouen is remarkable for the balance of its masses, Bourges for its interior height and glass, Le Mans for its examples of transition from roman-esque to gothic. Secondary cathedrals such as Bayeux, Lisieux, Évreux, and Coutances in Normandy have equal richness and charm, while those of Brittany are treasured for their rustic appearance. Many of these 'minor' edifices, too, were modelled on one of the greater buildings. There were 'families' of cathedrals, and one can trace on the map the descendants of Paris or of Rheims with all the exactness of a genealogical tree.

Nevertheless, gothic did not take root everywhere with equal speed and without resistance. In Burgundy romanesque at first held its own against, and then came to terms with, the new style. Farther south there was greater variety of form. The ogival arch was retained, but without flying buttresses; the side-aisles were omitted, as at Angers, or raised to a height equal with that of the central nave, as at Poitiers. Or again, e.g. at Angers, the bays of the nave-vaulting were given a curve almost as deep as that of a cupola. This union of wall and ogive, this compromise, so to speak, between the spirit of romanesque and that of gothic, produced splendid results in which we seem to find once more the majesty of Roman architecture. The rose cathedral of Albi is a masterpiece in this style, which yet produced erratic tendencies outside the true current of art and of its logical development. Perfection, however, remained characteristic of that happy land around which the kingdom of France had grown up and from which the spark of genius had been struck.

7. SCULPTURE, THE DAUGHTER OF ARCHITECTURE

But architecture was not the sole witness to that genius; its energy enlivened other arts, just as a mother guides the footsteps of her children. The first of these children was sculpture, also a technique of wood and stone, and always closely allied with architecture. Sculpture, however, was not so easy to revive; it had to start virtually from scratch. The tide of barbarian invasion had in some measure spared architecture; for men cannot do without houses nor Christians without churches. But the plastic art was looked upon by man as pagan, and had almost completely disappeared. For centuries the West had been incapable of carving a statue in the round; while Eastern influence, as well as that of ivories, reduced the art of relief to appliqué ornament that was not always without a certain charm. In Carolingian times some rather faltering attempts had been made to adorn the capitals of columns with stylistic plants and animals, poor imitations of Byzantine models. The goldsmith's craft was held in great esteem, and repoussé work, in which the relief was obtained by beating a sheet of metal to conform with a previously engraved design, heralded the first medieval bas-reliefs. Reliquary statues, especially in Auvergne, foreshadowed the pending reappearance of carved figures in the round; and shortly after the year 1000 we find a few amateur specimens of sculptured ornament, e.g. the Christ in Majesty surrounded by angels at St Genis des Fontaines at Roussillon.

Relief was henceforward a *sine qua non* of Christian art, sculpture began to flourish, and we might even say that the cathedral itself was bursting into flower. The capital, a remote copy of Corinthian models, added human figures to the geometrical, vegetable, and animal designs; all of which, however, were as yet awkward and half buried in the stone. An event of paramount importance now occurred. Walls, as we have seen, were enormously thick, and doorways were splayed. Architects suddenly conceived the brilliant idea of 'redeeming' these oblique surfaces with an arrangement of stepped pilasters one behind

N

the other, and these pilasters became statues in the shape of living men. The principle was first tried out in Languedoc, Burgundy, and the Île de France; but the pilasters on the Royal Porch at Chartres represent the earliest masterpieces of this wonderful invention.

Sculpture quickly spread to other parts of the building, notably the tympanum, a sector formed by two curvilinear branches and the lintel, which offered a fine surface upon which to depict the great scenes of sacred history. Arch-springs were also decorated, at first with simple geometrical patterns, then with figures taken from life. Romanesque and gothic doorways continued to be treated in this manner until the neo-classical revival. Animal forms were very seldom used to decorate the interior, but capitals were adorned with a variety of plants which gradually became more and more realistic. Sometimes, though not often, sculpture was used to set off an interior arch-spring or the base of a column; Semur-en-Auxois has magnificent examples of this kind. But it is above all on the exterior of Rheims cathedral that purely ornamental sculpture is found in works not accessible to the human eye. Photography, however, has collected the evidence of this labour accomplished for God's glory and for no other purpose.

Nevertheless, romanesque art, which conveys so powerful a sense of vitality, remained strictly subordinate to architecture; the sculptor made no effort at independence, he submitted to the requirements of the building as a whole.[1]   There is not an ornamental detail that is not associated with some architectural item; even what seems at first glance mere exuberance appears on closer scrutiny to have been intentional and conditioned by utility. Every figure in every doorway is carved from the column or pilaster itself; all the statuettes on arch-springs are part of the blocks which they adorn.[2]   That well-known and allegedly naïve 'stiffness' of the porch figures, e.g. at Chartres, was actually intended; their lines had to conform with the rigid parallel lines of the columns from which they were carved.

Where were these statues made? In the edifice itself, after the stones were in place? No. Everything was so carefully planned according to the architect's design, that all blocks were carved beforehand in the masons' sheds; and there is a picturesque window at Chartres showing men thus engaged. Many detailed sketches must have led up to the completed carving, sketches more precise than those found in Villard de Honnecourt's note-book. Each piece was marked so that it could be set in its appointed place: one vertical line, for instance, might indicate the first statue in the porch, two the second, and so on.

---

[1] Cf. Jean Alazard, 'Le sens de l'Équipe dans les chantiers de Cathédrales' in *Revue des deux Mondes*, 1st Nov. 1951.
[2] To remove the cathedral sculpture, the revolutionaries had only one means: since they could not detach them from the stone, they had to smash them with hammers.

Sculpture was therefore the offshoot of architecture in spirit but also in 'technique'; nor can we doubt that this subordination is largely responsible for the strong impression of unity with which the cathedral strikes us.

In course of time, however, a change took place corresponding to the constant progress of art. Sculptors remained obedient to technical demands, but they tended to overstep the previous limitations of their craft. Figures were still carved from the building-blocks, yet seem to be detached therefrom; draperies overflow the strict bounds of architectural lines; figurines in the arch-springs look as if they were attached to the stone rather than carved from it. If this development deprived the monument of some of its formal unity, sculpture gained in freedom, in perfection, and in beauty.

Romanesque sculpture belongs to the great awakening. Not all problems have been resolved, far from it; but life is everywhere present, ready to burst forth. Figures are still uncouth, but they wear the sturdy grace, the powerful charm of youth. Perfectly adapted to the spirit of the building, they represent an art inspired by meditation, by profound and simple faith. For all that, romanesque sculpture is still a decorative art, in which fantastic beasts, unknown plants, and intricate geometrical patterns mingle freely in mysterious harmony. It is the art of Vézelay (1120–34), of Autun and of Charlieu; the art of Moissac (1135) and Beaulieu (1140), in which ease and mystic inspiration seem closely linked; the art of St Benoît-sur-Loire (1095), one of the earliest churches in this style; the art, though with differences due to ancient survivals, of St Trophime and St Gilles, those Provençal jewels. It is also the sumptuous art of Notre-Dame la Grande at Poitiers. But the masterpiece of romanesque sculpture is, beyond doubt, the stupendous Royal Porch at Chartres, which was executed about 1140–60 and is to-day the pride of the gothic cathedral between whose towers it is contained. With forms now immobile as if hesitating, and now in motion as revealed by ruffled draperies, the sculpture of the Royal Porch is characteristic of an art which, though it had not yet achieved full mastery of its medium, was impelled by the purest spiritual motives.

The gothic revolution is no less apparent in sculpture than in architecture. Capitals representing scenes from Holy Scripture, fabulous beasts, and geometric patterns—the whole antiquated vocabulary, so to speak, of romanesque—were more or less abandoned; whatever was retained underwent modification. Sculpture entered into its own and made gigantic strides. Figures in the round covered every available surface, varying in size from a few inches to 13 or 16 feet. Although the progress of sculpture did not always keep pace with that of architecture, it is generally true to say that as each cathedral was built

technical advances were passed on to the next, and each new achievement served as the starting point of further experiment.   Innumerable
masterpieces stand as milestones marking the progress of sculpture
towards maturity; e.g. the statue of St Stephen at Sens, the two groups
on the transepts at Chartres, the few surviving specimens at Notre-
Dame (especially the tympanum devoted to the glory of Mary), and the
magnificent sculpture at Amiens, including the unforgettable 'Beau
Dieu.'   This progress was accomplished in small details: one sculptor
learned how to suggest physical movement; another how to represent a
smile, a bowed head, or a bent knee beneath flowing garments.   Time
and again we are reminded of the fact that it was precisely at the
moment when philosophy set man at the centre of knowledge, making
him the starting-point of its journey towards God, that sculpture
manifested this same humanistic tendency, even striving after individual
likenesses.   The high-water mark of this effort was attained at
Rheims—Rheims of the Virgin and Child and of the smiling Angel—
where art achieved unsurpassed freedom and truth, beyond which
there lay nothing but the risk of mere virtuosity.   Gothic carving,
with its manifold variety, is perhaps the sole European rival of Greek
sculpture in its heyday.   Sacred art never again reached the same level;
Christendom in the thirteenth century gave many a Phidias to the
West.

Medieval builders undoubtedly assigned an important place to
sculpture, but their motive in so doing was not simply aesthetic and
decorative.   A synod held at Arras about 1025 urged the representation on church walls of scenes from Holy Scripture, for 'this
enables illiterate people to learn what books cannot teach them.'   St
Gregory the Great had said the same thing in the sixth century, and
such was the intention of romanesque and gothic artists.

The cathedral has often been compared, especially since the days of
Victor Hugo, to a great stone book from which humbler folk could
learn, to a Bible of images speaking in a tongue that all could understand.   But one may fairly ask how so many people were able to
receive the message, to take an interest in all these details, which are
meaningless for the vast majority of men to-day.

To simplify the understanding of their iconography, artists employed a well-tried system.   Particular classes of persons were almost
invariably represented in the same way.   Saints, for example, were
easily recognized by a circular nimbus placed behind the head; and if
this aureole were stamped with a cross it indicated divinity.   Again,
God, Christ, the Apostles, and the angels were always shown barefooted.   There were also traditional portraits of certain great saints:
St Peter had fuzzy hair and a thick-set beard; St Paul was bald, but with
a long beard.   Furthermore, certain groups were generally placed in

the same position: at Chartres the figures on the north transept (the region of dull light) belonged to the Old Testament, while those of the New Testament were set in the full blaze of the south. In a group of Apostles, the one immediately on our Lord's right was invariably St Peter, on his left St Paul. In the Crucifixion, our Lady stood on the right of the Cross, St John on the left. Lastly, there was a whole series of symbols, so familiar that none could mistake them. Everyone knew, for instance, that an Apostle with keys in his hand was St Peter, the porter of heaven. A naked sword, a spiked wheel, a grid, and other instruments of execution were so many means of designating martyrs who had borne witness to God by dying in such and such a way; while a saint carrying his own head was a hero of Christ who had died by decapitation. The four celebrated living creatures, symbolic of the Evangelists, were equally familiar; and when four persons were represented astride the shoulders of four others, this represented the Evangelists carried by the four great Prophets, for the New Testament rests upon the Old. Thought was clothed in outward form; such was one of the leading ideas of an art in which man saw everything as the sign and symbol of heavenly mysteries.

Now what was the teaching offered by these Bibles in stone? Émile Mâle has shown clearly that it was based, generally speaking, on the great scholastic encyclopaedias, notably the four *Mirrors of the World* by Vincent of Beauvais. It represented, in fact, the whole history of the world and of man, a complete *résumé* of contemporary knowledge. Starting with the Creation, the Temptation, and the Fall, it followed the Old Testament, but with more emphasis upon the deeper and typical sense than upon the narrative and anecdotal element. Next came the series of our Lord's precursors, the Patriarchs and Prophets. There were also scenes of which the symbolical explanation referred to some aspect of dogma or the sacraments. For example, Melchisedech was shown as a priest holding a chalice, while the crossing of the Red Sea was a symbol of baptism, that miraculous water beyond which lies salvation. Finally, Christ Himself appears, and in many forms. On the tympanum of the central doorway we have Christ majestic and terrible, with the glorious light of the Last Judgment spread beneath His feet; Christ of the Gospels, almost every scene from which is depicted in one or other building; Christ of the Resurrection;[1] and Christ of the Ascension rising majestically into the air. Around him is a whole cortège of saints: first Mary, His beloved mother, to whom a

---

[1] The Crucifixion, however, is seldom depicted; it is found only at St Gilles du Gard, at Notre-Dame de Dijon, and, much later, at Rouen, Bayeux, Rheims, and Strasbourg. I am inclined to suggest, though this is only an hypothesis, that medieval artists disliked the idea of representing the Man-God's frightful suffering. This art, so profoundly religious, had a horror of all sentimentality, of all spectacular representation; it carefully avoided any claim to stir up emotion.

whole porch was frequently devoted, then the Apostles and Confessors. All these form an impressive whole consisting of hundreds and sometimes thousands of figures.

But the cathedral spoke to man. Its humanistic sculpture was intended to appeal directly to him, to associate him with the great work. In order to engage and hold his attention, he himself was represented under various aspects. Calendars showed the four seasons, and included the signs of the Zodiac to remind him that time is God's work. The liberal arts of grammar, arithmetic, rhetoric, music, etc., were also displayed in order that man's intelligence might share in all that gives glory to the Creator. Lastly, by presenting a series of easily recognizable characters, the Virtures and Vices, artists provided a whole catechism of moral law. The total result was coherent, varied, and accessible to all; its sole purpose was to lay hold upon man's soul in its most simple reality and raise it to God who is the summit of the spiritual life.

Such was the framework within which both romanesque and gothic sculptors worked. The discipline to which they submitted, so far from paralysing their creative power, rendered it still more free; 'art is born of constraint,' says Gide. Medieval craftsmen had no need to look for a programme and an ideology; they were far removed from the craving of 'modern' art to be original at any cost. Hence they were able, each according to the measure of his gifts, either to copy established models, or to create new forces, or at any rate to produce variations. It is difficult to know what most to admire in the iconography of that happy age, its imposing order or its marvellous diversity.

8. THE PLAY OF COLOUR

Sculpture was not the only art intended to instruct, interest, and move Christian people. The arts of colour played a part likewise, and were of great importance in the religious monuments of the Middle Ages. A leading French architect refers to the time 'when the cathedrals were white'; he meant well, no doubt, but he got his facts wrong! White they never were, even in the days of their pristine glory; nor were they of that sober grey which we have come to venerate as characteristic of the past. On the contrary, they were all brilliance and lustre, both outside and inside, a world in which light played over gold and every tint of the palette; a wonderful casket as it were, of which some notion is still conveyed by many a great altarpiece. Statues and bas-reliefs, too, were painted, or 'upholstered' as the saying was. Why upholstered? It sometimes happened, particularly in the interior of churches, that colour was glued on in sheets to make it adhere more firmly. Upholstering was a specialist job; it wa paid for separately, and often at very high rates. An Armenian visitor, Peter Martyr, who described Notre-Dame as it was in the fifteenth century, saw the cathedral not in its present austere robe of ashen grey, but gorgeous in purple, blue, and gold.

There was even a warm note about the pavement with its tiling of red clay and yellow slips, displaying rosettes, animals, and human beings, or at least some geometrical design whose repetition gave a beautiful effect. Later, towards the end of the thirteenth century, Arab influence resulted in the use of multi-coloured flagstones. But even where builders remained faithful to the old stone paving, patterned inlays of black lead (e.g. the famous Labyrinths already mentioned) lent a note of originality, a touch that broke the monotony of the floor.

During the romanesque period, the vast surfaces of walls and vaulting, rendered necessary by the architectural methods then in use, invited colour and provided a magnificent opportunity for display. The discovery of romanesque fresco-work is of fairly recent date; [1] the first specimens came to light less than a century ago, but its treasures continue to increase our admiration. The term 'fresco,' however, is not always quite exact. Besides painting 'in the fresh' (*al fresco*), where colour mixed with plaster was laid on a freshly prepared background, there was the 'distemper' process in which the coloured pigments were dissolved in water mixed with paste or some other adhesive material, and sometimes with wine to give greater brilliance. These methods of painting became general; while supplanting costly mosaics, they made it possible to cover huge surfaces, as well as to relieve the bare monotony of uniform vaulting and of wall-spaces that had only a few narrow windows.

Many examples of romanesque painting have been found wherever that style of architecture existed. They occur not only in the small sanctuaries of Catalonia, but also at St George of Oberzell (Reichenau), Schwarzheindorff, San Clemente at Rome, and Aquila cathedral; but above all in France where there are numerous specimens in many provinces—St Savin-sur-Gartempe, St Chef in Dauphiné, Tavant, and old Pouzauges. The list grows from year to year. These works, whose delightful archaism is blended curiously with an amazing virtuosity, and whose charm is everywhere so engaging, differ widely among themselves. Some shine with the brilliance of enamel, while others are intentionally subdued, almost monochrome. According to the influences to which artists were subject, some paintings (e.g. in

---

[1] The discovery is mainly due to Prosper Mérimée, the novelist and playwright who was also Inspector General of Historical Monuments. In the course of his duties he discovered the amazing frescoes at Saint-Savin (Vienne). At Paris, the best part of these treasures has been assembled in the form of minutely accurate copies which are housed at the Musée des Monuments français (Trocadéro).

the baptistery at Poitiers) remind us of Gallo-Roman mosaics; others (e.g. those in the cathedral at Puy with their short-haired figures) are reminiscent of Carolingian manuscripts; whereas at Berzé-la-Ville the whole scheme of decoration seems Byzantine. Many such works convey a sort of rustic or popular atmosphere, suggesting purely local inspiration and immemorial tradition. In other cases one senses foreign, erratic influences. At St Julien-de-Brionde, for instance, the olive-skinned, slit-eyed figures and dimly fanciful setting remind one irresistibly of Scythian art, as if some foreign painter had sojourned here, or some native artists had travelled in Asia long ago.

What were the themes of romanesque painting? Mostly the same as those used by the sculptors; they were taken principally from Holy Scripture and catechetical teaching. The colossal vaulting of the nave and porch at St Savin is filled with beautifully balanced scenes from Bible history, the Gospel, and the Apocalypse; at Berzé-la-Ville, Christ is enthroned among His saints; while at Tavant there is a 'psychomachy' or battle of the virtues and vices. The Bible of colour went hand in hand with, and sometimes preceded, the Bible of stone.

Painting occupied a less important place in the gothic age. The almost total disappearance of wall-space, the partitioning of vaulting, and above all the introduction of stained glass, tended to cramp its style. It was retained in the finest buildings, but for purely decorative purposes, using blue, red, and gold as if to outdo its rival glass, as may be seen in Viollet-le-Duc's exact reproductions in the Sainte Chapelle. Nevertheless, painting continued, and on a larger scale than has long been imagined. It is found in small country churches, as at Petit-Querilly, where scenes from the New Testament are painted in the compartments of the vaulting.

But by far the most common means of employing colour in gothic churches was that of glass. It is the glass which endows a cathedral with its vibrant atmosphere and that persuasive element so familiar to all who go to pray therein. Those cathedrals which have no stained glass leave one with an impression of nudity, of sterility, one might almost say of widowhood. One must have seen the sun set through the windows of Chartres to understand the contribution made by a technical discovery to the Christian heritage. A technical discovery? Perhaps not altogether so, for the first attempts at painting on glass may be dated long before the great period of gothic art. The very perfection of the earliest romanesque windows is clear proof that a whole tradition lay behind them; and the eleventh-century monk Theophilus, who wrote a famous *Treatise on Several Arts*, spoke of the French glass-makers as technicians already in possession of a long established craft. The use of coloured glass panels set in lead may have been known during the later Roman Empire. It is said to have survived in the

neighbourhood of Trèves and to have developed about the seventh
century under the influence of cloisonné gold-work and enamels, and
later under that of alabaster plaques hollowed out to receive bits of
coloured glass.   At all events, it was during the eleventh century that
men first sought to fill window-spaces with huge masses of colour, and
from that time stained glass was always associated with Christian
architecture.

It is hardly necessary to recall that a stained-glass window is not a
painting *on* glass; it is a painting made *with fragments of* glass, i.e. a
number of glass pieces assembled to form a whole and held together by
a network of lead.   It was therefore a difficult and subtle art, requiring
the highest technical skill together with outstanding artistic gifts.   It
was also a costly process.   Suger tells us that work on the glass for St
Denis involved throwing precious stones into the molten mass.   He
was clearly yielding to a taste for exaggeration, unless he was trying to
express in poetic language the cost of the windows and their extraordinary brilliance, like that of jewels.   In any case, to make, colour,
and roll the glass, then to cut it with hot iron (diamonds were not used
until the sixteenth century), and finally to mount it according to the
plan of enormous ready-made 'cartoons,' was a formidable task.
Master-craftsmen were at the head of mobile workshops; they moved
with their materials and their assistants from one building-site to
another, halting near forests which supplied them with the necessary
charcoal.   They seem to have been almost independent of the architect's surveillance, far more at any rate than were the sculptors, and
even free from ecclesiastical interference.   They had their own
methods, traditions, and secrets, of which we know little or nothing.

One of the many merits of romanesque, says Raymond Rey,[1] was
that it 'raised the craft of glass-making to the dignity of a monumental
art by subjecting it to the rule of style and formal structure.'   Henceforth the stained-glass window shared the honour of depicting and
interpreting Holy Scripture and the doctrine of the Church.   Who
set this work on foot?   Possibly Suger and his abbey of St Denis, or
the anonymous group of glass-painters at Chartres; we cannot be
certain.   In the church of the Trinity at Vendôme, in that of St Denis
at Jouhet in Indre, in the cathedral at Le Mans, and above all in the
great window of the choir at Poitiers, we can still admire these early
specimens of glass with their simple but deep colours, their figures as
yet stiff but perfectly balanced, and their incomparable brilliance.
The romanesque glass-painters seem to have preferred symbolic, and
then 'story-book,' windows.   These latter were divided into compartments and showed the several scenes from an episode taken from the
Gospel or from the life of a saint.   So large a heap of anecdote can be

[1] *L'Art roman et ses origines*, 1945.

N*

somewhat confusing, and even illegible, when it is set at any great height; but the shimmer of pattern and symbol, the gleam of background and border, lent unparalleled vigour to the sense of purity and the joy of light.   In presence of such windows one is reminded of those rich Persian carpets whose threads are sunbeams.

The gothic period marks the triumph of stained glass.   The technical achievements of architecture practically did away with walls, so that it was natural to devote the whole remaining space to luminous glass.   As the structure moved towards its logical perfection, so glass-painting became gradually more prominent until, in the lofty chamber of the Sainte-Chapelle, it virtually took the place of stone.   The iron braces which held the window in place now blended with the contours of medallions and figures, and this set artists on a new road.   Side by side with 'story-book' lights there appeared others devoted to a single figure and thus far more easily distinguished.   Nave windows received the image of Christ or His Blessed Mother, a row of Prophets or Apostles, a whole population similar to that which mounted guard in the porch.   At Chartres (cathedral of the Virgin 'de la Belle Verrière'), at Bourges, at Tours, and at Angers a vast array of stained glass helped sculpture to delight the eye and teach the mind of its beholders.   And when some unknown genius conceived the idea of setting rose windows high up, for instance, in the façades of the transept, light poured in and the cathedral at length appeared as a visible sign and promise, so to speak, of heaven.

9.   The Cathedral, House of the People and Summary of Medieval Art

A setting of this kind, so far removed from human dwelling places, could not but attract the faithful and fill their hearts with joy.   It was never empty.   The cathedral was the mother-church, where people flocked on great feast-days from every parish in the city.   The splendour of glass and sculpture, the stately pomp of liturgy, were there in plenty, for both rich and poor.   No charge was made for seats; there were no seats.   On winter days, of course, it must have been terribly cold, for no heating was provided.   Those who could afford to do so brought a footwarmer, or a hot-water bottle like the one sketched by Villard de Honnecourt, who designed it so that My Lord Bishop might 'fearlessly attend high mass.'

The cathedral, then, was in very truth the 'house of the people'; not in the lay and derogatory sense which some have given the phrase, as if the cathedral were a mere secular building, but simply as a place where men and women liked to forgather.   It is perfectly true that it was used from the beginning as a common-room, 'town parlour,' commercial exchange, and for many other purposes. That was eminently reasonable. Since there was no suitable hall of equal size, why not borrow it from God? Precisely because he was a Christian, medieval man was not frightened of God. He took liberties with Him, and with His house, that would horrify the twentieth century. Only the great ceremonies at St Peter's in Rome, with their enormous crowds acclaiming the Pope as he is borne in on the *sedia gestatoria*, can give the least idea of what a cathedral was like in the great days of the Middle Ages. One can no longer witness those scenes which were so familiar at places of pilgrimage—at Chartres, for instance, where good folk enjoyed a snack in the church or slept on the ground, 'making a night of it' as the old documents say.

As the people's house, the cathedral was ever at their disposal in all sorts of ways. One aspect revealed itself to none but learned men, who, being thoroughly acquainted with Scripture and theology, were able to interpret its symbols. But there was another simple, familiar, and popular aspect which gave confidence to the humblest. The same forms clothed in beauty, from which the learned derived lofty spiritual instruction, touched the hearts of simple folk by speaking to them of faith, hope, and love. They were all the more sensible of this language in that many of its elements were drawn from their own lives and were therefore close to their own thoughts. We have already mentioned 'calendars' in which the son of the soil saw himself engaged in his daily task, vine-dressing or reaping, warming himself at the hearth, or killing a pig. The flora and fauna displayed at innumerable points of the building consisted of everyday plants and animals, though mingled with a few freaks to amuse and rouse one's curiosity. The virtues and vices depicted as players in a comedy were no less striking. How the congregation must have smiled to see Cowardice, represented by a handsome but timid knight, fleeing from a hare; or Discord illustrated by a quarrel between a husband and his spouse, with the lady's distaff and her husband's tankard flying through the air! Here and there also were small bas-reliefs, carved as mere workshop pranks. The famous Booksellers' Porch at Rouen contains a whole series of them: a goose examining a urinal, a sow playing a hurdy-gurdy, etc. Laughter is the sign-manual of the human race, and the Church was too human to be scandalized thereby. Since everything centred upon the cathedral, she thought it only right that entertainment should not be overlooked.

We do not always appreciate the influence which contact with the cathedral must have exercised upon Christian folk. It is not in vain that a man, or a whole people, lives amid beauty; something penetrates into his soul, something that will stand up to vulgarity and dishonour. While providing men with moral and religious instruction, the cathedral also gave them the most relevant lessons in aesthetics.   An incomparable place of prayer, it was also a museum in which all forms of art were brought together.

Everything in the cathedral was made with an eye to beauty. Great attention was paid to the liturgical furnishings, and the wooden carving in the choir-stalls was hardly less elaborate than the stone sculpture of the façade.   At the end of the period, the 'Jubé,' a sort of bridge thrown across the nave at the entry to the choir, afforded an opportunity for some magnificent work.   Some of these structures are still in place; those at the priory of Bourget du Lac in Savoy and at Wechschburg between Leipzig and Chemnitz are sheer marvels.   The lateral aisles of Notre-Dame at Paris and at Bourget, together with a few fragments preserved in various museums, are perfect specimens of their kind.   The altar was simple, sometimes slightly ornamented on the front with some delicate piece of sculpture; but behind the sacrificial table hung curtains of material in correct liturgical colours according to the feast.   From the thirteenth century onwards, curtains were superseded by a sculptured and painted altar-piece, bright with gold.   This was the retable which became popular in the fourteenth century.   Finally, on the altar and the cantor's desk there lay open richly decorated missals and psalters.

Wandering through the nave, there was much to admire.   The tombs, for example, of bishops, lords, and ladies, the sight of which was no cause for sadness because death was represented as peaceful, the certainty of union with God.   Some of these tombs told the whole story of those whose mortal remains lay beneath, showing their years, their labours, and their daily occupations.   The tomb of an abbot of Aubazine in Corrèze showed the whole community, including the lay-brother who tended sheep.   More often the scene depicted was that of the funeral together with some religious subject, e.g. the Crucifixion, Last Judgment, or Coronation of Mary.

Many future art-forms—painting, jewellery, glass-work, and enamelling—owed their existence to the cathedral, to the unanimous longing of that age to put beauty at the service of God.   Enamelling had been popular in Carolingian days, and became most important in the twelfth century.   The chief centre was Limoges, whose workshops turned out astonishingly beautiful reliquaries, crosses, trinket boxes, plaques for bookbinding, caskets, and plain ornamental panels.   Even Byzantine mosaic was not more brilliant than the turquoise and lapis-lazuli blues, the purples and reds of this material which has lasted for centuries and still delights us with its unfading brightness.

On great feast days, the whole length of the nave was hung from pillar to pillar with huge and magnificent tapestries, whose heavy texture and deep colours blended admirably with both the stonework

and the glass. This art became increasingly popular from the beginning of the twelfth century (when the Bayeux Tapestry was made) and
helped to provide religious instruction with its scenes from Scripture
or the Lives of the Saints. Sens, Angers, Strasbourg, and the Chaise-
Dieu still provide us with specimens that enable us to appreciate the
original beauty of these furnishings with their few but perfect colours
and their invariably noble composition.

But all these things must not be considered as static, fixed, like so
many museum-pieces. All the arts fostered by the cathedral shared in
the living body of the liturgy, drawing sustenance from the Christian
sap that rose from the thousand invisible roots of the building. Indeed,
the cathedral found full expression only on great occasions. Such
were a Pontifical High Mass, the wedding or funeral of some important
personage, and, above all, the coronation, when Mother Church, as it
were, hallowed the mystic espousals of a king with a Christian nation.
A natural offshoot of the liturgy was the liturgical drama.[1] Starting
in the cathedral, it eventually moved out into the porch and marked the
rebirth of the theatre as a popular amusement and means of self-expres-
sion. Thus, in addition to many other achievements, the cathedral
was the first to organize entertainment.

Finally, the Church made use of music to perfect her spiritual
climate. The principles of Gregorian chant were laid down by St
Gregory the Great early in the seventh century. At Saint-Gall,
about the year 900, a monk-musician and poet, Notker the Stammerer,
had introduced the 'sequence,' a song based on the vocalization of the
'Alleluia.' Next, perhaps at St Martial at Limoges, composers added
the 'trope' which was suited to all parts of the sung Mass. Music
formed part of the *quadrivium* in universities, and was held in very
high esteem. It was the subject of treatises by eminent authorities,
among whom was the celebrated Guido d'Arezzo.[2] Polyphonic or
'measured' chant, for two and three voices, was introduced at Cluny
by Peter the Venerable early in the twelfth century, and was developed
during the thirteenth. St Bernard, however, condemned it as effemin-
ate and not conducive to piety. Rome, too, was of his opinion, and
plain-chant or 'Gregorian' remained the standard of Church music;
it was a perfect match for the organ, and endowed the ceremonies with
that strange sonority, now joyful, now poignant, which is still familiar.
No one has rendered finer homage to its serene, transcendent beauty

[1] Concerning which Émile Mâle has shown that it influenced the sculpture of the
cathedral by suggesting typical scenes.
[2] He is known to have invented the stave, or rather the ingenious mnemonic which
makes it possible to designate the notes. This mnemonic is taken from the hymn of St
John the Baptist, the half-lines of which begin with notes in ascending progression: *ut*
queant laxis / *re*sonare fibris / *mi*ra gestorum / *fa*muli tuorum / *sol*ve polluti / *la*bii reatum /
*Sancte Io*annes /.

than Mozart. 'I would,' he said, 'give all my work to have written the *Preface* of the Gregorian mass.'

Such was the cathedral in its heyday, on festivals when a whole population shared in the joy represented by its soaring vault, when a whole Christian people saw itself reflected in all that was most pure and most beautiful therein. Rodin thought to emulate the old sculptors with his *Porte d'Enfer*; but one day, glancing through some photographs of Chartres, he exclaimed: 'We are mere triflers!'

10. The Spread of Gothic

It need scarcely be said that gothic art was not confined to France; so great a fire could not but spread. The days have passed when romantic adorers of the ogival style proclaimed Cologne as its pattern and masterpiece. Cologne, so they maintained, was a stone copy of the teeming German forest. Others preferred the Duomo at Milan. Such opinions may still be found in the works of Michelet, and even of Montalembert, but they are out of date. To-day not even the most chauvinistic archaeologist denies the fruitful influence of French art on Germanic architecture, and, though less directly, upon English, Spanish, and Italian.

There is abundant evidence to show the presence of French architects on many foreign building-sites. We have already noticed Villard de Honnecourt in Hungary and William of Sens in England. At Wimfen-en-Thal, a document of 1268 refers to an architect who had come from Paris to build '*more francigeno,*' in the French style. Geoffrey of Noyon worked at Lincoln, Peter Fitzpiers at Toledo, Mathew of Anas at Prague, and Master Humbert at Colmar. When the Emperor Frederick II, a great devotee of the arts as well as of literature, wished to build or to restore a church, he would take no step before consulting Philip Chinard. His successor in Sicily, Charles of Anjou, invited another Frenchman, Peter of Angicourt, to visit the island. But these names are a mere handful compared with those we should like to know. Who were the French architects whose skill we admire at so many cross-roads in Greece and in the East? Who was the architect-monk who built what is undoubtedly the finest of all Cistercian naves, at Alcobaça in Portugal, about 1149? What is true of architecture applies also to sculpture; French stonemasons were in demand throughout Christendom. Traces of the Chartres sculptors have been discovered on the façade of Orvieto cathedral. The Swedish archives still contain a record of Stephen Bonneuil's arrival at Upsala in 1287; he travelled with a whole team of masons on a visit financed by Swedish students at Paris.

When French gothic left the borders of its native land, it naturally underwent certain modifications, compromising with local influences and sometimes employing materials other than stone. Imperial Germany was the principal beneficiary; it contains whole families of churches whose mother, or at least grandmother, was French. Limburg on the Lahn, for instance, is descended from Laon. Notre-Dame at Trèves, with its trefoil choir, was the first completely gothic church in Germany (1240–60), and derives from French models. The choir of Cologne was inspired by that of Amiens. French sculpture was so highly esteemed in imperial territory that traces of it are found everywhere. Looking at the statuary of Naumberg or Bamberg, one might imagine oneself at Rheims; that of Strasburg (whose nave is also sister to Amiens) irresistibly suggests the masterpieces of Chartres or Rheims. But notwithstanding its French origins, the Germanic cathedral retained its own peculiarities for better and for worse; it often gives an impression of being more the result of systematic determination than of creative impulse. Exact, logical, mathematical, rather than spontaneous, its very strength has an element of instability recalling the vagaries of imperial politics. Nevertheless, whether at Cologne, Strasburg, Friburg-im-Brisgau, or Ulm, one cannot but admire the soaring height, the bold proportions, the noble shape of towers and steeples.

The history of English gothic is somewhat different. So far from rejecting the ogive, England discovered it at the same time as, if not before, France; but she thought of it from another angle. Romanesque influences continued much longer than in France; they are apparent in 'Early English,' which was born at Durham. The new style was introduced here about 1250 and remained for some while distinctly French, e.g. at Canterbury, Chichester, Westminster, and Lincoln. Then it quickly took on special characteristics: triple lancet windows and sharply pointed arcades, as at Wells, Salisbury, and Exeter, lent it undeniable originality. However, the old Celtic love of curves and counter-curves did its best to associate with the demands of gothic mathematics. The 'Perpendicular' and 'Ornate' or curvilinear style found expression in an amazing outburst of superabundant decoration: the lines of the façade completely disappeared under a profusion of columns, blind arcades, and statues; the plan of the vaulting was concealed; and the vast window-bays of the original gothic were broken up into innumerable pools of light. It was an art of richness and almost excessive elaboration, which none the less produced some exquisite masterpieces such as Lichfield, which was known as 'Lady Cathedral.'

The Iberian Peninsula also yielded to this temptation of exuberance, but not in the same way. Just as she called in French military aid for the campaigns of the Reconquista, so Spain and Portugal invited

French architects to build churches in the territory recovered from Islam. First, the Cistercians introduced the ogive, not only at Alcobaça, but also at Poblet, Santa Cruz, and Las Huelgas. Then gothic cathedrals began to rise at Zamora, Salamanca, Barcelona, Leon, Burgos, Toledo, and Seville. In the newly established kingdom of Portugal, Lisbon, Oporto, Evora, and Faro in the south were obviously inspired by Paris or Bourges, Chartres or Rheims, and even Albi or Coutances, at any rate so far as the essential framework of the structure was concerned. The decoration, however, changed. True, French influence is apparent, for example, at St James of Compostella, where the 'Porch of Glory,' designed by a certain 'Master Mathew' (a Frenchman, no doubt), equalled its greatest rivals at Paris and Amiens; but the main trend was otherwise. For one thing, German and Arab influences were at work. There was a tendency to accentuate the play of light and shadow by making the sculpture stand right out from the stonework as if cast in metal; while monstrous animals, tangled bodies, and geometrical patterns swarmed over the walls. All this was very far removed from the original style, and ended by smothering architectural lines under a mass of ornament. Cathedrals such as Burgos and Toledo may disconcert a visitor who has come straight from Chartres or the Sainte-Chapelle; but no one can deny their strange and penetrating charm.

11. THE ITALIAN EXCEPTION AND THE GLORY OF GIOTTO

Italy was the one exception to the spread of gothic, an exception of capital importance since it was to influence the whole future. Italy, it is true, played her part in the great movement which, during the twelfth and thirteenth centuries, led Christendom to cover her land with churches. A violent earthquake in 1117, added to the constant peril of fire, was one of the determining factors in the Italian architectural movement. Wealthy cities such as Pisa, Genoa, Siena, Florence, Milan, Parma, and Bologna were glad of an opportunity to build for God; but they did so according to their own genius, trying at once to assert their powerful individuality and yet remain faithful to more ancient traditions, to an Italy that had once been mistress of the world and had not yet fallen prey to the bloody rivalries of Guelph and Ghibelline.

There was, however, a certain amount of gothic in Italy. French Cistercians introduced their sober architecture at Chiaravalle, Fossanuova, Casamari, and San Galgano;[1] and when the newly established mendicant Orders found themselves obliged to build numerous

---

[1] These four abbeys, built between 1171 and 1218, were sisters of Clairvaux and Fontfroide.

churches, they borrowed much from the primitive and austere gothic of Cîteaux. The double church at Assisi (1228–53), erected by Brother Elias in honour of St Francis, which now contains the Poverello's tomb, has gothic vaulting, but in the style of south-west France; it ignores the mathematics of flying-buttresses, which were at first omitted altogether. There were many Italian churches of this kind, where the ogival vaulting was allied with huge wall-surfaces, and where, so far from admitting light into the nave, the builders seem purposely to have shut it out. The great cathedrals built by wealthy cities, so austere and so restrained, were constructed on similar lines. They willingly adopted the gothic plan, which was more elaborate than that of the ancient and primitive basilica, and also the ogival roof; but the spirit of the building was altered. A mixture of colour in the abundant use of marble, as well as carving on the façade, which reminds one of casket-work, gave it an entirely different appearance. The cathedrals of Siena (1221), Orvieto (1290), and Florence (1296) have a majestic beauty comparable with that of their French contemporaries; but one feels as though one were in another climate.[1]

The fact is that these buildings are true to the land, to racial characteristics, to a whole long stretch of history. Another indication of this is the endurance of romanesque in Italy throughout the period when gothic naves were rising beyond the Alps; for example, San Lorenzo fuori le Mura at Rome is contemporary with Rouen. Lombard-romanesque compromised with the gothic colonnades, tending to crouch rather than to soar. At the very time when Notre-Dame was in process of construction, Pisa finished her Duomo and began the Campanile and Baptistery. Nothing illustrates more forcibly the difference between France and Italy than a comparison of these two monuments. The dome (cupola) modelled upon that of the Pantheon at Rome rather than on Byzantine types, appeared later on similar baptisteries. Poised by Brunelleschi on the crossing of the naves at Florence as the very sign and symbol of Heaven's vault, the dome is so essential a part of the edifice that in Italian the whole cathedral is named after it, *Il Duomo*.

Italian sculpture likewise gives evidence of this loyalty to tradition, of this same determination to open up a new path while making use of past experience. French influence there undoubtedly was, and French stonemasons very likely worked on Italian sites, but their influence was not decisive. The masters to whom Italian masons looked were partly Byzantine, but chiefly those anonymous Roman artists who had made sarcophagi. At the height of the thirteenth century, when the sculptors of Chartres and Rheims were acknowledged as teachers by

---

[1] Milan cathedral dates from the end of the fourteenth century, but its exuberance and astonishing richness make it the masterpiece of Italian gothic.

the rest of the world, the ancient bas-reliefs on Roman sarcophagi were studied by Niccolò Pisano (*d.* 1278). From them he learned to carve those amazing groups of crowded, ungainly figures which are yet full of life and seem, as it were, the outcome of some dramatic striving. But Italian sculpture did more than just develop its own aesthetic; it applied itself to parts of the cathedral to which artists had paid scant attention. The pulpit assumed extraordinary dimensions, almost like a small theatre, with projecting ambos, a profusion of lecterns supported by lions or eagles, and balustrades resembling embattlements. The whole thing was covered with bas- and high-reliefs of inexhaustible richness: Prophets and Apostles, Doctors and Evangelists, not to mention Angels and Devils, mingled with all the denizens of bestiary and herbal. Splendid examples of such pulpits may be seen in Siena cathedral, in the Baptistery and Duomo at Pisa, in the church at Orta, and in San Andrea at Pistoia. Next, the door itself (as distinct from the portal so dear to French artists) was wonderfully decorated. Here, it may be, the Italian sculptors were obeying some immemorial tradition, some mysterious discipline; for since biblical times 'the door' had always had a symbolic sense, and its opening signified the approach of God. The use of heavy ornamental door-leaves was derived from Byzantium, from the venerable Roman basilica of Santa Sabina, from Salerno, and from Hildesheim. They were decorated, so to speak, with whole chapters in bronze. And when the hour of the Renaissance struck, Andrea da Pisa and Ghiberti gave sublime shape to this tradition in those glorious doors at Florence which Michelangelo described as the 'Gates of Paradise.'

In consequence, Italian religious art was endowed with profoundly original characteristics, and a kind of bridge was established between ancient forms and those which the Renaissance was later to develop. This twofold nature was to become less pronounced in architecture and sculpture than in painting, a field in which Italy was to reign supreme. The permanence of romanesque, and the peculiar orientation of gothic in the peninsula, resulted in the nave continuing to possess enormous wall-surfaces. The fresco, which French gothic ousted in favour of stained glass, had therefore no reason to disappear. In a country where strong light does not call for abnormally large window-openings, mural painting thus continued on its way or, rather, took a new direction.

Italian mural painting begins with ancient models, looking back with Cimabue (1240–1301) not only to such masterpieces of Byzantine mosaic as those at Ravenna, but also to specimens which were then in process of installation at Venice and in Sicily, the two points of Italy's contact with the East.[1] With Cavallini (1250–1316) it looked back

[1] See Chapter X, section 6.

also to the Rome of Constantine. Thus early Italian romanesque frescoes of the traditional schools were the parents of later French examples, which, however, were perhaps more spontaneous and had more local variety.

But the beginning of the thirteenth century witnessed an event of the first importance: a man arose, a poet and a saint, who taught his contemporaries to love the life of nature, and who proclaimed, as none had done before him, the brotherhood of Christian hearts. His outlook was largely due to the influence of St Francis of Assisi; in him the Poverello's very soul laid hold upon all the resources of Romano-Byzantine technique to produce a genius. Such was the miracle of Giotto (1266–1337).

The truly unique level which this Florentine painter was to occupy in the history of Western art has been summed up in three lines of Dante:

> Credette Cimabue nella pittura
> tener lo campo, e ora ha Giotto il grido
> Che la forma colui obscura.

His appearance eclipsed the slavish imitators of ikons, and thereby set art upon the road to realism which it has never since wholly abandoned. 'To the abstract symbols of a vehement and rigid hagiography there succeeded concrete images of immediate experience, elementary and strong as the things they represent: shepherds, sheep, trees, rocks, the blue sky, the familiar world of a small herdsman, such as it is by nature and eternally when genius crystallizes it in the permanence of style.' [1] Before the intensity of his compositions one feels indeed that a new world was opened to mankind. Giotto stands alone; none of his contemporaries approach him, neither Simone Martini, nor Taddeo Gaddi, nor the Lorenzetti, nor even Orcagna, exquisite and pathetic as they can sometimes be. Giotto by himself may be considered no less important than the French sculptors who had rediscovered the secret of living form. Painting is his gift to us.

The very essence of genius is to be sought in the mystery of its appearance. What was the secret of the little Tuscan shepherd who used to pass the time engraving on a stone the outlines of his sheep, and who was accidentally discovered by Cimabue? Of course, he had outstanding gifts which drew immediate attention and on account of which he was invited at different times to Rome, Sicily, Padua, Rimini, Naples, Ravenna, and perhaps even beyond the confines of Italy, to the papal residence at Avignon. It is likewise clear that his versatility was equal to that of the greatest artists; he turned out not only mural paintings, but also studio pieces, e.g. crucifixes and altar-pictures, with

[1] Jean Leymarie.

astonishing regularity.   But he must have had something else besides.
No man can produce the greatest dramatic poem in paint, or give the
most beautiful symbols living form, without depth of soul and an
ardent craving for God.   Giotto, who has been represented as gay,
fond of the flesh-pots, a swiller of Chianti, and a master of repartee, bore
constantly in his soul the same mystic yearning which his contemporary
Dante interpreted in dramatic form.   The spiritual son of St Francis,
he expressed this yearning through hope and love.

Apart from a few isolated panels, viz. a crucifix at Padua, one at
Santa Maria Novella at Florence, the Madonna of the Offices, and the
Dormition of the Virgin at Berlin, only three of his compositions have
survived: the strikingly youthful Franciscan cycle at Assisi; the Life
of Christ and the Virgin in the Arena Chapel at Padua, the masterpiece
of his maturity; and the later groups at Santa Croce in Florence, with
their broader and more austere classicism.   Not all these immense
series have the same emotional power, and yet there is no scene in which
we cannot discern the deep faith and simplicity of heart that are characteristic of a true Christian.   At Assisi the 'Miracle of the Spring'
and the 'Preaching to the Birds' seem so perfectly in keeping with the
spirit of Il Poverello that one can almost feel the living presence of the
saint.   At the Arena our Lord's figure in the 'Resurrection of
Lazarus' radiates such supernatural vitality and splendour that one can
scarcely imagine a finer representation of the Man-God in His triumph
over death; while in the tragic scene of the 'Kiss of Judas' there is
revealed the whole wretchedness of man, an anguish caused by the
certainty of his fault and the weight of his disloyalty.

Thus, as the great days of the Middle Ages were about to close,
Christian genius, incarnate in a little Tuscan shepherd, gathered up its
most valuable heritage.   'The consciousness of the divine in human
nature,' the religion of God Incarnate, which had been served so
devotedly by the cathedral architects and stonemasons, proclaimed
itself under other forms but with no less compelling truth.   Later,
when art had turned aside from its path, such painters as Fra Angelico,
Signorelli, and Michelangelo, all of them more or less remote descendants of Giotto, would still bear witness to that consciousness and that
religion.

CHAPTER X

THE DECLINE OF SCHISMATIC BYZANTIUM

1. THE MORROW OF THE SCHISM

WHILE the West erected its memorial to one of the most prolific civilizations in all history, the East afforded a very different spectacle. Not that Byzantium bore no resemblance to her former self, as heir to the glories of Theodosius and Justinian, as the bastion whose walls and legal code had withstood the tide of barbarism, as the economic, spiritual, and political centre of the Mediterranean world. By the middle of the eleventh century, however, though she had many claims to respect and admiration, that vast Empire which the Macedonian dynasty had governed with so firm a hand no longer seemed responsive to an inward urge. The great ship continued on her course, shaken by one storm after another; but the past alone could not guarantee her future.

A portentous doom weighed heavily upon Byzantium, the schism of 1054. That misunderstanding, which had developed in the course of centuries between two halves of the Church, had many causes. First, there was a difference in rites and observances, more rigid and uniform in the East, more subject to variety in the West. Next, there were theological differences the importance of which was exaggerated by both camps. One of these had been provoked by the Western introduction of the *Filioque* clause into the Creed; another was the unwillingness of the Patriarch of Constantinople to recognize the primacy of the Roman See, mainly because he alone counted in the East since the territory of the other patriarchates had been completely or partially overrun by Moslem invasion. Lastly, the refined and scholarly Byzantines despised the uncouth westerners.

One man's ambition had brought about the rupture: Michael Caerularius, Patriarch of Constantinople. Abnormally intelligent, and possessed of subtlety that masked a will of steel, this man, who in his youth had hoped to don the purple slippers of the Basileus, was at length admitted to Holy Orders and transferred his ambitious dreams to the ecclesiastical plane. He longed to be sole head of a Church free from all control, with his jurisdiction covering every diocese of the East; and to attain his goal he had not hesitated to employ underhand dexterity, perfidy, and even violence. Insisting on what appeared to divide Christians one from another, describing the slightest differences of expression as heresy, and condemning as scandalous such innocent customs as that of shaving the beard, he had laboured with great skill to sow tares among the two parts of Christendom.   The West, and chiefly the Holy See, had unwisely overlooked the fact that not only did the patriarch desire a rupture, but that every inopportune exercise of authority played into his hands.   Rome had precipitated the crisis by sending as legates to Byzantium Cardinal Humbert and Frederick of Lorraine, two rough-and-ready characters who knew nothing of oriental subtlety.   Astuteness and cunning were opposed to abruptness and heavy-handed blundering under the disillusioned eye of the Emperor Constantine IX Monomachus, who cared more for literature and feminine charms than for theological dispute.   When Cardinal Humbert, thinking to break Caerularius, laid the Bull of excommunication on the high altar at Santa Sophia (16th July 1054), he had ensured the patriarch's victory.   Taking advantage of the indignation called forth by this gesture, Caerularius rallied almost the entire East, from the Basileus to the humblest workman, against barbarian and heretical Rome which had insulted the princes of the Holy Byzantine Church on their own doorstep; and on 24th July an oriental synod promulgated a series of canons which sealed the rupture.

But this rupture was not altogether fatal.   There were certainly profound differences between the Greeks and Latins, whose susceptibilities had been aroused.   Nor did the spiritual and moral outlook of the West coincide with the symbolical and eschatological attitude of the East.   But the two parts of Christendom were still united by links forged over a period of thirty generations.   At the beginning of the eleventh century there had even been signs of mutual understanding, for the twofold menace of the Normans and the Turks, increased popularity of pilgrimages to the Holy Land, and a better appreciation in the West of oriental spirituality had all helped the cause of unity. Constantine IX had entertained nothing but respect and goodwill towards the Roman pontiff.   What, then, brought about the conflict? Here we must recognize one of those instances, more frequent than is sometimes imagined, in which the personality and intentions of a single man are of decisive weight and can change the course of history.

Caerularius appeared to suffer here on earth a supernatural chastisement; though involved in the plot which brought Isaac Comnenus to power, he was soon embroiled with the Basileus.   Arrested on the latter's order, and slandered by every hack-writer in the sovereign's pay, he died of the brutal treatment meted out to him.   The oriental Church forthwith canonized him in recognition of his fight for independence.   None of all this, however, is of any consequence; the Seamless Robe was already rent, and nine centuries of devoted effort have so far failed to remedy a situation that no Christian can ignore, a situation for which the responsibility cannot be said to rest wholly on one side or the other, but whose weight Christ's brethren collectively must bear.

Looking back on the event, we recognize its dramatic character; what was the contemporary reaction? Did men realize the tragic and disastrous nature of the rift? Whatever Michael Caerularius may have intended, the very idea of schism horrified many believing souls. It is hard to read without emotion the letter written by Peter, the holy Patriarch of Antioch, to his colleague at Constantinople: 'I beg you,' he says, 'I beg and implore your Divine Beatitude, kneeling in spirit at your sacred knees, to yield under this blow and bow to circumstance. I tremble lest, while you endeavour to sew up the wound, it may turn to something worse, to schism; lest while you try to raise up what has been smitten down, a worse fall may be in store. Consider the obvious result of all this, I mean the yawning gulf that must ultimately separate from our holy Church that magnanimous and apostolic see; life henceforward will be filled with wickedness, and the whole world overturned. If the two queens of the earth are at loggerheads, then alas! abundant sorrow will reign everywhere; our armies will nowhere again be victorious.'

Peter of Antioch's noble and prophetic words were echoed by other prominent figures at a later date. George the Hagiorite declared before the Emperor Constantine Ducas, in 1064, that the Latin faith was not in error, since the use of fermented bread had been rendered necessary in order to prove to certain stray sheep that our Lord's Body was endowed with soul and reason, symbolized respectively by the yeast and salt mixed with the flour. John II, Metropolitan of Kiev, agreed that the false practices of which the Occidentals were accused did not affect dogma. Theophylact, Archbishop of Ochrida in Bulgaria, expressly stated, in his treatise *On the Errors of the Latins*, that these 'errors' could not possibly justify a schism; he sternly criticized the proud pretensions of Eastern theologians, and asserted that the root of the difference lay chiefly in personal and racial hatreds.

But along with these moderate opinions, unjust and extravagant views were put forward. The gulf of schism was deepened, as if purposely, by malevolence and stupidity. There were, at Byzantium, theologians and others who, since they were unable to understand the West and had no wish to do so, continued the work of Michael Caerularius, heaping up unfounded calumnies. It suffices to glance through any one of the innumerable treatises published at that time to appreciate the weakness and often the abject meanness of these accusations. The complaints voiced in one such pamphlet are no less than twenty-eight! The six major 'errors,' borrowed from the argument of Photius, concern azymes (i.e. the use of leavened or unleavened bread—a grave matter), the Procession of the Holy Ghost, confirmation administered separately from baptism, infractions of the lenten and Saturday fasts, and, finally, the celibacy of priests. But to these fundamental objections pamphleteers were driven by the same indignation to add a hotch-potch of others. They assured their readers that Latin priests behaved unbecomingly at divine office; that they were actually so lewd as to shave their beards; that the celebrant approached the altar with covered head (an absolutely scandalous business); that the faithful made the sign of the cross with five fingers, whereas everyone knew it should be done with only three; and lastly, that deceased bishops lay in state in their coffins with unjoined hands! It was upon such trashy grounds that the East henceforward judged the West.

Nevertheless, while these libels were propagated, the historical fact of schism does not seem to have been fully grasped. Among Byzantine historians, neither John Scylitzes, nor Michael of Attalia, nor even that great scholar Michael Psellos (who distinguished himself by first acting as public prosecutor in the case of Caerularius and then as his official panegyrist) refer to schism in so many words. We have to wait more than 150 years before a chronicler speaks of 'the conflicts which arose between the Patriarch Michael and the Latins.' This failure looks very much like a conspiracy of silence. It may perhaps be explained on the grounds that Orientals had long been used to theological quarrels and felt certain this was only one more, one no more important than the rest; but it is still more surprising to discover that the situation remained obscure even in the West. Cardinal Humbert drew up a report in which he boldly claimed to have vanquished the Patriarch, and allowed it to be understood that the imperial wind had blown from the right quarter. In the twelfth century, Cardinal Boso affirmed with the utmost simplicity that 'the business on which the legates went to Constantinople terminated amicably.' One might almost be dreaming! The illusion was not dissipated until later, when the situation appeared in its true light as a terrible disaster.

In practice, the schism did not altogether suspend relations between East and West. The commercial movement, which was going from strength to strength, brought Italian merchants to Byzantium; traders from Genoa and Amalfi established themselves on the Golden Horn, and were followed by Venetians as soon as the imperial Golden Bull of 1082 had opened all Byzantine ports to vessels of the Most Serene Republic free of customs dues. Very many westerners took service with the Basileus as mercenary soldiers, especially Germans, Englishmen, and, of course, Normans. These latter, among them Roussel de Bailleul, to whom we shall return, always thirsted for adventure in foreign lands. There were also numerous marriages between reigning families who belonged to different churches. Yaroslav the Wise, King of Kiev, was grandfather to most of the crowned heads of Europe; uncle to Philip I of Poland and Olaf III of Norway; father-in-law to Gytha, daughter of Harold of England, to Solomon of Hungary, and to Henry IV of Germany; while his great-grand-daughters were married to the sovereigns of Denmark and Norway. Seeking reconciliation with the Normans, the Basileus Michael VII married his son to a daughter of Robert Guiscard; and when Andronicus ascended the throne following the assassination of Alexius II, he straightway took to wife little Anne of France, daughter of Louis VII, who had been betrothed to his predecessor. The memory of these dynastic relations between East and West was preserved by the Capetian monarchs; for the Gospel-book used in the coronation service at Rheims had been brought to France by Queen Anne at the time of her marriage with Henri I, and the Christian name Philip, originally Byzantine, remained in the French royal family until modern times.

Even in the religious domain, some contacts survived the schism. Pilgrimage to the Holy Land included a halt at Constantinople to venerate, among a host of relics, the Shroud and Tunic, together with the veil and girdle of our Lady. Some churches of the Roman rite remained open in the capital, where there was even a Cluniac house known as La Charité. Moreover, certain Latins heard the call of the 'Great Mountain' and went to found a monastery on Athos under the special protection of the Basileus. Conversely, the Orientals were represented in the West by the best of all ambassadors, the saints. We need only recall the transfer of St Anthony's relics to the banks of the Rhône, or those of St Mamas to Langres, which was afterwards so proud of them. Among innumerable Byzantine monks who visited Monte Cassino or Rome for devotional reasons was good St Nicholas. He journeyed through the whole of Italy, carrying a wooden cross and crying 'Kyrie eleison!' before dying in 1094 at Trani on the Adriatic. He was canonized by the Western Church soon after his death.

Nevertheless, disagreement between East and West steadily increased. There was mutual suspicion, latent hostility, contempt, jealousy, and lack of understanding. Byzantium, however, suffered most from this rift. At a time when faith underlay every aspect of life, schism could not but entail consequences on the political plane. It destroyed all possibility of solid agreement between the Byzantine Empire and the newborn kingdoms of the West. This was all the more harmful inasmuch as Byzantium, at a moment when her vitals were secretly devoured by decadence, was obliged to resume her role as bastion of Europe against the marching hordes of Asia, a role which she had upheld for centuries but which henceforward she could not sustain alone.

2. BYZANTIUM IN THE GRIP OF FEUDAL ANARCHY

The period immediately following the schism was among the worst in Byzantine history. Many of the emperors, who followed one another in quick succession—there were thirteen within the space of forty years—ended their reigns with a hurried abdication, if not under torture and execution. Meanwhile, home politics went from bad to worse, imperilling the existence of the empire. The ambitions of the military aristocracy had long been evident, and the feudal process was no less apparent in the East than in the West. War-lords and heads of administration had only one desire, and that was to become legal owners of the territory entrusted to their care. The Macedonian emperors had been strong enough to oppose them; but their successors gave way, and there was rebellion, civil war, and anarchy.

For twenty-five years these vainglorious nobles were all-powerful. Having distinguished themselves on the field of battle, they intended to profit by their exploits. Such, for example, were Phocas, Comnenus, Scleros, Diogenes, Botaniates, Ducas; and they were joined by mercenary adventurers who had taken service with Byzantium. All of them found adherents on the plains of Anatolia, cosmopolitan bands of warriors fanatically devoted to their leaders, ready for anything provided they were well paid. Jealous of one another to the point of internecine strife, and sufficiently disloyal to compromise with an outside enemy in order to attain their ends, these war-lords fought over the prostrate empire until it was at the mercy of invaders.

What could the emperors do to stem the flood? With the excepception of two, Isaac Comnenus and Romanus Diogenes, who remained true soldiers on the throne, all followed the absurd policy initiated by Basil II of systematically weakening the army. Power was in the hands of a clique of palace eunuchs, philosophers, and theologians, of whom the least that can be said is that they were too weak to govern the state in such dangerous circumstances. One of their leading members was Michael Psellos, a former tax-collector who became first a doctor of philosophy, then preceptor and counsellor of emperors. These mandarins sought to undermine the soldiery, to withhold military supplies, and to disarm the fleet. Since the nobility appeared dangerous, it was proposed to supplant them with a hierarchy of officials, all of whom, even the emperor himself, would be appointed on the basis of examinations!

The warriors had recourse to arms, and for a whole quarter of a century there was an endless succession of revolts, seditions, and *pronunciamentos*. Every troop-leader felt the urge to carve out a handsome fief from which he could defy the basileus. Some of them

became heroes of exciting and picaresque epics.   The most curious of
these was Roussel de Bailleul, a Norman who had accompanied Robert
Guiscard to Sicily, and afterwards took service with the Byzantine
emperor.   He then turned traitor, negotiated with the Turks, and set
to work in his own interests, robbing Moslems and Christians alike.
Failing to take Constantinople, he was captured a first time, set free in
return for an enormous 'gratuity,' and allied himself with the worst of
the Turkish marauders, who ultimately betrayed him and turned him
over to his adversary.   His career was characteristic of that age.

Amid this confusion, a procession of emperors filed through the
Sacred Palace.   Not all of them were incapable; several of them had
intelligence and courage, but not the superhuman energy necessary to
break the turbulent ambitions of so many.   Constantine IX Monomachus, who died worn out in 1054, was followed by Michael VI
(1056–7), an aged madman, whose fame rests on a decree obliging all
his subjects to wear red hair.   Overthrown by a sedition, he promptly
had his head shaved and fled to a monastery to avoid a worse fate.   His
conqueror, Isaac Comnenus (1057–9), the first member of that
illustrious family to wear the purple, was a fine soldier and might have
re-established order; it was he, in fact, who freed the state from the
intrigues of the Patriarch Caerularius.   But police-work of this kind
was disagreeable to his mystic and neurasthenic soul, so that he too
disappeared into a monastery.   His friend Constantine X Ducas
(1059–67) was a literary type; he worked against the army and had the
good luck to die without seeing the consequences of his frenzied anti-
militarism.   But his successor Romanus IV Diogenes, another fine
soldier whom Constantine's widow had hurriedly espoused for the
sake of protection, paid dearly for his predecessor's insane policy.
He boldly assumed command of the army against the Turks, but was
defeated and taken prisoner at Mantzikert.   Henceforward the plunge
towards disaster became more rapid.   Michael VII (1071–8) disgraced
himself by subjecting his father-in-law to atrocious torments and at
once resumed the anti-militarist policy.   Meanwhile, however, on
every frontier, enemies were tearing from Byzantium shreds of living
flesh; for it was at this time that Roussel de Bailleul and many others
like him were making havoc in all four corners of the stricken empire.
In 1078 a general revolt of the army broke out, and Michael VII was
deprived both of his throne and of his wife by one of his greedy
warriors, Nicephorus III Botaniates (1078–81).   But the situation was
such that this brave soldier could do nothing to reform the army and
restore order to the state.   Sedition grew more frequent, and when the
most brilliant of the Anatolian generals, Alexius Comnenus, marched
on Constantinople, Botaniates also fled—into a monastery.   Alexius
was a strong, intelligent, and able man, resolved to drag his country

from the bloody filth in which she wallowed. It was high time; from the four cardinal points innumerable enemies were already on the march, those enemies which weak states invariably call forth.

3. ENEMIES FROM THE NORTH AND EAST: THE TURKS

For fifty years Byzantium had been a beleaguered place, obliged to keep constant watch upon her walls. Since the death of the last great 'Macedonian,' Basil II, whose terrible victories had won him the surname of 'Bulgaroctonos,' the manifold threat had not ceased to grow on every frontier. In 1025 the empire still included the Balkans as far as the Danube and the Drave, southern Italy, Syria, the whole of Anatolia, and Caucasian Armenia. What was left sixty years later? Look at the map opposite.

In the north the Bulgarians, having been crushed by Basil, had for some while remained calm; but other adversaries had taken their place in the everlasting assault of hungry steppes upon more fertile lands. Most restless of all were the Petchenegs, a Turkish people occupying territory north-west of the Black Sea between modern Rumania and the southern Veraine. About 1049 the officials at Constantinople had attempted to settle them in Thrace, but they had quickly resumed their depredations. Isaac Comnenus almost managed to subdue them; but the task was superhuman, and was further complicated by the help given to these enemies by the Paulician and Bogomilian heretics,[1] who had taken refuge in the mountains. And their forces were always increasing. Under Constantine Ducas there appeared a hitherto unknown variety of barbarians, the Uzes, a vast horde of about 600,000 souls, who overran the Balkan peninsula from north to south. Unable to conquer these savages, the emperors tried to enrol them in the Byzantine armies; but their doubtful loyalty made them more dangerous than useful, as Romanus Diogenes learned to his cost. The Uzes and Petchenegs were a suitable reservoir of manpower in the hands of rebellious generals; in 1078 they threatened the outskirts of the capital, which only managed to avoid the peril by loading them with gold.

These hammer-blows at the very gates of the fortress-city naturally encouraged others to pour through the breach and share the loot. The Hungarians had been Christian since the time of St Stephen (1000–1038), and had hitherto maintained friendly relations with Byzantium. In 1059, however, they allied themselves with the Petchenegs and launched an attack which was repulsed by Isaac Comnenus. They resumed hostilities during the reign of Constantine X, and took Belgrade in 1064. The Serbs, who had for long served as mercenaries

[1] For the Paulicians and Bogomils, see Chapter XIII, section 4.

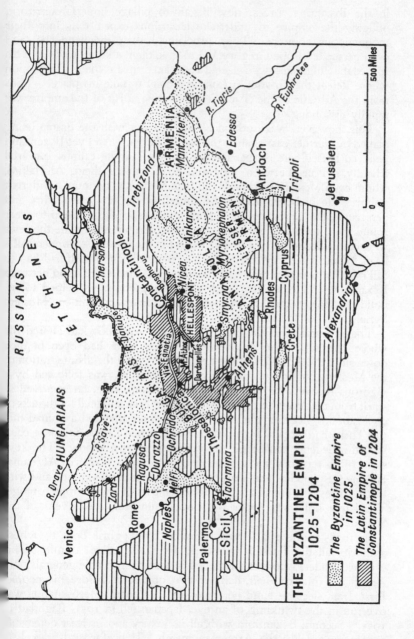

THE BYZANTINE EMPIRE
1025–1204

- :::: The Byzantine Empire in 1025
- ///// The Latin Empire of Constantinople in 1204

RUSSIANS

PETCHENEGS

HUNGARIANS

R. Drave

R. Save

Venice

Rome

Naples

Melfi

Palermo

Sicily

Taormina

Zara

Ragusa

Durazzo

Ochrida

SERBIANS

BULGARIANS

Via Egnatia

Thessalonica

Thessaly

Athens

M. Athos

Dardanelles

HELLESPONT

BOSPHORUS

Constantinople

Chersonese

Trebizond

Nicea

Ankara

Myriokephalon

Smyrna

Rhodes

Crete

Cyprus

ARMENIA

Mantziker

R. Tigris

R. Euphrates

Edessa

Antioch

Tripoli

Jerusalem

Alexandria

LESSER ARMENIA

R. Danube

R. Vardar

500 Miles

in the Byzantine forces, now began to pillage imperial territory, obliging the empire to undertake hazardous expeditions into their mountainous country. They proclaimed their independence, and even persuaded Pope Gregory VII to give them a king (1076). This roused the Bulgarians, who elected a Serbian prince as their 'Czar,' upon whose defeat they invited a Lombard chief to take his place. Thus from the Adriatic to the Black Sea the whole north of the empire was rapidly dissolving.

This, however, was nothing by comparison with the drama being played out farther east against the Seljuk Turks. And yet Byzantium believed herself safe in that quarter. The Fatimite caliphs appeared friendly. True, between 1009 and 1020, one of them, Al-Hakim, whom even Moslem historians call 'the Mad,' had adopted a different policy. He had demolished the church of the Holy Sepulchre and persecuted the Christians in all sorts of ways, obliging them to wear round their necks a copper cross weighing ten pounds, while the Jews were compelled to carry a similar weight in the form of a wooden calf's head. But this frenzy had not lasted; the madman himself had had to call it off for fear of reprisals. Relations were therefore good between Byzantium and Islam, so much so that the emperors helped to rebuild the Holy Sepulchre and sent corn to relieve a famine in Moslem Syria.

The appearance of the Turks about the year 1000 had altered the whole outlook. The decadence in which Islam had been bogged down since the Abbasids of the tenth century, and the disintegration of the Moslem Empire among provincial dynasties, was followed by a vigorous recovery headed by a young military race, far removed in spirit from the Arabs and Persians, who had been softened by the arts of civilization. Leaving the Aral steppes, where they led a nomad life, the Turks had already begun their march when Prince Seljuk, a chief haloed in legend, took their destiny into his own hands. The key stone of his territory was a quadrilaterial formed by Siberia, Afghanistan, the Caspian Sea, and Turkestan. His men, dull-skinned and with black, slit eyes, were strong, thick-set fellows of tremendous courage. The latent holy war broke out once again with the advent of the Seljuks.

In 1038–40 the attack was launched by Toghril Beg, to whose authority all the Turkish tribes had been obliged to submit. This excellent leader, who was succeeded in turn by two able generals, Alp Arslan and Malikh Shah, had set two objectives before his people. First, Iran, sleeping amid her roses and her poets: Mesopotamia was overrun in the twinkling of an eye, Ispahan fell in 1051, Baghdad in 1055. Second, Byzantium with all its luxury and its least defensible provinces, notably the Armenian march. Henceforward scarcely year passed without the Basileis having to ward off the blows of their indefatigable enemy.

The history of this struggle for the Middle East was marked by two great dramatic incidents, both of which left a deep impression on contemporary minds. In 1064 Christian Armenia collapsed. Had Byzantium done all she could to protect that distant but crucial bastion? Had there not been secret mistrust between the monophysite Armenians and the Byzantines who had harassed them over the question of a single nature in Christ? At all events, the ancient capital of Ani fell; a massacre followed, and the silver cross surmounting the dome of the cathedral was cut down for use as the threshold of a mosque. The majority of Armenians took refuge in Cappadocia and the foot-hills of Taurus, where they founded a new Armenia which will feature in the story of the crusades. Their fatherland was nothing more than a battle-field drenched in blood.

The other great act of the tragedy was the battle of Mantzikert (1071), where Romanus Diogenes met with catastrophe. A resolute leader, he tried to reconstitute his armies with Uze and Petcheneg mercenaries and Norman volunteers. For three years fortune seemed to smile on him: he carried out a number of successful operations east of Antioch and beyond Cappadocia, though without being able to prevent the enemy raiding as far as Iconium near the sea. In 1070 the Turks laid siege to Mantzikert north of Lake Van, one of the last Armenian cities still in Byzantine hands, and Romanus Diogenes hurried to the rescue. The action took place on 19th August 1071. Outmanoeuvred by the Turks, who pretended to withdraw in order to lure him into a prearranged trap, deserted during the battle by the Uzes and Petchenegs, who, as Asiatics, were unwilling to fight against their kindred, abandoned also, it may be, by Roussel de Bailleul, the unfortunate Emperor put up a heroic defence with a handful of his faithful subjects. In vain; he was taken prisoner by the Turks, but they had been so impressed by his courage that they treated him with the utmost respect.

Mantzikert is an all-important date, but one to which few Western historians refer. This Byzantine defeat had grave significance; it proved that the eastern empire was no longer capable of acting as the bastion of Christendom, a role which it had once been her glory to sustain. It was therefore necessary for the younger spirit of the West to carry arms to the threatened frontiers of the East. The rout of the Byzantine forces was answered by the crusades: 1095 was in the womb of 1071, and the vanquished Romanus Diogenes called to Godfrey de Bouillon.

As it happened, there was immediate recourse to the West. Michael II humbled himself so far as to ask Gregory VII for troops, and the

Pope replied by directing an appeal to the European sovereigns; but the embarrassment in which Christendom found herself, owing to the conflict between the papacy and Henry IV, rendered his appeal completely ineffective. Nevertheless, this episode foreshadowed the crusade.

By their victory at Mantzikert the Turks had gained direct access to the West, and they derived further advantage from growing dissension among the Byzantine leaders. Thrusting forward in all directions, they had nothing to do but exploit their successes, and in 1076 they entered Jerusalem. By 1078 they had occupied most of Asia Minor, with the result that their possessions were so intermingled with those of the Byzantines that they did in fact control the whole country. Moreover, Nicephorus Botaniates, convinced that money could do everything, dreamed of taking their regiments into his own pay. He established them on the Hellespont, on the Bosphorus, on the Propontis, at Nicea, at Nicomedia, and at Chalcedon. When, in 1081, Alexius Comnenus began his policy of restoration, Soliman the Turk, who was in theory his vassal, refused to recognize his authority and proclaimed himself independent. Nicea thereby became the first capital of the future Seljuk sultanate, which was to last until 1302. *Quos vult perdere* . . .

4. ENEMIES IN THE WEST AND SOUTH: THE NORMANS

The Turks, alas! were not the only peril. While the Basileis turned a blind eye to the Nordic hosts whom they still hoped to domesticate, the South and West produced another foe who would not be subdued. The Normans, those terrible pirates who had spread terror throughout the West during the ninth and tenth centuries, were again seeking fertile territory in which to settle as they had done in Normandy in 911. Their habit was to attack ill-defended regions, phrase which admirably described the rich lands of Apulia in Byzantine Italy.

While the Norsemen were still no more than pirates, the Mediterranean had not escaped their depredations; they had sacked Arles, Valence, and Nîmes, using the Île de Camargue as a depot for arms and booty. The Italian peninsula had also suffered from their raids, and chroniclers have preserved an amusing though surely mythical story concerning one of their chiefs. In order to gain entry into a town near Pisa, he pretended to be dead; the good citizens opened their gates to his coffin, from which he suddenly emerged, fully armed and grasping a battle-axe. However, Viking raids had been less frequent in the Mediterranean than elsewhere, because the Moslem fleet based on Andalusia kept watch upon the Straits of Gibraltar. If the Norman managed to obtain a foothold in Italy it was by methods similar to that of the Trojan horse, though somewhat different from the guile of Hastings.

Italy was torn with civil strife, and numerous military leaders were in need of troops. Since the country itself showed no enthusiasm to provide them, they invited mercenaries. The Normans liked nothing better than warfare, as one of their songs openly admitted: 'Our sole reason for being on earth is to pillage property and kill men.' Besides, they were proficient soldiers, as bold on land as at sea, able to mount cavalry raids on hundreds of places within reach of their headquarters, cunning tacticians, and hardy shock-troops. When the use of stirrups was adopted by the Normans in north-west France (c. 950), heavy-armed knights, sitting firmly in their saddles and riding in close order, had begun to play the same part in battle against infantry and light horse as is assigned to tanks in modern warfare. Norman armoured brigades could therefore do themselves justice in the pay of an Italian duke or count.

They were first employed in 1028 by some Lombard princes, and their superiority was such that a leader of ten men long passed as a kind of general. In 1029 the Duke of Naples rewarded a Norman soldier, one Rainulf, by giving him the city and lands of Aversa—a splendid example to other long-toothed pirates. Thenceforward, every Norman corporal dreamed of conquering Italian territory and setting himself up as a baron. Though feared and hated, the Normans intruded everywhere, simply because they were indispensable. The Byzantine civil service, the princes of Salerno and Capua, the city of Naples, even the popes and the abbots of Monte Cassino, all invoked their aid. Throughout the Cotentin and Pays d'Ouche, in every stronghold and in every necessitous household owing fealty to the Duke of Normandy, tales were told of brothers or cousins who had made their fortunes at the lance-point way down in the sunny lands. There was also a sentimental link between southern Italy and Normandy. It was believed that during the sixth century the Archangel Michael had appeared to some shepherds on Monte Gargano and left a red cloak as proof of his visit. Two hundred years later the relics of this sacred object had been brought by St Aubert to Norman Brittany, and deposited at Mont Saint Michel, where they were still preserved. So many excellent reasons could not but attract a current of emigration from Normandy to Italy, where a crowd of sturdy youths, with nothing on earth but their valour and taste for adventure, had nothing to lose and everything to gain. About 1030 the situation in the south was as follows. The whole of Sicily was in Moslem hands; Byzantium governed the 'theme of Langobardia' (Calabria together with the territories of Otranto and Apulia) through an official known as the

Catapan, and exercised nominal suzerainty over the three commercial republics of Gaeta, Naples, and Amalfi on the west coast, and the three Lombard principalities of Benevento, Capua, and Salerno. Within twenty-five years this situation had completely changed. The Macedonian basileis had taken arms against Saracen pirates in the eastern Mediterranean, and one such expedition, in 1036, had included three hundred Norman mercenaries under the Prince of Salerno. Among these were three brothers, William, Onfroy, and Dreux, whose courage soon passed into legend. Sons of Tancred de Hauteville, a small landowner in the Cotentin, they had found it impossible to eke out a livelihood on the paternal fief, and set out to seek their fortune.

A great future lay in store for the Hautevilles. Their story is an epic romance, lurid, abounding in rough feats of arms and entertaining pranks; but it is dominated by the ambition of these 'lads from Coutances,' as Jerome and John Tharaud are pleased to call them. Nothing is lacking, not even the most charming love affairs. There is beauty and poetry as well; for these terrible fellows might be described as Nordic Apollos, with clear brows, eyes of liquid moonstone, and blond as Wagnerian heros. But Byzantium had no worse enemy.

William (surnamed 'Iron-arm') and his brothers soon tired of serving the wily Greeks, who were always ready to betray their friends and give short measure when it came to pay. They decided to strike out on their own. In less than five years the Byzantines were driven from Apulia, and only just managed to retain their hold on a few ports, e.g. Bari and Trani, and the toe of Italy. William distributed the rest among his brothers and nephews, until southern Italy had been partitioned among a dozen ferocious Normans, not to mention a crowd of lesser vultures who seized an abbey here, a small district there.

It was at this juncture that there appeared a man, in many ways a genius, who was to inspire his countrymen with ambition on the grand scale. Robert Guiscard, another son of Tancred de Hauteville, began life as a brigand chief and raised himself to become founder of an empire. He was a stronger character than the other three, a first-rate soldier, and an outstanding politician. This magnificent creature was described by his contemporary, the Princess Anna Commena, who saw him after he had passed his sixtieth year, as 'taller than the tallest warriors, fresh-complexioned, fair-haired, broad-shouldered, bright-eyed, and so well proportioned from head to foot that he was a perfect model of beauty.' Surnamed 'le Guiscard,' the cunning, Robert at first received a cold welcome from his brothers; family feeling among the Hautevilles never took precedence of personal interests. But he quickly managed to carve out a small domain which was, to tell the truth, no more than a haunt of brigands. A fortunate marriage in 105 enabled him to cut a somewhat better figure, and from that time he never looked back.

Robert was assisted by the Pope, at first unintentionally. St Leo IX, while trying to halt the Norman advance, was taken prisoner by Guiscard, who was at that time allied with one of his compatriots, Richard of Aversa. The Sovereign Pontiff was treated with every mark of respect, but was obliged to recognize the rights of the pirates over such territory as was then in their hands. After the death of his brothers, in 1059, Robert became Duke of Apulia, and was already a person of consequence when Nicholas II decided to alter his system of alliances. Urged by Cardinal Hildebrand, the Pope sought to protect himself on the south while he confronted the Emperor.[1] He was disgusted with the Byzantines, who had just broken away from Rome, and invited Guiscard to become his protégé. At the Council of Melfi, in 1059—a memorable date for the Normans—Nicholas invested Richard of Aversa with the principality of Capua, and Robert with the duchy of Apulia, thereby conferring official dignity upon these one-time rascals.

Byzantium paid the price of their good fortune, and from 1060 onwards hardly a month went by without Guiscard making an attack upon what remained of imperial territory in the peninsula. War between the Normans and Byzantines lasted for twelve years. Gisolf, Prince of Salerno,[2] was driven from that city after a six months' siege [3] without receiving the least assistance from his protector Michael VII. The Basileus had cause to regret his failure, for it was soon his turn to be despoiled. The fall of Bari in 1071, after a siege lasting three years, followed by that of Brindisi, sounded the death-knell of Byzantine rule in Italy.

A new power of unlimited ambition was now established in the Mediterranean. While they were still engaged settling accounts with Byzantium, the indefatigable Normans found time, between 1060 and 1072, to take Sicily from the Moslems. This campaign started under the leadership of Roger, the last of the 'lads from Coutances,' who had been called in as a mercenary by an incautious emir at loggerheads with one of his colleagues. After some brilliant successes, the hot-headed

---

[1] See Chapter V, section 3.

[2] Guiscard had married Gisolf's daughter as his second wife.

[3] The capture of Salerno was the occasion of a pleasing episode in keeping with the manners of medieval warrior society. Here is how Jean Béraud-Villars describes it: Guiscard, by threats of horrible torture, deprived his brother-in-law of all his goods: gold, gems, precious objects, and even relics. The Prince of Salerno kept in his treasury a tooth of St Matthew which Guiscard specially coveted. He demanded its surrender, but the Lombard, who was passionately devoted to this talisman, had a Jew's tooth dragged out and presented it to his conqueror. But Robert saw through the trick and had Gisolf informed that unless he handed over the genuine tooth of the Apostle, he would have all his own teeth drawn next day. Gisolf did as requested.'

young man had tried to kick against the tutelage of his terrible brother; but he was defeated and obliged to stand down. The conquest of Sicily was resumed under the direction and for the benefit of Guiscard. It was completed by the fall of Palermo in 1072, and the Normans began that strange chapter of history during which, amid the beauty of gardens and of fountains, they accomplished a fascinating synthesis of all the elements of civilization left in that island by Greece, Rome, Byzantium, and Islam.

Based firmly upon southern Italy and Sicily, gazing from afar with mingled envy, admiration, and contempt upon Byzantium ablaze with wealth and glory, Guiscard had measured her real weakness.[1]   He, the son of a beggarly noble from Coutances, dreamed of an oriental empire; had not his daughter Helen been betrothed to the son of Michael Ducas? In 1081 he was preparing to realize his dream by force of arms when, at long last, a great man appeared on the Byzantine throne.

5. THE AGE OF THE COMNENI

When Alexius, the true founder of the Comnenian dynasty, assumed control of the empire, the situation was fraught with peril. Eastward, beyond the Bosphorus, the population of the capital could see the Turkish tents of camel-hair. Westward, the Normans were disembarking on the Adriatic seaboard, at the starting-point of the old Roman Via Egnatia, along which they had decided to march on Thessalonica and Byzantium. The Emperor's daughter Anna, in her historical poem *Alexiad*, tells us that 'he saw his kingdom in agony and on the point of death.' But Alexius was a magnificent soldier, of legendary courage, as well as a highly skilled and cunning diplomat. He was tall and handsome, capable of inspiring love no less than fear. Conqueror of Roussel de Bailleul, whom he had led captive before his master Michael Ducas and been rewarded with honours and the

---

[1] The fate of the Greek Church in southern Italy and Sicily raised a difficult question and contributed to the separation of East and West. Since the eighth century, Byzantine prelates and monks had laboured to propagate their liturgy, their calendar, their language, and their psalmody. Moslem occupation had undone all their efforts in Sicily, but oriental worship remained firmly established in Calabria at the time of the Norman conquest. Without waiting for instructions from their new masters, Basilian religious presumed to reopen their convents; St Bartholomew (1050–1133) and St Chremes were both canonized by the Latin Church. Their foundations were generously endowed. But the Normans imposed Roman jurisdiction; as vassals of the Holy See since 1059, they naturally chose all the metropolitans and a majority of bishops from the clergy of the Roman rite. The Byzantines were embittered. Their attitude may be judged from the case of Basil of Reggio. Duly enthroned by the Patriarch of Constantinople and no less duly expelled by the Normans, he was understandably dissatisfied with his uncomfortable position. He compromised himself by corresponding with the antipope Clement III, and after eleven years, disappointed by the Council of Melfi (1089), asked the Patriarch to transfer him to an uncontested see.

Emperor's own daughter in marriage, Alexius had reached the throne by way of adultery, conspiracy, and sedition—no new road.   Falling in love with the Basilissa, Mary of Alania, whose fascinating charms are still renowned, he had escaped the wrath of the old Emperor, put himself at the head of the Thracian troops, and deposed him.   His long reign (1081–1118) called a halt to the anarchy which for twenty-five years had been driving Byzantium headlong towards the abyss.

Alexius Comnenus faced up to the manifold danger with wonderful energy.   That from the West was most dangerous; so he negotiated a truce with Soliman, and even provided him with mercenaries.   Then he turned to deal with Guiscard who, considering himself a kinsman of Ducas by reason of the marriage between his daughter and the de-throned emperor's son, spoke of establishing himself in the capital. Some clever diplomatic moves preceded more vigorous operations. An enormous offering of 144,000 gold pieces gave the German Emperor to understand that he would do well to prevent Guiscard from overrunning Italy.   The Venetians hated the Normans, and agreed to employ their vessels against those of the Duke of Apulia; but like good business men they first obtained, as price of their inter-vention, the astounding privilege of buying and selling anywhere in the empire without payment of customs.   This was the starting point of the Republic's enormous wealth.   But it was all in vain.   Guis-card's armoured cavalry overthrew the Byzantine forces before Durazzo (October 1081), and Alexius escaped the massacre only by hiding among the rocks.   The way to the capital lay open, and the worst was expected, when Henry IV descended upon Italy, partly to settle accounts with Gregory VII, partly to assist Alexius, and obliged Guiscard to return.   While the Norman, in a frenzy of rage, was pil-laging the Eternal City, Comnenus was able to renew the struggle against Robert's eldest son, Bohemond, who was thrusting eastwards, wearing him down and exhausting his reserves until he lost heart and abandoned the expedition.   Guiscard's death, on 15th July 1085, put an end for the time being to the Norman peril.

But just then another danger reared its head: the Petchenegs were again marching from the north.   Assisted by heretical Greeks, Bulgarians, or Serbs, and allied with a Turkish corsair named Tzachas, they struck terror into the empire.   The winter of 1090–1 seemed to mark the end of Byzantium.   Then, quite suddenly, Alexius solved the problem.   For each barbarian a barbarian and a half!   His money and promises of booty launched the Polovtsi, or Cumans, from the Russian steppe against the Petchenegs.   The result was butchery; these ferocious hordes, who were 'defending civilization,' massacred with savage joy.   'Wonderful sight!' cries Anna Comnena, 'a whole nation exterminated with their women and children!'

Nevertheless, in his extreme anxiety, Alexius is said to have taken a new step heavy with consequences. Western chroniclers assert that he wrote to a French nobleman, Robert of Flanders, who had been his guest on the way back from the Holy Land, asking him to return with some knights to help the East. The authenticity of this letter has been strongly denied, but the intention was there beyond a doubt. It was a foolish move: why proclaim the weakness of a distant empire of whose riches the West already dreamed? At all events, the Emperor's letter, whether genuine or not, was one of the factors that brought about the crusades. About 1095, having got rid of the Petchenegs and the Normans, Alexius hoped to restore order in his realms; but the crusaders were already at the gate.

We shall have more to say [1] about the passage of this first crusade through the Byzantine empire: the amazing skill with which Alexius held its ravages in check; how he obtained from the crusaders an oath of vassalage for all the lands they might reconquer; and how he made war on Bohemond, Prince of Antioch, who had won himself too powerful a fief. This man of iron fought to the bitter end, subduing the Cumans, his former allies, attempting to roll back the Turks towards the interior of the Anatolian plateau, and even doing his best to curtail the exorbitant privileges of Italian merchants. When he died, he might well have been proud of his achievement: order had been re-established at home, the army and navy had been reformed, while the enemy stood at a respectful distance on the frontiers. Anna, his daughter and historiographer, did not exaggerate when she compared him to the heroes of Greek epic.

It so happened that the next two emperors who followed Alexius, his son John II Comnenus (1118–43) and his grandson Manuel Comnenus (1143–80), were able to exploit the advantages of his success against the forces of disintegration. And, strange to say, each of them succeeded quite peacefully to the throne.

John carried on his father's policy in every detail. This swarthy little man with jet-black eyes contrasts pleasantly with other emperors of the period. He was a remarkably fine soldier, brave to the point of rashness, but he was also modest and reserved, opposed to luxury, and thoroughly human. His efforts extended to every frontier. In the north, he attacked the Petchenegs on their own ground; they ceased to be a menace, and his victory was commemorated for generations with an annual feast. His diplomacy sought to ensure the presence of reliable ambassadors at the Serbian court. The Hungarians, who made bold to attack the empire, though the Empress herself was of their race, were beaten; and on the death of Stephen IV, in 1131, it was John Comnenus who appointed his successor.

[1] Chapter XI, section 3.

He was less successful against the Venetians, whose insolent claims he endeavoured to resist; his fleet was unable to prevent the Doge's vessels from taking Corfu, Chios, and Rhodes.   In the east, he confronted both the Turks, from whom he took several places on the Black Sea, and the Christian princes of Cilicia, who defied his authority and whose defeat was followed by John's triumphal entry into Antioch. Lastly, turning towards the west, he was filled with mounting wrath at the immense prestige enjoyed by Roger II (1101–54), a refined and subtle monarch who, as heir of his father Roger and his uncle Robert, had united southern Italy and Sicily, and who, taking advantage of the difficulties in which the Church found herself owing to the schism of Anacletus,[1] assumed the royal crown in 1130.   In order to prevent the Norman joining an alliance against him, John II not only reached an understanding with the German Emperors Lothair and Conrad III, but actually made a secret agreement with Roger's own subjects.   He may have been contemplating direct action when he was killed in a hunting accident (1143) at the age of fifty-five.

John II's policy, then, was the same as his father's.   The only thing for which he can be blamed is that he so weakened the Christian princes of Cilicia that a year after his death (1144) the Moslems were able to take Edessa.   This event, which resulted in the second crusade, was to have painful consequences for his son Manuel.   The new Emperor, a brave soldier whose stature and swarthy complexion made a deep impression on his people, had to face a difficult situation.   His great qualities unfortunately went hand in hand with a tendency to excess, which blinded him to the true state of his resources.   He appeared at first to adopt the policy of his father and grandfather.   He married — without much enthusiasm, says the chronicle—Conrad III's sister-in-law, the buxom Bertha of Sulzbach, 'whose solid charm depended solely on her shining virtue.'   In order to prevent Roger II making Corfu a permanent base for hostilities against Greece, he renewed his ties with Venice by a series of commercial agreements.   When the crusaders arrived in his territory, he showed extraordinary cunning, amounting perhaps to felony,[2] by dispatching them post haste into Anatolia, where the Turks lay in wait.   His principal mistake, however, was to believe that as soon as Roger II died he could regain a foothold in Italy and dominate the whole peninsula as his remote predecessors had done. He was wrong.   William I of Sicily (1154–66), busy though he was with his harem and building schemes, was not the man to be caught napping, as Manuel learned to his cost.   The Basileus attacked Ancona; whereupon a fleet of 140 Norman galleys descended upon Constantinople, acclaimed their leader under the very walls of the

[1] See the passage dealing with the Schism of Anacletus in Chapter III, section 7.
[2] See Chapter XI, section 5.

capital, and directed a hail of arrows through the palace windows. Manuel's ambition ended by embroiling him with the Venetians, who wanted him as their friend only so long as he was at a distance; it brought him into collision with Frederick Barbarossa, who had the same designs upon Italy as himself; and lastly, it caused him to neglect his eastern frontier. He had no difficulty in dealing with Renaud de Châtillon, Prince of Antioch, who broke his vassal's oath and was forced to beg pardon barefooted. But when the Turks resumed hostilities in 1176, the imperial army was cut to pieces in the defiles of Phrygia at Myriokephalon, and Asia Minor was lost for ever.

On Manuel's death, in 1180, the West had already been pacified by the Treaty of Venice between the Pope, the Emperor, and the Italian cities. It began to seem as though a decisive intervention in the East would be necessary; the stage was set for the drama of Constantinople and its fall to the crusaders.

Ruin was fast approaching. Events were precipitated by the minority of a twelve-year-old Basileus, Alexius II, and the regency of his mother, the beautiful and much-sought-after Empress Mary, as well as by the intrigues of numerous courtiers and officials of Western origin. A Kurdish leader named Saladin was in process of consolidating the Islamic Near-East preparatory to swooping on the Holy Land. In the south-west, William II of Sicily (1166–89), whom Manuel had offended by breaking off the engagement of his daughter with that prince, had resolved to be avenged upon the empire. Less than thirty years old, well educated, and highly civilized, he had the reputation of a first-class warrior. Moreover, at about this time there were terrible outbreaks of xenophobia in Constantinople. The mob, led by a gang of howling monks, massacred the Latins, burned their houses, and pillaged their goods; the papal legate, Cardinal John, had his head cut off and tied to a dog's tail. Meanwhile, a strong man who combined the qualities of a clever adventurer with those of a wild beast seized power, had Manuel's lovely widow strangled, and publicly trampled underfoot the corpse of his young nephew Alexius. Thus did Andronicus (1183–5), the last of the Comneni, inaugurate his reign.

The life of this man might have been taken from a history of the Italian Renaissance. Athletic, magnificent, looking little more than a youth at sixty, a tireless warrior, and a still more tireless lover of beauty in all its several manifestations, this twelfth-century Caesar Borgia combined the highest gifts with almost unimaginable wickedness. Within the space of two years Constantinople witnessed a splendid revival, but was also the scene of daily executions aggravated by tortures which cannot be set down. Andronicus hated the Latins; if he had taken no part in the massacre, he had certainly abetted it. He crowned his infamy by signing a treaty with Saladin whereby he undertook to help the Sultan conquer Palestine, which he already held as a fief of the Greek Empire. The West retaliated. In the spring of 1185 an enormous host of eighty thousand men and two hundred ships led by William II of Sicily moved against Byzantium. Durazzo fell, and a series of forced marches along the Egnatian Way brought the aggressors to Thessalonica, which they promptly invested. The town was defended by a few mercenary battalions; it was carried by storm, and so appalling was the massacre that even the contemporary world was horrified. Shut up in Byzantium, a prey to mortal dread, Andronicus, the proud saviour of yesteryear, became the public enemy. One of his favourites, Isaac Angelus, stirred the populace; Andronicus attempted to flee, but was captured and treated with at least equal cruelty to that in which he had himself indulged.[1]

Such was the end of the Comneni, a family that managed to stem the tide of disaster but was unable to prevent the decline. Constantinople was saved from the Norman attack by its own courage no less than by the fact that the enemy, laden with booty and softened by the Greek climate, could not exploit their victory at Thessalonica. Surprised at the passage of the Strymon (Strouma) by an army hastily levied among the Turks and Russians, the Normans were decisively beaten, and their fleet, having reached the Bosphorus, turned tail. Sicily was no longer a real menace to Byzantium; she too was sliding rapidly towards the abyss, Sicily where Tancred the Bastard (husband of Constance, daughter and heiress of Roger II) was in revolt against the Germans of

---

[1] One must read the account of his end in the Chronicle of Nicetas in order to understand the degradation to which even a Christian mob could descend when properly roused: 'He was imprisoned in the fortress of Anemas with a chain round his neck and irons on his feet; thus manacled, he was brought before Isaac and charged with all manner of crime. He was buffeted and kicked. His teeth were smashed and his hair torn out. Women whose husbands he had killed or blinded slapped his face. After that, one hand was cut off, he was castrated, and thrown back into the same prison without food or drink or any comfort. Some days later they put out one of his eyes and set him on a camel, bareheaded and clothed in nothing but a filthy tunic. All the lowest and vilest elements of the populace assembled to dishonour him with a last outburst of fury, leaving him with no shred of the dignity which had erstwhile surrounded him, nor any trace of the loyalty they had once sworn to observe. Some struck him on the head with sticks, others flung stones, others again pricked him with bodkins. One debauched female emptied a whole cauldron of hot water on his head. Indeed, there was no one who did not offer him some insult. When he had been thus led to the place where there are two columns supporting a bronze wolf and sow in the act of fighting, he was made to dismount from the camel and strung up by his feet. He endured these torments, and many others which I cannot name, with incredible constancy and wonderful presence of mind, saying nothing in the midst of that infuriated mob of persecutors, except: 'Lord, have pity on me; why do you trample on a broken reed? . . .' The popular fury being still unsatisfied with these monstrous cruelties, some tore off his tunic, another drove a sword into his entrails via his mouth. Two Italians, each taking a two-handled sword, ran him through with all their strength to see who had the best sword and who could use his best. He expired at length after so many torments, holding his hand to his mouth; some believed that he did so in order to drink the blood which flowed from one of his wounds.'

Henry IV, and where his son, the mysterious Frederick II, would soon realize his dreams.[1]   But it was no longer in south-west Italy that the danger lurked.

The family now raised to the Byzantine throne by mob-caprice, the Angeli, were a mediocre set.   The frivolous Isaac II (1185–95) gave free rein once more to feudal anarchy, burdened the country with taxes, and allowed Bulgarians and Turks to ravage imperial territory.   Overthrown by his brother, he was ritually blinded.   Alexius III (1195–1203) was even worse.   Insurrection broke out at all points.   The son of Isaac, another Alexius, profited by the arrival of the fourth crusade to have his father restored to the throne with himself as associate emperor. But strong nationalist feeling, justified by the behaviour of the crusaders, encouraged an ambitious member of the Ducas family, Alexius 'Mourzuphles'—'the man with joined eyebrows'—to have Alexius IV strangled, while the blind emperor was left to die in prison. Foolishly, since his forces were insignificant, Alexius V attempted to oppose the Western allies; but the only result was to provoke an appalling tragedy, the fall of Constantinople to the crusaders.   In 1204 the Byzantine Empire seemed to have perished, and a Latin empire was erected on its ruins.[2]

6.   The Glory of Byzantium in the Eleventh and Twelfth Centuries

Successive disasters, however, and increasing decadence had not affected the outward splendour or the daily life of Byzantium.   Cruel losses had been inflicted by the Turks, the Normans, and more insidiously by the Venetian traders; but wealth had for so long flowed into the Golden Horn that it continued to do so throughout the eleventh and twelfth centuries.   The Macedonian dynasty had established Byzantium upon firm economic bases and had enriched her with noble monuments.   In this respect, at any rate, the empire still existed. Froissart, who described the capital in the fourteenth century, diminished as it then was by the ravages of Western invaders, could not hide his astonishment at the wealth accumulated within its walls and at the artistic treasures that were everywhere to be seen.

Constantinople under the Comneni and Angeli was such as it had been in the preceding age.   The products of the whole Mediterranean world, including those regions in Moslem hands, were unloaded on the quays of its gigantic port; while caravans, setting out from the Trebizond gate for furthest Asia, Ethiopia, or the heart of Africa, brought back silk, ivory, furs, and perfumes.   Nor did the capital

---

[1] See Chapter V, section 7.   [2] See Chapter XI, section 8.

alone derive profit from this busy trade.   Thessalonica, a halting place
on the Adriatic route towards the Bosphorus, enjoyed similar good
fortune.   At the St Demetrius fair, in late October, a whole city of
tents, sheltering a hundred thousand souls, covered the plain of the
Vardar, where Spaniards mingled with Chinese, Mongols with
Ethiopians, and all the world rubbed shoulders.   Protected by high
walls begun by Theodosius in the fifth century, completed by Heraclius
in the seventh, and furnished with innumerable majestic towers by the
Comneni, Byzantium, at the hour when so many enemies looked to
share her spoils, could still believe the past had not yet gone.

Among her outstanding sons and daughters was Anna Comnena,
a princess of the blood, who had been nourished on Homer, Thucy-
dides, and Polybius.   Her long historical poem, *Alexiad*, describes the
principal events of her father's reign.   Other members of the nobility
who were also men of letters included Anna's husband Nicephorus
Bryennius; Isaac Comnenus, younger brother of John II, a learned
commentator on the *Odyssey*; the Emperor Manuel himself; and his
sister-in-law Irene, a pupil of the most illustrious and most beggarly
poet of his age, Theodore Prodromos, a sort of Verlaine with lodgings
at court.   Many chroniclers also laboured to exalt the glory of that
epoch.   Such were John Cinnamus, Michael and Nicetas Acominates,
and George Cedrenus; while Eustathius, Archbishop of Thessalonica,
of whom we shall have more to say from the religious standpoint,
proved himself 'the most brilliant light of the Byzantine world since
Michael Psellos.'

Art too spread its gorgeous mantle to hide secret sores.   Feudal
anarchy was followed by a splendid renaissance under the Comneni,
somewhat like that of the Macedonian epoch.   Alexius abandoned the
Sacred Palace for the castle of Blachernae on the Golden Horn, a
residence which he and his successors delighted to improve.   'Nothing
equals its external beauty,' says Eudes de Deuil, who accompanied
Louis VII on crusade.   'As for the interior, words fail; it is covered
with paintings done in gold and brilliant colours; the floor is paved
with marble in the most cunning patterns; and I cannot say wherein
lies its chief value and beauty, the richness of materials or the quality of
its ornament.'   In those immense halls with their golden colonnades,
seated upon a throne of chased gold, wearing the golden diadem set
with precious stones, the Basileus must indeed have appeared as the
living representative of Justinian and Theodosius.

But while they considered their own glory, these emperors did not
forget the majesty of God.   The age of the Comneni produced a
wealth of churches similar to that which, at the same time, was covering
the West.   In Constantinople itself the finest was that of the Pantocrator, destined as the burial place of the Comneni, of the Angeli, and

later of the Palaeologi.   Replicas of this masterpiece arose throughout
the empire: at Athens, at Thessalonica, even in Cyprus and Cappadocia, where many a church perched on some rocky height claimed
the Pantocrator as its model.   In the monastic republic of Mount
Athos, which was born and reached maturity in the previous era, architecture tended to become more refined.   There is a heaviness about the
church of the Great Lavra, but this gives place to a rare synthesis of
quiet strength and spiritual uplift at Ivirion, at Vatopedi, and above all
at the Serbian monastery of Khilandar.   The arrangement of brick-
work in this latter building is almost unique of its kind.   The same
period produced some wonderful refectories constructed on the plan of
a church, with a little apse for the superior's place, white marble tables
with plates hollowed out in the surface, and kitchens roofed with
cupolas which in turn are surmounted with open lanterns to let out the
smoke.   It is an imposing style of architecture, expressive of firm
faith, restrained and delicate, though not without a hint of pride.
Another example may be seen not far from Athens, on the old Sacred
Way to Eleusis, where stands the church of Daphne, a jewel of stone
and mosaic dedicated by the Greeks to the 'Dormition of the Virgin.'
It is now occupied by a community of French Cistercians and called
Dalfinet.

The ornamentation of these churches yielded nothing to that of their
predecessors; in a way, it is even more beautiful.   It remains somewhat ostentatious; but a noticeable return to hellenic conceptions, to
more temperate planning, and to a happy blend of Christian tradition
with that of antiquity, result in a simplification of lines and a love of
sculptural forms which are indicative of true genius.   Under theological influence, this art tended to symbolic conventionalism which is
not easily appreciated by a Westerner since he cannot grasp its meaning,
but whose intentional rigidity and fixed range of colouring seek only to
attain a point where creative inspiration transcends the world of sense
to touch the metaphysical and divine.   The mystical purpose, however, does not altogether exclude a certain amount of realism, whose
subtlety is all the more striking on account of its infrequent use.

It is from the art of the Comnenian period that we obtain our most
cogent evidence of the splendour of Byzantium, as well as of the
influence which her civilization continued to wield at an hour when she
was already doomed.   It has been said that the art born on the
Bosphorus determined the whole of European art at that epoch.   This
is clearly an exaggeration; but we have seen [1] its powerful impact upon
Western forms.   Romanesque derives from sumptuous Greek fabrics
the custom of depicting animals *affrontée* (to use an heraldic term)
on the capitals of pillars.   Whence the ornamentation of liturgical

[1] Chapter X, section 5.

vestments? The figure of St Michael in Puy cathedral is most probably wearing the hieratic costume of the basileis; nor is it unreasonable to suppose that the Christ in Majesty which Urban II saw above the choir at Cluny, when he consecrated the abbey church in 1095, resembled some Pantocrator ablaze in all the glory of his state. In the priory of Berzé-la-Ville, the pomp of the Byzantine court is forcibly suggested by a similar Christ, together with the figures of SS. Sergius and Blaise, and a procession of saints bearing a crown and heavily embroidered robes. The spacious backgrounds of bright blue found in many romanesque frescoes were almost certainly inspired by oriental mosaics. And who knows if we should ever have seen the strange cupolas of Saint-Front beneath the skies of Périgord without those of Santa Sophia?

Throughout the West, and under the most varied forms, the development of Byzantine art reveals the splendour of the old empire. It was from the Orient that Venetian traders brought back those precise aesthetic principles which enabled them to erect the basilica of St Mark. Begun in 976, after a fire which had destroyed the primitive church, its five cupolas seem like some vast block rolled from the Orient to the Adriatic shore. At the time of its consecration, in 1095, it lacked the familiar brilliance of gold and mosaic, which were added later; nor, as yet, was the entrance dominated by that bronze quadriga which the crusaders brought back from Constantinople after 1204. But the spirit of the building was such as we know it to-day; the nearby campanile was in course of construction, and the Doge's Palace, a distant rival of Blachernae, was being raised on wooden piles driven into the mud.

Venice was still friendly; but even among those whose hatred of Byzantium was mingled with admiration, oriental influences were profound and strongly marked. There are parts of Palermo, Monreale, and Cefalu where it is easy to imagine oneself in some quarter of old Constantinople. When the Sicilian kings desired to manifest their glory in stone, they felt they could not do better than employ Greek methods, and often enough Greek architects and artists. This, however, did not always prevent them from combining Byzantine forms with Islamic elements which had survived in the island after 150 years of Moslem rule. In 1132 Roger II built the famous Palatine chapel, perhaps the supreme masterpiece of oriental art, a jewel blazing with golden mosaics, ancient columns, and its ceiling in Moslem style, where Christ, His hand raised in blessing, seems to hesitate before so crushing a display of magnificence. Forty years later, in 1174, William II built the cathedral of Palermo; it has since been badly disfigured, but the great Sicilians still sleep beneath their tombs of porphyry and mosaic. In 1185, on a hill overlooking the bay, the same king built the basilica of Monreale.   He intended it as the burial-place of his family; and there he lies, watched by that colossal Panto-crator with which no Byzantine figure of our Lord can be compared. Byzantine art was also affected to some extent by Arabian influences, but the Arab lands received more from the Greeks than they themselves supplied.   Artists from Constantinople laboured in countries occupied by the Moslems.   Manuel Comnenus, for example, sent mosaic-workers to adorn the church of the Nativity at Bethlehem; while mosques such as that of the Ommayads at Damascus, and the celebrated mosque of Omar at Jerusalem, still preserve traces of work carried out by these 'infidels.'   In fact, the widespread use of mosaic by Islam seems to have originated in Byzantium.

The most distant regions on the outskirts of civilization reflected the glory of Byzantine art.   The most striking example is Russia.   After that very odd person St Vladimir had converted his fellow country-men to Christianity, his son, Yaroslav the Wise (1016–54), a sort of Russian Charlemagne, set about making Kiev a real capital, and this ambition was shared by all his successors.   There were close com-mercial and dynastic ties between Kiev and Constantinople; thus, Vladimir II married a Greek and was almost a Byzantine prince. Moreover, Kiev, with its cathedral of Holy Wisdom, its hundreds of churches, and its golden-roofed monastery of Mount St Michael, was a replica of Constantinople.   The mosaics of Holy Wisdom, made by Greeks in about 1054, included a Pantocrator and Panhagia which were exact copies from originals in Santa Sophia on the Bosphorus.   Kiev was a centre of Byzantine influence in the heart of Russian territory, and shed her light wherever the Slavs penetrated.   She had already been weakened by the attacks of northern tribes and Polovtsian raids when she was swept away in the Mongol invasion at the beginning of the thirteenth century; but the seed which she had planted in Holy Russia was destined to increase and multiply for centuries.   The ikons which her rulers purchased in the empire fixed the style of those made in Russia until modern times, the least of which bears irrefutable witness to the splendour of Byzantium.

7.   The Faith and Religious Customs of Byzantium

The keystone of Byzantine society, whose greatness none can fail to recognize, was the same as we have shown it to be in the West, viz. Christian faith.   Medieval Byzantines believed no less profoundly than, and in almost the same fashion as, their far-distant Catholic brethren.   Every Byzantine home had its ikon; Byzantine daily life, public and private, was subject to the Church; Byzantine missionaries were still, as they had always been, courageous mouthpieces of Christ;

Byzantine monasteries were ever full, and ever putting forth fresh shoots. Byzantium may well astonish and even shock us in many ways; but the fact remains that her essential Christianity cannot be denied.

When Alexius Comnenus ascended the throne, in 1081, under those dramatic circumstances which have already been described, the barbarian units serving as mercenaries in his army took advantage of the general disorder to pillage a number of churches during Holy Week. Public opinion treated their conduct as a criminal outrage, while the Emperor and his mother both declared that the very thought of it kept them awake at nights. A synod met to decide what penance was required to expiate so terrible a sin. For forty days the whole court, from the Basileus to the humblest servant, fasted, ate no meat or fish, and slept on the bare ground, while many people had themselves severely scourged. The Emperor set an example, wearing a hair-shirt next his skin and sleeping on the stone floor with a stone for his pillow. During that unforeseen Lenten period, no monastery in the empire led a more exemplary life than did the Sacred Palace. There you have a perfect example of Byzantine Christianity, its love of the spectacular, its violent manifestations of repentance, but also its genuine and admirable sincerity.

The faith, then, was present in every phase of Byzantine affairs, even when that presence was least apparent. Thus, in the Hippodrome, which was still the hub of collective life, all ceremonies and demonstrations, whether horse racing, theatrical performances, or public executions, began with a solemn blessing. The Basileus, standing in his box, made the sign of the Cross three times over the people with a fold of his gold-embroidered mantle.

To believe and to practise one's faith were not only moral and canonical obligations; they were imposed by the law of the land. The civil courts took cognizance of blasphemy, profanation, sacrilege, and several other crimes. An excommunicated person was almost inevitably imprisoned. Nor was it necessary to commit any of the graver sins in order to incur punishment; one had only to miss Mass on three successive Sundays! Those who sat or knelt during vespers on the vigils of great feasts were punished with a fine, for 'only he who prays standing honours the Resurrection.'

The leading characteristics of this faith were much the same as in the West. Among well-educated people it was lofty and well founded, nourished on Scripture and the Fathers, interested in metaphysical and eschatological theories rather than in moral and social effort. But among the common people, as well as among the more boorish elements of the clergy and monastic proletariat, it was often of low quality, full of superstition, free and easy in matters of conduct, and more concerned with rites than with evangelical principles.   It was, in fact, not unlike the religion of millions in the West.

The Byzantines also practised the cult of saints, whose relics formed a considerable part of their 'export trade.'   They firmly believed that a handful of sand impregnated with water from the miraculous fountain of St Saviour had power to ward off epilepsy; that St Theophrano's ring could cure gout; that to sleep in the church of 'SS. Anargyres, Cosmas, and Damian' had a definite therapeutic value; and so forth. Every home had its reliquary in the form of a model house, or church with cupolas, or even a head, an arm, or a leg.   With regard to the authenticity of relics, the good folk of Byzantium were no more critical than their neighbours in the West; they were absolutely certain that there, in the church, lay the mantle of the prophet Elias or the miraculous staff of Moses!

Apart from actual heresy, their faith was often adulterated with superstition and extremely doubtful practices.   Magic and astrology kept house with Christian principles.   The Patriarch Caerularius, for example, held spiritualistic seances with a medium named Dosithea, reports of which were drawn up by his secretaries.   Anna Comnena mentions astrology as among the 'sciences' of which Byzantium was proud; and the fact that her father Alexius rejected 'this superstition which substituted poisoned dreams for hope in God' shows that it was practised at his court.   There was a veritable swarm of sorcerers and witches, soothsayers and fortune-tellers, vendors of amulets and charms.   But the Orient held no monopoly in these, any more than in those liberties which believers took with Christian morality.   Many an Eastern council thundered against women who ogled men in church, against shopkeepers who tore pages from the liturgical books in order to sell the miniatures, against those who brought food and drink into consecrated buildings, against those who took up residence in churches with their wives and children.   But did the West afford a more edifying spectacle?

The real difference between Eastern and Western Christianity, apart from the question of obedience to Rome, lay wholly in externals.   The liturgy was far more complicated, detailed, and prolonged than in the West.   It was the so-called liturgy of St John Chrysostom, which had relegated that of St Basil to ten days in the year and that of the 'Presanctified' to Lent.   With its 'oblation' (*proskomidi*), its Mass of the catechumens preceded by the Little Entry and followed by the Mass of the faithful which opened with the Great Entry and went on for nearly an hour, the Byzantine Mass was three times as long as the most solemn occasions in the Western rite.[1]

Another difference appeared in the representation of the Divine

[1] See Chapter III, section 9.

Persons and of the saints. After the grave crisis which had threatened their extinction, ikons achieved enormous popularity and their style gradually became fixed. The ikon was a picture of God, of the Blessed Virgin, or of a saint. It was conceived and executed according to hard and fast rules, observing a prescribed system of lines and colouring determined by a fixed pattern of symbolism. In the religious life of Byzantium it played the same part as did sculpture in our cathedrals; it was intended alike for the humble and the learned, speaking to each in a different but equally cogent voice. The eleventh and twelfth centuries were a period of intense activity in the making of ikons, which were generally painted in distemper on wooden panels and heavily ornamented with gold. Sometimes, however, they consisted of fine mosaic-work, or were carved from soapstone or marble; the cheaper kinds might be made of terra cotta. At this period, also, it became customary not only to frame them in precious metals but actually to overlay them with gem-encrusted silver, so that only the faces and hands were left showing. Such too is the present-day technique.

Where the East did resemble the West was in the number of its clergy. Byzantium was full of priests; they swarmed everywhere, even in the emperor's entourage. 'Look after the priest and you will go to heaven,' said an old proverb, whose clerical origin it is impossible to doubt.

The secular clergy had sunk very low, if we may believe Alexius Comnenus, who took steps to improve it. 'Christian faith,' he said, 'is in peril, because the clergy go from bad to worse.' Accordingly, he drew up a complete plan of reform, re-enacting the disciplinary decrees of councils, requiring that priests should be more devout, better behaved, and properly instructed. It is worth noting that the prefect Pourianos conceived the idea of erecting a seminary, the 'School of St Nicholas,' where young men might 'study the sacred sciences before entering the priesthood.' The result of these measures was not particularly encouraging. The 'pappas' were recruited from the lower classes. Most of them were family men; for a cleric was allowed to marry before taking major orders, after which he had the right and even the obligation not to put away his wife. They lived among the people, who loved but had scant respect for them. In these circumstances it was impossible to hope for much.

The cream of the episcopate was drawn from the masters of the Patriarchal School or the Imperial University, but there was an increasing number of monastic prelates. Their standard of education and behaviour was far superior to that of their subordinates; some of them—John Mauropous, for example, Theophylact of Ochrida, the great Eustathius of Thessalonica, with his disciples Michael of Athens and Euthymius of Neopatras—were men of considerable learning and merit.   But too many bishops succumbed to the pleasures of the capital and the palace; not caring to reside in their provincial sees, too many of them became mere worldly politicians.

In this, as in the preceding epoch, the best of the clergy were monks. Religious were bound to celibacy, and were infinitely more faithful to Christian principles.   Unfortunately, however, the Byzantine monks were more isolated from the world than were their Western brethren, so that they could not help to leaven the Christian lump as did the Cistercians, Premonstratensians, Franciscans, and Dominicans.

There were well-filled monasteries, veritable hives of sanctity, all over the empire, sometimes on the outskirts of cities, but more often in remote places, where they formed small states within the State.   Several of these communities have survived intact and provide us with a direct notion of what monachism was in the days of the Basileis.   The most famous of all was Mount Athos, founded by St Athanasius of Laura, the 'Holy Mountain,' standing on a long finger of Chalcidice measuring twenty-eight miles from north to south.   Throughout the whole of this distance there were convents of all sizes, priories and hermits' huts; while anchorites spent lives of prayer and silence in caves hollowed out among cliffs that overlooked the sea.   For centuries there was a constant flow of monks to Athos.   Some of the older establishments, e.g. the Great Lavra (Laura), Vatopedi, Zographu, grew to an enormous size.   Others were of more recent date: one was founded by a group of princes, another by Russian ascetics, another by Georgians.   We have already mentioned Khilandar, built by Serbian princes, and the Latin monastery at Constantinople, which was under the patronage of traders from Amalfi.

Athos was not the only flourishing monastic republic.   Before the Turkish invasion there was one in Cappadocia, in the volcanic region near Caesarea, where the convents were partly excavated from the rock. In Thessaly, on a steep spur of the Pindus range broken up by erosion into precipitous ledges and sharp peaks, stand the Meteors, well known to tourists.   They can only be reached by a net attached to the end of a rope which the brethren haul up on a winch.   At Patmos the holy monk Chrysodulus, who had been driven from Cappadocia by the Turks, tried, with the support of Alexius Comnenus, to establish a model monastery on the very spot where St John was believed to have written his Apocalypse.   And even in the heart of Arabia the Moslems permitted the foundation of monasteries in the solitudes of Sinai, not far from that mountain upon which Moses received the Tables of the Law.

It cannot be denied that all was far from well in these Byzantine convents, where indifference took its toll as it had done elsewhere. The same deplorable results as in the West were produced by lay interference.   This was often more flagrant than in Europe, for the lay 'owner' would come and install himself in the monastery together with his wife and children.   Many communities were ill-disciplined and lazy.   There were some pretty scandals at Mount Athos.   On one occasion certain monks appeared over-anxious to mind the sheep, and it was discovered that a number of women had disguised themselves as shepherds. . . .   More than once the emperors expressed their indignation; seven gyrovagues, for instance, were rounded up by the imperial police in the streets of Constantinople, and Alexius threatened to have their eyes gouged out if they continued to wander abroad without leave.   Some of the bishops also tried their hand at the difficult task of monastic reform, notably Eustathius of Thessalonica (1179–92). This great man wrote a treatise or, rather, a pamphlet on *The Improvement of Monastic Life*, which incidentally makes delightful reading; but the hatred he thereby incurred obliged him to flee for his life.

It would, nevertheless, be a mistake to regard Byzantine monachism simply as an institution cut off from the life of the people and sunk in that pious egotism which too frequently goes hand in hand with moral laxity.   Oriental monks quite often undertook remarkable works of charity.   They were entrusted by the Comneni with the running not only of newly established homes for old people, but also of those travellers' hospices whose buildings may still be seen in many of the Balkan passes and where, according to a decree of Alexius, 'the fire should be kept burning night and day.'   Monks also had complete charge of the magnificent hospital of the Pantocrator,[1] which entailed work similar to that done by the Antonines and Holy Ghost order in Europe.   Public assistance, of which there were numerous centres, was controlled by a cleric.   He had generally been superior of a monastery, and was known as the 'Orphanotrophe,' i.e. guardian of orphans.   There were also houses for the blind, others for incurables, and others for the plague-stricken.   Christian charity among the Byzantines did not fall short of that practised in the West.

This may be a suitable place in which to point out a marked difference between the two halves of the Church.   Charitable organizations in the West sprang in large measure from the Church; many layfolk, notably kings, took part in their foundation, but we cannot say that the initiative was theirs.   It was the same in the spiritual domain with regard to the matter of reform; the Church preferred to handle this alone, without secular aid.   In Byzantium, on the other hand, nearly all large-scale or necessary undertakings were initiated by the emperors.

[1] The regulations of this institution have survived.   It gives directions for the disinfecting of clothes when a patient was admitted, and for the issue of bedding and shirts; it tells us how the doctors specialized as 'pathologists,' surgeons, etc., and even states that there were women doctors for childbirth.   We also learn how the pharmacy, the bursary, and the almonry were run.   All this was far in advance of the time.

The Basileis built churches and founded hospitals; they took steps to recall monks to their obedience, and to see that clerics passed through a seminary. Here we touch on the outstanding and immemorial characteristic of the Byzantine East. Caesaropapism may justly be considered its worst fault; religion was subjected to political influences, and the things that belonged to Caesar were inextricably bound up with those that belonged to God.

For generations the emperors had concerned themselves with theology; indeed theology had always been an affair of State at Byzantium. One writer calmly observes that 'on questions concerning sacred things no one may express an opinion, except the Doctors of the Church and the emperors.' The basileis of the eleventh and twelfth centuries clung to this privilege. Every one of them signed at least one decree deciding a matter of faith or morals, and not one of them failed to preside in person over a council. Manuel Comnenus was an enthusiastic amateur in this field. 'His reign,' says an historian,[1] 'was one long religious orgy.' A certain Demetrius of Lampe put forward a dangerous theory as to relations between the Father and the Son. The Basileus knew no rest until he had confounded him; he himself searched for arguments and quotations wherewith to crush the villain, and imposed his opinion on the grounds that 'the emperor cannot err'! The palace was continually interfering in matters of discipline and administration. In practice, no bishop was appointed without approval signified by the Master, who, moreover, had the right to alter ecclesiastical boundaries; and it often happened that a prelate was deposed out of hand for having given offence. The emperor even controlled the liturgical calendar; Manuel Comnenus revised it from end to end because he thought there were too many holidays. There is something almost scandalous in those lectures addressed by the basileis, whose own lives were often far from exemplary, to archbishops, metropolitans, and religious superiors. However well-intentioned it may have been, secular interference—just when the papacy was doing its utmost to escape from such control—was nothing short of disastrous.

One fact, however, calls for our notice, something quite new in Byzantium: there was a fresh current of opinion opposed to such interference. One clerical pamphleteer, Nicetas Choniates, poked fun at those princes who, 'not content with governing an empire, believe themselves endowed with the wisdom of Solomon in the affairs of God.' Solomon in this case was Manuel Comnenus.

But the real and increasingly powerful centre of resistance to imperial authority was the patriarchate, especially that of Constantinople, which had emerged predominant when other sees were swept away. The

[1] Chalandon, *Jean II et Manuel Comnène.*

Patriarch was naturally chosen by the emperor, who in the course of a solemn ceremony 'announced' the new prelate's name to the crowd, and then 'promoted,' i.e. invested him with his charge in presence of the senate. The formula of nomination was characteristic: 'Divine grace and our authority which proceeds therefrom have decided to promote the Right Reverend N. to the patriarchate.' The consecration was performed eight days later by a metropolitan in the cathedral church of Santa Sophia; and the ceremonial ended with the new Patriarch handing the emperor a written oath of loyalty. But no sooner had this Patriarch been appointed than he became an important figure with whom the Basileus must remain on good terms. His Holiness the Oecumenical Patriarch, Archbishop of New Rome, commanded limitless respect. Any attack on his person was considered sacrilege and punished as such. Bishops and metropolitans could be appointed only with his approval, and imperial edicts, known as 'Golden Bulls,' were signed and sealed by him. The people were therefore inclined to invoke the Patriarch's jurisdiction against abuses of imperial authority; and it was always easy for him to play the politician however unwilling he might be to do so. Very many of the patriarchs were in direct correspondence with the high offices of state, carried on secret negotiations with the worst enemies of the regime, and worked against the emperor. Michael Caerularius, for example, was in turn the friend of Michael VI (whom he brought to power) and then of his adversary. At first the favourite of Isaac Comnenus, he afterwards became a nuisance to that monarch and quarrelled with him.

This latent antagonism of the two powers increased as the empire declined, and was particularly noticeable in the grave matter of relations between Byzantium and Rome. Whereas the emperors, in their capacity as statesmen, more than once showed themselves in favour of reconciliation with the Latins, whose military strength might have proved useful even at the cost of a few dogmatic concessions, the patriarchs, representing a popular and fanatical chauvinism, were openly hostile to any such agreement. Indeed, one of the motives which caused Caerularius to precipitate the schism was his indignation at the sight of Constantine IX allying himself with the Pope against the Normans. His successors adopted the same attitude, opposing every effort to reconcile their Church with the Holy See, which 'stank of impiety,' and to which one of them said that he preferred the Moslems. Thus, from 1054, when the rupture occurred, until 1204, when the crusaders took Constantinople, the patriarchs played an underhand but decisive part in the history of relations between East and West. Nor can it be denied that their activity was altogether at variance with the best interests of Christ's Church.

8.   ATTEMPTS AT RECONCILIATION

The schism occurred in 1054, and it remained to be seen whether conversations would be resumed.   The question was undecided for one hundred and fifty years; political and theological complications made it impossible to solve, nor did the military disaster of 1204 help to cut the Gordian knot.   There were, however, approaches from both sides.   In 1057 the former legate, Frederick of Lorraine, who became Pope Stephen IX on 3rd August in that year, tried to reopen talks with Byzantium.   His anxiety was no doubt due as much to Norman ascendancy as to theological misunderstanding.   He appointed three ambassadors to visit Constantinople; but bad weather prevented their embarkation, and when Stephen died on 29th March 1058 these diplomats were still in Italy.   They never set sail, and the Patriarch Caerularius thus escaped the ordeal of a disputation with an embassy far better informed than that sent out in 1054, and which would almost certainly have won over a statesman like Isaac Comnenus to a policy of union with the Holy See against the Normans.

Failure likewise attended a mission sent by Alexander II in 1071 to Michael VII Ducas, who had invited the Sovereign Pontiff to make a careful study of questions separating East and West.   The powerful Michael Psellos, who had been completely won over to the cause of schism, who had put himself forward as the official panegyrist of Caerularius, and who was backed by the Patriarch, found no difficulty in dissuading the Emperor from listening to the tempter's voice.   It required nothing less than the disaster of Mantzikert in the same year to bring the imperial palace to a different view.   Deprived of a splendid army and paralysed by internal dissension, Byzantium could do nothing to prevent the Turks from overrunning Asia Minor.   Realizing the advantage of re-establishing contact with the West, Ducas sent two monks to congratulate Gregory VII on his election.   That great Pope desired reunion of the Churches; he seized this opportunity, and straightway took the initiative.   His first reply (9th July 1073) made reference only to a spiritual *rapprochement*; but, probably at the suggestion of his agent Dominic, patriarch of Grado, he decided that the best means of obtaining such a reconciliation was to send military aid, which would lay Byzantium under an obligation to the Latins. The idea of a crusade did not take shape for another twenty years; but it was conceived by this act of Gregory's genius, and he was pre-occupied with the colossal plan throughout 1074.   Having revealed his purpose to the Count of Burgundy and to William I of Sicily, he issued a Bull calling on his loyal subjects to defend Constantinople. He then made his peace with Henry IV, and proposed to leave the

Church under that Emperor's protection while he himself took command of the army.   'We are particularly encouraged,' he added, 'by
the fact (i) that the Church of Constantinople, which is separated from
Ourselves on the question of the Holy Spirit, desires peace with the
Apostolic See; (ii) that the Armenians are fast embracing the Catholic
faith; and (iii) that the majority of Orientals desire that the faith of the
Apostle Peter shall decide between conflicting opinions.'   The purpose
of the Holy See is nowhere better explained.   But this laudable project
came to nothing, and we hear no more about it after 1075.   Gregory
may have feared what Guiscard might do in his absence; or the
recruiting of an army may have encountered insuperable difficulties.
At all events, the recrudescence of the quarrel with Henry IV would
soon have put paid to Rome's eastern policy.

Henceforward antagonism between the two capitals went from bad
to worse.   When Michael VII was dethroned, the Pope excommunicated his successor, Nicephorus Botaniates.   On learning that the ex-
emperor had taken refuge with the Normans, he asked the bishops to
lend him their aid, without realizing, however, that the whole thing
was a ruse on the part of Guiscard (whose daughter had been betrothed
to Michael's son) in order to establish a claim to the imperial territories.
Bohemond landed in Epirus almost simultaneously with the accession
of Alexius I.   The new sovereign could not but feel resentment against
Rome.   We have seen how he allied himself with Henry IV and paid
him to attack the papal states; at the same time, he ordered all Latin
places of worship at Constantinople to be closed.   It is therefore not
surprising to find Anna Comnena speaking harsh words of Gregory
and of the Holy See in general.   After scoffing at the titles 'Sovereign
Pontiff' and 'Vicar of Christ,' she goes on to say: 'This is nothing but
arrogance on their part; for when the seat of empire was transferred to
our imperial city, together with the senate and civil service, the first
rank in the episcopal hierarchy was likewise transferred.   Moreover,
the basileis have always given precedence to the bishopric of Constantinople; above all, the Council of Chalcedon raised the Bishop of
Constantinople to the summit of the hierarchy and made all dioceses
subject to him.'

Such was the attitude confronting Urban II when he ascended the
throne of St Peter in 1088.   He was particularly worried by his own
isolation in face of a temporary understanding between the two
emperors.   The antipope Clement III was employing the good offices
of the Metropolitan of Kiev and of Basil, the Greek Archbishop of
Reggio, to effect a reconciliation with the East.   Urban, therefore,
decided to forestall his rival and felt that a bold step was most likely to
succeed.   Early in 1088 he complained that offices in the Latin rite
were no longer celebrated at Constantinople, and that his own name

had been erased from the diptychs. It was the first time that the question of schism (though that word was not used) had been raised. Harassed by the dangers threatening his country, Alexius Comnenus saw the value of such an opening; but in order to win greater freedom for manœuvre, he replied that he would do nothing without the approval of a council, to which he invited the Pope and his theologians, and at which it was proposed to discuss the bread used in the sacrifice of the Mass, one of the principal subjects of controversy. But the religious question was little more than a pretext; what most people had in mind was the improvement of a disastrous political situation. The synod met in September 1089; Urban II was not present, and for a good reason. Having fled for refuge to an island in the Tiber, he was obliged to leave Clement III not only to govern Rome but to hold a council in St Peter's. Alexius, however, overcame the ill will of his prelates so far as to obtain from the synod a recognition that no official decision had been taken to erase the Pope's name from the diptychs; and he had the Latin sanctuaries reopened. The debate on the real questions at issue never began; and even the conciliatory Theophylact of Ochrida, whose book appeared at this time, wrote that for his part he could never accept the *Filioque* clause. But at least the tension was relaxed.

In point of fact the higher Greek clergy had no wish to go further. A significant letter was addressed to the Pope by Nicephorus III Grammaticus, in which he reproached Urban II with having failed to notify Constantinople of his election, as was the custom among patriarchs, and in which he addressed him as 'My very dear and most venerable brother,' as if they were equals. At the same time Nicephorus informed the Patriarch of Jerusalem that he would never offer unleavened bread in the Eucharistic sacrifice. Firm adherence to a theory that the five patriarchs were autonomous, and hostility to alleged innovations by the Latins, were the main objections offered by the religious leaders of Byzantium to attempts at reunion; they were insensible to the wound of schism. The papacy, on the other hand, though it sincerely desired reconciliation, was not prepared to discuss in council those beliefs of which it considered itself to be the depositary; it looked for filial submission on the part of the Easterns rather than for the subtleties of their theologians. A solution might have been possible had the Byzantine emperor chosen to intervene. So close were the ties subordinating the Eastern Church to the Basileus that an exercise of imperial authority would have sufficed to overcome many obstacles. As things turned out, the launching of a crusade naturally inspired the emperors with lasting hostility towards the West; from now on, the question of reunion was seen in a new light.

As we have remarked, Alexius I made several appeals to the West for military aid.   But whether he was begging the Count of Flanders to provide him with 500 knights, as happened in 1081 when the Petchenegs threatened Adrianople, or was addressing a more general request to the Pope, he intended simply to hire mercenaries for the defence of Constantinople, or, at the most, to regain some territories in Asia Minor which had been overrun by the Turks.   It was for this purpose alone that his ambassadors attended the Council of Piacenza and 'earnestly solicited help for the defence of Holy Church.'   Urban II readily granted their request.

It is unfortunately open to doubt whether this military aid was conducive to reunion of the Churches.   The motive of the first crusade—not the only motive, of course, but still an important one—was certainly to relieve the pressure on Byzantium and to reinforce the Eastern frontier after the defeat of Mantzikert; but the Orientals cannot be blamed for having failed to recognize this motive.   The terms in which the crusade was preached; the sermons in which there was much talk of conquering Jerusalem, but little of friendly help for Byzantium; the part played by Rome and her legates; the overlapping of the crusaders' lofty purpose with the politics of the Eastern Empire; all this could not but alarm the Basileus who, moreover, did not like the prospect of these foreigners overrunning his territory.   The event, indeed, was worse than anticipated; contact between the refined Byzantines and the rough warriors from Europe soon gave rise to misunderstanding, suspicion, and open hostility.   It was not long before the Orientals were calling the crusaders 'rapacious beasts,' and the crusaders had some grounds for their belief that the Byzantines were not to be trusted.

In such circumstances there could be small hope of reconciliation, which was rendered more difficult by the introduction of Latin clergy into the free states established by the crusaders.   These priests were generally ill-disposed towards their oriental colleagues, whom they regarded as atrocious nonconformists, while the foundation of numerous Latin monasteries annoyed the Greek monks.   Several incidents revealed the latent antagonism.   Take, for example, the case of John V, Patriarch of Antioch.   Having been evicted by the Turks, he was at first held in great respect by the crusaders, who restored him to his see, rebuilt all the plundered churches, and divided them equally among the two sets of clergy.   But he was soon the object of underhand attacks by Latin prelates, chief among whom was Daimbert of Pisa, the turbulent Roman patriarch of Jerusalem.   Accordingly, he sought refuge in Constantinople, and left his see to a Frenchman, Bernard of Valentinois.

In spite of all these difficulties, to which they were by no means blind, the popes and several of the basileis continued to seek an opening.   At the Council of 1088 Urban II had the Latin thesis on the Procession of the Holy Ghost expounded by St Anselm, the great Archbishop of Canterbury; and so moderate and clear was the holy doctor's exposition that several Greek bishops accepted it.   At this period also Alexius Comnenus was on friendly terms with the abbot of Monte Cassino, with whom he studied ways and means towards an understanding.   Four years later Urban II was succeeded by Paschal II, to whom the Bishop of Barcelona delivered a letter from the Basileus; and when Henry V descended upon Italy and threw the Pope into prison (1111), Alexius protested vigorously against the ill-treatment to which the Holy Father was subjected.   Indeed, he went so far as to notify the Pope that he was prepared to come to Rome and receive the imperial crown at his hands.   Reconciliation seemed assured: Paschal II wrote a favourable reply, and the Basileus spoke of ending the schism.   In March 1112 it was proposed to hold a council, and pre-liminary discussions were to take place between the Archbishop of Milan and some Byzantine prelates.   But at this point deadlock was reached; for although union appeared easy from the diplomatic point of view, it was found to be impossible on theological grounds.   The archbishop was adamant, demanding unqualified submission by the schismatics before talks could begin; the Orientals redoubled their quibbling; and Alexius died before any solution could be reached.

With the second crusade friction between East and West revived. There is reason to suspect that Manuel Comnenus, who mistrusted Conrad III and his Germans, conspired against them with the Turks. His relations with the French under Louis VII were so bad that some of the Capetian's entourage spoke of nothing less than taking Constantinople; hearing which, Manuel hatched a plot which was to ship-wreck the whole expedition.   In the diplomatic game which lasted during the next thirty years, reunion of the Churches was tabled more than once; but such talk was a mere bargaining point, not a sincere effort at reconciliation.   During the pontificate of Adrian IV, Manuel regained a footing in Ancona, and was prepared to scatter his gold, his troops, and the independence of the patriarchate in order to recover the Norman lands in Italy.   In 1167 he made approaches to Alexander III, who needed his assistance against Frederick Barbarossa.   Two cardinals were appointed to discuss theological questions with representatives of the Greek Church, but they put forward a curious demand that the capital of Empire should be transferred to Rome.   The spiritual and political problems were in fact so closely interwoven that no solution was possible.

It was during this interlude that the anti-foreign riots broke out at Constantinople in 1182.   We have already seen how the populace, exasperated by the growing influence of the Latins with the Empress

Dowager, massacred thousands of Western Christians including the papal legate, Cardinal John.   Reprisals were carried out by the Western fleet, which committed no less abominable crimes on the coasts of the Hellespont and Archipelago.   Thenceforward, no matter what the diplomats might do to reopen conversations with a view to healing the schism, irreparable harm had been done.   An idea began to gain ground throughout the West that a solution lay in armed force alone, that Byzantine pride must be broken and the oriental Church given masters who would bring her to heel.   Byzantium, exasperated and horrified at the outrages committed by the Normans in Thessalonica, asked themselves whether an understanding with Islam might not be better policy; and Isaac II Angelus agreed with Saladin that a mosque which had been built on the shores of the Bosphorus should have its own duly appointed muezzins.   Only Celestine III would not abandon hope; he made advances to the Basileus, but without success.

That was the situation in 1198 when Innocent III, the greatest political genius of his age, ascended the papal throne.   His attitude towards this unhappy business was as noble, his thought as profound, as it was in everything he handled.   In his eyes, the crusade and the reunion of the churches were closely linked.   He believed that the Eastern empire could survive only by taking part in the struggle against Islam, and that harmony could be achieved only by submission to papal authority.   In August 1198 the Pope signified his intentions to the Basileus and the Patriarch, inviting them to 'humility before God.'   But Alexius III lacked intelligence and underestimated the peril.   He replied that 'the hour appointed by God had not yet struck' and, with some insolence, asked the Pope to 'leave things to Providence.'   Meanwhile, the Patriarch John dispatched a long pamphlet to Rome in which he pretended to refute the Holy See's claim to universal primacy.   Innocent III replied with a gentle reminder of St Peter's primacy among the Apostles, and suggested that an oecumenical council should meet to decide the question.   It is quite certain that the Pope only awaited some conciliatory move from the other side before carrying the matter a stage further.

But the Roman curia had no control over events; those who maintained that force alone could determine the Byzantine issue began to obtain the upper hand.   The claimant Alexius IV announced that, if he were restored to his throne, he would not only submit to the Pope's authority but would also—this was still more attractive to many members of the expedition—pay 200,000 silver marks and support 500 knights at Jerusalem.   In the meantime, representatives of Alexius III came to Rome with counter-proposals.   Despite this bitter wrangling, Innocent remained firm, refusing to allow his crusade to become entangled in Byzantine intrigue; but the strength of armed force and of Venetian money prevailed. When the crusaders stormed Jerusalem on 13th August 1204 and established a Latin empire, reunion, which seemed so near to fulfilment, was indefinitely postponed. That which might have been the salvation of Byzantium involved her in total ruin.

CHAPTER XI

THE CRUSADES

1. THE APPEAL OF CLERMONT, 1095

IT was at Clermont in Auvergne that the great adventure started, the most amazing episode in the history of medieval Christendom. On 18th November 1095 a council met at Clermont, the Pope himself presiding. During the first nine days the bishops, abbots, and other prelates discussed such urgent matters as reform and relations with the troublesome German Emperor Henry IV. Suddenly, on the tenth day, as if he had waited for his plan to reach full maturity, the Vicar of Christ rose to speak of something very different. He referred to the Sepulchre in which Jesus had lain for three days before His glorious Resurrection; he described this most sacred of all spots, towards which so many pilgrims had directed their weary footsteps and their hopes, but which was now in the hands of infidels, profaned and virtually inaccessible. Was Jerusalem to remain captive? The Pope concluded in a voice that expressed the whole fervour of his soul: 'Men of God, men chosen and blessed among all, combine your forces! Take the road to the Holy Sepulchre assured of the imperishable glory that awaits you in God's kingdom. Let each one deny himself and take the Cross!'

He who thus, in few phrases, had given Europe a new destiny was a Frenchman, Eudes de Châtillon, a former monk of Cluny, who had become Pope seven years earlier with the name of Urban II.[1] The political situation was such as might easily have daunted the stoutest heart: others might have considered it unlikely that Christendom would engage in so perilous an undertaking, especially when it was suggested by a Pope who was himself defied by an antipope backed by the most powerful sovereign of that age. But Urban II considered his project as no earthly affair; it was one of those supernatural calls, like that of the last trumpet, to which no Christian could remain deaf.

Urban was not the first to conceive this plan,[2] though no one had yet tried to give it shape. Soon after the year 1000, Sylvester II had exclaimed: 'Soldiers of Christ, arise!' Next, when the terrible Hakim

---

[1] On Urban II see Chapter V, section 4, and Chapter IV, section 5. His statue overlooks the Marne below Épernay.

[2] On the origin of the idea of a crusade see Carl Erdmann, *Die Entstehung des Kreuzzugsdedankens* (1935), and E. Delaruelle's article 'Essai sur la formation de l'idée de Croisade' in the *Bulletin de l'Histoire ecclésiastique*, 1944, p. 12.

destroyed the church of the Holy Sepulchre in 1010, Sergius IV had
launched an appeal prophetic of that delivered at Clermont.   Lastly,
on the eve of his death, Gregory VII had spoken of forming a
Christian league against Islam, and had uttered words tantamount to a
promise: 'I would rather risk my life to deliver the Holy Places than
govern the universe.'   But at the end of the eleventh century circumstances called no more for words, but for action.

The event which determined the papacy to act was the Turkish
invasion; and that decision, more than any other, was taken cautiously
after long and careful weighing of the pros and cons.   For some time
after the Arabs had conquered Palestine four hundred years earlier,
there was a *modus vivendi* between them and Christendom, and pilgrims
were able without much difficulty to visit the Sepulchre, which was in
the care of Christian clergy.   But since the year 1000 the situation had
altered: an atmosphere of tolerant indolence had given place to a
revival of the Holy War.   This was due to the appearance of the
Seljuk Turks.   Not that they were more cruel or less civilized than
other Moslems—indeed the crusaders recognized their generosity and
chivalry—but they were a young people, on the flood tide of expansion,
fanatical devotees of Islamic law, and knowing nothing of tacit under-
standings with the enemy.   When they took Jerusalem, in 1076, the
dreadful news was spread that pilgrimage was no longer possible, that
a poll-tax had been imposed by the Turks on visitors to the Holy Land,
and that many of them had been molested, robbed, and even reduced
to slavery.   One Peter of Achery, returning from this unpleasant
journey, was full of horror-stories.

Urban's principal motive was to deliver the Tomb, so that the
faithful might be free to go and pray there.   The project was already
in the air, many westerners already dreamed of it; and the papacy, well
informed, as always, may have been aware that the situation in Asia was
singularly favourable to its realization.   Since the death of its third
sultan, Malikh-Shah (1072–92), the Seljuk empire had broken up into
four parts: Persia, where his sons were fighting for the throne; Syria,
where two of his nephews reigned in fraternal hostility at Aleppo and
Damascus; and finally Asia Minor, which, from Nicea to Konieh, was
in the hands of a younger member of the family.   Moreover, the
Arabs in Egypt hated the Turks, who looked upon them as heretics.
The disunion of Islam would be of great advantage to the Christian
enterprise.

Concern for the Holy Sepulchre was not the only motive behind
Urban's decision.   There were several others, explicit or presumable.
The defeat of Mantzikert in 1071, when Romanus Diogenes was taken
prisoner, opened a wide breach in the rampart established by Byzantium against attack from Asia, and the West naturally felt obliged to

reinforce the East at so vital a point. It was rumoured that the Basileus Alexius Comnenus had renewed the appeal addressed by his predecessor to Gregory VII, and had written to Count Robert of Flanders asking for military assistance.[1] In the opinion of Urban II, to help Byzantium was to obey an elementary law of fraternal charity, to ward off a danger threatening the whole of Christendom, and even perhaps to go some way towards healing the schism—a work which never ceased to preoccupy the Holy See.

But there was another and more fundamental reason: the Church had tried for centuries to abolish violence, though with only partial success; she was wise enough to realize the impossibility of changing lions into lambs.   The best means, therefore, to restrict the use of force in Christendom was to direct it towards some higher and sacred end. In his address to the Council of Clermont, Urban II made no secret of this idea, for he invited even brigands to become soldiers of Christ.   A psycho-analyst has said that the crusades provided an outlet for inhibited passion, and Western morality certainly profited thereby.

Such, then, were the motives which determined Urban II to launch Christendom on this adventure.   Had he other and secret reasons? Did he believe that the crusade might afford a unique opportunity of establishing, by means different from those of Gregory VII, the *de facto* primacy of Rome over the Christian world?   It so happened that in 1095 the German Emperor, the King of France, and the King of England were all three outside the Church for various reasons, and excommunicated persons were not allowed to take the Cross. Looking back upon events, we realize that the Pope's political ambition, or what appears as such, was but a means to the establishment of God's reign on earth, to man's possession of a City not made with hands.

As for those who heard the appeal of Clermont, it would be idle to suggest that all of them obeyed in a spirit of selfless devotion; there is no doubt that worldly motives played a part.   Urban II made express reference to one of these: the over-population of a country like France where there was no room for the new-born generation. On the economic plane also there was the temptation to acquire the gold and precious materials in which the East abounded.   The great Italian ports of Genoa, Pisa, and Venice kept this end in view, and the history of the crusade has its maritime and commercial aspect,[2] which, though not particularly edifying, must not be overlooked. Again, youthful barons and impoverished younger sons of good family were pleased with the idea of acquiring on Moslem territory those fiefs which niggardly Fate denied them in Europe.   Add to these motives a thirst for adventure, a need to pass the boundaries of a

---

[1] Chapter X, section 5.
[2] Cf. G. Lacour-Gayet, *Histoire du commerce*, vol. ii, p. 289.

narrow world, the eternal image of the East—not forgetting that of foreign princesses—and one has a more or less complete list of the human, all too human, causes of the crusade. But it would be unfair to suppose that they were the primary and determining causes. If, to use Péguy's words, 'policy' was bound up with 'mysticism,' even if 'mysticism was reduced to policy,' it must not be forgotten that the crusade was a *mystical* fact, in the true sense of that word. It was the manifestation of a spiritual impulse springing from the noblest depths of man's soul, the heroic expression of a faith which found no satisfaction unless in sacrifice, an answer to the call of God.

2. THE APPEAL IS ANSWERED

Those present at the Council of Clermont reacted with extraordinary enthusiasm and a wonderful upsurge of faith. We are able, from various sources, to reconstruct the scene as that great assembly rose to its feet and answered the Pope's call with a tremendous shout 'God wills it so!' Urban himself took up these words and made them the watchword of the expedition. Crosses were forthwith cut from mantles or curtains, and sewn on to the right shoulder of volunteers. All that is to-day most impressive in mass-movements, e.g. political meetings or world-pilgrimages, may give us some idea of that human tide. On the evening of 27th November there was no more red stuff in Clermont; some therefore had a cross tattooed on their shoulder, and in some cases were branded with red-hot iron. 'Many,' says Michelet, 'were suddenly wearied of all that they had loved; barons left their castles, artisans their crafts, and peasants their fields, toiling and suffering to preserve from sacrilegious profanation the ten square feet of earth in which the body of their God had lain for a few hours.'

The movement spread from Clermont to all the provinces of France. On leaving the council, Urban II halted in several towns to renew his appeal, while missionaries travelled far and wide, winning adherents wherever they preached. This holy contagion quickly reached Flanders, Italy, England, and Scandinavia. To all those who took the Cross the Church granted a special blessing, remission of Purgatory, suspension or even cancellation of their debts, and protection for their families and property while they were absent. The departure was fixed for 15th August in the following year under the direction of the Bishop of Puy, Adhemar de Monteil, heir to the princes of Royat. His appointment was intended to show that the expedition had no other purpose than to serve God.

Michelet rightly says that the expedition included men of all ages and of every rank. The Church did her best to restrain this torrent of fervour by curbing thoughtless enthusiasm; those who wished to enrol had first to obtain the approval of their parish-priest, and monks could only do so with permission of their superiors. A vow to go on crusade was declared irrevocable and subject to canonical sanctions; to break it entailed excommunication. But these precautions did not suffice to prevent the enlistment of adventurers, vagabonds, and social misfits, as well as of ne'er-do-wells, politicians, and brigands. Every crusade, except perhaps the third, had its quota of wives, children, and traders, not to mention a whole crowd of loose women. The history of the crusades, indeed, is full of episodes that reveal the worst side of human nature: egotism, unbridled lust, frightful cruelty, and rapacity. This, however, is not at all surprising; you cannot excite large human groups without stirring the bad with the good.

Nor must we expect to find the leaders themselves all first-rate types, all saints. There certainly were men of that calibre, and in surprising numbers; but alongside such true servants of God as Godfrey de Bouillon, Baldwin IV (the little leper-king), and St Louis, alongside such genuine leaders as Baldwin II, there were unscrupulous adventurers like Renaud of Châtillon, scheming politicians like Bohemond the Norman, incompetents like Guy de Lusignan, even cowards and downright traitors. Although we shall find many examples of sublime unselfishness, the attitude of the maritime traders and in some cases, alas, of the Templars themselves, was worse than that of Shylock.

These human defects, however, help to put the crusade in its proper perspective: it was no romance of the Round Table. Though a splendid enterprise, it was fundamentally human as, on a smaller scale, was the cathedral. René Grousset, the most eminent French historian of the crusades, has described them as an 'epic'; and one instinctively calls to mind the great epic heroes, when we read of men who were prepared to fight though outnumbered by forty to one and whose physical strength was demonstrated by extraordinary, if brutal, feats of swordsmanship and otherwise. But if the crusading host had consisted entirely of such giants, the drama would hold little interest except as legend. Our main concern is with the nameless mass, the rank and file, for whom the crusades were the greatest of all Christian adventures, notwithstanding the presence in their midst of so many scoundrels.

France played a leading part in the crusades. Guibert de Nogent's celebrated formula, 'Gesta Dei per Francos,' must not be interpreted as a mere piece of jingoism, for in Palestine and Syria the word 'Franks' was applied to all westerners regardless of the land of each one's origin. Besides, the majority of those who took the Cross were Frenchmen. 'Those Frenchmen are unnatural,' said the troubadour Marcabru, 'who refuse to interest themselves in God's affairs.' France had the largest population; the appeal had been launched on French soil by a French Pope; Cluny, which inspired the papacy, was a French institution; it was in France that chivalry had attained its perfection; and the barons of France had long experience of warfare against the Moslems in Spain, where they had taken part in the Reconquista. All these factors helped to make Frenchmen the most numerous and often the best of the crusaders.

So, in 1095, Christendom set out upon the march. A glorious chapter of history had opened; it was to last until the end of the twelfth century, and the tall shadow of the crusader may be detected behind all the events—political and religious, spiritual and artistic—of that period. It is usual to speak of eight crusades; but large or small groups of men left Europe every year, sometimes unarmed and led not by soldiers but by monks, for whom the call of the Holy Land was so strong that they were prone to act impetuously and without sufficient forethought.

3.   THE FIRST CRUSADE

The first wave of this tide was so strong that the Church could neither restrain it nor direct it according to her plans, and the 'popular' crusade met with disaster. Among the missionaries who preached the message of Clermont the most famous was Peter the Hermit. A Picard from Amiens, he was a man of burning faith, a kind of hairy prophet, clothed in rough homespun, emaciated by his austerities. He had a remarkable way of talking to the common people in their own language, and was immediately recognized as one sent by God. Wherever he spoke, crowds flocked to him from all sides, and even pulled out the hairs of his mule as relics! Were they going to leave to the rich and powerful, he asked, the honour of delivering the Holy Land? He was answered with a tremendous outburst of faith combined with that popular craving for a more just and brotherly society, freed from the tutelage of money and violence, which characterizes the whole medieval period and which found expression now in the communal movement, now in the apostolate of a Robert d'Arbrissel, now in the teaching of the Friars Minor, and now in bloody risings. There was also an element of base credulity—endless talk of signs in the heavens, or falling stars, and prophecies. Deliverance was at hand! It was time therefore to start.

These hapless folk, of both sexes and all ages, even the sick and the infirm, accordingly set out. To bear witness for God was more important than fighting, and the best witnesses, surely, are those who die for His holy name. They sold for next to nothing all that they possessed, and oxen shod like horses were harnessed to carts laden with baggage and children. It was exactly like a tribal migration. French

Flemings, Italians, and Germans formed the majority, but there were also Scotsmen and a few Englishmen. The 'army' consisted of four divisions: one led by Peter the Hermit; an Italian division whose leader is unknown; one commanded by an impoverished knight nicknamed 'Walter the Penniless,' whose party consisted of exactly eight gentlemen as poor as himself; and lastly, the Germans under Volkmar Gottschalk and von Lusingen, who, after massacring Jews in the Rhineland and Bohemia, were annihilated in Hungary.

The People's Crusade set off in the late spring of 1096. 'Is that Jerusalem?' they would ask, whenever they caught sight of the smallest fortified township. They were soon in difficulties: how were these thousands of emigrants to be provisioned? By wholesale pillage, of course; and the suspicion which greeted their arrival in Byzantine territory was fully justified by their sack of Belgrade, the chief imperial city after Constantinople. Alexius Comnenus ordered his Cuman and turcopole cavalry to keep an eye on them; and when he beheld this seething mass at the gates of his capital, he hurriedly provided ships and had them transported to Kibotos on the Sea of Marmora, which the Picard peasants named Civitot. The Turks were not far away. At first they paid little attention to this motley crowd of pilgrims; but about the middle of October, Walter's men decided to try their mettle—with appalling consequences. Cut down and overwhelmed with a hail of arrows, the unfortunate host fell back in such disorder that the Seljuk cavalry had difficulty in forcing a passage through their ranks and wreaking a worse vengeance. Only a few thousand, including Peter the Hermit, managed to escape. The Byzantines once more put them on board ship, and they joined the feudal forces whose arrival had just been announced.

For meanwhile the nobility had made careful preparations. Their military leaders, acting on advice from Rome, meant to take no chances. There were four tactical groups, each of which had been ordered to follow a different route; they were to meet at Constantinople and enter Asia together. Estimates of the numbers vary between 50,000 and 500,000.[1] In any case, it is certain that these large bodies must have dwindled month by month. At the fall of Nicea, the crusading army appears to have numbered no more than 30,000 men, and before Jerusalem it amounted to scarcely two divisions.

The first group consisted of Belgians, northern French, Lorrainers, and Germans. Their leader was Godfrey de Bouillon, Duke of Basse-Lorraine, a man of spotless character and splendid physique. Tall, broad-chested, stately, of superhuman strength and courage, he was yet

[1] The numbers of the crusading forces and of medieval armies in general present a difficult problem. The most detailed and careful study is Ferdinand Lot's *L'art militaire et les armées au Moyen Âge* (2 vols., Paris, 1946).

chaste, liberal, and a model of Christian piety; the very prototype of a crusader and almost a saint.[1] With him was his brother Baldwin of Boulogne; a brave warrior, but more of a politician than Godfrey, he was probably inspired by more material interests. Hugh of Vermandois, brother of Philip I, commanded troops from central France as well as the Norman brigade recruited by Robert Curthose (son of William the Conqueror), the vassals of Count Stephen of Blois, and those of Count Robert II of Flanders. Hugh was a great lord, elegant and refined, but a diplomat rather than a soldier. The southern French were led by Raymond of St Gilles, Count of Toulouse and Marquis of Provence, a complex personality. He had already been on pilgrimage to Jerusalem, had fought in Spain, and was the first great nobleman to take the Cross; but he had been bitterly disappointed by the nomination of Bishop Adhemar as commander-in-chief of the crusade. Though capable of sublime heroism, Raymond had also an unfortunate way of side-tracking danger, but his deep-seated faith and devotion to God's cause cannot be denied. The fourth and last group was a 'commando' unit raised by Bohemond of Taranto, son of Guiscard, who had caused the Basileus a good deal of anxiety between 1081 and 1085. It is just possible that these Normans felt a genuine desire to obey the Pope's call; but it is hard not to believe that they regarded the crusade no less as a means of satisfying their voracious appetites.

The first group set out in August 1096 and followed the Danube valley, where the Hungarians, forewarned by the passage of the 'popular' crusade, demanded hostages before they would allow free passage. Godfrey's division, moving in good order and observing strict discipline, reached Constantinople in December. The advance guard of the second division was already there. Hugh had received the banner of St Peter from the Pope in Rome. Taking ship at Bari, he had landed at Durazzo and crossed the Balkans, where the Byzantine officials had watched his progress with such close attention that his circumstances were little better than open arrest. Raymond's force from Provence and Languedoc, accompanied by the papal legate, started in October and travelled via northern Italy and the Balkans, where their relations with the Croats and Dalmatians were cordial to a degree. As for the Normans, they set out during the winter along a road they knew so well—the Egnatian Way, by which they had travelled ten years earlier not as crusaders but as mortal enemies of Byzantium. The four divisions linked up at Constantinople in

---

[1] We may obtain some notion of the complicated state of Christendom at the height of the Quarrel of Investitures by recalling that Godfrey de Bouillon had sided with Henry IV against the Pope and that he had taken part in the sack of Rome, an achievement of which, says Alberic of Trois Fontaines, he was so ashamed that for several days he was stricken with fever and it was then that he vowed to take the Cross.

August 1097, an event which afforded the Basileus small cause for rejoicing.

Alexius Comnenus was in an awkward position. He was troubled at the sight of these forces gathered beneath his walls, and not without reason. But what could he do to oppose them? He had only a few brigades of turcopoles, Cumans, and Petchenegs, whom the iron-clad cavalry of the West would brush aside like flies. On the other hand, he was a good diplomat, and realized that these pestiferous allies might be profitably employed against the Turks, provided they would agree to fight under his direction. Moreover, to give the Basileus his due, he was an excellent Christian and desired at all costs to avoid a war between his co-religionists on the Moslem's doorstep. Could he prevent a clash that must otherwise soon take place between his subjects and the Western armies? Anna Comnena tells us what Byzantium thought of the crusaders. She does not hide her own contempt for these people; she represents them as avaricious and talkative, unstable and impudent, brave and cruel; and she condemns their childish wonder at the sight of gold, precious stones, and silk. She looked upon them, in fact, as barbarians. The Europeans, on their side, knew nothing of the Greeks, and could not understand their intrigues, their delays, or their way of life. The priests and religious, with whom their ranks were crowded, assured them that the Byzantines were schismatics, enemies of the Holy Roman Church, which generally meant that they were henchmen of Satan, little more than gallows-birds. Nor was it long before every misfortune that overtook the crusade was attributed to the perfidious Greeks.

In these circumstances, Alexius behaved with great diplomatic skill. Combining the utmost politeness with underhand force, loading some of their chiefs with presents while he prevented the revictualling of their army, he managed to obtain an advantage which his numerical strength could not have afforded him. After weeks of negotiation, Godfrey de Bouillon, Prince of the Holy Roman Empire and soldier of the Pope, knelt before the schismatic, swore to recognize him as his overlord in respect of whatever lands he recovered from the infidel, and undertook to restore all such territory to the Byzantines. Alexius thereupon raised him up, embraced him, declared that he adopted him as a son, and offered him magnificent horses together with caskets full of gold. Most of the other generals followed Godfrey's example. Hugh of Vermandois agreed to do so because Byzantium appealed to his natural refinement. Bohemond, an incorrigible realist, looked to the generosity of Alexius for a handsome domain; and in fact the Basileus heaped him with gifts and promised him a fief, without, however, granting him the hoped-for title 'Grand Domestic of the Orient.' Only one refused outright to take a feudal oath: Raymond

The Crusades

of St Gilles, who argued that if the Holy Land were freed by the Pope's men, it should belong to none but the Pope. On that point the turbulent Provençal would not yield an inch.

Having reached agreement with the four crusading divisions, Comnenus hurried to provide the necessary shipping to transport them to the Asian shore, and this was done in the spring of 1097. In order to reach Syria, the gateway to the Holy Land, the crusaders had to march right across Asia Minor, which was ruled by the Seljukid of Anatolia. Sixteen years earlier the weakness of Nicephorus Botaniates had actually allowed the Turks to occupy Nicea, which they had made their capital; and Nicea was the first objective of the Western armies. Their courage and dash, assisted by Byzantine artillery and a bold manœuvre by the fleet, carried all before them (14th May–19th June 1097). But when the crusaders made their final assault and saw the imperial standard floating on the walls of Nicea, many believed they had been cheated; nor was this impression removed by the booty which was turned over to them as a sop to their indignation.

But this disappointment was only the beginning of their trials. The wild plains of Anatolia were already in the grip of summer heat, which caused untold suffering among the iron-clad chivalry of the West. Supplies ran short, and to meet this problem the army split into two corps: the Normans from Sicily and France under Bohemond, the remainder under Godfrey de Bouillon and Raymond of St Gilles. The Turks were now in a position to crush the two formations separately. At Dorylaeum, on 1st July, the Normans suddenly found themselves surrounded by the mounted hosts of Asia. Caught in a storm of arrows, they were scarcely able to re-group and stand their ground, and only the lightning intervention of Godfrey saved the day. In answer to their appeal, he moved so rapidly that he himself reached the battle-field with a mere fifty knights. The main body came up not long afterwards. While Adhemar of Monteil carried out a flanking movement, Godfrey overwhelmed the Turkish forces, and only a few thousand panic-stricken fugitives managed to regain the mountains. An enormous booty fell into the crusaders' hands; the military superiority of Christendom over Islam was established for a hundred years to come; and the disgrace of Mantzikert had been effaced.

This splendid feat of arms opened the way to the Holy Land but did not eliminate every obstacle. Crossing the plateau, a desert region studded with saltpans and unhealthy marshes, proved a veritable Calvary. There was bitterness among the leaders; God's service was hard and paid small profits. Baldwin and Tancred, having attempted to occupy Cilicia and disputed its possession, soon deserted the army and went to try their fortune in the neighbourhood of Edessa. When the crusaders reached the Taurus they were given a friendly welcome by some Armenian Christians who had taken refuge in that mountain-ous district after the ruin of their country.[1]　This was a stroke of good fortune; their knowledge of local geography and their ingenuity was to stand the invading army in good stead.

On 20th October the vanguard under Bohemond encamped before Antioch.　They were deeply impressed by that great city, which had been the second capital of the Church, after Jerusalem and before Rome, one-time residence of both St Peter and St Paul.　Here, on the banks of Orontes, the disciples of Jesus had first been called 'Chris-tians.'　No assault was possible so long as the place was in Turkish hands, and they prepared to besiege it.　But this was no easy matter, for although the crusaders were skilled in mass attack they had little knowledge of engineering.　The siege dragged on for eight months, and might have done so still longer had not a Genoese and Byzantine fleet arrived with sappers and carpenters who erected a wooden castle over against the walls.　The intelligence and determination of the Armenians saved the Christian army from starving to death during this long ordeal, but pestilence wrought havoc against which they were altogether powerless.

Meanwhile, it was learned that Baldwin had struck lucky.　The Armenian prince Thoros had chosen him as his son-in-law and heir, a timely sedition had carried off that monarch, and Baldwin had been installed at Edessa as the first European ruler in the East.　Success of this kind inevitably begat jealousy.　Bohemond had similar designs on Antioch, but his ambition at least served the common cause.　Having obtained a promise that the town should be his, he conspired with some Armenians, who opened the gates to him on 2nd June 1098.　And he was only just in time; for two days later the Emir Kourbouqa of Mosul appeared with a relieving force.　This was the third time that Islam had tried to save Antioch; the first two attempts, on 31st December and 9th February, had been easily frustrated, but the present occasion was far more serious.　The besiegers were now themselves besieged; they were exhausted and on the verge of despair.　Only a miracle could save them.　When that miracle occurred, many people, including the legate, refused to believe it; but the rank and file did believe it—which was what really mattered.　On 14th June, in conse-quence of a dream vouchsafed to a Provençal pilgrim named Peter Barthélemy, there was discovered under the floor of a church the very lance which had pierced our Lord's side.　Thrilled by so remarkable an event, the crusaders made a mass sortie on 28th June, and Kour-bouqa only just managed to escape with his life.

This third victory delivered the Holy Land to the invaders, but they were in no hurry to follow up their advantage.　They dawdled on the

[1] See Chapter X, section 3.

banks of the Orontes until mid January, growing ever more peevish and therefore prone to intrigue. Adhemar of Monteil, the spiritual director of the crusade, had died on 1st August, and his outstanding qualities of leadership were sorely missed. The Pope was invited to come and take command in person, but was naturally unable to accept. The military commanders differed as to strategy: some were in favour of marching straight for Jerusalem, while others thought they ought first to break the power of Islam in Iraq and Egypt. Rival interests were more than ever apparent. Bohemond announced his decision to remain at Antioch, which was now his property, a decision which more than satisfied Raymond of St Gilles. Alexius Comnenus viewed with some anxiety the erection of Latin fiefs which seemed to care little for his suzerainty, and he began to think that it might be best not to ruin the Moslems altogether. Accordingly, he made a secret pact with the Fatimites in Egypt, and when Hugh of Vermandois came as ambassador asking him to lead his troops against Jerusalem, he excused himself. There was discontent in the religious field also. The crusaders at first treated the Greek Patriarch of Antioch with every mark of respect, rebuilt churches, repaired the ikons, and restored the clergy. But they were soon annoyed to learn that the Greeks were openly criticizing their customs and beliefs; mutual hostility became more pronounced; and the latest refusal of Alexius convinced them that the Byzantines were no longer to be trusted. The situation was indeed grave. The Patriarch John V left for Constantinople and was succeeded by a Latin Patriarch, Bernard of Valentinois.

The rank and file of the army, backed by the pilgrim host, roused their officers and obliged them to renew the march on Jerusalem. The fiery Raymond of St Gilles set an example: barefooted, he took the southward road on 13th January; but six months elapsed before the first Christian knelt beside the Tomb—a long time for a journey of 312 miles. The fact is that, although the crusaders were still inspired by holy fervour, a natural weariness had begun to overtake them. Their heavy losses were not made good by reinforcements.[1] Realists began to think it was time to enjoy what they had won, to establish themselves in the beautiful Lebanese 'riviera' where spring was so delightful, and Godfrey de Bouillon had much difficulty in preventing Raymond of St Gilles from settling in this way at Tortosa. From the military standpoint, however, things seemed to have improved. The emirs of Beirut, Tyre, and Acre surrendered on their approach; while the Maronites, a hub of resistance to Islam, lent valuable aid. The European advance guard met with practically no resistance; Gaston of Béarn and Robert of Flanders entered Ramleh without drawing their

---

[1] These were sometimes considerable, as when Guynemer of Boulogne arrived with 20,000 Scandinavians.

P*

swords, and a hundred knights under Tancred and Baldwin of Bourg (Godfrey's cousin) reached Bethlehem, where Greek and Syriac Christians welcomed them with tears of joy.

At length, on 7th June, the army came within sight of Jerusalem. Before this city whose name had been a kind of supernatural watchword, in this countryside which evoked such vivid memories of their God, the Christians forgot their differences and sufferings, and proved themselves worthy of their calling. 'When they heard the name of Jerusalem,' says the chronicler, 'they could not restrain their tears. Falling upon their knees, they gave thanks to God for having enabled them to reach the goal of their pilgrimage, the Holy City where our Lord had chosen to save the world. Moving indeed were the sobs that rose from all those people. They advanced until the walls and towers of the city were distinctly visible. Then they raised their hands towards heaven as if in gratitude, and humbly kissed the ground.'

The siege, however, was difficult. Jerusalem had been occupied by the Moslems of Egypt, who had relieved the Turks and entrusted its defence to a Sudanese garrison. The first assault came to nothing. But it so happened that some Genoese sailors had landed siege material at Jaffa. Wooden towers were constructed and pushed up against the walls, while catapults hurled enormous blocks of stone. While these operations were in progress, the crusaders, with Godfrey at their head, recalling the miracle which had enabled Joshua to capture Jericho, and improving human skill with supernatural means, walked barefooted in an enormous procession round the city. The general assault took place on Friday, 15th July 1099. Every leader played his part: Godfrey built a bridge from one of the towers to the wall; Tancred and Robert Curthose threw themselves into a breach made by a battering ram. By evening Jerusalem was in the hands of the crusaders.

But, as if to emphasize that God's work had been accomplished by man, poor sinful man, the conquest of Jerusalem was marked with hideous carnage, of which the victors themselves were afterwards ashamed. The noble Raymond of St Gilles protected his prisoners, but thousands of others behaved themselves like butchers. At the Mosque of Omar, which stands on the site of the temple, there was such slaughter that the blood ran ankle-deep. Hours passed before the intoxication of unbridled rage gave place once more to Christian faith. Towards dusk the conquerors, now washed and recovered from their insane fury, climbed the Via Dolorosa barefooted, devoutly kissing each place where Christ had fallen. Then they flung themselves on the ground before the Holy Sepulchre, their arms stretched out crosswise, and lay there a long while, happy if exhausted.

4. THE LATIN KINGDOM OF JERUSALEM

Having taken Jerusalem, a number of crusaders thought they had fulfilled their vow and decided to return home. But there was no question of abandoning the Holy Land. Someone would have to be found who was prepared to stay on with a handful of troops in order to hold Palestine, which was but partially subdued and surrounded with enemies. None was better qualified for this task than Godfrey de Bouillon; he had shown matchless courage, his goodness and firmness were well known, and he was the most perfect Christian of them all. In spite of ill-tempered reserve on the part of Raymond of St Gilles, Godfrey was elected by the barons. According to tradition, he refused the title of king, not wishing to assume a golden diadem where his Redeemer had worn a crown of thorns. The true king of Jerusalem was Christ in the person of His Vicar; he, Godfrey, would be content with the more modest style 'Attorney of the Holy Sepulchre.' Such grand humility completes the portrait of a great crusader, who died in the following year, on 18th July 1100. His brother Baldwin, less scrupulous, became the first Latin king of Jerusalem.

This kingdom was destined to endure the vicissitudes of almost two hundred years, thanks to the intelligence and steadfastness of its first three titled sovereigns, Baldwin I (1100–18), his cousin Baldwin II (1118–31), and the latter's son-in-law Fulk of Anjou (1131–43). There was something of the Capetians in these rulers, who consolidated their territory, strove to establish their kingdom on the seaboard, and were able to impose their authority upon noblemen whose dominant virtue was not obedience.

The feudal regime had taken root in the East to the detriment of central authority which was so badly needed. Enormous fiefs had been created. Those of Edessa and Antioch dated from before the fall of Jerusalem. Raymond of St Gilles, for want of a royal throne, had installed himself as Count of Tripoli. There was also the principality of Galilee, baronies such as Lesser Armenia, and a number of siegniories, e.g. Beirut, Sidon, Tyre, and Nauplus. In theory, the king could not act without his council of vassals and officers of the crown; his revenue was derived from his personal domain and customs dues.

The Latin kingdom appears, at first sight, a mere copy of the Western monarchies, but in some respects it was a distinct improvement thereupon. For one thing, it had a first-rate judicial system. The high court enjoyed legislative powers and acted as the supreme tribunal. We possess a collection of its decisions known as the *Assizes of Jerusalem*, a famous document which throws much light upon medieval law. In cities the Viscount represented the central

government and administered criminal justice; but a court of twelve
burgesses decided lawsuits between members of their own class, while
mixed tribunals dealt with cases between burgesses and nobles.   There
were also special tribunals, e.g. the *Fonde* which took cognizance of
commercial suits, and the *Chaîne* for maritime causes.

From the religious point of view, an already involved situation was
further complicated by the Western regime.   The Holy Land was a
tangle of sects, including all those which had been driven from
Byzantium—Monophysites, Nestorians, Jacobites, and many more.
All recognized the nominal supremacy of the Roman Church, which
showed itself tolerant and friendly; it was, in fact, at this date that
different parts of the church of the Holy Sepulchre were assigned to
recognized Christian sects, one taking an altar, another a chapel, and so
forth.   The Patriarch of Jerusalem was the spiritual head, with four
archbishops dependent on him as follows: Caesarea with the suffragan
of Samaria; Tyre with the bishoprics of Acre, Paneas, Sidon, and
Beirut; Tiberias with Nazareth; and Montreal or Petra with the
bishopric of Jericho and the convent of Sinai.   Hebron, Lydda, and
Bethlehem were dioceses immediately subject to Jerusalem.   Antioch
was a separate patriarchate with the three archbishoprics of Tarsus,
Edessa, and Apamea.   There were, of course, numerous monasteries:
Mount Sion, La Latine, Mount Olivet, Josaphat, and the Holy
Sepulchre stood side by side with such Greek houses as St Sabbas.

The Latin kingdom of Jerusalem, then, was no mere copy but an
original creation.   Differences between it and the kingdoms of
western Europe became more marked as time went on, and not always
for the best.   With a speed that can surprise only those who do
not know the conservatism of the East and how quickly a westerner
'goes native' in 'colonial' countries, the crusaders grew so acclimatized
as to become virtually orientals.   Godfrey de Bouillon had lived with
monastic austerity, but King Baldwin sat on his throne wearing a gold-
embroidered burnous.   His beard was long like that of an Eastern
monarch; a gilded shield was carried before him; and he sat cross-
legged on a carpet to receive ambassadors who were required to
prostrate in his presence.   His chaplain, Foucher of Chartres, mentions
this phenomenon quite cheerfully and with complete candour.   'Here
we are, Europeans, become natives of the East.   He who was once an
Italian or Frenchman is now a Galilean or Palestinian.   We have
already forgotten our places of origin.   Here, one man owns his house
and servants as naturally as if they were his immemorial inheritance.
Another has married a Syrian, an Armenian, or even a baptized Saracen,
and lives with his native in-laws.   We use the several languages of the
country as circumstances dictate.'   The good man proceeds to tell us
quite frankly the reason of this absorption: 'He who in Europe owned

not so much as a village is lord of a whole city out here. He who was worth no more than a few pence now disposes of a fortune. Why should we return to the West when we have all we desire here?'

What he does not say, however, is that luxury, a life of ease, and contact with more 'advanced' civilization (in every sense of that word) exercised a disastrous moral influence on the crusaders, and still more so on their descendants. Nor was the intermingling of races always desirable when judged by its results. Too many half-breeds lost the characteristics of their Western ancestors. Adultery and broken marriage were also current coin, and one king of Jerusalem actually had two wives! This moral laxity extended also to the clergy, and reforming measures taken at the assizes of Nauplus remained a dead letter. Although the faith was theoretically unimpaired, many compromised not only as regards the Ten Commandments, but even in matters of doctrine, and numerous Christians dabbled in the religion of Mahomet.

This state of affairs was not calculated to endow the Latin kingdom with that unbreakable unity which was essential, if only to withstand the enemy. The young state was doomed to endless trouble, particularly through shortage of men. Europeans were never more than a small minority of overlords and merchants who controlled the natives; immigration schemes were all doomed to failure. In 1101, for example, the largest of these 'immigrant crusades' arrived at Constantinople and was taken in hand by Raymond of St Gilles; but they were massacred soon afterwards in the plains of Anatolia. Baldwin II conceived an ingenious idea of attracting to Palestine all Greek and Syriac Christians scattered about that part of the world; but his scheme was not equivalent to a steady flow of European immigrants, which remained insignificant to the very end. Practically speaking, the Latins held only the towns; the desert was still occupied by the Saracens, who ravaged the countryside right up to the city walls. Palestine had, therefore, to exist on a wartime basis, bristling with enormous strongholds whose garrisons must at every moment be prepared to resist Moslem invasion.

Besides its absolute numerical inferiority, the kingdom was also handicapped by its recruiting methods. Following ordinary feudal principles, the king summoned his vassals, who met to consider the royal proclamation, and then came—or did not come—to place themselves under his orders. Every thinking man realized that a standing army was indispensable, but the question was how to find the money. The King of Jerusalem was by no means wealthy, at the most he could maintain a few Turkish squadrons.

It was in order to supply this need that there arose a curious institution known as the Military Orders. The idea was simply to form a body of men who would consider themselves as knights of God, ready to serve Christ in arms, and, if need be, lay down their lives for Him. At the same time, they would be true monks bound by vows of poverty, chastity, and obedience. It is possible that the idea was borrowed from the *Ribats* of Islam. At all events, it helped to realize the noblest ideals of medieval Christendom. Two military Orders played a prominent part in the history of the Latin kingdom : the Templars and Hospitallers. The Templars were founded by Hugh de Payens in 1118, and were so called because they had established their head-quarters in the mosque of El Aqsâ on the site of Solomon's Temple. The order consisted of chaplains and knights (all of whom were of noble blood), and of servants or sergeant-commoners. They wore a voluminous white cloak derived from the Cistercian cowl, and before long this was adorned with a large red cross. The Hospitallers of St John likewise bore a red cross, but on a black mantle. They were originally a charitable Order devoted to the care of pilgrims, and had been established some time before the first crusade by Gerard of Martigues. The Hospitallers were transformed into a military Order about 1120 by Raymond of Puy, who entrusted them with the protec-tion of the Holy Sepulchre.[1] These two Orders provided the kingdom with what it had hitherto lacked, viz. a permanent army whose heroism and spirit of self-sacrifice were for a long time beyond praise. Both built huge fortresses whose imposing ruins may still be seen on many a hilltop. Tortosa, Toron, Chastel Blanc, and Le Chastel belonged to the Templars; Marjat, Chastel Rouge, Gibelin, and the famed Krak des Chevaliers to the Hospitallers. How was it that even these *corps d'élite* so rapidly declined? Between the Templars and Hospitallers holy emulation soon turned to bitter jealousy. These monastic soldiers, especially the Templars, becoming rich and proud, abandoned discipline for arrogance and even worse. In some cases they preferred money to the welfare of Christendom, and St Louis was obliged to inflict public humiliation for their downright treachery. Here was another example of oriental influence upon European institutions.[2]

Numerical weakness and a bad system of recruiting, which was not entirely counterbalanced by the institution of military Orders, were not the only difficulties confronting the Latin kingdom. Even in the West the feudal system tended towards anarchy ; and that tendency was

---

[1] The Teutonic Order, founded in 1122 as a charitable institution by the burgesses of Bremen and Lübeck, also became a military Order in 1190, but did little work in the Holy Land. We shall find them (Chapter XII) opposing the barbarians in eastern Europe. The Order of the Holy Sepulchre likewise dates from the time of Godfrey de Bouillon. According to tradition, it is much older, having been founded in Carolingian days and even in those of the Empress Helena. But its final constitutions were granted by Pope Urban II.

[2] For the end of the Templars see Chapter XIV. What remained of their Order was absorbed by the Hospitallers, who survive to-day as the Knights of Malta.

still more pronounced in a country where it had not resulted from historical necessity, but had been applied from without in consequence of jealousy among the nobles, all of whom believed that the King of Jerusalem was no more exalted than themselves.   Mutual animosity sometimes developed into internecine strife, for the barons had no sense of unity in face of Islam.

The Church herself often took part in these complicated intrigues. Instead of upholding the monarchy with all her strength, as she was even then doing in France, she treated it as a child in need of care and discipline, making the king feel that he had no existence apart from her. It is true that the Latin kingdom produced a few saintly prelates, but there were many more whose purpose was material rather than super-natural, and whose conduct cannot be described as exemplary.   Im-mediately after the taking of Jerusalem, Robert Curthose's chaplain, Arnoul Malecorne, was elected Patriarch.   A scheming cleric, his life was so far removed from sanctity that he had to be deposed.   Daim-bert, Archbishop of Pisa, succeeded him or, rather, stepped uninvited into his shoes.   But this did not mend matters, for the Pisan was just as ambitious, even more brutal, and quite unscrupulous where money was concerned; he was, in fact, a politician.   His first act was to suggest that Godfrey de Bouillon should clear out from Jerusalam where, he said, only the patriarchal authority should reside.   The kings were destined to suffer as much embarrassment from influential churchmen as from the most powerful barons.

Another cause of weakness stemmed from the impossibility of forming a united Graeco-Latin front against the Moslems, and it must be admitted that in this respect Byzantium was more to blame.   The basileis had every reason to be annoyed at the conduct of certain barons who scorned the emperor's suzerainty over their fiefs, although it had been clearly recognized in oaths sworn at Constantinople; and some of them took strong measures.   Thus, in 1138, John Comnenus arrived, in the course of a campaign, with a powerful force on the Orontes.   Finding Raymond of Antioch in no hurry to assist him, he humiliated that warrior by entering the city on horseback and obliging him to go on foot as his squire.   Such manifestations of authority were no doubt justified; but the fact remains that Byzantium never really took part in the crusade, although her intervention might have proved decisive; never really supported the Latins; regularly failed to crush the Turks, even when she had the chance; and even entered into highly suspect relations with certain Moslem chiefs.

The policy of the Latins towards Islam was so involved that it helped in no small measure to weaken them.   The crusaders were obliged by force of circumstances to maintain some sort of relations with their enemies.   They soon came to recognize the Turks as a brave and chivalrous race, and mutual esteem grew up. The Latins, however, were fully aware of rivalry between various Moslem states. Instead of treating Islam as a whole, they proposed to make use of these dissensions by playing off one faction against the other. Such a policy, in the hands of a far-sighted king like Fulk, was quite successful; but the barons quickly evolved their own private schemes, allying themselves with emirs, sharing in the quarrels of Islam, and, still worse, inviting the latter to take sides in their own feudal disputes. There is record of a battle between the Emir Djwali and the Seljukid of Aleppo, in which the former was assisted by Latin troops under Baldwin du Bourg and Jocelin de Courtenay, while his enemy's forces included Normans led by Tancred of Taranto!

Shameful proceedings of this kind make it even more surprising that the Latin kingdom endured for so long. That she did so was due partly to the first-rate ability of her early rulers, but also to the weakness of Islam, which was a prey to the worst form of anarchy. As soon as the situation was reversed, as soon as the Latin rulers grew weak at a time when strong men arose determined to revive the Empire of Mahomet, Godfrey de Bouillon's dream vanished into thin air. It was a dream that had never been founded on reality.

5. The Second Crusade

On 13th December 1143 Edessa, which included all Christian territory in the north-west of the kingdom, was taken by the Moslems. Fulk, third King of Jerusalem, had died a month previously, leaving two little boys as his heirs. This terrible warning did not go unheeded.

Until then, and in spite of numerous obstacles, the Latins had maintained their superiority. Baldwin I had seized every port from Caesarea to Acre and Sidon, thus assuring free communication with Europe. Baldwin II had consolidated these gains, though not without increasing difficulties, and Tyre had fallen to his arms in 1124. But the Seljuks now had a splendid leader in the atabeg Zengi. Baldwin had once defeated him at Aleppo, but was afterwards his prisoner for a year. During Fulk's reign it had become clear that a point of equilibrium had been reached. Whereas the Latins could make no further progress, the Moslems were in a position to take advantage of their gradual decline. The fall of Edessa was glaring evidence of this truth.

When Baldwin, Count of Hainaut, succeeded to the throne, his title passed to Jocelin de Courtenay, whose exploits had already won him legendary renown. The latter's son, Jocelin II, resembled him no more than did his maternal forbears who had come from the mountains of Armenia. He spent his time in drunkenness and lechery, caring nothing for the defence of his city, where, in any case, he never resided.

Despite a heroic resistance by Archbishop Hugh, Zengi took Edessa
in less than a month. Raymond of Antioch had been called upon for
help; but he was only too pleased to watch the embarrassment of a
neighbour with whom he was at loggerheads, and declined to assist.
His behaviour was that of a madman, and the disunion of the Latins
ended as might have been foreseen. The city was taken amid scenes
of dreadful carnage. Two years later, as the result of a palace revolution in which Zengi was assassinated, the Armenians of Edessa drove
out the Moslems and recalled their former count. Zengi's son,
Nureddin, hurried to recapture it, and Jocelin II escaped defeat and
butchery almost alone, thanks to the speed of his horse.

Christendom looked upon the fall of Edessa as nothing short of a
disaster: the Holy Land itself was threatened. After some delay, due
to his own difficulties, Pope Eugenius III called for a new crusade (1st
December 1145). His appeal roused little enthusiasm; nor did a
moving Christmas sermon, preached before the whole court at Bourges
by Bishop Geoffrey of Langres, persuade one great nobleman to undertake the hazards that were now recognized as inseparable from such an
enterprise. Then St Bernard intervened. His burning words spoken
at Vézelay on Easter Sunday, 1146, kindled a flame that seemed at first
to outshine the fervour of Clermont fifty years before.[1] The second
crusade began under the joint command of Conrad III and Louis VII.
The French king, indeed, had been among its most enthusiastic
advocates.

'Come, generous soldiers,' cried St Bernard, 'gird up your loins!
Do not betray your king! What do I say? Do not betray the King
of Heaven for whose sake your own sovereign embarks upon so
arduous a journey!' So arduous a journey. The saint could not have
spoken more truthfully; it was to prove more arduous than he thought.
The first crusade had been well organized; its leaders, though not
always agreed among themselves, had recognized the legate's authority.
In the second, each of the two kings desired to go his own way instead
of pooling his resources, and preparations were inadequate. Conrad
III was the first to reach Constantinople after a perilous march across
Hungary. He was welcomed by Manuel Comnenus,[2] who had
married his sister-in-law and, like him, detested the Normans. Unfortunately, however, Conrad was not able to prevent his troops from
pillaging and provoking the Greeks in a thousand ways. The
Basileus, therefore, arranged for their transport to Asia, but gave them
no further assistance. Did he do worse? Did he warn the Sultan of
Konieh, with whom he was on friendly terms? This rumour was
current among the Latins, with whom Byzantine treachery was now so

[1] On St Bernard's part in preaching the second crusade, see Chapter III, section 7.
[2] See Chapter X, section 5.

proverbial that they even accused the Greeks of having sold them poisoned flour. On 26th October 1147 the Germans were surprised and annihilated at Dorylaeum by an enormous Turkish army.

Simultaneously, Louis VII arrived at Constantinople, where the French actually proposed to storm the capital. Manuel now had recourse to stratagem, and gave out that the Germans had won some brilliant victories. Just as he had expected and intended, the French were eager to share in this harvest of laurels. But they were badly disillusioned. Hemmed in on the coast of Asia Minor, they paid heavily for their success on the Meander before suffering an overwhelming defeat at Laodicea. The folly of their leaders had cost the crusaders dear; meanwhile, however, those same leaders left their troops to be massacred by the Turks and embarked for Syria.

In the spring of 1148 it seemed that operations would be resumed by the young King Baldwin III, who was regarded, even by his enemy Nureddin, as 'a prince who has no equal.' Louis VII and Conrad joined him at Tiberias, and it seemed that the Christians might at last act in concert. Louis and Conrad were jealous of one another. They could not understand the complicated intrigues of Palestine, and persuaded themselves that, instead of driving on Aleppo and Edessa, it would be better to attack the Emir of Damascus, although his policy had for long been one of collaboration with the Latins. Over all hung no spirit of heroic brotherhood in arms but a cloud of discord, not to mention the scandalous conduct of Queen Eleanor of France, rumours of which had begun to reach the Holy Land. Damascus was taken; but while the conquerors indulged their insatiable greed, the garrison pulled themselves together and Nureddin hastened to their relief. The farce was now complete. The two monarchs re-embarked, wondering whom they should blame for their failure, Eugenius III, the Greeks, the Templars, or St Bernard. Anyone would do, so long as it was not themselves. Some weeks later Raymond of Antioch was killed, and Nureddin continued his advance. The Abbot of Clairvaux talked in vain of yet another crusade, while Suger drew up plans. The West had lost confidence both in itself and in its purpose; the Holy Land, it seemed, must henceforth fight alone.

6. SALADIN AND JERUSALEM

Thirty years would bring the Latin kingdom to the brink of ruin, but it is surprising she enjoyed so long a respite. Nureddin must have realized that the apathetic West would be slow to intervene and that Byzantium would never stir. Why, then, did he not hurl himself upon Jerusalem? Because one man stood between him and the city, Baldwin III (1143–62), whom René Grousset calls 'the model of a

European ruler.' Intelligent, unyielding, brave, and cunning, the young king stood his ground at every point. Although harassed by the dissensions which his own mother stirred up among his subjects and by fresh anxieties due to Renaud of Châtillon, who had just married Constance, the youthful heiress of Antioch, Baldwin managed for a time to prevent Nureddin from seizing Damascus. He defeated a Turcoman army, and took Ascalon after a bitter siege. Eventually, however, the Turkish chieftain stormed Damascus and made it his capital (April 1154). The peril was approaching step by step. Manuel Comnenus's marriage with Mary, daughter of Raymond of Antioch, seemed to presage better times; but disunion continued to frustrate all efforts. A brilliant victory was won on the shores of Lake Tiberias, thanks to a heroic charge by the Templars, but it could not be followed up. Baldwin III died soon afterwards at the age of thirty-two, so suddenly that there was whisper of poison. Fate seemed resolved that no king of Palestine should live long enough to accomplish his task.

Baldwin's brother Amaury (1162–74) was by no means his equal. Certainly, he was just as brave; in wisdom and piety he even surpassed the late king. But avarice obscured his political sense, and he wasted time appealing to the West. His army steadily decreased, and he could do little or nothing to oppose the Moslems, who raided right up to the walls of Krak. Then a new menace arose from Egypt, where the Fatimite government was crumbling to pieces and none knew what might take its place. Nureddin sent his able lieutenant Chirkuh to the banks of the Nile; Amaury went there in person. But the clumsiness of the Latins, their inability to reach an understanding with Byzantium, as well as the avarice of Amaury, who asked the Caliph for exorbitant sums of money, produced the exact result which it had been hoped to avoid: Egypt was occupied by the Turks. When Amaury was carried off by typhus in 1174, at the age of thirty-nine, the Latin kingdom was clearly in grave danger; for Islam had found a leader in Saladin who would unite her and revive the Holy War.

Saladin was a Kurd, nephew and (in 1169) heir of the vizier Chirkuh who had overrun Egypt. He had determined to build a kingdom, and had no vulgar ambition. Like Alexander, Caesar, and Charlemagne, he seemed destined to combine vast territories into an organic whole, to shape a civilization and direct its footsteps. He was a man of steel, trenchant and supple, a statesman of the first rank and a person of absolute integrity. He impressed even the Christians as a pattern of chivalry. Richard Cœur de Lion was his friend, and Dante places him in that special part of hell where, under a kindly light, are assembled those pure souls whose misfortune it was not to have known Jesus. After ridding himself of the Fatimite Caliph of Egypt, Saladin soon

liquidated the heirs of Nureddin.   Damascus yielded to his arms;
Egypt and Syria became one kingdom.   The schism was ended
between the Shiites of Egypt and the rest of Islam, which was Sunnite.
There was now a Moslem empire, compact and governed by the firmest
of hands.   The situation had been catastrophically reversed.

The Latin kingdom was about to undergo its hardest trial.   The
grievous story reads like a chapter from some *geste*; it might indeed
have been taken from the *Grail Quest*.   Amaury's son Baldwin IV was
a young man full of charm and vivacity, high-souled and of infinite
refinement.   Learned as a clerk and brave as the bravest knight, he
gave promise of great things to come.   But the evil destiny of his
house was not slow to strike.   One day, while he was at play, the ball
fell among some thorns.   In searching for it, Baldwin scratched his
arms; but although he had drawn blood, he astonished everyone by
remarking quietly that he could feel nothing.   The symptom could
mean only one thing, leprosy.   The prince was a leper.   Ointments,
drugs, and treatment of all kinds proved useless.   The reign of this
child (1174–83) was one long agony: corruption devoured his flesh, his
eyes disappeared, and his nerve-centres were paralysed.   Yet notwithstanding the certainty of a most dreadful death, Baldwin faced his
enemies with a fortitude and superhuman courage that can only be
explained by his Christian faith.   So long as he could sit a horse he led
his troops, and even won a resounding victory at Montgisard though
he had only 300 against 30,000 men.   When his strength failed, he had
himself carried into battle in a litter so that his troops could see him in
their midst.   His subjects, however, worried him far more than the
enemy.   There were, for instance, the bloody feuds of Renaud of
Châtillon, who was first in conflict with the Byzantines and then
attacked Turkish caravans in time of truce.   There was also open
intrigue concerning the succession, his sister Sibyl and her parvenu
husband Guy de Lusignan striving with the king's former tutor,
Raymond III of Tripoli.   Once more he obliged Saladin to retreat
from before the Krak du Moab; but his life was nearing its end, his
tortured body waited for a merciful deliverance.   He died at the age of
twenty-four and was buried near the Holy Sepulchre.   It has been
said that he lived only to atone for the pettiness and villainy of his
household, and it is indeed surprising that the Church has never
officially recognized his sanctity.

Final disaster was not long delayed.   His nephew Baldwin V died a
year later, aged six, and was succeeded by Guy de Lusignan and Sibyl,
a handsome but insignificant young man wedded to a pretty but somewhat crazy woman.   Between them and Raymond III of Tripoli there
soon developed a struggle in which every ambitious spirit of that time
played his part: the Patriarch of Jerusalem, the Grand Master of the

Temple, Jocelin III de Courtenay, and, of course, Renaud of Châtillon. Saladin had been waiting for just such an opportunity. On 4th July 1187, at a place now called Hattin among the stark hills that look down on Tiberias, the Latins, who had neither drunk nor watered their horses for several hours and gasped beneath their heavy armour, were encircled by the Kurd's swiftly moving army. Blinded by dust and by the smoke rising from dry grass to which the Turks had set fire, the knights could do nothing but save their honour. Those who were not killed were taken prisoner, among them King Guy, whom Saladin treated kindly, and Renaud of Châtillon, whom, on the contrary, he struck down with his own sword. The conqueror was now irresistible. Acre, Sidon, Ascalon, and Nazareth fell to him one after another. Only sea-girt Tyre held out; but on 2nd October 1187 Jerusalem opened its gates.[1] On top of the dome of the former mosque of Omar, which had been converted into a church, there stood a golden cross. The Moslems cut it down: 'Allah is great . . .'

7. The West against Saladin: the Third Crusade

Jerusalem had fallen. Only the shores of Syria with the cities of Tyre, Antioch, and Tripoli were in Christian hands; and the port of Acre was closed to Western shipping. Thus was a century of achievement nullified.

A great cry of sorrow and indignation rose from the whole of Christendom, led by the Italian Marquis Conrad of Montferrat. Arriving before Acre just after Saladin had taken that city, he was surprised not to be welcomed by its bells, until suddenly he noticed the standard of Islam floating on the towers. He promptly withdrew to Tyre, where he roused the population, set about preparing an immediate counter-offensive, and sent couriers to Europe with a request for help in order to save the fatherland of Christ. Rome was horrified by the disaster. News reached Urban II on 18th October, and two days later he lay dead. His successor, Gregory VIII, issued an urgent appeal but died on 17th December. Clement III took effective measures to provide for another crusade: a tax of 10 per cent known as the 'Saladin tithe' was imposed on all revenues, including the income of ecclesiastical benefices; and a personal invitation to take the Cross was sent to the three most powerful sovereigns of that period, Frederick Barbarossa, Philip Augustus of France, and Henry II of England, who

---

[1] During negotiations for its surrender the Templars and Hospitallers showed incredible hardness of heart by refusing their gold to unfortunate captives whom Saladin had agreed to set free on payment of ransom. Another painful incident occurred at Alexandria, where Venetian and Pisan sailors at first refused to take on board Christian refugees liberated by Saladin; they agreed to do so only when the Kurd held them personally responsible for the fate of their brothers in Christ.

was soon afterwards succeeded by his son Richard.   All three accepted,
though not for exclusively religious reasons.   The kings of France and
England had adopted an authoritarian policy with which many feudal
lords were discontented.   Barbarossa, having joined the crusade, stood
forth as head of the nobility, which was all part of his plan; [1] and in
order that this 'Carolingian' alliance of Pope and Emperor should not
unite the baronage against them, the two kings decided, come what
might, to follow Frederick's example.   Three crowns were enough—
in fact too many.

No crusade was better planned than was the third (1189).   Its three
commanders were real war-leaders; mobilization was methodical; and
strategic routes were worked out.   The Germans, especially, gave
proof of their natural genius for organization.   The approach of these
gigantic armoured columns caused the East to tremble, not only Saladin
but the whole Byzantine Empire which, after five dramatic years since
the death of Manuel Comnenus, was now governed by Isaac Angelus.
Outwardly, his relations with Frederick Barbarossa were good;
inwardly, he mistrusted the man who had married his son to the heiress
of Sicily.   He agreed with Saladin to expel the Latins from Constantinople, to allow the presence of muezzins in his capital, and to
hinder the advance of the crusaders.   The Turks, on their part, undertook (rather vaguely) to give back the Holy Places.   This Machiavellianism soon became known, and with catastrophic results.   Frederick
launched the Serbs and Wallachians against Byzantium; his troops
occupied a number of Greek cities; and when he learned that the
Basileus had imprisoned his ambassadors, he threatened to seize
Constantinople.   Isaac gave way, promised all that he was asked, and
surrendered carefully chosen hostages.

Barbarossa advanced into Asia Minor at lightning speed.   A springtime filled with victories seemed as a garland of flowers about the
invincible emperor's head.   Konieh, the Seljuk capital, fell within five
days, and the Taurus was crossed without difficulty, though Saladin
destroyed every place that he abandoned.   'It might have been
written,' says the chronicler Ibn-al-Athis, 'that Syria and Egypt no
more belong to Islam, had not Allah deigned to show clemency towards
his faithful servants by causing the German king to perish.'   For, on
10th June 1190, while bathing in the icy waters of a little Cilician river
called Selef, a tributary of the Cydnus, Frederick was seized with
apoplexy and drowned.   His peoples refused for a long time to believe
that he had met so miserable an end.   He was not dead, they pretended,
but hidden in a cavern of the Taurus.   Seated before a table (that of the
Grail, perhaps) he waited until it was time to take his sword again and
deliver the Sepulchre; meanwhile his fine beard had grown three times

[1] See Chapter V, section 6.

round the stone slab.   The truth was less poetic.   No sooner was
Frederick dead than his army disbanded; only a few units rejoined the
other expeditionary forces before Acre.

Philip Augustus and Richard (who in the course of this campaign
earned his nickname 'Cœur de Lion') had made their own arrangements.   They had once been friends, for the French king had supported Richard against his father Henry II.   But on succeeding to the
throne, the young prince showed himself as determined a champion of
English interests as his predecessor had been; and the breaking-off of
his engagement to Alice of France had incurred Philip's displeasure.
It was therefore as rivals rather than as allies that the two kings
embarked on the crusade.   They joined forces at Vézelay [1] in July
1190, and made their final preparations: they would meet again in
Sicily.   The winter passed amid confused intrigue.   In the spring,
Richard left Philip to attack Acre single-handed and went off to settle
a personal grudge against the Byzantines.   Assisted by Guy de
Lusignan, King of Jerusalem, whom Saladin had set free,[2] he captured
Cyprus and then turned his attention to the Holy Land.

The siege of Acre dragged on month after month, for the Christians
were too few to take the place by storm or to prevent it receiving
supplies.   Saladin, on the other hand, did not feel himself strong
enough to smash this wall of steel-clad warriors.   The camp had
become a fair where merchants and bankers drove a thriving trade, and
there were constant amusements, which the Moslems themselves
attended between one battle and the next.   At last, on 12th July,
Philip and Richard forgot their differences and carried the town by
assault; after which the King of France announced that he had fulfilled
his vow and embarked for home.

Richard Cœur de Lion was now left alone to carry on hostilities as
best he could.   Though an indifferent statesman and by nature passionate, in battle he was a giant whose courage made of him an epic
hero.   Nothing, however, was more inconsistent than his attitude to
war.   On one occasion he had 3,000 Saracen captives savagely put to
death; on another, he made approaches to Saladin and ultimately
became his firm friend.   Some Christians admired him, others detested

[1] We are told that the combined armies numbered 100,000 men.   Now we know on
unimpeachable evidence that Philip Augustus paid the Genoese for transporting 650
knights, twice that number of esquires, and three or four times as many foot-soldiers;
making a total of 1,950 cavalry and 6,000 or 8,000 infantry.   Richard Cœur de Lion may
be supposed to have had between 11,000 and 15,000 men, only a tenth of whom were
cavalry, certainly no more.   Frederick Barbarossa's force cannot be placed at more than
2,000 cavalry and twice as many esquires, while it is known that the Emperor reduced the
number of camp servants to a minimum, keeping only valets, cooks, and grooms, all of
whom were indispensable.

[2] Guy de Lusignan afterwards received the throne of Cyprus from Richard.   His
dynasty reigned for a long while in the island, encouraging literature and the arts.   The
kingdom of Cyprus lasted until 1378, when it was destroyed by the Genoese.

him for his arrogance.   He had also some peculiar whims, knighting Saladin's brother, for example, and offering him baptism together with the hand of his sister and the crown of Jerusalem!   His brilliant victories were all in vain, but his relations with the Kurd were so cordial that he obtained from him a treaty guaranteeing all Christians free access to the Holy Places.   Then he too set out for home; but his journey was interrupted by an unfortunate adventure.   He fell into the hands of Leopold, Duke of Austria, whom he had recently offended and by whom he was delivered to Henry VI.   That Emperor, in defiance of all law, kept him in captivity for thirty months.

Thus the best organized of all the crusades ended in fiasco, or at least in check.   It had restored to the Latins the whole coastline of Syria and Palestine, and Saladin's death in 1193 had removed the gravest threat to the Holy Land.   But Jerusalem was not yet delivered; nor had Richard Cœur de Lion the urge to go and pray there, since he could not go as conqueror.   Was the crusading spirit still alive? Certainly it was.   In spite of many disappointments, there were still thousands of pious or ambitious men anxious to rekindle the flame. In Palestine itself that spirit was embodied in the brave and wise Henri de Champagne; in Europe it was represented by the young Emperor Henry VI, who revived his father's plan to make Sicily the base of an all-out assault on Islam and Byzantium.[1]   But mistrust between Germans and Sicilians on the one hand and the Latins of Syria on the other defeated their common purpose; and the emperor's premature death put an end to the whole scheme.   Had the West still a leader capable of taking up the threads of this gigantic enterprise? History replied with Innocent III.

8. THE FOURTH CRUSADE

He who was destined to carry the Church to the summit of her power inevitably desired to resume the crusade and go down to posterity as the Pope who delivered the Holy Sepulchre.   His Ghibelline adversaries even accused him of treating the crusade as a convenient means of imposing his authority, of meddling in the affairs of independent sovereigns, and of levying exorbitant taxes.   Still stronger, no doubt, was his legitimate desire to free the Holy Land, to win a decisive victory for the Church; personal ambition went hand in hand with his sense of the dignity of the Apostolic See.   Innocent inveighed against selfish princes 'who are less willing to suffer for Christ than was Christ for them,' and against the clergy who refused our Lord a glass of water when he asked for it.

The enthusiasm on this occasion was not what it had been at

[1] See Chapter V, section 7.

Clermont or at Vézelay. Kings hesitated to embark on an adventure of whose cost they were only too well aware. Besides, Richard and Philip Augustus had just been at war with one another, and the latter was excommunicated for matrimonial reasons. Only the decadent nobility in search of fiefs were tempted to obey the call. Taking advantage of a tournament, Fulk, the parish priest of Neuilly, persuaded a group of knights from Champagne to swear the crusader's oath, while Abbot Martin of Paris had a like success at Basel. The expedition set out in April 1201, under the command of Thibaut III, Count of Champagne. Its principal leaders were Baldwin, Count of Flanders; the Count of St Pol; Simon de Montfort, who afterwards distinguished himself in the Albigensian crusade; [1] Geoffrey de Villehardouin, who has left a long and delightful account of the adventure; and Boniface of Montferrat, who took the place of Thibaut on his death ten months later.

The first question was, how to reach the Holy Land. Experience during the third crusade had proved the sea route best; the next step was to obtain shipping. For this purpose they approached Venice, the leading maritime power; but the Venetians fought shy. The octogenarian but vigorous Doge, Henry Dandolo, had a quicker eye to business than any of them. He took the Cross, to the tune of 85,000 gold marks and half the conquered territory, which he considered fair payment for the hire of his ships. At the end of some weeks, 36,000 marks were still unpaid. The crusaders were encamped on the island of St Nicholas, and Dandolo kept them short of supplies until they were hungry enough to understand. The Venetians, it appeared, would forgive them this accursed debt on one straightforward condition: they must take Zara, the Republic's competitor on the Dalmatian coast. So it was done. 'Instead of winning back the Holy Land,' cried Innocent III, 'you have thirsted for the blood of your brethren. Satan the arch-deceiver has seduced you'; and he notified the ringleaders that they were excommunicate. .

The crusaders were now joined by young Alexius, son of the dethroned Basileus Isaac Angelus [2] whose eyes had been put out by order of Alexius III. Was it by chance and on his own initiative that the young man came to ask for his father's restoration to the throne? In return for this favour he offered 200,000 marks, supplies, troops, payment of all the crusaders' debts, and even an end to the schism. Since he was brother-in-law to Philip of Swabia, himself excommunicate and hostile towards the Pope,[3] it seemed not unlikely that the scheme had been worked out between them and the notorious Ghibelline Boniface of Montferrat, lest a victorious campaign in Palestine

---

[1] See Chapter XIII, section 7.   [2] See Chapter X section 5.
[3] See Chapter V, section 7.

should complete the triumph of Innocent III. The troops, indeed, were quite willing to march against Byzantium, the home of traitors, thieves, and murderers, who had massacred the Latins in 1182 and deserved chastisement on that account. The Venetians dreamed of conquering new markets in the East. There were thus few members of the expedition unwilling to turn aside from their original goal; Simon de Montfort was almost the only leader who protested.

Although Innocent III was not informed, he may have had an inkling; for when lifting the excommunication he had addressed the crusaders in these words: 'Please God your repentance is sincere; may He prevent a repetition of your sin! A recidivist is no penitent, but a liar, a dog that returns to its own vomit.' But when this warning reached Zara the expedition was already on its way to Byzantium; the Pope was grief-stricken and prepared to excommunicate them anew.

The arrival of the crusaders before Constantinople is described in a celebrated passage of Villehardouin:

> Then had those on board the ships and galleys and transports (*huissiers* [1]) full sight of Constantinople; and they took port and anchored their vessels. Now you may know that those who had never before seen Constantinople looked upon it very earnestly, for they never thought there could be in all the world so rich a city; and they marked the high walls and strong towers that enclosed it round about, and the rich palaces, and mighty churches—of which there were so many that no one would have believed it who had not seen it with his eyes—and the height and the length of that city which above all others was sovereign. [2]

The chronicler is frank enough to confess that 'no man there was of such hardihood but his flesh trembled.' Success, however, was not long delayed. The city was carried by assault on 17th July 1203, Alexius III fled, and Isaac was restored to the throne along with his son as Alexius IV.

Relations between the inhabitants and the occupying power were as might have been expected: the crusaders showed themselves arrogant and vexatious, the Byzantines loathed them in return. The subjects of Isaac I and Alexius IV had good reason to believe that their masters were exploiting them for the benefit of the Latins, and a furious outburst at the beginning of 1204 resulted in the proclamation as Alexius V of an agitator, one Ducas nicknamed 'Mourzuphles,' who liquidated the two basileis.

The indignant crusaders determined to retaliate, and Constantinople was besieged and carried by storm for a second time, on 13th April 1204. The city was reduced in three days, but those days were filled with horror. The account written by Nicetas Acominates gives some

---

[1] Ships fitted with large doors (*huis*) rather like modern landing-craft.
[2] The translation is by Sir Frank Marzials from *Memoirs of the Crusades* (Everyman's Library), which also contains Joinville's Chronicle—(Tr.).

idea of the crusaders' conduct. 'They broke the holy images worshipped by the faithful. They threw the relics of martyrs into places which I dare not name. In the great church [Santa Sophia], they smashed the high altar, which was made of precious materials, and shared the fragments among themselves. They stabled their horses there; stole the sacred vessels; tore wrought gold and silver from the pulpit, throne, and doors. A public prostitute sat in the patriarchal chair and sang an obscene song. . . .' The Greek did not exaggerate; for when Innocent III was told of this abominable episode he was moved to anger and wrote to the same effect: 'These soldiers of Christ who should have turned their swords against the infidel have steeped them in Christian blood. They spared neither religion, nor age, nor sex. They openly committed adultery, fornication, incest. . . . They stripped the altars of silver, violated the sanctuaries, carried off ikons, crosses, and relics.' Such was the achievement of an expedition of whose glory Innocent had dreamed.

The taking of Constantinople was no less disastrous from the political viewpoint. The Latins, with one terrible blow of their mailed fist, had laid low Byzantium, the last outpost of resistance to the Asiatic threat. Could they themselves protect the Bosphorus? When Mourzuphles was overthrown, the crusaders decided that one of themselves should be chosen in his place. Who was it to be? Dandolo was anxious to accept, but they would have none of him. Boniface of Montferrat was too powerful, especially as he had created some sort of title for himself by marrying Isaac's widow and appointing himself guardian of his son Manuel. Baldwin of Flanders was a safe choice: he was accordingly elected 'Emperor of Romania,' and the papal legate officiated at his coronation.

The idea of establishing the feudal system in the East was utterly absurd. Having no roots in that part of the world, it was no better than legalized plunder. Everyone wanted a share in the spoils: Montferrat became King of Thessalonica; Villehardouin established the principality of Achaea; there were counts of Thebes, marquesses of Corinth, lords and then dukes of Athens, all of whom were theoretically vassals of the Emperor but really independent. Venice, of course, was not forgotten; she had occupied every strong point on the coast, and her Doge assumed the proud title 'Lord of three quarters of the Greek empire,' which he continued to bear until the fifteenth century. The bronze horses which had been the glory of the Hippodrome were sent to St Mark's, where they may still be seen; and it need hardly be said that the Most Serene Republic refused point blank to recognize the Emperor as its overlord. This crumbling of Western strength was not the only deplorable result of partition. By deflecting the current of immigration towards Greece and Byzantium, the Latin empire dried up the small trickle that had hitherto reached the Holy Land, thus weakening still further the kingdom of Jerusalem. The fourth crusade, in fact, was a catastrophe.

The history of the Latin empire is one long story of decline. Seven emperors succeeded one another in less than forty years, swept away by a mounting tide of enemies. All those greedy peoples whom the Comneni had only just managed to hold at arm's length showed their heads again. The Bulgars were first to attack; in 1206 they captured Baldwin I, who died in prison. Nor had the Greeks accepted their fate. Members of the families of Angelus and Comnenus established themselves on the plateaux of Asia Minor or in the Balkans, and made life difficult for the Latins. The 'despots of Epirus,' in particular, harassed the kingdom of Thessalonica, whose capital they eventually stormed in 1227. At Nicea, Theodore Lascaris, who was related both to the Angeli and to the Comneni, resumed the imperial title; and it was not long before all those who resented the Latin occupation crossed the Bosphorus to join him. A prosperous and well-governed state was now opposed to the puppet-empire of Romania. John Vatatzes, son-in-law of Theodore Lascaris, overran Thrace in 1222, superseded the Epirots in Thessalonica, and even united with the Bulgarians to threaten Constantinople. Meanwhile, Baldwin II (1237–61) spent his time begging assistance from the West, but his plea fell upon deaf ears. In 1258 a great general, Michael Palaeologus, succeeded to the empire of Nicea. On 25th July 1261 he appeared before Constantinople; the city threw open its gates, and Baldwin II decamped. A few Western lordships remained scattered about Greece; but the Latin empire, founded on the violation of an oath sworn to God, had vanished from the earth.

There was a moment when Innocent III hoped that the Latin occupation of Constantinople might help to improve the religious situation. When his indignation passed, the Pope began to feel that, since every occurrence is subject to Divine providence, there must be a silver lining to this cloud, perhaps an end of schism for which his predecessors had longed. The Emperor Baldwin actually invited him to come and celebrate the reconciliation of Christendom in 'the imperial city'; a Latin patriarch was elected in the person of Thomas Morosini, though without papal approval; and Cistercian monasteries, together with commanderies of the Templars and Hospitallers, sprang up throughout the East.

Hopeless muddle soon resulted. Latin clerics had no control over their native flocks, and disagreed among themselves. The Arch-bishops of Patras and Thessalonica refused to obey the patriarch, claiming that their sees were far more ancient than his. The Military Orders, here as elsewhere, quarrelled both with one another and also with the priests and monks.   Negotiations begun by a papal legate, the Cardinal of St Suzanna, broke down.   The resistance, headed by Michael Acominates, Greek Archbishop of Athens, received secret support from the people of Nicea.   A new legate, the domineering Spanish cardinal Pelagius, resolved to try stern measures: he imprisoned those of the Greek clergy who would not submit, closed their churches, and drove the religious from their monasteries.   But the Emperor himself, Henry of Flanders, intervened.   Hopes of reaching an understanding had not yet been abandoned.   There were theological discussions, and even talk of a marriage between a Lascaris and a Courtenay, the latter a niece of the Latin emperor; but all to no avail. Innocent IV made one final effort about 1250.   Seeing the Latin empire falling to pieces, he sent the General of the Franciscans, John of Parma, to Nicea with instructions to negotiate a settlement.   John Vatatzes, who coveted the Byzantine throne, lent a willing ear; but the two skilful diplomats both died.   Alexander IV failed to take advantage of the accession of Michael Palaeologus, who was looking for support, and there was nothing more to be done.   Force prevailed; two years later the Greeks returned to Byzantium, and the prospect of an early reunion disappeared.

9.   THE MONGOL TERROR

In the meantime there occurred a terrible and monstrous happening, which, though it did not immediately affect the Holy Land, had noticeable repercussions on the crusade.   While the Latins were storming Constantinople, events were taking place in the heart of Asia which came within an inch of overwhelming Europe.   Just as the Huns had done centuries ago, other horsemen had set out from the steppes to attack the golden cities of China, of Persia, and of the West.   The Mongols, a new people, had revived the ancient dreams of Attila, and their ruler, Temoudjin, was a yet greater captain than the fifth-century conqueror.   He is famous in history as Genghis Khan (1162–1227).

Leaving the highlands around Lake Baikal, the Mongols had obeyed a mysterious instinct which from time to time launches one of these yellow peoples on a career of unlimited conquest.   Thick-set, powerfully built, broad-faced, snub-nosed, slit-eyed, 'the hairs so few upon their cheeks that they can easily be counted,' their heads shaven except for a crown of hair done up in plaits behind their ears, clothed in undressed skins and a jacket which they never washed, these people were not pleasant guests to see coming over the horizon.   Mounted on stocky horses that were not much to look at but could gallop at terrific speed and stay apparently for ever, these riders with their deadly bows were strangely ubiquitous; they had a way of appearing quite suddenly at one time in places hundreds of miles apart. Their sinister and well-merited reputation preceded them, for they would often massacre an entire population including not only women and children, but cats and dogs as well. On the other hand, strange to say, their organization was first-rate: they had a sound financial system (using paper money), a highly efficient network of postal relays, and an excellent commissariat. They came very near to accomplishing the dream of Asiatic domination.

In 1202, as the fourth crusade was leaving Venice, Genghis Khan was subduing the Tatars of Manchuria; those Tatars whose name, by some extraordinary confusion, the West altered to 'Tartars' and applied it to the Mongols themselves. In 1209 he completed the conquest of Mongolia. Two years later he launched his hordes against the fertile land of China, subjugated the Sung dynasty, razed Pekin, and did not hesitate to ruin 10,000,000 peasant-farmers by his taxes and requisitions. Turning westward, he threw himself upon Turkestan, Afghanistan, and Persia; took Bokhara and Samarkand amid scenes of indescribable horror; crossed the Urals, and skirted the Caspian Sea. His final raid in 1224—fortunately it was indeed the last!—carried him through southern Russia, where he annihilated the Polovtsi and over-threw the cavalry of the princes of Kiev. Death caught up with him in 1227; no other power could stop him. He left an enormous empire stretching from Korea to the Volga, and from Baikal to Tibet. It was the largest Asiatic empire ever known, exceeding by far the territories of Byzantium and Germany. His sons carried on his work, haunted by the same idea: the Mongols must possess the earth, their capital Karakorum should be the capital of the world. One of them, Batu, beginning where his father had left off, started for Europe. In 1236-7 he swept down on Kiev, wiped it off the map, then overran Volynia and Galicia. At this point he halted and settled down in the empire of the Golden Horde, a cosy little realm extending from the Urals to the Danube. Four years passed and the yellow horsemen were again in the saddle, led this time by the invincible Sabutai, who never accompanied his men into battle but directed operations from a distance and with consummate skill. Poland, the Ukraine, and Hungary were attacked, Vienna was in peril; the Mongols passed along the Adriatic, and Europe awaited the *coup de grâce*. Nor was western Europe alone involved. One of Temoudjin's sons governed the steppes of Asia, another Turkestan, another Persia, the last two of which had been won from Islam. The Byzantine empire of Nicea, the Latin kingdom of Jerusalem, even the empire of Mahomet, all were alive to the same threat. The enigmatic shadow of the rider from the steppes mounted on his pony, bow in hand, loomed large against the background of oriental politics.

The intervention of this terrible foe in the complicated relations of Greeks, Latins, and Moslems was rendered even more astonishing by one remarkable fact. Some of these appalling nomads, who never tired of massacre, were actually Christians. Nestorian missionaries had converted Huns, Turks, Chinese, and Mongols. Many of them acted as secretaries to the yellow chieftains, and devised alphabets to suit their dialects. Genghis Khan's entourage included Nestorians of pure Mongol race but properly baptized. Nestorian influence had likewise penetrated to the courts of his sons. Tchormaghan, for example, the Mongol conqueror of Persia, had two Nestorian brothers-in-law, and in the course of his campaigns he was always anxious to spare the Christians. All these sons of Genghis, on the other hand, detested the Moslems, who were not only hostile to the name of Christ but had been the only peoples seriously to oppose their expansion towards the south and west. One question, therefore, called for an answer: Could Christian unity prevail between Europeans and these curious baptized folk from the depths of Asia? There were those in both camps who thought it could.

10. ABORTIVE AND FALSE CRUSADES

The lamentable failure of the fourth crusade had not discouraged all men of goodwill. At the beginning of the thirteenth century that great Christian dream was still something more than a game for business men and politicians, as was proved in 1212 by the 'Children's Crusade,' one of the most touching manifestations of loyalty to Christ. In obedience to the call of a humble shepherd-boy, Stephen of Cloyes near Vendôme, thousands of adolescents came forward and took the Cross. No one doubted that our Lord had appeared to Stephen and handed him a written order to deliver the Sepulchre: innocent children would do what warriors had been unable to accomplish. As in the days of Peter the Hermit, crowds flocked about Stephen. Philip Augustus forbade the crusade, but preparations went ahead: it travelled across France and reached Marseilles, which Stephen entered in a magnificent chariot. Here the young crusaders embarked in seven galleys; two were shipwrecked, two others ran ashore in Algeria—whether through accident or sabotage is uncertain—and the passengers were sold into slavery. Another children's crusade was organized at Cologne by a youth named Nicholas; it crossed the Alps but petered out through hunger and exhaustion on the roads of Italy. 'These children put us to shame,' murmured Innocent III when he learned the facts; 'we sleep while they set to work.'

The Pope, however, was by no means disheartened. Although sick and weary, he showed superhuman energy when there was question of a crusade, sending out one appeal after another, and appointing public prayers. At the Lateran Council in 1215 he decreed extraordinary measures, notably the prohibition of all tournaments and wars between Christians, as well as a new tax which he himself paid together with every one of his cardinals. Young Frederick II, John of England, and Andrew of Hungary promised to take the Cross. The great Pope's death in July 1216 delayed the project; but his successor Honorius III, at the request of Archbishop William of Tyre, who visited Rome for that purpose, at once took up the reins. A holy priest named Jacques de Vitry was appointed Archbishop of Acre; and he went out to try and stir enthusiasm in the Latin East, which he found, it seems, in a state of wellnigh hopeless decadence. Such was the beginning of the fifth crusade.

John Lackland was dead; Frederick II, always fond of mental reservations, went back on his word; and only Andrew of Hungary set off, in September 1217, with Leopold, Duke of Antioch. John of Brienne, King of Jerusalem, Hugh de Lusignan, King of Cyprus, and Prince Bohemond IV of Antioch-Tripoli were already mobilized. The only efficient leader among them was John of Brienne, a first-class strategist and statesman. But the King of Hungary would not obey him. For four months he campaigned alone in the neighbourhood of Mt Tabor; then, disappointed at being unable to bring the Moslems to pitched-battle, he embarked for home, followed by a writ of excommunication.

It was at this juncture that Brienne prepared to attack Egypt, an excellent idea inherited from Amaury. The plan was to take Alexandria or Damietta and negotiate its exchange for Jerusalem. There was a fair chance of success. In May 1218 the crusaders effected a brilliant landing and encamped before Damietta. Every counter-attack was defeated by John's gallantry. In 1219 the sultan expressed his willingness to hand over Jerusalem provided the siege were raised. But now another evil genius intervened: the legate Pelagius, that self-important Spaniard who had behaved so foolishly at Constantinople. Like Andrew of Hungary, he was stoutly opposed to a unified command, and would not hear of losing Damietta, even as the price of Jerusalem. He declared in the Church's name that Damietta must be taken *as well as* Jerusalem; anyone who thought otherwise was a traitor and a felon! John of Brienne was exasperated, but gave way before what he supposed was the Pope's wish. As a matter of fact, when Honorius III learned what had happened, he blamed his representative. Damietta was taken on 5th November 1219; but the stupid warrior-cardinal allowed himself to be shut up in the city. Cut off from Palestine by Egyptian corsairs and then by the annual flooding of the Nile, he tried to escape by marching on Cairo. His way was blocked by the stronghold of Mansurah, and his army had to retreat in the middle of summer, knee-deep in water and ravaged by fever. Fortunately the sultan allowed him to withdraw his troops in return for the surrender of Damietta. Another crusade had been turned into a farce by the incompetence of its leaders.[1]

The sultan had been moved to clemency by a rumour that Frederick II was proposing to sail East,[2] and the Moslem had strong reasons for not wishing to fall foul of him.

It was fifteen years since that remarkable emperor had sworn to take the Cross; but oaths of that kind carried little weight with him. His godfather, Innocent III, and his former tutor, Honorius III, had both placed blind trust in him—a fact of which he had taken full advantage. He had struck a rich mine of plausible excuses and fallacious arguments for delaying the fulfilment of his vow. Frederick, though a Christian king, was irresistibly attracted by every aspect of Islamic civilization. He lived like an oriental despot in his court at Palermo, surrounding himself with Moslem scholars and artists, not forgetting a bevy of Eastern women. Whether he retained his faith in Christ, whether he was a believer or an atheist, remains an insoluble problem. He was on terms of closest friendship with the Egyptian sultan, Melik-el-Kâmil, exchanging with him magnificent embassies and costly presents, and even knighting one of his aides-de-camp. Surely so notorious an Islamophil could only be coming East as a welcome visitor to hear the muezzins chant on fine clear evenings.

In order to interest Frederick in the affairs of the Holy Land, the barons decided to offer him the crown of Jerusalem. All his ancestors had dreamed of such an honour, and Frederick had no intention of refusing. However, John of Brienne, who was now a very old man, had a young daughter Isabel; so it was agreed that the Emperor should marry her and succeed John. Frederick's first concern was to get rid of his father-in-law, which he did in the most scurvy fashion, and thus became sole master of the kingdom. But still he delayed to take the Cross, until the new Pope, Gregory IX, less indulgent or less credulous than Innocent and Honorius, excommunicated him.

Frederick II immediately set sail (28th June 1228). The situation was paradoxical in the extreme: an excommunicated crusader! Godfrey de Bouillon might well have turned in his grave. But the most astonishing fact remains, that this impious and so-called sixth crusade actually succeeded. 'He's no crusader, he's a pirate!' roared the Pope; but Frederick hit the mark where all others had failed. He was

---

[1] It was during the fifth crusade that St Francis of Assisi went as a missionary to preach the Gospel in Egypt. The saint wished to substitute the way of love for that of force. (*See* Chapter XII, section 4.)

[2] On Frederick II, *see* Chapter V, section 7.

condemned by Gregory, who sent a party of Franciscans to proclaim the excommunication throughout Palestine; he was also on the worst possible terms with the baronage, whom he exasperated by his arrogance; and yet he brought off a curious diplomatic triumph. By a treaty, signed in February 1229, his friend Melik-el-Kâmil agreed to hand over the Holy City (excluding the mosque of Omar), Nazareth, and all towns and villages lying on the Jerusalem–Acre and Jerusalem–Jaffa roads. The sultan also freed his Christian captives. The faithful of both religions might henceforth go and pray in the Holy Places. At the same time, the two sovereigns signed a ten-year offensive and defensive alliance against all enemies whatsoever, present and future. Frederick entered Jerusalem on 17th March. Next day the Patriarch laid his capital under interdict; and the day after that the Emperor crowned himself 'to the sole clash of arms' in the church of the Holy Sepulchre. It was indeed a fantastic business.

But can we really blame this extraordinary man who brought the Cross back to Jerusalem? Since no solution could be arrived at by force, why find fault with diplomacy? Besides, the Mongol invasion, which threatened the whole East and would soon imperil Europe as well, obliged those responsible for the two greatest empires to unite against barbarism on the march. The truth is that Frederick's policy of religious tolerance was far in advance of his time; it appeared as treason, impiety, and sacrilege. At the very moment when he was restoring Jerusalem to the Christians, the papal forces and those of his father-in-law John of Brienne were attacking his possessions in Sicily, and he had to return with all speed. But when Gregory IX received full information about arrangements in the Holy Land, he understood the advantages of Frederick's policy, and lifted the excommunication by the treaty of San Germano in July 1229.[1]

The aged Pope, however, who was approaching his hundredth year, felt the impossibility of prolonging so ambiguous a situation, and he decided to fit out one more crusade. This expedition of 1239 was a poets' crusade, led by two well-known troubadours, Philip of Nanteuil and the charming Thibaut IV of Champagne, who wrote such delightful verses to honour Blanche of Castile. It was a romantic ride during which the barons amused themselves with crazy feats of daring. One of these ended in disaster when a French corps, foolishly sent into action by its commander, Henri de Bar, was cut to pieces. But Islam was now divided between two of Saladin's nephews, Ayyub (Sultan of Egypt) and Ismaïl (Sultan of Damascus); so that the Western army by dealing first with one and then with the other, was able, for all its strange goings-on, to recover large tracts of Palestine, notably Galilee

[1] Not, however, for long. The struggle between the Pope and Emperor was resumed and ended, as we have seen, in Frederick's overthrow. (*See* Chapter V, section 7.)

and Ascalon. By 1240, in fact, the kingdom had returned almost to its original size; but that could not last. No sooner had the minstrels returned home than Ayyub overcame his rival, and Islam began to resent the presence of Latins who were constantly meddling in its affairs. The Templars had supported one of his rebellious vassals, and the Sultan of Egypt struck. The Latin kingdom was in full decline, without a leader, and in the throes of anarchy. Ayyub let loose upon it one of the least civilized of Turkish tribes, the Khwarizmians, whom the Mongols had driven from their homes. At that time, moreover, Christendom was in hopeless confusion; the yellow horsemen had appeared in Poland and Silesia, Hungary and Croatia, and even the Pope did not know what to do. On the eve of his death Gregory IX had proclaimed a crusade against John Vatatzes and the Byzantines of Nicea who were harassing the feeble emperors of Constantinople. Soon after his accession Innocent IV decided to reach a settlement with Byzantium and announced a fresh crusade against Islam. In Italy the bloody struggle between Guelfs and Ghibellines was at its height. The fall of Jerusalem on 23rd April 1244, and its sack by the Khwarizmians was followed in quick succession by that of Tiberias and Ascalon. But just as the world seemed about to end, there appeared St Louis.

11. A Saint on Crusade

A man who from childhood upwards had sought to live in the sight of God [1] could not remain outside the most splendid of all medieval Christian enterprises. He had always thought of himself as directly concerned in God's affairs. He was the king of the Cathedral; so also he would be king of the Crusade. Through him the crusades were to resume that dignity, that holiness of purpose and of conduct which they had long since abandoned. St Louis's efforts ended in defeat; but they gave to Almighty God a gift which that true Christian had always dreamed of offering him, the testimony of blood.

Late in 1244 St Louis was seriously ill and swore to take the Cross if he recovered. He did so, and immediately set about the fulfilment of his vow. The new Pope, Innocent IV, who had been elected eighteen months previously, was a staunch supporter of the crusade. At the famous Council of Lyons, in 1245, he had decreed its revival and arranged to finance it with a system of fresh taxes. Who would take part? Not Frederick; he had been excommunicated and deposed by the council, which talked of supplanting him on the imperial throne. Not Henry III of England; he was hoping that the absence of the French king would afford him an opportunity for revenge. Secret

[1] On St Louis, see Chapter VII, section 8.

talks on the state of Christendom were held at Cluny between the Pope and the Capetian, with no one else present, except Blanche of Castile; and Louis must have realized in the course of these conversations that almost the whole weight of the crusade would fall upon his shoulders. This, however, did not deter him.

Meanwhile, the oriental chess-board seemed to promise Christendom a fairly simple game. Islam was in peril: the Mongols had occupied the whole of Persia between 1235 and 1239; with the fall of Erzerum in 1242 they had fastened their hold upon the Caucasus; and they were now threatening Asia Minor, where the Armenians of Taurus had prudently agreed to become their vassals in April 1244. Again, the fratricidal strife between Damascus and Cairo grew ever more violent, and in the spring of 1245 Egyptian troops with their terrible Khwariz-mian mercenaries were besieging the Syrian capital. The papacy learned of these events. But it was uncertain whether a man like St Louis could handle the situation; oriental intrigue was not exactly in his line.

Our knowledge of the crusade is based on the testimony of a staff officer who took part in it, John, Sire de Joinville, seneschal of Champagne. *The Book of the holy words and good deeds of our saintly King Louis* throws vivid light upon the hero. For Joinville was not only a courteous knight and an eloquent story-teller; he had a keen eye for true greatness. Indeed, as we follow his account of the crusade and its dramatic vicissitudes, we realize that from the strategic and diplomatic points of view it had been badly organized. Material arrangements were somewhat better; for the island of Cyprus had been chosen as base of operations, and the Genoese and Venetians kept it plentifully supplied. The fenland town of Aigues-Mortes was named as the port of departure. The rest was in God's hands.

The crusade was preached in March 1247 by the Pope's legate Eudes de Châteauroux. Louis's three brothers joined up, together with many great lords of France, Flanders, Brittany, and Burgundy, as well as King Haakon of Norway. The gentry followed suit, though sometimes without much enthusiasm. St Louis embarked on this warlike expedition with mystic joy, as if it were a pilgrimage. He even set up a commission whose duty it was to hear the complaints of his subjects, so that he could leave the country sure of justice being done in his absence. Barefoot, wearing a coarse tunic, carrying the pilgrim's scrip and staff, he visited numerous abbeys, praying the saints to watch over his enterprise. Finally he arranged that Madame Blanche should hold authority over the realm while he was away; she was to be advised in military matters by the Count of Poitiers, and thus the kingdom would be in good hands. On 25th August the royal fleet, consisting of thirty-eight vessels, sailed from Aigues-Mortes, while a thousand voices hymned the *Veni Creator*.

After a perilous journey, in the course of which, says Joinville, they circled Stromboli for three days, they arrived at Cyprus. Henry I received the King of France in his capital at Nicosia with all that pomp of which the Lusignans were past-masters. But much time was wasted in discussion as to whether they should make straight for Palestine or go first to Egypt; and it was during this sojourn that an unlooked-for event occurred. Louis made contact with the Mongols and thought of negotiating with them. The Pope had already tried to establish relations with these terrible conquerors from Asia. A Franciscan missionary, John of Plan-Carpin, and the Dominican Ascelin had carried papal messages to the khans of the Volga and Persia, and even to the Great Khan himself, whom they visited in his capital at Kara-korum.[1] At the same time, the King of Armenia sent his own brother to the Mongol ruler. In due course St Louis welcomed two oriental Christians with an offer of collaboration from Eidjigidai, Mongol high commissioner of the Caucasus region, who suggested that they should make a concerted attack on the Moslems. He was far from despising this offer, and sent back three missionaries with rich presents, including a tent in the form of a chapel adorned with images of our Lady and the saints. St Louis treated apologetics as part and parcel of diplomacy. What good would have been an alliance with the Nestorian Mongols? It might have helped to defeat the Turks; but it would also have ruined a whole civilization in favour of barbarism, a fact he appears to have overlooked. At all events, the negotiations proved abortive.

At length, on 4th June 1249, a great fleet arrived before Damietta and the army landed. St Louis did not wait to muster his troops, but launched an immediate attack, striding towards the shore fully armed and with the water up to his arm-pits, so keen he was to tread enemy ground. It is little short of miraculous that so imprudent an operation should have succeeded. Surprised by this attack, the Moslems did no more than skirmish, and Damietta fell. The crusaders had reason to believe that Providence was on their side; but they did not exploit their victory by marching on Alexandria or Cairo. Under pretext of awaiting reinforcements, which were then on their way under his brother Alphonse of Poitiers, St Louis allowed a month to pass, during which time his barons became demoralized. When these reinforce-ments arrived, on 20th November, and notwithstanding the difficulty of crossing the Delta, he ordered an advance on Cairo (known to the crusaders as 'Babylon'), simply because he had been told it was the Moslem capital. Meanwhile, the Egyptians had rallied. Their best general, Emir Fakreddin, had chosen the citadel of Mansurah as his base, for it enabled him to command the Delta. This damp region, a network of canals, was an ideal centre of resistance; the crusaders

[1] On John of Plan-Carpin and other missionaries to Asia, *see* Chapter XII, section 5.

had no engineers or bridge builders, and could not cross the canals
unless they built dams.   Farther on they found the enemy drawn up
before Mansurah on the opposite bank, and proceeded to dam the river
under a hail of arrows and a bombardment of Greek fire (the secret of
which the Moslems had learned from Byzantium), while the Egyptians
on the other side dug new trenches.   Men and months were wasted in
this way; epidemic also took its toll.   At length, however, a bedouin
spy revealed the existence of a ford.   Fakreddin was taken by surprise
and killed; the Egyptians evacuated Mansurah and their camp, which
were occupied by the crusaders in the belief that they had conquered.

Alas! they were quickly disillusioned.   The Moslems at once
launched a series of counter-attacks.   The Christian positions were
encircled, deprived of communications with Damietta, and subjected to
furious assaults.   The crusaders were in a critical situation, which was
aggravated by famine as well as by scurvy and typhus.   An attempt
was made to negotiate, but the enemy's demands were unacceptable.
Only one course remained: they must attempt to fight their way
through to Damietta.   St Louis was so badly afflicted with dysentery
that he could no longer stand upright; but he remained calm, energetic,
and sublime as ever.   He refused to go on board one of the ships which
would try to reach Damietta, for he had resolved to lead the terrible
retreat in person.   The enemy gave chase, pouring across a bridge of
boats under the command of the Emir Baibars (nicknamed 'the Crossbowman'), a gigantic blue-eyed Turk from Russia.   The Christian
rearguard fought heroically and with heavy casualties, but in vain: the
army was lost.   The king's brothers and the great barons surrendered.
The victors found St Louis lying utterly exhausted in a humble cottage;
they took him prisoner while, upon the Nile as in the plain, they
massacred or rounded up the remnants of the glorious seventh crusade
(8th February 1250).

It was a terrible ordeal; but through ordeal a Christian proves his
worth, and St Louis now showed of what stuff he was made.   While a
prisoner in Mansurah, he was cured by the sultan's physicians, but he
also learned the full extent of the disaster.   His whole army had been
slaughtered by the Egyptians, excepting only a few from whom they
could expect a heavy ransom.   Still, he did not despair: he still had
God (who is ever close to those in suffering, and in whom he now lived
more than ever before), saying his office like a monk and impressing
the Moslems with his untroubled piety.   Moreover, he still held
Damietta where lay the queen.   A pretty but frivolous woman, she
now rose to the occasion, issuing orders to the barons and resolved to
die rather than capitulate.

Besides, the Egyptians were not ferocious when the heat of battle
had died down.   Relations that were almost friendly grew up between

them and their prisoners. Many became interested in the Christian religion; Joinville, for instance, was visited in his tent by an old man who questioned him at length upon the mysteries of the Redemption and Resurrection. This, however, did not prevent occasional outbreaks of fury. St Louis was threatened with horrible tortures unless his wife surrendered Damietta, threats to which he listened with supreme indifference. It was, in fact, this imperturbability which so impressed the Moslems that they began at last to speak of negotiation. In return for Damietta and a ransom of 100,000 gold bezants, they would free the king and the remnants of his army. At the end of April 1250 what was left of the crusade embarked for Acre.

St Louis spent another four years in the East, believing that he had not fulfilled his vow. During that time he was *de facto* head of the Latin kingdom, and was regarded in all neighbouring countries as a legendary figure, the very image of a just and wise king—St Louis of the Oak at Vincennes. The sultan respected his judgment and forgave him such part of his debt as had not yet been paid. His friendship was sought by the Old Man of the Mountain, leader of the Assassins, a dreaded sect of fanatics who used their daggers for the slightest reason and without the least compunction. Administrative duties, however, were merely incidental to St Louis; the essential task was his pilgrimage in the footsteps of Christ, and he was able to receive Communion at Nazareth. There was a brief moment when he thought that Moslem dissensions would allow him to intervene between Aleppo and Cairo, and thus to recover Jerusalem. But the two sultans composed their differences and would agree to no such terms. St Louis was bitterly disappointed; he refused the offer of a safe-conduct to visit the Holy City, not wishing to be indebted to the Infidels for the happiness of praying at the Tomb which he had failed to deliver.

He now began to think of returning home, for there was alarming news from France. The kingdom had recently been disturbed by a strange popular movement known as the 'shepherd's crusade,' led by a half-witted demagogue calling himself the 'Master of Hungary.' Blanche of Castile was dead, and the truce with England was liable to be broken off at any moment. The king's brothers were urging him in letter after letter to return, and St Louis finally consented. But before leaving, he wished to prepare against the future. In May 1253 he sent the Franciscan William of Roubrouck to the Mongols in the twofold capacity of missionary and secret-service agent. Next, he refortified the most strategic points of the little kingdom. Then, in April 1254 he embarked, certain of returning before long at the head of a new crusade which would achieve final victory.

12. THE END OF A GREAT DREAM

St Louis never abandoned the hopes with which he came back from the Holy Land.   Those nearest to him saw clearly that behind every one of his decisions lay a resolve to set out once more with the cross sewn upon his mantle, and, if necessary, to die for Christ.   Every piece of news that reached him from the East seemed like a call from God. In Palestine the Venetians and Genoese were at daggers drawn, involving the barons in their bloody strife in full view of the Moslems. At Byzantium the Latin emperor Baldwin II was overthrown and superseded by Michael Palaeologus.   But the decisive trumpet-call sounded in his ears soon after the recapture of Constantinople by the Greeks, when the Near East was in dire peril.

In 1260 the Mongols, under Hulagu, Khan of Persia and grandson of Genghis, renewed their assault on Islam.   They had taken Bagdad and overrun Mesopotamia in 1258.   In three months (January–March 1260) they occupied Syria, and Saladin's dynasty vanished in the cyclone.   Bohemond VI of Antioch-Tripoli and Hethum the Great, king of the Armenian Taurus, prudently joined forces with the yellow men, whose generalissimo, Kitbouqua, was a Nestorian Christian. It seemed that Jerusalem might yet be delivered by an allied force of Latins and Asiatic nomads.   Some historians even refer to a 'Mongol crusade.'   But this policy was rejected by the barons of Acre, either through fear of the invaders or through jealousy of their northern colleagues.   All but one of them preferred an agreement with the Moslems of Egypt.   Thanks to which the Mamelukes, under Baibars 'the Crossbowman,' were able to halt the attack in Galilee, pursue the Mongols into Mesopotamia, and force them back into Persia with results that were not slow to appear.   Baibars, who now controlled Egypt and Syria, was proclaimed sultan in place of his master, whom he quickly assassinated, and then turned on the Christians.   Armenian Taurus was occupied, followed by Caesarea, Aesouf, principal strongholds of the Templars, Jaffa, and lastly Antioch.   When St Louis died before Tunis, Baibars was gradually reducing the Krak des Chevaliers, and Acre, where Jaime I of Aragon had established himself in 1268, remained as the only Christian fortress.

The Mameluke invasion of Palestine horrified Christendom.   Alexander IV and Urban IV both talked of resuming the crusade.   But they did so without much conviction, since the originator of the scheme was Manfred, King of Sicily, whom they mistrusted.   As for St Louis, he had already made up his mind.   Though still ailing and exhausted after his ordeal in Egypt, he set no value upon life weighed in the balance against so noble a design.   During Lent, 1267, he once again took the crusader's oath upon the Crown of Thorns and a fragment of the True Cross, the most sacred of all relics preserved in his capital. Protests made by Joinville and other counsellors could not dissuade him; the baronage yielded to his importunities and followed suit.

Charles of Anjou, the king's brother, now took a hand. He was a man of great charm and high intelligence, a skilled diplomat and ambitious idealist, whose plans were not unworthy of Caesar or Napoleon. Charles had been invested with the crown of Sicily by the Pope, and having defeated Manfred at Benevento, he set about a vast scheme of matrimonial alliances whose purpose was nothing less than to establish himself as successor to Baldwin II, the Catholic emperor of Byzantium. The crusade which the Angevin wished to revive was not the seventh but the fourth. In face of this threat, Michael Palaeologus sent messengers to Rome, begging the Holy Father to prevent such an attack. 'If you fear the Latins,' Clement IV replied, 'return to the bosom of the Church.' Negotiations were reopened, and once again there was talk of ending the schism. But Clement died on 29th November 1268, and Charles, assisted by the Germans, managed to prolong the papal interregnum for three years. Michael Palaeologus watched the growing storm. Seeing the Angevin negotiate with the enemies of Byzantium—Serbs, Hungarians, and Bulgars—he turned to the King of France and invited him to arbitrate on the question of reunion. St Louis could only regard an expedition against Byzantium as an unthinkable diversion, and Charles received from his elder brother an order to abandon his intrigues and to join the true crusade.

What happened then? Did the two brothers strike a kind of bargain? Since the successful intervention of the Normans in North Africa, the Sultan of Tunis had been a vassal of Palermo; but he was heavily in arrears of tribute. Did Charles, as heir of the Norman kings, ask his brother to settle this matter in return for his agreeing to take part in the crusade? Did he point out that a rich place like Tunis would make an excellent base of operations? Did he take advantage of the saint's Christian sentiments to persuade him that the Sultan of Tunis was only awaiting an opportunity to embrace the Christian faith with all his people? 'Ah!' cried St Louis, 'may the day come when I shall see myself the sponsor and second father of such a godchild!' At all events, the eighth crusade set sail for Tunis on 11th July 1270.[1]

The disastrous failure and the misery it entailed are well known. The expedition, like that against Egypt, began with a deceptively easy landing. Then it was bogged down in the humid plain of Carthage, unable to march on Tunis and held at arm's length by Berber cavalry.

[1] The abortive negotiations with Venice provide us with accurate figures for St Louis's second crusade.   It included about 10,000 souls, of whom 7,300 were fighting men, for at this date neither esquires nor pages fought.

Q*

Soon it was swallowed up in total inertia beneath the overwhelming heat of a Tunisian summer.   Epidemic broke out, as once before on the banks of the Nile.   St Louis's son, little John-Tristram, died, and was quickly followed by the papal legate.   The crusaders' camp was ravaged by cholera, and the king himself was stricken down.

His death-scene, even now, has power to stir emotion.   Knowing that he would never again rise from his bed, Louis prepared to meet his fate with the serenity of a martyr.   He took all necessary steps for the maintenance of order when he should be gone.   For his son's benefit he dictated that sublime work known as his *Instructions*, wherein all his descendants would find precepts for the government of men.   He took almost a month to die.   At the end he could no longer speak, but his lips moved feebly when the priests around him recited the prayers for those *in extremis*.   On the evening before his death he managed to speak a few words, asking for Holy Communion and desiring to be laid on the ground, upon a bed of ashes with his arms in the form of a cross.   He was heard to murmur in a curiously distinct voice: 'Introibo in domum tuum, adorabo ad templum sanctum tuum et confitebor nomini tuo.'   Then his head fell back.   It was 25st August 1270, the day chosen by the Church to celebrate his memory.   As Louis de Poissy had lived, so he died, in God's service—the last of the crusaders.

The failure at Tunis, which Charles of Anjou's arrival and diplomatic skill could not prevent from becoming a disaster, sounded the death-knell of the crusades.   Henceforward the history of the Latin kingdom in the East is but the story of a march towards death.   Moral decadence rapidly increased; everywhere there was hostility between Templars and Hospitallers, between the 'oriental' and the 'Roman' party, between lords and commons.   There were pitiless civil wars in which, for example, we find Bohemond VI of Antioch having one of his rebellious vassals walled up alive.

Islam watched and waited; the despairing West seemed no longer to care about the Holy Land.   The intervention of the brave Prince Edward (afterwards Edward I) of England gave it a few years respite, but no advantage was taken of his achievement.   In vain the Mongol khan of Persia, Abaqa, sent embassy after embassy to Europe, imploring Edward I, Gregory X, and the fathers of the Council of Lyons in 1274 to join him in an attack upon the Moslem world.   No one dared to take the initiative.   Jaime I had evacuated Acre in order to fight the Moors in Spain.   Charles of Anjou was busy elsewhere and sent an insignificant force.   Even the death of their great adversary Baibars in 1277 could not shake the Christians out of their lethargy.   When Abaqa resumed the offensive against Syria in 1281, his Mongols were supported only by Christians from Armenia and Palestine, and the sultan Qalaoun hurled them back beyond the Euphrates. A few months later the Sicilian Vespers (1282) broke the Angevin power and hamstrung the one man who could still have taken the Cross.

Sidon, Haifa, Beirut, Tripoli, and Acre were the sole places now in Latin hands, and Qalaoun prepared to take them one by one. The single hope now lay in an alliance with the Mongols. Abaqa's successor, Arghun, suggested as much to Pope Honorius IV and Philip the Fair in 1284–5. His envoy, the Nestorian monk Rabban Sauma, was well received in Europe, but nothing was done, and two years later Islam returned to the attack. Tripoli fell in 1289 after a terrible siege which ended in appalling massacre; Acre was the last remaining bastion.

Here the crusaders wrote the final page of their glorious history. Completely encircled, ceaselessly bombarded by a large battery of catapults, starving, and deprived of all succour, they held out for six weeks with no hope but to save their honour. The end of this last little island of Christianity, swept by the tide of Islam, was worthy of its past. One epic counter-attack, one desperate sortie followed another; Templars and Hospitallers were reconciled at the approach of death and bore themselves as heroes. When, on 18th May 1291, the Arab trumpets sounded the assault, the Grand Master of the Hospital, John of Villers, and the Grand Master of the Temple, William of Beaujeu, stood side by side to defend the Gate of St Anthony. Side by side they fell. The Marshal of the Temple, Matheo of Clermont, rose and fell on the wave of attackers, laying about him with might and main, laying a road of corpses until he too was overwhelmed. Of the Templars, ten survived; of the Hospitallers, seven; of the Teutonic Knights, not one. The victorious Mamelukes slaughtered all on whom they could lay hands, especially priests, and Christendom was proud to learn that a group of Dominicans had died on their knees chanting the *Salve Regina*.[1] All that was left of the crusaders' kingdom was the tiny island of Rouaud off Tortosa, which the Templars held until 1303.

13. THE BALANCE-SHEET OF THE CRUSADES

The crusades had ended in failure; but was that failure complete? To all appearances the balance was disastrous: so much suffering, so many sacrifices for so little. France alone had lost thousands of men

---

[1] Chroniclers have estimated that Acre was defended by anything between 25,000 and 40,000 men against 120,000 to 600,000 Moslems! But Acre cannot have had more than 20,000 inhabitants (a large number for that period), of whom, say, two-thirds took part in the fighting. The Moslems certainly outnumbered them, but to nothing like the extent that has been alleged.

in these expeditions to the Holy Land,[1] and the treasuries of Christendom were exhausted. Materially speaking, none of the ends in view had been achieved. The Holy Sepulchre had not been delivered. There were still a number of religious houses in Jerusalem, and pilgrimages became somewhat easier; but such advantages might have been accomplished at less cost by negotiation. It was, in fact, this procedure to which the papacy had recourse in the fourteenth century, when Roland of Anjou was persuaded to buy the Holy Places from the Moslems, and when Clement VI entrusted them to Franciscan guardianship in 1342.

Nor had a reunion of the Churches been effected, although at one time this had seemed almost to have been accomplished. Michael Palaeologus, when threatened by Charles of Anjou (who attacked Albania soon after the debacle at Tunis), had sent the Patriarch Beccos to Gregory X in hopes of ending the schism. He had declared himself ready to accept the Roman Creed together with the *Filioque* clause, to recognize the use of unleavened bread, and to acknowledge the Pope's primacy. At the Council of Lyons in 1274 the reconciliation seemed complete; and the Greek prelates had sung mass in St John's cathedral, repeating the *Filioque* three times so that there should be no doubt about their sincerity. But this was merely a political manœuvre. The Greek clergy remained hostile to the Latins, to this pontiff who 'sustained impiety,' to 'this veritable wolf in the fold.' Photius and Caerularius were praised from the pulpits of oriental churches. Already in 1278 Nicholas III noticed an evident reluctance to give effect to the decision of Lyons. With Martin IV, who was devoted to the Angevin cause, pretence was abandoned; he supported an alliance between Charles, Philip de Courtenay, and Venice against the 'so-called emperor of the Greeks.' Andronicus II, on succeeding his father, had drawn the unavoidable conclusion; he had exiled Beccos and other partisans of reunion, and financed the anti-French revolt which ended in the 'Sicilian Vespers.' Victorious Islam beheld the scandal of continued schism.

But if the great adventure of the crusades was in many respects disappointing, can we say that it was useless and harmful? No. The crusades, more than any other event in medieval history, enabled Christendom to become conscious of its own fundamental unity. Notwithstanding differences of race and nationality, men felt the existence of a higher unity, a kind of spiritual association, with the Pope at its head and the little kingdom of Palestine as the fatherland and

[1] It is difficult to estimate these numbers exactly. Except in the beginning, the masses took no part; the leaders would not be encumbered with them, and we know that there was little emigration from west to east. At all events, the nobility suffered the heaviest losses; when the hecatombs of the Hundred Years War were added, the aristocracy almost annihilated and a new nobility took its place.

symbolic link. That is why the crusades, despite their failure, can be considered as one of the outstanding achievements of the medieval Church. Many of the actors in this drama gave evidence of moral bankruptcy, but the best of them were true witnesses to Christian faith and morals.

This large-scale shifting of peoples, this tremendous ferment, was to have all kinds of results. From the ethnical point of view, there was an importation of Western elements into the East, and consequent racial admixture. In the Turkish cemeteries at Konieh and Antalya we still find tombs bearing French or Flemish names. East and West, Islam and Christendom, learned to know one another. The esteem and friendship of the Turks, a chivalrous enemy, towards the Latins has endured until this day. France, who had been the 'Sword of Christ' and had poured out most of her blood, derived a moral advantage from her sacrifices. Her prestige in Syria and Egypt and the spread of her language in those countries were due to the crusades, which were also responsible for the introduction of many novelties to the West. Great upheavals of this kind react upon even the smallest details of social life and its accompaniments—items of dress, food, etc. Saffron, shallots (Ascalon onions), camlets (materials made from camel-hair), as also the use of tents, 'damascened' blades, and caftans appear to have had such an origin. It was also most probably in the East that hereditary arms were first used, for many heraldic terms are derived from Arabic. Architecture [1] and music likewise owe much to these new influences which, however, must not be exaggerated.[2] Generally speaking, the crusades opened up wider horizons for the West, but was that altogether an advantage? In its discovery of another civilization, another religion, another system of morality,[3]

[1] Conversely, Western architecture exercised a good deal of influence on the East. The churches of the Holy Sepulchre, St Anne of Jerusalem, and Tortosa recall the styles of Burgundy and Auvergne; later on the mosques were similarly affected. Moslem military architecture borrowed from Latin technique.

[2] These secondary results of the crusades have long been exaggerated. Leprosy was believed to have been brought back by the crusaders, who were also alleged to have imported maize, buckwheat, apricots, and even cats. Recent studies have shown that this was not so; these errors arose before it was discovered that long before the crusades there were important contacts between the eastern Mediterranean basin and the coasts of Italy and Provence through the medium of pilgrims and sailors. The statement regarding maize relied upon a document of 1204 which has been proved a forgery; maize, in fact, came from America after Columbus. The apricot had already been brought by the Arabs to Spain. The first reference to buckwheat occurs in a document of 1436 (cf. R. Grant, *L'Agriculture au Moyen Âge*, 1951). As for the tradition which connects the Rosary with those rings of amber beads which the Orientals are constantly fingering, the article 'Chapelet' by Dom Leclerq in his *Dictionnaire d'archéologie* shows that this form of prayer was used in England before 1095. Besides, we know very little about the strictly religious consequences of the crusades. All that can be said for certain is that a few elements in the Carmelite liturgy are of oriental origin.

[3] To say nothing of the method of depilation which came from the East at that period and raises a number of questions.

feudal Christendom was subject to disrupting influences. For it was on the morrow of the crusades that there appeared the first symptoms of a great doctrinal crisis.

The crusades helped in other ways also to prepare the modern world, the Europe of the Renaissance and Reformation. The enormous increase of money and the taste for luxury acquired in the East, as well as the commercial growth of the Italian ports, were to alter the whole social system. New economic currents came into being, by-passing Byzantium and Russian Kiev to follow the routes Genoa–Marseilles–Lyons, or Venice–Switzerland–Champagne, to Bruges and London. Socially, the crusades marked the beginning of the end of the nobility; the crusaders involved themselves in debt in order to finance their journeys, and were often obliged to sell land to their vassals or enfranchisement to their serfs. The same results were sometimes brought about in a more touching way, as in the case of the lord of St Phalle near Sens. Taken prisoner with St Louis, he was ransomed by the voluntary subscriptions of his peasants, all of whom he freed on his return. Lastly, the kings profited by the absence of their more powerful subjects to increase their authority.

Thus, to some extent, the modern world emerged from the most typically medieval enterprise. For a long, long time, however, the West was to look back with nostalgia upon the crusades. At the beginning of the fourteenth century, Charles of Valois, husband of Catherine de Courtenay, and Basileus *in partibus*, dreamed of taking the famous road once more. Treatises on the *Recovery of the Holy Land* were published by such writers as the Franciscan Fidenzio of Padua and Pierre Dubois, whose political and financial schemes were combined with a lively Christian sense. In 1327 the Avignon Pope John XXII called for a crusade, but in vain.[1] In 1334 Philip of Valois signed an agreement for a crusade with Venice, Cyprus, and the Hospitallers, a project from which the Capetians were deterred by the Hundred Years War. But in the East, the last and heroic Latin king of Cyprus, Peter of Lusignan, with his 'Order of the Sword,' inflicted heavy losses on the Turks before he perished together with his kingdom by a traitor's dagger (1369). Even so, the crusading spirit had not altogether disappeared. At the height of the Great Schism it inspired those young knights who died for Christ at Nicopolis in 1397. And when Joan of Arc wrote her famous letter to Talbot, she appealed to the same spirit in begging him to desist from fratricidal strife and help the French revive the great adventure in God's service.

In the heart of every man born of Christ the crusades remain a glorious memory; and it is significant that the very word 'crusade'

---

[1] It is pleasant to learn that the Christians of Greenland responded to this appeal and sent a cargo of furs and walrus tusks to help finance the expedition.

still suggests a heroic enterprise undertaken for some pure and lofty purpose. As long as Christianity endures on earth, as long as there exists a civilization from which Christian principles have not been wholly banished, there will be men to treasure these pages of sanctity and heroism inscribed by the crusaders with their blood.[1]

[1] Judgments on the crusades vary considerably, even among Christian historians. M. Olichos in *missions* is somewhat hesitant. B. de Vaulx is not very enthusiastic in his *Histoire des missions catholiques*, and the conclusion reached in Funk-Brentano's little book *Les Croisades* is frankly pessimistic.

CHAPTER XII

THE HOLY WAR OF THE MISSIONS

1. CHRISTIAN EXPANSION IN THE WEST

THE crusades in the East were not the only manifestation of the Holy War for Christ. There were earlier undertakings which continued and succeeded long after the crusades were over. When times no longer favoured military expeditions under the sign of the Cross, that same Cross continued to enlarge its field of influence, no longer by the baron's sword but in the hands of poor and unarmed missionaries.[1]

There are several ways of explaining Christianity's power of expansion. It expresses the vitality of medieval society both in the spiritual and in the political domain. What colonization and emigration have been for our modern world, such were the several forms of the Holy War for Europeans from the eleventh to the thirteenth century. Such, too, were a number of military expeditions, e.g. the Norman conquest of England and the occupation of southern Italy and Sicily by Robert Guiscard and his men.

It expresses also that intolerance of boundaries which we cannot so easily appreciate and of which pilgrimages are another example. Medieval man is often represented as attached to the land, rooted in his allotment or fief; but he was always ready to travel. He would set out for Compostella or the crusades regardless of discomfort and inconvenience; and even though the number of travellers was small as compared with the population as a whole, the movement affected all classes and every country. The history of travel in the Middle Ages has scarcely been outlined, and may never be completely written; but those episodes of which we have record are convincing. At the Great Khan's court, William of Rubrouk met a Parisian goldsmith whose brother kept a shop on the Pont-Neuf, and when Jacques Cartier arrived in Canada he was astonished to find Red Indians making the sign of the Cross, which they claimed to have learned from their ancestors.

It need scarcely be said that a Christian purpose was never absent from these journeys and mass movements. The longing to win souls for Christ, to obey His parting order, 'Go ye and teach all nations,' went hand in hand with less disinterested motives. The expansion of Christendom, in a word, was the net result of these individual

[1] See Chapter I, section 4.

wanderings, even though the means which they employed may sometimes appear totally unchristian.

2. THE RECONQUISTA

Throughout the Middle Ages and well into modern times the Christians of Spain and other Western lands waged a thrilling struggle to win back the Peninsula from Islam. There were, it is true, many regrettable chapters in this story, which is darkened by appalling violence and insatiable greed, by bitterness and ferocity. The two adversaries often gave way to abominable and wellnigh unbelievable cruelty. There was an emir, for example, who kept his enemies' severed heads in a chest for the mere pleasure of taking a peep at them now and again; there was also an unfortunate cadi whom the Cid Campeador actually roasted alive by throwing him into a ditch full of burning logs. But alongside these horrors, the history of the Reconquista includes many sublime deeds in which heroism and self-sacrifice are found together, in which men are inspired by the loftiest ideals, considering life less precious than God's honour. All the passions, high and low, chivalrous idealism as well as sordid realism and sexual dissipation, sought an outlet in these wars which prove, even more vividly than does the history of the crusades, that medieval Christianity was at once superhuman and all too human.

The whole enterprise was based on a specifically religious purpose. Territorial gains and losses were naturally at stake, but the two opponents were far more concerned with extending or protecting the home of a living faith. 'The Moors cried "Mahomet!" the Christians cried "St James!"' says the *Poema del Cid*. The history of the Reconquista, as much as, and perhaps even more than, that of the crusades, is the history of a conflict between two religions, of one Holy War against another, of the Cross against the Crescent. The Church had understood and encouraged it as such from the beginning. In 1063, for instance, Alexander II granted a general indulgence to French knights who went to the assistance of their Spanish brethren.[1] The Reconquista foreshadowed the crusades and formed a sort of appendix thereto; it was considered no less meritorious to fight in Spain than in Palestine. Nor was the papacy alone in fostering the Reconquista. The great religious Orders gladly associated themselves with the undertaking, and their monasteries helped the Cross to take root in lands recovered by the soldiers. The monks of Cluny established themselves in the Peninsula in 1033 and provided numerous bishops.

[1] This was the 'Bull of the Crusade,' starting with the words *Eos qui in Ispaniam*. There is an interesting commentary upon it by R. Naz in *Dictionnaire de droit canonique*, section XXII, column 774 ff.

Cîteaux followed a hundred years later. All Christendom, indeed, could not but concern itself with a contest upon whose issue depended the fate of one of its favourite pilgrimages. The 'Baron St James' was believed to charge at the head of Christian armies, and the popularity of Compostella itself was closely linked with the success of this holy war against Islam.[1]

Thousands obeyed the Church's call and went to fight the Moors in Spain. All sorts of motives continued for three centuries to inspire a

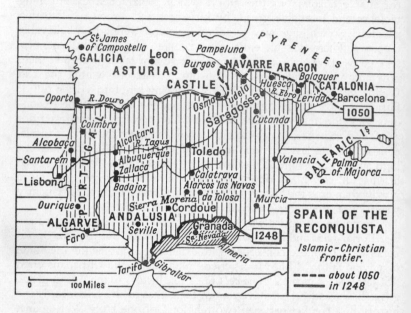

SPAIN OF THE RECONQUISTA

Islamic-Christian frontier.

- - - - about 1050
——— in 1248

constant stream of volunteers, such as the desire to gain indulgences, hope of obtaining lands, love of adventure, and even mere taste for war. France played a leading part, and was even somewhat embarrassing to her Spanish neighbour. There were Frenchmen from every walk of life and from every district, among whom we find the great names of Talleyrand, Turenne, and D'Albret. There were also nobles from the south (Languedoc and Provence), many of whom had territorial or matrimonial interests beyond the Pyrenees. The Reconquista was at once a Christian enterprise, an expression of Spanish patriotism in which France took a leading share, and a means whereby the inhabitants of the Peninsula not only wrote a magnificent epic but became aware of themselves and of their destiny.

The country had been dominated by Islam for 350 years, and the

[1] See Chapter II section 10.

terrible flood that had reached the threshold of Poitou, where it was halted by Charles Martel, had remained to cover four-fifths of the Iberian Peninsula.   But Christian Spain was sprung from the blood of St Hermenegild, and though submerged by the infidel tide she refused to drown.   Even in those areas where the Moslems were all-powerful the 'mozarabic' Christians clung to their faith.   About the year 850 they had even produced a number of martyrs: Archbishop Eulogius, the priest Fraefectus, and two charming girls, Maria and Flora, who shed their blood at Cordova at the age of twenty.   Christian life had survived; the vanquished had obtained recognition for their statute, which was known as the 'Law of the Visigoths,' and ensured its application by officials called Protectors.   Moreover, there were still bishops, who continued to hold councils; and a few monastic communities, descended from St Germain-des-Prés and Gorse, had managed to survive.   Nevertheless, it must be frankly admitted that these Christian nuclei were in a constant state of decline, contaminated by the manners of Islam, consisting on the one hand of hotheads who dreamed of martyrdom and on the other of trimmers ready for compromise.   They were sorely in need of help from without.

Meanwhile, perched among the mountains in the north, a number of petty kingdoms, richer in courage than in cash, had preserved their independence and would later provide the starting point of the Reconquista.   On the eve of the eleventh century the frontier between the Moslem and Christian zones started on the Atlantic seaboard and followed the Douro upstream as far as Osma, whence it ran northwards to a point south of Pampeluna, and from there to Barcelona on the Mediterranean.   North of this line lay the chain of Catholic States as follows: (1) Asturias, founded by Pelagius, later extended to the Douro and united with Galicia, with its capital at Leon; (2) the County of Castile, which was in a fair way to becoming a full-fledged state; (3) Navarre, including the Pyrenean counties and stretching to the upper Ebro; (4) Aragon, which was for long attached to Navarre, but had become a kingdom by means of succession; and (5) Catalonia, the ancient 'march' of Charlemagne, which was now a feudatory county of the French king.   All these little states, though energetic and determined, had one grave defect: they were too often disunited. Their complicated dynastic histories had been and continued to be stained by fratricidal strife; and their disunion would have been fatal to the Reconquista had Islam itself not been worse affected.

Moslem Spain had attained its zenith in 929, when the Arab-Syrian dynasty of the Ommayad had taken the imperial title of Caliph.   It dominated almost the whole of North Africa beyond the Straits of Gibraltar.   Cordova was the Ommayad capital, a noble city celebrated for her schools and artists, whose wonderful mosque still bears witness

to her glory.   Granada and Seville were scarcely less magnificent.
For many years the caliphate of Cordova had refrained from aggression; it had merely kept an eye upon the frontier through a line of
'ribats' or fortified monasteries.   But shortly before the year 1000 the
northern Christians had been gravely alarmed when the terrible Al
Mansur launched a general attack, took Compostélla in 997, and razed
the whole place, excepting only the tomb of St James.   About 1050,
however, the situation had improved.   Several provinces had become
detached from Cordova, where the caliphs dreamed away their days in
poetry and sensuality; and in 1031 the caliphate itself gave place to a
federation of twenty-three small states known as 'Taifas.'   The
Christians now had the advantage if they chose to take it.

One man did so choose, Ferdinand I, King of Castile (1028–65).
Profiting by Moslem divisions, he laid siege in turn to the taifas of
Toledo, Saragossa, and Badajos, and frightened Motadid, the voluptu-
ous King of Seville, into submission.   On his death, one of his three
sons, Alfonso VI, determined the succession by making war on his
brothers (1065–1109) and resumed the offensive.   He enlisted the
services of Burgundian knights, fellow countrymen of his wife Constance.   Next, he appealed to the monks of Cluny and to Pope
Gregory VII, who preached a crusade in his favour.   Alfonso pressed
the Moslems hard.   For seven years his armoured cavalry, similar to
those depicted in the Bayeux tapestry, struck at one taifa after another
—Saragossa, Valencia, Granada, and Seville.   Toledo, a city dear to
Christian hearts, fell in 1085 after a siege of twenty-five months.
Alfonso occupied the whole of Castile between the Douro and the
Tagus; having come from the north as a petty king, he now bore the
proud title 'Toleti Imperii rex et magnificus triumphator.'   On the
shore of Tarifa, at the exact spot where the first squadrons of Islam had
disembarked in the eighth century, he spurred his horse into the sea,
crying, as if about to launch an attack on Africa, 'I have reached the
uttermost point of Spain.'

These splendid feats of arms were desultory and sporadic, but their
effect upon Islam was remarkable: everywhere the emirs yielded.
Troops from Navarre and Aragon swept down upon Tudela, Castilians upon Saragossa.   Moslem rule in Spain seemed on the point of
collapse when an event occurred to alter the whole situation.   Eighteen
hundred miles from Europe, in the southern Sahara, there had been
a religious revolution (1035).   One Abdullah-ibn-Yasin, on a pilgrimage to Mecca, had accomplished a reform among the Tuaregs,
desert nomads whose manners and ferocity were comparable with
those of Mahomet's Bedouins or the Mongols of Genghis Khan.
These strange fanatics, skilled camel-drivers and invincible horsemen,
covering the lower half of their faces with a blue veil as a protection

against sand, had crossed the desert and invaded the fertile lands of Maghreb. They looked upon war chiefly as a matter of religion, as an act of faith. Their intention was to bring back the Moslems to the strict religion of the Prophet and to chastise those who were lax. These Puritans of the desert were organized in communities that were at once religious and military. They have been described as Islamic Templars. Their proper name was *al-mourâbitoun* (Marabouts), a word which the Christians rendered as *Almoravides*. In 1055 they captured Tafilet, then Sous and the whole of southern Morocco. On the death of Ibn Yasin, in 1059, their new leader, Youssuf-ibn-Tachfin, showed himself still more enterprising. He crossed the Atlas, overran northern Morocco, and soon afterwards took possession of Oudjda, Tlemcen, Oran, and Ouarsenis. By 1082 he had reached the walls of Algiers.

Alarmed by the successes of Alfonso VI, the emirs of Spain cast frightened looks toward the victorious Almoravids, although they were not unaware of the danger that might overtake their little states if they called in such terrible allies. But Motamid spoke for them all when he declared that he 'would rather look after camels in Maghreb than pigs in Castile.'

It was the end of June 1086, and from this moment the situation in the Peninsula was completely reversed. The Christians found themselves confronted not by the helpless taifas, but by a splendid warrior-people, inspired with the conviction that they were the mouthpiece of the Prophet, and unencumbered with such business or matrimonial alliances as nearly all the emirs had contracted with the Christians. In the space of a few years the Almoravids not only liquidated the taifas, but imposed their rigid authority and Puritanism on Spain. Alfonso VI, who had ventured unwisely across the Tagus, was surprised by Youssuf on 23rd October 1086, at Zalacca between Badajoz and Albuquerque. The Spaniards were confounded by the attack of these veiled horsemen with their scar-faced Negro and Algerian Bedouin auxiliaries; their chargers were scared by the din of tom-toms and the sight of camels. Alfonso escaped with a handful of men and made for Toledo, while the Tuaregs decapitated the remainder and formed their heads into enormous pyramids, from the top of which muezzins called the faithful to evening prayer. There was no longer any question of driving out the Moslems, but of saving what was left of Christian Spain. Organized resistance was summed up in one name, embodied in one man, whom history and poetry know as the Cid Campeador. Literature has idealized and thereby distorted his character. His real name was Rodrigo de Bivar, a country gentleman from Old Castile. He was certainly a hero, brave as a lion and eager for war. But he was an adventurer who often failed to distinguish his private interests from those of Christendom; a soul full of contradictions, in which the most revolting brutality was found side by side with real love for the poor and genuine humility.   Having quarrelled with Alfonso VI, whom he suspected of murdering his brother, he took service with the Emir of Saragossa against the Moslem king of Lerida (an ally of the Count of Barcelona), and distinguished himself in the struggle against the Almoravids.   Rodrigo's outstanding achievement was the capture of Valencia in 1094 after a twenty months' siege.   He restored the bishopric and converted the mosque into a cathedral.   His might and prowess thrilled the whole of Spain, and he became the living symbol of resistance to the foreigner.   Christian latinists called him *Campidoctor* (master of war); the Moslems knew him as the *Sid* (lord). Once again he managed, though not without difficulty, to halt an offensive at Bairen; and when he died, on 10th July 1099, he was mourned by the entire Peninsula.   Soon afterwards, when Valencia was abandoned, his courageous widow, Chimena, bore the great soldier's remains in a shroud ornamented with gold; and it was said that the sight alone of this funeral procession scattered the enemy.

The enthusiasm inspired by the Cid was felt throughout the Peninsula.   The Spaniards and their numerous French allies had at first been unable to withstand the Almoravids, but now they rallied and counter-attacked.   They marched on Huesca, Balaguer, and the mouth of the Tagus, where they recovered Santarem, Lisbon, and Cintra. Moslem territory was overrun in a series of extensive forays as far as Almeria and Murcia.   But the situation continued to fluctuate, for the Almoravides also dispatched raiding parties throughout Spain.   In 1108 Temyn, son of the aged Youssuf, took Ucles.   In 1111 he launched a sweeping attack upon Portugal from Evora to Lisbon and Oporto, taking from Count Henry of Burgundy the fruits of twenty years endeavour.   In 1114 the Moors occupied the Balearic islands and attacked Barcelona, which was saved only by the arrival of an army from beyond the Pyrenees.

The situation was reversed by a new Christian leader, Alfonso I of Aragon, surnamed the Fighter (1104-34).   His courage and determination won a number of splendid victories and made a deep impression on his fellow countrymen.   Saragossa was taken in 1118, and the enemy crushed at Cutanda in 1120.   A great raid in 1125 and 1126 brought him by way of Valencia and Murcia to Cordova and Granada in the heart of the Andalusian kingdom.   He too, like his great predecessor, was able to ride his horse into the sea, looking across towards Africa; and when he died, in 1134, soon after his one and only defeat, he had proved to Spain that the Almoravids were not invincible.

Once more, however, a religious and political interlude changed the state of affairs. Just as the Almoravids had come to power through a religious reform, so they came to grief through the same means. Many Moslems accused them of being narrow-minded Puritans, formalists, and materialists who emptied the Koranic revelation of its spiritual content. The opposition was led by a mahdi named Mohammed-ibn-Toumart whose 'confessors of divine unity' (*al-mohades*) preached a holy war against the Almoravids. During 1122 they swept Morocco with fire and sword, and by 1146, after an orgy of bloodshed, it was entirely in their hands.

The Christians of Spain might have profited by this situation if they had been able to unite. The Almoravids were on the decline; their morale had been lowered not only by the Almohads, but also by the easy-going Andalusian way of life. Alfonso VII of Castile proclaimed himself 'Emperor of Spain,' exacted vague oaths of fidelity from the grandees of Aragon and elsewhere, and also raided as far as Cordova. But the offensive which might have won the day was never mounted, and the Almohades were allowed to overrun Spain during the year 1145.

The war now became more violent. While the Almohads encountered serious difficulties in subjugating the remnants of the Almoravids, Christendom took the offensive. In the West, Portugal made her glorious début upon the stage of history with Alfonso-Henry, grandson of the Duke of Burgundy, great-grandson of Robert, King of France, and grandson on his mother's side of Alfonso VI. He defeated the Moors at Ourique in 1134, was proclaimed king by his troops, and recovered Lisbon once for all in 1147 with the assistance of an Anglo-French fleet. Then he crossed the Tagus, extended his dominions to the frontiers of Algarve, and was recognized as king by Pope Alexander III in 1170. To the north-west, Aragonese as well as Catalans and Castilians, though bound by no formal treaty, were agreed as to the future partition of Spain. They launched a general offensive, which was halted only by the strategic skill of the Almohad leader Yakub at the battle of Alarcos in 1195, a victory which marked the climax of Almohad power in Spain.

The beginning of the thirteenth century found Innocent III upon the papal throne. Archbishop Rodrigo Ximenes of Toledo recruited a large army which included volunteers from every part of Christendom, and the Pope supported the crusade in Spain as he had done in the East. It was led by three kings, Sancho V of Navarre, Pedro II of Aragon, and Alfonso VIII of Castile. The several units mustered at Toledo in June 1212, crossed the Sierra Morena, and found Islam drawn up for battle. Seated upon a shield and wearing a green turban, Yakub directed operations from a hilltop. The Moslems attacked to the rhythmic beat of drums; the armoured wall of knights wavered for a moment, then rallied and bore down on the Almohad pikemen, who were quickly thrown into disorder and cut to pieces. Among the loot was the Caliph's standard, azure with gold stars, which was hung up in Toledo cathedral. The battle of Las Navas da Tolosa was fought on 16th July 1212, and the Spanish Church has since commemorated this 'triumph of the Cross' with an annual feast.

We need not be surprised to find the Church taking part in these savage battles. Our modern sensibility may be shocked to discover the Archbishop of Narbonne and the Primate of Toledo assisting at the carnage of Las Navas, and thanking God as they rode over the battlefield strewn with Moslem corpses. But such were the manners of that age, and the campaigns in the Holy Land provide many similar examples. We must also recognize the pre-eminent part played by the Church in this wholly secular contest. The Reconquista could scarcely have succeeded without her. So many Christian princes who had practically gone native were ready to compromise with the Moors; so many of their subjects would have preferred semi-apostasy to disastrous heroism. Bishops, priests, and monks, however, repeatedly stirred the zeal of nobles and of their troops, and managed, though with great difficulty, to endow the soldiers and politicians with a single sense of dedication.

The most striking evidence of the Church's part in the Reconquista is her creation of the Spanish military Orders. It has been maintained that these were first suggested to Alfonso the Fighter by the *ribats* of Islam; and we know that he founded the Order of Knights of St Saviour, who wore a white mantle charged with a *cross patonce gules*. But the renown of the military Orders of the Holy Land quickly spread to Spain, and a king of Barcelona wore the habit of a Templar on his death-bed. Two gentlemen of Salamanca gathered a party of their friends in an orchard of pear-trees and established the Order of St Julian of the Pear-tree. A few years later, in 1156, its headquarters were moved to Alcantara on the Tagus. The Order was renamed after that city; its reputation increased, and its golden shield, charged with a *cross floretty purpure*, was distinguished on many a field. In 1158, when the Templars decided they could no longer hold Calatrava, two monks—St Raymund, Abbot of Fitero, and Brother Diego Velasquez—resolved to defend the place themselves. They were soon joined by a body of faithful knights, whose arms—*or a cross floretty gules and two shackles sable*—was likewise renowned in battle. The Knights of Santiago, established in 1161 and reorganized by the Holy See in 1176, were originally intended to protect pilgrims and provide hospices on the roads to Compostella; but they too were often called upon to fight, which they did with unsurpassed heroism. The military Orders of Alcantara, Calatrava, and St James were each subject to its respective Master, supreme Council, and Commander. They were destined to play a decisive part in the Reconquista during the thirteenth century,[1] and embodied all that was noblest in the soul of Christian Spain.

The victory of Las Navas marked the end of Almohad power. Jaime I of Aragon, 'the Conqueror,' recovered the Balearic islands, and, with the aid of some English and French crusaders, he drove the Moslems from Valencia in 1238. Meanwhile, Castile and Leon were united under Ferdinand III, the Saint (1217–52), a great king, a man of iron, and a true Christian, who was determined to liberate Andalusia. Proclaiming himself 'knight of Christ, servant of God, and standard-bearer of the Lord St James,' he gave the Reconquista its true character as a Christian Holy War. Cordova fell in 1236 after a siege of several months; it had belonged to Islam for 525 years, and was never again lost. The bells of St James of Compostella, which Al Mansur had carried away in 997 on the backs of Christian captives, were returned to the Galician sanctuary—on Moslem backs this time. The Almohad commandant of Granada saved himself by doing homage to Ferdinand and helping him to take Seville (1248). Nothing now stood in the conqueror's way but the charming little kingdom of Granada at the foot of the Sierra Nevada. It yielded in due course, and Ferdinand was meditating a blow at the enemy in Africa when death found him out in 1252. He died serenely, stripped of his royal ornaments, the penitent's rope about his neck, a blessed candle in his hand, murmuring the *Te Deum* in his agony.

Ferdinand III brought to an end the medieval chapter of the Reconquista. It was in his day that Spain built her cathedrals, founded her universities, produced St Dominic, and became, in fact, a first-rate Christian power.

3. CHRISTIAN EXPANSION TOWARDS THE NORTH AND EAST

The same expanding force which enabled Christendom to drive the Moslems to the uttermost limits of the Iberian Peninsula caused her to look eastward and to extend her sway over lands that were still pagan. What the Germans call 'drang nach Osten' began long ago when Celtic missionaries gradually penetrated the heathen forests, and when St Boniface shed his blood to win Germany for Christ. The victorious campaigns of Charlemagne, during which clerics followed in the wake of his armies, had been a step in the right direction; but they had relied upon conversion by force—a questionable

[1] So decisive that the first care of Ferdinand the Catholic, after driving the Moors from Spain in 1492, was to submit the military orders to royal authority: the king himself was in future their Grand Master.

method, to say the least.   Christian Germany was now the starting-point for new conquests; the drive to the east tended to become an exclusively German undertaking, and the means of evangelization were too often those which Charlemagne had used to incorporate the Saxons in his Christian empire.   Besides the oriental and Spanish crusades, then, there was another in north-eastern Europe, character-ized by all the violence and mistaken strategy of those pious but formidable expeditions.

The conversion of Scandinavia forms a single exception to the preponderance of German missionaries and the use of force.   After St Anscar's failure in the middle of the ninth century, the conversion of the Nordic countries had been the work of their own kings.   The ancient Vikings had been quick to realize that baptism would enhance their status in the civilized world; both Harold Bluetooth of Denmark and St Olaf of Norway had brought their territories within the orbit of Christendom.   The great Canute (1016–35), whose empire comprised most of Scandinavia and part of the British Isles, had also worked for the spread of Christianity.   About the year 1000, the new religion had been officially recognized in Iceland, where Isleif Gissurson was consecrated bishop by Adalbert of Bremen in 1056.   The evangeliza-tion of Sweden was slower, but followed the same pattern; and about 1080 King Inge applied to Rome for the erection of two episcopal sees in his realm.

The predominant part taken by the Scandinavians in the conversion of their own countries had this advantage, that there was no break in their history.   Their national traditions, instead of disappearing as happened in Germany, were incorporated with the new customs. Christian poems, lives of saints, and pilgrim guides, all written in the vernacular, took their place side by side with the Eddas and Sagas. The winter merry-making was identified with the festival of Christmas, and children even received at baptism names derived from those of ancient pagan gods.

This gentle imposition of Christianity caused Scandinavia to draw closer to the West.   When, in 1060, King Harold the Stern of Norway quarrelled with the Archbishop of Bremen, to whose jurisdiction he was subject, he remembered his own service in the Varangian Guards at Constantinople, and sent for a number of Greek prelates.   Traces of that influence are discovered as far afield as Iceland.   But the move-ment came to nothing, and the young churches of the north clung to Rome.   Many Swedes, Norwegians, and Danes went on pilgrimage to Compostella, Rome, or Mont Saint-Michel; while the register of visitors to Reichenau Abbey contains 670 Scandinavian names within a period of less than 200 years.   There were many students from these countries at the University of Paris, and in 1183 the North sent numerous volunteers to help Portugal against the Moors. Some years later a Scandinavian crusade reached the Holy Land just after Saladin had taken Jerusalem. Having played an important part in the recovery of Sidon, it passed through Constantinople and Germany, and reached Scandinavia, where King Sigurd had lately founded Stockholm. The Nordic lands became true Christian centres with their own metropolitans. Lund was created an archbishopric in 1104, Trondjhem in 1152, and Upsala in 1164. The clergy too were active, and Bishop Absalom guided the policy of Denmark from 1182 until 1201.

Scandinavian Christians wished in their turn to spread the Gospel. In Greenland the bear- and seal-hunters formed a small community of their own. From 1126 they numbered about 3,000, and had a bishop at Gadhar, where the cathedral was 82 ft long. Traces of them have been found in the Far North at 72°. The 'Vinland' of Scandinavian legend has never been exactly identified; but it certainly had a small Christian colony, for a bishop sailed there in 1121. The Scandinavians intervened likewise on the coast of Finland, a well-known pirate base. Here, more drastic methods were required. About 1157 the holy King Eric of Sweden left the island of Gotland at the head of a large army. He was accompanied by Bishop Henry of Upsala, who was martyred and buried at Abo, and became patron saint of the young Finnish community. Christianity was finally established in Finland by the Dominicans in the thirteenth century.

Meanwhile, on the shores of the Baltic, from Jutland to the Gulf of Riga, other methods were employed; for the problem there was not quite the same as in Scandinavia. At that time the Germanic world, belonging to the Holy Roman Empire, was bounded by a line drawn roughly as follows: lower Elbe–middle Oder–Riesengebirge–Sudetenland. It included Bohemia, whose population was Czech but which had belonged to Germany since its conversion; belonged, that is, inasmuch as the bishopric of Prague was suffragan to Mainz. Even after the accession of its first king, Ottokar I, in 1198, Bohemia remained part of the Empire, of which its monarch was an Elector. Farther east, there were two more Catholic states. Poland, an outer bastion of Christianity, extended beyond the Vistula. Converted through the influence of St Dombrovska, it was developed by Boleslav the Mighty (992–1025), who made it into a kingdom. Again, the Finnish or Turco-Mongol peoples of Hungary had formed part of Christendom since the baptism of King St Stephen (996–1038), and there was thus established on the Middle Danube a vigorous state which would afterwards seek to embrace Croatia, Dalmatia, Transylvania, and Wallachia. Hungary, in fact, was another bastion of Christianity towards the east.

Beyond these areas, where Catholicism was firmly implanted, lay extensive pagan lands, especially the whole of north-east Germany, where the Wends, the Obotrites of Mecklenburg, the Pomeranians, the Prussians between the Vistula and Niemen, the Livonians, Letts, Lithuanians, and Finns were known to the West under the general appellation of 'Wends.' Still farther east, a district four times the size of France was occupied by the principality of Novgorod-Kiev. It was inhabited by Slavs who were afterwards called Russians.

Converted in the tenth century by Princess Olga and her grandson Vladimir the Saint (987), Russia had had its Charlemagne in Yaroslav the Wise (1015–54),[1] and had become a leading power. The metropolis of Kiev, a trade centre on the road from the Baltic to the Straits, had the appearance of a regular capital. It seemed to rival the illustrious city on the Bosphorus with its own cathedral of Holy Wisdom, its hundreds of churches, and the priceless treasures of its monasteries. The Russians had received the Gospel from Byzantine missionaries; and Kiev looked to Constantinople for administrators, for bishops, and frequently for wives. Russian Christianity therefore evolved apart from the West, and its isolation was gradually completed by the schism of 1054. At the beginning of the eleventh century, in border regions where Greeks and Catholics met, there had already been fierce rivalry between Latin and oriental missionaries. German monks sent out by the Emperor Otto I had been obliged to withdraw by the arrival of Byzantine Russians.

This rivalry, however, grew less and ultimately disappeared, because political events prevented Russia from exerting her former influence. Yaroslav's empire fell to pieces more rapidly than that of Charlemagne; southern Russia was overwhelmed from the north; while Kiev was sacked in 1169 and again in 1202 by the Polovtsi. Suzdal (the future principality of Moscow) declared its independence, so did Galicia. Above all, the Mongol invasion in the thirteenth century[2] struck a mortal blow at the principality of Novgorod-Kiev. Genghis Khan's raid in 1224 and Batu's invasion (1236–40) ended in the establishment of the Golden Horde on the Volga and in the final subjection of the Russians to the Mongols. Kiev was ruined. The Franciscan Jean Plan-Carpin, who visited the place, tells us that no more than two hundred houses remained. Russia was now but a small tributary vassal of the Golden Horde, and could no longer share in the spread of Christianity. Her place was taken first by the Poles, but to a greater extent by the Germans, who compelled the heathens of the Baltic to accept Christianity, and occupied the territory between that sea and Russia.

The evangelization of the Slavs in northern and eastern Germany, which had made considerable headway during the tenth century,

---

[1] See Chapter X, section 6.   [2] See Chapter XI, section 9.

thanks to St Adalbert of Hamburg, came to a standstill at the beginning
of Henry IV's reign, when that emperor dismissed the prelate.   Paganism raised its head once more, and in 1066 Gottschalk, prince of the
Obotrites and friend of St Adalbert, was assassinated.   The empire,
engaged in mortal conflict with the papacy, did nothing.   Bishops
could no longer reside in their dioceses; and the Slavs, not content with

CHRISTIAN
EXPANSION
ON THE
BALTIC

fighting Christianity at home, attacked other Catholic areas (notably
Saxony), destroying churches and capturing priests, whom they
crucified or mutilated in the most horrible fashion.   By 1110 the
situation was so grave that the Duke of Saxony led a punitive expedition into Slav territory.

The Christians, however, did not despair, and Polish missionaries
were sent by Boleslav III to Pomerania.   Starting from Gniezno,
they travelled fearlessly into the most hostile regions, and by about 1122
they had managed to erect bishoprics on the lower Vistula.   Two
years later, Bishop Otto of Bamberg informed King Boleslav that he

would make himself responsible for the conversion of Western Pomerania on the Oder. In 1124–5 he moved in great pomp from Pyritz to Stettin, taking with him liturgical vestments and rich plate in order to impress the heathen. His biographers assure us that he baptized no fewer than 22,000 persons; too many, no doubt, for within three years most of them had returned to paganism. With the accession of Lothair of Saxony in 1125 the Empire began to take fresh interest in evangelization. His work was carried on by his son-in-law Conrad III (1138–52) and by his grand-nephew Frederick Barbarossa (1152–90), both of whom were adversaries of the Pope.

From about 1125 the Germans identified evangelization with territorial expansion, from which the feudal lords, particularly the young Saxon Duke Henry the Lion and the Margrave Albert the Bear, derived substantial benefit. At first the procedure followed was that of the mission. Otto of Bamberg visited the Wends and the country around Stettin which he had by-passed on his former journey; while St Norbert,[1] after his appointment as Archbishop of Magdeburg and with the aid of his canons regular at Marienkloster, set to work on a still larger scale.

But the results appear to have been disappointing. In Pomerania, the Christian prince Wratislav was assassinated. Henry, son of Gottschalk, spent a long life fighting paganism among the Obotrites, but on his death two heathen lords seized power. Even the magnificent efforts of St Benno of Meissen among the Wends, of St Vicelin, Bishop of Oldenburg, among the Obotrites, together with the patient endeavours of Cistercians and Premonstratensians, impressed many German rulers as inadequate, and an idea steadily gained ground that the pagans would never be converted unless by force of arms.

In 1147, when preaching the second crusade in Germany, St Bernard found the nobility unenthusiastic for an expedition to Palestine. He therefore assured them that a northern crusade would be equally meritorious, and the 'Crusade against the Wends' was decided at the Council of Frankfort. This recourse to arms was probably a mistake. At all events the army, consisting of Saxons, Swabians, Czechs, and Poles, accomplished very little; it stirred up anti-Christian hatred, and such conversions as were made did not endure.

Albert the Bear now took a hand. Having decided to occupy pagan territory, he presented himself to the people not as an enemy but as their protector. Taking with him colonists from Holland, Germany, and Flanders, he made steady progress until, in 1150, he was able to re-establish the bishopric of Havelberg, thus preparing the way for the 'March of Brandenburg' which his descendants were to make so important a part of Germany. At the same time, notwithstanding the

[1] See Chapter IV, section 4.

disapproval and even resistance of earlier missionaries, Henry the Lion, Duke of Saxony, settled at Lübeck, founded Rostock, and rebuilt Mecklenburg. The principal date in this advance to the Baltic is 1202; it marks the foundation of Riga, which became the starting-point of all future expansion.

About the end of the twelfth century the twofold work of colonization and missionary endeavour had made large inroads upon pagan areas. But there was still much to do. The missionaries established in Livonia by an Augustinian canon named Meinhard were in such danger that it became necessary to mount a regular crusade (1199–1204) with the approval of Pope Innocent III. The most savage of all these heathen folk were the Prussians,[1] at whose hands St Adalbert of Prague had suffered martyrdom in 997.[2] A Cistercian monk, one Christian, from the monastery of Oliva, did heroic work among them, but without permanent results; for he was obliged to leave Prussia in 1216 by a sudden outburst of unparalleled violence throughout the pagan countries lying between the Baltic and the mountains of Bohemia. This state of affairs lasted for some twenty-five years. Christendom learned with horror that in one place 20,000 of the faithful had been massacred; elsewhere 5,000 had been reduced to slavery; while Christian virgins, crowned with flowers, had been sacrificed to evil spirits. It was surely no coincidence that at this very time, about three years before the Khwarizmians took Jerusalem, the Mongols were ravaging central Europe, crushing the Poles and Germans at Leignitz, and overwhelming the forces of Bela IV in Hungary.

Immediate action was called for; and he who determined the West to crush the northern pagans was none other than Frederick II, the same emperor who was to engage in mortal combat with the Holy See and, though excommunicate, to lead the fifth crusade. But at this stage he had not quarrelled with the Pope, to whom he could therefore look for assistance; and in 1230 the Franciscans, Dominicans, Cistercians, and Premonstratensians were directed by papal Bull to preach a Nordic crusade.

The active element in this Christian undertaking to liquidate the pagans of the north was the Order of Teutonic Knights which had been created in the Holy Land. An Order of hospitallers intended to provide for German pilgrims, it was originally known as the 'Order of our Lady of the Germans at Jerusalem,' and might have been described as a poor relation of the Templars and Hospitallers. After the death of Barbarossa in 1190, Frederick of Swabia joined Guy de Lusignan

[1] The Prussians, kinsmen of the Letts and Lithuanians, were not of Germanic stock. The habit of confusing the Prussians with the Germans is modern and dates from the government of Germany by the Hohenzollerns, rulers of Brandenburg. The true Prussians were in fact wiped out and replaced with Germans.

[2] He must be distinguished from his namesake of Hamburg.

before Acre and conceived the idea of transforming this institution into a military Order modelled upon that of the Hospitallers. Henry von Walpot, its first master, obtained approval from Rome, and the white mantle and black cross of the Teutonic Knights appeared thenceforward on many a battle-field. Until 1225 these warriors fought in the East, where, indeed, they did such good service that their numbers fell to twelve, and the authorities decided that in future two knights must always remain on the reserve list to ensure the Order's continuance. The new grand master, Hermann von Salza, a personal friend of Frederick II, realizing perhaps that Palestine could not much longer withstand the hordes of Islam, dispatched his subjects to the north. Another Order, that of the Swordbearers, modelled likewise on those of Palestine, had been founded in 1208 by Bishop Albert at Riga for service in Livonia and Courland. They too wrote a fair, though shorter, page of medieval history. After their defeat by the Russians, in 1237, they combined with the Teutonic Knights who had taken charge of operations in the north at Bishop Christian's request. Fifty-seven years were needed to overcome Prussian resistance. It was a war of extermination, for which the Teutonic Knights enlisted men from all over Germany, and even Czechs. A fully organized crusade began in 1230. Wherever they were successful, the Knights obliged their defeated enemies to build those formidable and imposing castles which can still be seen at Malbork, Kwidzym, Thorn, Kaliningrad, and at several other points—a line of fortresses whose purpose was to prevent counter-attack. The wisdom of these measures became clear during the Prussian offensive of 1251–73. The Duke of Pomerania, who had been so imprudent as to assist the revolted pagans, was chastised unmercifully. The Lithuanians, who, in a bitterly contested action, had killed 150 Knights, were slaughtered left, right, and centre. No means were barred that might help to break resistance, not even treachery in the form of murdering an enemy who had been invited to negotiate over the dinner table. At length, after many set-backs, marvellous endurance, and unbelievable tenacity, the Teutonic Order gained the upper hand. In 1283 the Grand Master Hartman von Heldrunge launched a decisive attack against Sburdo, the last resistance leader, who is said to have asked for baptism and even to have enrolled himself among the Knights. Pomerania surrendered at the same time.

What are we to think of these terrible mopping-up operations carried out by the great German military Order? The heroism of the Knights is beyond question; it was sublime not only in the pagan lands of the Baltic, but also in action against the Mongols, where many of them fell, as well as in Transylvania whither they were summoned by the Hungarian kings. But their ferocity is no less undeniable. A whole people vanished beneath their hammer-blows. Not one Prussian survived; the country was repeopled with German colonists. Surely some other means could have been found; surely it was not necessary to exterminate a pagan race in order to eradicate paganism. It was a sad ending to a glorious chapter of 'Christian' history.

4. St Francis of Assisi, Father of the Missions

One man at least had come to the conclusion that force was not the best method. The great saint who, at the beginning of the thirteenth century, had laboured so hard to bring back Christian life to its original purity could not but long to spread the Gospel by love rather than by violence. St Francis of Assisi [1] wished to revive the old apostolic tradition of unarmed missionaries, their hearts filled with charity and tenderness.

Jacques de Vitry tells how the crusaders, when besieging Damietta in 1219, witnessed the arrival in mid July of 'a simple and unlettered man, but pleasant and dear to God as to men, Father Francis, founder of the Order of Minors.' The general chapter of 1219 had decided to send brethren to heathen lands. Brother Giles went to Tunis; others steered for Morocco where they would find the palm of martyrdom; while Francis himself, no less anxious to shed his blood for Christ, started for the East. So many had wished to accompany him that he had chosen twelve by drawing lots. These included Bro. Illuminatus, Bro. Peter of Catana, Bro. Leonard, and Bro. Barbaro, one of his first disciples.

The spectacle presented by the crusading army was not one to cheer the heart of a saint. The leaders were all at sixes and sevens, the most disgraceful licentiousness prevailed among the troops, and the camp was thronged with whores. Moreover, the Christians were experiencing one set-back after another. On 29th August, when they proposed to make a final assault, the Poverello warned them that by doing so they would run headlong into disaster; and in fact they lost 6,000 men.

He remained with the army for several months, and his apostolate at first brought forth rich fruit. Since the failure of their assault, he had been looked upon as one inspired by God. Such was his courage and generosity that the knights regarded him as a pattern of chivalry, and he quickly won recruits. 'This Order, which grows so rapidly,' says Jacques de Vitry, 'reminds one of the primitive Church, for its members live exactly as did the Apostles. Master Régnier, prior of St Michel, has joined them, so has our priest Colin the Englishman,

---

[1] For St Francis's journey to the East, and for his place in the history of the crusades, see also Chapter IV, section 8, and Chapter XI, section 10.

R

and Dom Matthew to whom I had given the cure of La Sainte-Chapelle. Michael, Henry the Cantor, and several others, whose names I forget have done the same.'

But such happy results achieved among Christians could not satisfy the apostolic heart of Francis, and the camp soon learned that he, who sang so pleasantly of Christ, was actually proposing to visit the Infidels themselves. Most of the soldiers thought it a huge joke: how perfectly ridiculous to preach charity and brotherhood to these Moors who had just announced that anyone who brought in a Christian head would receive a gold bezant! The dictatorial Cardinal Pelagius, who had lately arrived with reinforcements, left Francis in no doubt that such also was his view. He did not dare to forbid the attempt, knowing that Francis was *persona grata* at Rome, but he emphatically disclaimed all responsibility.

Together with Bro. Illuminatus, the saint walked over to the enemy lines, chanting these verses from Psalm xxii: 'Even though I be in the shadow of death, I shall fear nothing, Lord, for Thou art with me.' Naturally, as soon as the Moslems caught sight of the two friars, they rushed furiously upon them. 'Sultan! Sultan!' cried Francis at the top of his voice. The guards, believing they had come to ask for a truce, clapped them in irons and led them to their camp. Questioned, the saint replied quite simply that he would like a chat with the sultan, to explain the teaching of Christ.

The Sultan of Egypt at that time was Melik-el-Kâmil, Frederick II's friend. Curious, though somewhat sceptical, he was quite ready to discuss with a Christian scholar the relative merits of the Koran and the Gospel, and therefore directed his attendants to bring in these unexpected messengers. By way of a little fun he had spread before him a carpet embroidered with crosses, so that the two Christians would have to tread upon their sacred symbol—which St Francis did without the least hesitation. 'Gracious me!' jeered the sultan, 'so you trample on the Cross of Christ!' 'Do you not know,' replied Francis, 'that on Calvary there were three crosses, one for Christ and two for the thieves? We adore the one; you can have the other two, and if you care to strew them on the ground why should we hesitate to trample on them?'

After this introduction, the two men were soon on friendly terms, and Melik-el-Kâmil even suggested that Francis should remain with him. 'Certainly I will,' answered the latter, 'if you will become a Christian!' And to prove the infinite superiority of his God he offered to undergo a trial. 'Heat a large oven; your priests and I will get into it, and you can judge by what happens which of our two religions is more holy and true!' Surprised, but under no illusions as to the heroic virtue of his own people, El-Kâmil replied: 'I don't really think my priests would much care to get into an oven.' 'Very well,' retorted Francis, 'I'll get in by myself. If I die, you can put it down to my sins; but if the divine power protects me, will you swear to recognize Christ as true God and Saviour?' The sultan had much difficulty in persuading him that as a leader in Islam he could not very well ask for baptism. He wished to load his extraordinary visitor with presents; but Francis refused them all, except a small twopenny-halfpenny horn which would do to announce a sermon.

Melik-el-Kâmil had him escorted back to the crusaders' camp with every mark of respect. On taking leave of him he said: 'Do not forget me in your prayers; and may God, through your intercession, reveal to me the faith that is most pleasing in His sight.'

5. TRAVELS AND ADVENTURES OF MISSIONARIES IN ASIA

This first attempt at evangelization on infidel soil had definitely not succeeded. But it was not, properly speaking, a failure; in fact, as an indication of what was to come, it was of capital importance. Zeal for the conversion of those who knew not the Gospel, once so ardent but now somewhat cooled, was reawakened by the Poverello and his teaching. The Benedictines might remain in their cloisters; the Dominicans and Franciscans would carry on their missionary work. St Dominic, inspired by the same ideal, had originally visited Rome in order to lay before Innocent III a project for evangelizing the Cumans. Later, he had preached in Denmark; and every subsequent master-general of the Order was anxious to propagate the faith.

The mendicants sought to base their missionary work upon solid doctrinal and scientific foundations, as witness St Thomas's *Summa Contra Gentiles* and *Rationes Fidei contra Saracenos*. Among Franciscan writings, Roger Bacon's *Geographical Survey of the Holy Land* and, later, Raymond Lull's *Ars Generalis* (a *summa* intended for the conversion of infidels) had the same end in view. The prominent place occupied by the mendicants in the medieval Church was to have far-reaching consequences. The popes, though continuing to encourage the crusades, were keen supporters of the mission, and came to look upon it as of more importance. 'We believe,' wrote Gregory IX in 1238, 'that in the eyes of the Redeemer it is just as good to bring infidels to confess the divine Word as to crush their falsehood by force of arms.'

This first chapter in the story of what may be called the modern missions was chiefly the work, then, of Dominicans and Franciscans. In Europe the sons of St Dominic, undeterred by their initial set-back, realized their founder's dream and managed, about 1227, to establish Christianity among the Cumans, whose territory lay between the

Carpathians and the Volga; but the Mongol invasion thirteen years later put a tragic end to their achievement.   Missions were also established in the Baltic lands at the time of the 'Nordic crusades,' and Pope Innocent IV appointed a special legate to supervise them.   Another great Dominican, St Hyacinth, settled at Kiev in 1222.   The influence of his monastery was such that the Pope thought of creating a Russian bishopric, and a group of catholic priests and monks set out in 1238. They descended upon southern Russia and the Ukraine, working hard among the natives who had relapsed into paganism, and thereby laying the foundations of what was to become the Uniate Ukrainian Church. Nor did these missionaries withhold their labours from the Mongols on the lower Volga, the Don, and the Donetz.   Records tell us that about 1290 certain Mongol princesses were baptized as Catholics by the Franciscans, and that the Great Khan ordered the restoration of a bell which the Moslems had stolen from a Catholic church.   In 1333 Pope John XXII wrote to the Khan Ozbeg, notwithstanding the conversion of that ruler to Islam, thanking him for his goodwill toward the Catholics; and in the following year Benedict XII sent a Franciscan, John of Marignolli, as ambassador with magnificent presents to the khan.

But it was chiefly in Asia that the new Orders distinguished themselves.   At first they were concerned only with the Near East and its borderland.   On the morrow of their founder's 'mission' the Franciscans established themselves firmly in Palestine, where St Francis had left Bro. Benedict of Arezzo in charge of the province of Romania. From there they spread throughout the Orient: there was a Franciscan house at Jerusalem and one at Constantinople.   The Dominicans followed in their wake, erected the province of Cyprus, and settled communities both in Greece and at Constantinople.   The two mendicant Orders soon penetrated deeper into the Asiatic continent, towards Aleppo and Damascus, Bagdad, Armenia, and Persia.   The zeal of these new apostles seemed to know no bounds.   They worked not only among the Moslems, but also among schismatic and heretical Christians, making contact with the Jacobites, Nestorians, and Armenians.   The Maronites were Lebanese Christians who had bravely withstood Islam; but after the sixth oecumenical council in 681 they had separated themselves from both Byzantium and Rome. They made overtures to the Holy See soon after the passage of the crusaders through their country, submitted in 1182, and were recognized by Innocent III as an independent community with their own primate, two archbishops, and three bishops.   In 1237 the Dominican prior of Jerusalem, who was in touch with them, declared that they were perfectly faithful members of the Catholic and Roman Church. Such results augured well for the future.

A remarkable chapter in missionary history forms a gloss, so to speak, upon that of the crusades, a picturesque and adventurous chapter telling of journeys into Mongol lands.[1] In 1241 the Asiatic horsemen shattered the last elements of Christian resistance at Leignitz, and this bloody disaster moved the papacy to think of a crusade. It was preached by Franciscans and Dominicans at the bidding of Gregory IX, who, together with the Landgrave of Thuringia and the King of Bohemia, strove to win the Germans to their cause. Innocent IV began his pontificate on the same note. At the Council of Lyons in 1245, and in a letter to the Teutonic Knights in 1248, he still spoke of a 'crusade against the Tartars.' But not quite so urgently. He had learned that some of these terrible nomads, and a good many of their womenfolk, were Christians; heretics, no doubt, but baptized all the same. Christendom began to dream of these barbarian princesses who had led their husbands to the faith, of these savage kings who had caused their people to receive baptism. Might there not be among them a new Clotilde or Clovis? To this pious hope was added the strategic purpose of gaining new allies who might help to turn the tables upon Islam. A new policy was therefore tried with a view to the conversion of the 'Tartars.'

Christian ambassadors were accordingly dispatched to the Mongols, partly as preachers and partly as diplomats. The first of these embassies was led by John of Plan-Carpin, a Franciscan. Starting from Lyons in 1245, and travelling by way of Germany, Poland, and Russia, he reached the capital of Batu, Khan of the Lower Volga. From there he continued eastward, passed south of Lake Balkash, and at length arrived, in July 1246, at the Great Khan Guyük's camp near Karakorum. John was welcomed by the lord of the Mongols, who was friendly to the Nestorians, and talked with several Mongolian Christians; but the result was disappointing. In a letter preserved in the Vatican archives, the Great Khan ordered the Pope to submit to him as 'master of divine law throughout the world.' Another and simultaneous embassy-mission, led by the Franciscan Brother Laurence of Portugal, proved equally futile. But the Church was not to be discouraged. Ascelin, a canon of Lyons, visited the Mongol governor of Transcaucasia; he was rather more successful, inasmuch as he was accompanied on his return journey by two envoys with a letter suggesting an alliance against Islam. A similar proposal was made to Guyük in 1248 by King Hetum I through his brother Sempad, Constable of Armenia.

All these approaches, however, were on the diplomatic and strategic level, as was also the curious episode of St Louis's correspondence with the Mongols.[2] The ambassadors whom Louis received at Cyprus in

[1] On the origins of the Mongols see Chapter XI, section 9.
[2] See Chapter XI, section 11.

1248 brought no more than a proposal to combine against Islam.   The
Capetian must have taken it seriously, for he decided to reply; but he
must also have been thinking more Christian thoughts, since his
answer was carried not by diplomats but by three Dominican friars,
Andrew and Guy de Longjumeau and John of Carcassonne.   Unfortunately, Guyük's widow pretended to believe that the King of France
was offering his submission.   She replied by sending rich gifts accompanied by a letter requiring St Louis to swear an oath of fealty, and
when the Dominicans rejoined him at Caesarea, in 1251, they had to
admit partial failure.

Nevertheless, Bro. Andrew de Longjumeau returned from this
disappointing embassy with fresh information about Christian influence
in Mongol territory.   The new khan's mother was a Nestorian, as
were several of her women.   Sartaq, the young khan of the Lower
Volga, was also reported to have embraced Nestorianism.   St Louis
already had visions of the cross, blessed by Roman missionaries,
standing amid the nomad tents.   Instead of ambassadors, friars though
they might be, would he not do better by sending real missionaries
carrying no official mandate but merely a letter of introduction?   The
result of these deliberations was the most extraordinary mission of the
thirteenth century.   Its leader, William of Rubrouck, was a sturdy
Franciscan, born near St Omer; he was accompanied by Bro. Bartholomew, a gaunt and sallow Italian from Cremona.   Their story is a
strange commentary upon the mysterious East in the Middle Ages, and
also upon the reaction of two westerners to their experiences in that
far-distant land.

Having studied the best available geographers, Ptolemy and Isidore
of Seville, the two friars left Constantinople in May 1253.   They
frankly avow that as they plunged into Asia it was as if 'the gates of
hell had closed behind them.'   Everything about these people whom
they had been ordered to baptize was unfamiliar: the colour of their
skin, their physique, their dress, their language, and even their diet.
This latter consisted of fermented mares' milk, and the Fleming, who
preferred beer, says that the first cup of it made him sweat profusely.
Reaching the lower Volga, they were welcomed by Sartaq, who, to
their great surprise, was quite well informed about Western affairs and
had them escorted to the capital of the Great Khan Mongka.   It was a
peculiar journey, and the two Franciscans kept their eyes wide open.
They came across a town where the inhabitants spoke Persian, a
Buddhist community, vast deserts, mighty rivers; but what impressed
them above all was the fact that in even the most outlandish places they
found Mongol troops guarding the wells—tangible proof of the Great
Khan's power.   At last, in January 1254, they reached the master's
tent.   It was hung with cloth of gold, and there was a fire heaped up

with thorns, wormwood roots, and cow-dung.   Round about lay a
city of tents, where the friars were astonished to find a woman named
Paquette, a native of Metz, who was married to a Russian architect.
They also encountered a Parisian goldsmith, one Guillaume Boucher,
who made all kinds of marvellous gold instruments for the Mongol.
The khan received them with the utmost courtesy, and the Nestorian
members of his court invited the Franciscans on Easter Sunday to sing
the divine office before a beautiful statue of our Lady fashioned by
Guillaume 'in the French style.'   Karakorum was then the scene of a
public debate at which the two friars were invited to expound their
teaching in presence of Moslem doctors, Nestorian priests, and
Buddhist philosophers.   Of these three groups, the Nestorians showed
themselves least friendly, emphasizing those points wherein they
differed from the Catholics.   Sergius, an Armenian weaver who passed
himself off as a priest, was frightened by the prospect of losing all that
he had gained, and intrigued against the Franciscans.   Moreover, the
lives led by these Nestorians often left much to be desired; and the
Mongol chieftains tended to look upon all Christians with the same
contempt in which they held such people.   'God has given you a rule,'
said the Great Khan one day to the two missionaries, 'and you Christians do not observe it.   Now we have soothsayers, and we do all that
they tell us.'   There the discussions ended, and with them all hope of
converting the nomads.   Mongka parted from his guests on friendly
terms, supplying them with provisions for their journey and assuring
them they would always be welcome if they chose to return.   He also
handed them the usual letter calling upon the Christian king to recognize the Great Khan as 'lord and sovereign of the earth, and son of
God.'   Rubrouck and Bartholomew retraced their steps in the summer
of 1254, sorry to have achieved so little.

All together, these attempts by the Catholics to penetrate Asia had
met with small success.   However, they had not been entirely fruitless.
They taught the West not to regard the heart of Asia as an inaccessible
terra incognita, but as a possible field for future missionaries—and
business men!   Contact between Christians and Mongols was not
completely severed.   Thus, in 1258 the Khan of Persia wrote to Pope
Honorius IV, inviting him to resume the crusade and reminding him
that the Mongols had always been friendly towards the Christians.
In 1287 a Nestorian monk, an Ouigur named Rabban Sauma, was sent
by another khan from China to the West.   In Paris he saw Philip the
Fair; at Bordeaux he met Edward I of England; while Pope Nicholas
IV accorded him a place of honour in the Holy Week ceremonies at
Rome and gave him communion with his own hand.   Such meetings
may not have produced immediate results; but at least they showed that
Asia was not closed to the missionaries of Christ.

There was further evidence of this fact in 1295, when Venice witnessed the return of a commercial family which had spent thirty-five years travelling on business in that immense continent, whose uttermost boundaries they had reached.   Marco Polo, with his father and uncle, had journeyed through Mesopotamia, Persia, and Khorassan; from there they had struggled across the Pamirs, and followed the silk route to Kashgar, 'city of beautiful gardens,' and thence to Lob-Nor and the Ongut steppe.   Finally, they had entered China (which they called 'Cathay') and received a friendly welcome from the Mongol khan. They had taken part in Mongol warfare and explored the Chinese empire as far as Yunnan and Fukien.   Marco Polo had also been included in an embassy from the Khan of China to Ceylon.   From his lively narrative the Western world discovered both the treasures and the disappointments of Asia.

Christian interest in the Yellow Continent did not subside.   While merchants, especially Italians, left for China and even made fortunes there, evangelization was resumed.   In 1289 Nicholas IV, who had learned from Rabban Sauma the importance of the Nestorian communities, decided to send out a mission led by John of Montecorvino, an Italian Franciscan.   Its success was quite unexpected.   The friars landed in the Indies near Meliapur, baptized several thousand natives, and erected a number of bishoprics.   On his arrival at Pekin in 1294, one of John's fellow countrymen, who had settled there as a trader, gave him land on which he built two churches.   The Franciscan also converted more than 10,000 Tartars, including the prince of the Onguts, who became his protector, and the latter's son, who took the Christian name John.   The psalter was translated into Mongolian.   In 1307 Clement V appointed Montecorvino Archbishop of Pekin, and soon afterwards sent out other Franciscans to act as his suffragans.   It seemed that the whole of Mongolia was about to become Catholic. When the Chinese emperor went to war, he asked the archbishop's blessing and devoutly kissed the Cross.   Catholic bishops established themselves in many places between the Crimea and Fukien, and the khans even granted them pensions.

The popes continued to send out new teams.   The most famous of these was one led by Odoric of Pordenone (1265–1331) who worked in Persia, then in India, where he recovered the relics of St Thomas of Tolentino and three other Franciscans whom the Moslems had put to death in 1322.   He also visited Malabar, where he found a community of those 'Christians of St Thomas' who were almost as old as Christianity itself.   Next, he travelled through Ceylon and Java; landed at Canton, where he was amazed to find a cathedral built by brethren of his Order; and finally reached Pekin, where he was overwhelmed by the splendour of the imperial palace.   From him we learn that there were Catholic processions at the emperor's court; that the emperor attended Mass, during which he was incensed by the archbishop; and that the missionaries were invited to imperial hunting-parties, at which they rode with the khan on his elephant.   By about 1350, therefore, evangelization seemed to have been crowned with success.   The Franciscans attended to China and the steppes, while the Dominicans looked after Armenia and Persia with their *Societas Peregrinorum propter Christum* (founded in 1321) and its dependent body, the United Brethren, a former Basilian congregation which had adopted the Dominican rule.

It was not long, however (1363–8), before the end of Mongol rule in China struck a mortal blow at the Catholic missions.   The Ming dynasty supported a nationalist revival which sought to do away with everything that had been favoured by those whom they had supplanted. In 1370 Urban V appointed another archbishop of Pekin—a professor of the Sorbonne—and a legate for the whole of China; but Asia, trembling beneath the shock of the Mongol collapse, was already abandoning Christianity.

6.   Missions in Africa: Raymond Lull

Northern Africa as well as Asia interested the West.   Christian institutions were still a living memory in Africa, where men still read St Augustine and spoke of the martyrs Cyprian, Perpetua, and Felicity. Surely the tide of Islam must one day recede from those lands which had once belonged to Christ.   It was well known that small Christian communities had survived at Tleman, Ceuta, Carthage, and in Tripolitania; but they were almost swallowed up in darkness.

There were, however, two countries whose geographical position concentrated their attention upon Africa.   The history of Spain had been intimately bound up with that of Algeria, and from her shores would sail the greatest of all medieval missionaries.   The Norman kingdom of Sicily had inherited a largely Moslem culture, and her southern coast looked across to Tunisia.   It was, in fact, from Sicily that the first expeditions against Africa set out at the beginning of the twelfth century.   Roger II led one of these (1118–23), but without much success.   He tried again in 1135, and managed to gain a foothold in Tunisia and Tripolitania, where he found a few Christian centres. But he could not withstand the Almohad counter-attack in 1152, and was obliged to withdraw.   His grandson William II adopted a similar policy, made raid after raid on Tunisia, and compelled it to pay him tribute in 1180.[1]

[1] This right of tribute, which passed along with the Norman heritage to Charles of Anjou, was the immediate cause of St Louis's crusade in Tunisia. (*See* Chapter XI, section 12.)

R*

The purpose of these operations was political and commercial rather than religious; but since Eugenius III encouraged Roger in his design, it is possible that when the Norman kings set foot in Africa they intended to benefit Christendom as well as themselves. Such contacts with Islam in Africa helped to arouse general interest in that continent. Many Italian, Spanish, and Portuguese theologians looked upon the Moslems as a heretical Christian sect rather like the Arians,[1] and this belief was partly responsible for the missionary drive in Africa.

In 1214 St Francis of Assisi talked of visiting Morocco, and actually set out on foot. Sickness obliged him to turn back; but when he embarked for the Holy Land five years later, he sent two of his brethren, Giles and Elias, to Tunisia. They were most unwelcome to the Christian merchants at Tunis, who feared that their preaching might ruin trade and therefore sent them packing. Bro. Giles was bitterly disappointed thus to have escaped the crown of martyrdom.

But it was not long before Africa contributed her share of martyrs to the Order of St Francis. At about the time that their holy founder started for the East, five brethren, Otho, Berard, Peter, Accursus, and Adjutus, left the Portiuncula for Morocco. Their heroic faith became apparent in the course of their journey through Spain. At Seville, which was still in Moorish hands, they entered a mosque and preached against the Koran, which earned them an immediate flogging. Calling at the palace, they were received by the king, whom they informed with the same quiet confidence that they had come to tell him that he must 'renounce Mahomet, a vile slave of the Devil'; and they only just managed to escape death by hanging, decapitation, or defenestration. Thrown into prison, they tried to convert their jailers, until at last the crafty monarch announced that he would not grant these five hotheads the privilege of martyrdom, and sent them on their way to Morocco.

Here they indulged the same divine folly and were summoned before the 'miramolin' Abu-Yakub, who represented the Almohad sultan. Though half naked and in chains, the five humble friars did not lose heart. 'Who are you?' 'Disciples of Brother Francis.' 'What are you doing here?' 'He has sent us across the world to preach the way of truth.' 'What is this way?' Whereupon, Bro. Otho, who was a priest, recited the *Credo* and began to explain it point by point. But as soon as he said that Jesus is the incarnate Son of God, the miramolin lost his temper: ''Tis the Devil has sent you to tell me such things!' he roared, and summoned his executioners. Throughout that night the five unfortunate missionaries were flogged to blood, dragged by the throat over cobble-stones, drenched in boiling oil and then with vinegar. But they continued to pray aloud, exhorting

---

[1] This idea reappeared in 1578 in a proclamation by Don Sebastian, king of Portugal, to the inhabitants of Morocco.

one another to remain steadfast. Next day, 16th February 1220, the Moslem had them once again led before him; some of them had their entrails hanging out. Did they continue to despise the Koran? Did they still believe in their God? All replied that there is only one truth, the Gospel. 'I'm going to kill you!' shouted the Moor. 'Do what you like with our bodies,' they replied; 'our souls are in God's keeping.' These were their last words. Abu-Yakub called for a sword, and with his own hand cut off their heads. When Francis heard the news at Damietta, 'Praise be to God!' he cried, 'now indeed I know that I have five Friars Minor.'

At about this time the Dominicans also set foot in Africa. There is record of them at Tunis before 1230, and in Morocco about 1225, when a Bull of Honorius III authorized them to impose and absolve from excommunication in that country. One of them, Bro. Dominic of Fez, who had been appointed Bishop of that city, suffered martyrdom there in 1232. This pioneer blood, however, was not shed in vain; for the Moslems realized that they could not rid themselves of men who, as soon as one hero fell, another took his place. After 1233 they tolerated the presence of bishops; and Gregory IX believed that evangelization had advanced so far that he addressed a Bull to the Sultan of Morocco inviting him to embrace the Christian faith.

As a matter of fact, the conversion of Morocco was a very slow process. Generations were required to understand Islam, to meet its arguments, and to win its confidence. One man, a Spaniard, understood Islam perfectly. At that time the Iberian Peninsula, a mosaic of peoples and religions which had perforce to reach some basis of agreement, favoured the growth of an idea that conversion is best achieved by preaching. It was significant that over the shrine of Ferdinand III in the royal chapel at Seville hung an inscription in Latin, Arabic, Hebrew, and Spanish. St Raymond of Pennaforte first conceived the idea of approaching Islam in a spirit of understanding and love, and of speaking to them in their own language. An eminent jurist and all-round scholar,[1] Raymond was also an attractive personality. He decided to found two Dominican convents at Murcia and Tunis [2] for the training of missionaries to Moslem countries, where students would learn Arabic and become familiar with the Koran. His idea was taken up and expanded by Raymond Lull (1235–1316), one of the most interesting characters in the history of medieval missions.

The life of Raymond Lull is like some tremendous epic: full of adventure, danger, love of Earth, and love of God. The hero himself was possessed of a colossal intellect and encyclopaedic knowledge; he was ready to go anywhere in search of mystery. His genius was

[1] See Chapter VI, section 8.
[2] The Bey of Tunis, as we shall see, was more or less under Christian influence.

perhaps incomplete and disorderly, but it was wholly devoted to practical apologetics and to the spread of God's kingdom.

This man, who meditated in the prow of a ship in the roads of Palma (Majorca) on the vigil of our Lady's Assumption in 1314, this handsome old man with a white beard, clad in the homespun of a Franciscan tertiary, was well known to the crowd of idlers on the quays, renowned for his learning as for his holiness.   He is commonly spoken of as 'Blessed Raymond' or *Doctor Illuminatus*; an aura of mingled truth and legend envelops him.   No one knows exactly at what age he died, whether at eighty or one hundred years.   Some said that he had discovered the philosopher's stone and the secret of prolonging life. Before his conversion, he is known to have written many books of romance and light verse; afterwards, hymns and treatises on theology, philosophy, and mysticism.   He is said to have travelled all over the world, and to have been received by kings in the four corners of Europe, even amid the mists of England.   He had five audiences with the Pope, and made pilgrimages not only to Compostella and many French shrines, but also to the Holy Sepulchre.   Now we watch him as he sets out once more for his beloved Africa, where he had already endured much for the name of Christ, and where, no doubt, he hoped to suffer martyrdom.

This Catalan with a soul of fire was born at Palma in 1235.   From youth upwards he displayed brilliant gifts and a keen enjoyment of life. At first it seemed unlikely that this fever would lead his steps into the way of God.   He was a troubadour, a lover of song and gallantry, who would be recalled to moral rectitude neither by the advice of princes nor by love for his wife.   He tells us in his romance *Blanquerna* that one evening, towards dusk, he beheld on a sudden his future self turn round and lift towards him a hideous face devoured by cancer.   Whether the incident is true or imaginary, the fact remains that he forthwith renounced his wanderings, his gallant verses, and his carefree ways. Like Pascal, he resolved during those hours of pain and darkness to reorientate his life, and he held fast to that determination throughout half a century.   His later poetry proclaims nothing but sincere repentance.   'Am I worthy to praise thee, my God, I who have sinned so often?   I am but a troubadour, but still I love Thee.'   Even in his wayward days 'Raymond the Fool' had loved the God of pardon. Henceforward that love became a supernatural longing for One who had smitten his heart as He did that of Saul on the road to Damascus. This longing is expressed in page after page of his writings, which remind us of the great St Teresa: 'Say, fool, what would'st thou do if thy Beloved ceased to love thee?—I would still love so as not to die; for not to love is death, and love is life.'

And so God's troubadour employed himself in the service of Love.

Men awaited the Gospel not only beneath his very eyes in Spain, which had recently been liberated by the Christian armies, but also in Africa just across the water. The pattern of his life's work was clear, and on several occasions, whilst in ecstasy, he beheld our Lord Himself, who confirmed him in his chosen path. He was well acquainted with the Moslems: he had met many of them, and knew their language so well that he wrote books in Arabic. A vast plan was taking shape in his mind. Like St Raymond of Pennaforte, of whose advice he had the benefit, he would train missionaries in schools and colleges where they would study oriental languages; he would prepare summaries of Christian faith in the idioms of those peoples whom he hoped to convert; and lastly (for this intellectual knew well that 'without blood there is no redemption') he would expose himself to martyrdom as the supreme evidence of his devotion to Christ.

He spent years submitting this plan to kings and popes. He knocked at every door, whether he were welcome or not, and King Jaime of Catalonia founded the College of Miramar for the training of thirteen Friars Minor on the lines laid down by Raymond Lull. At Rome, he submitted to Nicholas II a daring questionnaire from which it appeared that 'Christians are responsible for the Infidel's ignorance concerning sound Catholic faith.' He also explained to Celestine V how important it was to convert the Tartars; for this man of the world was well informed as to existing contacts between the Mongols and the West, and his 'plan for recovering the Holy Land' included a Mongol alliance. Boniface VIII and Philip the Fair, just as they were going to engage in mortal conflict, received from Lull what amounted to a demand that they should get together and bring light to peoples plunged in darkness. The movement set on foot by this extraordinary man bore fruit; for the universities of Paris, Oxford, Bologna, and Salamanca instituted Chairs of Arabic, Greek, Hebrew, and Chaldean. Raymond Lull could congratulate himself that the first two points of his programme had been at least partially realized. To the third, that of personal witness, he would himself now give effect.

In 1292 he sailed for Tunis, where he knew he would find small Christian communities, consisting chiefly of resident merchants. But the experience of Bros. Giles and Elias had proved that these gentry were hostile to outspoken preachers. They kept themselves to themselves; their relations with the Moors were of a strictly business nature, and excluded any attempt to gain their souls. Lull intended to follow a very different course. Dressed as an Islamic sage, he would mingle with the crowds that always gathered around a poet or preacher on street corners and other public places.

He acted in this way for several weeks, spoke on every possible occasion, and even argued with Moslem professors in their own schools.

But one day, when he had clearly outwitted an adversary, the latter became angry, determined to be revenged, and immediately denounced him to the authorities as a Christian. Raymond Lull was tried as a blasphemer and condemned to death. It seemed that the hour had come when the Franciscan tertiary must bear bloody witness to his faith in Christ. Such, however, was not to be: our Lord, it appeared, had further need of him. An influential citizen of Tunis, who had heard him speak, intervened in his favour. He was granted his life, but received a merciless flogging (in which he rejoiced, thinking of his Master at the pillar), and, still quivering with pain, was put on board a Genoese ship which was about to set sail. But his enemies had not reckoned with his indomitable courage: hardly had night fallen than he dived into the sea and swam ashore, resolved to continue his apostolate.

Having tried once, he would try again. Besides, even had he refrained on grounds of worldly wisdom, God would surely have constrained him. He returned to Majorca in order to rest and recuperate his strength; but he now began to wonder if it might not be better to spend his time writing books than to run the risk of labouring in Africa. One day, while he was meditating in a little wood, a hermit stood before him and discussed this problem: he must take no notice of difficulties or of apparent set-backs, God wished only for his testimony; all the rest would be added unto him.

He set out once again, though no one would agree to share his peril. King Jaime suggested that he should remain in the Balearic islands and Spain, where there was much good work to be done. But that was not what God had ordered him to do. This time he landed at Bougie in Algeria. He showed no caution, no restraint; it seemed he was in a hurry for martyrdom, and he began to attack the doctrine of Mahomet in public places. Again he was arrested; the Genoese and Catalan merchants saw to it that he was less harshly treated; and he spent six months imprisonment writing a long Arabic treatise against the faith of Islam. At the end of that period he was deported; but his ship was wrecked off the coast of Italy, and he lost all his belongings, including the precious manuscript. Providence seemed wrath with him.

He made two more journeys. On the final occasion he was a very old man, the venerable figure whom we have described praying in the bow at Palma, ready to set sail. Knowing that his strength was almost exhausted, Raymund made his will and arranged for the translation of his books into the principal oriental languages. For the last time he landed from a Catalan merchantman in his beloved Africa, of whose conversion he had not despaired. King Jaime understood the importance of his mission, and wrote to the King of Tunis asking that Raymond should be well received. Thanks to this letter, he was made 'Procurator of the Infidels' and was able to go unmolested for a whole year. Then one of his pupils was sent out to assist him. He knew that the end could not be far off, and watched the approach of death with heroic determination. He continued to speak, to write numerous treatises on Moslem teaching, and to proclaim Christ. But one day, in June 1316, an agitator roused the populace, who beat him up and left him for dead. Had some Genoese sailors not intervened, he would have expired where he lay.

He was carried on board ship, regretting only that he had not suffered martyrdom on African soil. His strength failed rapidly; it became evident that he was past help, and he died as the ship approached Majorca. He was laid to rest in his native isle, an heroic witness to missionary zeal, the forerunner of those who would long afterwards bring back to Africa the Cross and love of Christ.

Such was Raymond Lull, the 'Fool of God.' He himself defined his place in the history of Christian expansion. At a time when the crusading spirit was giving place to the more peaceful methods advocated by St Francis, the Franciscan of Majorca laid down their guiding principle: 'I see worldly knights going overseas to the Holy Land, hoping to regain it by force; but their energy is spent long before they have attained their goal. I have therefore come to the conclusion that this victory cannot be won, Lord, except in the way that You taught Your Apostles, i.e. by love, prayer, and tears. Holy religious knights must therefore take the road; they must preach the truth of the Passion to the Infidels, and do for love of You what You did for love of them.'

7. The West Alone is not the Church of Christ

Teaching such as that of Raymond Lull recalled the Church to her original purity. The crusades may have been intended to win the East for Christ; but they were also looked upon by those who took part in them as a means of Western expansion, and that is why their grandeur was marred by so much cruelty and self-interest. Henceforward, the missionary ideal was something altogether different. No matter from what country they came, the heralds of the Gospel considered themselves in the service of the Church alone; and the Church was one in Christ, notwithstanding schism and internal differences.

Besides, Western Christendom was not alone in working for the kingdom of God. No picture of Christian expansion is complete without some notice of the non-Roman churches which, though schismatic, were no less offshoots of the great tree sprung from the grain of mustard seed.

In an earlier age Byzantium had done much to spread the word of God. She had helped to convert many countries, including Russia; and, though now enfeebled, she had not altogether abandoned the work

of evangelization.   Even after the tragedy of 1204, she continued to
send out missionaries, some of whom started from Nicea, whither the
remnants of the empire had fled.   Bishoprics of the Greek rite were
established also in the most remote provinces.   A group of Byzantine
and Russian missionaries went as far·as the Baltic lands; but opposition
on the part of their Teutonic rivals made it impossible for them to hold
their own.   Monachism, which had always been the strongest means
of proselytism in the East, continued to flourish.   New convents,
hermitages, and chapels were constantly being built; and during the
twelfth century there were Greek monasteries even in southern Italy,
which was subject to the Normans and later to the Holy Roman
Empire.

Within the Byzantine Church's sphere of influence, notwithstanding
frequent local opposition to the basileis, there were many countries
which derived their spiritual nourishment from the roots of Greek
Christianity.   Bulgaria, whose King Boris was baptized in 863, had
hesitated for some time between Byzantium and Rome, but had eventually recognized the jurisdiction of Constantinople when Basil II
incorporated that country in the Eastern Empire (1019).   After several
attempts at independence the Bulgarians, assisted by the Rumanians
and Serbs, managed to regain their liberty under Caloian, about 1185.
The new state sought to free itself from the patriarchate, and seemed
for a moment on the point of submitting to Rome.   Negotiations
were opened with Innocent III, and a Bulgarian patriarch was enthroned
by the papal legate at Tirnovo in 1204.   But there was no lasting
reconciliation.   The Tsar, John Assen, alarmed by the presence of
Latins at Constantinople, was soon at war with them; he broke away
from Rome, and Bulgaria resumed relations with Byzantium.   Reunion
was again discussed, and agreement reached, at the Council of Constantinople in 1277; but there were fanatical adherents of Orthodoxy in
Bulgaria, and the independent patriarchate looked for its spiritual life
to Byzantium until it was swept away by the Turks in 1393.

The Serbs, who had established themselves in the northern Balkans
during the seventh century, had been baptized by Roman missionaries
two hundred years later; but their conversion proved transient and
was undertaken for a second time by Greek missionaries.   During the
eleventh century Serbia was torn between two influences: the eastern
areas were subject to Byzantium, the west and south looked to Rome.
It was Gregory VI who, in 1078, conferred the crown on Prince
Michael of Dioclea.   Soon afterwards Stephen I Nemanya united
some small principalities and adopted the Byzantine rite for his Church.
He died so holy a death as a monk of Khilandar, on Mt Athos, that the
Serbs still revere him as a saint under his monastic name, Simeon.
But he did not recognize the schism, and maintained friendly relations

with the Pope.   The fact remains, however, that Greek influence penetrated deeper and deeper into the Serbian kingdom, and Stephen's third son, who was also a monk of Khilandar, exercised a powerful influence upon the religious life of his country.   Proclaimed Patriarch of Serbia by the Basileus of Nicea, Theodore Lascaris, he immediately declared his independence and obtained a decree that the Serbian patriarch should henceforward be consecrated by his own suffragans. All the same, tension between East and West continued in Serbia, and it was not until the second half of the thirteenth century that the country finally became schismatic, though the Croats, a kindred people farther to the west, remained fervent Catholics.   Here, again, the influence of the Greek Orient had been strong, and Mount Athos continued as one of the chief centres of Serbian spirituality.

The same religious fervour may be traced in numerous 'little churches,' whose quaintness does not alter the fact that, in spite of grave doctrinal errors and unimaginable difficulties, they represented Christianity in far-distant regions.   Each of these churches had its martyrs, and each has left documents which, heresy notwithstanding, bear splendid testimony to its love of Christ.   Such was the Georgian Church, which stood in constant danger from the incursions of Byzantines, Persians, Arabs, and Turks.   At one moment it was tempted to embrace the monophysite heresy, but was soon brought back to the true faith and reformed in the eleventh century by its great king, David the Restorer.   It was remarkable for its intense faith, of which there is ample evidence in the beautiful monastery of Ivirion and that of the Iberians on Mount Athos.   Its monks spread all over the East as far as Sinai, founding convents that were centres of flourishing religious life and theological studies.   The Georgian Church remained in communion with Rome until the middle of the thirteenth century, and then lapsed gradually into schism.

The Armenian Church adopted monophysitism.   In the ninth century it suffered severely under the Arabs, then under the Byzantines, who occupied a large part of the country in 1045.   But it taught the world a lesson in heroic resistance.   When the Armenians were driven from their homes by the Turks in 1064, many of them settled in the Taurus and founded a small kingdom which was to play an important part at the time of the crusades.   They continued friendly towards Rome, holding frequent discussions on reunion; and though they remained independent, Greek influence had to compete with opposition from the Western Church, especially from the Dominicans.

In Mesopotamia the Jacobite Church, which had also embraced monophysitism, began by welcoming the Moslems, who rid them of the Byzantines.   Subjected in turn to Mohammedan persecution, rent by one crisis after another, hemmed in between Greeks and Turks, they hailed the crusading army as their deliverers. But when fortune ceased to smile upon the Western invaders, the Jacobites suffered cruelly for their former friendship. Yet, in spite of persecution, internal rivalry, and apostasy, their Church did not disappear; at the end of the thirteenth century it still had nearly 100 bishops in Syria and Mesopotamia subject to the Patriarch or Maphrian of Mosul.

In Egypt, the monothelite Coptic Church was likewise initially well disposed towards the Moslems, but was soon betrayed. Saladin, in particular, excluded Christians from all public offices, and forbade the use of crosses and bells. Persecution became more severe; murder, pillage, and the destruction of churches became everyday occurrences which ended under Mameluke rule in a regular butchery of Christians (1302). Ill-treated, obliged to wear a badge of infamy on their dress, the Coptic Christians continued on their way, and have survived into the twentieth century. The Ethiopian Church, far away in Africa, had its own peculiarities which, none the less, went hand in hand with intense religious life. The monasteries, containing thousands of monks, were so important that their abbot-general was head of the whole Church; and they sent out a continual stream of missionaries who preached among pagans in the heart of the dark continent.

The legend of Prester John's kingdom, which so fascinated the West, may have originated in Christian Ethiopia. It may, on the other hand, be traced to the Nestorian Church, whose remarkable influence in Asia we have already noticed. In the thirteenth century it counted no fewer than twenty metropolitan sees and two hundred bishoprics in Persia, Mesopotamia, Khorassan, Turkestan, India, China, and Mongolia; but it was annihilated by the victory of the Ming in China and by the invasion of Tamerlane in the fourteenth century. The Nestorian Church was heretical both in faith and morals, but for centuries it kept Christianity alive in several places where it no longer exists.

The Christian seed-time had yielded a hundredfold. The grain scattered by the Sower had sprung up (with the inevitable tares) in many regions of the earth. When we remember those great harvests gathered in by Rome and Byzantium we ought surely to think with gratitude of those little plots of corn thriving among stones and thickets up and down the world.

CHAPTER XIII

HERESY, THE RIFT IN CHRISTENDOM

1. The Meaning and Scope of Heresy

MEDIEVAL Christendom was an imposing monument, solid and well balanced; but there were hidden cracks that needed careful watching if serious damage was to be avoided. These cracks took the form of heresies, i.e. doctrinal errors, sedition and revolt against the authority of Holy Church. On several occasions, and in varying degrees, they split the edifice of Christian society and called for the most drastic measures.

Heresy is as old as the Church. No sooner had the Gospel seed been sown, than tares were found growing with the corn. The sand of the amphitheatre had scarcely drunk the martyrs' blood when the horror of persecution was increased by differences among Christians themselves. During the first four centuries there was a long list of errors, from the Gnostics and Montanists to the Donatists and Manichaeans. During the barbarian epoch, heresy appears to have been confined mainly to the East, but there it knew no bounds: Monophysitism, Monothelitism, Nestorianism, and many another body of strange beliefs had interfered with the deposit of faith. Popes, councils, and even the secular arm had striven against these false doctrines, which were continually revived in face of tradition and authority. During this early period the West had encountered no form of heresy except Pelagianism. Towards the end of the tenth century a number of others had appeared in rudimentary shape, but a hundred years later the problem became serious.

The causes of heresy were manifold. In some cases it retained the doctrinal and theological characteristics belonging to earlier forms; for discussion of religious matters was a constant attraction to those minds which were beginning to discover the excitement of ideas in general. But there were other motives in addition to this intellectual craving; heresy often emerged as a condemnation of the Church's morality. This was something almost wholly new; it arose from protests against the scandalous behaviour of a section of the clergy. Extreme anxiety over the Church's peril was shared by popes, bishops, and many monks, all of whom were eager for reform. Gregory VII, St Bernard, St Francis of Assisi, and St Dominic all dedicated themselves to labour for the Church's welfare, but without overstepping her sacred boundary-marks. Weaker minds and mere hotheads, on the other hand, refused obedience to the 'unfaithful hireling,' and returned to what they looked upon as the truth delivered by Christ. Many of these heretical currents, therefore, originated in a purpose no less praiseworthy than that which inspired the saints; but for that very reason they became all the more dangerous once they had begun to flow.

Christian society reacted quickly and, as it were, instinctively against such doctrines and the movements to which they gave rise. One might almost say that the masses reacted more speedily and with greater violence than did the Church herself in the persons of her rulers. For heresy appeared as an insult to faith, to all that was best and most essential in medieval society. Since religion was an integral part of human life, any attack upon it was a mortal blow at man's heart and threatened his existence. Those believers in whose eyes eternal salvation was the only thing that ultimately mattered could obviously not tolerate the blasphemy of heretics, who risked calling down upon all and sundry the wrath of God. Very often, therefore, it was public opinion that demanded exemplary punishment for the guilty, and sometimes inflicted such punishment without reference to authority. At Soissons, for example, in 1120, when the Bishop hesitated to burn some heretics, they were seized by the mob, who piled up the faggots of their own accord. At Cologne, St Bernard was unable to prevent the people dragging some Cathars from prison and cutting their throats. At St Gilles, Pierre de Bruys was literally torn to pieces. There were hundreds of similar cases.

Another reason for stern methods against heresy was more sub-conscious perhaps, but no less compelling. The whole political and social regime was based upon faith; social and political institutions rested on the Creed. Heresy was therefore considered as an attack not only upon man's inmost life, but also upon the established order. Thus, when the Albigensians declared that they condemned the taking of an oath, they were threatening the whole feudal regime which, as we have seen, depended on an oath. The very concept of Christendom led medieval society to regard heresy as the most dangerous form of anarchy. 'There is nothing strange,' says Mgr Arquillière, 'in the fact that Christendom saw in heresy the spectre of its own destruction; for to embrace heresy is to mutilate the figure of Christ, to parody the Church's teaching, to misunderstand the authority of God present in His Church, to inflict a mortal wound upon society, and to imperil the whole Christian world.' [1] No penalty seemed too severe for these

---

[1] The anti-social and revolutionary character of heresy explains why excommunicated sovereigns and even those of little faith, e.g. Frederick II and Manfred of Sicily, were stern opponents of heresy.

revolutionaries: they were burned at the stake, as were poisoners and those who practised witchcraft.

2. THE MINOR SECTS

It must be admitted that some heresies never passed beyond ecclesiastical circles, and therefore had a relatively small circulation. Such, at the beginning of our period, was the error of Berengar, head of the school at Tours, a pious canon of austere life, and a strong opponent of simony. At the same time, he was a brilliant theologian and one of the first, long before St Thomas, to understand that reason might be used in theology. His application of this principle to the doctrine of the Holy Eucharist was disastrous, for it caused him to deny transubstantiation. The bread and wine, he maintained, were only symbolic *even after their consecration.* Berengar was denounced, harried by Cardinal Hildebrand (afterwards Pope Gregory VII), summoned before the Council of Vercelli, and then before the Lateran Council in 1059. Violently attacked by Lanfranc, he had recourse to some wonderfully skilful argument, twisting and turning and making at least a show of submission. By these subterfuges he managed to escape with nothing worse than the condemnation of his teaching. Berengar died reconciled with the Church, a model of repentance. He had caused no widespread trouble; unlike the later theories of Abélard, his doctrine did not affect the masses, but was rather a battle-ground of specialists.

It was otherwise with those doctrines (if we may so describe a heap of notions and ideas many of which were childish and incoherent) whose champions had the gift of demagogy at a time when simple folk were too easily aroused. In point of fact, it is hard to find one's way about the maze of movements which interlocked with one another, used analogous terminologies, and were all characterized by a similar emotionalism. We can, however, distinguish three types. The latest of these included a number of apocalyptic sects properly so called, which appeared mainly in the thirteenth century and to which we shall presently return. The second comprised pantheistic systems of various kinds, some of which involved the most unseemly behaviour. Last, and most numerous, was a group of errors that in one way or another foreshadowed the Protestant Reformation.

At the end of the twelfth century Amaury Bène, a pantheist and former professor of theology at Paris, taught that, because God is everything and since each man, sharing in Christ's divinity, is the living incarnation of the Holy Ghost, therefore we have no need of sacraments, and, better still, we cannot sin, because each of us is God! Alarmed by the progress of this comfortable doctrine, the Bishop of

---

[1] See Chapter III, section 6, and Chapter VIII, section 6.

Paris prosecuted Amaury, who was condemned by Innocent III and agreed to retract. But his pupils survived him and were condemned at the request of Philip Augustus in 1210. Banned in France, this heresy reached Switzerland and the Rhineland. It was fostered by a professor at Strasburg, one Ortlich, who founded the 'Brethren of the Free Spirit,' and became progressively extravagant: no need of sacraments, of authority, or of moral laws; the Holy Ghost is all in all! Nothing was forbidden to the adherents of this sect, which even preached community of wives. From it there stemmed the 'Turlupins' at Paris, the 'Adamites' (forerunners of our modern nudists) in Austria, and the 'Luciferians' of Magdeburg, who practised sorcery. Every one of these vagaries relied upon a single verse of Scripture, in which St John (iv. 24) says that we 'must adore God in spirit and in truth.' They were severely dealt with in every land.

Such outlandish aberrations, and the revolting practices to which they gave rise, limited their appeal. Others were more serious, because their consequences were more far-reaching and their protagonists often led irreproachable lives. These were the heresies that claimed to reform the Church from without, by rejecting her authority and hierarchical structure, and by appealing as it were from an institution riddled with abuses to one of their own creation, pure, lofty, and undoubtedly divine.

The first of such 'reformers' was an ex-monk, a Belgian named Tanchelin who lived early in the twelfth century. Though practically illiterate, he had a ready tongue and knew how to excite a crowd. Nor did he disdain the arts of stage-management to make an impression. Representing himself as a bishop sent expressly by the Pope, he would appear in public covered in gold lace and escorted by guards wearing brilliant uniform. On every possible occasion, and with the utmost modesty, he would proclaim himself 'betrothed of the Virgin, son of God, and twin brother of Christ.' Naturally, he too claimed direct inspiration from the Holy Ghost and rejected the sacraments. But his most successful line was to denounce the conduct of certain clerics; and the enthusiasm of his audience invariably reached its climax when he exhorted them not to pay their tithes. As a matter of fact, his morals and those of his friends seem to have been no better than those of the clergy whom he castigated, and he was as ready as the next man to take money to finance his theatrical displays. The sect made considerable progress in the Rhineland, Holland, and Belgium. Denounced by St Norbert, Tanchelin was tracked down, arrested, and assassinated in 1124 by one of his disciples whose behaviour he had criticized. His organization, being devoid of doctrinal bases, soon collapsed.

But ideas of this kind were 'in the air,' and men of Tanchelin's

stamp were not uncommon at that date.   Not long after his death, one
Eon de l'Étoile embarked on a similar adventure in Brittany.   He had
one sure means of convincing the mob: does not the *Credo* say '*per eum
qui venturus est judicare vivos et mortuos*'?   *Eum?*   Why of course,
Eon!   This argument won him adherents from the whole area between
Brittany and Gascony, until one day he tried preaching at Rheims,
where he was arrested and imprisoned for the remainder of his life.

Almost simultaneous, but far more serious, was the heresy of Peter
de Bruys, a learned priest and first-rate orator whose private life was
above reproach, but a fanatic, a formidable sectarian, whose powerful
voice and wild gesticulations made a deep impression on the crowds
whom he addressed.   His teaching was complicated and not altogether
coherent: he claimed that infant baptism was of no effect, and (like the
Anabaptists) that adults should be rebaptized; that bread and wine
have never been transubstantiated, except by Christ in person on the
single occasion of the Last Supper; that the dead derive no benefit from
the prayers and alms of the living; and finally that statues, crosses, and
churches are absolutely useless.   One may fairly ask what was left of
Christianity, of which this firebrand claimed to be the only true representative.   But as he seasoned his peculiar theology with attacks upon
the clergy, objecting to their authority, to their ownership of property,
and to their receipt of tithes, he enjoyed a measure of success from
Provence to Gascony.   St Bernard, Peter the Venerable, and even
Abélard, denounced him as the most dangerous of heretics.   He came
to a horrible end.   On Good Friday 1124, at St Gilles du Gard, he
dared to insult the Catholics by having meat roasted over a great fire
made of all the crosses he had been able to collect.   But he was seized
and torn to pieces by an angry mob who roasted the gobbets at his
own fire.

Peter's teaching, however, did not die with him; it was taken over
and enlarged by his friend Henry of Lausanne, a handsome fellow with
an easy and persuasive tongue.   His bearing was dignified, his conduct
simple and austere.   He wore plain homespun, went bare-footed, and
slept on the bare ground—all of which, St Bernard assures us, was mere
hypocrisy.   The essence of his preaching was a virulent attack upon
the Church, which he denounced as a heap of filth, a cesspool of fornication.   Wherever he went, places of worship were burned, crosses
were overthrown, and priests molested.   It is amazing that for twenty
years he was able to carry on these exploits notwithstanding several
condemnations, retractions, and relapses.   He was finally overthrown
by St Bernard and died in prison.   But the very success of such
propaganda shows not only in what danger the Church stood, but also
how dimly the common folk perceived the difference between genuine
reform and its distorted image.

They perceived it even less clearly in the movement set on foot by Arnold of Brescia, a pious canon who had once impressed those who knew him with the purity of his life and his sincere love of poverty. How did he fall into rebellion and heresy? It is difficult to say; his whole character is an enigma. Pride and political ambition may perhaps account for his behaviour. He disapproved of the Church's wealth, demanded the confiscation of all ecclesiastical property, and joined in open conflict even with those who, though partisans of reform and friends of poverty, could not advocate a remedy which would in the circumstances have ruined the Church. The quarrel soon reached its climax. At Brescia, Arnold roused the people against their Bishop. Driven from Italy to France and from there to Bohemia, he attracted large crowds wherever he stopped, and formed them into a kind of revolutionary Band of Poverty. As we have seen,[1] Arnold finished as idol of the Romans and leader of their insurrectionary and anti-papal commune until he was destroyed through the intervention of Frederick Barbarossa.

Although the work of such agitators as Peter of Bruys, Henry of Lausanne, and Arnold of Brescia had been limited, it was none the less symptomatic. It shows how necessary was reform in the Church, and it explains the success of two great heresies which embodied similar aspirations on a far greater scale, and of which Peter, Henry, and Arnold were the forerunners.

3. THE WALDENSES

Peter de Vaux (Valdo or Valdès), a Dauphinois resident at Lyons, was an upright man and a fervent Christian. Like many others in the middle of the twelfth century, he felt a longing to return to the living sources of the Gospel, to bring the Church back to her first fervour and original purity. After a successful career in business, he resolved to devote time and money to spreading knowledge of the Holy Scriptures, of which he himself was a keen student. Together with two priest-friends, he undertook the colossal task of translating the Bible into vernacular, and in course of their conversations these three men had frequent occasion to regret that the Church was no longer what she had been in Apostolic times, that she no longer gave ear to her Master's counsels of self-sacrifice as practised by St Alexis, for instance, whose life they read with mounting excitement in a famous contemporary poem. Originally, then, Waldensianism was very similar to the great manifestations of zealous faith which were set on foot by Dominic Guzman and the Poverello of Assisi. But this enthusiasm quickly took a wrong turning.

[1] See Chapter V, section 6.

In 1170, or thereabouts, an event occurred which Valdo took to be a sign from God: one of the canons engaged in translating the Bible was accidentally killed. Surely, thought Valdo, the Lord had employed this tragic means as an indication that in order to please Him it was not enough to run a goose-quill over yards of parchment. Peter forthwith sold all his goods, distributed their proceeds among the poor, abandoned his wife, and made up his mind that he would dedicate himself wholly to Christ. So there he was, clothed like St John the Baptist and wearing *sabots* (whence his followers were often called *Insabatati*), standing in the public squares at Lyons and neighbouring cities, crying his message of penance and poverty, denouncing the excessive wealth of the Church and the disgraceful conduct of the clergy. Such language, as we have seen, always found an audience, and there were thousands of these unofficial prophets. Groups of people soon gathered around Peter, living as he lived and passing on his message. They called themselves *Humiliati* or *Poor Men of Lyons*, but the people named them 'Waldenses' after their founder.

The Church might have used this movement for her own ends, and Innocent III came to regret that he had not done so. But personal questions and blunders on both sides made this impossible. The Archbishop of Lyons, worried at the thought of uncommissioned and often uneducated laymen venturing to expound the Scriptures, forbade them to preach. Valdo appealed to Pope Lucius III, who confirmed the Archbishop's decision. Things now went from bad to worse. The heretic proudly declined, in the first place, to recognize any authority superior to what he believed to be 'his' truth; and what had perhaps been mere misunderstanding developed into open revolt. The founder of the new sect declared that the clergy had no right to speak in God's name; that every Christian was a depositary of the Holy Ghost (a belief common to numerous heresies at that time), so that all were entitled to comment on Scripture; that in any case there was no trace of a priesthood in the Gospel; and that men are sanctified not collectively as members of a Church, but individually, alone under the eye of God. In many respects the Waldenses foreshadowed Protestantism.

It is characteristic of all heresies that, once the initial error has been elevated to the rank of dogma, they go farther and farther astray. The Waldenses certainly intended to remain Christians; indeed they claimed to be the only ones faithful to the primitive ideal. But their cavilling led them to deny the Real Presence in the Holy Eucharist, to abandon the Mass, except once a year on Maundy Thursday in commemoration of the Last Supper, and to recognize only one prayer— the *Our Father*. At the same time the anti-social nature of their teaching became more pronounced. Not only did they deny the

Church's right to own property, but they treated every oath as blasphemy, condemned even defensive warfare, and would not allow the courts to punish criminals, on the ground that their offences had nothing to do with God. Puritanism of this kind was equivalent to anarchy.

The result was that many worthy people were seduced by the Waldensian missionaries, and the movement acquired sectarian organization. Its leaders were highly respected and influential men, who led lives of absolute chastity and subsisted on alms. At first they were called 'Beards'; but the example of the Cathars soon caused them to be known as 'The Perfect' or 'Pure Ones,' who met twice a year in a chapter or *majoral*. It was these 'Beards' who conferred remission of sin in a kind of sacrament which was no longer called penance but *melioramentum* (improvement). The rest of the members, or 'believers,' were urged to follow the example of their chiefs; and indeed the Waldenses as a whole lived austere and worthy lives, free from the charge of licentiousness which the Cathars had deserved.

The sect spread first through Lyonnais, Dauphiné, Provence, and even Languedoc, where they were often confused with the Cathars, at any rate by the general public. The ecclesiastical authorities, however, never lost sight of the distinction, and, according to the legate Peter of Vaux-de-Cernay, regarded them as 'much less perverse.' Small but fervent Waldensian communities gained firm footing in the Alpine valleys. Driven from Lyons, they likewise found a home in Italy, where they were known as the 'Poor Men of Lombardy' and held aloof from the French sect in certain matters of dogma. They also found their way to Germany, and even to Spain, where Alfonso II of Aragon treated them with some severity. Finally, they reached Bohemia and Poland.

Until the fourteenth century the Church waged no systematic campaign against them as she did against the Cathars, and Innocent III never abandoned hope of bringing back the best of their leaders to the fold. That great Pope even encouraged the 'Humiliati' of Lombardy, whose external life closely resembled the Waldenses, with whom they were not seldom identified. He even lent his support to Durand of Huerca, a former Waldensian who remained in the Catholic Church after the sect's condemnation and established a sort of lay community calling themselves 'Poor Catholics.'[1] The Church took stern measures only where Waldensian propaganda became aggressive or threatened the clergy. In such cases they were persecuted throughout the thirteenth century, e.g. in Provence, Tarentaise, and Embrunois, as well as in Piedmont and Lombardy, the Rhineland, and Bohemia.

Waldensian puritanism was never completely extirpated in the same

---

[1] See Chapter IV, section 7.

way as was Albigensian Catharism.   During the middle years of the
fourteenth century there were numerous high valleys in the Alps
where it was so strongly entrenched that the Inquisitors were often met
with armed opposition; and it survived into modern times in the shape
of those Alpine communities which later merged with Protestantism.
In Bohemia, too, the Poor Men of Lyons were absorbed by the
Hussites.   The popular songs of Upper Lombardy and the Romansh
valleys still speak of 'the man of God who wished to live poor and
naked like Jesus'; and, since it is not known what became of Valdo
after his expulsion from Dauphiné about 1185, they tell us that God
simply called him to Heaven.

4.   FROM MANICHAEISM TO CATHARISM

The Waldensian heresy was still in some sense Christian.   Its
doctrine was part of those 'Christian truths gone mad' of which G. K.
Chesterton says the world is full.   But there was another and very
different heresy, the most dangerous of all those which confronted the
medieval Church, one which still enjoys gloomy celebrity as Catharism
or Albigensianism.

The essential ideas and principles in this case had nothing Christian
about them.   It was a resurgence, after many centuries of underground
wandering, of the old dualist current which had originated long ago in
far-off Mazdean Iran.

In the third century of our era the ancient doctrine of two inimical
principles had been given new life by a prophet named Mani or Manes,
who, according to the fashion of that age, had made a syncretism from
all sorts of disparate elements, and expressed it in verse that was not
devoid of charm.   This body of teaching included fragments of
Judaeo-Christianity capable of leading simple minds astray.   Manes,
who died in 276, was probably executed by order of King Sapor II of
Iran at the request of the Zoroastrian clergy.   His sect spread over
large areas of the Roman world, and in 290 it was the victim of a terrible
but ineffective persecution under the Emperor Diocletian.   Manichaeism became increasingly popular, helped by the simplicity of its central
dogmas, by its claim to provide simple answers to all the great
problems, and by its accommodating system of morality.   When
Christianity triumphed over paganism in the first quarter of the fourth
century, this 'plague from the East' constituted a serious threat.   St
Augustine, who had himself been a Manichaean in his youth, made
strenuous efforts to curb the progress of the sect in Africa; but he failed
to extirpate it, and traces of the heresy survived almost everywhere
from beginning to end of the barbarian epoch.   It had reappeared
frequently, and under various shapes, mainly in the Eastern Empire.

In the seventh century we have the Paulicians, whose name may have been derived from Paul of Samosata, one of their founders, whose mother was a Manichaean. Their doctrine claimed to be Christian, and even posed as the only genuine form of Christianity; but it was in fact dualist after the Iranian pattern. The Paulicians affirmed that our world is the scene of battle between two powers: on one hand the Heavenly Father in three persons, Lord of heaven and of the angels; on the other, the Creator or Demiurge, god of evil and of all that is on earth. Their heyday was the ninth century, when they were led by Sergius Tychicus and numbered seven dioceses with Corinth as their mother-church. Michael the Stammerer may have been a Paulician, but the Macedonian dynasty kept a close watch upon this sect. It consisted chiefly of warlike mountaineers, and the basileis hesitated between two courses: whether to settle them on the frontiers as mercenary troops, or to destroy them by force. The first solution proved dangerous, because the Paulicians allied themselves with the barbarians against whom they were supposed to fight. The second was therefore adopted, and by the eleventh century the last remaining nests of dualism in Asia Minor had been virtually annihilated.

Meanwhile, dualism had put forth a new branch in the Balkan lands, among the Bulgarians and Graeco-Slavs. This was the Bogomil heresy, which derived its name from a Greek priest, Bogomil, who lived in the tenth century under Tsar Peter of Bulgaria. The word itself means 'friend of God.' Their teaching was a mixture of Paulician dualism and elements of old Slavonic paganism, which latter also recognized two principles—Bielbog and Tchernobog, the gods respectively of white and black. Though using Christian terminology, the Bogomils rejected the Trinity, the Incarnation, Baptism, and the Cross. According to them, prayer was all that mattered, especially the *Our Father*. Their purpose was to assist the white god in heaven against the black god who created the earth. They condemned marriage and all fleshly intercourse since it perpetuates creation.

The sect made rapid strides, and the young Bulgarian Church never managed to arrest it. The Eastern emperors also devoted a good deal of attention to this heresy, especially Alexius Comnenus, who was the hero of an amusing story. Bogomil was succeeded as head of his sect by one Basil, whom Alexius summoned to the palace and told him he was so impressed by the beauty of his teaching that he thought of embracing it. The astonished Basil was delighted; he not only explained the doctrine and organization of his Church at considerable length, but named all its friends and sympathizers. Nothing was wanting to this enthusiastic sermon, which was interspersed with execrations against the Orthodox Church and its ikons. Meanwhile, behind a large curtain, the members of a tribunal sat listening while their secretaries took notes. The curtain was suddenly withdrawn, and Basil must have looked a little foolish. But he was not subdued; no, the angels of light would protect him, neither fire nor sword could come near him.

Alexius Comnenus was no bloodthirsty tyrant; he did not order the holy man's immediate execution, but merely imprisoned him together with the leading members of his sect. It was not until some years later, under pressure of public opinion and the demands of the clergy in face of Basil's contumacy, that he allowed the heretic to be burned. Alexius himself considered it better to reason with the Bogomils; accordingly he sent them missionaries and had a treatise (*The Dogmatic Armour*) compiled to refute their errors. But these Bogomils were accused, on good grounds, of siding with all the empire's enemies. Towards the end of the twelfth century they were subjected to violence not only in Byzantine territory, but also in Bulgaria and Serbia, and many of them died at the stake. They accordingly took refuge in Bosnia, where, in about 1200, they converted the Khan Koulin with some 10,000 of his subjects, and established an official church which lasted until the fourteenth century through a long period of gradual decline. Travel from Bosnia to Montenegro, from Herzegovina to Dalmatia, and you will still find churches built by the Bogomiles. Their frescoes bear witness to a strange inspiration, imposing and barbaric, full of giants with enormous right hands and of fabulous beasts which seem to derive from Scythian Asia.[1]

From Dalmatia Manichaeism spread westward through Provence, Aquitaine, and Languedoc. Passing through northern Italy, Albigensianism was confused with a popular movement known as the 'Pataria,' whose members were denominated 'Patarines.' It is clear that their remote forebears were known, for they were also called 'Populicians,' a manifest corruption of 'Paulicians.' These facts, however, do not prove that every Manichaean current reappearing in the West had a common source in the East? The revival of ancient dualism may have been spontaneous, corresponding to a natural tendency of the human mind, or it may have been due to the influence of Arabs who had preserved the traditions of African Manichaeaism.

5. CATHARISM, TRANSCENDENT ANARCHY

The 'Catharist' or 'Albigensian' heresy appeared fully fledged at the beginning of the twelfth century. Before we inquire into the nature of its doctrines, we shall do well to remember that, as the later

[1] Some remarkable specimens were shown at the Exhibition of Yugoslav Art at Paris in 1950.

partisans of Catharism rightly insisted, it is difficult to learn the truth about a religious movement when the only surviving documents were written by its adversaries.   We should hardly accept Moslem accounts as a true picture of Christianity, or judge Catholicism from Protestant opinion.   Our knowledge of the Cathars is derived from notes taken at their interrogation and from the papal Bulls or conciliar decrees which condemned them.   Admittedly, that is not altogether satisfactory; but it is worth noting that the evidence of these documents considered as a whole is unanimous, and it is often possible to show that there can be no question of collusion.   Moreover, some of the most violent opponents of the sect must have been well informed, since they themselves had once belonged to it.   The inquisitors Raynier Sacconi and Bonacorsi, for example, had both been Catharist bishops.

The heresy appears from these sources as a peculiar synthesis based upon Manichaean dualism but with a superstructure derived from many other systems.   There was a layer of Docetism, a very early heresy which denied the reality of the Incarnation.   There was also a certain amount of Gnosticism, that mysterious doctrine full of strange and lofty speculations, which had flourished in Egypt and throughout the Near East during the first centuries of the Christian era.   Finally, there were traces of Hinduism, e.g. the belief in metempsychosis; for, says an inquisitor, 'the Cathars never kill an animal or winged thing, believing as they do that the brute beasts are inhabited by the spirits of men who have died outside their sect.'   It is not easy to find one's way about a doctrinal system in which myth and dogma are so closely interwoven.

Dualism was the essential foundation.   In the world as we know it, said the dualists, there are two opposing principles: Perfect and Imperfect, Absolute and Relative, Eternal and Temporal, Good and Evil, Spirit and Matter.   Why this opposition?   Because the world is the scene of battle between two gods, the god of Good and the god of Evil, whom the Iranians named respectively Ormuzd and Ahriman. All agree as to the nature of the first: he is infinitely pure, infinitely perfect, infinitely good, the plenitude of Spirit.   As to the other, whom they called Satan or Lucibel or Lucifer, opinions differed: some held that he was a real god, absolutely distinct from the good; others conceived him as a creature who had been led by pride into revolt and wickedness.

To this essential duality there corresponded a twofold creation. The good god created the invisible world of perfect spirits; the evil god created the visible world of matter, in which sin resides.   How was man born?   Lucibel, having brought forth the world from nothing, wished to people it.   He made bodies from mud, then, after lying in wait for a very long time in the woods of heaven, he managed to capture a few pure spirits and entice them into these earthen vessels.

By the attraction of concupiscence he caused the first of these creatures to have carnal intercourse, and every time a child is born the Evil One encloses in its body the soul of a fallen angel.

The good god, however, took pity on his angels imprisoned here below. Having decided to send them his word by the voice of a messenger, he assembled his faithful angels and invited them to undertake this difficult mission. All refused, except one, Jesus, whom God thenceforward called his son. Jesus descended upon earth, but since he was a pure spirit he could have no contact with matter; he only *appeared* to take human flesh in the body of a woman, it was only in *appearance* that he lived, suffered, and died. Before the coming of Jesus, men had lived in frightful darkness which was sustained by the prophets of the Old Law, servants of the god who made the world, of the cruel god Jehovah. But Jesus taught all men to renounce the earth, the flesh, and even life itself in order to become pure spirits and regain their lost fatherland or heaven.

The world, then, as a battleground between two gods, was a place in which man must strive to detach himself from all that is material, carnal, and terrestrial. Only thus could he serve the good god. At the end of time, when Lucibel's last creation had thrown off its carnal vesture, everything impure would have disappeared; every spirit would have resumed its place in the celestial harmony; there would be no hell, no lost souls, but all (after a certain number of purificatory reincarnations) would be saved.

It is scarcely necessary to observe how far such teaching was removed from Christianity. The whole grandeur of Christian revelation was abolished. The Incarnation, Passion, and Resurrection were meaningless. Human life was no longer sanctified or exalted by the example of our Divine Model, the Incarnate Son of God. The body was a mere bundle of rags which we should try to shuffle off. The spiritual demands of this doctrine were altogether inhuman, and even attacked life itself. The very scriptural and theological foundations crumbled, since the Old Testament was Satan's word.

A terminology retaining some Christian elements barely concealed the antithesis of Christianity. The ideal was to strive with one's whole being towards heaven, rejecting earth and flesh; but it was an ideal to which many devoted themselves heart and soul. These people were called 'the Pure,' 'the Perfect,' or (from the Greek word) 'Cathars.' This latter term was used to designate the sect as a whole, their heresy was known as 'Catharism.' The Perfect possessed no worldly goods whatsoever; they also abstained from marriage and from all carnal delights. Their asceticism was extreme, for they ate neither meat nor anything derived from an animal. If they were already married, they put away their spouses and observed absolute continence.

Some of them lived like fakirs or Hindu hermits, lost in a transcendent dream, 'motionless as a tree-trunk, insensible to all around them.' The majority were engaged in an apostolate of preaching and example which certainly made a deep impression on the masses. Only the Perfect would be saved; they alone would escape the servitude of matter; they alone would find, after death, the sphere of pure Spirit and of the good God. Some of them had so powerful a yearning to attain so blissful a condition that they chose to die. This was the sacred suicide (*endura*), which, though not expressly commanded by the sect, was greatly admired; it was effected by poison, by unlimited fasting, or by pneumonia voluntarily contracted through exposure to cold after a very hot bath.

The Perfect were initiated by a kind of sacrament known as *Consolamentum* which included the imposition of hands and of the Gospels on the aspirant's head. It formed a definite contract from which there could be no turning back. Once 'consoled,' the initiate had to live up to his undertaking; for the Spirit of God had descended upon him, implanting supernatural reality and leaving only the appearance of flesh. It was for this reason that many adherents of the sect hesitated before so thorough-going a renunciation and postponed the ceremony of 'consolation' until the hour of death.

Meanwhile, pending this final (and somewhat gratuitous) sacrifice, members who were not Perfect were numbered in the ranks of 'believers,' who might do almost anything they wished in this vale of tears from which they had not the good sense to depart. They could eat meat, and there were even butchers among their ranks. They could continue to enter Catholic churches and receive the sacraments. They could marry and have carnal intercourse, even outside marriage. Christian morality and plain common decency was no more an obstacle to these ideas than was faith. Believers were required to do no more than to abstain from whatever might make them party to the development of earthly society, Satan's daughter. They were forbidden, for example, to take an oath, because oaths were taken in the name of a god who was not the true one, and they had also to avoid anything in the nature of military service.

The worship of the Cathars, it need hardly be said, was in keeping with their metaphysical, theological, and moral teaching. All the external manifestations of Christian cult were proscribed: no crosses, images, or relics were allowed. The faithful gathered at least once a week for a ceremony at which one of the Perfect read a passage of the New Testament and gave it a suitable interpretation. The congregation then recited the only 'spiritual' prayer, the *Our Father*. An occasional sacred meal, more like the primitive agape than the Eucharist, pretended to commemorate the Last Supper: each of those present received a piece of blessed bread, which was taken home and kept in a precious vessel. The Cathars were not particularly logical, and in some places they aped the Catholic Church by instituting a form of confession, in which the faithful accused themselves of sins against the dogma and discipline of their sect.

Their purpose was clear: to combat the Church by imitating her institutions. They were organized into 'churches' or dioceses, each of which was in charge of a Catharist bishop assisted by an 'elder son' and a 'younger son' from whom his successor was chosen. These bishops met in regular councils and were in oecumenical relations with all Manichaean churches of the East and West. Locally, believers were directed by 'deacons' whose duties were similar to those of a Catholic priest. Christian festivals were also retained, though differently interpreted. Pentecost celebrated God's foundation of the Church of Spiritual Truth, Christmas commemorated the coming of God's Spirit into the world.

How are we to judge of such doctrine? It is very difficult to be fair towards men so peculiar and ideas so abstruse. There can be no doubt that some of the Perfect were endowed with high and lofty spiritual aspirations, and that many of them treated God's call, which they pretended to have heard, with the utmost seriousness. It is no less certain that the self-sacrifice which many of them practised, their asceticism and their true fraternal charity, put to shame some of the Catholic clergy who had no respect whatsoever for our Lord's precepts. However, this does not mean to say that Catharism was the right solution to the problems which confronted the medieval Church.

These heretics were both fundamentally antichristian and fundamentally antisocial—transcendent anarchists. Antichristian, they strove not to reform but to destroy the Church of Christ, which they regarded as the 'handmaiden of evil' and the 'synagogue of Satan.' Did they not reject all those traditions, moral laws, practices, and institutions upon which the Church had built a stable society? Did they not condemn the whole clergy, without distinction of good and bad, as 'unable to remove the world's ordure since they were equally befouled?' Antisocial, they denied and would have annihilated society. 'Everything under the sun and moon is but corruption and confession,' said Limosus Negro, one of the Perfect. A society of the Perfect, had such a thing been feasible, would immediately have destroyed itself by ritual suicide and total virginity. Although it was not feasible, since the Perfect were by good fortune a small minority, their radical indifference to all earthly things led to the rejection of every moral principle and to the free play of every human passion.

The American historian of the Inquisition, H. C. Lea, whose book cannot by the widest stretch of imagination be considered favourable

S

to Catholicism, says of the Cathars: 'If a majority of the faithful had adopted their beliefs, Europe would have been reduced to primitive savagery; it was not merely a revolt against the Church but the abdication of man before nature.'   Another Protestant, Paul Labatier, in his celebrated *Life of St Francis of Assisi*, is yet more severe.   'The papacy,' he writes, 'has not always been on the side of reaction and obscurantism; thus when it crushed the Cathars, its victory was a triumph of good sense and reason.'   He goes on to say that 'the persecution endured by the heretics must not be allowed to engage our sympathy to the extent of upsetting our judgment.'   It is from this point of view that we must judge the terrible fate which overtook Catharism in the South of France.   By destroying it, the Church laid low a dangerous power which, had it triumphed, would have ruined not only herself but also that civilization of which she was the mainstay.

6. THE SOUTH OF FRANCE A PREY TO HERESY

Nor was this peril a mere figment of imagination.   During the twelfth century it constituted a mortal threat.   The heresy was gaining ground over enormous areas of Christendom, and nothing seemed able to stop it.   The two regions most seriously affected were Italy and southern France.   Emerging from Lombardy, the Patarins spread through the peninsula as far as the papal states and Calabria.   They were firmly entrenched at Ferrara, Verona, Rimini, and Treviso, and they drove the Catholic clergy from Piacenza.   At the beginning of the thirteenth century, just after his coronation, Otto IV was horrified to learn that in Rome itself there was a school where Catharism was taught in broad daylight; and it is also a fact that the Podestà of Assisi at that date was a Patarin!

The situation was still worse in the South of France, especially in what is now called Languedoc, the district of Toulouse up to the Pyrenees, and Albi from which the heresy was afterwards named.   In the 'refined and frivolous' south, Christianity had by no means the same vigour as it enjoyed in the north.   The towns were too rich, and life was too easy.   Religion was pervaded with an atmosphere of carelessness, with a spirit of tolerance that amounted to indifference. The Jews were admitted everywhere, even to high public office.   Men were more preoccupied with courts of love and gallant poetry than with metaphysical certainties.

In such a climate the Church had grown thoroughly effete.   Nowhere was vice so widespread or so openly practised.   Simony was found on all sides, and many of the clergy led lives that were nothing short of scandalous.   The principles of reform were almost unknown for the University of Paris had no counterpart at Toulouse to prepare its members for ecclesiastical responsibility, and too many worldly prelates carried the faults of their caste to episcopal thrones. The progress of Catharism was therefore wellnigh inevitable. A simple comparison between the lives of certain clerics and those of the Perfect sufficed to win adherents. Besides, the clergy, from top to bottom of the social scale, were often related to or friendly with heretics. An abbot of Alet, who had been appointed by the secular overlord, declared himself a member of the sect. The abbot of St Volusian at Foix had a brother and sister who were both Cathars; so had the abbot of St Papoul. The same was also true of several bishops, and parish priests naturally followed their superiors' example. Many of them accepted hospitality from the Perfect and sometimes took part in their ceremonies. One tolerant priest heard the confession of a 'believer' who wished to return to the Church, then challenged him to a game of chess, lost all he had, staked the man's penance—and lost again! Threatened from within and thrown back on weak defences, the Church in southern France gave way.

The most serious thing was that the civil authorities had been won over to heresy, which disheartened the saner elements. The vast majority of landowners were in league with the Cathars, and every noble family had at least one member among their ranks. Upper-class children were educated in Manichaean schools; widows and unmarried daughters entered convents established by the Perfect. The spiritual ferment that stirred the whole of Christendom, the desire for a purer life, seemed to make no progress except by way of heresy. There were, of course, other and less edifying motives, such as were partly responsible at a later date for the spread of Protestantism. The barons, for instance, found in heresy a splendid excuse for seizing the goods of the Church.

The greatest nobles did not, for the most part, declare themselves heretics; they managed to avoid excommunication by playing a double game. Thus Raymond VI of Toulouse, a refined and sceptical prince, always sensual and often cruel, was attended both by priests and by members of the Perfect, in order, no doubt, to make sure of heaven. But he and his vassals did not hesitate to pillage religious houses, to burn churches (sometimes with the congregation inside), or to drive recalcitrant bishops from their sees. The wife of Raymond-Roger de Foix had been 'consoled,' and his sister Esclairmonde had turned her castle at Fanjeaux into a Catharist seminary. He called himself a Catholic, but could not keep his hands off ecclesiastical possessions. The Trencavel viscounts of Béziers and Carcassonne were reputed heretics, and did so little to hide the fact that they endowed the Cathars with property they had recently taken from the Bishop of Albi. As for the gentry, most of them had links with heresy. And since there was none of the traditional antagonism between the towns and the nobility in southern France, all the urban centres were riddled with Catharism, excepting Narbonne, Montpellier, and Nîmes, where Catholicism still prevailed.

The gravity of the situation was admirably described by Henry, abbot of Clairvaux: 'It was commonly believed at Toulouse that if we had delayed to take action for another three years, there would scarcely have been anyone left in that neighbourhood familiar with the name of Jesus Christ.' He wrote these words in 1177; imagine the peril thirty years later when Christendom, tired of meekness, ceased to temporize and struck her blow.

This last point is one to be borne in mind, for it is generally overlooked: the Church behaved with marvellous patience towards the 'Albigenses.' During fifty years she employed no arms but those of charity, preaching, and public debate. A spiritual crusade preceded military operations, and it was only because the first made no headway that the papacy was literally forced to adopt the second.

It was in 1119, at a council held at Toulouse, that the danger of this heresy was first pointed out and the zealots excommunicated. But these measures do not appear to have hindered its progress; for in 1147 Eugenius III, who had come to France to preach the second crusade, expressed his amazement at what he had learned. A mission was then dispatched for the twofold purpose of bringing back heretics to the true faith and the clergy to a better mode of life. It included Cardinal Alberic, Geoffrey, Bishop of Chartres, and St Bernard. 'The basilicas have no congregations, the congregations no priests, and the priests no honour; there are only Christians without Christ,' lamented the great Cistercian when he reached Languedoc. Boldly he set about his task, and his personal prestige together with the brilliance of his language seems in many places to have made some impression. But the results were not lasting. As soon as he left, the heretics regained their influence, and at Verfeil he was even prevented from speaking. He founded Cistercian houses in the affected provinces: Grandsilve and Fontfroide were as sea-walls against the tide of Catharism. Had he been able to remain, he might have dealt a serious blow to the heresy; but he was summoned elsewhere by other duties, and neither the memory of his miracles nor that of his words sufficed to restore the situation.

At the Council of Lyons, in 1163, Alexander III referred to this situation in strong terms. The bishops and secular princes of 'Albigensian' districts were forbidden to protect or to tolerate the heretics, and were even instructed to confiscate their goods. To which Raymond VI of Toulouse replied, in a letter no less painful than sincere, that the heretics had become so strong that he 'neither could

nor dared repress the evil.' A fresh cry of alarm was raised by the third
Lateran Council in 1179, when the faithful were called upon to take
arms against the heretics and were promised indulgences. The legate
Henry of Albano, a former Cistercian, led a military expedition against
Roger II Trencavel, and forced him to release the Bishop of Albi; but
as soon as he departed Catharism flourished once again. Each of
Alexander III's five successors drew attention to the danger, but none
of them was in a position to do much about it.

On this point, as on many another, Innocent III gave the Church
some definite policy, and during the first year of his pontificate (1198)
he announced his determination to combat heresy. In Italy he
decreed that the Cathars were to be excluded from public office and
their property confiscated; but he was hindered by differences with the
Empire, which made it necessary to look for allies among cities teeming
with heretics. In southern France he felt more free and took vigorous
measures. His first legates, two Cistercians named Rainier and Guy,
encountered so many difficulties that they had to be recalled. Undeterred by this initial set-back, he immediately replaced them with two
other Cistercians from the monastery of Fontfroide, Peter of Castelnau and Raoul. They met with no better success; for the unfriendly
attitude of the nobility and some of the bishops rendered their efforts
useless, and they talked of throwing in their hand. Innocent, however, was by no means prepared to surrender; he instructed them to
stay where they were, and sent out a third legate in the person of
Arnaud, abbot of Cîteaux. Anti-catharist measures were strengthened: the Cistercians were ordered to combat the heresy by means of
public sermons and disputations, while the great barons were warned
that if they continued to abet heresy the Pope would urge the King of
France to seize their goods. This threat, however, proved ineffective;
Raymond VI swore to expel the heretics, but he made no move to do so.

It was at this juncture that St Dominic appeared on the scene.[1]
Passing through southern France on his way to Rome, he became
convinced that the Church must alter her methods. The legates
believed it necessary for the fulfilment of their mission to uphold their
dignity by travelling with a splendid retinue. Accordingly, they
arrived at the scene of debate with magnificent horses and numerous
servants, whereas their opponents came as poor men and on foot. In
his conversations with the legates, St Dominic found them disheartened,
and he suggested they might obtain better results if they too went,
'like their Divine Master, in all humility, on foot, without pomp or
money, like the Apostles.' The saint laid this admirable though
revolutionary idea before the Pope, who enthusiastically agreed.
He expounded his thesis, at the Council of Montpellier in 1206.

[1] See Chapter IV, section 9.

Then, resolved to preach by example, he sent home his horses and domestics, and took the road barefoot to beg his bread. The result was encouraging. Debates, at which the Cistercian legates had failed to impress, were conducted on a larger scale; and the first Dominicans began little by little to score over their adversaries in these tournaments of theological eloquence. At Montréal, for example, after fifteen days of discussion, they made one hundred and fifty conversions. The Lord Himself appeared to assist His own, for at Fanjeaux—as depicted in a celebrated picture by Fra Angelico in the Louvre—the Catharist books were destroyed in an ordeal by fire, while a memoir written by St Dominic was ejected from the flames with such violence that it rose to the ceiling-timbers, which were set on fire. The most important of these debates was held in the spring of 1207 at Pamiers, a Catharist and Waldensian stronghold, from which the Catholics emerged triumphant.

But notwithstanding St Dominic's efforts, the net result was small. Peter of Vaux-de-Cernay and William of Puylaurens, who chronicled the story, do not hide the fact that little was achieved; while the troubadour of the *Chanson de la Croisade* says frankly that 'all these folk considered sermons as so many rotten apples.' In view of this partial defeat, and the determination of the common people to persevere in heresy, the barons, especially the cunning Raymond VI of Toulouse, sided with the Cathars. Christendom was beginning to think that it might be necessary to use force when a tragic and decisive incident occurred.

7. THE ALBIGENSIAN CRUSADE

On 13th January 1208 the legate Peter of Castelnau and the Bishop of Conserans were leaving St Gilles, where they had once more attempted to persuade Raymond VI of Toulouse to withdraw his support from the heretics. The interview had come to nothing, and the two prelates set out with these words ringing in their ears: 'Wherever you go, whether by land or water, take care: I shall be watching you!' After spending the night in a hostelry on the right bank of the Rhône, they said Mass early on the morning of the 14th, and were preparing to cross the river when an old soldier rushed at them with a lance. Peter of Castelnau was mortally wounded and died soon afterwards, having just had time to pardon his murderer, a former cavalryman from Beaucaire and a minor vassal of Count Raymond.

This crime roused the whole of Christendom against its apparent instigator, as the murder of St Thomas Becket by Henry II's men had done thirty years earlier. Raymond VI was a paltry fellow. He had inherited the defects of his great-grandfather, Raymond IV of St Gilles, who had played so complex a part during the first crusade.

Impulsive, unstable, and, it must be admitted, lacking in candour, he had little of his ancestor's energy or courage. The manner in which he frequently deserted his friends throws an ugly light upon his character. No one, least of all Pope Innocent III, doubted that he was responsible for this crime, though the fact could not be proved. Rome, therefore, determined to launch a crusade against the heretics.

Papal emissaries preached in northern France throughout the year 1208. The same rights, indulgences, and honours would be granted to those who took arms against the Cathars and their feudal allies as were enjoyed by those who went on crusade to the Holy Land. The nobles of the South would no doubt defend themselves, so that the expedition could not be described exactly as a holiday trip; but it seemed likely to be less troublesome than the Eastern campaigns, and was not expected to last for more than forty days. Besides, it would prove extremely lucrative; for the heretics' property had been declared 'unprotected,' which meant to say that anyone was entitled to take possession of it. Lured by this prospect, many unlanded gentry in the north felt a keen desire to do battle for the faith. Raymond of Toulouse watched the appalling tempest gather, and decided to give way. He informed the Pope that if His Holiness would send a legate more acceptable than Abbot Arnaud of Cîteaux, he, Raymond, would submit. Bishop Milou was appointed, and the count began negotiations with truly edifying humility. In order to be freed from excommunication, he was prepared to do all that the legate asked: he would promise obedience to the Pope, give up seven of his castles, and take the Cross against the heretics in his own territory. But by mid June 1209 it was impossible to prevent the storm, and the chief result of this manœuvre was to leave Raymond II Trencavel, Viscount of Béziers, Albi, and Carcassone, with Raymond-Roger I, Count of Foix, alone to face the consequences.

The crusading army assembled at Lyons, and their departure was fixed for 24th June. Philip Augustus, who was then at war with England, had turned a deaf ear to the Pope's appeal, but allowed his vassals to take the Cross. The expedition was led by nobles of varying degree together with a number of bishops and metropolitans. Chief among these were the Duke of Burgundy, the Count of Nevers, the Count of St Pol, and such vassals of Raymond VI as the Count of Poitiers and Valentinois. Some chroniclers assess the crusading force at 50,000, others at 500,000. The first figure seems more probable, but it included more non-combatants than soldiers. The approach of so large an army was a grave threat to the south; for it was more than likely that the northerners would behave as foreign conquerors. Here was a civilization higher than their own, wealthy cities and splendid castles, a people whose physique astonished them and of whose language they were ignorant. The Pope had given express orders: they must extirpate the heresy, drive the Albigenses from their strongholds, and re-establish the authority of the Church; but they were not to solve the Catharist problem by wholesale massacre or to pillage the country's wealth. It soon became clear, however, that the religious authorities were unable to restrain the torrent which

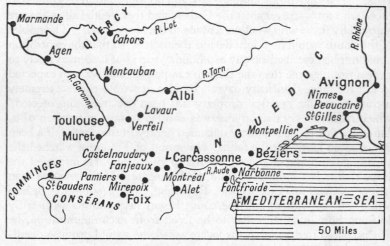

The Albigensian Crusade

they had themselves unleashed. The supreme command was held, in theory, by the two legates Arnaud and Milou; but the instinct of murder and every base passion took control.

Thus opened what is perhaps one of the most regrettable and most disturbing pages in the history of the medieval Church. It was necessary because of the terrifying progress of heresy, but it could have been less ferocious and less devastating. True, the horrors of the Albigensian crusade have often been exaggerated by historians and pamphleteers anxious to make the Church responsible for the crimes committed by these 'northern barbarians.' But the large number of atrocities makes it impossible for us to recall the undertaking with any degree of satisfaction.

The summer of 1209, then, witnessed a 'lightning crusade' which passed down the Rhône to a point beyond Nîmes somewhat in the manner of a route march. There was no resistance; towns and cities opened their gates to welcome the 'crusader' Raymond VI, who had joined the main body with a large cross on his breast. The drama opened at Béziers, which belonged to young Raymond-Roger, twenty-four-year-old heir of the Trencavels. He was prepared to submit, but the invaders could scarcely disband their army without striking a decisive blow at the heretics. His offer to surrender was rejected, and while Raymond-Roger hurried to prepare the defences of his capital at Carcassonne, the crusaders attacked Béziers. Havoc was let loose. Entering the city by surprise, the rank and file began a massacre which the nobles were powerless to prevent. Nothing could restrain the drunken troops from carnage: women and children, faithful Catholics, even priests and canons, were slaughtered indiscriminately.[1] The number of those slain may have been exaggerated;[2] but it was certainly very large, and the sack of Béziers remains one of the most shameful memories of a war waged in the name of Jesus Christ.

The episode, however, was nowhere repeated on so large a scale. Nothing similar happened at Carcassonne, which, though strongly fortified, was taken by surprise. Raymond-Roger was made prisoner; but it is still uncertain whether he was teacherously seized during a parley, or whether he volunteered as a hostage to save his people. At all events, there was no general massacre, only a form of pillage which is to-day called 'requisitioning.' Two heretical centres had now fallen, and Catharism had suffered a grievous set-back.

The period of forty days was drawing to an end. Someone must be found to administer the unfortunate young Trencavel's property, and after prolonged discussion the choice fell upon Simon de Montfort. This man was a native of the Norman Vexin, with estates in the neighbourhood of Paris, Conflans, Épernon, and Houdan. He was also Earl of Leicester and suzerain of Montfort l'Amaury, whose name his family bore. Simon, then, was no penniless adventurer. At the age of forty-five he was strong in mind and body, brave to the point of rashness, a Christian of exemplary faith, prepared, if necessary, to give his life for the Church. He was neither more nor less cruel than the majority of his contemporaries, despite the fact that he has been represented as a bloodthirsty monster. Rather, he was 'a soldier who fought for his faith without regard to himself or to others.' Having assumed control of Raymond-Roger's territory according to feudal law, he proceeded, together with a handful of loyal Catholics and some four thousand troops, to undertake sole responsibility for the crusade as well as for the struggle against heresy.

His first task was to complete the conquest of the Viscounty of Béziers. Albi fell, and Simon turned upon the Count of Foix, another

---

[1] As with most historical sayings, there is no truth in the famous words attributed to one of the legates: 'Kill the lot! God will find His own!' They were invented by Cesarius of Heisterbach near Boom in his account of the 'miraculous' capture of Béziers.

[2] Peter of Vaux-de-Cernay states that 7,000 persons were killed in the church of the Madeleine, which can scarcely hold 1,000. Even 1,000 corpses is far too many.

S*

friend of the Cathars. Pamiers and Mirepoix were taken in due course and entrusted to his friend Guy de Levis, marshal of the little army. In the first days of September 1209 a new stage was marked by the defection of Raymond VI. The Count of Toulouse, having broken all his promises, was excommunicated by a council at Avignon and his territory laid under interdict. Hurrying to Rome, he appealed to the Pope and distressed him with an account of the horrors he had witnessed; but he was condemned outright by two more councils to which he had been summoned. This time, supported by the Counts of Foix, Béziers, and Comminges, he decided to resist. The affair was now seen in a different light: henceforward it was a struggle between the people of the south and these armoured missionaries from the north.

A regular war broke out, for which Simon de Montfort received reinforcements from Flanders, Lorraine, and Germany. After taking Lavaur (1211) and various castles, in the course of which campaign he massacred several small groups of heretics, he tried in vain to capture Toulouse. Then he turned on the enemy forces, defeated them at Castelnaudary, and entered St Gaudens. By the end of 1212 he had overrun Quercy and Agenais as well as the territory of Foix and Comminges. Raymond VI held little more than Toulouse and Montauban.

Simon's brilliant successes alarmed Pope Innocent III, who began asking himself whether this formidable soldier of Christ was working exclusively for the glory of Mother Church, and whether his methods would produce the right results. King Peter II of Aragon, brother-in-law to the Count of Toulouse, feared the creation of a powerful state so near his own frontier. He prepared to act as intermediary between the two opponents, and was strongly encouraged by the Pope, who, when negotiations broke down and the King of Aragon drew his sword in defence of Toulouse, did not protest.

But this coalition of Aragon and the South of France was powerless against Simon, who was riding the full tide of victory. It met with disaster at the battle of Muret (10th–12th September 1213): King Peter was killed in action, and his allies fled pell-mell from the field. Simon de Montfort then scoured the countryside, taking Marmande, Montauban, Narbonne, and finally Toulouse. On 8th January 1215 a council assembled at Montpellier proclaimed the victor prince of the conquered territory, and asked the Pope to confirm their choice.

Innocent III took this as a sign that things were getting out of hand, and postponed his decision until the Lateran Council which he summoned for the following November. Meanwhile, he opposed the intended expropriation of all the vanquished; and when the Count of Toulouse arrived in Rome, he received a most paternal welcome from the Holy Father, whose noble character recoiled before measures that were little less than daylight robbery and who no doubt realized the folly of driving the lords of southern France to desperation. He preferred a policy of appeasement, but the bishops assured him that to reinstate the local nobility would be to revive heresy. The Pope yielded to their arguments, though not before he had guaranteed the rights of Raymond's wife and son.

Innocent had been far-sighted. The decision of the Lateran Council to establish the northern barons for good and all in place of the former landowners provoked an outburst of fury in the south. A few of these 'Frenchmen' made themselves loved and respected, but the vast majority were thoroughly detested. 'Whatever you do,' said the aged Pope to Raymond VI, who had come to take leave of him after the council, 'whatever you do, God grant you may begin well and finish better!' Was this an invitation to renew hostilities? No sooner was Innocent III dead than the South of France rose as one man. Simon was busy enlarging his conquests on the left bank of the Rhône, and the old Count of Toulouse, aided by his young son Raymond VII, launched a general offensive. Montfort replied with a direct attack on his capital, but was killed when a stone hurled by a mangonel struck him on the head (25th June 1218). His son Amaury was quite unfitted to succeed him in so difficult a command, and the army retreated on Carcassonne.

Would the whole war have to be fought again? The southern lords had recovered most of their property; would they return to heresy? The Cathars too had renewed their activity, and Pope Honorius III, who had succeeded Innocent, was seriously alarmed. He begged the assistance of Philip Augustus, who had fewer anxieties since the defeat of John 'Lackland' and his allies at Bouvines. The time had come for the French king to chew the chestnuts which others had pulled out of the fire, and this religious undertaking proved to be one of the most fruitful political enterprises ever handled by the Capetian dynasty. Troops under the Dauphin Louis (afterwards Louis VIII) reached the south in 1219. After six weeks they had failed to capture Toulouse, and withdrew; but Amaury de Montfort in Carcassonne, having lost nearly all his possessions and having no taste for further resistance, offered to cede his rights to the French king.

Philip Augustus had died in the meantime, and Louis VIII accepted Amaury's offer. The papal legates, as well as two councils at Paris and Bourges, implored him to embark on another full-scale crusade against Raymond VII of Toulouse, who was even more friendly than his father towards the heretics, and had been excommunicated on that account. The expedition started in June 1226, and the fall of Avignon was followed by that of Béziers and Carcassonne. A swarm of native priests and monks preceded the royal army, inviting the population to submit; order was quickly re-established, and an assembly at Pamiers delivered to the French king all lands belonging to the heretics. The death of Louis VIII delayed a full settlement, but the south was exhausted; its rulers understood that royal sovereignty was the best possible solution. Raymond VII was anxious for reconciliation with the Church. His daughter Joan married Louis IX's brother Alfonso, whom she succeeded; while Raymond himself offered the county of Avignon to the Pope, and some of his personal property to the French crown. Blanche of Castile and Cardinal St Angelo, as legate, signed the agreement at Paris on 12th April 1229.

After twenty years of almost uninterrupted warfare, the 'Albigensian crusade' ended in victory for the Church and even more so for the royal house of Capet. Christianity was saved from the peril which had threatened to overwhelm it. Catharism had ceased to pride itself as mistress of southern France; its leaders, hunted down by the Inquisition, were obliged to go into hiding or to flee. The hoped-for result had therefore been attained: public safety had been secured, but alas! at the cost of much blood and of many tears. The South of France has never quite recovered.

8. THE INQUISITION

At the very mention of this name hideous images arise; soft-hearted folk and sticklers for justice begin to feel uneasy. Nevertheless, we must ignore the ravings of propaganda and the more or less wilful confusion of both time and place. Far too many people were burned at the stake, but not so many as is commonly supposed. The medieval Inquisition had no Torquemada. To understand that tribunal and its work, we must imagine ourselves face to face with the peril threatening Christian society, the foundations of which were being slowly undermined. The Inquisition was established to counteract this danger. It was, in the strict sense, a tribunal to protect the public safety of Christendom; hence its severity.

Forcible suppression of heresy was not invented by the Church. She had always looked upon heresy as treason against the Divine Majesty, but she never demanded the application of those dreadful punishments which were incurred by all traitors under Roman Law. During the first three centuries she had recourse only to persuasion and spiritual sanctions. It was the Christian emperors, Constantine and his successors, who first inflicted temporal punishment in the shape of fines, imprisonment, and flogging, upon Manichaean and Donatist rebels against the true faith. The first great heresy-trial to end in a capital sentence was that of the Spaniard Priscillian; and it caused Pope Siricius, St Ambrose, and St Martin of Tours to protest in the very strongest terms. St Augustine took a slightly different view. He was a firm believer in tolerance towards heretics, especially the Manichaeans; but he realized that heresy was an attack on the bases of Christian society, which must accordingly defend itself. While advocating some degree of moderation, he considered the death penalty justified in extreme cases. St John Chrysostom, on the other hand, used to say that 'to kill a heretic is to introduce upon earth an inexpiable crime.'

Curiously enough, the Merovingian and Carolingian periods, which cannot at any rate be called squeamish, never attempted to drown heresy in blood. That was simply because religious nonconformity was not sufficiently widespread to constitute a real danger, and the Arians were believed to be on the point of conversion. The monk Gottschalk, who was convicted of heresy in the middle of the ninth century, was simply condemned to a flogging. What caused a more violent reaction was the reappearance of Manichaean dualism, the fundamentally antisocial character of which we have already seen. Even so, this greater harshness was the work of secular princes. It was Robert the Pious, for example, who had heretics burned at Orléans in 1022; it was the emperor Henry III who had others hanged at Goslar thirty years later. Until the middle of the twelfth century all executions of heretics were ordered by the civil authority, often under pressure from fanatical mobs. The Church objected to this form of murder and even more to summary executions, as was made clear time after time by the doctors and popes. 'Faith is the work of persuasion,' wrote St Bernard, 'it cannot be imposed by force'; and when he heard that some heretics had been burned at Cologne, he wisely added that it was absurd to create 'false martyrs' in this way.

Numerous conciliar enactments, while excommunicating heretics and forbidding Christians to give them asylum, refused to allow the death sentence. Spiritual penalties and, if need be, a moderate degree of temporal punishment, were held to be sufficient.

How was it, then, that, late in the twelfth century, the Church was led to establish a special court for the discovery of heretics; and why did that institution so soon adopt violent methods? It was because the sudden increase of heresy roused a keener sense of danger. When society was incorporated with the Church to form a spiritual and temporal entity known as 'Christendom,' Christianity made itself answerable for collective life as a whole, for public order, and for the fundamentals of civilization. Her legal system, however, was not equipped for such a task.[1] To seek out and repress spiritual anarchy, therefore, the Church devised a special instrument which was called the 'Inquisition.'

[1] See Chapter VI, section 8.

The idea emerged at the second Lateran Council in 1139, at a moment of grave crisis. Catharist Manichaeism was gaining ground every-where; Henry of Lausanne was at work in France, Arnold of Brescia in Italy, and Abélard was a disturbing influence among the under-graduates of Paris. It was proposed that the Church should hence-forward deliver trouble-makers to the 'secular arm,' in order to prevent them doing further damage. At the third Lateran Council in 1179 this idea began to take shape, and in 1184, by agreement with Frederick Barbarossa, an assembly met at Verona under the presidency of Lucius III. It drew up a regular constitution dealing with every aspect of the problem, setting out the various classes of heretics, laying down the judicial forms to which they were subject, and defining the penalties applicable to them and to their accomplices. Every diocese was to maintain a number of reliable clerics whose duty it would be to track down heresy and warn the civil authorities. The Constitution of 1184 is generally considered to have founded the Inquisition.

As yet it was a rudimentary affair; time would show whether or not it were adequate. What, for example, would happen if the bishops themselves were indulgent towards heresy? Rome soon woke up to the ambiguity of this situation. An Inquisition of legates was first added to, then substituted for, the diocesan tribunals. It was entrusted, as we have seen, to the Cistercians, and heretics who had been turned over to the secular arm were treated with extreme severity. In northern France, Philip Augustus showed himself a zealous upholder of the Inquisition; so did Frederick II, who, though half atheist, gave orders that anyone condemned as a heretic by the Church should be burned alive or have his tongue cut out.

The Albigensian affair strengthened the Inquisition. Local councils held at Avignon in 1209 and at Montpellier in 1215 re-enacted the constitution of Verona; and these measures were elaborated by the fourth Lateran Council in 1215, which made recourse to the secular arm obligatory. At the same time the armed intervention of the crusaders sealed the collaboration of the religious authorities with the civil power. But Catharism, at which so heavy a blow had thus been struck, went underground, disguised itself, and became a secret society whose thousands of members, scattered through every land, were extremely difficult to find. Bishops, abbots, legates, and all the clergy were reminded of their duty to be vigilant, to track down suspects, and denounce them. It was also provided that any house in which a heretic was taken could be forthwith destroyed, and that any bailiff who proved slack could be dismissed; while families and even whole villages could be held collectively responsible. But the Cathars were all the harder to detect in that they behaved as Christians and were shielded by numerous well-wishers.

And so, in 1231, immediately after the Albigensian crusade, Gregory IX decided to transform the Inquisition into a separate organ, independent of the bishops and even of the legates, and to establish permanent tribunals whose sole task would be to carry on the struggle against the secret forces of heresy. The Franciscans and Dominicans had already done good work in the South of France; they had great authority with the masses, and many of the finest intellects in Christendom were to be found among their ranks. A series of decretals was therefore addressed to them between 1231 and 1234, and the monastic Inquisition took its place in history. In 1235 the first inquisitor-general for the kingdom of France was appointed. He was Robert le Bougre, a Dominican, whose surname was derived from the fact that he had once been a 'bougre,' i.e. a Cathar.

Henceforward the Inquisition was in the hands of religious, who won for it its present notoriety by accepting every accusation and denunciation indiscriminately, by employing torture to extract confessions, and by automatically condemning its victims to the most hideous of penalties. Such, at any rate, is the belief of most people; but the facts are altogether different. From many points of view the Inquisition did behave atrociously, but it was not entirely evil. Its procedure is well known through a whole series of papal Bulls and other authoritative documents, but mainly through such formularies and manuals as were prepared by St Raymond of Pennaforte, the great Spanish canonist, and Bernard Gui, one of the most celebrated Inquisitors at the beginning of the fourteenth century. Reference to these sources gives a slightly less horrifying picture.

Let us imagine the tribunal at work. A party of Franciscan or Dominican inquisitors have reached some district where heresy is believed to be rife. They number at least three or four, one of whom will act as president. Summoning the population to the church, along with the bishop and clergy, they begin with a solemn sermon, adjuring everyone to assist them and inviting the rebels to seek God's pardon. So far, then, the Inquisition appears as little more than an extension of the tribunal of penance whose merciful and supernatural purpose it shares.[1] This purpose is expressed in judicial terms by the 'edict of faith' and the 'edict of grace' which the Inquisitors now proclaim. The first orders every Christian, on pain of excommunication, to name whomsoever is regarded as a heretic, including those who are merely suspect. The second grants rebels a period of from two to four weeks within which to come forward and confess their sin. If their heresy has caused no scandal, they will simply be given a penance; if it is notorious, they will have the benefit of an indulgence and will

---

[1] Léon E. Halkin, *Initiation à la critique historique*, 1951.

merely be condemned to make a pilgrimage or to spend a few days detention, probably in a religious house.

At the end of this period of grace, the whole business takes on a new look.   Denunciations have poured in as a result of the edict of faith, and the Inquisitors have held discussions with what Gregory IX calls 'discreet persons,' of sound faith and morals; but it has been made quite clear that heresy must not be made a false pretext for satisfying private enmities.

A host of passions, more or less openly avowed, was let loose on such occasions, and the Inquisitors must have found it difficult to separate the wheat from the tares.   Before long, in fact, it was found necessary to keep secret the names of those who supplied information; and even then more than one who had helped the inquiry ended some dark night with a dagger in his back or at the bottom of a ravine.

Whether designated by public rumour or denounced by an individual, the suspect is hauled before the tribunal for questioning. But we must pause here to consider an awkward question: Had he the right to be represented by counsel?   Most historians of the Inquisition reply in the negative, taking their stand on the Bull *Si adversus nos* of Innocent III, which forbade advocates and notaries to assist heretics. In Bernard Gui's manual, also, we read that the Inquisitors should proceed 'without the clamour of advocates.'   It seems, however, that this rule was frequently disregarded, and that the tribunal often allowed defendants to engage legal assistance; for there are numerous cases in which counsel undoubtedly appeared.   We know, for instance, that Joan of Arc's judges, one of whom was an Inquisitor, asked her if she wished for such aid, and that she refused.   In another Inquisitor's manual, that of Eymeric, we read these words which give the lie to Bernard Gui: 'Defendants must not be deprived of legal aid; on the contrary, they must be allowed attorneys and advocates, provided these are honest men, not suspect of heresy, and of unquestioned faith.'

Standing then before the tribunal, the defendant undergoes a long and searching interrogation.   He is not told who has provided evidence against him, for there is always danger of bloody reprisals, but the evidence itself is explained to him and he may try to refute it. If he manages to do so, things may go badly for the man who denounced him; for it is the rule that if bad faith be proved, the calumniator shall be condemned to the same penalty which the accused would otherwise have incurred.   In theory, the defendant has a right to bring forward witnesses in his own behalf; but few can be so heroic as to expose themselves for another's sake to the risk of being charged with heresy.

Upon what is the accusation based?   There are four possible reasons. First, open heresy: the defendant may have been denounced as a Cathar, either as one of the Perfect or even as a mere 'believer.' Second, he may, without actually belonging to the sect, have shown sympathy towards it, e.g. by genuflecting before the Perfect. Third, he may have sheltered a known heretic on at least two occasions, or have defended the rebels in public. Finally (and this aggravated the offence), he may once have abjured error and then relapsed.

To whichever category the defendant belongs, he can always endeavour to mitigate the severity of the tribunal by admitting his guilt, and is even advised to do so. The procedure of this avowal is almost the same as that for sacramental confession, and may well get him off with nothing worse than a canonical penance. But it may be that the accused will not confess, in which case the Inquisitors will try to make him contradict himself or to repudiate his heretical beliefs. He may also be subjected to a test which will show him up. Suppose, for instance, he is charged with Catharism, he may be confronted with a dog and told to cut its throat. The sect believes in metempsychosis, so he is in a dilemma: he must either betray himself or violate his convictions. The accused may also be reminded of the terrible fate awaiting him if he perseveres in heresy: imprisonment for life, or death by fire. He is left long to think things over in his cell on a diet of bread and water. Finally, if all these means fail, recourse may be had to torture.

This feature of the Inquisition has been most violently exploited by writers hostile to the Church; and no one can fail to be disgusted by the participation of religious in such abominable scenes. Hitherto the Church had been opposed to methods of this kind, but from the beginning of the thirteenth century she followed a trend initiated by the revival of Roman Law, and acted on the principles of secular jurisprudence. The 'question,' or preventive torture, which was intended to extract a confession, figures in some Italian laws about 1220. Innocent IV's Bull *Ad extirpenda* (1252) authorized and controlled its use by ecclesiastical tribunals. Alexander IV, in 1260, and Urban IV, in 1262, decided that the Inquisitors should themselves attend these horrible proceedings.

Suppose the unhappy defendant is condemned to undergo torture. What form will this take? Generally speaking, the Inquisitors have a choice of four methods, of which simple flogging is the most lenient. The rack is worse; here the victim is attached to a wooden frame with his legs and arms tied to a jack, the least movement of which will dislocate his joints. The strappado is a kind of diabolical game in which the accused is hauled up by rope to the top of a very high gibbet and then dropped to within a few inches of the ground. Finally there is the ordeal of burning coals, which requires no description.

These cruelties were revolting, and were rendered still more so by the apparatus of justice which surrounded them. We can only hope, for the honour of the Church, that such cases were not numerous.

Let us now imagine that a confession has been extracted. But before sentence is passed we must delay in order to notice the *boni viri*, good men and true. Innocent IV, who authorized the use of torture, was also the founder of this 'jury.' Varying in numbers from two to twenty, it consisted of sound Catholics who took part in the interrogations and gave their opinion. 'In the matter of such grave accusations,' said the Pope, 'we must proceed with the greatest care.'

And now we come to judgment day, when the verdict is proclaimed with no end of pomp and ceremony. It probably takes place in the main square before an immense gathering of people. The Chief Inquisitor delivers a sermon, which is also the sentence of the court, and often pauses to exhort his hearers to proclaim their faith which has been outraged. This is the *act of faith* (Spanish *auto-da-fé*) which came to have so terrible a meaning.

The accused has been found guilty of heresy. What will the penalty be? One of three kinds. (1) Imprisonment may be for life or for a shorter period, and of a severity proportionate to the gravity of the crime; the *murus strictus*, detention in a small, dark cell, and often in chains, is most dreaded. (2) If the crime is still greater and the scandal flagrant, the victim will be 'delivered to the secular arm.'

This shameful formula must leave us under no illusion whatsoever: it is no use arguing with Joseph de Maistre that only the civil power was responsible for the death of those turned over to it. The Inquisitors were perfectly well aware that in delivering a man to the secular arm they were sending him to his death. The Church's traditional horror of blood led her to adopt this procedure, but the result was known in advance. Besides, there were papal Bulls expressly commanding the secular authority to execute heretics so delivered. The usual penalty was the stake, that penalty which the Roman emperors had devised for the Manichaeans, which Robert the Pious had revived after the famous Orléans trial, and which had become so firmly established that most juridical treatises and constitutions refer to it as quite normal. The Church accepted it, and we may be shocked at her severity. On the other hand, she withheld the accessory pains often inflicted by civil courts—preliminary branding with red-hot iron, breaking on the wheel, etc.

Finally (3), any of these major penalties will almost inevitably involve the condemned in the confiscation of his goods, which will affect every member of his family; but there seem to have been frequent dispensations from this rule so that the innocent should not suffer.

The Inquisition, with all its cruelty, is perhaps the least attractive element of medieval Christianity. Must we therefore denounce the Church and condemn the institution outright as sheer barbarism? Rather we should try to understand it from the medieval point of view. St Thomas says that, by common consent, 'to corrupt the faith which is the life of the soul is far worse than to issue false coinage'; and the civil law undoubtedly punished coiners with the utmost severity. Besides, the Inquisition worked in an age when men were much less sensitive than to-day, more uncouth, and more resistant to pain; an age in which life was not surrounded with that hypocritical respect which the twentieth century proclaims so loudly and yet so continually denies. The Inquisition, even at its worst, was as nothing when compared with modern totalitarian regimes; its prisons were not so numerous as our concentration camps, and the gas chamber has claimed many more victims than the stake.

True, there were undeniable abuses on the part of the Inquisition, especially when it was taken over by the secular powers, as happened in the time of Philip the Fair and under the Spanish kings. But many documents attest the Church's anxiety to prevent such abuses: papal instructions directed provincials of the mendicant Orders to depose Inquisitors whose cruelty had outraged public opinion, and numerous appeals to Rome ended in the acquittal of condemned persons.

Figures are likewise eloquent, and prove that defendants were by no means inevitably destined to the stake. Out of 930 sentences pronounced by Bernard Gui over a period of fifteen years, 139 were acquittals, 132 canonical penances, 152 orders to go on pilgrimage, 307 imprisonments, and only 42 'deliveries to the secular arm.' The number, of course, is large, much too large; but one cannot help asking whether the proportion of capital sentences has not been larger under some modern 'legal' systems. The Inquisition was a weapon forged by circumstances, its use an unfortunate necessity called forth by present danger. But its powers were seldom abused, at any rate during the Middle Ages; and although we may dislike the institution, we can at least understand and appreciate its real value.

One question remains: Was the Inquisition effective? The answer varies from one case and one district to another. There can be no doubt that these tribunals managed to suppress Catharism, which they hunted down not only in southern France, but also in Italy, until scarcely a trace of it remained. But the Waldensian heresy, as we have seen, was far more tenacious. Notwithstanding the efforts of a long line of Inquisitors, it persisted in the high Alpine valleys and has never quite disappeared. Considered as an instrument of search and repression, the Inquisition was powerless to prevent the rise of new heresies whose hidden causes lay outside its view. By the beginning of the fourteenth century it had attained tremendous importance, being established in almost every country and enjoying the active support of kings; but it could not halt the encroachment of intellectual unrest upon Catholic faith and the birth of error in new forms. Heresy, as St Paul had foreseen, is part of the normal history of religion. It arises from the dangerous though necessary privilege of freedom. Violence is of no avail against this constant danger which itself proceeds from the prerogatives granted by Almighty God to man.

CHAPTER XIV

THE END OF CHRISTENDOM

1. The Hermit on St Peter's Throne

THE story of Celestine V's pontificate is peculiar, to say the least; and if it were not based on documents whose authenticity cannot be impugned, one might be inclined to treat it as a legend. In July 1294 the see of Peter had been vacant for more than two years since the death of Nicholas IV. The eleven cardinals, of whom the Sacred College then consisted, could not agree. They had been obliged to leave Rome, which was prey to murderous factions, and had taken up residence in the gloomy episcopal palace at Perugia. But the rival clans of Colonna and Orsini had transferred their quarrels to that ancient Etruscan hill-town, and the conclave came to nothing. The Church was growing sick and tired of the whole business.

Suddenly the crowd which awaited the great news saw three cardinals emerge from the palace. With a retinue of clergy and men at arms they reached the city gate and took the mountain road. Where were they going? The truth was quickly known. Somewhere in the *maquis* of Abruzzi, on the side of Mt Majella, there lived an old hermit, one Peter Morone, the eleventh child of a peasant family. As a youth he had joined the Order of St Benedict and had afterwards co-operated with a few friends in establishing the 'Celestines,' a new branch of the great Benedictine tree, devoted mainly to contemplation. He was now eighty years old, and had spent most of his life in a wretched hovel that was partly a cave, living on herbs and water, clothed in a plain homespun tunic. It was said that our Lord had visited him in ecstasy. At all events, he was pure of heart; in fact he was a saint.

The eleven cardinals had, let us say, a somewhat different view of life. What, then, persuaded them to seek out this man and offer him the tiara? We cannot be certain: ambiguous and contradictory motives were at work. Each of the opposing factions may have believed that they could manœuvre this gentle old man to suit their own ends. Or the conclave may have been influenced by fear of wrath and chastisement: the people's indignation was all too clear; maybe the ire of God also, for it was rumoured that the hermit of Mt Majella had had a terrible vision in which he saw those eleven guilty men burning in hell.   Nor can we rule out the voice of conscience which was still so strong that even prelate-politicians could not fail to hear it.   A thousand voices gave utterance to Christendom's longing for a just and holy leader, for that 'angelic pastor' of whom Roger Bacon had spoken, for that 'evangelical pope' whose coming had been eagerly awaited since Joachim of Flora dreamed his dreams.   Who could better fulfil those dreams than the holy ascetic of Abruzzi?

So it was that on 27th July 1294 an extraordinary procession entered the little town of Aquila.   Cardinals, bishops, and a swarm of lesser clergy escorted a rather shabby old man who rode upon a donkey, his eyes closed, absorbed in prayer.   Charles II of Anjou and his son Charles Martel, who had recently been crowned King of Hungary, held the bridle.   More than 20,000 onlookers shouted their approval and spread garments or branches in the way, just as another crowd had done one Sunday morning centuries before.   It seemed that a new chapter of history was about to open, that Sanctity incarnate would direct the affairs of Earth.   The *Eternal Gospel* was read by thousands, and there was much talk of an era in which the Holy Spirit would govern the world.   Now, surely, that era had begun.

As things turned out, however, this odd pontificate was a farce. No sooner had he been crowned as Celestine V than the poor old hermit became the plaything of political forces, a fact which he was too simple-hearted to realize.   Under pretext of assuring his safety, Charles II invited him to reside at Naples and promised to provide him with a cell just like the one on Mt Majella.   Actually, of course, the Capetian intended to use him as a means towards the subjugation of Sicily.[1] What could the holy pontiff have done in these circumstances?   'What will you do, Peter Morone?' asks the Franciscan poet Jacopone da Todi.   'You are put to the proof, and we shall see the work for which a life of contemplation has prepared you.   If you disappoint the world's hopes, a curse will follow.'

Alas! poor Celestine was virtually in chains, and for all his sim-plicity he could not fail to understand his situation.   Dread was mingled with regret for his beloved solitude, dread of damnation; and his remorse was stimulated by Cardinal Benedict Gaetani, an intelli-gent and strong-willed character, a realist who did not believe it possible to save the Church by appointing a mere figurehead to govern her.   At the saint's dictation—so, at least, he assures us—he drew up a grandly worded petition whereby the Pope humbly begged the Sacred College to give him a successor.   On 13th December 1294, arrayed in full pontificals, Celestine V read this document before a huge congrega-tion.   Then he descended from his throne, stripped himself of his insignia, laid aside the tiara and Fisherman's ring, and seated himself

[1] See Chapter V, section 8.

upon the ground like a beggar. 'You flee this place which wise men and fools alike desire to attain!' cried Cardinal Matteo Orsini.

Eleven days later, on 24th December, the conclave met at Naples and elected Benedict Gaetani, who took the name of Boniface VIII. As for Celestine—'the coward of the great refusal,' as Dante unjustly calls him—he wished to return to his mountain, but was not allowed to do so. Boniface VIII was not going to risk the factions making use of him. He was likewise prevented from taking ship for Greece, and a narrow cell in the castle of Fumone was assigned to the unfortunate hermit who was freed by death in 1296. He was canonized by Clement V in 1313, when he was no longer an embarrassment.

2. UNREST

This strange episode, in which genuinely spiritual ambitions were inextricably bound up with obvious intrigues, is evidence of the crisis which imperilled Europe towards the end of the thirteenth century. This crisis was to grow greater from year to year until, about 1350, the very foundations of Christendom were falling into dust. But the Church had already survived numerous crises; why, then, should this one prove more serious, so serious, in fact, that it marked the closing of an epoch?

The truth is that men could no longer feel sure of anything. Perhaps, also, the Church was tired by her efforts to maintain and even to strengthen her hold upon the West; maybe she had exhausted her vitality in so many noble enterprises. At all events, it was clear in every domain that the inner urge was no longer what it had been; there was less flame, less fervour. A man had only to look around him to see that.

First, the popes succeeded one another too quickly to be of much effect. The Holy See was often vacant for disturbingly long periods (a total of ten years between 1241 and 1305), and the papacy itself was soon to leave Rome for Avignon. Even the crusades were a thing of the past; oceans of blood had been shed, but the Holy Sepulchre was still in infidel hands, and Acre had fallen in 1291. The energy of the cathedral-builders was beginning to flag. Workshops remained open and splendid edifices were nearing completion; but there was no longer the enthusiasm of those days when volunteers from all classes used to lend a hand carrying stones, and when collectors for the building funds were welcome everywhere. The missions still bore witness to the imperishable life of Christianity, and were even at that time penetrating the most inaccessible regions of Africa and Asia; but this great work was almost unknown to the general public.

There was an even greater peril. The force of human gravity was once again at work: the Christian lump had once more lost its leaven, and the clergy were returning to their old ways. True, results had been achieved on which there was no going back. There were no more married priests; but since the clergy were too few and were, perforce, recruited from a society whose own morals tended to grow lax, many of them gave scandal by their indifference. Negligence in the fulfilment of duty was another widespread evil: there was too much nepotism in the appointment of bishops, there were too many prebendal canons, too many absentee parish priests who seldom said Mass. When a prince of the Church possessed four or five bishoprics and three or four abbeys, it was difficult to see how he could have the spiritual interests of all his flock at heart.

Herein lay the real danger. Love of lucre was the gangrene of the clergy. It was the characteristic vice of that age, one which the great city merchants had raised to the dignity of a principle, and which penetrated all classes of society, not excepting the papal palace. The same greed for money was found among the higher clergy, too many of whom seemed bent on chasing benefices, one cardinal being said to possess no fewer than twenty-three. And so on down to the bottom of the scale, where a proletariat of vicars, etc., was also consumed with the leprosy of gain, because it was so poor and had to fight over crumbs fallen from the tables of the great.

There is abundant evidence of this clerical rapacity. We have Jacopone da Todi addressing Celestine V: 'Mistrust beneficiaries ever thirsty for prebends; their thirst no beverage can assuage!' We have Dante hurling this rebuke at the popes of his time: 'You have made yourself a god of gold and silver; what difference is there between you and the idolater, except that he adores one god and you a hundred?' (*Inferno*, xix. 112.) Again, we hear Cardinal Jean le Moyne pass this stern judgment on the prelates: 'To-day, none of them, or alas! very few, bother to lead their flocks to pasture. On the contrary, all think of shearing or milking them; they care for the wool and the milk, but not for the sheep.' These unhappy truths find ironical echo in popular fable and in the *Roman de Renart*.

Worst of all, the same crisis affected the religious Orders which had so courageously rescued the Church at the beginning of the thirteenth century. When Jacopone da Todi wrote: 'O little-cherished poverty, few men have espoused thee to the point of renouncing a proffered bishopric,' every one of his Franciscan brethren knew exactly what he meant. The ideal of poverty was withering away, and religious found themselves caught up by force of circumstances in worldly affairs. The stream of vocations, too, gradually dried up until about 1350, when the situation became grave. More disastrous yet was the crisis of authority. The affair of the Franciscan 'Spirituals' is perhaps the most

striking example, but it existed in most Orders, notably the Premonstratensians, whose members 'exempted' themselves from obedience
to their superiors. The success of the great Orders exposed them to
the temptation of riches, against which the Poverello had had to fight.
There were too many fine convents, too many monastic churches
which sought to emulate the magnificence of the more splendid parish-
churches and cathedrals; while the most bitter rivalry existed in this
connection not only between one Order and another, but even between
different houses of the same congregation. Besides, the prestige of
the monks themselves had reached a very low ebb, as appears from
the criticism of a publicist named Pierre Dubois who wrote at the
beginning of the fourteenth century.

The situation may be summed up as follows. For centuries the
Church had been responsible for the culture of Christendom; but
she herself was now in danger of being swallowed up by this profane,
money-ridden civilization, as she had almost been engulfed by feudalism
before the Gregorian reform. The equilibrium had been broken
between the creative effort of civilization and the Christian ideal of
renouncing Earth for Heaven. A reform was therefore indispensable,
and the best minds said as much. Thus, William le Maire of Angers:
'The Church must be reformed entirely, in her head as well as in her
members.' So too William Durand, Bishop of Mende, writing in
1311: 'If this most necessary reform is not accomplished, things will
go from bad to worse, and all this evil will be imputed to the Holy
Father, to his cardinals, and to his council.' Such appeals were soon
to find thunderous echo in the inspired voice of St Catherine of Siena.
Reform was needed, but was it possible?

This crisis within the Church had serious consequences, for it
brought about general unrest, a ferment analogous to those which
occur in decomposing liquids. Old errors reappeared all over
Europe without any contact between the various groups responsible
for them. The Brothers of the Free Spirit were not dead; they
reawoke in Germany, Italy, and elsewhere, as did the minor heretical
sects of Turlupins, Adamites, etc. 'Every married woman who does
not weep for her lost virginity will be damned,' said some. 'There
are two pernicious words, "mine" and "thine"; they must be suppressed,' affirmed others, who advocated an integral communism.
The *Begards*,[1] a group once characterized by genuine piety, now

[1] The little-known *Begard* movement, with its female branch of *Béguines*, was certainly
widespread in the Middle Ages and tended to heresy late in its long history. About the
end of the twelfth century there appeared in the Low Countries communities of women,
half secular, half religious, whose members took a vow of chastity, devoted themselves to
prayer and nursing the sick, wore a grey habit, but were free to leave the association.
They were called *Béguines*, whence, probably, our word 'bigot.' The movement spread
to France, Germany, and Italy. Men followed their example and were called *Béguins* or

consisted of hotheads who went about crying '*Brod durch Gott!*' and the Waldenses, whom the Inquisition had failed to stamp out, emerged once more from their Alpine valleys. Among new heresies that sprang up at this time were the Apostolic Brethren, founded by an unfrocked Franciscan named Segarelli who denounced the Church as the 'lair of Satan, the den of demon Money,' and foretold its approaching doom. These people infested a wide area in the neighbourhood of Parma. Their founder was arrested and burned, together with his most fervent disciples; but the movement continued under the direction of Fra Dolcino, and did so much harm in the province of Vercelli that the bishop mounted a regular crusade which only achieved its purpose in 1307, after two years of armed conflict.

These symptoms were alarming, for the doctrinal errors which underlay them clearly supplied a spiritual need. Many good Christians asked themselves whether the ills afflicting Christendom were not portents; whether they did not herald chastisement; whether the Church as a temporal institution had not betrayed her trust; whether it might not be necessary to build another and purer society, nearer to God, in which the Holy Ghost would rule the world not through a clerical hierarchy, but directly, by the immediate attraction of His law. A whole world of more or less apocalyptic dreams drank at these sources which intoxicated weaker spirits, and for these latter Joachim of Flora was an inexhaustible well-spring.

It will be remembered [1] that Joachim was an honest and pious Cistercian who had given proof of the highest virtue, but had far too vivid an imagination together with a dangerous leaning towards illuminism. Many of his contemporaries regarded him as a saint and made much of his theories, although the fourth Lateran Council had condemned his views on the Trinity. His prophecies, however, had not been condemned. In accordance with his tripartite theory of man's history, he announced that the revelation of the Father and of the Son would be followed by the final revelation of the Holy Ghost. Then everything would be perfect, every blot on human nature would

---

Begards. Their way of life was bound by no hard and fast rules; some gave themselves to manual labour, others to begging. The Church called them 'Continents.' Some communities affiliated with the Third Orders of St Dominic and St Francis for purposes of spiritual direction. But at the end of the thirteenth century they turned towards the Franciscan 'Spirituals' in Southern France and Italy, while in the Rhineland they were soon contaminated by the pantheistic doctrines of the Brothers of the Free Spirit. In 1311 the Council of Vienne ordered the suppression of all communities of Begards and Béguines. But ten years later inquiries carried out chiefly by the Belgian bishops had rehabilitated most of the Béguine communities, and John XXII confined himself to the abolition of those communities which had been won over to heretical ideas. Béguines and Begards continued to flourish during the fourteenth and fifteenth centuries. But they were not free from heretical contagion, and the Church kept a watchful eye upon them.

[1] See Chapter IV, section 6.

disappear, and the precepts of the *Eternal Gospel* would be accomplished. With curious precision, Joachim named the year 1260 as the beginning of the Third Person's reign, which would last until the end of the world.

These ideas, which very properly involved the obligation to do penance, became known throughout Christendom; and since they helped to encourage reform, the authorities had done nothing to oppose them. But in the prophetic year, 1260, they were taken up once more and amplified by certain Franciscans who called themselves 'Spirituals.' We have already seen that in the lifetime of St Francis, and even more so after his death, the question arose as to whether an enormous congregation could continue to live in that state of sublime anarchy which was the ideal of its founder. Surely the Rule required adaptation. This had been done, but there was still a tendency in the Order to demand a strict application of the Rule, a craving on the part of the 'Spirituals' for total renunciation and heroic poverty. Their principal spokesman in the mid-thirteenth century was Gerard of Borgo San Donnino, who not only pushed these ideas to their logical conclusion, denouncing any and every kind of ownership on the part of religious, but also produced a strange medley of themes derived both from the Franciscans and from Joachim of Flora. In a work entitled *Introduction to the Eternal Gospel*, he announced that the third age of humanity would be that of St Francis, that the Poverello was 'the angel of the sixth seal' mentioned in the Apocalypse, and that they, the Franciscan 'Spirituals,' would soon rule the whole earth and establish the kingdom of God therein.

Although Alexander IV had condemned these follies in 1255, and although St Bonaventure had done his best to keep the Order on a middle course, the 'Spirituals' continued to make headway. Their leaders were Peter John Olive in Languedoc, Ubertino da Casale in Tuscany, and Angelo Clarens in the March of Ancona. Celestine V authorized the 'Spirituals' to form a distinct branch of the Franciscan Order, but Boniface VIII revoked the permission and bade them return immediately to the fold. A great number refused to do so, and a remarkable surge of enthusiasm now took hold of the 'Spirituals' (henceforth known contemptuously as *fraticelli*). It was translated into sublime and vehement poetry by Jacopone da Todi, but the sincere and generous aspiration of the 'Spirituals' towards a purer form of Christianity led to deplorable rebellion and gave rise to some intolerable insults against the Church. Worse still, in their conflict with the papacy, these 'Spirituals' took side with the Colonna against Boniface VIII, and later with Louis of Bavaria against John XXII.

Treated henceforth as rebels and heretics, the 'Spirituals' came under the notice of the Inquisition, and those of Ancona were condemned, notwithstanding the real holiness of many of their number. When the minister-general, Gaufredi, read the verdict, he murmured: 'Would that we were all guilty of this crime'; but it was surely not for love of poverty that they had been censured. The Tuscan 'Spirituals' were next on the list; but the most serious episode of the whole affair took place in Languedoc, where the *fraticelli* were badly tainted with Catharism. In 1316 and the following year mass trials were held at Narbonne, Béziers, and Marseilles, among the most illustrious victims of which was a Franciscan named Bernard Délicieux. Before being sentenced to imprisonment for life he openly criticized the Inquisition, and several of his brethren were burned.

The movement, however, did not entirely die out. Moving farther and farther away from the established Church, whose destruction by Heaven they continually invoked, the 'Spirituals' reappeared in several guises during the early fourteenth century. From them descended the Lombards, a sect founded in 1322 on the Rhine by a Dutchman, one Lollard Walter, who was arrested and burned. They were still a living force when Protestantism first emerged.

The 'Spirituals,' however, were not entirely harmful to the Church. Even within the Order of St Francis there were holy souls who tried to practise their ideals without embracing their errors. Thus, about 1334, John da Valle and, above all, Blessed Paoluccio of Trinci, initiated the *Observance* movement which sixty years later received a powerful impulse from St Bernardine of Siena. In a more general way too the movement brought about a mystical revival, the importance of which we shall presently see. All the same, the trouble was deep-rooted and showed to what extent the soul of Christendom was disturbed. The situation was extremely dangerous, for it coincided with an intellectual ferment.

3. THE INTELLECTUAL CRISIS

For the immediate cause of this crisis we must look to the history of culture and to the Church's part therein. We have seen that 'Mother Church,' as guide of man's intelligence, had taught her children to reflect, to wrestle with the great problems, and to construct philosophical systems. But in course of time she suffered the fate of most teachers, who see their pupils, on reaching adult age, take wing and fly in a direction opposite to that which they have been advised to follow.[1] Reason, which the Church had taught men how to use, tended to rebel against those very principles in whose service it had formerly been most loyal. Jurisprudence, which the Church had done much to revive,

---

[1] This has been emphasized several times in the course of Chapter VIII. 'My best pupil,' Renan used to say, 'is the one who first leaves go of my hand.'

claimed independence of ecclesiastical authority. There was thus a noticeable atmosphere of rebellion in every department of thought, even when the externals of obedience continued to be observed. And many new forces helped to thicken that atmosphere: bourgeois pride took advantage of increasing wealth, while the young monarchies, in pursuit of their ambitions, disliked ecclesiastical tutelage.

Unfortunately, at the beginning of the fourteenth century, the Church had no one to locate the danger-spots, to demolish the theories of her opponents, and to integrate what good they possessed in a new Christian synthesis. There was sore need of another Aquinas, but he was not forthcoming. Theology, once mistress of the sciences, was in a state which one scholar [1] has described as 'general decadence.' Philosophy and theology were still taught in the universities, but with nothing like the mastery of a former epoch. The various schools— Albertism, Thomism, and Scotism—continued on their several ways, but their systems had become mere dogmatism, employing set formulae by way of argument. Among the Thomists, who represented the most complete body of doctrine, there was no first-rate scholar apart from Hervé de Nédellec. Too many schoolmen were outmoded fanatics, so convinced that their predecessors had said all that was to be said that they dared not add one jot or tittle of their own, but confined themselves to the development of secondary matters and to the exhibition of their personal erudition and dialectical virtuosity. The advantage was now with those who, though professing Christianity, had ceased to derive inspiration from Christian principles and sought answers to the major problems outside the framework of revealed truth.

Men were digging into new positions which would be those of the 'modern world.' Hitherto it had been universally admitted that intellectual effort must be subject to superior control and directed to a single supreme end—the knowledge of God. Opinions might differ as to the means, especially as to the part played by reason; but the principles were firmly established, and all the cultural sciences sheltered behind theological walls. Meanwhile, inside this noble edifice, there had been minds at work—often unconsciously—destroying its foundations. Duns Scotus by insisting on the intuitive and mystical elements of knowledge at the expense of reason, and Roger Bacon by investigating more deeply than any of his predecessors the role of criticism in research,[2] had both helped to upset the balance between reason and faith. Durand of St Pourçain, Bishop of Puy and then of Meaux, was almost a rationalist. The life of thought was called in question as never before. Can the intellect lay hold upon reality? What is the value of reasoning? Is faith truly the *alpha* and *omega* of intellectual

---

[1] Fr Cayré in his well-known manual of Patrology.
[2] On Duns Scotus, *see* Chapter VIII, section 9; on Roger Bacon, ibid., section 11.

effort? Is there no conflict between revealed truth and science? Such questions as these were causing uneasiness in the minds of men at the end of the thirteenth century. But so far from confining themselves to destructive criticism, the most eminent thinkers were trying to leave it behind and to create a general theory of knowledge.

Among all these followers of the *via moderna* (a phrase then coming into use), the most remarkable was William of Occam (1298–1349), an English Franciscan, first a student and then professor in the University of Oxford. His abnormally penetrating mind was endowed with an insatiable thirst for knowledge; his intellect approached genius in the fields of both analysis and synthesis. But he lacked the sense of discipline, of permanence. His work lay in questioning everything. This profound thinker, who was on more or less friendly terms with the 'Spirituals' and sided with Louis of Bavaria against the Holy See, acted as a solvent, so to speak, upon every subject with which he came in contact. Although he usually took care to disguise his thought in the ambiguous garb of dialogue, his ideas were censured by the papacy; but he was not to be deterred. What were these theories? Occam had been educated on the principles of Duns Scotus, many of which he quickly repudiated but exaggerated those which he retained. Powerfully influenced, likewise, by other Oxford professors who were devotees of physical science and mathematics, he argued that nothing could serve as a foundation of knowledge except the evidence of sense and what followed necessarily therefrom. Hence the concrete, the singular, the individual, must take precedence of general ideas, classes, and universals, which are only verbal signposts. His empiricism tended to destroy the whole of traditional metaphysics by depriving it of its proper object, the universal. According to Occam, it was impossible to demonstrate either the spiritual nature of the soul or the existence of God. Morality depended entirely on the will of man, which must not allow itself to be influenced by concepts which have no foundation in reality. Christianity was thereby reduced to a mere shadow. Nevertheless, Occam posed as a true Christian; he claimed to reach by faith all those truths which were inaccessible to his philosophical and theological system; a supernatural theology, unrelated to intellectual activity, explained everything by the will of God. On the one hand, therefore, he propounded an absolute empiricism closely akin to modern existentialism; on the other hand, fideism. How far removed from the splendid syntheses of an earlier age!

Occam's influence was considerable. It might have been said that the Christian intellect now experienced a kind of malicious pleasure in rejecting all those things whereby it had hitherto lived and had its being. Oxford was naturally Occamist, and the Englishman's theories were introduced to Paris by Jean Buridan (*d.* 1358), rector of the Sorbonne. The religious Orders were also involved, and repeated condemnations were of no avail. Occam's theses, especially the application of his principles to the theology of the sacraments and of the Church, reappeared in systems more clearly heretical, e.g. that of his compatriot John Wyclif (c. 1320–84), a forerunner of the Protestant Reformation. John Huss gave them new life, and Luther proclaimed himself an Occamist.

Notwithstanding the harm done to faith by this current of thought, there can be no doubt that its consequences were largely beneficial to the intellectual progress of mankind; it fertilized the sciences by freeing them from subjection to ecclesiastical authority. Bacon and Occam taught men to observe, to experiment, and to exclude philosophical prejudice from research. Their teaching, in fact, initiated a great period of scientific discovery. Buridan, who studied the mechanical theories of Aristotle, set modern physics on its feet, and came near to solving the problem of weight. Twenty years later Bishop Albert of Saxe, followed by Nicolas Oresme, Bishop of Lisieux, went farther in this direction, heralding the science of modern astronomy and even that of analytical geometry; while natural history and geography received fresh impulse from the narratives of Marco Polo and other travellers.

Like all great human crises, this spiritual upheaval brought with it creative opportunities no less than grave perils. The same is true in the realm of art. Few masterpieces were produced. Inspiration was affected. Artists began to show a certain tendency towards artificiality, towards affectation, and, before long, towards over-elaboration. Architecture led the way, and those magnificent buildings, in which wealth of ornament could not detract from their essential unity and simplicity, gave place to the 'flamboyant,' to virtuosity for its own sake, and even to vulgarity. Architects were determined to exhibit their impeccable technique at all costs, in and out of season. Hence those dreary constructions, not unlike geometrical diagrams, launched into the air with an abundance of curves and counter-curves, heavily ornamented porches and windows, balustrades and towers.

Those arts which had been, so to speak, the pupils of architecture began to strike out on their own. Sculptors, as masters of their particular craft, were not prepared to go on playing second fiddle to the masons. Instead of confining themselves to work on the cathedrals, they would supply the wants of private clients who were building fine town residences and sumptuous tombs. Painters turned their backs on the walls of churches in favour of the easel; besides, they now looked for inspiration to the real and picturesque instead of to mere size or to the mystic urge.

This 'laicization' of thought was responsible for a phenomenon of capital importance—the revival of Roman Law. We have seen [1] how the Church, in her universities or at least through the work of her professors, rescued the ancient legal treatises from oblivion. Bologna was the chief centre of these studies. But the revival entailed serious risks, similar to those encountered in other fields. While Canon Law was founded on divine ordinances and ecclesiastical tradition, Roman Law claimed to be sufficient unto itself and quite independent of Scripture. The Bolognese professor Accorso (*d.* 1260) made this perfectly clear; nor was it long before the whole field of jurisprudence ceased to be watered by the Gospel stream. Take the case of marriage. To the notion of a sacrament involving the free consent of two persons for the realization of their end there was added ('substituted' might be a better word) the purely human notion of a contract entailing material stipulations. And this same laicization had dire consequences in yet another sphere, that of the Church' relation with the civil power. When the jurists endeavoured to substitute their own principles, or rather those of the Roman Empire, for the only principles which Christendom then considered valid, there was a violent upheaval which brought the Church into collision with new forces on the flood-tide of their development.

4. The Destruction of Christian Unity

The political crisis was to some extent determined, and undoubtedly aggravated, by the rupture which now became apparent in the unity of Christendom itself. The intellectual crisis meant death to that vigorous organic unity with its rigid hierarchies and orderly methods so familiar to the medieval mind. By abandoning its former principles it tended to fall apart. [2]

The splendid picture of a united intellectual society traversed from end to end of Christendom by vital currents—in which there was constant and fruitful interchange of men and ideas, in which Latin, the liturgical language, served as an international vehicle of thought; this picture, which for three centuries had represented actual fact, was now fast fading, though there was evidence that the state of affairs it represented had not entirely ceased to be. Jerome of Prague, for instance, passed from the university of his native city to those of Paris, Oxford, Cologne, and Heidelberg, to continue his education in Hungary,

[1] Chapter VIII, section 10.

[2] It is true that, even when the spiritual unity lay in ruins, there was still a measure of cultural unity whose secret, however, was soon to be found in the rediscovery of antiquity rather than in Christian tradition. The work of recovering the great classics, begun towards the end of the twelfth century, was still in progress at the beginning of the fourteenth and assumed the character of a campaign against the 'barbarian products' of the Middle Ages; it was regarded as such by Petrarch (1304–74), a champion of Latin literature. But even this cultural unity was already threatened from every direction.

Austria, Poland, and even Lithuania.   Again, oil-painting, which was to have so distinguished a history, preserved a manifestly international character.   What had vanished was that splendid geographical unity of intellect in which all the great centres played their appointed parts and acted one upon another as do the elements of harmony.

One highly significant event was the rapid failure of Paris University, whose star was declining even while it continued to attract such minds as that of Master Eckhart.   There were disturbing rumours about the value of its degrees.   Above all, it could no longer claim pre-eminence; the Quartier Latin was no longer the sole nursery of fashionable ideas and revolutionary theories.   Oxford, with Bacon, Duns Scotus, and Occam, was no less illustrious.   The University of Prague, established in 1348, would soon take pride of place in central Europe; Coimbra and Salamanca in the Iberian Peninsula were flourishing as never before; and the weakening of Paris became still more marked when the Hundred Years War destroyed the political ascendancy which France had held for twenty decades.

The bonds of intellectual unity were slackened in yet another way. Throughout the Middle Ages its representatives had been drawn almost exclusively from among the clergy.   It is true to say that every thinker of importance between 1050 and about 1300 was either a priest or a monk.   With the fourteenth century a change set in, very gradually at first but with mounting impetus.   Laymen (middle-class folk for the most part) entered the field of intellect, and Buridan was the first Rector of Paris who was not a cleric.   Non-specialist works of all kinds, including theological treatises, were now written for the use of educated laymen.   The whole perspective was undergoing a slow but fundamental transformation.

Another phenomenon of 'laicization' was the definite emergence of national languages.   Since the middle of the thirteenth century Latin had had to compete with vernacular, which became more and more prominent as if in obedience to some natural law working from within. Even those who, like Dante, regretted that the language of Virgil was no longer the living symbol of Western unity helped to supersede it. German continued to gain ground in Teutonic countries, and Old German was the language used in the Great Saxon Chronicle of 1248. In France, the chronicles of Villehardouin and Joinville had shown the fine literary use that could be made of a language described by Bernardo Latini as 'the most delectable.'   Fabliaux, the Roman de la Rose, the Roman de Renart, and other works bore witness likewise to the vitality of French.   The first official document written in English was the proclamation of Henry III in 1258.   In Spain, from 1150 onwards, many royal texts were drawn up in Spanish, which was used almost exclusively by about 1300.   At the beginning of the fourteenth century

T

vernacular seemed firmly entrenched everywhere. Nicolas Oresme would soon be writing in French, Lopez de Ayala in Spanish, and the mystic Ruysbroek in Dutch.

This linguistic revolution was the symbol of another, more fundamental and of graver consequence—the awakening of nationalism. Having subdued the feudal nobility, the kings endeavoured to build powerful states resting securely on national consciousness; while the commercial rivalry of trading groups was often attended with violence, and no less frequently extended beyond their own frontiers. Many causes, some less worthy than others, helped to remind the various peoples of their individual characteristics, of their common interests, and of their common loyalties. This partitioning, which was not merely political but also cultural and even religious, threatened Europe and would soon tear her to pieces.

Thus, on the threshold of the fourteenth century, Christendom found herself prey to the forces of disruption. It seemed she must be overwhelmed by her own betrayals and by the enemy from without. So thought many clear-headed observers. In a book written about 1308–13 on the fall of the Roman Empire, in which he took a peep into the future, Abbot Engelbert of Admont distinguished three kinds of 'secession' according to the thought of St Paul (2 Thess. ii. 3): the mind without faith; the Christian community severed from the Holy See; and the kingdoms rejecting the old order of unity to follow each its own way in isolation. These symptoms appeared to him as heralds of antichrist, of the end of the world. It was in truth the end of *a* world.

5.   THE STRUGGLE FOR PRIMACY: BONIFACE VIII

Only in this setting is it possible to understand the fresh struggle now joined between the papacy and the secular powers on the twofold level of ideology and politics. The *casus belli* was nothing new, for the whole medieval period had been loud with the clamour of this debate as to the primacy.[1]   The fundamental idea upon which the popes had insisted was, in substance, this: Because the end of society is the kingdom of God, and because the criterion of all human activity is the Word of God, therefore the Pope, as Vicar of Christ, enjoys a legal right of control over those who have been entrusted with the government of men. But was this right limited to the spiritual domain? Did it not also extend in some measure to the temporal sphere in which the secular powers ignore the commandments of God and the superior interests of the Church? The theory of 'Two Swords' had led to some confusion between the two orders, and Innocent III had not

[1] Chapter V, section 5.

hesitated to write: 'The Church's liberty is nowhere better assured than in those places where she enjoys full power as well in temporal as in spiritual matters.' At the Council of Lyons, in 1245, Innocent IV had proclaimed that Christ, true King and true Priest according to the order of Melchisedech, had transmitted His kingship *as well as* His priesthood to Peter and his successors, who merely delegated part of their authority to temporal sovereigns. The canonist Henry of Susa repeated this doctrine in his *Summa Aurea*.

So far, in the course of this dispute, the Holy See had been opposed by none except the emperors; and, since the fall of the Hohenstaufen, the imperial crown of Germany could no longer be considered a particularly dangerous rival. The situation altered with the emergence of the western monarchies. Their kings had muzzled the nobility, and had established their authority over town and country alike; the national clergy were their allies; and the civilizing functions of the Church were now claimed by the State. The State, or rather its servants, an educated group of laymen, were more or less jealous of the Church; for the triumph of the State meant their own personal success. These new kingdoms, the most powerful and advanced among which was France, had no wish to dominate the whole of Christendom, but were determined to exercise a perfectly free hand within their own frontiers. Their leaders considered themselves sufficiently grown up to stand on their own legs independently of Mother Church.

A new theory was therefore evolved, founded at once on Scripture and on Roman Law. Power was said to be held *directly* from God, not transmitted through the Pope; and the notion of an all-powerful state was borrowed from the ancient world. These ideas became current through several channels. They were first formulated by some theologians at Paris who had resolved to oppose the Roman Curia, and a small work entitled *Questio in utramque partem*, written about 1260, affirmed with a wealth of argument that the King of France was in no way dependent on the papacy. Another pamphlet asserted that 'before there were any clergy there was a king of France who had the care of his realm and could make laws.' Not long after this, an eminent Dominican at Paris, one Jean Quidort, maintained that the State is founded upon natural law; that it can reach its objective without Christian government by applying the dictates of reason and elementary morality; and that the Church's business is with man's supernatural end. Quidort went still further and asked whether the Christian people might not take a direct share in the conduct of ecclesiastical affairs, and whether the people's sovereignty is not the basis of all power, even clerical! Questions such as these were a favourite topic of discussion at the beginning of the fourteenth century, and they were given a strong polemical tone in a little book called

Dispute between a cleric and a soldier, which argued that 'the king is above the laws, customs, and liberties; he is responsible to God alone.' Peter Dubois, a clever but muddle-headed thinker, developed similar ideas, and went so far as to claim that the Church should be governed by the State, because only the State can effect the necessary reform. More important, these theories were adopted by professional lawyers and royal counsellors, who embodied them in formulae borrowed from Roman Law, which, of its very nature, ignored the rights of the Church. Philip the Fair's ministers Peter Flotte and William de Nogaret, the first lawyers to become Chancellors, were both professors of Roman jurisprudence.

The papacy defended itself against these adversaries who sought to undermine its authority and to deny it all right of action outside the purely spiritual domain. Advocates of papal power replied to those who upheld the State's omnipotence, and the debate became increasingly acrimonious. Giles of Rome wrote as follows: 'No one can in full justice hold a field or a vineyard from anyone at all except in submission to the Church and through the Church.' The more cautious and moderate James of Viterbo recognized natural law as the basis of secular power, but claimed that this power had no value unless subject to spiritual authority, because the Church, as guardian of truth, has a plenitude of power (*plenitudo potestatis*) over all temporal rulers. Augusto Trionfo was even more outspoken: 'The Sovereign Pontiff himself does not know the extent of his supreme authority.' Above all, there was Alvarez Pelayo, a Spanish Franciscan, who formulated these theses most explicitly in his *De planctu ecclesiae* (1330): 'The Pope governs all, rules all, disposes of all, decides all at his discretion. He may deprive anyone of his rights as he sees fit. Every spiritual and every temporal thing is subject to the Church.' All these defenders of papal prerogatives undoubtedly intended to safeguard the spiritual authority; but they did not express themselves very well, nor could they escape from the social and political conditions of their age. Neither the Council of Trent nor Leo XIII made any such claims when they defined Catholic teaching on the pre-eminence of the Church.

Now it was all too easy to exploit certain kinds of language, and these attempts to bolster the Holy See's position suffered in consequence. The other camp produced a number of theorists who were infinitely more dangerous than their predecessors. Most formidable was Marsilius of Padua, whose book *Defender of the Peace* (1324) caused a great stir at the time when Pope John XXII was embroiled with Louis of Bavaria. In a remarkable synthesis, which included the earlier anti-papal arguments, he proposed a system of government according to which the Church would have no power except on the spiritual plane; authority would reside in the people, who would delegate it to someone of their own choice. This meant that general councils (in which laymen would take part), and not the Pope, were judges in matters of faith. Marsilius went on to deny that the Pope is St Peter's successor and that all priests enjoy the powers of Christ. This conception of the Church as a mere doctrine, as distinct from a society, tended to destroy the very foundations of Christendom; but though condemned, it continued to find favour. Occam's theory was more restrained, at least in its mode of expression. He recognized the Pope's primacy of jurisdiction in temporal affairs, but affirmed that the power of princes rested on natural law. In the event of conflict between the two powers, or in the event of papal authority running amok, the whole Church, i.e. the faithful as a single unit, would step in and heal the breach. Occam was, in effect, advocating those conciliar theories which assumed such importance in the second half of the fourteenth century.

The fact that theories of this kind were so widely supported is proof of a serious decline of papal authority and of a change in the idea of Christendom. The extent of this decadence was further emphasized by a series of grave political occurrences which coincided with the ideological debate. The protagonist and the victim of these events was Pope Boniface VIII [1] (1294–1303), the former Cardinal Benedict Gaetani who had succeeded Celestine V.

It is difficult to understand or to describe this man whose character was so complex and whose true outlines have been blurred by the venom of his adversaries. Descended from an aristocratic Spanish family, related to Innocent III, Gregory IX, and Alexander IV, Boniface was tall and stately. The purity of his morals cannot be doubted, notwithstanding assertions to the contrary. Determined and courageous, he was capable of noble fortitude in adversity; he was certainly more a man of action than a mystic. But he was by nature excitable, domineering, unsuited to diplomacy, and liable to ride roughshod over those who disagreed with him. He had a way of translating prudent thought into violent conduct. In his thirst for glory he overlooked the strength of those arrayed against his throne, forgetting that the days of Gregory VII and Innocent III were past.

Boniface VIII was about fifty years of age when he assumed responsibility for the Church. Crowned at Rome on 23rd January 1295, he let it be known by an unwonted pomp of ceremonial that he meant to have a great pontificate. Europe was in a sorry state. The 'Spirituals' were causing trouble with their whispers that Celestine's abdication was void and nullified the election of his successor. Hardly less

---

[1] For a more favourable picture of this pope than has hitherto been fashionable, *see* Gabriel Le Bras, 'Boniface VIII, symphoniste et modérateur,' in *Mélanges Halphen*, 1951, p. 383.

irksome was the King of Naples with his patronizing attitude towards the Holy See. At Rome the Colonna factions, led by two members of the Sacred College, were intriguing to such an extent that it later became necessary to depose both cardinals. The King of France had just adopted a financial policy that could not but damage the Church's interests. Even in Denmark, King Eric was persecuting the clergy. And as if these trials were not enough, Christendom was ravaged by fire and sword: France against England; Adolf of Nassau against Albert of Austria in Germany; in Italy, Genoa against Pisa, Pisa against Florence; Anjou disputing Sicily with Aragon; Guelphs and Ghibellines at daggers drawn everywhere.

It was soon apparent that the efforts of Boniface to restore peace were doomed to failure; but he still hoped to revive the prestige of the Church so that she might once more stand forth as arbiter of Europe. A serious attempt was made at moral reform by reorganizing the papal administration, as well as by insisting upon the rights of ecclesiastical jurisdiction which too many rulers tended to ignore. In order to consolidate and strengthen these measures, Boniface decided, as had his predecessor Innocent III, to summon a great council at Rome and to embody the principles of his activity in the celebrated Bull *Unam Sanctam* (1302). The more important formulae discoverable in this document are as follows: (1) There is only one Church, outside which there is no salvation. (2) The Church has only one Head, Christ, who has delegated His authority to His vicar, the successor of St Peter. (3) The Pope has two swords, one spiritual, the other temporal; the first is wielded by the Church, i.e. by the Pope, for the good of souls, the second is entrusted to kings, who may not use it except in the higher interests of Christianity and under the Pope's direction. (4) The temporal is subject to the spiritual, which may pass judgment upon it if it goes astray. Consequently (5) no one can be saved unless he willingly submits to the Pope. There was nothing new about this Bull, either in its form or in its content. It defined, for the first time and in dogmatic terms, the teaching which had been generally accepted from the days of St Bernard to those of St Thomas Aquinas. It made no reference to direct papal intervention in temporal affairs; it did not even condemn the thesis of a state founded upon natural law. In short, its terms were so restrained, so general, that modern theologians find no difficulty in reconciling it with their own teaching, and it continues to bind Catholics even in the altered climate of to-day.

But the circumstances in which the Bull was promulgated took the wind out of its sails. In the year 1300, following an ancient Jewish tradition, Boniface VIII proclaimed the whole succeeding twelve-month a period of special graces and remission of sin available to all those who visited Rome and prayed in the great basilicas. This first jubilee was a tremendous success;[1] crowds flocked to the Eternal City, and it seemed that all Christendom, recovered from its long sickness, was gathered around the Sovereign Pontiff. The Pope, however, may have observed that there was not one king among the pilgrims. Chroniclers tell us that on several occasions Boniface appeared in public wearing the imperial insignia and with two swords borne before him, while heralds cried: 'I am Caesar! I am the Emperor!' At all events, it was on this occasion that he fixed the design of the tiara. It was to be one ell in height, in memory of the standard used by Noah when he built the Ark of salvation. It was to be circular, like the macrocosm. In addition to the golden circlet and denticulation crowned with fleurs-de-lis, which already adorned the base, it was to have another diadem half-way from the summit to signify the two powers. In such a setting the Bull *Unam Sanctam* was bound to be looked upon as an instrument of papal imperialism. So, indeed, it was regarded in France, where five years previously a painful conflict had developed between the sovereign and the papacy.

6. PHILIP THE FAIR AND THE OUTRAGE OF ANAGNI

Philip IV (1285–1314), whose noble bearing and handsome features caused him to be named 'the Fair,' was in many respects, both physical and moral, very like his grandfather St Louis, whom he claimed to consider as his model. Nothing could be more unjust than to see him as another Frederick II; for he had a lively faith, attending Mass every day, wearing a hair-shirt, and taking the discipline. He was also recognized as charitable and kindly towards the poor. Beneath a calm exterior, however, lay a violent temperament, prone to icy wrath, of which pride was the moving principle. No one has ever decided the standard of his intelligence, whether he was the plaything of his entourage, or whether his ministers were mere pawns in his own complicated and daring game.

Be that as it may, he advanced a number of professional lawyers, in whose hands he appeared to leave the reins of government. These were Peter Flotte, William de Nogaret, and Enguerrand de Marigny, all of whom had been trained in the science of Roman Law, all of whom were of lower- or middle-class origin and fanatical servants of the State. Their motto was, 'The Prince's good pleasure has the force of law.'

Now Boniface VIII underestimated the Capetian's strength. Former conflicts between the see of Peter and a number of crowned heads had terminated in Rome's favour; but the Pope should have realized that the kings of France, good Christians though they were, had no

[1] See Chapter II, section 10.

inclination—as had John 'Lackland,' for example—to allow the papacy to interfere with their administration.   Philip Augustus and even St Louis had made that fact perfectly clear.[1]   Still less, then, would a man like Philip IV be so disposed.

The first incident concerned a question of money.   By vote of the provincial synods, the king had obtained a tax of one-tenth of the revenues of the clergy.   A few malcontents complained to Rome, and Boniface VIII, breathing fire and brimstone, promulgated the Bull *Clericis laïcos* forbidding princes to demand and the clergy to pay taxes without permission of the Holy See, on pain of excommunication (February 1296).   Philip and his lawyers were angered by the offensive terms of this Bull, which was unsound in law since it failed to distinguish between royal contributions and those legally due from the clergy by virtue of their holding fiefs.   The reply was not long delayed.   In August 1296 two royal ordinances forbade (*a*) the export of money and precious objects without government permission, which dried up the stream of offerings to the Holy See, and (*b*) the unauthorized residence of aliens in France, which clearly affected papal legates, alms-collectors, and all those Italians who held benefices in the kingdom. Boniface protested indignantly in a second Bull, but could make no impression upon Philip.   Indeed, the French clergy assembled at Rheims wrote to the Pope asking him to revoke his Bull.   Rome now awoke to the danger.   The intrigues of the Colonna had reached such a point that Boniface had no wish to increase the number of his adversaries.   He gave way, toned down the provisions of *Clericis laïcos*, and even called upon the clergy of France to pay as required. This reconciliation was cemented by the canonization of St Louis on 11th April 1297.

Fundamentally, however, there had been no change.   The two opponents were keeping watch on one another.   Boniface VIII made no objection when the Flemings, who were at war with France, wrote him a letter in which these words occurred: 'You who are sovereign of the French kingdom in temporal as well as spiritual affairs'; and listened with satisfaction while a cardinal informed him from the pulpit of St John Lateran that he was the spiritual and temporal overlord of all overlords.   At about this time Philip received two legates who came to urge a truce with the King of England.   He told them that 'the temporal government of the kingdom belonged to himself alone, and in this matter he recognized no superior; in the spiritual domain, he was, like his predecessors, a true son of the Church.'   No one could have distinguished more clearly between the king and the private individual, between the function of the State and that of the Church.

But smoke was already rising from another fire.   In July 1295, for

[1] See Chapter V, section 10.

administrative reasons, Boniface had separated the district of Pamiers from Toulouse and made it an independent diocese. He had done so without consulting the King of France, which was not particularly diplomatic. Worse still, he had appointed to the new see an abbot named Bernard Saisset, whose anti-French sentiments were well known. Rumour said that the bishop was conspiring with the Counts of Foix and Comminges to detach the Pyrenean South from France, and also that he spoke of the king in abusive terms, calling him a coiner, a bastard, and a good many worse things besides. Intoxicated with the success of his Jubilee Year (1300), Boniface upheld Saisset. In July 1301, Philip had the bishop arrested and brought to Senlis; this was contrary to Canon Law, and the prisoner appealed to the Pope. The royal jurists sent a long indictment to Rome, accusing Saisset of every conceivable crime. They even charged him with teaching heretical doctrines and of insulting the Holy Father in public. He was certainly innocent of these two charges, and the very extravagance of the indictment made it worthless.

Boniface VIII replied with the Bull *Ausculta fili*, demanding the bishop's release and summoning the king to attend in person or by proxy a council to be held at Rome. The tone of this Bull was moderate, but the Pope touched a sore spot with these words: 'Those who assure you that you have no superior, and that you are not subject to the supreme hierarchy of the Church, are deceiving you; they are outside the fold of the Good Shepherd.' The lawyers were furious; and the chronicler tells us that the Bull was snatched from the legate by the Count of Artois as he was on the point of handing it to the king. The ministers took care that its contents should not become known in France. Instead, two apocryphal documents were circulated, couched in such arrogant terms that they could not but inflame public opinion against the Holy See, which was now subjected to a campaign of libels. Finally, Peter Flotte convoked an assembly at Rheims; it included all classes of the nation, even the Third Estate, and was the first meeting of what was afterwards known as the states general. Flotte's purpose was to strengthen his own hand against Rome; the clergy were embarrassed, but eventually sided with the king.

It was now a case of open warfare. Boniface VIII determined to stand fast to the bitter end, all the more so because Philip the Fair had just been defeated by the Flemings at Courtrai (July 1302), where Flotte and the Count of Artois had lost their lives. The Pope went so far as to declare in full Consistory: 'If the King of France does not behave himself properly I shall have the unpleasant duty to depose him like a little boy.' The council met at Rome a few weeks later. Notwithstanding opposition on the part of Philip's government, it was attended by four French archbishops, thirty-five bishops, and six

T*

abbots.   As stated above, the Bull *Unam Sanctam* was bound in the circumstances to appear as a manifesto of papal imperialism directed against the king.

Philip could not take this lying down; but his conduct, suggested by Nogaret, was abominable.   It was not sufficient to invoke feudal and natural law against the Pope; he must be denounced as unworthy to occupy the throne of Peter on account of his evil habits and unsound faith, and then summoned before a council which would depose him. In Italy the 'Spirituals' and the Colonna clique lent a willing hand. In France two assemblies were held during the spring of 1303, in which Nogaret, who was now chancellor, slandered the Pope at great length and begged the king to order the arrest of this false prophet, this simoniac, this blasphemer.   Boniface VIII tried to defend himself by calling upon the Aragonese in Sicily and Albert of Austria.   It was too late; his enemies had forestalled him.   The French people, deceived by the propaganda of the jurists, were solidly behind their king, who was supported by the Ghibellines in Italy; and even at the papal court the conspirators had accomplices among the cardinals.

The outrage was perpetrated by Nogaret himself and Sciarra Colonna.   On 7th September 1303 six hundred cavalry and 1,500 infantry attacked the little town of Anagni where Boniface had taken refuge.   The lilies of France were carried alongside the banner of St Peter, as if to show that France was fighting for the Church.   The troops marched on the castle and set fire to the doors of the cathedral, through which they gained entry to the precincts.   Then, while the soldiers gave themselves up to pillage, Nogaret and Sciarra hurried to the papal apartments.   Abandoned by all except two cardinals, the Pope awaited his aggressors.   Wearing liturgical vestments and the tiara, he knelt in prayer.   According to a very doubtful tradition, Sciarra struck him in the face; it was no more than a symbolic blow, but an atrocious insult all the same.   'Here is my neck, here is my head . . .' murmured Boniface.   Nogaret intervened and formally directed him to summon a council which would give him judgment. The Pope refused; whereupon he was informed that he was a prisoner in his own palace pending his removal to France.

Nogaret's plan, however, was frustrated.   While the troops were removing their spoils from Anagni, a faithful cardinal managed to rouse the populace; and the Frenchmen took to their heels followed by loud cries of 'Long live the Pope!   Death to the foreigners!'   Four hundred Roman knights escorted Boniface VIII back to the Eternal City; but the outrage had so overwhelmed the aged pontiff that he reached home a broken man, and died a month later on 11th October 1303.

This tragedy struck a mortal blow at the concept of Christendom. The old order, founded on the supremacy of the Church as arbiter no less in the temporal than in the spiritual domain, was extinguished by Nogaret. We may blame Boniface VIII for his intransigence and his blunders, but the truth is more grave. His mistake lay in wishing to remain a medieval pope like Innocent III at a time when a new conception of the world was emerging under the impulse of young, ambitious states. The papacy would henceforward have to reckon with this new ideology, not, of course, by abandoning her principles, but by applying them in other ways. An era of nationalism was beginning.

Benedict XI (1303–4) took immediate steps to reach an understanding with Philip, who was freed from excommunication, together with his ministers, excepting Nogaret. Clemency was shown even to Colonna, and the Bull *Clericis laïcos* was amended in favour of princes; but Benedict followed the example of his predecessor in refusing to summon a council. This was a fundamental issue, and he chose to leave Rome rather than to obey the factions. He died after a pontificate of eight months, and was so venerated by the people that the Church soon raised him to her altars. His death was said to have been due to indigestion brought on by eating figs; but there was talk of poison, and the villain of Anagni was not above suspicion. Three years later, another tragedy would show the world what to expect from 'reasons of state.'

7. The Drama of the Templars

The affair of the Templars began in 1305. One Esquieu de Floyran, a native of Béziers, approached certain members of the French king's council and laid before them a long list of accusations against the Order of the Temple. Nogaret pricked his ears: the Temple was rich, and that sufficed to interest him. Two years later, on 12th October 1307, the funeral of Charles de Valois's wife was attended by the Grand Master, who had no suspicion of what was to follow. Next day all the French Templars were arrested, and the royal police could congratulate themselves upon a famous haul.

There followed a sudden outburst of propaganda in which it was not hard to detect the lawyer's hand. Monstrous accusations were levelled at the knights. It was alleged that on the day of their initiation they spat upon the crucifix; that they adored idols; that they indulged in homosexual orgies; that they were shameless speculators and dishonest business men. This final charge was the only one founded upon fact. History has done justice to the others; there is not a shred of evidence in any shape or form to support them. How was it that the glorious militia, founded at the height of the crusades and under the aegis of St Bernard, had fallen so low? Had not the Templars given proof of their unsullied heroism at Acre twenty years before?

True, but the Order had already a somewhat shady reputation in most countries. Under careful administration throughout a period of two hundred years they had amassed enormous riches, and during the last crusades they had acted as heaven-sent bankers. After the loss of the Holy Land they had continued their financial operations, and many nobles, many traders, and even many states were in their debt. Few debtors love their creditors, and public opinion was prepared to back the jurists of Philip the Fair in their attack upon the Temple.

Each of these last crusades helped to widen the gulf between the Order and Western Chivalry. Worn out in the struggle against the Infidel, the Templars missed no opportunity to criticize the often absurd strategy of the crusaders; while the diplomatic relations which they had been led to establish with the Moslems roused suspicion of compromise and even of high treason. Another cause of complaint was their undeniable pride and their proneness to disobedience, for which they had been severely criticized by St Louis as well as by Frederick II. Finally, an aura of mystery with which they surrounded their rites and ceremonies—'through mere stupidity,' as one of them admitted—gave them the appearance of a secret society, thereby tending to confirm even the most obscene and unjustified of rumours. The king's police were in a very strong position.

Dumbfounded by their unexpected arrest, powerless in the face of legal intrigue, these warriors submitted to the worst humiliation. They were told that the Pope had abandoned them, that the king was their friend and had their best interests at heart; but in addition to Philip's agents they were confronted with a body of royal Inquisitors. What should, what could they do? Placed in the dilemma of having either to confess their guilt in order to obtain pardon, or else to be condemned to a hideous death, many of them, including the grand master Jacques de Molay, thought it best to plead guilty. This was exactly what the jurists were waiting for: these admissions would enable them to be rid of the Order once and for all.

But, as things turned out, the affair was prolonged for seven years. After their initial surprise, a number of the Templars retracted their confessions. The aged Pope Clement V, despite his failing health, made a vigorous protest against the royal proceedings, which had ignored the 'right of clergy,' and announced that he was taking the case into his own hands. He entrusted the investigation to the bishops and to a board of Inquisitors to be appointed by himself. The Order's ultimate fate would be decided by a council.

Since the ecclesiastical courts declined to use torture, all the accused now withdrew their confessions. Philip the Fair and his jurists were annoyed by this turn of events. The prolonged and scrupulous investigation did not suit them in the least; they wished for a spectacular trial on the grand scale, and therefore had recourse to the same means they had employed against Boniface VIII. An assembly of the states was convoked at Tours, where the king's representatives obtained a decree suppressing the Order. Thus armed, Nogaret brought pressure to bear upon the Pope, reminding him in no ambiguous terms of all that the French Crown had done for the Church, and, incidentally, that it would be useless for him to oppose the sovereign's will, 'unless he wished to hear a different language.' Clement V hesitated, as sick men invariably do, until, at a favourable moment, some of the knights were brought before him and repeated their confessions. Whereupon he directed the various governments to take immediate proceedings against the Temple.

Still the French government was not satisfied, for a succession of trials up and down Europe was slowly bringing truth to light. The heads of the Order were beginning to waver, but a fair number of members protested in open court the innocence of their brotherhood, while several horrified their judges with an account of the tortures under which they had been obliged to confess. A decisive blow was necessary, and Enguerrand de Marigny undertook to deliver it. His brother, the Archbishop of Sens, summoned a provincial council, before which fifty-four Templars were made to appear. They were allowed no opportunity to defend themselves, but were condemned as 'relapsed,' for having previously retracted their confessions. Next day, on the outskirts of the Bois de Vincennes, these unfortunate men were slowly roasted alive, protesting their innocence to the very last. With four exceptions, the remaining prisoners hurried to admit their guilt; 'I would have confessed to having murdered God,' cried one of them.

The foregoing events took place in 1310, and it was in this atmosphere of terrorism that a council met next year at Vienne in Dauphiné to decide the future of the Templars. The courts of England, Spain, Germany, and Portugal had returned verdicts of 'Not guilty,' as had the ecclesiastical tribunals; but Philip came in person to preside over the council's deliberations. Clement V was at death's door, and he yielded. His Bull *Vox in excelso* decreed the dissolution of the Order, which was described as 'guilty of admitted scandals, odious to King Philip [!], useless to the Holy Land'; and Christian governments were invited to take steps for its suppression.[1] Philip the Fair had achieved what he had set out to do, but not so the lawyers. Most of the Templars were in prison or had been 'reconciled,' i.e. they had been laicized or had joined other congregations. · It remained, therefore, to deal with the grand master and his deputy, so that the king

---

[1] Portugal alone refused, and the order survived in that country as the 'Militia of Christ.' Later, it assisted Henry the Navigator to undertake his great voyages of discovery.

might be seen by all to have had the last word, and no further retractactions might bring his judicial system into disrepute. Jacques de Molay and Geoffroy de Charnay appealed to the Pope, but all in vain: Clement V dared not even reply. On 19th March 1314 they were brought out in front of Notre-Dame at Paris, in presence of three cardinals, many prelates, and an enormous crowd. Here they were sentenced to life imprisonment. Then, these men who had proved themselves such indifferent leaders, whose fruitless cunning and clumsy manœuvring had done so much disservice to their Order, acted once more and for the last time as true knights. 'We are not guilty,' they cried, 'of the charges alleged against us, but we *are* guilty of having basely betrayed the Order to save our own lives. The Order is pure, the Order is holy; the accusations are absurd, and our confessions false.' Philip the Fair could not accept such a blow. That same evening, after having been declared 'relapsed,' the two heads of the Temple mounted the stake with indomitable courage, redeeming at the eleventh hour their sins and shortcomings. The Pope and the king both died before the year was out; and it was unanimously agreed among the common people that Jacques de Molay, when on the point of death, had summoned them before the judgment seat of God.

A good deal of mystery still surrounds the tragedy of the Templars. Avarice hardly suffices to account for the venom shown toward them by the royal government.[1] It may be that the young Capetian monarchy dared not harbour an organization which had its headquarters outside France, in Cyprus, and which, with its enormous wealth and its connection with all the leading families, might endanger the State. Tradition still maintains that the Temple was in fact a secret society; and it is related that, as Louis XVI's head was severed by the guillotine, an unknown voice was heard to cry: 'Jacques de Molay, you are avenged!'

From the Christian point of view this drama had regrettable consequences. A glorious chapter in the history of Christendom was closed, and it is surely no mere coincidence that the Templars were done to death by Philip the Fair, the same monarch who had outraged the Pope. Besides, the manner in which this miserable affair was handled, not to mention the weakness of Clement V, left an indelible impression that the Holy See had become a mere toy in the hands of the French kings since leaving Rome for Avignon.[2]

---

[1] In any case, their suppression was not so profitable as it might have been, since the Hospitallers also received a share of the booty.

[2] On the historical plane alone, the tragedy of the Temple marks a stage in the decline of feudal society, in the abasement of that noble chivalry which was becoming more and more useless, and which, just at this time, was proving its inability to withstand the new type of army at Courtrai, in Flanders (1302), at Morgarten in Switzerland (1315), at Crecy (1346), and in other great battles of the Hundred Years War.

8. THE PAPACY AT AVIGNON

The Popes of the twelfth and thirteenth centuries had been nomads. They had spent a large part of their time in the hill-towns overlooking the Roman Campagna, in various cities west of the Apennines between Perugia and Naples, and even in France. When Innocent IV fled from Frederick II, he resided for seven years at Lyons, where Gregory IX had held the fourteenth oecumenical council. Between 1100 and 1304 the papacy had spent a total of 122 years away from Rome; for the anarchical state of Italy, the turbulence of the Roman mob, and recurrent Germanic invasions had prevented any kind of stability. The idea of preparing a refuge beyond the Alps had perhaps been in the mind of Innocent III when, on the eve of the Albigensian crusade, he requested Raymond VI of Toulouse to hand over seven castles in Provence, which were afterwards surrendered to Philip III in exchange for the Comtat-Venaissin. The presence of the papal court in French territory was therefore nothing new. What was unusual was the papacy's absence from Italy during a period of seventy-two years (1304–76), more than sixty of which were passed in the city of Avignon (1309–76). So long a sojourn, however, had not originally been intended; it was due to a variety of circumstances.

On the death of Benedict XI (7th July 1304) the papal states were in hopeless confusion. Defied by the independent spirit of the towns, by the disloyalty of vassals, and by the ambition of local adventurers, the Pope's authority seemed little more than nominal; and this was a small-scale picture of Italy as a whole. The house of Anjou, established at Naples, was at war with the King of the Romans (a permanent candidate for the Imperial crown) and also with the Aragonese in Sicily; Florence was besieging the Ghibellines in Pistoia; Venice coveted the papal city of Ferrara; while Milan watched with anxiety the rising star of Visconti, the first of many such unscrupulous tyrants. The cardinals assembled at Perugia had good reason to talk of 'storm-clouds threatening Peter's barque with shipwreck.'

But a more disturbing shadow loomed over the conclave, that of Philip the Fair, who pursued his hatred of Boniface VIII even beyond the tomb, and demanded a trial for the condemnation of his memory. Benedict XI had tried in vain to separate the French king from Nogaret by lifting the former's excommunication and leaving the minister under censure. The conclave was divided on the attitude to be adopted towards the 'Elder Daughter of the Church.' Ten Italian cardinals, led by the dean, Matteo Orsini, were determined to protect the memory of Boniface; six others, led by the dean's own nephew, Napoleon Orsini, wished for reconciliation with France, even at the cost of summoning a council.

The conclave, which opened on 18th July, dragged on and on; but the rule of fasting on bread and water after the ninth day, as laid down in 1274, was not applied. December came in without any member of the Sacred College having obtained the necessary two-thirds of the votes; and it was then that Napoleon Orsini suggested the election of a prelate who was not a cardinal. The 'Bonifacians' put forward the name of Bertrand de Got, Archbishop of Bordeaux, who was supposed to be moderate in his views. The 'French' clique hesitated for a while; but they eventually supported his candidature after long and complicated negotiations, in which Philip took so active a part that he was rumoured to have had a secret meeting with the archbishop and to have imposed certain conditions. At all events, it was only when news reached Perugia of the Capetian's willingness that the conclave dared to elect Bertrand on 5th June 1305.

The new Pope took the name of Clement V. He announced his intention to be crowned at Vienne in Dauphiné, in imperial territory, after which he would return to Rome. On further consideration, however, he began to feel distinctly uneasy. He decided to put first things first, and terminate the conflict with Philip before crossing the Alps; then he would try to confirm the uncertain peace concluded between England and France in 1303, and to launch another crusade. With this first end in view, he approached Philip's ambassadors and made two important concessions, altering the place of his coronation from Vienne to Lyons (a city controlled by France) and creating a batch of nine cardinals, all of whom were French.

Clement V was no man of iron. He had the natural liveliness, easy tongue, and refinement of the Gascons; but these amiable qualities were of little use against the icy Philip and his lawyers. During recent events he had managed to play a double game, taking part in the anti-Boniface assembly of the French clergy, and then attending the council at Rome; but this desire to please everyone degenerated into lamentable weakness when it came to dealing with Philip the Fair. His undiscriminating generosity, moreover, was turned to the advantage of a greedy family, and almost nothing was done at the papal court without the intervention of some cardinal-nephew who was more or less in the pay of France. So, when an ambassador arrived from Paris, the unfortunate Pope, who was also suffering from cancer of the bowel, could refuse practically nothing. He was like one bewitched.[1]

Meanwhile, Clement V had not fulfilled his promise to return to Italy; he was too deeply engrossed in French affairs. Philip was

[1] The affair of the Templars revealed the full extent of Clement's weakness. He was rightly indignant at the abuse of the royal power, but he had not the courage to resist the cold violence of the king. Nor is it impossible that the Pope's abandonment of the Templars was one half of a political bargain: Philip did in fact drop his demand for the posthumous trial of Boniface, and that painful episode was forgotten.

pressing him to abandon the Templars; and it may be that, after an interview with the king at Poitiers, he foresaw danger in remaining on French soil. Comtat-Venaissin was papal property; it would assure him at least a semblance of freedom, and he made up his mind accordingly. Avignon belonged to the Marquis of Provence, a vassal of the French Crown; but Clement took up residence there in a Dominican convent, at the same time reserving for himself a place of retirement in the priory of Groseau among the green foothills of Ventoux. This arrangement was not intended to be permanent; and when the Council of Vienne had given judgment in the case of the Templars, the Pope once more spoke of returning to Rome. But the Eternal City was in the throes of civil war. So successfully had the Guelphs stirred popular passion against Henry of Luxembourg (1308–14), newly elected King of the Romans, that the latter could not be crowned in St Peter's and had to be content with St John Lateran. Indignant, he appealed to the Aragonese of Sicily. In these circumstances there could be no question of the Holy See's return. Besides, Clement's disease was making rapid strides, and he was now but a shadow of his former self. As a last hope of regaining strength, he asked to be taken to his native Gascony; but he died on the way at Roquemar, on the west bank of the Rhône (20th April 1314), leaving behind him an unenviable heritage.

Clement had set the Church on a perilous course by throwing in her lot with that of France. French affairs now occupied first place in papal policy; indeed, the archives of the Apostolic Chancellery contain as many documents concerning the one kingdom of France as those referring to the rest of Christendom, and of 134 cardinals created between 1305 and 1376 no fewer than 133 were French. On six occasions these cardinals elected one of their own number, and whenever there was question of returning to Rome, they invariably showed hesitation. Nor were their fears unjustified. It became customary to fill the court with relatives and fellow countrymen of the Pope: the Gascon team was followed by other groups from Quercy and Limousin, which formed the reigning Pope's entourage and often displayed considerable talent in high office. Clement V had looked upon Avignon as no more than a temporary lodging, but with John XXII that lodging looked like becoming a permanent residence.

The election of Jacques Duèse, on 7th August 1316, terminated an interregnum which had lasted for more than two years. The conclave which met at Carpentras was dispersed by armed bands employed by the Got faction. But it succeeded, not without difficulty, in reassembling at Lyons, and eventually chose a frail old man of seventy years, who, it was thought, would get in nobody's way. But his slender body housed the soul of a leader endowed with first-rate ability together with remarkable energy and breadth of view.   The pontificate of John XXII lasted for eighteen years, and the Holy Father's activity during that period is almost incredible.   No sooner had he been elected than he gave orders that the episcopal palace at Avignon be made ready for his immediate occupation, and that all government departments be transferred there.   It was an understandable decision; for the Guelphs had just been defeated at Montecatini, and there was no immediate prospect of returning to Italy.

Avignon, situated in papal territory, was a dependency of a Provençal family with whom John XXII was on the best of terms; connected with France by the famous bridge of St Benezet, it was a most useful watch-tower.   The bishop's house stood on the southern slope of the Rocher des Doms, a limestone escarpment overlooking the Rhône, together with the cathedral of Notre-Dame and the old castle of the commune.   The town itself lay to the south.   In order to obtain more space, John XXII purchased an orchard and some buildings on the hill, as well as the little church of St Stephen which was to become his private chapel.   Corner-towers and walls enclosing a covered walk formed an irregular quadrilateral which resembled a fortress rather than a palace.   The Pope's modest apartments being small, the chancellery and other government offices found what accommodation they could in the city until the necessary buildings were restored or newly built at Bedarrides, Noves, Barbentane, Sorgues, and Châteauneuf.   All this was very inconvenient; but it was only temporary, and John XXII had probably not yet given up hope of being able to return to Italy.

Proof of his ultimate intention lay in the fact that he continued to interest himself in Italian politics.   To restore order in the papal states, it was first necessary to subdue the Ghibellines who held the Lombard cities, particularly Milan, where Matteo Visconti had established a regular dictatorship.   The Pope believed that he could do this, and dispatched a legate at the head of an army of mercenaries and Neapolitans, while the Curia denounced his enemies as heretics.   But Louis IV of Bavaria, King of Germany (1314–47), who had just strengthened his position by defeating his Habsburg rival Frederick the Fair, renewed the claims of his predecessors.   The conflict between the priesthood and the empire thus entered upon a new phase.   Those who, like Marsilius and Occam, maintained the independence of states as against the Church, prepared to justify this policy by arguments; while the 'Spirituals,' condemned by the Holy See, worked hard to rouse the masses against Pope John.   Louis, who had been excommunicated, descended upon Italy and rallied the Ghibellines.   He was crowned at Rome, and forthwith sold the tiara by auction to a monk named Peter of Rieti, the antipope Nicholas V.

Meanwhile, a difference between the papacy and Edward III of England on the subject of taxation, which had started under Clement V, had taken an unsatisfactory turn. The situation was grave indeed, but it became still worse. The Italian Ghibellines were soon embroiled with the Germans; the anti-pope, driven from Rome under a hail of brickbats, thought of nothing but obtaining pardon; and John XXII was preparing yet another campaign in Italy when he died at the age of ninety. The immediate problem confronting his next two successors was whether to continue his policy in the hope of returning to Italy. The peace-loving and thrifty Benedict XII (1334–42) sought reconciliation with the Ghibellines, after which he meant to entrust the defence of the Church's interests to Taddeo Pepoli, who had recently occupied Bologna. But disorder was spreading everywhere: the Romagna and March of Ancona were in a state of hopeless anarchy. At Rome the great families had fortified a number of ancient ruins, and were using the Colosseum, the Palatine, the Arch of Titus, and the Theatre of Marcellus as bases of regular warfare.

The situation degenerated still further under Clement VI (1342–52). The Malatesta were adding to their possessions in the neighbourhood of Rimini; the sceptical and ostentatious Giovanni Visconti, ruler and Archbishop of Milan, was negotiating the purchase of Bologna; and the French 'rectors' of the papal states were looked upon with hatred and contempt. An amazing episode now occurred in the Eternal City. One Cola di Rienzi, who was legally the son of an innkeeper, but who may have been a bastard of Henry VII, declared himself inspired by the Third Person of the Trinity to regenerate Rome. An able demagogue, he styled himself 'the humble envoy of the People against the dogs and serpents of the Capitol.' He managed to seize power on 19th May 1347, and brought the aristocrats to their senses. A magnificent ceremony took place amid popular acclamation. Rienzi, seated in the Capitol, proclaimed himself sole emperor. He then proceeded to the basalt cistern, in which Constantine was supposed to have been baptized by St Sylvester, bathed therein, and announced that through him Rome had been cleansed of her sins. Seven of the highest prelates then placed upon his head seven crowns to symbolize the gifts of the Holy Ghost; after which, pointing his sword north, south, east, and west, 'The whole world is mine!' he cried. But the Roman nobles, whose lives Rienzi had spared with unwonted generosity, soon regained the upper hand. The masses grew tired of his continual and costly exhibitions, and Cola now discovered the true worth of popular enthusiasm. In 1354 he was deposed, hacked to pieces by an infuriated mob, and finally burned on the tomb of Augustus. The ghosts of antiquity were certainly abroad in Rome.

It is not difficult to understand that in such circumstances the popes felt no inclination to risk their necks in Italy. Accordingly, in 1348, they negotiated the purchase of Avignon from Joan of Naples, heiress of Provence, and resolved to turn the palace into a more comfortable home. In April 1335 Benedict XII had invited his fellow countryman, Pierre Poisson, to build a new tower for the use of the Sovereign Pontiff and his household. This was the Tower of the Angels, 140 feet high and joined to the east wing by two buildings. Hitherto the private apartments of John XXII had been quite unassuming. Poisson demolished large parts of them and began the more stately edifice which we see to-day. Half monastery, half fortress, this castle has a certain grandeur. The central court retains its cloister; the interior decoration is modest, with sculptured vines on a blue background; and there is a tower at each corner. The two highest of these cover the north side. One is known as the Tour Campane because it contained a bell; the other, the Tour des Trouilles, is 170 feet high and forms a solid bastion.

This austere group of buildings bore the stamp of the man who had conceived it. Jacques Fournier, born of humble parents in the County of Foix, was a former Cistercian, a great persecutor of heretics, hard on himself as on others, unyielding, and parsimonious. As Benedict XII, he preserved the habits of a monk on the Apostolic throne. His successor, Clement VI (Pierre Roger, a native of Limousin), was altogether different—affable and easy-going, with the manners of a gentleman. He had been in turn abbot of Fécamp, Bishop of Arras, Archbishop of Sens and then of Rouen. 'My predecessors,' he used to say with a twinkle in his eye, 'did not know how to live as popes should do!' Highly intelligent, a hard worker, and a man of wide culture, he was the most magnificent of the Avignon popes. Abandoning all hope of returning to Rome, he resolved to complete and improve the palace. As a fortress it was not sufficiently strong; as a papal residence it was inconvenient and unimpressive. These defects were remedied by the architect Jean de Loubières, who designed the Wardrobe Tower, the Tower of St Laurence, and a building 170 feet long containing the Hall of Audience and a new chapel with ogival vaulting. The grand entrance with its guard-room and portcullis was in the western façade.

The interior was richly decorated, but most of this ornament has unfortunately disappeared; it was the work of an illustrious group of Italian and French artists, including Matteo Giovanetti of Viterbo and, almost certainly, Simone Martini. What little survives gives us some idea of the beauty of the whole: scenes from the lives of St Martial and St John the Baptist, figures of prophets and sibyls, but above all, on the third floor of the Wardrobe Tower, a wonderful starred ceiling and some exquisite hunting scenes reminiscent of Persian miniatures.

These original designs were destined to have a great influence, especially on tapestry.

Let us try to imagine the papal court in its austere yet princely setting. Contrary to well-worn tradition, there was no excessive luxury; only the sacred liturgy was attended with a gorgeous display of ceremonial. But the Avignon popes, all of whom had been more or less accustomed to the French administrative system, added to the number of official departments and staffed them with a huge army of clerics, most of whom were extremely able men. There were also about 400 domestics, noble squires, serjeants-at-arms, porters, chamberlains, and huntsmen of various classes. To these we must add the Pope's innumerable relatives together with their friends and relations. All these people formed a busy little world of their own, intriguing and quarrelling, but doing their appointed work. The population of Avignon was further swelled by a crowd of place-hunters as well as by the many tradesmen and artificers who supplied the papal court. Wood from Geneva, wine from Burgundy, salt from Languedoc, corn from France; all these were unloaded at the foot of the Rocher des Doms, and stored in warehouses along the riverside.

It is commonly believed that the residence of the popes at Avignon did untold harm to the Church, but that is an exaggeration. There can be no doubt that, by removing from the turmoil of Italy, the Holy See avoided an extremely dangerous situation. Far from being 'bishops of the French court,' these popes were all conscious of the universality of the Church and of her greatness. From Clement V to Clement VI, all did their best to encourage the missionaries who were propagating the Catholic faith in the most distant lands; and it was the court of Avignon which established the hierarchy in Persia and China. All cherished a hope of reviving the crusades, and several of them attempted to do so. If the result of their efforts amounted to very little a few naval raids and the occupation of Smyrna—that was the fault of Christendom as a whole, not of the popes themselves. Their diplomacy often ran parallel with that of France, but was always distinct therefrom; and their endeavours to prevent the Hundred Years War were inspired by the loftiest Christian principles. Their independence was manifest likewise in their opposition to a custom whereby the kings of England and of France enjoyed the revenues of vacant bishoprics, and disposed of certain benefices dependent thereon. In 1337 a strongly worded protest on this subject was sent from Avignon to Paris; and although the Statute of Provisors (1351) and that of *Praemunire* (1353) had affirmed the views of the English Crown with regard to benefices, the Holy See obtained an assurance from Edward III that he would not apply the Acts voted by Parliament. In face of Germanic claims also, these Avignon popes used the proud language that might have been expected from the heirs of Innocent III. The renewed struggle between the priesthood and the empire ended in a victory for the Pope. Louis of Bavaria was vanquished ('for the honour of the Church,' said Clement VI), and his successor Charles of Moravia, a friend of the papacy, was recognized by the whole of Germany after 1347.

It is true that the residence at Avignon had other consequences not so favourable to the Apostolic See, which had to face the Italian anarchy unaided, and which was soon afterwards denied a voice in the affairs of Germany by the celebrated Golden Bull of 1356. But it is difficult to see what other policy could have been adopted at that time and under those circumstances. Above all, the Avignon popes deserve credit for their work in perfecting the administration of the Church, whose four great departments—the Chancellery, the Camera, the Tribunal of the Rota, and the Penitentiary—were reorganized and given clearly defined duties. The archives of the papacy at Avignon are preserved in the Vatican Library; they include 456 volumes of letters, 43 of petitions, account-books, and bundles of documents, which represent an extraordinarily high degree of efficiency.

Fortified by this strong central administration, the papacy tended more and more to intervene in ecclesiastical appointments and the allocation of benefices. The principle that every ecclesiastical charge is at the disposal of the Holy See had been laid down by Clement IV in 1265; but it was chiefly after their removal to Avignon that the popes seized every opportunity to exercise the privileges hitherto enjoyed by the electors of bishops and abbots and by collectors of benefices. The system of 'reserves,' which had operated from time immemorial in certain dioceses and was gradually extended to others, led the Holy See to impose its own choice in an ever greater number of cases. Nothing is more significant in this connection than the following three sets of figures: in the single diocese of Liége, John XXII intervened on 496 occasions; Benedict XII, within a period of less than eight years (1334–42), distributed more than 4,000 benefices in France; and out of fifty-eight French bishops appointed during that time, only nine were chosen by cathedral chapters. It is safe to say, then, that this policy— which another Avignon pope, Gregory XI, made into a hard and fast rule in the case of archbishoprics and abbacies—strengthened the papal authority to a considerable extent and prepared it for still further advances.

Such methods, on the other hand, inevitably gave rise to ill-feeling. Charges and benefices were too frequently given to clerics of the papal court, a fact which caused much discontent; no Spaniard, for instance, liked to see Frenchmen as beneficiary canons in his country. Apart from these nominations, there were taxes to be paid: common services, i.e. one-third of the revenues of prelates; annates, or one year's fruits, for lesser benefices; and the confiscation of movable goods belonging to deceased clerics.   In addition, there were tithe rent charges, procurations, quit-rents, and Peter's pence.   Collectors were appointed to gather these dues; a financial administration was set up with fixed areas, or 'collectories'; and a central department was established, whose operations were no less complicated than those of the banking houses with which it maintained close contact.   These measures caused the Avignon popes to be accused of rapacity and with sordid greed.[1]

The Church's critics were legion, and extremely voluble.   A good many of them were Italians who were aggrieved to see the Pope so far from Rome.   Dante rebuked Clement V for having married the Church to the kingdom of France; and all are familiar with Petrarch's indictment against 'the hell of the living, the cesspool of vices, the sewer of Earth, the most vile-smelling of cities.'[2]   One day there was found nailed up on a cardinal's front door a 'letter from Lucifer,' in which the master of hell congratulated the Sacred College for having worked so well on his behalf; and while we must allow for the polemical purpose of these diatribes, we cannot deny that they contained an element of truth.

Still worse, the papacy's absence from Rome seemed like treason in the eyes of Christendom.   Even though the city of Peter were in the throes of anarchy, it was still rich in tradition and symbolic power, against which nothing could prevail.   The holy city, whose sanctuary had welcomed such vast crowds in the Jubilee year of 1300, could not remain the widow of St Peter's successor.   Hence there grew up the striking image of the 'Babylonian captivity,' of a papacy held prisoner by dark and terrible forces, an image with which the Christian world afterwards became familiar through the inspired utterances of St Brigit of Sweden and St Catherine of Siena.   However understandable and even excusable the sojourn of the popes at Avignon may have been, it was looked upon as an indication of divine wrath, and is certainly evidence of the Church's decadence during the fourteenth century.

9.   THE AGONY OF THE MID-FOURTEENTH CENTURY

There were many such omens about the year 1350; for the dismemberment of Christendom, which had long been foreseen, was passing

[1] It is only fair to set John XXII's annual income of 228,000 florins alongside the 546,000 of Edward II of England, the 600,000 of Robert of Naples, and the 785,000 of Philip VI of France.   But all this fiscal apparatus seemed unbecoming in the Church. (On questions of money at the court of Avignon, see Yves Renouard, *Les relations des papes d'Avignon et des compagnies commerciales et bancaires*, 1941.)

[2] Some of these attacks were written by theorists who upheld the rights of the State; e.g. Marsilius of Padua, who accused the Avignon popes and their court of every vice in order to bring the papal power into disrepute.

into the realm of fact.   The struggle of the papacy with the Empire had been resumed.   Anjou and Aragon were ravaging southern Italy with fire and sword in an attempt to determine its possession, while the rest of the peninsula was given over to the horrors of civil war.   Germany was in a state of chaos; the Swiss peasants were fighting the German horsemen; and the Spanish nobility were doing their best to destroy the royal authority in that land.   As if all this were not enough, the Hundred Years War had broken out, and its consequences were to prove more disastrous than those of any previous conflict.

The *casus belli* was one of those dynastic quarrels which had confronted the two kingdoms on several occasions in earlier centuries. The three sons of Philip the Fair—Louis X, Philip V, and Charles IV —all died young and without male issue.   A plenary assembly of the French barons twice refused to confer the crown upon Edward III of England, son of Isabella of France, who was herself daughter of Philip the Fair.   They had declared his candidature contrary to 'the common custom of France, which did not allow a woman to succeed to the kingdom.'   Edward did not at first choose to take umbrage at this refusal; for in 1328 he did homage for Guienne and Ponthieu at the coronation of Philip VI de Valois, nephew of Philip the Fair and great-grandson of St Louis.

But there were far deeper causes of antagonism between the two young Western monarchies.   To begin with, the presence of English domains in French territory were all very well so long as the feudal tie was a reality; but they appeared unnatural with the advent of new political formulae tending to centralization.   Powerful economic causes were also at work.   France, for instance, could not endure to see the port of Bordeaux, a great market of wine and corn, controlled by London.   Both powers, too, had an eye on Flanders, where Bruges stood at the junction of trade-routes from Venice, the Baltic, and Spain.   More fundamental still was the natural enmity between two nations, each of whom coveted the hegemony of the West.

The Hundred Years War began in 1338, and immediately took on a character of unwonted violence.   There was no question of a mere feudal conflict; the peoples themselves were more deeply involved than ever before, and a new national sentiment was abroad.   Large areas of western Europe were also implicated.   On the side of England stood the Emperor Louis of Bavaria together with the Counts of Holland and Zeeland.   France was assisted by the blind King John of Bohemia, the Count of Luxembourg, the Prince-Bishop of Liége, and various lords.   Flanders, a stake in the struggle, had embraced the cause of England, who furnished her with wool; she had been persuaded to do so by James van Arteveld, who exploited the misery resulting from the stoppage of imports.

France soon had cause to tremble at the might of her adversary. Her king was an indifferent statesman whose undoubted courage lacked the control of reason, and within twelve years she had suffered heavy losses. Her fleet was destroyed at Sluys in 1340, leaving England mistress of the seas; and every year since then one French province or another had been subject to attack. Most serious was the defeat of Crécy (1346), where the English bowmen crushed the out-of-date French cavalry. Calais was taken, and only the pity of Queen Philippa of Hainaut had prevented Edward III from putting to death Eustache de St Pierre and the heroic burghers who surrendered themselves as hostages. The Popes had been powerless to stop this conflict; and on the death of Philip VI, in 1350, France was in sorry straits.

The East also was in grave danger. Since Michael Palaeologus (1258–82) drove the Latins from Constantinople,[1] the Byzantine Empire had become a mere shadow of its old self. The traditional ceremonial had been restored, but that meant very little. Reduced to the north-west of Asia Minor, Thrace, and a part of Macedonia, with a few strongpoints in Peloponnesus and a nominal suzerainty over Epirus, Byzantium stood by and watched Bulgars, Serbs, and, above all, the Ottoman Turks devour her former territories. Nor, indeed, did her rule extend over all the Greeks, for the State of Trebizond rejected her authority; Venice occupied the archipelago; while Genoa held Chios together with many ports on the Black Sea and in Anatolia.

The dynasty of the Palaeologi had been trying for ninety years to oppose the forces of destiny with heroic desperation, but internal crises and discord had prevailed. Michael VIII, who had checked the ambition of Charles of Anjou and Sicily, was succeeded by Andronicus II the Elder (1282–1328), a very different type of man, whose grandson, Andronicus III the Younger, assisted by a high official named John Cantacuzene, seized Constantinople and had himself crowned in 1328. On his death, in 1341, Cantacuzene sought recognition as sole heir in place of the little Palaeologus, who was only ten years of age; and so well did he go about it that John V Palaeologus was faced with a usurper styling himself John VI. This anarchy, which lasted throughout the reign of John V and gave rise to episodes worthy of an adventure story, ended with the total collapse of authority, as Bulgarian, Serbian, Turkish, and even Spanish commandos were called in to help dispute the throne.

Danger from without was visibly increasing. Stephen Dushan, a first-rate leader, became kral or ruler of the Serbs in 1331. He defeated the Bulgars and gradually built up, from fragments of the Eastern Empire, a 'Greater Serbia' stretching from the Danube to the Adriatic

[1] See Chapter XI, section 8.

and Aegean. The stronghold of Seres, between Thessalonica and Constantinople, fell into the hands of Stephen, who was forthwith crowned at Uskub in 1346 as 'Emperor of the Serbs and Rumanians.' He was recognized by the religious superiors on Mount Athos, and proclaimed the Bishop of Okhrida Patriarch of an autonomous Serbian Church. In 1350 no one realized the weakness of this stupendous edifice or foresaw that five years later, after Stephen's death, it would fall to pieces.

Far more serious was the Turkish peril. The Seljuks, dislodged by the Mongol invaders, had been superseded by their kinsmen the Ottomans, who, from the rank of petty emirs, had managed to raise themselves by the end of the thirteenth century to the position of powerful monarchs. Osman (*d.* 1326), founder of the Osmanli dynasty, had made Asia Minor a Turkish bastion. His son Orkhan followed in his footsteps, and was the first sovereign to establish a professional army which could be put into the field without delay. This was the famous Corps of Janissaries. Brusa fell to their arms in 1326, Nicea in 1329, Nicomedia in 1337; and from the walls of Byzantium they could be seen beyond the Straits, ready to leap across whensoever they might choose. The Palaeologi had tried to hold them at bay, but had not sufficient troops. The young Basileus Michael, who had been made joint sovereign by his father Andronicus II, had been defeated; and the only successful counter-offensive was that led by a German *condottiere* named Roger of Flor. At the head of some Catalan bandits, he obliged the Ottomans to retreat; but his claims became so exorbitant that the emperor got rid of him by having him murdered at a banquet. About 1350 the Ottoman Turks crossed the Straits, supported by Cantacuzene who pretended to be using them against his rival John V. Thrace was overrun; Gallipoli became a Turkish fortress; and the whole of Europe wondered where this offensive would stop, whether Serbia and Hungary would not also be engulfed. The Yellow Peril began to haunt the minds of men,

The only satisfactory result of this latest tragedy was to draw the Byzantines nearer to the West, i.e. to the papacy. Hopes of reunion had vanished since the attempt of Michael VIII, which ended in the decisions of Lyons.[1] Beccos had never ceased to proclaim the urgent necessity of a settlement; and this was desired by a considerable party at Byzantium (including a number of clear-headed politicians who considered Western aid essential if the Ottomans were to be halted), by intellectuals who had read the Catholic thinkers and had even translated St Thomas Aquinas, and by certain empresses of Western origin who were unwilling renegades from the Roman faith, such as Anne of Savoy, regent for young John V. Catholic influence was at work even

---

[1] See Chapter XI, section 13.

in the Palace of Blachernae through the efforts of a Calabrian monk, Barlaam, and of a French Carmelite, Peter Thomas, who converted the boy-emperor. The advocates of reunion, however, met with resistance from the Greek clergy. 'Rather the turban than the tiara!' yelled these fanatics. Moreover, the ambassadors who came to the West to discuss reunion with Robert of Anjou at Naples, with Philip the Fair at Paris, and with Benedict XII at Avignon, put forward unacceptable conditions. To have granted their request for a new council which should include representatives of the Byzantine clergy would have looked like disavowing the decisions of Lyons. They called likewise for an expedition against the Turks, but this was altogether impossible considering the international situation. In 1337, with a view to bolstering his position, John Cantacuzene gave many assurances of his devotion; but this was no more than a tide of words. The rift between West and East continued as yet one more tragic symbol of Christendom's dismemberment.

The Turkish menace was still remote, and the Anglo-French war, at any rate in its early stages, was limited to a small area of the west. But there were other causes of anxiety, from which no country and no class escaped. An economic crisis had been gradually developing during the past fifty years, for the expansion of medieval economy was at an end. Progress, which had until now been continuous in every field, was brought to a standstill, as well in agriculture, where enfranchisement of the serfs had gone forward simultaneously with the clearing of uncultivated areas, as in commerce and industry, which had been so flourishing during the thirteenth century. The great colonizing movement also seemed exhausted. The fairs began to decline in Champagne and elsewhere, and there was a succession of unfortunate bankruptcies. In 1327 and 1343 the banking houses of Usani, Corsini, Bardi, and half a dozen others failed. Apart from Bruges, the great Flemish cities were in decline. Florence, Genoa, and Venice held their own, but were soon affected by Ottoman depredations and by troubles due to the Hundred Years War. Everywhere there was stagnation.

To meet these difficulties, which were increased from one decade to another by the expenses of war, recourse was had to palliatives similar to those employed by modern states, including monetary manipulations, for which Philip the Fair has been severely blamed. Though unable to print bank-notes, he arrived at the same result (inflation) by altering the value of gold pieces. Excessive regimentation was also tried: governments made orders, and professional bodies poured forth a flood of rules and regulations. Bureaucrats had a fine time controlling the distribution of raw materials, the maximum size of contracts, the standard of wages, the length of working hours, and the processes of manufacture. The freedom of international commerce was shackled for fear of competition, and the corporative system became rigid. This iron system of controls resulted, as do all such methods, in sclerosis.

The fossilization of society, the slowing down of an economy which had reached its zenith, was accompanied by another phenomenon which helped to aggravate the situation: a decline in the birth-rate. After the year 1000, the rising tide of population had sustained the whole of medieval society.[1] From the beginning of the thirteenth century it had steadily receded. English statistics, which are very full, show a marked falling-off in the birth-rate after 1250: from 1300 to 1328 the population increased slightly, but diminished by half between the latter date and 1420. In France, a simple comparison is eloquent: whereas the kingdom had 4,400,000 hearths in 1328, the same territory numbered only 4,800,000 in 1789.

In many respects this reduction of the birth-rate is as hard to explain as the preceding rise; it is connected, perhaps, with physiological laws about which we know little. But accidental causes intervened also, some of them with terrible effect.

The fourteenth century was, in fact, a period of spectacular calamities. These were not due solely to the follies of mankind, to foreign and civil wars which are so harmful to the common people; for Heaven itself now seemed to take a hand. In the autumn of 1315, following a bad harvest everywhere, famine began to take its toll; and, as the two summers of 1316 and 1317 were equally unfortunate, it assumed gigantic proportions. Scenes were repeated which had been described three centuries earlier by Raoul Glaber—emaciated children, peasants gnawing the bark of trees, and even some cases of cannibalism. Some chance figures preserved by the city of Ypres reveal the extent of this scourge: in a city of 20,000 inhabitants, nearly three thousand corpses were buried between 1st May and mid October 1316.

Famine, however, was nothing compared with the disaster which overtook Europe in 1347 and lasted for thirty months. The Black Death, which has left an undying memory of its horror, is described in hideous detail by Boccaccio in his *Decameron*. The sickness began in the East, where it caused frightful havoc. It arrived in the West with unabated fury, and neither hygienic measures nor public prayers could arrest it. The first symptoms were the appearance under the arm-pits of tumours, which grew to the size of an egg. Swellings quickly appeared on other parts of the body, or the skin became smeared with horrible black and white patches. In either of these cases, death was certain; it generally took place on the third day without any sign of

---

[1] See Chapter I, section 5. On the decline of economic life, we await Perron's study, *À l'origine d'une economie contractée: Les crises du XIV*⁰ *siècle*. Meanwhile, see Lacourt-Gayet in his *Histoire du commerce*.

fever. Contagion was immediate: to touch the clothes of an affected person was sufficient to contract the disease. Even animals were affected, and, it seems, more rapidly than men; for a story was told about some pigs which stirred a heap of contaminated rubbish with their snouts, and were dead within an hour. All Europe lived through two and a half years of terror.

Countless documents provide us with information as to the dire effects of this calamity on population. In five months, according to Boccaccio, Florence and its suburbs lost 100,000 citizens. In the Burgundian village of Givry, where the annual death-rate was forty, the numbers for 1348 were 650. At Soisy-sur-Seine, out of 140 families only six remained. At Amiens there were said to have been 17,000 deaths. At Avignon, from 25th January to 27th April 1348, 62,000 persons, representing half the population, are alleged to have died; and since the charnel houses were full to overflowing, the Pope gave permission for burial in the papal cemetery, where, in March and April, 11,000 corpses were interred. One might continue indefinitely with this sinister enumeration. No country escaped the disaster, which reached as far as Iceland. Even allowing for the usual exaggerations of the chroniclers,[1] we may safely say that one-third of the population of Europe was exterminated.

The Black Death (1348–50) marks a turning-point in the history of Europe. It ended the wonderful surge of vitality which had brought society to its highest summits; henceforward Christendom was a broken reed. The great age of the Cathedral and the Crusade ended in putrefaction and in horror.

10. PROFOUND CHANGES IN THE CHRISTIAN SOUL

The consequences of these various misfortunes weighed no less heavily on men's minds. Medieval man had been joyous, confident in

[1] Are their figures any more reliable than in the case of military estimates? The mortality stated here for Florence and Avignon probably exceeded the total population of those cities; and it is unlikely that the population of Avignon was 120,000. On the other hand, there are official documents which give exact figures, e.g. the parish-register of Givry. We also know that 94 members of the Curia died, out of 450, and that some religious houses in which contagion was rapid were decimated. 133 out of 140 Dominicans perished at Montpellier, 153 out of 160 at Maguelonne; the Franciscans at Marseilles and Carcassonne were wiped out altogether. But country places were far less severely hit, and some districts escaped altogether (*see* V. Renouard, 'La peste noire de 1348–1350' in *Revue de Paris*, March, 1950, pp. 107–19). In his *Histoire artistique des Ordres mendiants* (1939), Louis Gillet has shown in striking fashion the immense effects of the plague. 'The flower of humanity was suddenly cut down. Two whole generations were swept away. There was a lacuna, a hiatus in history. England changed her language: French, the language of the baronage, was absorbed in the maternal idiom. Building everywhere came to a halt. This rent in time marks the end of the Middle Ages. It was, as one chronicler wrote, like the beginning of another period of the world.'

life, sustained by hope.   He was no longer so.[1]   Its violence notwithstanding, medieval humanity had been a brotherly society; that too was
no more.   In face of mortal danger, charity and friendship and such
deeper sentiments as family love lost their hold.   'The sick died without
their relatives, and without priests,' says a chronicler, 'and if a man
hastened to bury the dead, it was not through pity, but through fear of
contagion.'   War, increasing anarchy, and the complexity of international relations, wherein men might well wonder where their duty
lay, were not calculated to restrain human passions.

In fact, there was a growing sense of exasperation, to which the Jews
fell victim in many places.   During the period 1336-8 a terrible wave
of anti-Semitism swept over Germany, caused, no doubt, by economic
difficulties.   During the Black Death they were accused of poisoning
wells, of purposely contaminating food; and there were so many
pogroms, especially in the Rhineland and Italy, that the Pope decreed
excommunication for anyone who burned a Jew.   But the merchants
of the Ghettos were not the only ones against whom this sense of
exasperation was directed.   There was also a good deal of social
agitation which, for at least a century, gave rise to a host of dangerous
elements: vagabond scholars, 'fleecers,' 'coquillards,' and 'caimans'
who infested France long after the end of the Hundred Years War;
outcasts of every shape and shade, of whom Villon was to be the
immortal spokesman.

There were many other signs of unrest.   The ordered universe,
lucid and coherent, felt its foundations tremble, and anguish spread
through every vein.   The passage of a comet in 1315 terrified people
in all lands.   In 1325 Saturn and Jupiter were in conjunction, which
was taken as an evil omen.   Then, in 1341, there occured a total solar
eclipse.   All these things inevitably gave rise to talk about the end of
the world.   But nothing is more significant of this spiritual change
than the transformation of art.   The peaceful simplicity of romanesque
and gothic sculpture was superseded by a new striving after the
emotional.   Classic examples of this tendency are the weeping angels
who mount guard over Calvary and the Deposition from the Cross in
the Arena chapel at Padua.   At Rouen, in 1310, the Passion appeared
for the first time on the tympanum of a cathedral, and artists soon
became obsessed with death.   To the peaceful recumbent figures on
the old tombs there succeeded hideous images of rotting corpses, with
empty eye-sockets and bowels devoured by worms.   'Danses
macabres' became fashionable in literature as in painting, where death
began to be represented under the form of a skeleton carrying a scythe.

---

[1] You will search in vain for one pessimistic note in the whole of medieval literature.
Hamlet, Alceste, the 'Mal de siècle,' and the black dreams of atheist existentialism are
modern products.

There are masterpieces on this theme in the Campo Santo at Pisa, at the Chaise-Dieu, at Basle, and at Strasbourg; but they are far removed from the inspiration of earlier medieval sculpture.

From the religious point of view, this agony of the mid-fourteenth century had important consequences. It is in times of distress that man experiences an access of fervour, that his voice seems to carry more conviction when he cries: 'O Crux, ave, spes unica . . .' So it was at the period in question; there was indeed a blaze of faith. The chronicler Gilles le Muisis, speaking of life at Tournai during the plague, remarks, not without a touch of irony, that 'people who had been living as husband and wife hurried to regularize their position,' and that 'merchants had to shape dice into paternoster beads.' [1] The interest taken in the Passion of Christ since St Francis of Assisi grew at this time to enormous proportions: St Bonaventure's *Meditations on the Passion*, which were translated into many languages, and a *Life of Jesus* by the Carthusian Ludolph of Saxony were extremely popular. Mysticism made striking progress with Master Eckhart and (somewhat later) Tauler, foreshadowing that vast current which, in the fourteenth and fifteenth centuries, would inundate the Christian soul and reach its high-water mark in the *Imitation of Christ*. But this mysticism was of a kind very different from that which flourished in the best period of the Middle Ages. Formerly there was equilibrium between the contemplative and the active life, as with St Bernard; between mystical knowledge and speculative theology, as with St Thomas Aquinas. Henceforward, mysticism tended to become sufficient unto itself, to shut itself away in the cloister, to be its own end.

But by no means all the consequences of this spiritual restlessness were fortunate. Many weak minds failed to acquire an increase of faith; indeed, their fervour went astray. Old heresies, such as that of the Brethren of the Free Spirit, took on new life about 1350. Error likewise reared its head among the Begards and in certain houses of Béguines. The whole atmosphere was more favourable to superstition, which was always a blot on the medieval soul. From the beginning of the fourteenth century sorcery was rampant even in the highest classes of society, and some Inquisitors were actually students of astrology! An abundant literature grew up denouncing sorcerers and witches, a literature which included such famous works as the *Struggle against Witchcraft*, by Arnauld de Villeneuve, a papal physician.

Discontent was widespread; and if one final proof be needed, it may be found in the conduct of the 'Penitents' and 'Flagellants.' Froissart says that they appeared on the morrow of the Black Death. In fact,

---

[1] True, he goes on to say that once the epidemic was over there was 'a regular orgy of merrymaking.'

the movement started somewhat earlier, though it received a powerful impulse from that epidemic. Divine wrath weighed heavy on the world! Penance! Penance! Expiation and sacrifice! Bands of these crazy folk wandered the high roads, refusing to sleep in the same place on two consecutive nights. They wore a mantle adorned with two red crosses, walking two by two, with crucifix and banners at their head, and scourge in hand. They would assemble in some public place, strip to the waist, form a circle, and lie prostrate for some while. Then, at a given signal, they would rise and lash themselves to blood with scourges made of leather thongs tipped with small bronze crosses, howling incessantly 'Kyrie eleison.' Performances took place twice every twenty-four hours, one of them at night, and the strange pilgrimage lasted for thirty days. Fanatics of this kind travelled all over Europe, causing so much trouble that they were condemned by Clement VI, who ordered the arrest of their leaders. But his measures were ineffective, and the Flagellants continued for a long while afterwards.

11. The Balance Sheet of Christendom: 1350

We must not, however, be deceived by such alarming pictures. They may cast a shadow upon medieval Christendom, but they cannot affect its true greatness. Undeniable flaws in the Church at about this time do not detract from the results obtained by ten generations of faithful souls and inscribed for ever in the balance-sheet of history.

From the geographical standpoint alone those results are impressive. In three centuries Christianity had won control of practically the whole of Europe, and had caused the Gospel seed to flourish in distant lands where no one had dreamed in 1050 that it could be sown.

Islam, the most dreaded enemy of the Cross, had been rolled back on the continent. In Spain, south of the Guadalquivir, the Moslems now held nothing but the Sierra Nevada overlooking Granada and its circlet of well-watered gardens, Almeira, and Malaga. Sicily, occupied in turn by Normans, Angevins, and Aragonese, had been secure against any Moslem counter-offensive for two centuries. In these two countries, once subject to Arab rule, there remained only such elements as could contribute to the progress of art and thought, the memory of ancient philosophy and science, and supreme technical skill.

Northwards, Christianity had made some important gains. By the end of the eleventh century it had penetrated no farther than the west bank of the Elbe and southern Scandinavia; now the whole Baltic region was dotted with Christian communities. An irresistible urge had carried the faith from the Elbe to the Vistula, submerging the

Wends, taking in Poland, annexing Prussia, and even reaching Finland. Since 1309 the grand master of the Teutonic Order, resident at Marienburg on the Lower Vistula, had been preparing an offensive against Lithuania, a pagan centre in Christian territory. The whole of Scandinavia had been converted; there was a regular network of parishes, and the Scandinavian hierarchy exercised jurisdiction over all inhabited territory as far as those icy solitudes visited from time to time by a few Lapland tribes. The islands to the north of Scotland, as well as the shores of Iceland and Greenland, had likewise received Christian colonies whose bishops dwelt in the heart of polar mists at Hólar, Skálhot, and Gardhar.

The lands that were afterwards to be known collectively as 'Russia' had been converted by Byzantine missionaries; but they had suffered severely since the middle of the thirteenth century under the Golden Horde. The principality of Kiev lay in ruins; but religious and national life had taken refuge in Ruthenia, in the republics of Pskov on Lake Peipus and of Novgorod on Lake Ilmen. Meanwhile, a number of small principalities had grown up in the forest clearings, where colonists from Novgorod had intermarried with the natives to produce a type called 'greater Russians.' Such was Vladimir, whither the patriarch Maximus moved in 1300 when he was driven from Kiev; such, above all, was Moscow, to which city the patriarchal see was finally transferred in 1326.

The prospects of Christianity appeared less favourable in the southeast, where Byzantium, failing in her task and inaccessible to Western aid, could do nothing to halt the progress of the Ottoman squadrons. Herein lay the worst danger; for, while Christian Bulgaria had already been reduced to a shadow, Stephen Dushan's 'Greater Serbia,' which seemed to form a bastion against the Turkish advance, was a mere illusion.

Europe, then, was almost entirely Christian. Within the aforesaid limits, paganism had virtually disappeared; there was no need to fear its return, except in the form of superstition, unchristian morals, and constantly recurring heresies. But against these more insidious perils the Church was now on her guard, and the Inquisition provided her with a weapon of defence.

Christianity had also occupied new bases outside Europe, although her boldest undertaking, the crusade, had failed.[1] Her most easterly position was the kingdom of Lesser Armenia at the foot of the Taurus range, which survived the Moslem threat for another twenty-five years, thanks to a Mongol alliance. Cyprus was in the hands of the Lusignans; Rhodes had been governed by the Hospitallers since 1310; Venice held ports in the Archipelago and Morea, Genoa in Chios and

---

[1] Acre, the last Christian stronghold in the Holy Land, had fallen in 1291.

Lesbos. A younger son of the house of Anjou ruled in the Peloponnese, while the Duchy of Athens had been occupied by a band of Catalan mercenaries. All these formed an outer ring of defences in face of the Turkish peril.

It was not, however, in the domain of force that the Church had so much cause for optimism. Vast horizons had been opened up by the missions. This noble work had been given new life by St Francis of Assisi, and the astonishing adventures of Nestorian missionaries in Mongolia seemed to augur well for their Catholic brethren. The papacy, helped by the mendicant Orders, could congratulate itself upon some surprising gains. Preachers had been sent out in the wake of merchants, and the study of oriental languages had been encouraged. In Persia, where Catholics and Nestorians had been reconciled in 1288, the city of Sultanyeh became an archiepiscopal see in 1318, with the Dominican Franco of Perugia as first metropolitan. Six suffragan dioceses had also been erected, and there were bishops at the foot of Ararat as well as at Tiflis in Georgia. Better still, China had opened her doors to Christ, and Clement V had made John of Montecorvino Archbishop of Pekin with half a dozen suffragans. The Dominicans were hard at work in India, where Jordan of Sévérac had received the diocese of Gulam in 1330. The future certainly appeared to hold great promise, especially when it was learned that the work of Franciscan martyrs and of Raymond Lull was about to bear fruit in Africa.

Such results speak for themselves; but they are scarcely comparable with those obtained in fields that have nothing to do with geographical expansion.

Within a period of three centuries the Church had proved herself the leading force in society, of which she was both guide and arbiter. She had entered upon this role during the barbarian epoch, with high courage, certainly, though in a manner that was bound to land her in difficulties and give rise to controversy. But she had fulfilled her self-appointed task with supreme skill and to the general satisfaction of mankind. Even at the end of this era, when her leaders and many of her members were severely criticized, when her authority was openly defied, when she was gradually ceasing to be identified with the West, she remained a very great power. And the high standards expected of her are proof that men still felt the need of her greatness, a feeling, perhaps, amounting to nostalgia.

Her power rested upon an organization comparable with, if not superior to, that of the foremost European states. The rough and ready methods of an earlier age had given place to solid institutions. The papacy, as we have seen, delegated much of its administrative burden to the College of Cardinals, which was created for that purpose; it kept in touch with the Church abroad through a network of legations; relied to a great extent for the execution of its wishes upon the co-operation of the mendicant Orders; and took into its own hands the appointment of bishops.   From these measures the Holy See gained incalculable benefits, which it still enjoys.   The Church had embodied her principles in Canon Law, while the Inquisition, for all its defects, provided an efficient means of control.   She had her own finances and her own social works.   Her diplomatic corps was carefully chosen, and her archives were among the best kept at that time.

But these advantages were not used simply as a means to power. Generally speaking, they were made to serve those higher principles which tend to perfect our nature.   The saint and the knight were presented as superior types, and, thanks to the Church's influence, came to be looked upon as such.   It was likewise due to the Church that the moral law was recognized as sacred and inviolable, even in the act of sin.   In spite of terrible crises, she effected a certain refinement of manners, giving to the world a little more justice and love.   One of the chief consequences of her effort may be seen on the social plane, where she contributed more than anyone else to the abolition of servile labour and to the recognition of individual rights.[1]

The Church had always been realistic, taking the world as she found it, notwithstanding her ambition to make it a better place. Between 1050 and 1350 she had realized those great syntheses of which Christian intellectuals had dreamed since the patristic age.   Now she could offer a philosophical system, a conception of the world, as rich and as valuable as those which she had inherited, a system which included all that was best in ancient thought.   The whole corpus of modern learning derives from universities founded by the Church, from methods evolved by her children.

During that period, also, Christian art attained its zenith.   Before then it had been feeling its way.   Except in the East, where it had followed the road mapped out by Rome, it had walked as if uncertain and afraid.   But these three hundred years were an epoch of great creative audacity, during which Christianity expressed itself with much originality, with a power of invention and synthesis the like of which has never since been seen.   The cathedral, with its vertical lines suggestive of a soul at prayer, with its precise mathematics and regular design, with its innumerable forms directed to a single end at once human and divine, was concrete evidence of the Church's greatness, to which it still bears witness.[2]

All these results were achieved within a single framework; all

---

[1] We, who complain of the high cost of living, should appreciate the efforts of those social theologians who evolved the notion of a 'just price.'   And let us not forget that it is our irreligious age that has founded the eighth sacrament, that of property.

[2] Urban development owes much to the Church, whose gardens and religious houses preserved a modicum of open space within the narrow confines of city walls.

flowed from one motive principle, the idea of Christendom.[1] Medieval man built the cathedrals, compiled the *summae*, embarked on the crusades, spread and intensified the Gospel message; while the Church's power reached heights hitherto unexplored, and she herself became the guide of human thought. Why so? Because the men and women of that age were firmly convinced that Christianity could be given an outward form, a form in which Christian principles would be embodied in institutions; in which the spiritual would correspond with a system of political and social grades; in which Christian men and women, recognizing the unity of that form, would fulfil the obligations imposed on them by faith; in which the City of the World would prefigure the City of God.

By the middle of the fourteenth century this ideal was no longer founded in reality, it had ceased to inspire the collective conscience of Christians and to help them as a single unit towards their goal. Though not yet dead, Christendom had been mortally wounded, and would be superseded within a hundred years by a wholly different concept of the world.

Can this failure be explained? To some extent it can, but not completely. There is no doubt that at the beginning of the century in question too many Christians, even among the higher clergy, were found wanting, unfaithful to their vocation. Evidence of decline was apparent in frantic chasing after benefices, in the increased financial demands of the Curia, and in the growing preoccupation of clergymen with temporal affairs. But the Church had already survived more than one similar crisis, and, thanks to repeated efforts, had emerged from each more youthful and more vigorous. How was it, then, that reforms initiated at the beginning of the fourteenth century and continued after 1350 did not suffice to regenerate Christendom and avoid the terrible upheaval of the Protestant revolution?

Some historians have blamed the very essence of Christendom, which, as we saw in the last section of Chapter I, harboured the seeds of its own decay. For the Church was too closely linked with the fate of secular society; the spiritual was too much concerned with questions that were not within its province. Too many people, otherwise sincere, confused the interests of Christ with those of the historico-social complex which was Christendom. On the other hand, there were not wanting those who saw the impending danger and tried to forestall it. Why did they fail? In previous centuries St Bernard, then St Francis and St Dominic, had managed to extricate the Church

---

[1] See Chapter I, section 9. Note that the idea of unity deriving from that of Christendom survived the latter. Pierre Dubois proposes in place of Christendom a secular society of European nations, a United States of Europe. (*See* Bernard Voyenne, *Petite histoire de l'idée européenne*, 1952.)

from her difficulties; why were no such men forthcoming in the early fourteenth century? Why did those who talked loudest of reform choose the way of anarchy and even of heresy?

The third cause of Christendom's decline was an intellectual revolt against the data of Revelation, against the very idea of the human race as an organic unity controlled by faith. The development of rationalism in every department of thought, and the appearance of nationalism which was to some extent its consequence, undermined the floor of Christendom. It is not enough to blame human pride and to see this phenomenon as the work of Satan. Why did men feel the need of spiritual nourishment other than that whereby they had existed until now?

Perhaps the answer to these questions is one that transcends those founded upon direct historical observation. The three facts to which we have just drawn attention reveal an undeniable lowering of vitality in the Christian soul, which therefore lacked strength to accomplish yet one more reform, to free itself from the trammels of this world, and to win the loyalty of mankind. Maybe it was simply that medieval society, which had emerged from the fiery furnace of a barbarian age, had grown feeble after a triumphant career of three hundred years. Earthly successes are always transient; having attained their zenith, they start immediately to decline. And this is even more true in the case of a human society whose end is not temporal glory, whose Master chose to conquer the world by defeat and death. Some philosophers of history—Spengler, Toynbee, Sokorin, and others—maintain that communities are subject to laws akin to those which govern individuals, that a time of youth and fulfilment necessarily gives place to old age and death. They may be right, especially when they associate a certain form of spiritual behaviour with each of these phases. Medieval Christendom had enjoyed its time of youth and faith, of vital urge and spiritual uplift. In a different age, and in many respects, a new equilibrium had to be found.

The Church of Christ would have a part to play in this new world. Though a divine institution carrying the promise of eternity, she sometimes appeared closely associated with this or that form of human society; but in fact she transcended them all. She never identified herself with the Roman Empire. Rather, the Empire relied upon her for support in its declining years. And when that Empire collapsed, she managed to steer an independent course amid the chaos of barbarism; nor was she taken prisoner by that form of civilization to which she herself had contributed the noblest elements.

She was destined to play the part of guide in that new world which came to birth after a period of woeful confusion. She would effect a new synthesis between the transient facts of history and the eternal principles of Christ. The somewhat incoherent agitation of the 'Spirituals' and a revival of mysticism would breathe fresh life into Christian sentiment, adapting it to the new kind of man, the man of modern times, who, though less sociable, more interior, and more refined, was still a believer. As the nations became conscious of themselves and abandoned the old dream of formal unity, the Church would concern herself with a more spiritual type of unity. She would continue her task within the framework of local patriotisms, and at length baptize the new-born sentiment of nationalism in the blood of Joan of Arc. When modern man, seeking more distant horizons, set out to discover the world, the Church would send her missionaries in company with the conquistadors, and the fervour of new Christian communities would make good her losses to Protestantism. With the advent of new critical understanding and means to knowledge, she would adopt all that was of value in this ferment to clarify her dogmas, to improve her methods, and to strengthen her organization. Christendom might be on the point of death; but the Council of Trent, in no uncertain terms, would proclaim the Church's future role on earth.

The misfortune is that this attempt to realize a new synthesis was not made two centuries earlier. What would have happened if a pope like Pius V had undertaken to restore Christian values about 1350; if the Catechism of the Council of Trent had stolen a march on the Reformers; if St Ignatius of Loyola had been contemporary with Jacopone da Todi, Occam, and Wyclif? The grain sown by Christ in good soil never dies, for such is His promise; but human error may sometimes delay its germination.

12. THE LAST WITNESS: DANTE

As medieval Christendom plunged into the abyss, a cry went up, stronger, perhaps, and more moving than any that had yet been heard. This voice gave utterance in immortal language to the sublimity of the Christian ideal and to the age-long Christian message.

He whose cry was to echo down the centuries and bear witness, even in our own day, to medieval culture, stood, as do all creative geniuses, at a turning-point of history. One part of him was deeply rooted in the past, another looked boldly to the future. He fashioned one of the most perfect of those national languages which were at that time in process of development. Through him literature took a decisive step towards its present-day pattern, analysis of the individual soul and knowledge of its hidden psychology. But the material element of his work was drawn from the immediate past which he resurrected and glorified. Everything essential therein proceeds in substance from the ideal laid down, from the experience acquired, by Christian generations of the great epoch. Two poetic streams had risen during the Middle Ages: one initiated by the Franciscans; the other scholarly, flowing from the troubadours and the courts of love. Those two currents were to unite in the *dolce stil nuovo* which he presented for the admiration of the world in a series of immortal verses. The *summae* compiled by medieval philosophers and theologians, and the cathedrals, those great compendia of stone and glass, called for a poetic *summa* in order to perfect the threefold pattern.

Its author was Dante Alighieri, born in the spring of 1265 at Florence, where he spent his childhood. He knew sorrow early; for his mother died when he was very young, his father remarried, and he saw his country drenched in the blood of internecine warfare. The merest trifle was made to excuse a fight in Tuscany, which to this extent reflected the state of Italy as a whole. Guelphs and Ghibellines were reviving ancient feuds; upstart bourgeois and aristocratic cliques were rivals for power and wealth; while an exasperated people were ever prepared to rise against their oppressors. It was from his memory of these things that the poet called up an image of the Arno 'flowing less with water than with blood.'

One day, however, this unhappy childhood was enlightened by a heavenly sunbeam. Later, in the *Vita Nuova* (1292), he described how, at the age of nine years, he met a little girl of his own age, named Beatrice, and how from that hour he was in love with her for all eternity. 'One might have said,' he murmured, 'that she had come on earth to show us the nature of a miracle.' This childish love so completely filled Dante's heart that nothing could ever tear him from it. Nor, indeed, had it to endure the wear and tear of life, the merciless erosion caused by habit and daily contact. Beatrice died young; but she became an imperishable image, the symbol of all that is loftiest and purest in man's soul. She was actually identified with uncreated Wisdom, which sometimes reveals itself to mortals in mystical contemplation, in the lightning-flash of genius, or in the overwhelming sweetness of a spring morning.

It was in order to rejoin Beatrice in the empyrean, where her everlasting youth was confounded with ineffable knowledge, that Dante gave himself entirely to the study of all that human intelligence could at that time acquire. Arts and sciences, philosophy and theology, nothing escaped his joyous longing. Valuable friendships guided him in this untiring search: the charming and melancholy poet Guido Cavalcanti, the musician Casella, the sublime painter Giotto, the theologian Bro. Remigio da Girolami (himself a disciple of St Thomas), and, above all, his 'dear and kind' old master Brunetto whom, in the fifteenth canto of the *Inferno*, he thanks in moving terms for having taught him 'how man makes himself eternal.' At the age of twenty-four his education was complete.

But at Florence, towards the end of the thirteenth century, it was impossible for a young intellectual to pursue in peace the task of personal perfection. If not by choice, then by force of circumstance, he was caught up in the flow of events. Besides, Dante was never one to stand apart from a struggle when truth was at stake. For him, principles were incarnate beings and errors had the faces of men. At the age of twenty-four he fought as a loyal Guelph against the Ghibel-lines of Arezzo, and then joined an expedition against Pisa. He was destined to share throughout his life in political warfare, from which his passionate temperament and unyielding determination allowed him no means of escape. He was married when about thirty years old to a certain Gemma Donati, of whom he required no more than that she should be the mother of his children, and whom he nowhere mentions in his works. He was also enrolled in the guild of physicians, one of the most honourable in the scale of Arts. These qualifications might have enabled Alighieri at another time and in another place to live as a comfortable bourgeois, devoting his nights and dreams to literature; though his work would surely have suffered in consequence. But events, which are the manifestation of God's Providence, tore him from such an easy-going existence and exposed him to all the vicissi-tudes of a wandering life.

In 1300 he was elected prior of the city, i.e. one of the council of six persons who administered its affairs, and he found himself in a mael-strom of violence and intrigue. The Florentine Guelphs at that time were split into two factions. True, the whole Guelph party sided with the Church and was traditionally opposed to imperial ascendancy in Italy; but one faction, the 'Whites,' resented the pressure brought to bear upon their city by the overweening Boniface VIII through his legate, Cardinal Matteo d'Aquasparta. The 'Blacks' were whole-heartedly for the Pope and even wished to help his ally, Charles II of Naples, recover Sicily.

In the Jubilee year of 1300, also, Florence resolved to send an official delegation to Rome, and Dante was offered a place therein. He accepted, partly, perhaps, to get a closer look at Boniface VIII and the Curia, partly, no doubt, to avoid suspicion of cowardice—for his enemies could take advantage of his absence. 'If I remain,' he asked, 'who will go; but if I go, who will remain?' He had judged aright. The 'Blacks' seized power and called in Charles II; the pacification of Florence was attended with a spate of decrees, and many of the 'Whites' were arrested and exiled. In January 1302 Dante was driven from his native city, cast from 'the fair sheepfold wherein I used to sleep, a lamb.' (*Paradiso*, xxv. 2.)

He lived henceforward as an outcast, always troubled by 'the bitter taste of another's bread, the hard road of another's stair'; and so it was to be for the remaining twenty years of his life. It was a dreadful fate, to be torn from one's country and turned loose upon the highways of the world; he was a 'displaced person.' But such cruelty is characteristic of mankind. It caused Dante the most bitter suffering: he had learned the invariable degradation of political wrangling. He had longed 'to form a party on his own,' but that is a pleasure for which politicians generally charge too high a price. He travelled to Verona, Lucca, Ravenna, and even, maybe, to Paris, a wanderer on earth, having no homeland but his inner self where he accomplished a work of genius. Florence gave him one chance to return, but at the price of intolerable humiliation in the shape of public penance to be done in the cathedral. 'That is not my way of returning home,' he replied.

Eventually, he went to live at Ravenna, the gentle, dreamy city of mosaics, where a wealthy man, one Guido Novella da Polenta (nephew to Francesca da Rimini, the sinner whom he has immortalized), took him under his protection. The sufferings of exile, the privations, the bitterness, and perhaps the insidious marsh-fever, had engraved his features with fascinating beauty. Boccaccio tells us that, as his literary work became known, people who saw his tragic and sombre form go by would say to one another: 'There's a man who has been to hell and come back again.' He, the poet, was deprived of all earthly joys. He had seen his enemy Boniface VIII succumb to Nogaret's blow, and cried out in horror at this sudden collapse of Peter's throne. He had likewise beheld the arrival of Henry VII in Italy, not to restore peace, as he had hoped, but to foster anarchy. There remained only a transcendent hope and, as he says in the closing lines of his poem, 'that love which moves the Sun and the other stars.' Offered the post of ambassador at Venice, he accepted, although his strength was ebbing rapidly; for was not the service of peace the service of Almighty God?

Dante died at Ravenna on 14th September 1321, and that noble city which had sweetened his exile was determined to retain his body. When his name became celebrated, Florence, his ungrateful fatherland, tried to recover it, but in vain. So there he lies, close to the church of St Francis, where he had so often prayed, in a tiny garden filled with cool shade and with silence. Far removed from the strife and suffering of earth, as in the sublime vision born of his imagination, beyond the circles of hell and the mount of expiation, he has, no doubt, attained to everlasting peace, to the seven stages of heaven where, at the summit, dwells the Lamb.

His principal work, the *Divine Comedy*, was written during the last years of his life, after he had reached the age of fifty, when knowledge of men and experience of events had taught him to hope in God alone.

U*

Consisting of three parts—*Inferno, Purgatorio,* and *Paradiso*—this famous work is one of the most tremendous achievements in all the literature of the world. Like many a great monument of human thought, it has its fanatical devotees, its tireless scholiasts; but the general public admires it from farther off and without pretending to penetrate its secrets, confining themselves to a few episodes which are part of the common culture of the West.

It must be admitted that the *Divine Comedy* is in many ways a difficult work, because Dante was determined to pack into it all the knowledge he had been able to acquire, and to load that knowledge with arid dissertations on botany, alchemy, mineralogy, and physiology, or with abstract philosophical and theological speculation. It is difficult also on account of its numerous allusions to facts and people of that age, allusions which have no secrets from the learned but which escape those readers who are not familiar with the history of the *Trecento.* Finally, it is a difficult work because of its constant use of allegory. The poet intentionally concealed his thoughts—'that difficult enigma,' he says in Canto XXXIII of the *Purgatorio*—by recourse to an esotericism which innumerable scholars have, for six centuries, attempted to elucidate in commentaries which contradict one another in the most disconcerting fashion.

The fact remains, however, that in spite of obscurity and occasional monotony, the *Divine Comedy* is a fascinating work, an intellectual universe so wonderful that it is hard to know how any man could have conceived it. The beauty of language, the rhythmic cadences, the definitive exactness of so many formulae, and above all that interior breath, that vital urge which drives the poem along, even through interminable declamations, until it reaches a land of light and incomparable fullness—all these qualities make the *Divine Comedy* a unique achievement, one of the three or four priceless jewels in Europe's crown.

Notwithstanding a host of symbols and obscurities, the general meaning of the poem is clear. It is the description of a journey claimed to have been made by the author in Holy Week, 1300, through Hell, Purgatory, and Heaven. He describes those whom he met on the road, the facts which he learned, and his own meditations on this marvellous experience. The descriptive passages are so extraordinarily precise that it has been possible to draw maps and plans and to build models of that country beyond the grave. But across the background formed by this strange geography, a perpetual shifting of figures, episodes, and allusions transforms each region into a dreamland forest where the most resplendent images succeed nightmare visions.

The theme was not original. Many ancient writers, e.g. Homer and Virgil, had pictured the living visiting the dead. There were also Moslem poems describing journeys through heaven and hell; and Celtic monks of the barbarian epoch, in the feverish solitude of their convents, had written many another such tale around the persons of St Brendan or St Patrick. But upon this common ground Dante erected a monumental structure, combining the profound truth of man's destiny with all that the Middle Ages had discovered about eternal realities, and resting the whole of his romantic story upon theological foundations.

Dante himself is the hero of the *Divine Comedy*; the background is his own experience, the story of his conversion. Wandering in 'the dark forest' of vice, he almost stumbles into hell where so many unfortunates pay the price of sin. Saved from damnation through the intervention of our Lady, he gradually discovers the way of light by climbing the painful mount of Purgatory. Two providential beings come to assist him on this journey: Virgil, representing human reason freed from the yoke of passion, and Beatrice, who stands both for ineffable love and for revealed truth. Thanks to them, he is able to reach the place of all peace and of all justice, Paradise. The poem is essentially autobiographical. He whom we follow on this curious road is a man like unto ourselves. Like him, we are shaken by the gusts of hell, we feel the breath of fire in which the damned are burning. With him we share the proud sorrows of sinful love. With him also we rise to light and certainty. He is a man speaking to men with human voice; and herein his poem bears a close resemblance to the cathedral. Like every cathedral, the *Divine Comedy* is built on the human scale. The Last Judgment over the cathedral door warns the soul of its peril, as does the *Inferno*, and then leads it with an escort of saints to the great Rose Window where the angelic choirs are ranged about the majesty of God. The poet is directed by our Lord Himself to 'rescue those who live on earth in a state of misery and lead them to the state of bliss.' It is to all his mortal brethren that he cries his awful warning. The *Divine Comedy* is not merely the autobiography of an exiled Florentine at Ravenna giving vent to his bitterness and hate; it is the story of the soul's journey from the slavery of sin to the liberty of the sons of light, of intelligence enlightened by faith and discovering immortal truth disguised in mortal shape.

The historical framework within which this mighty adventure unfolds is none other than that society of which the poet had direct experience: Christendom. The events to which he refers are those of Christian history; the protagonists of his fantastic work are men who had played a part therein. The problems he is so anxious to solve are those which troubled the whole Christian world. His ideal is the same as that which inspired reforming popes, saints, crusaders, and great thinkers; it is the ideal of a hierarchic order upon earth corresponding to the perfect harmony of heaven. Dante, like his contemporary Andrea da Firenze, in the fresco at Santa Maria Novella, wished to depict the civilization of Christendom at a moment when it was collapsing under stress.

Dante's anxiety for Christendom led him to concentrate his attention on the Church as supernatural guide of that society and keystone of its existence. No literary work has ever been so completely concerned with the Church as is the *Divine Comedy*. None has spoken with more fervour and tenderness of the Spouse of Christ than he who is so often quoted for his invective against some of her prelates and some of her institutions. He was her devoted and unwavering son; he wished to see her absolutely pure, absolutely beautiful, strictly faithful to her Master's precepts, freed from the filth wherewith human weakness defiles the Vessel of Election.

His genius and prophetic insight saw the perils to which the Church was then exposed. Amid the bloody conflicts of his age, he realized that Christendom was passing through a crisis, that her very existence was in danger. The Church seemed to him no longer to obey the law of Christ. Involved as he had been in pitiless strife, he was sometimes unfair, blaming those who had not deserved his censure. But was he wrong in the last resort? His protest was that of the 'Spirituals'— of whom he was never one—but it was also that of some of the best Christians then alive. It heralded St Catherine of Siena's indignation.

The tragedy, in his eyes, was that the Church, instead of proving herself the unassailable witness of things spiritual, the mouthpiece of God, had become bogged down in things of Earth. In the twenty-seventh Canto of the *Paradiso*, St Peter tells Dante:

'The Spouse of Christ was not reared upon my blood, and that of Linus and of Cletus, that she might then be used for gain of gold.' It was against this fundamental treason that he took his stand, even to the point of unfairness.

His work is thus a tremendous clamour against those who betray the ideal of Christianity, against those 'ravening wolves in the guise of shepherds,' against those who 'make a god of gold and silver,' against prelates with richly caparisoned horses, and against all those who, by their silence, make themselves accomplices of evil, decking their sermons with witticism and buffoonery instead of recalling the faithful to their sacred duties. The Popes and members of the Curia, whom he expressly names, appeared to him responsible for this state of affairs: Rome, 'where Christ, day in day out, is put to sale' (*Paradiso*, XVII. 51), and later Avignon, where, as vassals of the kings of France, the popes did nothing to prevent the infamy that played unchecked around them. Does that mean to say that Dante, the Guelph, was an enemy of the papacy? No. He had 'respect for the sovereign keys.' He recognized the Pope as our Lord's representative on earth; he even compared Boniface VIII, insulted by Nogaret, to another Christ; and in one passage it is even possible to detect the doctrine of papal infallibility.[1]

What he desired was a papacy freed from earthly shackles in order to lead and care for the baptized. He believed that the Church had committed a fundamental error by accepting the 'Donation of Constantine,' the existence of which he no more doubted than did most of his contemporaries. 'Ah Constantine! to how much ill gave birth, not thy conversion, but that dower which the first rich Father took from thee!' (*Inferno*, XIX. 115–17.) Temporal interests had led the popes to take a hand in worldly business, and thereby to compromise their integrity. 'The Church of Rome, by confounding two powers in herself, falls into the mire, and fouls herself together with her burden.' (*Purgatorio*, XVI. 127–9.)

What was the solution to this grave problem? At one time Dante thought the world would recover if the two swords could be separated, if the Church could be confined within her proper domain and the temporal sphere entrusted to the Emperor, who was the traditional embodiment of unity. That is why Dante, the Guelph, called for the intervention of the Germans in Italy, not (as has been suggested) because he had become a partisan of Henry VII, but because the end for which he hoped seemed to justify this means. Events proved him wrong. Instead of appreciating his high responsibility, the emperor showed a lust for power, greed of gain, weakness, and incapacity to oppose Clement V. What, then, of the splendid image of which Dante dreamed—that image which had haunted so many minds since the Carolingian era, that dream of a universal monarchy, of a world governed spiritually by the Pope and temporally by a Caesar in obedience to the precepts of Christ? Was it a mere decoy? Now that this hope had been disappointed, what remained?

Men could still remind themselves that in face of eternity all earthly associations are vain, that Christian policy has ultimately to deal with a kingdom not of this world. The true mediators, therefore, the true guides to whom the poet finally entrusted himself, were not worldly powers, but privileged souls on whom the Spirit of God had descended: Virgil, reason purified; Beatrice, mystical knowledge; and all those who have escaped from the bondage of sinful nature to attain the full stature of humanity—the saints who are the real heads of the Church.[2]

---

[1] *Paradiso*, v. 73, 80, *vide infra*.

[2] It is significant that foremost among the saints who lead him to the Virgin Mary he has placed St Bernard of Clairvaux, who was, as we have seen and without any doubt, the most perfect representative of those virtues which ennobled medieval Christianity.

Only they can lead the Spouse of Christ into the light, and it is because there are so many of them that we can still have hope. The human side of the Church may be defiled; but no matter, if she continue to preach her message. A liberator will one day arise, whose coming Dante prophesied in the shape of a mysterious personage, the *Veltro*, the 'Greyhound,' whose identity has been much discussed but who may possibly be none other than Christ intervening directly in history.

Thus the essential lesson of the *Divine Comedy* is simply an appeal to the Christian conscience. 'If the world to-day goeth astray,' says Marco Lombardo to Dante on the third terrace of the Mount of Expiation, 'in you is the cause, in you be it sought.' (*Purgatorio*, XVI. 82, 83.) The drama of Christendom is played out in her soul, where each one of us feels himself torn between longing for the light and connivance with the powers of darkness, while the Hound of Heaven goes in chase of men. The true goal, the effort necessary above all others, is to remind men that they are not on earth for the sake of its pleasures, to rouse the consciences of those who lie benumbed in sleep.

> Ye Christians be more sedate in moving,
> not like a feather unto every wind;
> nor think that every water cleanseth you.
> Ye have the old and New Testament
> and the shepherd of the Church to guide you;
> let this suffice you unto your salvation.
> If sorry greed proclaim aught else to you,
> be men, not senseless sheep.
>
> *Paradiso*. V, 73–80.

It is a pure and simple lesson, which the Church had taught her children throughout the period of Cathedral and Crusade, just as she had done during the barbarian night and in the heroic days of the Apostles and Martyrs. Echoing that lesson, Dante expressed in noble language the same thoughts uttered by the mystics in their prayers, by craftsmen in their churches, by the theologians in their writings, and by crusaders in the shedding of their blood.

'*Metanoeite!* be ye transformed in mind!' Such is the keynote of Christian faith, whereby man rises above himself and makes himself eternal; such is the word that passeth not away, that sums up the whole history of the Church. For since she was entrusted with the Beatitudes on a hill in Galilee, what has she done all down the centuries but repeat this word, calling men back from the transitory forms in which earthly societies are revealed, to the permanent requirements of their faith?

CHRONOLOGICAL TABLE

Italics are used to indicate the principal events in each column.

DATE	HISTORY OF THE CHURCH	POLITICAL AND SOCIAL EVENTS	ARTS AND LETTERS

ELEVENTH CENTURY

DATE	HISTORY OF THE CHURCH	POLITICAL AND SOCIAL EVENTS	ARTS AND LETTERS
1050		The Turks in the Near East, Henri I reigning in France since 1031.	Abbey church, Conques (1030–80), St Hilaire, Poitiers (1045–80). (Sta Maria, Ripoll, 1031.)
1054	*The Greek Schism. Death of Pope St Leo IX.*	Council of Narbonne codifying the 'Truce of God.' Death of Yaroslav the Wise, king of Kiev.	
1055	Victor II (1055–7).	Death of Zoe, Empress of the East.	
1056		Overthrow of the Macedonian dynasty at Byzantium. Death of the German emperor, Henry III. Accession of Henry IV (1056–1106).	
1057	Cardinal Humbert publishes *Against Simoniacs*. Stephen IX, Pope (1057–8).	Robert Guiscard, Duke of Apulia (1057–85). Isaac Comnenus at Byzantium (1057–9).	
1059	*Decree of Nicholas II (Pope 1058–61) on the election of popes by the cardinals.*	Constantine X Ducas Emperor of Byzantium (1059–67). The Almoravids in Morocco.	
1060		Philip I, King of France (1060–1108).	
1061	Alexander II (1061–1073).		
1062			The Trinity, Caen (1062–83).
1063	Alexander II grants an indulgence to the 'crusaders' of Spain.		San Miniato, Florence, consecrated (1063). Pisa Cathedral begun (1063–1119).
1064		The Turks take Armenia.	St Stephen, Caen (1064–87).
1065		Death of Ferdinand I, the Great, of Castile, and accession of Alfonso VI (1065–1109).	St Mary, Cologne, consecrated (1065).
1066	Pagan revolt in Baltic lands.	*Norman Conquest of England.* William I of England (1066–87).	
1067		Romanus IV Diogenes, Emperor of Byzantium (1067–71).	
1071		*The Byzantines crushed by the Turks at Mantzikert.*	

611

DATE	HISTORY OF THE CHURCH	POLITICAL AND SOCIAL EVENTS	ARTS AND LETTERS
1072			Lincoln Cathedral (1072–92).
1073	*Election of Gregory VII (29 June).*		
1074	Decrees against simony and Nicolaïsm.		
1075	St Robert founds Molesmes. Gregory VII condemns lay investiture.		
1076		Henry IV rebels against the Pope. The Turks enter Jerusalem.	St Sernin, Toulouse (1076–1119).
1077	Stephen de Muret founds the future Order of Grandmont.	*Canossa (25th Jan. 1077).*	
1078		The Turks occupy Asia Minor.	Cathedral of St James of Compostella (1078–1128); St Trophime, Arles (1078–1220).
1080	Conversion of Sweden.		St Benoit sur Loire (1080–1108).
1081		Accession of Alexius Comnenus (1081–1118).	
1084	St Bruno founds the Charterhouse.		
1085	*Death of Gregory VII.*	*Toledo recovered from Islam.*	
1086	Victor III (1086–7).	The Almoravids in Spain.	
1087		Death of William the Conqueror. William II Rufus, King of England (1087–1100).	
1088	Urban II (1088–99).		*Abbey church of Cluny (1088–1109).*
1090	*Birth of St Bernard.*		
1093			Durham Cathedral (1093–1130). Abbey of Maria Lach (1093–1156).
1094		*Valencia captured by Cid Campeador.*	
1095	*Urban II, at Clermont, preaches the first crusade.* Foundation of the Antonines.	Campaigns of Boleslav III of Poland in Pomerania.	Cathedral of St Mark, Venice (1095–1500).
1096	Robert of Arbrissel founds the Order of Fontevrault.		Vézelay (1096–1132).
1098	*Foundation of Cîteaux.*		
1099	Paschal II (1099-1108). *Capture of Jerusalem by the crusaders.*	Foundation of the Latin kingdom of Jerusalem. Death of Cid Campeador.	Modena Cathedral (1099–1184). St Clement at Rome (1099–1118).

DATE	HISTORY OF THE CHURCH	POLITICAL AND SOCIAL EVENTS	ART AND LETTERS
		TWELFTH CENTURY	
1100		Henry I, Beauclerk, King of England (1100–35).	The cloister at Moissac. Mayence Cathedral (1100–1234).
1101		Roger II of Sicily (1101–54).	Angoulême Cathedral (1101–28).
1104		Alfonso I of Aragon, the Battler (1104–34).	
1106		Henry V of Germany (1106–25).	
1108	William of Champeaux founds St Victor.	Louis VI, King of France (1108–1137).	
1112	St Bernard enters Citeaux.	Dramatic 'commune' of Laon.	
1113		Vladimir II, Prince of Kiev (1113–25).	
1115	*St Bernard* founds Clairvaux.		Gothic attempts at Morienval.
1116			St Gilles du Gard (1116–80).
1118	*Foundation of the Templars.*	John II Comnenus (1118–43).	
1119	Callixtus II (1119–1124).		
1120	The Hospitallers become a military Order.		The *Chanson de Roland.* The sculptures at Vézelay. St Front, Périgueux (1120–73). Autun Cathedral (1120–1178). St Zeno, Verona (1120–78). Salamanca Cathedral (1120–78).
1121	St Norbert founds Prémontré.		
1122	Peter the Venerable, Abbot of Cluny (1122–56). Suger, Abbot of St Denis. Concordat of Worms. End of the Quarrel of Investitures.	The Almohads in Morocco.	
1123	Ninth Oecumenical Council (Lateran).	*The 'Truce of God' made binding on the whole Church.*	
1124	Death of the heretic Pierre de Bruys.		
1125		Lothair of Saxony, Emperor (1125–38).	
1126	Creation of a bishopric in Greenland.		
1130	Death of Honorius II; election of Innocent II; schism of Anacletus.		Gothic abbey of Fontenay (1130–47). Romanesque cathedral of Parma (1130–50).

DATE	HISTORY OF THE CHURCH	POLITICAL AND SOCIAL EVENTS	ART AND LETTERS
1130			St Stephen's Cathedral, Sens, gothic (1130–64).
1132			Palatine chapel, Palermo.
1134		Victory of Alfonso-Henry of Portugal at Ourique.	
1135		Stephen of Blois, King of England (1135–54).	Sculpture at Moissac.
1137		Louis VII, King of France (1137–80).	Abbey church of St Denis, gothic (1137–89).
1137		Conrad III, Emperor (1138–52).	
1139			Death of the jurist Irnerius.
1140			Sculpture of the Royal Porch, Chartres.
1141	Council of Sens: St Bernard confounds Abélard.		
1142			Gratian publishes his treatise on Canon Law.
1143		Baldwin III of Jerusalem (1143–1162).	
1144	Lucius II (1144–5).	Manuel Comnenus (1143–80).	
1145	Election of Eugenius III (1145–57), a Cistercian monk.	Edessa retaken by the Turks.	St Bernard's *De Consideratione*. Angers Cathedral (1145–1230).
1146	*Easter Sunday, at Vézelay, St Bernard preaches the second crusade.*	At Rome, demagogic dictatorship of Arnold of Brescia.	
1147		Retaking of Lisbon by Alfonso-Henry of Portugal. 'Crusade' on the Baltic.	
1148			Many Cistercian abbey churches in primitive gothic.
1150		Progress of Albert the Bear in Brandenburg and of Henry the Lion to Lubeck.	Mans Cathedral (1150–1300). Zamora Cathedral (romanesque, 1150–1174). Noyon Cathedral (1151–1220).
1152		*Frederick Barbarossa, King of Germany, Emperor* (1152–90).	
1153	*Death of St Bernard* (20th Aug.). Anastasius IV (1153–4).		Senlis Cathedral (1153–91).
1154	Adrian IV (1154–9).	Henry II Plantagenet, King of England (1154–89).	
1155		Adrian IV declares the right of serfs to marry freely.	
1156	Foundation of the Order of Alcantara.		

DATE	HISTORY OF THE CHURCH	POLITICAL AND SOCIAL EVENTS	ART AND LETTERS
1158	Foundation of the Order of Calatrava.		
1159	Alexander III (1159–1181).		
1160			Laon Cathedral (1160–1207). Cistercian abbey of Pontigny (1160–1180).
1161	Foundation of the Order of St James.		
1162			Poitiers Cathedral (1162–1271).
1163			Notre-Dame de Paris begun (1163–1260).
1165	About this date the Catharist heresy appeared in S. France.		
1167			Between 1150 and 1200, successive redactions of Tristam and Iseult.
1168			Sens Cathedral (numerous subsequent alterations).
1169		Sack of Kiev.	
1170	Martyrdom of St Thomas Becket. Rise of the Waldensian heresy.		
1171	Birth of St Dominic.		
1174	Canonization of St Bernard.	Baldwin IV of Jerusalem, the leper king (1174–83).	Basilica of Monreale near Palermo.
1175			Soissons Cathedral (1175–1212) and Canterbury (1175–1192).
1176		Frederick Barbarossa defeated at Legnano by the Italian urban leagues. Venetian defeat at Myriokephalon, Asia Minor finally becomes Turkish.	
1179	Third Lateran Council. Decree requiring two-thirds majority for the election of a pope. Appeal against the Cathars.	Portugal becomes a kingdom. The Church condemns tournaments.	Education made obligatory in all dioceses.
1180		Philip Augustus, King of France (1180–1223).	Cathedrals of Agde (1180–1300) and Wells (1180–1239).
1181	Lucius III (1181–5).	Andronicus Comnenus (1182–1185).	
1182	Birth of St Francis of Assisi. The Maronites return to the Roman Church.		

DATE	HISTORY OF THE CHURCH	POLITICAL AND SOCIAL EVENTS	ARTS AND LETTERS
1184	The Assembly of Verona institutes the Inquisition (episcopal).		St Benezet builds the bridge at Avignon.
1185	Urban III (1185–7).	Isaac Angelus (1185–95).	Palermo Cathedral.
1187	Clement III (1187–1191).	*Disaster of Tiberias, Saladin retakes Jerusalem.*	
1189	The third crusade.	Richard Cœur de Lion, King of England (1189–99).	
1190	Foundation (in the Holy Land) of the Teutonic Knights.	Death of Frederick Barbarossa; Henry VI of Germany (1190–1197).	Portuguese abbey of Alcobaça (1190–1220). Cathedrals of Leon (1190–1271) and Bamberg (1190–1274).
1191	Celestine III (1191–1198).		
1192			Bourges Cathedral (1192–1270).
1194			*Chartres Cathedral* (1194–1260).
1195		*Enfranchisement of serfs by the church becomes more frequent.* At Byzantium, Alexius III Angelus (1195–1203).	
1197		Frederick II, King of the Romans.	
1198	*Election of Innocent III* (8th Jan.). St John of Matha founds the Order of Trinitarians.		
1199		John 'Lackland,' King of England (1199–1216).	

THIRTEENTH CENTURY

DATE	HISTORY OF THE CHURCH	POLITICAL AND SOCIAL EVENTS	ARTS AND LETTERS
1201	The Inquisition entrusted to papal legates.		
1202	Innocent III launches the *fourth crusade.*	Foundation of Riga.	Death of Joachim of Flora. Rouen Cathedral (1202–1300).
1203		At Byzantium, overthrow of the Angelus family.	
1204		*Constantinople taken by the crusaders;* foundation of the Latin Empire of the East.	
1205	Innocent III reveals to Bishop Diego and St Dominic their true mission.	At Nicaea, the Greek Emperor Theodore Lascaris. Poland becomes a kingdom.	
1207	St Dominic founds Notre-Dame de Prouille.		
1208	Murder of the legate Peter of Castelnau.		

DATE	HISTORY OF THE CHURCH	POLITICAL AND SOCIAL EVENTS	ARTS AND LETTERS
1209	Foundation of the Carmelites. Beginning of the Albigensian Crusade.	Otto of Brunswick crowned Emperor.	
1210	*Innocent III gives verbal approval to St Francis's undertaking.*		*Miracles de la Vierge* composed.
1212	St Clare founds the Poor Clares.	Great victory of the Christians of Spain at *Las Navas da Tolosa.*	
1213	Foundation of the charitable Order of the Holy Spirit.	Victory of Simon de Montfort over Peter of Aragon at Muret.	
1214		*Bouvines.*	*Rheims Cathedral* (1214–1300). Birth of Roger Bacon.
1215	Twelfth Oecumenical Council (Fourth Lateran). *Approval of the Friars Minor (Franciscans).*	The Great Charter in England. The Church condemns judicial duels.	*Official foundation of Paris University.*
1216	*Death of Innocent III,* election of Honorius III. *Foundation of the Order of Friars Preachers* (Dominicans). Pagan revival in the Baltic lands.	Henry III, King of England (1216–72).	
1217		Ferdinand III of Castile, the saint (1217–52).	Le Mans Cathedral (1217–54).
1218	Fifth crusade, John de Brienne in Egypt.	*Frederick II, King of Germany then Emperor* (1218–50). Simon de Montfort killed before Toulouse.	
1219	St Francis of Assisi in Egypt.		
1220	The Franciscan martyrs of Morocco.		Amiens Cathedral (1220–70). Cathedrals of Salisbury (1220–66) and Brussels (1220–73).
1221	*Death of St Dominic* (6th Aug.).		
1222	The Dominican St Hyacinth forms a convent at Kiev.	John Vatatzes, Greek Emperor of Nicea.	
1223	Foundation of the Servites. And, by St Peter Nolasco, of the Order of Mercy.	Louis VIII, King of France (1223–6).	
1224	St Francis receives the Stigmata.	Genghis Khan invades Russia.	Mont St Michel, chief gothic parts.
1225		The Teutonic Knights fight in the West.	Beginning of the *Roman de la Rose.*

DATE	HISTORY OF THE CHURCH	POLITICAL AND SOCIAL EVENTS	ARTS AND LETTERS
1226	*Death of St Francis* (3rd Oct.).	St Louis, *Louis IX, King of France* (1226–70).	Burgos Cathedral (1226–60).
1227	Death of Honorius III. Cardinal Hugolin becomes Gregory IX.		Cathedrals of Trèves (1227–53) and Toledo (1227–1418).
1228	Canonization of St Francis.		Church of St Francis at Assisi (1228–33).
1229	The 'false crusade' of Frederick II succeeds: Jerusalem surrendered to the Christians.	The S. of France is attached to the Capetian domain.	
1230		The 'Crusade' of the Teutonic Knights in the Baltic lands.	About 1230, renaissance of Roman Law.
1231	Gregory IX entrusts the Inquisition to the mendicant Orders.		
1233	Year of the 'Great Devotion.'		
1234	Canonization of St Dominic.		Raymund of Peñafort publishes his treatise on Canon Law.
1236			Great period of the Rheims sculptors.
1237		The Mongols in S. Russia.	
1238		Great Mongol invasion of Turkestan and Persia.	
1240			Birth of Cimabue (1240–1301).
1241	Death of Gregory IX, the papal see vacant for two years.	*The Mongols in Central Europe: Christian defeat at Liebnitz.*	Villard de Honnecourt working in Hungary.
1243	Innocent IV (1243–1254).		The Sainte-Chapelle, Paris (1243–8).
1244	*Final loss of Jerusalem.*		
1245	The Council of Lyons deposes Frederick II.	John of Plan-Carpin travels in Asia.	Westminster Abbey (1245–68).
1247			Beauvais Cathedral (1247–72).
1248		Longjumeau's embassy to the Mongols.	*The Bees*, a satiric work by Th. de Chantimpré.
			Cologne Cathedral (1248 – nineteenth century).
1250	Failure of the seventh crusade: *St Louis captive in Egypt.*	In the Empire, the Great Interregnum.	Expansion of English gothic.
			Cathedrals of Siena (1250–1326), Upsala in Sweden (1250–1435), and Strasbourg (1250–1318).

DATE	HISTORY OF THE CHURCH	POLITICAL AND SOCIAL EVENTS	ARTS AND LETTERS
1252	Innocent IV authorizes the use of torture by the Inquisition but institutes a jury of good men and true.		
1253		William of Rubrouk travels among the Mongols.	
1254	Alexander IV (1254–1261).		
1255	Condemnation of the 'Spirituals.'		
1256	Union of the Augustinians in a single Order.		
1257	*St Bonaventure, Minister General of the Franciscans.*		
1258		Michael VIII Palaeologus, Byzantine emperor. The Mongols take Bagdad. The Provisions of Oxford.	
1260		St Louis expressly forbids the judicial duel. The Mongols in Syria.	Death of Accorso, the Bolognese jurist.
1261	Urban IV (1261–4).	*The Greeks drive the Latins from Constantinople.* Michael VIII Palaeologus (1261–82).	
1263		Anti-clerical revolt at Cologne.	
1265	Clement IV (1265–8).	Travels of Marco Polo in Asia (to 1295).	*St Thomas Aquinas begins the 'Summa.'* Birth of Dante and Duns Scotus. Roger Bacon publishes *Opus Majus.*
1266		Conradin, last descendant of Frederick II, dies on the scaffold.	*Birth of Giotto.*
1268			
1270	Failure of the eighth crusade.	*Death of St Louis at Tunis,* accession of Philip III the Hardy.	Exeter Cathedral (1270–1370).
1271	St Gregory X (1271–1276).		
1272		Edward I, King of England (1272–1307).	
1273		Rudolf of Habsburg, Emperor (1273–91).	Limoges Cathedral (1273–1329).
1274	Council of Lyons, *Decree instituting the Conclave.*		Deaths of St Bonaventure and St Thomas Aquinas.
1275			Ratisbon Cathedral (1275–1524).
1276	Innocent V.		
1277	Nicholas III (1277–1280).		
1278			Death of Nicolo Pisano.

DATE	HISTORY OF THE CHURCH	POLITICAL AND SOCIAL EVENTS	ARTS AND LETTERS
1281	Martin IV (1281–5).	Last Mongol attack on Moslem Syria.	
1282		The Sicilian Vespers. Andronicus II the Elder, Emperor of Byzantium (1282–1328).	Albi Cathedral (1282–1480).
1283	Prussia forcibly converted by the Teutonic Knights.		
1284			Collapse of Beauvais Cathedral. Death of Roger Bacon.
1285	Honorius IV (1285–1287).	Philip IV the Fair, King of France (1285–1314).	
1287		Mongol embassy in the West.	
1288	Nicholas IV (1288–1292).		
1289	John of Montecorvino leaves for China.		
1290			Orvieto Cathedral (1290–1320).
1291	*End of the Christian Holy Land; fall of Acre.*	Albert I, Emperor (1291–1308).	York Minister (1291–1342).
1292	Papal interregnum of two years.		The *Vita Nuova* of Dante.
1294	St Celestine, the hermit-Pope. Accession of Boniface III.		
1296			The Duomo, Florence.
1298		Albert I, German Emperor (1298–1308).	

FOURTEENTH CENTURY

DATE	HISTORY OF THE CHURCH	POLITICAL AND SOCIAL EVENTS	ARTS AND LETTERS
1300	*First 'Holy Year' (Jubilee).*		End of the *Roman de la Rose*, third cycle of the *Roman de Renart*.
1301			About 1300, many works for and against the papacy.
1302	Bull *Unam Sanctam*.	Philip the Fair beaten by the Flemings at Courtrai.	
1303	*The Outrage of Anagni and death of Boniface VIII.* Missionary journeys of Raymond Lull in Africa (to his death in 1316). Benedict XII (1303–1304).		
1304			Birth of Petrarch (*d.* 1374).
1305	Clement V (1305–14).		

DATE	HISTORY OF THE CHURCH	POLITICAL AND SOCIAL EVENTS	ARTS AND LETTERS
1307	*Montecorvino, Archbishop of Pekin.* Arrest of the Templars in France.	Edward II, King of England (1307–27).	
1308		Henry VII of Luxemburg, Emperor (1308–13).	Death of Duns Scotus.
1309	*The papacy moves to Avignon.*		
1310			The Passion sculptured for the first time on a cathedral tympanum (Rouen).
1314	Execution of the Templars. Death of Clement V.	Louis IV of Bavaria, Emperor (1313–47). In France, death of Philip the Fair and accession of Louis X le Hutin (1314–16).	
1315		The great famine of 1315–16.	
1316	Election of John XXII (1316–34). Repression of the 'Spirituals.'	Philip V the Long, King of France (1316–22).	Dante writing the *Divine Comedy*.
1317			The *Corpus Juris Canonici* fixes the Church's legal code for 600 years.
1318	Constitution of a Catholic hierarchy in Persia.		St Ouen, Rouen (1318–1537).
1321			Death of Dante.
1322	The 'Lollard' sect.	Charles IV the Fair (1322–8).	
1324			Birth of Wyclif. Marsilius of Padua's *Defender of the Peace*.
1326	The Russian patriarchal see transferred to Moscow.	Death of Osman, accession of the sultan Orkhan.	
1327		Edward II of England deposed and killed. Edward III king.	
1328		*Philip VI of Valois, King of France* (1318–50). At Byzantium, John VI Cantacuzene (1328–41), and John V Palaeologus.	
1329		Nicea captured by the Ottoman Turks.	
1330	Creation of Catholic dioceses in India.		Alvarez de Pelayo's *De Planctu Ecclesiae*.
1331		Stephen Dushan in Serbia.	
1334	Benedict XII (1334–1342).		
1335			Construction of the palace at Avignon.
1337			*Death of Giotto.*

DATE	HISTORY OF THE CHURCH	POLITICAL AND SOCIAL EVENTS	ARTS AND LETTERS
1338		Beginning of the Hundred Years War.	
1339			Vienna Cathedral (1339–59).
1340		Naval defeat of the French at Sluys.	
1342	Clement VI (1342–1352).		
1344			Prague Cathedral (1344–86).
1346		Charles of Moravia, Emperor. French defeat at Crecy.	
1347		The Black Death (30 months). At Rome, Rienzi's *coup d'état*.	
1348	The papacy buys Avignon.		Foundation of Prague University.
1349			Death of William of Occam (born 1298).
1350		The Turks enter Europe.	
1353			Andrea da Firenze's fresco at S. Maria Novella.
1356		The Golden Bull excludes the Pope from all share in the imperial election.	

INDEX

INDEX

Aarhus, 10
Abaqa, 478(*bis*)
Abbasids, 402
Abdu-Allah-ibn-Yasin, 488 f.
Abélard, 56, 87, 98 ff., 101, 189, 260, 312, 316(*bis*), 322 f., 325, 340, 521, 523, 546; and Héloise, 289, 306, 307, 322 f.
Åbo, 495
Abruzzi, 553 f.
Absalom, Bishop, 495
Abu-Yakub, 510
Accorso, 564
Accursus, 339
Achaea, 463
Achard, 110
Acominates, Michael, 415; Nicetas, 415
Acre, 445, 448, 452, 457(*bis*), 459, 468, 470, 475, 476(*bis*), 479 and n., 499
Adalberon, Archbishop, 222, 266, 349
Adalbert of Bremen, 494
Adalbert, St, of Hamburg, 497; of Prague, 499
Adam of St Victor, 49
Adamites, 522, 557
Adela of Turin, 262
Adelard of Bath, 317
Adhemar, Bishop, of Monteil, 49n., 436, 440, 443, 445
Adjutus, Bro., 510
Adolf of Nassau, 570
Adrian IV, Pope, 199 ff., 265, 430
Adrian V, Pope, 203
Adrianople, 429
Adriatic, 397, 402, 415, 417, 466
Aegean, 12, 590
Aegean Isles, 8
Aelred, St, 48
Aesouf, 476
Afghanistan, 402, 466
Africa, 414; mission in, 509
Africa, North, 12, 477, 487, 492, 509, 527
Agde, 351
Agen, 37
Agenais, 298, 542
Agnes, Empress, 173(*bis*)
Agobard, 184, 279
Ahriman, 530
Aigues-Mortes, 472
Aimery Picaud, 66n.
Aimon, Abbot of Pierre-sur-Dives, 355; Archbishop of Bourges, 276
Airanes, 370
Aix-en-Provence, 5
Aix-la-Chapelle, 193n., 207

Alan of Lille, 52n., 114, 325
Alarcos, 491
Albania, 480
Alberic, Cardinal, 536
Alberic, founder of Citeaux, 81, 127
Albert, Bishop, founder of Swordbearers, 500
Albert, Bishop of Saxe, 563
Albert of Hapsburg, 75
Albert the Bear, 498(*bis*)
Albert the Great, St, 27, 44, 309, 315, 316, 325, 326(*bis*), 329, 340, 341, 342
Albi, 373, 388, 534, 535, 541; Bishop of, 537
Albigenses, 45, 99, 137, 150, 197, 520, 527, 529, 536, 538–44, 546 f. *See also* Catharism
Albret (family), 486
Albuquerque, 489
Alcantara, Order of, 492
Alcobaça, 386, 388
Alcuin, 184, 307, 318
Alet, Abbot of, 535
Aleth, mother of St Bernard, 77 ff.
Alexander II, Pope, 121, 122, 123, 426, 485
Alexander III, Pope, 28, 45n., 115, 192 ff., 214, 223, 224, 225, 233, 235, 242, 254, 338, 370, 430, 491, 536
Alexander IV, Pope, 310, 311, 329, 330, 465, 476, 549, 559
Alexander of Hales, 310, 316, 326, 327(*bis*), 342
Alexandria (Egypt), 64n., 468, 473; (Italy), 193(*bis*)
Alexius I Comnenus, 399, 404, 408 ff., 419, 421 ff., 427, 428, 430, 435, 439, 441(*bis*), 443, 445, 528 ff.
Alexius II Comnenus, 397, 412
Alexius III Angelus, 414, 431(*bis*), 461 f.
Alexius IV Angelus, 414, 431, 461 f.
Alexius V Ducas, 414, 462
Alfonso I of Aragon, 490
Alfonso II of Aragon, 526
Alfonso VI of Castile, 488, 491
Alfonso VII of Castile, 491
Alfonso VIII of Castile, 491
Alfonso I of Portugal, 214
Alfonso II of Portugal, 214
Alfonso-Henry of Portugal, 491
Algarve, 491
Algeria, 467, 509, 514
Algiers, 489(*bis*)
Al-Hakim, 402
Al-Mansur, 488, 493
Alma Redemptoris Mater, 49

Almeria, 490
Almohads, 491 f., 493
Almoravids, 4, 489(bis), 490(bis), 491
Alp Arslan, 402
Alphonse of Poitiers, 473
Alvarez Pelayo, 568
Amadour, St, 36
Amalfi, 9, 396, 406, 422
Amaury, 455; A. Bène, 521 f.
Amiens, 3, 6, 90, 347, 351, 354, 357, 359, 369n., 370, 371, 372(bis), 376, 387(bis), 388, 438, 593
Anacletus II, antipope, 103–5, 132, 187, 188, 411n.
Anagni, outrage of, 571–5
Anatolia, 398, 400, 410 f., 433, 449
Ancona, 411, 430, 559
Andalusia, 404, 490 f., 493
Andrea da Firenze, 1, 2, 608
Andrea, Giovanni, 5
Andrew of Hungary, 468
Andrew of Longjumeau, 506(bis)
Andronicus I Comnenus, 397, 412 f.
Andronicus II Palaeologus, 480, 589 f.
Andronicus III Palaeologus, 589
Angela of Foligno, Bl., 44
Angelico, Fra, 392
Angelo Clarens, 559
Angers, 313, 351, 372, 382, 385
Angoulême, 365
Ani, 403
Anjou, 22, 23, 363
Anna Comnena, Princess, 406, 408 f., 410, 415, 420, 427, 441
Anscar, St, 494
Anselm, St, of Bec, 27, 43, 48, 49, 181, 215, 306(bis), 320 f., 323, 340, 430; of Lucca, 285 f.
Antalya, 481
Anthony, St, the Hermit, 40n., 46, 254, 397; of Padua, 51n., 52, 163
Antioch, 12, 403, 410, 411 f., 444(bis), 445(bis), 447 f., 455, 457, 476
Antonines, 254, 423
Apamea, 448
Apollonia, St, 46
Apostolic Brethren, 558
Apulia, 404 f., 409
Aquasparta, Cardinal Matteo d', 604
Aquila, 379
Aquileia, 9, 11
Aquitaine, 104(bis), 529
Arabia, 422
Arabs, 16, 402, 418, 434(bis), 481n.
Aragon, 214, 476, 487, 491, 588; Alfonso I of, 490; Alfonso II of, 526; Pedro II of, 214, 491, 542
Ararat, Mt, 598
Architecture, 563; gothic, 366–73; romanesque, 361–6

Ardent, Raoul, 51
Arezzo, 504, 604
Arghun, 479
Aristotle, 164, 263, 318, 319, 324, 325 f., 326, 328, 331, 332 f., 340, 563
Arles, 9, 189, 304, 364 f., 404
Armenia, 12, 400, 402 f., 447, 452, 473, 478, 504 f., 517
Armenians, 403(bis), 427, 444(bis), 448, 453, 472, 504, 517
Arnaud, Bishop of Cîteaux, 537, 539
Arnauld de Villeneuve, 40, 595
Arnold of Brescia, 99n., 133, 189, 190 f., 208, 524
Arnoul Malecorne, 451
Arras, 19, 376
Arteveld, James van, 588
Artois, Count of, 573 f.
Ascalon, 455, 457, 471, 481
Ascelin, 473, 505
Asia, 380, 397, 414, 434, 439, 443(bis), 453, 503–9
Asia Minor, 8, 404, 412, 426, 429, 434, 443, 454, 458, 464, 472, 528, 590
Assassins, 475
Assen, Tsar John, of Bulgaria, 516
Assisi, 143, 145, 389, 392(bis)
Asturias, 487
Athanasius of Laura, St, 422
Athens, 416(bis), 463, 465
Athos, Mt, 40n., 416, 422 f., 516 f., 517, 590
Atlas, Mt, 489
Aubazine, 384
Aubert, St, 405
Auch, 9
Augustine, St, 7, 38, 63, 79, 113, 115, 130, 153, 162, 184, 237, 263, 287, 318, 320, 509, 527, 545
Augustinians, 162, 498
Augusto Trionfo, 568
Aulnay, 364
Ausculta Fili, 573
Austria, 522
Autun, 39, 363 f., 375
Auvergne, 350, 363
Auxerre, 350
Averroes, 317, 326(bis), 333n.
Aversa, 405; Richard of, 407(bis)
Avicenna, 317, 326
Avignon, 131, 190, 205, 226 f., 240, 245, 251n., 391, 482, 542, 544, 546, 555, 579–587, 584 (palace), 593 and n., 608
Avila, 305
Ayyub, 470 f.

Bacon, Roger, 3, 33n., 316, 318, 325, 341–3, 503, 554, 561, 565
Bagdad, 12
Baikal, Lake, 465 f.

Bairen, 490
Balaguer, 490
Baldwin I of Constantinople, 461, 463, 464
Baldwin II of Constantinople, 37, 464, 476 f.
Baldwin I of Jerusalem, 447 f., 452
Baldwin II of Jerusalem, 437, 447, 449, 452
Baldwin III of Jerusalem, 452, 454 f.
Baldwin IV of Jerusalem, 437, 456
Baldwin V of Jerusalem, 456
Baldwin of Boulogne, 440, 443 f.
Baldwin of Bourg, 446, 452
Balearic Islands, 490, 493
Balkans, 11, 400(bis), 440(bis), 464
Balkash, Lake, 505
Baltic, 3, 10, 13, 14, 495, 496(bis), 498–500, 503
Bamberg, 366, 387
Barbaro, Bro., 501
Barbarossa, see Frederick I
Barcelona, 388, 430, 487, 490(bis)
Bari, 406 f., 440
Barlaam, a Calabrian monk, 591
Bartholomew, Bro., 506 f.
Bartholomew, St, 46
Basel, 129, 251, 461
Basil, St, 420
Basil II 'Bulgaroctonos', 398, 400, 516
Basil, Archbishop of Reggio, 427
Basse-Lorraine, 439
Batu, Khan, 466, 496(bis), 505
Bayeux, 372, 377n., 488
Beaucaire, 19, 538
Beaulieu, 375
Beaune, 364
Beauvais, 347, 372
Bec, 320(bis), 362
Beccos, Patriarch, 480(bis), 590
Bede the Venerable, St, 56
Bedouins, 488 f.
Begards, 557 and n. 595
Béguines, 557n., 595
Beirut, 445, 447 f., 479
Bela IV, 499
Belgium, 439, 522
Belgrade, 400, 439
Benedict, St, 7, 119, 126 f., 128, 148, 237, 249, 268
Benedict XI, Pope, 575, 579
Benedict XII, Pope, 504, 583 f., 586
Benedict of Arezzo, Bro., 504
Benedictines, 11, 42, 46, 161, 239, 248 f., 250, 503
Benevento, 9
Benno, St, 498
Béraud-Villars, Jean, 407n.
Berbers, 477
Berengar, 62, 98, 320, 321, 521
Bergen, 365
Berlin, 392
Bernard of Clairvaux, St, 3, 5, 7, 32, 41 f.,
43, 47–9, 51, 58, 76–115, 119 f., 128 f.,
138(bis), 149, 185, 189, 207, 221, 222,
242, 254, 277, 306, 322, 324, 353, 385,
453, 454, 498, 523(bis), 536, 545, 609n.
Bernard of Menthon, St, 257
Bernard of Valentinois, 429, 445
Bernard-Délicieux, 560
Bernardine of Siena, St, 560
Berzé-la-Ville, 380(bis), 417
Bethlehem, 67, 418, 446, 448
Béziers, 535, 541 f., 544, 560
Bible, The, 44 f., 376 f.; translators, 524 f.
Bielbog, 528
Blachernae, 415, 417, 591
Black Death, 15, 592 f., 595
Black Friars, see Dominicans
Black Sea, 402, 411, 589
Blaise, St, 46(bis), 417
Blanche of Castile, 290, 291, 298, 309, 470,
472(bis), 475, 544
Boccaccio, 592 f., 605
Bogomils, 400n., 528 f.
Bohemia, 10, 189, 214, 254, 314, 439, 495,
499, 504, 524, 526 f.
Bohemond, Prince of Antioch, 410, 427,
437, 441, 443 f.
Bohemond IV of Antioch-Tripoli, 468
Bohemond VI of Antioch-Tripoli, 476, 478
Bohemond of Taranto, 440, 445
Boileau, Étienne, 295 f.
Bokhara, 466
Boleslav I, the Mighty, 11, 495
Boleslav II, 216n.
Boleslav III, 497
Bologna, 157 f., 243 and n., 254, 307 f.,
312, 314, 338 f., 388, 564. See also
Universities
Bolsena, miracle of, 34, 48
Bonacorsi, 530
Bonaventure, St, 3, 27, 34, 43, 47, 49, 51,
160, 310, 325(bis), 326, 327 f., 336, 342,
559, 595
Boniface, St, 493
Boniface VIII, Pope, 68, 186, 226, 243, 254,
278, 297, 513, 555, 559(bis), 566–75, 579,
604 f., 690
Boniface of Montferrat, 461(bis), 463
Bonneuil, Stephen, 386
Bordeaux, 9, 233, 236, 507, 588
Boris, King of Bulgaria, 11
Bosnia, 529
Boso, Cardinal, 396
Bosphorus, 404, 408, 413, 415 f., 418, 431,
463 f.
Bossuet, 51, 115, 297
Boucher, Guillaume, 506
Bougie, 514
Boulogne, 440, 445n.
Bourbon-Lancy, 364
Bourges, 9, 351, 371, 372, 382, 388, 453

Bourget du Lac, 384
Bouvines, battle of, 22, 25 f., 197, 291
Brandenburg, 10, 498
Bremen, 450n., 494
Brendan, St, 607
Brenner Pass, 19
Brethren of the Cross, 255
Brethren of the Free Spirit, 522, 557 and n.,
   595
Bridge-building, 250 f.
Bridget, St, 43, 587
Brindisi, 407
Brioude, 363
British Isles, 10, 494
Brittany, 372, 405, 472, 523; Dukes of, 9
Bruges, 588, 591
Brunelleschi, 389
Brunetto, 603
Bruno of Cologne, St, 120, 126
Bruno of Querfurt, 11
Bruys, Pierre de, 520, 523
Buddhists, 507
Bulgaria (Bulgarians, or Bulgars), 11, 395,
   400, 402, 409, 414, 464, 477, 516, 528 f.,
   589(bis), 597
Burchard of Worms, 39, 265, 338
Burgos, 388(bis)
Burgundy, 9, 21, 77, 189, 299, 352, 364(bis),
   365, 372, 374, 472, 481n., 491
Burgundy, Henry, Count of, 420 490
Buridan, Jean, 562 f., 565
Byzantium (Byzantines), 8, 10 f., 19, 29,
   62, 349, 390, 393 f., 395, 396 f., 398–432,
   434 f., 441, 445, 451, 456, 458, 459, 462,
   464(bis), 471, 482, 496, 515 f.

Caen, 352, 363, 365
Caerularius, Michael, 393 ff., 399, 420, 425,
   480
Caesar Borgia, 412
Caesar of Arles, 51
Caesarea, 422, 448, 452, 476, 505
Cahors, 314, 365
Cairo, 468, 472, 473(bis), 475
Calabria, 405, 408n.
Calais, 589
Calatrava, Order of, 492
Calixtus II, Pope, 132, 133(bis), 182, 187,
   217
Calo, Peter, 46
Calvin, 88, 115
Calvoian, 516
Camaldoli, 122, 125
Cambridge, 314
Cambronne, 370
Canada, 484
Canon Law, 242, 244, 338
Canons, 233
Canossa, 75, 178 f.

Canterbury, 70, 216, 217, 228, 306, 320,
   321, 335, 339, 357, 365, 387
Canticle of the Sun, 148
Canton 508
Canute, 10, 494
Capet, house of, 9, 18, 19, 20, 21, 22 f., 94,
   210, 212, 217, 397, 482, 544
Capet, Hugh, 21
Cappadocia, 403(bis), 416, 422(bis)
Capua, 9, 405 ff.
Carcassonne, 535, 541, 543 f.
Cardinals, Sacred College of, 173 f., 223,
   553, 570, 580, 587, 598 f.
Carmelites, 162, 481n.
Carthage, 477, 509
Carthusians, 43, 126 f., 251
Cartier, Jacques, 484
Casamari, 388
Casella, 603
Casimir I, 11
Caspian Sea, 402, 466
Cassiodorus, 318
Castelnaudary, 542
Castile, 151, 487, 488, 489, 491, 493
Catalans (Catalonia), 379, 487, 491
Catana, 501
Catapan 406
Catharism (Cathars), 150, 154, 520, 526,
   527, 529–35, 537 f., 539, 541, 543, 544,
   546 f., 549, 551 f., 560. See also Albigenses
Cathedrals, 58 f., 110, 231, 252, 296 f.,
   347–92, 599, 607
Catherine of Siena, St, 557, 587, 608
Caucasus, 472 f.
Caumont, Arcisse de, 363
Cavalini, 390
Cefalu, 417
Celestine III, Pope, 431
Celestine V, Pope, St, 513, 553 f., 556, 559
Ceuta, 509
Ceylon, 508
Chaise-Dieu, The, 385
Chalcedon, 404; Council of, 427
Chalcidice, 402
Champagne, 19, 402
Chanson de Roland, 284, 343, 344
Charlemagne, 15, 17, 21, 29, 73, 123, 169,
   171, 184, 186, 189, 240, 243, 305, 307,
   487, 493 f.
Charles I of Anjou, 295 f., 299, 300, 386,
   477 f., 480, 589
Charles II of Anjou, 554
Charles IV of France, 23
Charles II of Naples, 604
Charles Martel, 487
Charles Martel, King of Hungary, 554
Charles of Moravia, 586
Charles of Valois, 482
Charlieu, 375
Charter of Charity, 84

Chartres, 3, 6, 27, 38, 40, 46, 49, 70, 182, 207, 211, 231, 243, 255, 267, 306 f., 308, 322, 338, 347 f., 351, 355, 356, 368, 370 f., 374(*bis*), 375 ff., 380, 382, 383, 386, 387 ff.
Chastel, Le, 450
Chastel Blanc, 450
Chastel Rouge, 450
Chemnitz, 384
Chester, 365
Chiaravalle, 388
Chichester, 387
Chimena, 490
China, 12, 415, 465 f., 467, 507(*bis*), 508, 518
Chinard, Philip, 386
Chios, 411
Chirkuh, 455(*bis*)
Christian, Bishop, 500
Christian of Oliva, 499
Christopher, St, 251
Chrysodulus, a monk, 422
Church and State, 167 ff., 423 f., 566–9
Cid Campeador, 485, 489 f.
Cid, Poema del, 485
Cilicia, 12, 411(*bis*)
Cimabue, 390 f.
Cinnamus, John, 415
Cintra, 490
Cistercians, 42, 49, 80, 109, 114, 128 f., 135, 136, 140, 150, 161, 231, 353, 370, 388(*bis*), 416, 422, 464, 498, 499(*bis*), 536 ff., 558
Citeaux, 80 f., 82, 127 f., 140, 150, 306, 389, 486
Clairvaux, 83–6, 114
Clement III, Pope, 218, 278, 408n., 427 f., 457
Clement IV, Pope, 330, 342, 477, 586
Clement V, Pope, 343, 508, 555, 576 ff., 580 f., 587, 609
Clement VI, Pope, 480, 583, 584 f.
Clericis Laicos, 572, 575
Clermont, 181, 280, 364, 438, 453; Council of, 277, 279, 433, 435
Clotilde, 505
Clovis, 169 f., 211, 505
Cluny, 13, 97, 108, 119, 122(*bis*), 125, 129 f., 135, 221, 254, 306, 352, 363, 364, 370, 385, 397, 417, 433, 438, 472, 485, 488
Coimbra, 311, 314, 565
Colin the Englishman, 501
Colmar, 467
Cologne, 19, 192, 208(*bis*), 326, 336, 363, 386, 387, 467, 520, 564. *See also* Universities
Colonna, 553, 559, 570, 572, 574 f.
Columba, St, 119
Comminges, 542; Count of, 573
Comneni, the, 408–15. *See also* Alexius; Andronicus; Isaac; John; Manuel
Compiègne, 370
Compostella, Santiago di, 12, 36, 64 f., 67,

69 f., 257, 344, 350, 365, 388, 484, 486, 488, 492, 494
Conques, 37, 363, 365
Conrad II, 65
Conrad III, 107, 111, 187, 411(*bis*), 430, 453(*bis*), 497
Conrad of Saxony, 49
Conradin, 25
Conserans, Bishop of, 538
Constance of Antioch, 455
Constance of Burgundy, 488
Constance of Sicily, 195, 196, 198, 413
Constantine IX Monomachus, 394, 399, 425
Constantine X Ducas, 395, 399, 400(*bis*)
Constantine the Great, 226(*bis*), 390; Donation of, 609
Constantinople, 6, 37(*bis*), 214, 248, 308, 393(*bis*), 396 f., 399(*bis*), 400, 411 f., 414, 417(*bis*), 418(*bis*), 423, 425, 427, 429(*bis*), 430(*bis*), 439(*bis*), 440(*bis*), 449, 453, 458(*bis*), 462, 471, 476, 494, 496, 504, 516, 589
Constantinople, Latin empire of, 463, 476
Copts, 12, 517 f.
Cordova, 13, 289, 317, 487(*bis*), 488, 490 f., 493
Corfu, 411(*bis*)
Corinth, 463, 528
Coronation, 210 f., 214
Corrèze, 384
Cotentin, 405 f.
Coucy, De, 71, 260, 262, 295
Courland, 500
Courtenay, Catherine de, 482
Courtrai, 573, 578n.
Coutances, 373, 388, 406, 407, 408
Cracow, 514
Crécy, 589
Cremona, 506
Crimea, 508
Crispin, St, 46
Croatia and Croats, 471, 495
Cruciferi, the, 254
Crusade, the First, 410, 429, 433 ff.; the Second, 106 f., 111, 430, 452–7; the Third, 457–60; the Fourth, 460–5; the Sixth, 469 f.; the Seventh, 471 ff.; the Eighth, 477; the Children's, 467
Cumans, 149, 409 f., 439, 441, 503
Cutanda, 490
Cydnus, 458
Cyprian, St, 170
Cyprus, 416, 459n., 468, 472 f., 482(*bis*), 504 f., 578
Cyril and Methodius, Sts, 10
Czechs, 495, 498, 500

Daimbert, Archbishop of Pisa, 429, 450
Dalmatia, 440, 461, 495, 529

x

Dalphinet, 416
Damascus, 418, 434, 454, 455(bis), 456, 470, 472, 504
Damietta, 468 f., 473 ff., 501
Dandolo, Henry, 461, 463
Dante, 3, 47, 68 f., 112, 119, 346, 391, 392, 455, 555, 556, 565, 587, 602–10
Danube, 400, 466, 495
Daphne, 416
Dauphiné, 379, 526 f.
David of Augsburg, 44
David the Restorer, 517
Decameron, 592
De Consideratione, 100, 138
De Miraculis, 38
Decretals, the False, 184, 243
Demetrius, St, 415
Demetrius of Lampe, 424
Denmark (Danes), 10, 11, 189, 214, 366, 397, 493, 494, 495, 503, 570
Deschamps, Eustache, 33, 212
Dies Irae, 62, 315
Dijon, 365
Dioclea, 516
Divine Comedy, 605–10
Djwali, Emir, 452
Docetism, 530
Dolcimo, Fra, 558
Dombrovska, St, 11, 495
Dominic, Patriarch of Grado, 426
Dominic, St, 1, 7, 41, 44, 49, 51, 113, 119, 120, 140, 149–58, 221, 493, 503, 524, 537 f.
Dominic of Fez, Bro, 511
Dominicans (Black Friars, Friars Preachers), 42 f., 46, 51n., 58, 62, 153 ff., 155 f., 157, 158 ff., 221, 239, 295, 325, 335 f., 422, 479, 495, 499, 503–9, 511, 517, 538, 547, 593n., 598. See also Mendicant Orders
Donati, Gemma, 604
Donatists, 519
Dosithea, 420
Dubois, Pierre, 482, 557, 568, 600n.
Duccio, 1
Duèse, Jacques, see John XXII
Duns Scotus, 316, 336 f., 561 f., 565
Durand, Bishop of Mende, 557
Durand of Huerca, 526
Durand of St Pourçain, 561
Durazzo, 409, 413, 440
Durham, 307, 365, 369, 387

Eadmer, 49
Eckhart, Master, 565, 595
Edessa, 106, 411, 443, 444, 447 f., 452(bis), 453(bis), 454
Edward I, 24, 478, 507
Edward II, 24, 587n.
Edward III, 583, 585, 588 f.

Egypt, 434, 445(bis), 446, 455 f., 458, 468, 469n., 470 f., 481, 502, 517
Eidjigidai, 473
Eleanor of Aquitaine, 22, 23, 215
Elias, Bro., 510, 513
Elizabeth, St, of Hungary, 258, 358; of Schönau, 136; of Thuringia, 147
Engelbert of Admont, 566
England, 9, 13, 18, 20 21, 23 f., 25, 157, 190, 214 f., 298 f., 365, 386, 387, 396, 435, 436, 439, 458, 484, 493, 589
Enguerrand de Marigny, 571, 577
Eon de l'Étoile, 523
Epirus, 427, 464
Eric, King, 495, 570
Erzerum, 472
Eternal Gospel, 559
Ethiopia, 12, 414, 415, 518
Eudes de Châteauroux, 472
Eudes de Châtillon, 181, 433, 437
Eudes de Deuil, 415
Eudes Rigaud, Archbishop, 232n.
Eugenius III, Pope, 95 f., 106, 114, 133, 187, 189(bis), 190, 453, 454, 536
Eugenius IV, Pope, 206
Eulogius, Archbishop, 487
Eustache de St Pierre, 589
Eustathius, Archbishop of Thessalonica, 415, 421, 423
Euthymius of Neopatras, 421
Evora, 388, 490
Évreux, 365, 372
Exeter, 387
Eymeric, 548

Faith, St, 37
Fakreddin, Emir, 473 f.
Famagusta, 358
Fanjeaux, 535, 538
Faro, 388
Fatimites, 402, 445, 455
Fécamp, 365
Fénelon, 369
Ferdinand I of Castile, 488
Ferdinand III of Castile and Leon, 493, 511
Ferrara, 579
Feudalism, 15 ff.
Fidenzio of Padua, 482
Fiesole, 365
Finland, 495, 496
Fitzpiers, Peter, 386
Flagellants, 595 f.
Flanders, 19, 299, 410, 429, 436, 440, 472, 498, 578n., 588
Florence, 1(bis), 34, 68, 245, 263, 264, 365, 388, 389(bis), 390, 392, 579 591, 593 and n., 603 f., 605
Foix, 535(bis); Count of, 573
Fontaines, 77, 85 f.

Fontenay, 370
Fontevrault, 364
Fontfroide, 370, 536, 537
Fossanuova, 330, 388
Foucher of Chartres, 448
France, 9, 10, 16, 18, 19, 20(bis), 21 f., 23, 25, 70, 146, 190, 206 f., 208, 217 ff., 246, 267, 296, 351, 369, 370, 373, 379, 387 f., 389, 435, 436, 437 f., 440, 443, 454, 458, 472, 481, 485, 486, 493, 496, 534, 565
Francesca da Rimini, 605
Francis, St, of Assisi, 7, 42, 44, 48, 49, 51, 59, 71, 113, 120, 140–9, 155, 221, 253, 389, 391 f., 392, 469n., 500–3, 510, 515, 557, 595; of Sales, 44, 84
Franciscans (Friars Minor; Grey Friars), 42 f., 142, 145, 146 f., 158 ff., 209, 221, 239, 291, 295, 325, 326, 327, 335 f., 422, 438, 480, 482, 496, 499, 501, 503–9, 510, 513, 547, 593n., 598. See also Mendicant Orders
Frankfort, Council of, 498
Frederick I Barbarossa, 3, 25, 184, 186–94, 275, 306, 412, 430, 457 f., 459n., 497, 499, 546
Frederick II, 3, 25, 166, 198–202, 218, 225, 229, 241, 244, 262, 298, 386, 414, 468, 469 f., 499(bis), 502, 520n., 546
Frederick of Lorraine, 394, 426
Friars Minor, see Franciscans
Friars Preachers, see Dominicans
Friburg-im-Brisgau, 387
Friends of God, 44
Froissart, 414, 495
Fukien, 508(bis)
Fulk of Anjou, 447, 452(bis)
Fulk of Neuilly, 51, 256, 461

Gaddi, Taddeo, 391
Gaeta, 406
Gaetani, Cardinal Benedict, 554 f.
Galahad, 112, 284, 293, 345
Galicia, 466, 487, 496
Galilee, 470, 476, 610
Gallipoli, 590
Gardhar, 495
Gascons and Gascony, 523, 580 f.
Gaston of Béarn, 445
Gaufredi, 560
Geneviève, St, 46
Genghis Khan, 201, 465–7, 476, 488, 496
Genoa and Genoese, 13, 19, 138, 200, 201, 388, 396, 435, 444, 446, 459n., 472, 476, 482, 514, 591
Geoffrey, Bishop of Chartres, 536
Geoffrey, Bishop of Langres, 453
Geoffrey of Noyon, 386
Geoffroy de Charnay, 578
George, St, 46

George Cedrenus, 415
George the Hagiorite, 395
Georgia, 422, 517, 593
Gerard of Borgo San Donnino, 559
Gerard of Martigues, 450
Germans and Germany, 9(bis), 18, 20(bis), 25, 146, 173 f., 182, 187, 197, 200, 207 f., 365, 369, 387, 396, 413, 439(bis), 454, 458, 460, 493 ff., 496(bis), 498(bis), 499 and n., 526, 609
Gerona, 365
Gertrude, St, 43
Ghent, 19
Ghibellines, 187, 188, 197, 200, 204, 388, 460, 461, 471, 574, 579, 582 f., 603 f.
Ghiberti, 5, 390
Ghirlandaio, 1
Gibelin, 450
Gibraltar, 407, 487
Gide, André, 378
Giles, Bro., 501, 510, 513
Giles of Rome, 568
Gilles le Muisis, 595
Gillet, Louis, 363
Giotto, 3, 391 f., 603
Giovio, Paolo, 5
Gissurson, Isleif, 494
Givry, 593
Glaber, Raoul, 13, 14, 592
Gniezno, 11, 497
Gnosticism, 519, 530
Goad of Love, 50
Godfrey de Bouillon, 106, 281, 403, 437, 439, 440(bis), 441, 443(bis), 445, 446(bis), 447, 448, 450, 451, 452
Goldast, 5
Golden Horde, 466, 496
Golden Horn, 396, 414 f.
Golden Legend, 36
Golden Letter, 43
Gorse, 487
Gotland, 495
Gottschalk, Bishop of Puy, 12, 69; Prince of the Obotrites, 497 f.; provost of the Premonstratensians, 102; a Saxon monk, 320, 545
Grado, 426
Graeco-Slavs, 523
Grail, the Holy, 112, 284, 293, 344
Granada, 488(bis), 490, 493
Grande Chartreuse, 97
Grandsilve, 536
Gratian, 243, 265, 273, 286, 338
Greece (Greeks), 8, 394, 406, 408, 409, 417, 418(bis), 441(bis), 445, 453, 454, 463, 464, 467, 476, 480, 496, 504
Greek language, 317 f.
Greenland, 10, 495, 597
Gregory I, the Great, Pope, St, 376, 385
Gregory VI, Pope, 225, 516

Gregory VII (Hildebrand), Pope, St, 3, 28, 40, 58, 95, 120, 121–5, 130, 133, 136, 173, 175–81, 183 f., 185, 222, 224, 225, 228, 263, 276, 402 f., 407, 409, 426 f., 434, 435(*bis*), 488, 521
Gregory VIII, Pope, 457
Gregory IX, Pope, 147, 162, 165, 200, 207, 225, 243, 278, 298, 310, 326, 339n., 469, 470 f., 503 f., 510, 547 f.
Gregory X, Pope, 330, 477, 480
Gregory XI, Pope, 586
Grenoble, 362
Grey Friars, *see* Franciscans
Grosseteste, Robert, 318
Grousset, René, 437, 454
Guelfs, 187 f., 197, 204, 388, 471, 581 f., 603 f.
Guernes of Pont-Saint-Maxence, 46
Gui, Bernard, 547 f., 551
Guibert of Nogent, 51, 437
Guido d'Arezzo, 385
Guido Cavalcanti, 603
Guido Novella da Polenta, 605
Guigo, 43, 126
Guilds, 269 f.
Guillaume d'Orange, 344(*bis*)
Guiscard, Bohemond, 409, 427, 440
Guiscard, Robert, 8, 174, 177, 180, 397, 399, 406–8, 409, 484
Gundhild of Denmark, 10
Guy, Bernard, 46
Guy de Longjumeau, 505
Guy de Lusignan, 437, 456(*bis*), 457, 459 and n., 499
Guynemer of Boulogne, 445n.
Guyük, Great Khan, 473, 505
Gytha, daughter of Harold (Eng.), 397

Haakon, King of Denmark, 40
Haakon, King of Norway, 472
Haifa, 479
Hakim, 433
Hamburg, 10
Harold Bluetooth, 494
Harold the Stern, 494
Hartman von Heldrunge, 500
Hastings, Battle of, 405
Hattin, 457
Hauteville, Dreux de, 406
Hauteville, Onfroy de, 406
Hauteville, Roger de, 407
Hauteville, Tancred de, 188, 406(*bis*)
Hauteville, William de, 406
Havelberg, 498
Hebron, 448
Heerwagen, John, 5
Heidelberg, 314, 564. *See also* Universities
Helena, Empress, 450
Hellespont, 401, 431

Heloïse, *see* Abélard
Henri I (Fr.), 21
Henri IV (Fr.), 7
Henri de Bar, 470
Henri de Champagne, 460
Henry I (Eng.), 23, 215
Henry II (Eng.), 23, 215 f., 241, 457, 459
Henry III (Eng.), 24, 217, 298, 565
Henry II (Ger.), 24, 275
Henry III (Ger.), 173, 545
Henry IV (Ger.), 25, 123, 173, 176 ff., 182, 184, 187, 262, 397, 404, 409, 414, 426, 427(*bis*), 433, 497
Henry V (Ger.), 182, 187, 430
Henry VI (Ger.), 25, 195 f., 460(*bis*)
Henry VII (Ger.), 25, 605, 609
Henry I (Lusignan), 473
Henry of Albano, 537
Henry the Cantor, 501
Henry of Clairvaux, 536
Henry of Flanders, 465
Henry of Langerstein, 44
Henry of Lausanne, 523, 546
Henry, son of Gottschalk, 498
Henry of Susa, 567
Henry of Upsala, Bishop, 495
Henry the Lion, 498
Henry von Walpot, 499
Heraclius, 415
Heresy, 519–52
Heretics, fate of, 545, 550 f.
Herman of Valenciennes, 45
Hermann von Salza, 499
Hermann-Joseph, Bl., 49
Hermenegild, 487
Hermits, 40n., 533; of St Augustine, 162
Hervé de Nédellec, 561
Herzegovina, 529
Hethum the Great, King, 476
Hilary, St, 51
Hildebert, 52
Hildegarde, St, 136
Hildesheim, 390
Hincmar, 320
Hirschau, 353
Hohenstaufen (family), 25, 187, 202, 567
Hohenzollerns, 499n.
Holidays, 59 f., 270, 424
Holland, 498, 522
Holy Land (Palestine), 29, 67, 161 f., 410, 412, 413, 437, 438, 443, 447 f., 449, 453 f., 459 f., 470, 476, 478, 480, 485, 498, 499 f.
Holy Sepulchre, 3, 13, 64, 67, 106, 284, 402(*bis*), 433(*bis*), 434(*bis*), 446, 447 f., 450, 456, 458, 460, 470, 480, 555; Church of the, 481n.; Order of the, 450n.
Holy Year, 68, 69, 73
Honorius II, Pope, 103, 111, 187, 188
Honorius III, Pope, 121, 153 f., 165, 200, 233, 244, 279, 468(*bis*), 469, 510, 543

Honorius IV, Pope, 479, 507
Honorius of Autun, 44, 51, 110, 287
Hospitallers, 254, 255, 257, 450(*bis*) and n., 464, 478, 479, 482, 499, 578n., 597
Hospitals and hospices, 255, 257 f., 292, 423
Hubert, St, 46
Huesca, 290
Hugh des Fosses, 43, 132
Hugh of Lincoln, St, 27
Hugh de Lusignan, 468
Hugh de Payens, 450
Hugh of St Victor, 42 f., 53, 138, 307, 324, 326, 339
Hugh of Vermandois, 440(*bis*), 441, 445
Hulagu, 476
Humbert, Cardinal, 123(*bis*), 394, 396; Master, 386
Humiliati, 139, 146, 525
Hundred Years War, 588
Hungary (Hungarians), 8, 11, 14, 16, 19, 26, 189, 214, 400, 410, 439, 440, 453, 466, 471, 477, 495, 499, 500
Huns, 467
Huss, John, 563
Hussites, 527
Hyacinth, St, 504

Iberian Peninsula, 12, 26, 387, 485 ff., 493
Ibn-al-Athis, 458
Iceland, 10, 494(*bis*), 593, 597
Iconium, 407
Ignatius of Antioch, St, 48
Ignatius of Loyola, St, 602
Île de Camargue, 404
Île de France, 369, 374
Illuminatus, Bro., 501 f.
Imitation of Christ, The, 55, 58, 115, 595
India, 364, 598
Indians, Red, 484
Indre, 381
Inge, King, 384
Innocent II, Pope, 3, 103, 115, 133, 160, 187, 206, 233
Innocent III, Pope, 3, 28, 32, 45, 51, 73, 115, 119, 120, 121, 135(*bis*), 137–40, 146, 149 f., 153 f., 165, 185, 186, 196, 207, 208, 213, 214 f., 217, 218–26, 229, 233, 242 f., 247, 256, 272, 278, 299, 309, 431(*bis*), 460, 461 ff., 467, 469, 491, 499, 503 f., 516, 522, 525, 537, 539, 548, 566 f.
Innocent IV, Pope, 72, 162, 165 and n., 201, 218, 223, 242, 245, 255, 297, 310, 311, 465, 471(*bis*) and f., 503, 504, 549 f., 567
Inquisition, the, 164, 314, 530, 544–52
Intellectual crisis, 560–4
Investitures, quarrel of, 31, 168–73, 175 ff., 183 ff.

Iran (Persia), 12, 402, 434, 465 ff., 472, 476, 504, 527
Iraq, 445
Ireland, 9
Irene, Empress, 415
Irnerius, 338(*bis*)
Isaac I Angelus, 413 f., 458, 461 f.
Isaac II Angelus, 431
Isaac I Comnenus, 394, 398 ff., 415, 425 f.
Isaac II Comnenus, 414
Isidore of Seville, St, 184, 318, 506
Islam, 11, 13, 19, 64, 200, 317(*bis*), 388, 402, 408, 412, 418, 431(*bis*), 434(*bis*), 443 f., 445(*bis*), 450, 541 f., 455, 457 f., 466, 471, 472, 476, 478 f., 480, 485, 486 f., 488, 491, 493, 500, 596
Ismail, 470
Ispahan, 402
Issoire, 363
Italy (Italians), 9, 10, 19(*bis*), 20(*bis*), 24, 25, 208, 246, 388 f., 404 ff., 411 f., 430, 436, 439, 440, 471, 481n., 484, 508
Ivirion, monastery, 416, 517

Jacobites, 12, 448, 504, 517
Jacopone da Todi, 554, 556, 559
Jaffa, 446, 470, 476
Jaime I of Aragon, 476, 478, 493
Jaime, King of Catalonia, 513 f.
James, St, 69, 485. *See also* Compostella
James of Milan, 50
James of Viterbo, 568
Janissaries, 590
Java, 508
Jean de Meung, 345 f.
Jericho, 446, 448
Jerome of Prague, 564 f.
Jerusalem (Holy City), 61, 64 f., 67, 70, 98, 106, 200, 202, 214, 218, 254, 255, 418, 428, 429, 431 f., 433 f., 439(*bis*), 440, 444 f., 446(*bis*), 447, 457, 460, 470, 471, 475, 480, 499
Jerusalem, Latin kingdom of, 447–52, 471, 475, 478
Jews, 99, 272n., 317, 402, 409, 534, 594
Joachim of Flora, 43, 136, 554, 558 f.
Joan of Arc, St, 6, 482, 548, 602
Jocelin I de Courtenay, Count of Hainaut, 452
Jocelin II de Courtenay, Count of Hainaut, 452 f.
Jocelin III de Courtenay, Count of Hainaut, 457
John the Apostle, St, 377, 422
John the Baptist, St, 46, 385n.
John Chrysostom, St, 420, 545
John the Hospitaller, St, 46
John VIII, Pope, 10, 28
John XII, Pope, 172

John XXII, Pope, 47, 243, 278, 482, 504, 557n., 559, 568, 581 f., 583, 586, 587n.
John II Comnenus, Byzantine emperor, 410 f., 415, 451
John V Palaeologus, Byzantine emperor, 589 f.
'John VI,' Byzantine usurper, 589
John, King of England, 24, 25, 214 f., 216 f., 468(bis)
John V, Patriarch of Antioch, 429, 445
John II, Metropolitan of Kiev, 395
John Cantacuzene, 589 ff.
John of Bohemia, King, 588; of Fécamp, 41, 48; of Marignolli, 504; of Montecorvino, 508(bis); of Parma, 465; of Plan-Carpin, 473; of Salisbury, 27, 40, 306, 307, 325; of San Gemignano, 52n.; of Severac, 598; da Valle, 560; of Villers, 479
John Scylitzes, 396
John Vatatzes, 464 f., 471
Joinville, Sire de, 290n., 291 f., 295, 472 f., 475, 477
Josaphat, monastery of, 448
Jouhet, 381
Jubilee year, 571, 573, 604
Juliana, St, 48
Jumièges, 365(bis)
Junius, Adrian, 5
Jurisprudence, 338 f.
Justice, ecclesiastical, 240–4; administration of, 296
Justinian, 393, 415
Jutland, 495

Karakorum, 466, 505 f.
Kashgar, 507
Khilander, monastery of, 416, 422, 516
Khorassan, 507, 518
Khwarizmians, 471(bis), 472, 499
Kibotos, 439
Kiev, principality of, 214, 418, 597; city of, 418, 466, 482, 496, 504
Kitbouqa, 476
Knights of St Saviour, 492
Koulin, Khan, 529
Kourbouqa, Emir of Mosul, 444

Labour, dignity of, 267–70
Lanfranc, 320(bis), 521
Langobardia, theme of, 405
Langres, 397
Langton, Stephen, 48, 217
Languedoc, 150, 152, 364, 374, 440, 486, 526, 529, 534, 559
Laon, 206, 322, 350, 351, 370 f., 387
Lapland, 597

Las Huelgas, 388
Lateran Council of 1179: 537; of 1215: 37, 146, 161, 468, 546, 558
Lateran Palace, 226
Latin, use of, 315, 564 f.
Lauda Sion, 48, 62, 331
Laurence, Bro., 505
Lavra, the Great, 416, 422
Lazar houses, 255 f.
Legates, papal, 227 f., 412, 440, 465, 478, 516, 537(bis), 538, 572
Legnano, 193 f.
Leicester, 541
Leignitz, 499, 504
Leipzig, 384
Le Mans, 351(bis), 372, 381
Leo IX, Pope, St, 407
Leon, 365, 388, 487, 493
Leonard, Bro., 501
Leonardo da Pisa, 317, 340
Leopold, Duke of Antioch, 468; Duke of Austria, 460
Leprosy, 481n.
Lesbos, 598
Letts, 496, 499n.
Leyser, Polycarp, 5
Libraries and copyists, 302–4
Lichfield, 387
Life of Otto of Bamberg, 53
Life of St Malachy, 99
Lille, 19
Limburg, 386
Limoges, 36, 306, 350, 352, 365, 384, 385
Limosus Negro, 533
Lincoln, 363, 365, 386, 387
Lisbon, 388, 490(bis), 491
Lisieux, 372, 563
Lithuania, 496, 499n., 500, 565, 597
Liturgy, 60–3
Lives of the Saints, 36
Livonia, 496, 498, 500
Lob-Nor, 507
Lollard, Walter, 560
Lombards (Lombardy), 16, 19, 190 f., 405, 406, 527
'Lombards, the', a sect, 560
London, 264, 313, 482, 588
Lopez de Ayala, 565
Lorenzetti, 391
Lorraine, 21, 439
Lothair, 103 ff., 411, 498
Lotharingia, 9
Louis VI (Fr.), 94, 217, 276
Louis VII (Fr.), 3, 21, 22, 23, 74 f., 94, 103, 106 f., 111, 190, 193, 206, 215, 255, 267n., 397, 415, 430, 453, 454
Louis VIII (Fr.), 22, 291, 543 f.
Louis IX (Fr.), St, 3(bis), 22, 29, 37, 41, 44, 58, 62, 147, 164, 166, 201, 210, 217, 224, 255, 256(bis), 260, 262, 267n., 269, 277,

281, 286, 290–300, 437, 450, 471–5, 476, 477 f., 482, 505 f., 544, 576
Louis X (Fr.), 23
Louis IV of Bavaria, 25, 559, 562, 568, 582, 586, 588
Love, 285–90
Lübeck, 450n., 498
Lucca, 365, 605
Luciferians, 522
Lucius III, Pope, 525, 546
Ludmilla, St, 10
Ludolph of Saxony, 595
Lund, 230, 495
Lusignans, 563
Lusingen, von, 439
Luther, Martin, 115, 284, 563
Luxembourg, Count of, 588
Lydda, 448
Lyonnais, 526
Lyons, 9, 19, 202, 217(bis), 223 f., 229, 232 f., 235, 247, 263, 272, 298, 327, 482, 505(bis), 524 f., 539; University of, 313
Lyons, Council of, in 1163: 536; in 1245: 165, 471, 505, 567; in 1274; 165, 330, 478, 480

Macedonia, 8, 406, 589
Macedonian dynasty, 414 f., 528
Magdeburg, 11, 498, 522
Maghreb, 489(bis)
Magna Carta, 214, 217
Mahomet, 449, 452, 466, 485, 488, 489(bis), 510, 514
Maimonides, 317, 326
Maine, 22
Mainz (Mayence), 10, 19, 366, 495
Malabar, 508
Malachy, St, 113; Life of St Malachy, 99
Malbork, 500
Mâle, Émile, 38, 377, 385n.
Malikh-Shah, 402, 434
Mamas, St, 397
Mamelukes, 476(bis), 479, 518
Manchuria, 466
Manfred, King of Sicily, 476 f., 520n.
Mani or Manes, 527
Manichaeans, 519, 527 ff., 533, 535, 550
Mansurah, 469, 473 f.
Mantua, 202, 206
Mantzikert, 399, 403(bis), 404, 426, 429, 434, 443
Manuel Comnenus, 410 ff., 415, 418, 424 (bis), 430, 453–5
Maphrian of Mosul, 518
Marabouts, 489
Marcabu, 437
Marco Lombardo, 610
Marco Polo, 507 f., 563
Maria and Flora, martyrs, 487

Marienkloster, 498
Marjat, 450
Mark, St, 46
Maronites, 12, 445, 504
Marriage (matrimony), 54, 261 f., 285, 293 f., 564
Marseilles, 19, 317, 364, 467, 482, 560
Marsilius of Padua, 568 f., 582, 537n.
Martial, St, 36
Martin, St, 46, 71
Martin IV, Pope, 225, 480
Martin, Abbot of Rheims, 461
Martini, Simone, 391
Mary of Alania, 409
Mary Magdalene, St, 70 f.
'Master of Hungary,' the, 475
Matheo of Clermont, 479
Mathew of Anas, 386
Matilda, Countess, 178, 180, 181, 192, 220n., 320n.
Matthew, St, 407n.
Matthew, Dom, 502
Mauropous, John, 421
Mecca, 488
Mechtild of Hackeborn, St, 47
Mecklenburg, 496, 498
Medard, St, 46
Meinhard, 499
Melchite Church, 12
Melfi, 407, 408n.
Meliapur, 508
Melik-el-Kâmil, 469 f., 502(bis)
Melitene, 12
Mendicant Orders, 32, 43, 145, 155, 158, 163 f., 201, 237, 239, 253, 388 f., 503, 599. See also Dominicans; Franciscans
Merovingians, 4, 6
Merswin, Rulman, 44
Mesopotamia, 12, 402, 476(bis), 517
Messina, 19
Michael, the Archangel, 46, 405, 417
Michael II, the Stammerer, Byzantine emperor, 528
Michael VI, Byzantine emperor, 399, 425
Michael VII, Ducas, Byzantine emperor, 397, 398, 399, 403, 407, 408(bis), 409, 425
Michael VIII Palaeologus, Byzantine emperor, 464 f., 476, 477(bis), 480, 589 f.
Michael Acominates, Archbishop of Athens, 421, 465
Michael of Attalia, 396
Michael of Dioclea, King of Serbia, 516
Michelangelo, 390, 392
Michelet, Jules, 386, 436
Mieczlaw, Duke, 11
Milan, 9, 181, 188, 191, 192, 193, 357, 365, 386, 388, 579; Archbishop of, 430
Military orders, 450, 464 f., 492 f.
Milou, Bishop, 539
Ming dynasty, 509, 518

Miramar, 513
Missions to heathen, 484–518
Modena, 365
Mohammed-ibn-Toumart, 491
Moissac, 364, 369, 375
Molay, Jacques de, 576, 578
Molesmes, 127
Monachism (monasticism), 9(bis), 10, 14, 40n., 42, 125, 236, 422, 423, 515 f.
Monarchy, 16 ff., 209–19
Monasteries (monks), 10, 82–6, 109, 125, 237 ff., 249 ff., 272n., 301, 311, 422 f., 429, 448, 499, 517 f., 607
Money, 270–4, 556
Mongka, Great Khan, 506 f.
Mongolia (Mongols), 12, 415, 418, 465–7, 471 ff., 475 f., 478(bis), 479, 488, 496, 499 f., 503–5, 508, 509, 590
Monophysites (monophysitism), 12, 448, 517, 519
Monothelites (monothelitism), 12, 517, 519
Monreale, 417 f.
Montanists, 519
Monte Cassino, 105, 329, 397, 405, 430
Monte Gargano, 405
Montenegro, 11, 529
Montferrat, Conrad of, 457
Montfort, Simon de, 541 f., 461 f.
Montisgard, 456
Montpellier, 308, 313, 339 f., 536 f., 543, 546
Montréal, 448, 538
Mont Saint-Michel, 65, 71, 351, 405, 494
Moors, 478, 486, 490 f., 493n., 495, 501, 513
Moravia, 10
Moriental Abbey, 370
Morocco, 489, 491, 501, 510 f.
Morosini, Thomas, 464
Mortemer, 21
Moscow, 496, 597
Moslems, 12, 19, 64, 69, 139, 180, 199, 262, 293, 393, 399, 402, 404 f., 407, 411, 414, 417(bis), 418, 422, 425, 434, 438, 445, 446, 449, 451(bis), 452(bis), 453, 455, 459, 467 f., 473 f., 476(bis), 479 f., 487 ff., 502, 508, 596
Motadid, 488
Motamid, 489
Mount St Michael, monastery at Kiev 418
Mourzuphles, 462 f.
Moyne, Cardinal Jean le, 556
Munich, 207
Murcia, 490(bis)
Muret, 542
Myriokephalon, 412

Naples, 9, 214, 329, 330, 391, 405(bis), 406, 554
Narbonne, 9, 317, 536, 542, 560; University of, 314; Archbishop of, 492

Naumberg, 387
Nauplus, 447, 449
Navarre, 487 f., 491
Nazareth, 448, 457, 470, 475
Nestorians (Nestorianism), 12, 29, 448, 467, 473, 476, 479, 505, 506 ff., 518, 519, 598
Nicea, 404, 434, 439, 443, 464, 465 f., 515, 517
Nicephorus III Botaniates, Byzantine emperor, 398, 399, 404, 427, 443
Nicephorus III Grammaticus, Patriarch of Constantinople, 428
Nicephorus Bryennius, 415
Nicetas Acominates, chronicler, 413n., 462 f.
Nicetas Choniates, chronicler, 424
Nicholas, St, a Byzantine monk, 397
Nicholas II, Pope, 173 f., 226, 407, 513
Nicholas III, Pope, 480
Nicholas IV, Pope, 342, 507 f., 553
Nicholas V, Pope, 115, 278
Nicholas of Bari, St, 37
Nicholas of Gerran, 52n.
Nicomedia, 404
Nicopolis, 482
Nicosia, 473
Nîmes, 404, 536
Nogaret, William of, 568, 571, 574, 575, 577, 605, 609
Norbert, St, 44, 51, 120, 131 f., 498, 522
Nordström, Johan, 5 f.
Normandy, 22, 231, 352, 363, 365, 366, 372, 404, 405(bis)
Normans, 8(bis), 13, 14, 16, 19, 24, 174, 177, 188, 214, 263, 317, 394, 396, 397, 403, 404–8, 409, 413, 414, 425 f., 427, 431, 440(bis), 443, 452, 453, 477, 484, 516
Norway, 198, 397, 472, 494
Notker, 385
Notre-Dame (churches so called), 71 (list); Dijon, 377n.; Paris, 50, 350, 355, 359n., 371(bis), 376, 379, 384, 389; Poitiers, 375; Trèves, 387
Novgorod, 597
Novgorod-Kiev, principality, 496(bis)
Noyon, 351, 370 f., 386
Nureddin, 453–6

Oberzell, 379
Oblates, 221
Obotrites, 496 ff.
Occam, William of, 209, 229, 337, 562 f., 565, 569, 582, 602
Oderic of Pordenone, 508
Olaf of Norway, St, 10, 494
Olaf III of Norway, 397
Olaf of Sweden, 10
Oldenburg, 498
Old Man of the Mountain, 475

Olga, Princess, 496
Olivet, Mount, 448
Omar, mosque of (El Aqsâ), 418, 446, 457, 470
Ommayads, 418, 487
Ongut, 507 f.
Oporto, 388, 490
Oran, 489
Orcagna, 1, 391
Orcival, 363
Oresme, Nicolas, Bishop of Lisieux, 563, 565
Orkhan, 590
Orléans, 211n., 267, 306, 313, 339 and n.
Ormuzd, 530
Orontes, 444 f., 451
Orsini, 579 f.
Orta, 390
Ortlich, 522
Orvieto, 34, 386, 389
Osma, 487, 590
Osmanli dynasty, 590
Otranto, 405
Otto I, 496
Otto III the Great, 9, 29, 171 f., 186
Otto IV, 25, 197 f., 534
Otto of Bamberg, Bishop, 497 f.
Ottokar I, 495
Ottomans, 590. See also Turks
Ouarsenis, 489
Oudjda, 489
Ouistreham, 365
Ourique, 491
Oxford, 314, 317 f., 335 336, 562, 565. See also Universities
Ozbeg, Khan, 504

Padua, 314, 326, 391, 392, 594
Palaeologi, 416, 498 f. See also John; Michael
Palermo, 314, 408, 417(bis), 469, 477
Palestine, see Holy Land
Palma (Majorca), 511 f., 515
Pamiers, 573
Pamirs, 508
Pampeluna, 487
Paneas, 448
Paoluccio of Trinci, 560
Papal primacy, 183–6
Paquette of Metz, 507
Paray-le-Monial, 364 f.
Paris, 9, 13, 21, 27, 50, 52n., 66, 85, 157, 164, 212, 241, 246, 255, 258(bis), 262, 270, 303, 306(bis), 308, 317, 326(bis), 327, 329, 336, 355, 369, 371(bis), 379n., 386, 388. See also Universities
Parma, 363, 365, 558
Parsifal, 112, 284, 293

Paschal II, Pope, 121, 133 f., 181 f., 430
Patarines, 189, 529, 534
Patmos, 422
Patras, 462
Patrick, St, 607
Paul, St, 376 f., 444
Paul of the Desert, St, 40n.
Paul of Samosata, 528
Paulicians, 400n., 528 f.
Pavia, 188, 214, 338
'Peace of God,' 275
Pedro II of Aragon, 491, 542
Pekin, 466, 508(bis)
Pelagianism, 519
Pelagius, Cardinal, 465, 468
Pelagius, founder of Asturias, 487
Périgord, 364, 417
Périgueux, 363 f.
Peroun, 11
Persia, see Iran
Perugia, 553, 579 f.
Petchenegs, 400(bis), 409 f., 429, 441
Peter, St, 9, 64, 69, 183, 376, 377, 427(bis), 431, 440, 444
Peter, Bro., 501
Peter, Tsar, 528
Peter of Achery, 434; of Agincourt, 386; of Antioch, 395; of Blois, 325; of Castelnau, 537 f.; of Limoges, 52n.; of Lusignan, 482; de Vaux, 524; of Vaux-de-Cernay, 526, 538, 541n.
Peter the Bald, 51
Peter the Hermit, 51, 256, 438, 439(bis)
Peter the Venerable, 38, 43, 101, 125, 129(bis), 306(bis), 352, 385, 523
Peter Barthélemy, 444
Peter Damian, St, 58, 86, 119, 122 f., 138, 222, 320
Peter Flotte, 568, 571, 573(bis)
Peter John Olive, 559
Peter Lombard, 53 f., 324, 329, 331
Peter Martyr, 379
Peter Morone, 553
Peter Thomas, 591
Peterborough, 369
Peter's Pence, 244, 587
Petit-Querilly, 380
Petra, 448
Petrarch, 587
Philibert de l'Orme, 369
Philip I (Fr.), 21, 74, 123, 176, 181, 215, 261, 440
Philip II Augustus (Fr.), 22, 24,*25, 74, 197, 207, 213, 218 f., 241, 264, 269, 277n., 291, 298, 309, 339, 457, 459(bis) and n., 461, 467, 522, 543, 546
Philip III (Fr.), 22, 579
Philip IV the Fair (Fr.), 22, 111 f., 219, 246, 296, 339, 479, 507, 513, 551, 568, 571–5, 576–8, 579, 588

Philip V (Fr.), 23
Philip VI (Fr.), 482, 587n., 588 f.
Philip I (Poland), 397
Philip de Courtenay, 480
Philip of Bonne Espérance, 44, 49; of Nanteuil, 470; of Swabia, 461
Phocas, 398
Photius, 395, 480
Phrygia, 412
Piacenza, 534; Council of, 429
Picards, 438 f.
Pico della Mirandola, 5
Pilgrims, 26, 63–72, 257, 313, 394, 397, 433, 434, 472, 480, 494, 499, 571
Pisa, 13, 19, 188, 363, 365, 388, 389, 390, 404, 429, 435, 595, 604
Pisano, Niccolò, 390
Pistoia, 390
Pius VIII, Pope, 115
Plan-Carpin, John of, 473, 496, 505
Plato, 263, 317, 319, 324, 326, 334
Poblet, 388
Poème de Carité, 16
Poitiers, 362, 364, 372, 375, 380, 381; Count of, 472, 539
Poitou, 22, 363, 487
Poland (Poles), 11, 189, 214, 216n., 230, 366, 466, 471, 495, 496, 498, 499, 526
Polovsti, 409, 418, 466, 496
Pomerania, 496, 497 f., 500
Pontaubert, 364
Pontigny, 370
Poor Catholics, 526
Poor Clares, 146
Poor Men of Lombardy, 526
Poor-relief, 253 f.
Pope and emperor, 1, 105, 133, 134, 137, 189–94, 339, 404, 412, 433, 458, 588. See also Investitures
Popes and bishops, 232 f.
Popes, election of, 173 f., 223; dress of, 225 f.; work of, 224 ff., 227
Portugal, 21, 197, 214, 251, 311, 364, 386, 387, 388, 490 f., 495, 505
Pouzauges, 379
Praefectus, a priest, 487
Prague, 10, 314, 386, 565
Prayer, 56 f.
Premonstratensians, 44, 97, 131 f., 135, 139, 149, 161, 422, 498, 499, 557
Prester John, 518
Priests and parishes, 234–6, 421
Prostitutes, reclamation of, 256 f.
Provence, 19, 364, 375, 440(bis), 481n., 486, 523, 526, 529
Prussia, 496, 499, 500
Psellos, Michael, 308, 396, 398, 415, 426
Ptolemy (geographer), 506
Pyritz, 497

Qualaoun, 479(bis)
Quidort, Jean, 567

Rabanus Maurus, 318
Rainulf, 405
Ramleh, 445
Ransomers, 258
Raoul, a Cistercian, 537
Ratisbon, 10
Ravenna, 9, 192, 307, 338, 349, 390, 391, 605; Council of, 61
Raymond, St, Abbot of Fitero, 492
Raymond Lull, Bl., 76, 317, 341, 503, 511, 515, 598
Raymond Nonnatus, St, 257 f.
Raymond of Antioch, 451, 453–5
Raymond of Pennaforte, St, 243, 258, 279, 338, 511, 513, 547
Raymond of Puy, 450
Raymond III of Tripoli, 456(bis)
Raymond IV of St Gilles, Count of Toulouse and Tripoli, 440(bis), 441–3, 445(bis), 446, 447(bis), 449, 538
Raymond VI of Toulouse, 535 ff., 538(bis), 539(bis), 541 ff.
Raymond VII of Toulouse, 544
Raymond-Roger de Foix, 535, 539, 541 f.
Raynier Sacconi, 530
Reason and faith, 319 ff., 326, 333 f., 360 ff.
Recluse of Mollieu, the, 16
Recluses, 40n.
Reconquista, 14, 76, 387, 438, 485–93
Reggio, 427
Regnier, Prior of St Michel, 501
Regular clergy, 236–40
Reichenau, 379, 494
Relics, 37, 397, 405, 407n., 420, 477
Remigio da Girolami, 603
Renaud de Châtillon, 412, 437, 455 ff.
Rey, Raymond, 381
Rheims, 3, 6, 9, 38, 206 f., 210 f., 228, 266, 272, 306, 347, 350 f., 352, 357, 368, 369n., 370–2, 374, 376, 377n., 387, 389, 397, 572, 573
Rhineland, 439, 522
Rhodes, 411, 597
Ribe, 10
Richard I, King of England, 24, 195, 278, 455
Richard of St Laurent, 44, 49
Richard of St Victor, 49, 324
Rienzi, Cola de, 583
Riesengebirge, 495
Riga, 495, 498, 500
Rimini, 491
Robert of Arbrissel, 132, 438
Robert le Bougre, 547
Robert Curthose, 440, 446, 451
Robert of Flanders, 410, 440, 445

Robert II the Pious (Fr.), 9, 21
Rocamadour, 36
Roch, St, 256
Roger II of Sicily, 104 f., 188, 195, 262, 411(bis), 413, 417, 509
Roger II of Trencavel, 537, 539
Roger de Flor, 590
Roland of Anjou, 480
Roman law, 243, 338 f., 564, 567 f.
Roman de la Rose, 345 f., 565
Roman de Renart, 556, 565
Romania, 463 f., 504
Romanus IV Diogenes, 398, 399, 400, 403, 434
Rome (Eternal City), 9, 64 f., 67(bis), 68 f., 70, 123, 146, 157, 188, 189, 190, 196, 263, 331, 338, 365, 379, 389, 409, 431, 440, 444, 583, 608
Romuald, St, 119, 125
Rosary, the, 50, 56 and n., 481n.
Roscelin, 321, 322
Rostock, 498
Rouaud (island), 479
Rouen, 9, 117, 240n., 262, 371, 372, 377n., 383, 389, 594
Roussel de Bailleul, 396, 399(bis), 403, 408
Royan, 436
Rudolph, Emperor, 25
Rumanians, 516
Russia (Russians), 11, 413, 418(bis), 422, 496, 500, 515, 597
Rutebœuf, 33
Ruthenia, 597
Ruysbroek, 565

Sabatier, Paul, 534
Sabutai, 466
St Denis, abbey of, 350, 352, 353, 354, 357, 370, 381
Saint-Étienne, church at, 365
Saint-Front, 417
Saint-Gall, 385
St Germain-des-Près, 487
St Julian, Order of, 492
St Lazarus, Order of, 255
St Mark's (Venice), 417, 463
St Nicholas, island of, 461
St Papoul, abbey, 535
St Peter's (Rome), 68, 180 f., 191, 214, 226, 362, 369, 383, 428
Saint-Pierre-sur-Dives, 365
Saint-Pol, Count of, 461
St Sabbas, monastery, 448
St Sernin, church of, at Toulouse, 363, 365
St Volusian, abbey, 535
Sainte Chapelle, 3, 37, 380, 382, 388, 501
Saintes, 364 f.
Saintes-Maries, 364
Saisset, Bernard, 573

Saladin, 218, 412, 413, 431, 455, 457(bis), 458–60, 476, 517
Salamanca, 314, 318, 363, 388, 565
Salerno, 9, 124, 181, 188, 228, 307 f., 314, 340, 390, 405, 406, 407n.
Salisbury, 387
Salve Regina, 49, 91, 479
Salzburg, 10
Samaria, 448
Samarkand, 466
San Galgano, abbey, 388
Sancho V of Navarre, 491
Sant' Ambrogio (Florence), 34
Santa Cruz, 388
Santa Maria Novella (Florence), 1, 2n.
Santa Sophia (Constantinople), 394, 417 f., 425, 463
Santarem, 490
Sapor II of Persia, 527
Saracens, 14, 406, 448 f.
Saragossa, 488(bis), 490
Sardinia, 19
Sartaq, 506(bis)
Saulieu, 364
Sauma, Rabban, 479, 507 f.
Savonarola, 163
Savoy, 384
Saxony (Saxons), 10, 366, 493, 497(bis), 498
Scandinavia, 10, 13, 436, 445n., 494 f., 597
Schism between East and West, 393 ff., 425 f., 482
Schleswig, 10
Scholasticism, 318, 319–37
Schwarzheindorff, 379
Science, medieval, 339–43
Scotland, 9, 439, 597
Scylitzes, see John Scylitzes
Scythia, 380, 400, 529
Segarelli, 558
Segovia, 365
Selef, river, 458
Seljuk, Prince, 402
Seljukid of Anatolia, the, 443; of Aleppo, 452
Seljuks, 11 f., 402, 404, 434, 590. See also Turks
Sempad, Constable of Armenia, 505
Sens, 9, 351, 370 f., 376, 385, 482; Council of, 101
Serbia (Serbs), 11, 214, 400, 409, 410, 416, 422, 458, 477, 516(bis), 529, 589(bis), 597
Seres, 590
Serfs, 264–7, 295
Sergius, St, 417
Sergius III, Pope, 172
Sergius IV, Pope, 434
Sergius, an Armenian, 507
Sergius Tychicus, 528
Sermons, 50 ff.
Sernin, St, 36

Seville, 388, 488(bis), 493, 510
Shiites, 456
Siberia, 402
Sicilian Vespers, 204, 479, 480
Sicily, 12, 13, 21, 166, 177, 181, 191, 195 f.,
 199, 204, 214, 317, 365, 386, 390 f., 405,
 407, 408, 411 f., 413, 417, 443, 458 f., 460,
 470, 476, 477, 484, 509, 596
Sick, care of the, 254 ff.
Sidon, 447 f., 452, 457, 479, 495
Siena, 388 f., 390
Sierra Morena, 491, 493
Sigier of Brabant, 27
Signorelli, Luca, 392
Sigurd, King of Sweden, 495
Silesia, 471
Simeon, St (formerly Stephen I Nemanya
 of Serbia), 516
Sinai, 422, 448, 517
Sion, Mount, 448
Skalhot, 597
Slavs, 10, 11, 418, 496(bis), 497
Sluys, 589
Smyrna, 585
Soissons, 520
Soisy-sur-Seine, 593
Soliman the Turk, 404, 409
Sorbon, Robert de, 292, 296, 312(bis), 313
Sorbonne, the, 509, 563
Spain, 3, 4, 12 f., 14, 27, 69, 76, 146, 157,
 176, 214, 234, 364, 365, 387, 438, 440,
 478, 481n., 485(bis), 486, 487 ff., 509,
 526, 596
Spire, 363, 366
'Spirituals,' 556 f., 557n., 559 f., 574, 582,
 602, 609
Stabat Mater, 50, 62, 315
Stephen I of Hungary, St, 11, 214, 376, 400,
 495
Stephen IX, Pope, 426
Stephen I Nemanya (Serbia), afterwards St
 Simeon, 516
Stephen IV (Bulgaria), 410
Stephen of Blois, 23, 440; of Cloyes, 467
Stephen Dushan (Serbia), 589 f., 597
Stephen Harding, St, 82, 83, 127 f.
Stettin, 497, 498
Stockholm, 495
Strasbourg, 368, 377n., 385, 387, 522, 595
Sudan, 446
Sudetenland, 495
Suger, Abbot of St Denis, 96 f., 107, 109 f.,
 111, 113, 130, 217, 222, 350, 352 f., 370,
 381(bis)
Sully, Eudes de, 269
Sully, Maurice de, 51, 222, 350, 354
Summa Aurea, 567
Summa Theologica, 3, 32, 331 f.
Sunnites, 456
Suzdal, 496

Swabians, 498
Sweden, 10, 198, 366, 494 f.
Switzerland, 157, 189, 257, 482, 522, 578n.
'Swordbearers,' 500
Sylvester II, Pope, 433
Syria, 12, 21, 317, 400, 402, 434, 437, 443,
 448, 454, 456, 457, 458, 460, 476, 478, 481

Tabor, Mount, 468
Tafilet, 489
Tagus, 488 f., 490 f., 492
Taifas, 488
Talbot, 482
Tamerlane, 518
Tanchelin, 522
Tancred, 443, 446
Tancred of Taranto, 452
Tancred the Bastard, 413
Tarifa, 488
Tauler, 595
Tavant, 397 f.
Tchernobog, 528
Tchormaghan, 467
Temoudjin, 465 f.
Tempier, Bishop of Paris, 333n., 335
Templars, 111 f., 257, 361, 450(bis), 454 f.,
 464, 471, 476, 478, 479, 489, 492, 499,
 575–8, 580n., 581; Grand Master of the,
 456 f., 479, 575; Marshal of the, 479. See
 also Military Orders
Temyn, 490
Teutonic Knights, 200, 201, 479, 499 f.,
 504; Grand Master of the, 500, 597. See
 also Military Orders
Tharaud, Jerome and John, 406
Theodore Lascaris, 464, 516
Theodore Prodromos, 415
Theophilus, a monk, 380
Theophylact, Archbishop of Ochrida, 395,
 421(bis), 428
Thessalonica, 408, 413, 415 f., 421, 423, 431,
 463 f.
Thibaut, Count of Blois, 260
Thibaut II, Count of Champagne, 102, 113
Thibaut III, Count of Champagne, 461
Thibaut IV, Count of Champagne, 290, 470
Thibaut V, Count of Champagne, 299
Thomas the Apostle, St, 46, 508
Thomas à Becket, St, 24, 46, 70, 168, 215,
 216
Thomas Aquinas, St, 3, 7, 27, 32, 34(bis), 44,
 48, 51, 56, 157, 159, 164, 212, 225, 273n.,
 286, 310, 312, 315(bis), 316, 323, 325, 327,
 329–36, 503, 551
Thomas de Chantimpré, 120
Thomas of Tolentino, St, 508
Thorn, 500
Thoros, Armenian prince, 444
Thrace, 8, 400, 409, 464, 589

Thuringia, 147, 504
Tiara, papal, 571
Tiberias, 448, 454, 457, 471; Lake of, 455
Tibet, 466
Tiflis, 598
Tirnovo, 516
Tithes, 245, 247
Tleman, 509
Tlemcen, 489
Toghril Beg, 402
Toledo, 264, 307, 308, 317(bis), 323, 386, 388(bis), 488 f., 491(bis), 492
Tolosas, Las Navas da, 492
Toron, 450
Tortosa, 445, 450, 479, 481n.
Torture, 260 f., 549 f.
Toulouse, 36, 313, 317, 339, 350, 352, 363, 365, 440, 534, 536, 542 f., 573
Tournai, 366
Tours, 9, 130, 339n., 365, 382, 521, 577
Towns, growth of, 205–9
Trade and commerce, 273 f.
Trani, 397, 406
Transcaucasia, 505
Transylvania, 11, 26, 495, 500
Treatise on Several Arts, 380
Trebizond, 414, 589
Trencavel viscounts of Béziers and Carcassonne, 535
Trèves, 380
Trinitarians, Order of, 139, 258
Tripoli, 447, 457, 479(bis)
Tripolitania, 509
Tristram and Iseult, 289, 345
Trondjhem, 495
Troyes, 351, 355, 358
Truce of God, 276 f.
Tuaregs, 288 f.
Tudela, 488
Tunis, 476, 477(bis), 480, 501, 513
Tunisia, 509
Turcomans, 455
Turkestan, 402, 466(bis), 518
Turks, 8, 29, 67, 106, 278, 394, 399(bis), 400, 402(bis), 403, 410–14, 422(bis), 426, 429 f., 434(bis), 439, 441, 443(bis), 444, 446, 451, 454(bis), 457 f., 467, 481, 482, 516 f., 589 f. See also Ottomans; Seljuks
Turlupins, 522, 557
Tuscany, 19, 559, 603
Tyre, 445, 447 f., 452, 457(bis)
Tzachas, 409

Ubertino da Casale, 559
Ucles, 490
Ukraine, 11, 466, 503
Ulm, 368, 387
Unam Sanctam, 570 f.
United Brethren, 508

Universities, 308–14; Bologna, 318, 513; Cologne, 564 f.; Heidelberg, 565; Oxford, 318, 513, 562, 564; Paris, 316, 318, 330, 335, 494, 515, 564, 565; Salamanca, 318, 513
Upsala, 386, 494
Urban II, Pope, 28, 51, 131, 181(bis), 215, 228, 277, 280, 417, 427–30, 433, 435(bis), 436, 457
Urban III, Pope, 195, 265
Urban IV, Pope, 34, 222, 233, 330, 476, 549
Urban V, Pope, 509
Uskub, 590
Usury, 271 f.
Uzes, 400(bis), 403(bis)

Valdès or Valdo, see Peter de Vaux
Valence, 404
Valentinois, 539
Vallombrosa, 122, 125
Valois, 22
Van, Lake, 403
Varangian Guards, 494
Vardar, 415
Vatatzes, see John Vatatzes
Vatopedi, 416, 422
Velasquez, Bro. Diego, 492
Veltro, 610
Vendôme, 381
Venice (Venetians), 19, 188, 193, 200, 273, 390, 409, 411, 412, 414, 417, 432, 435, 461 f., 463, 472, 476, 480, 482, 507, 579, 591, 605
Veni Creator, 48, 472
Veni, Sancte Spiritus, 48
Vercelli, 558; Council of, 521
Verfeil, 536
Vermandois, 22
Vernacular literature, rise of, 343–6, 565
Verona, 365, 546, 605
Vézelay, 38, 135, 206, 267, 352, 363, 364 f., 375, 453, 459
Vicelin, St, 498
Vienna, 314, 359, 466
Vienne, 9, 379n., 577, 580 f.
Villard de Honnecourt, 358, 359, 371, 374, 382, 386
Villehardouin, 461 ff.
Villon, François, 594
Vincennes, 241, 475, 577
Vincent of Beauvais, 46, 325 f., 341, 377
Vincent of Saragossa, St, 37
Violence, Church opposed to, 274–80
Viollet-le-Duc, 363, 369, 380
Visconti, Giovanni, Archbishop of Milan, 583
Visconti, Matteo, 582
Vita Nuova, 603

Vitry, Jacques de, 207(*bis*), 285, 286, 295, 468, 501(*bis*)
Vladimir I of Kiev, St, 418, 496
Vladimir II of Kiev, 418
Volynia, 466
Voragine, Jacobus de, 36, 46

Waldenses, 45, 136 f., 146, 524–7, 552, 558
Wales, 9
Wallachia, 458, 495
Walter the Penniless, 439(*bis*)
Walter of St Maurice, 44
Watt, Joachim von, 5
Wechschburg, 384
Welf, house of, 187. *See also* Guelfs
Wells (Somerset), 387
Wenceslaus, St, 10
Wends, 10, 111, 496, 498(*bis*), 597
Westminster, 387
Wibert, Archbishop of Ravenna, 180
William I of Sicily, 411, 426
William II of Sicily, 412 f., 417, 509
William I, the Conqueror (Eng.), 23, 122, 176, 215, 255, 262, 278, 440
William II Rugus (Eng.), 23, 181, 215
William of Auvergne, 326; of Beaujeu, 479; of Champeaux, 43, 83, 84, 131, 306, 322, 324; of Mailly, 52n.; of Puylaurens, 538; of Rubrouk, 475, 484, 506 f.; of St Pathus, 290n., 292; of St Thierry, 43, 87,
97, 100, 114 f.; of Sens, 386; of Tyre, Archbishop, 468
William le Maire of Angers, 557
Wimfen-en-Tal, 386
Winchester, 365
Wolfram von Eschenbach, 112, 284
Worms, 178, 340, 363; Concordat of, 183
Wratislav, 498
Wyclif, John, 209, 563

Ximenes, Rodrigo, Archbishop of Toledo, 491

Yakub Almohad, 491(*bis*)
Yaroslav the Wise, 397, 418, 496(*bis*)
Youssouf-ibn-Tachfin, 489(*bis*)
Ypres, 19, 592
Yunnan, 508
Yves of Chartres, 211n., 338, 340
Yvetot, kingdom of, 17

Zalacca, 489
Zamora, 388
Zara, 461 f.
Zengi, 452 f.
Zographu, 422
Zoroastrians, 527